HANDBOOK OF RESEARCH ON INTERNATIONAL ADVERTISING

T0313725

To those who have suffered and to those who continue to suffer from the Great East Japan Earthquake.

Handbook of Research on International Advertising

Edited by

Shintaro Okazaki

Associate Professor, Universidad Autónoma de Madrid, Spain

Edward Elgar

Cheltenham, UK • Northampton, MA, USA

Published by
Edward Elgar Publishing Limited
The Lypiatts
15 Lansdown Road
Cheltenham
Glos GL50 2JA
UK

Edward Elgar Publishing, Inc.
William Pratt House
9 Dewey Court
Northampton
Massachusetts 01060
USA

Paperback edition 2014

A catalogue record for this book
is available from the British Library

Library of Congress Control Number: 2011932885

ISBN 978 1 84844 858 2 (cased)
       978 1 78347 601 5 (paperback)

Typeset by Servis Filmsetting Ltd, Stockport, Cheshire
Printed in Great Britain by Berforts Information Press Ltd

Contents

PART VII   SOCIAL INTERACTION

PART VIII   IMC AND THE GLOBAL MARKET

About the editor

Shintaro Okazaki received his PhD from the Universidad Autónoma de Madrid (Spain) where he works as Associate Professor of Marketing in the College of Economics and Business Administration. Dr Okazaki's research focuses on international advertising, global branding, mobile commerce, consumer generated media, and information privacy concerns. His work has appeared in the *Journal of Advertising, Journal of Advertising Research, International Journal of Advertising, Journal of International Marketing, Journal of Business Research, Journal of World Business, Psychology & Marketing, European Journal of Marketing, International Marketing Review, Tourism Management, Information & Management, Online Information Review, Journal of Computer-Mediated Communication, Computers in Human Behavior* and *Internet Research*, among others. He serves on the editorial boards of the *Journal of Advertising* (Associate Editor), *Journal of Advertising Research, International Journal of Advertising, Journal of Public Policy & Marketing, International Marketing Review, Journal of Interactive Advertising, Asian Journal of Communication, Electronic Markets, Internet Research, Journal of Electronic Commerce Research, Journal of Marketing Communications* (former Deputy Editor), and *Journal of International Consumer Marketing*, among others. He is a former Deputy Editor of the *Journal of Marketing Communications*. Dr Okazaki is also on the Executive Board of the European Advertising Academy (EAA). His awards include the 2007 Best Reviewer from the *International Journal of Advertising*, and the 2008 Best Academic of the Year from the Mobile Marketing Association and the 2010 Best Paper Award of the *Journal of Advertising*.

Contributors

Russell Belk is Kraft Foods Canada Chair in Marketing at the Schulich School of Business at York University. He is Past President of the International Association of Marketing and Development, and is a Fellow and Past President of the Association for Consumer Research. He has received the Paul D. Converse Award, the Sheth Foundation/*Journal of Consumer Research* Award for Long Term Contribution to Consumer Research, two Fulbright Fellowships, and honorary professorships on four continents. He has over 500 publications; they involve the meanings of possessions, collecting, gift-giving, materialism and global consumer culture. His work is often cultural, visual and interpretive.

Ling Bith-Hong is an Associate Professor in the Department of Marketing at the National Chung Hsing University (Taiwan). She received her PhD from the University of Hawaii at Manoa (USA) and was a Research Fellow at the Yoshida Hideo Foundation (Japan) and the University of Adelaide (Australia). Bith-Hong's professional expertise and research are in the areas of international marketing, food and wine marketing, and applied economics. Her research work has been published in *Australasian Marketing Journal*, *Aquaculture Economics and Management*, *Agricultural Economics*, *Aquaculture Research*, and others.

Ivana Bušljeta Banks is a PhD candidate at the University of Antwerp. She is a Senior Lecturer at the Zagreb School of Economics and Management, teaching Business Communication and Promotion & Advertising courses. Her research interests include advertising effectiveness, cross-cultural advertising, the use of rhetorics in advertising, ethics in advertising, services marketing, and new marketing communications media. She has presented her work at a number of conferences, such as the European Marketing Academy Conference, the International Conference on Research in Advertising, and the International Conference on Corporate Social Responsibility, and has published in the *Social Responsibility Journal*.

C. Luke Bowen is a Managing Partner of Evil Genius Beer Company, a Pennsylvania based craft brewery. Previously, he worked as a Business Fellow Graduate Research Assistant in the Villanova School of Business. Luke graduated from Villanova University in 2010 with an MBA in Strategic Management. His research interests are in the areas of marketing strategy and strategic planning.

Shu-Chuan Chu is an Assistant Professor in the College of Communication at DePaul University, USA. She received her PhD from the University of Texas at Austin. Her research interests include social media, electronic word-of-mouth and cross-cultural consumer behavior. Her work has appeared (or is forthcoming) in the *Journal of Global Marketing, International Journal of Advertising, Journal of Interactive Advertising, Journal of Marketing Communications, Journal of International Consumer Marketing, Chinese Journal of Communication,* and *International Journal of Internet Marketing and Advertising,* among others. Her work has also appeared in books such as *Handbook of Research on Digital Media and Advertising: User Generated Content Consumption, Computer-Mediated Communication across Cultures: International Interactions in Online Environments,* and *Advances in Advertising Research (vol. II).* Dr Chu has been a Visiting Professor at Xiamen University in China and is currently the Chair of the International Advertising Education Committee (IAEC) at the American Academy of Advertising.

C. Samuel Craig is the Catherine and Peter Kellner Professor, Professor of Marketing and International Business, and Director of the Entertainment, Media and Technology Program at New York University's Stern School of Business. He received his PhD from the Ohio State University. Prior to joining New York University, Professor Craig taught at Cornell University. He is co-author, along with Susan Douglas, of *International Marketing Research,* 3rd edition, and *Global Marketing Strategy.* He and Professor Douglas have received four 'best article' awards from the *Journal of International Marketing.* His research interests focus on the entertainment industry, global marketing strategy and methodological issues in international marketing research.

Mary Sully de Luque received her PhD in Organizational Behavior at the University of Nebraska. She is currently an Assistant Professor of Management at the Thunderbird School of Global Management. Previously, she was a Senior Fellow at the Wharton School working with the GLOBE project. Mary's research interests include the influence of culture on leadership, feedback processes in the work environment, and talent management. Her work has been published in *Administrative Science Quarterly, Academy of Management Review,* and *JIBS,* among others. She currently serves on four editorial review boards and has received many awards for her scholarship.

Patrick De Pelsmacker received his PhD from Ghent University (Belgium). He is Professor of Marketing at the University of Antwerp. His current research interests include advertising effectiveness, new marketing communication formats, branding, cross-cultural advertising and branding, ethical consumer behavior and social marketing. His work has been published in, amongst others, *Journal of Advertising, International Journal of Advertising, Journal of Advertising Research, Journal of Interactive Advertising, Journal of Interactive Marketing, Psychology and Marketing, International Marketing Review, Marketing Letters, Journal of Consumer Affairs, Journal of Business Research, Journal of Business Ethics, Cyberpsychology, Behaviour and Social Networking,* and *Accident Analysis and Prevention.* He is on the editorial board of *Journal of Advertising* (Associate Editor), *Journal of Business Research, International Journal of Advertising* and *Journal of Public Policy & Marketing.*

Sandra Diehl is Associate Professor of Media and Communication at Klagenfurt University, Austria. She received her PhD from Saarland University, Germany. Her current research interests include international advertising, mobile Internet, health communication, pharmaceutical advertising and new media. She is currently board member and treasurer of the European Advertising Academy. She serves on the editorial boards of the *Journal of Marketing Communication* and the *Journal of the Global Academy of Marketing Science.*

Susan P. Douglas was the Paganelli-Bull Professor of Marketing and International Business at New York University's Stern School of Business. She passed away suddenly in early January 2011. She received her PhD from the University of Pennsylvania. Prior to joining New York University, Professor Douglas taught at Centre-HEC, Jouy-en-Josas, France, and was a faculty member of the European Institute for Advanced Studies in Management in Brussels. A Past President of the European Marketing Academy, and former Vice President of the Academy of International Business, Professor Douglas was elected a Fellow of the Academy of International Business in 1991 and was Dean of the Fellows from 1999 to 2002. She was made a Fellow of the European Marketing Academy in 2002 and chaired the Fellows from 2002 to 2005.

Martin Eisend is Professor of Marketing at European University Viadrina in Frankfurt (Oder), Germany. He earned a doctoral degree at Freie University Berlin, Germany. His research activities center on marketing communication and methods of empirical generalization. His research has been published in *Journal of the Academy of Marketing Science, International Journal of Research in Marketing, Marketing Letters, Journal of Advertising,* and other journals.

Louisa Ha is a Professor and Chair of the Department of Telecommunications at Bowling Green State University, Ohio, USA and

Associate Editor of *Journalism and Mass Communication Quarterly*. Her edited book, *Webcasting Worldwide: Business Models of an Emerging Global Medium*, received the AEJMC 2007 Robert Picard Award for Books and Monographs in Media Management and Economics. She is also the recipient of the 2006 Barry Sherman Teaching Award in Media Management and Economics. She received her PhD in Mass Media from Michigan State University. Her research interests are media technologies and business models, international advertising, online advertising and audience research.

Jörg Henseler is Associate Professor of Marketing at the Institute for Management Research, Nijmegen School of Management, Radboud University Nijmegen, the Netherlands. He is also Visiting Professor at the Higher Institute of Statistics and Information Management (ISEGI), Universidade Nova de Lisboa, Portugal. Dr Henseler is an expert on partial least squares (PLS) path modeling, an exploratory and predictive form of structural equation modeling. He has published in academic journals such as the *International Journal of Research in Marketing and Structural Equation Modeling*, and he has edited two books on PLS (for a full list of publications see http://www.henseler.com/publications.html).

Robert J. House received his PhD in Management from Ohio State University. He was appointed the Joseph Frank Bernstein Endowed Chair of Organization Studies at the Wharton School of the University of Pennsylvania in 1988. He has published over 130 journal articles and has received the Award for Distinguished Scholarly Contribution to Management, conferred by the Academy of Management. He is a Fellow of the Academy of Management, the American Psychological Association, and the Society for Industrial/Organizational Psychology. He was the principal investigator of the Global Leadership and Organizational Behavior Effectiveness (GLOBE) Study from 1993 to 2003. Dr House's research interests include leadership, personality, power in organizations, and the implications of cross-cultural variation for effective leadership and organizational performance.

Kenichi Ito received his Master's degree in Psychology from the University of Alberta, Canada, where he is currently a PhD student in the social and cultural psychology program. His research interests include cross-cultural comparisons of perception and cognition. His work has been accepted for publication in the *Journal of Cross-Cultural Psychology*.

Jeffrey K. Johnson received his PhD from Michigan State University. Dr Johnson works as a World War II historian at the Joint POW/

MIA Accounting Command in Honolulu, Hawaii. His current research interests include the creation of social and cultural narratives. His work has been published in the *Journal of Popular Culture*, *Popular Culture Review*, and *Advertising & Society Review*. His first monograph is entitled *American Advertising in Poland: A Study of Cultural Interactions Since 1990*. He is currently working on a book-length study of comic book superheroes and US history. He can be reached at phoboes2000@yahoo. com.

Sara Kamal (PhD, the University of Texas at Austin) is an Assistant Professor of Marketing Communications at the American University in Dubai, United Arab Emirates. Her research interests are the economic effects of advertising, new media and cross-cultural consumer behavior. Kamal's research has appeared in the *International Journal of Advertising*, *Journal of Interactive Advertising* and in books such as *Computer-Mediated Communication across Cultures: International Interactions in Online Environments*, and *Advances in Advertising Research (vol. II)*. She has also presented her work at various conferences including the American Advertising Academy (AAA) and the Association for Education in Journalism and Mass Communication (AEJMC). Email: skamal@aud.edu.

Philip J. Kitchen is Dean at the Faculty of Business, Brock University, Canada, where he is also tenured Professor of Marketing (2010). Previously he was Director of the Research Centre for Marketing, Communications, and International Strategy (CMCIS) and Chair of Strategic Marketing at Hull University Business School (2001–2010). He is also Affiliated Research Professor of Marketing at the ESC Rennes School of Business, France. He is the Founder and Editor of the *Journal of Marketing Communications*. Has published 13 books and over 100 papers in leading journals around the world. Listed as one of the 'The Top 50 Gurus who have Influenced the Future of Marketing', *Marketing Business*, December 2003, pp. 12–16, he is a Fellow of CIM, RSA, and HEA, and a Member of the ALCS, Institute of Directors and Institute of Marketing Science (USA).

Silke Knoll is a PhD student at the European University Viadrina in Frankfurt (Oder), Germany. Her thesis deals with marketing's influence on consumers' quality of life. Further research interests include consumers' trust in marketing and gender roles in advertising.

Carrie La Ferle received her PhD from the University of Texas-Austin. She is a Professor in the Temerlin Advertising Institute at SMU in Dallas. Her research examines how culture impacts advertising effectiveness and is published widely, including the *Journal of Advertising*. Dr La Ferle has been a Visiting Fellow at NTU in Singapore and is the recipient of several grants, the Teacher-Scholar Award from Michigan State University, and the President's Associates Award from SMU. Within the AAA, she has held positions from Newsletter Editor to VP. Dr La Ferle sits on several editorial review boards and has lived in Canada, Japan and Singapore.

Ashok K. Lalwani is an Associate Professor of Marketing at Indiana University, Bloomington. He holds a PhD in Marketing from the University of Illinois, Urbana-Champaign, an MS in Marketing from the National University of Singapore, as well as from the University of Florida, and an Engineering degree from the Indian Institute of Technology (IIT), New Delhi. He has taught marketing courses at Temasek Polytechnic, Singapore, The University of Illinois at Urbana-Champaign, and the University of Texas at San Antonio. He also held an executive position in the marketing division of a multinational firm. Ashok is interested in understanding how consumers' cultural values shape their judgments, behaviors and responses. Another research stream examines biases in consumers' price perceptions. He has published more than a dozen articles in scholarly journals such as *Journal of Consumer Research*, *Journal of Personality and Social Psychology*, and *Journal of Consumer Psychology*. Ashok has won numerous awards for his research and teaching. He is the recipient of the President's Distinguished Award for Research Achievement, and the Dean's Research Excellence Award, both at the University of Texas at San Antonio. More recently, his co-authored paper titled 'The Horizontal/Vertical Distinction in Cross-Cultural Consumer Research' was one of the top 20 most cited articles in the *Journal of Consumer Psychology*, 2006–2011. He was also on the list of excellent instructors (top 10 percent campus-wide rated as outstanding), at the University of Illinois at Urbana-Champaign.

Wei-Na Lee received her PhD from the University of Illinois at Urbana-Champaign. Her research examines the role of culture in every aspect of persuasive communication. Her work has been published in various book chapters, conference proceedings, and the *Journal of Advertising*, *Journal of Advertising Research*, *Psychology & Marketing*, *Journal of International Marketing*, *Journal of Business Research*, *International Journal of Advertising*, and *Journal of Computer-Mediated Communication*, among others. She co-edited the book *Diversity in Advertising* (2005, Lawrence Erlbaum). She is a three-time recipient of the American Academy of Advertising Research Fellowship. She is currently the Editor of the *Journal of Advertising*.

Carolyn A. Lin received her PhD from Michigan State University. Dr Lin's current research interests include the content, uses and effects of digital advertising, social marketing, health marketing and new media technologies. Her work has been published in the *Journal of Advertising*, *Journal of Advertising Research*, *International Journal of Advertising*, *Journal of Broadcasting & Electronic Media*, *Journalism & Mass Communication Quarterly*, *Human Communication Research*, *Health Communication*, *Journal of Health Communication* and elsewhere. She serves on the editorial boards of the *Journal of Advertising*, *Journal of Interactive Advertising*, *Journal of Broadcasting & Electronic Media*, *Journalism & Mass Communication Quarterly*, among others. Dr Lin is the Founder of the Communication Technology Division at the Association for Education in Journalism & Mass Communication.

Yuping Liu-Thompkins received her PhD from Rutgers University. She is Associate Professor of Marketing and E. V. Williams Faculty Fellow at Old Dominion University, and a 2010–2012 Fellow of the Society for New Communications Research. With a personal passion for technology, Dr Liu-Thompkins' research focuses on the intersection among marketing, technology, and consumer psychology. Her main research areas include Internet marketing and customer loyalty. Dr Liu-Thompkins' publications have appeared in *Journal of Marketing*, *Journal of Advertising*, and *Journal of Advertising Research*, among others. She is also an editorial review board member for *Journal of Marketing Communications*.

Inés López received her PhD from the University of Murcia, Spain. She is an Assistant Professor at the Miguel Hernández University. Dr Lopez's current research focuses on the role of emotions in consumers' behavior both from an intra- and an inter-personal point of view. Her work has been published in *Electronic Commerce Research & Applications*, *Ecological Economics*, among others, and presented at conferences such as ACR, SCP, EMAC, La Londe and ICORIA. She has been awarded for the Best Working Paper from the Society for Consumer Psychology in 2011.

Manuela López is a PhD student at the University of Murcia (Spain) with a pre-doctoral scholarship from the Spanish Ministry of Education. Her research interests focus on the influence of e-WOM in consumer behavior. She has presented her work at international conferences such as the International Conference on Research in Advertising (ICORIA) and the International Product Development Management Conference (IPDM).

Takahiko Masuda is an Associate Professor of the Department of Psychology, the University of Alberta, Canada. He received his PhD from the University of Michigan in 2003. His current research interests include cultural variations in perceptual and cognitive processes between East Asians, Asian immigrants in Canada, and North Americans. His work has been published in *Journal of Personality and Social Psychology*, *Personality and Social Psychology Bulletin*, *Journal of Experimental Psychology*, *Cognitive Science*, *Psychological Science*, and *Proceedings of the National Academy of Sciences of the United States of America*. He serves on the editorial boards of *Personality and Social Psychology Bulletin* and *Journal of Cross-Cultural Psychology*.

Brent McKenzie is an Associate Professor in the Department of Marketing and Consumer Studies, at the University of Guelph, in Canada and received his PhD in Marketing from Griffith University in Australia. He is a leading expert on retail trade in the Baltic States. Dr McKenzie's work has been published in such venues as the *Retail Digest*, and the *Journal of Business Research*. He was the recipient of the 2006 and 2010 Emerging Scholars Award by the Association for the Advancement of Baltic Studies, and sits on the editorial board of the *Baltic Journal of Management*, the *Journal of Education, Knowledge & Economy*, and the *Estonian Business Review*.

Makoto Mizuno is an Associate Professor of Marketing in the School of Commerce, Meiji University in Tokyo, Japan. He received his PhD in Economics from the University of Tokyo, Japan. His current research interests include social interaction and preference formation of consumers, marketing communication using social media, etc. His works have been published in *International Journal of Industrial Organization*, *Advances in Complex Sciences*, *European Journal of Operational Research*, and others. After working in the advertising industry for almost 20 years, he moved to academia.

Barbara Mueller is Professor of Advertising in the School of Journalism and Media Studies at San Diego State University. She received her PhD in Communications from the University of Washington. In addition to a multitude of articles in academic journals, such as the *Journal of Advertising*, *Journal of Advertising Research*, *Journal of International Marketing*, *International Journal of Advertising*, *Advances in International Marketing* and *International Marketing Review*, she is author of *Dynamics of International Advertising: Theoretical and Practical Perspectives*, 2nd edition, Peter Lang, 2011; *Communicating with the Multicultural Consumer: Theoretical and Practical Perspectives*, Peter Lang, 2008; and co-author (with Katherine Toland Frith) of *Advertising and Societies*, 2nd edition, Peter Lang, 2010. Her research interests focus on the role of culture in commercial communications.

Ayşegül Özsomer is Associate Professor of Marketing at Koç University, Istanbul, Turkey. She received her PhD in Marketing from Michigan State University and has conducted research, taught and consulted in the USA before joining Koç University in 1997. Her research focuses on (a) global marketing strategy with a particular emphasis on standardization-adaptation issues, (b) global brand management, and (c) market orientation and its relation to firm performance. She has published in top scholarly journals including the *Journal of Marketing, International Journal of Research in Marketing*, and *Journal of International Marketing.* Dr Özsomer was a Visiting Scholar at the marketing department of UCLA in 2002–2003 and the University of Michigan, Ann Arbor in 2008–2009.

Narda R. Quigley is an Associate Professor of Management at the Villanova School of Business (Villanova University, Pennsylvania, USA). She received her PhD in Organizational Behavior from the University of Maryland, College Park, after which she completed a post-doctoral appointment working with Dr Robert J. House and the GLOBE Project at the Wharton School. Her research interests include work groups and teams, personality, motivation, and emergent and cross-cultural leadership. Dr Quigley's work has been published in *Organization Science, Organizational Behavior and Human Decision Processes*, and *Organizational Research Methods*, among others. She currently serves on the editorial review board of *Group and Organization Management.*

Christian M. Ringle is Professor and Managing Director of the Institute for Human Resource Management and Organizations (HRMO) at Hamburg University of Technology (TUHH) and is a Visiting Professor of the University of Newcastle (Australia). He received his PhD from the University of Hamburg. Dr Ringle's research addresses strategic management, human resource management and organizations, marketing and quantitative methods for business and market research. He has published in top scholarly journals such as the *International Journal of Research in Marketing, Journal of the Academy of Marketing Science,* and *Journal of Service Research* (for a full list of publications see www.tuhh.de/hrmo). Moreover, Dr Ringle is an expert in PLS-SEM and co-developer of the SmartPLS software (www.smartpls.de).

Salvador Ruiz is a Professor of Marketing at the University of Murcia (Spain). Dr Ruiz's current research interests include the effects of information and emotions in consumer behavior and family decision making. His work has been published in *Electronic Commerce Research & Applications, Journal of Advertising, Journal of Business Ethics, Journal of Business Research, Journal of Interactive Marketing*, and *European Journal of*

Marketing. His awards include the Best Working Paper from the Society for Consumer Psychology in 2011 and the best paper published in 2009 in Revista Española de Investigación en Marketing.

Marko Sarstedt is Assistant Professor at the Ludwig-Maximilians-University, Munich, Germany. His main research interest is in the application and advancement of PLS path modeling to further the understanding of consumer behavior and to improve marketing decision making. His research has been published in several international journals, including *Journal of the Academy of Marketing Science*, *Journal of Business Research*, *Journal of World Business*, *Long Range Planning*, and *Journal of Advertising Research*, and he has served as a consultant for various companies.

Manfred Schwaiger is Professor of Business Administration at Ludwig-Maximilians-University, Munich (LMU). He received his PhD from Augsburg University and has published numerous articles on corporate reputation and communications management, among others, in *Journal of the Academy of Marketing Science*, *Journal of Advertising Research*, *European Journal of Marketing* and *Schmalenbach Business Review*. He is editorial review board member of the *Journal for Public Policy and Marketing*, the *Journal of Advertising*, and the *International Journal of Advertising*. He received Best Paper Awards from the European Institute for Advanced Studies in Management (EIASM) and the Association for Marketing & Health Care Research, among others.

Sawa Senzaki received her Master's degree in Psychology from the University of Alberta, Canada, where she is currently pursuing her PhD in the social and cultural psychology program. Her research interests include cultural variation in visual perception, and the development of such culturally unique perspectives.

Sharon Shavitt is the Walter H. Stellner Professor of Marketing at the University of Illinois at Urbana-Champaign, where she has been on the faculty since 1987. Shavitt has written and lectured extensively on consumer psychology. Her multidisciplinary research program focuses primarily on the cultural factors affecting consumer motivations, responses to advertising, and survey response behaviors. Her publications have appeared in *Journal of Consumer Research*, *Journal of Consumer Psychology*, *Journal of Advertising*, *Journal of Personality and Social Psychology*, and *Journal of Experimental Social Psychology*, among other outlets. Shavitt is President of the Association for Consumer Research. She previously served as co-Chair of the Association for Consumer Research 2008 conference, the largest international consumer research conference. She has also been Associate Editor of the *Journal of Consumer Psychology*.

María Sicilia received her PhD from the University of Murcia, Spain, where she now works as an Associate Professor of Marketing. Her articles have appeared in the *Journal of Business Research, Journal of Advertising, Journal of Interactive Marketing, Electronic Commerce Research and Applications*, and *European Journal of Marketing*. Her research interests are focused on advertising and consumer behavior.

Hirokazu Takada is Professor of Marketing and International Business, Zicklin School of Business, Baruch College, the City University of New York. He received his PhD from the Krannert Graduate School of Management, Purdue University, Indiana. Dr Takada's current research interests include analysis of diffusion of new products, country of origin effects, international marketing research, and advertising research. His work has been published in *Journal of Marketing, International Journal of Marketing, Journal of Business Research, Journal of Applied Statistics*, and others.

Charles R. Taylor is the John A. Murphy Professor of Marketing at Villanova University. He also serves as Senior Research Fellow in the Center for Marketing and Public Policy Research. Professor Taylor is a Past President of the American Academy of Advertising. He currently serves as the Editor in Chief of *International Journal of Advertising*, which is published by the World Advertising Resource Center. He previously served as Associate Editor of *Journal of Public Policy and Marketing* and *Journal of Advertising*. Dr Taylor's primary research interests are in the areas of international advertising and advertising regulation. He has published numerous articles in leading journals and serves on several editorial review boards. Taylor's research has received 'Best Article' awards at *Journal of Advertising, Journal of International Marketing*, and *Journal of Macromarketing*. Professor Taylor has taught courses in Korea, Austria, China, Germany and the Czech Republic, has served as a Fulbright Senior Scholar and has given speeches or lectures at many leading universities.

Ralf Terlutter is Professor of Marketing and International Management and Head of the Department of Business Management at Klagenfurt University, Austria. He received his PhD from Saarland University, Germany. His research areas include international advertising, advertising and children, pharmaceutical advertising, and advertising and new media. He is currently President of the European Advertising Academy and Vice-Dean of the Faculty of Business and Economics at Klagenfurt University.

Marwa Tourky is a Teaching Assistant in the Business Administration Department at Faculty of Commerce, Tanta University, Egypt and a Doctoral Researcher at Hull University Business School, UK, where she was supervised by Dean Kitchen. She holds a BSc in Business Administration from Tanat University, Egypt, and an MRes from Hull University Business School, UK. She has presented several papers in leading international marketing conferences such as IMTC, AM, BAM, and CMC. Her research interests incorporate corporate identity management, corporate and marketing communications, corporate branding, image and reputation, corporate social responsibility and business ethics.

Huaitang Wang is a Research Analyst at the Faculty of Extension, the University of Alberta, Canada. He received his PhD degree in Psychology from the University of Alberta in 2010. He has published articles in East Asian psychology journals.

Jinnie Jinyoung Yoo is currently a PhD Candidate in Advertising at the University of Texas at Austin. Her research interests include cross-cultural and multicultural advertising with a focus on diverse cultural cues in advertising messages, cross-cultural consumer behavior and psychology, and global branding.

Yang Zhang is an Assistant Professor at the School of Business Administration in the Northeast (Dongbei) University of Finance and Economics of China. She received her PhD from the University of Science and Technology of China and her current research interests include corporate reputation, brands and intellectual capital. Her work has been published in *Communicative Business*, *International Journal of Business Research*, and *Management World*, among others. She received Best Dissertation Awards from Xiamen University in China.

Xin Zhao is Assistant Professor of Marketing at the University of Nebraska-Lincoln. He received his PhD in Marketing from the David Eccles School of Business at the University of Utah. He studies consumer culture, advertising, and branding issues in emerging economies from a sociocultural and historical perspective. He has conducted extensive fieldwork in China. His research has appeared in the *Journal of Consumer Research*, *Journal of Advertising*, *Advances in Consumer Research*, and *European Advances in Consumer Research*. His work on Chinese advertising was the winner of the 2003 ACR-Sheth Dissertation Competition and the runner-up of the 2009 Sidney Levy Dissertation Award.

Foreword

Shintaro Okazaki's *Handbook of Research in International Advertising* is an anthology of 23 chapters by top scholars from around the world. The authors are internationally renowned from the fields of marketing, advertising, psychology and communication. The book provides their collective research insights and wisdom on international advertising on a range of topics from gender to branding, from data collection to IMC, and from cognitive psychology to Russian advertising.

Reflections are provided on the leading research themes within international advertising and the book manages to successfully balance the impact of digital and traditional media in relation to current and future theory and practice. Several new cultural paradigms are introduced and, while some of these are well known in the management literature, such as GLOBE, many have not previously been formulated as bases for cross-cultural advertising. Furthermore, the book refreshes and updates our views of the variables that have traditionally been explored in international advertising such as agency, consumer socialization, gender and issues of trust. For scholars, the *Handbook* gives useful and practical tips for conducting international advertising research by drawing our attention to a variety of methodological issues including, amongst others, sampling, partial least square, and cultural equivalence.

This multifaceted collection provides sharp insights for both expert and novice international advertising researchers. Dr Okazaki has provided us with a first-class reference for international advertising students and scholars as well as people with a broad interest in this intriguing field of study.

Douglas West
Executive Editor, *Journal of Advertising Research*
Professor of Marketing
Birkbeck, University of London, UK

Preface

The creation of a scholarly network resembles knitting a quilt – we personally and individually find threads and create layers of collaborative works. This book, *Handbook of Research in International Advertising*, grew out of such a network, which I am fortunate enough to have established over the past year. Leading academics from a wide range of countries each generously agreed to contribute a chapter, and to offer their precious insights on diverse subjects in international advertising research. I am now pleased to present this work to our community.

The chapters in this book address issues about the ways in which researchers grasp original ideas, generate rich theory, or advance the state of the art from new perspectives. Throughout the project, this book was intended to overcome three important challenges that may maximize our contribution to the shaping and the working of our increasingly complex world.

The first challenge was to offer new insights into diverse cutting-edge topics. I wanted to establish whether there was something we had not seen or learned in the past in terms of theories, methods or implications. Both the country and the expertise of each author are also so diverse. I recruited top researchers from relatively distinct fields of interest. As editor of this *Handbook*, I wanted to include such diversity for a good reason: often, our differences in terms of scientific discipline, research methods, interpretations, or managerial applications can become a rich source of inspiration. While such diversity is an important asset we possess, it has sometimes been neglected because of practical problems or preconceived ideas.

The second challenge was to introduce new cultural theories as an alternative worldview. Cultures differ in their definitions of the human environment, including novelty, hazard, opportunity, attack, gratification and loss, while, at a general level, they also resemble each other; thus people tend to perceive and respond to them similarly and appropriately. To date, however, only limited theories can be applied to our market classification. This book contains several chapters that have challenged this point by examining new cultural paradigms. This approach is consistent with recent reviews by thought leaders who collectively urge the need for new theories in cultural explanations.

Ever-changing world markets also provide us with fascinating opportunities for our research. The third challenge was to incorporate those visions and insights into areas that have not yet been touched in prior international advertising research. For example, this book includes digital media, retrospective research and consumer psychology, along with some methodological issues.

This *Handbook* would never have been possible without the help and guidance of many people. My sincere appreciation goes to Ben Booth (Commissioning Editor) of Edward Elgar Publishing, who has been instrumental in publishing this book. I am deeply indebted to Elizabeth Clack (Senior Desk Editor) for her support, encouragement, and patience throughout the production process. Special thanks also go to Professor Susan Douglas, who passed away in January 2011. In memory, I appreciated her willingness to work on the chapter, and her commitment to it, which was co-authored and gratefully completed by Professor Craig.

Finally, I hope that readers will find this *Handbook* helpful for setting guidelines, or for refreshing ideas for conducting international advertising research. Different people may encounter this book at different stages of their professional careers. I hope that this *Handbook* will take you through a journey called research, by providing a path, expanding your visions, and encouraging you to find opportunities along the way.

Shintaro Okazaki
Editor
Madrid, May 2011

PART I

LEADING THOUGHTS

1 Best practices for cross-cultural advertising research: are the rules being followed?
Charles R. Taylor and C. Luke Bowen

INTRODUCTION

Over the years it has been observed that the body of research on international advertising has faced some limitations based on the relatively limited use of advanced theories, study designs and analytical techniques (Miracle 1984; Moriarty and Duncan 1991; Zinkhan 1994; Taylor 2002, 2005). While this does not suggest that significant strides have not been made in better understanding global advertising, it does suggest a need for researchers interested in this topic to be attentive to such issues. Moreover, a recent article by Ford, Mueller and Taylor (2010) is evocative of progress being made on some key issues in international advertising research. The primary purpose of this chapter is to outline several suggestions or guidelines for conducting effective cross-cultural advertising research. An additional goal is to examine whether such guidelines have been followed over the past five years in research conducted in leading marketing and advertising journals. To this end, a content analysis of studies is conducted.

The chapter's scope is limited to cross-cultural studies that have focused on an issue related to advertising and promotion. Thus, to be included in the content analysis, a study must collect and report data from at least two countries. Individual country studies are not included in the analysis. The next section of the chapter will focus on identifying some key guidelines for cross-cultural advertising researchers. It should be noted at the outset that the goal of the content analysis is to assess the collective adherence to the guidelines. Furthermore, the goal is neither to critique individual studies, nor to promote the idea that each individual study needs to adhere to every guideline in order to make a contribution. However, monitoring the degree to which several of these issues are being addressed does allow for an assessment of overall progress being made in advancing the international advertising field.

GUIDELINES FOR RESEARCHERS

Several different suggestions for advancing the field have been made by prior researchers. Much of the following discussion will draw on the summary provided by Taylor (2005), supplemented by some additional studies. Major suggestions have been made in the following areas:

- geographic scope of studies;
- compelling rationale for selection of countries;
- use of cross-national research teams;
- use of cross-disciplinary research teams;
- use of a wide range of data collection techniques;
- need for more multi-method studies;
- need for stronger theory bases;
- wider use of various analytical techniques;
- need for equivalent measurement instruments;
- need for post hoc equivalence test;
- need for assessment of cultural differences on samples;
- need for more studies of general populations (vs. students).

These issues will now be outlined individually and research questions posed.

Geographic Scope of Studies

Taylor (2005) observed a need for more studies on cross-cultural advertising that focused on contexts other than the U.S. vs. Japan or the U.S. vs. major countries in the EU. Fam and Grohs (2007) further noted that studies of values expressed in advertising normally took the form of comparing the U.S. and a foreign country, or else using a cluster of countries. While it is somewhat understandable that long developed and large economies would receive much attention, the aforementioned recommendation by Fam and Grohs is in the interest of the field, especially given the growth of the BRICs and several newly developing nations. As a result it is worth examining which countries are commonly included in comparative studies.

RQ1: What countries/regions have been most frequently compared in cross-national advertising studies?

Compelling Rationale for Selection of Countries

Too often in the past, countries included in cross-cultural research have been chosen for reasons of convenience as opposed to providing a strong basis for hypothesis testing. It has previously been observed that cultural dimensions (Milner 2005), economic development level (e.g., Pollay and Mittal 1993) and social factors (Yang 2000; Davila and Rojas Mendez 2001) can be predictors of the type of advertising used. These and other factors can be used as a basis for developing hypotheses.

As a general rule, there should be a compelling reason why two or more specific countries are compared. While studies in which data is collected from a very large number of countries are an exception in some instances, those with a more limited number of countries examined should closely match the theoretical base for the study with the countries in which data is collected. For example, if a researcher is interested in testing differences in individualism/collectivism, it makes sense to include countries that vary significantly on this dimension. Alternatively, if a consumer behavior theory such as the elaboration likelihood model is tested, it may make sense to test countries at different levels of economic development in order to help assess the robustness of the theory.

RQ2: To what extent are cross-national advertising studies providing compelling rationale for countries included in the data set?

Use of Cross-National and Cross-Functional Research Teams

Miracle (1984) observed that the use of more cross-national research teams would provide broader perspectives on international marketing research. It makes good sense that in attempts to provide broadly applicable theory, contributions from individuals from different countries can lend themselves to strong theory development. Similarly, cross-functional teams of researchers likely have an advantage in integrating perspectives from different research disciplines to help advance knowledge. As a result, it is worthwhile to examine the following questions:

RQ3a: How common is the use of cross-national research teams in cross-cultural advertising research?
RQ3b: How common is the use of cross-functional research teams in cross-cultural advertising research?

Data Collection Techniques Used

Prior discussions of the international advertising literature have focused on the relatively high proportion of conceptual papers and content analyses that have been conducted. Taylor (2005) specifically cited a shortage of survey studies and experiments. He noted that much research in the international advertising area had been descriptive, focusing on what types of advertising exists as opposed to developing deeper insights as to why certain advertising strategies and executions are effective. Okazaki and Mueller (2007) also noted a shortage of experiments, indicating that there is pressing need for more of this type of study. It was also noted that more multi-method studies would be valuable as well:

> RQ4a: Have a wide variety of data collection techniques been used in cross-cultural advertising research?
> RQ4b: Are surveys commonly used in cross-cultural advertising research?
> RQ4c: Are experiments commonly used in cross-cultural advertising research?
> RQ4d: Are multi-method studies frequently used in cross-national advertising research?

Theoretical Bases

Some authors have argued that culture and advertising are intrinsically linked (e.g., Schudson 1984). However, other researchers have found that cultural differences matter more under certain circumstances, such as product type and the degree to which the product is used collectively (Han and Shavitt 1994). Moreover, there has clearly been a trend toward more global marketing, suggesting that it is at least worth testing whether some generalizable theories hold across cultures.

While cultural dimensions can form a valid basis from which to predict cross-national differences in some instances, prior literature has been characterized by only limited application of theories applied in single country studies of marketing phenomena. In addition to consumer behavior theories and communications theories, recent years have seen the development of other perspectives drawn from management and international business, such as resource advantage theory, global consumer culture theory (and the global/local/foreign consumer culture positioning framework, see Alden, Steenkamp and Batra 1999), and global marketing strategy theory (Zou and Cavusgil 2005). Taylor (2002) called for more studies testing the cross-cultural applicability of general theories. With the recent advancement and application of international business frameworks, it is particularly useful to look at the extent to which various theoretical bases are being applied. Thus:

> RQ5a: Which theoretical perspectives have been applied most often to cross-national advertising research?

RQ5b: Have traditional consumer behavior theories and other theories from communications, psychology and sociology been widely applied?

Analytical Technique Used

Early studies of cross-cultural advertising were either conceptual or descriptive, owing in part to their largely descriptive nature, leading to only limited application of advanced analytical techniques. As technology and analytical techniques have advanced, it has become more feasible to collect large cross-national data sets. As a result, it is more realistic to expect that a wider range of analytical techniques would begin to be applied to cross-national advertising studies. This would lead to the expectation that techniques that can help more effectively analyze certain types of data, such as structural equations modeling, would be used more frequently. It is also the case that some researchers (e.g., Thompson 1997) have called for more cross-cultural studies using qualitative techniques. As with most research disciplines, a mix of major analytical techniques being used (assuming they are properly applied to the task at hand) is likely a positive state of affairs.

RQ6: Which analytical techniques are most commonly applied in cross-national advertising studies?

Back-translations and Equivalence Tests

Craig and Douglas (2005) in their textbook *International Marketing Research* have long advocated following appropriate procedures to ensure equivalence of data collected in multiple countries, including following a translation and back-translation process (see also Brislin 1980 and Miracle 1988). While there is now a significant science surrounding effective translation of survey instruments (see Harkness et al. 2003), failure to back-translate should now be viewed as a fundamental flaw in cross-cultural research.

While there are multiple possible post hoc techniques for measuring equivalence, Steenkamp and Baumgartner's (1998) approach, which employs confirmatory factor analysis, appears to have become the standard for cross-cultural research in marketing. This approach looks at three particularly critical forms of equivalence: configural, metric and scalar. Ewing, Salzberger and Sinkovics (2005) also proposed a Raasche-based technique for measuring cross-cultural equivalence that can be employed. Regardless of the method, it is important that these forms of equivalence be analyzed in order to assess data quality in addition to allowing researchers to include only those items where equivalence is established in subsequent analyses.

RQ7: In what proportion of cross-national studies are appropriate translation/back-translation procedures being followed?

RQ8: In what proportion of cross-national studies are appropriate post hoc equivalence tests being conducted?

Verifying the Existence of Cultural Differences

As observed by Taylor (2005), in cases where cultural variables are used as a basis for predictions it is advisable to collect data from the sample on the cultural dimensions used, especially given the ready availability of scales used by Hofstede (1980) and House et al. (2006). This is particularly applicable in cases where sub-groups in a society, such as students, are used for data collection. In this way, the real existence of the hypothesized difference can be verified (Taylor 2005). Moreover, it can allow for testing of individual level differences in the data set.

RQ9: What proportion of cross-national advertising studies that use cultural variables for hypotheses are collecting data on the cultural dimensions used?

Types of Subject

In the past, a disproportionate number of the cross-national studies have used student subject as opposed to a sample from the broader population. The use of student samples has been justified based on accessibility and greater homogeneity of the group (e.g., Calder, Phillips and Tybout 1977; Chan et al. 2007). While this is not surprising given the greater difficulty associated with collecting data from multiple countries, it has been observed (e.g., Moriarty and Duncan 1991; Zinkhan 1994) that the general research stream would benefit from more studies using non-student samples.

RQ10: To what extent are non-student subjects vs. student subjects used in cross-national advertising research?

METHODOLOGY

A content analysis of articles appearing from January 2005 to December 2010 in 11 major marketing, advertising and international business journals for which cross-national advertising papers would be appropriate submissions was conducted. An additional criterion was that the journal needed to be listed in the SSCI citation index. The resulting list of journals included four general marketing journals: *Journal of Marketing*, *Journal of Marketing Research*, *Journal of Consumer Research* and *Marketing Science*; three advertising journals: *Journal of Advertising*, *International Journal of Advertising* and *Journal of Advertising Research*; and three journals with an international marketing or business focus: *Journal of International Business Studies*, *Journal of International Marketing* and *International Marketing Review*.

A graduate research assistant with a strong background in research methodology was trained extensively by the lead author. A data coding instrument was developed based on prior literature on international research methods. In addition to publication, countries, whether there was a stated rationale for the countries selected; primary rationale for selection of countries; use of cross-national and cross-disciplinary research teams; primary data collection technique; theory base; analytical technique; use of back-translation; use of post hoc equivalence test; measurement of cultural factors; application of individual difference measures; and type of subject were the primary variables coded.

RESULTS AND DISCUSSION

While reliability was not measured for the entire sample, as it primarily involves simple classification, the lead author coded 20 studies independently to assure that there were not systematic differences in coding of some of the items and found no significant discrepancies. The literature search found 51 studies that collected cross-national data on an advertising topic.

Journal Coverage

Table 1.1 shows the breakdown of articles by journal. As can be seen, four journals, the *International Journal of Advertising* (24 percent), *Journal of Advertising* (22 percent), *International Marketing Review* (22 percent), and *Journal of Advertising Research* (20 percent) accounted for 88 percent of the papers published on cross-national advertising in these journals. In spite of their focus on international business/marketing topics, *Journal of International Business Studies* published just one (2 percent) cross-national article on advertising in the six-year period analyzed and *Journal of International Marketing* just three (6 percent). The four general marketing journals together published just four articles on this topic, with two in *Journal of Marketing*, one in *Journal of Marketing Research*, and none in *Journal of Consumer Research* or *Marketing Science*. One thing that is

Table 1.1   Frequency by journal

	Number	Percentage
Journal of Advertising	11	22%
Journal of Advertising Research	10	20%
International Journal of Advertising	12	24%
International Marketing Review	11	22%
Journal of International Marketing	3	6%
Journal of Marketing	2	4%
Journal of Marketing Research	1	2%
Journal of Consumer Research	0	0%
Marketing Science	0	0%
Journal of International Business Studies	1	2%

Table 1.2   Countries studied

	Number	Percentage
North America vs. Asia	13	25%
Europe vs. Asia	4	8%
North America vs. Europe	6	12%
Latin America vs. Asia	0	0%
Latin America vs. Europe	0	0%
Latin America vs. North America	0	0%
Three or more continents	16	31%
Other	12	24%

clear from this data is that the top advertising journals regularly publish cross-national studies.

RQ1: Geographic Scope

As can be seen in Table 1.2, the single most common geographic scope in the 51 studies reviewed was "three or more continents", with 16 studies (31 percent) falling into this category. This was followed by North American vs. Asia with 13 (25 percent) and North America vs. Europe comparisons with six studies (12 percent). It is notable that while some of "three or more continents" studies focused on Latin America, no two-way studies included Latin America, which appears to be an understudied region. In general these results suggest improvement in scope of studies over that reported by Taylor (2005). It is clear that North America vs. Asian studies, while still very common, no longer dominate the literature. Nevertheless,

Table 1.3   *State rationale for country selection*

	Number	Percentage
Yes	43	84%
No	8	16%

Table 1.4   *Cross-national research team*

	Number	Percentage
Yes	26	51%
No	25	49%

more studies with a direct focus on understudied regions, including Latin America, the Middle East and Africa, could add to the literature.

RQ2: Compelling Rationale for Countries

Table 1.3 shows that 43 or 84.3 percent of the studies reviewed did provide a compelling rationale for the selection of countries in the study. Just eight (15.7 percent) did not do so. This finding is suggestive of the criterion of "rule" being largely followed by academic researchers conducting cross-national studies. While it may seem to be a very basic issue, this finding appears to represent a considerable improvement over previous decades, as both Miracle (1984) and Zinkhan (1991) called for convenience to become less of a factor in country selection in cross-national advertising research.

RQ3: Use of Cross-National and Cross-Functional Research Teams

As shown in Table 1.4, 26, or just over half (51 percent), of the studies were conducted by cross-national research teams. Cross-functional research teams were a bit less common, with 39 percent of the studies including researchers from different disciplines. Both of these figures are encouraging in terms of researchers from different countries and different disciplines working together on cross-national advertising research. The fact that more than half of studies in these prestigious journals are conducted by cross-national research teams is suggestive that this is a common practice. It can be persuasively argued that this is a positive development in that multiple perspectives on cross-national research can produce deep insights.

    While cross-functional teams did not account for a majority of the

Table 1.5   Cross-functional research team

	Number	Percentage
Yes	20	39%
No	31	61%

Table 1.6   Both cross-national and cross-functional research team

	Number	Percentage
Yes	16	31%
No	35	69%

cross-national advertising studies conducted over the past six years, the fact that nearly 40 percent of the studies used such teams (see Table 1.5) is encouraging and represents an improvement over previous time periods (Miracle 1984; Taylor 2005). Again, different perspectives are brought to the research, providing the potential for different and new perspectives to advance the literature. This is not to say that all studies need to be conducted by cross-functional teams to produce valuable contributions; rather that having a significant number of studies that do so is worthwhile and desirable for the discipline.

Table 1.6 shows that 16 or 31 percent of the studies were conducted by a research team that was both cross-national and cross-functional. This is further evidence that progress has been made in this area.

RQ4: Data Collection Techniques Used

RQ4a asked whether a wide variety of data collection techniques are being used in cross-national advertising research. As shown in Table 1.7, content analyses are still the most frequently used analytical technique, with 18 (35.3 percent) of the studies using this method. However, it is notable that surveys came a close second, with 17 (33.3 percent) studies, followed by experiments, at nine studies (17.6 percent). A smaller number of studies used secondary data analysis and qualitative approaches. No studies were purely conceptual in nature. Based on these results, it is clear that a variety of analytical techniques is being used.

While content analysis was still the most frequently used technique, it is clear that surveys are now used with almost equal frequency, thus supporting RQ4b, which asked whether surveys are commonly used in cross-national advertising research. Similarly, the answer to question RQ4c,

Table 1.7   Data collection technique

	Number	Percentage
Content Analysis	18	35%
Experiment	9	18%
Survey	17	33%
Conceptual	0	0%
Qualitative	3	6%
Secondary Data Analysis	4	8%
Other	0	0%

which asked if experiments are commonly used in cross-national advertising research, is in the affirmative.

In analyzing these results, it is worth drawing a comparison to Taylor's (2005) analysis of the previous ten years of cross-national articles in *Journal of Advertising*. Interestingly, content analyses accounted for a very large percentage of studies (34 percent), as found here. Meanwhile, surveys accounted for just 22 percent of studies and experiments accounted for 25 percent of the studies. While the Taylor (2005) analysis is from a single journal, it is nonetheless apparent that the proportion of content analysis has remained relatively stable while the proportion of studies that are surveys has increased. Meanwhile, and somewhat surprisingly, experiments account for just 16.6 percent of studies. Thus, while the overall results are indicative of a wide variety of data collection techniques being used, content analyses still likely account for a higher proportion of studies that would be ideal. Granted, content analyses that examine a new or unique phenomenon can help identify a useful framework or describe an existing state of affairs. However, the technique has the weakness of not being effective in testing theories or providing evidence of the underlying process that explains why the phenomenon being investigated occurs.

The increase in the proportion of studies that used survey data over the past six years is an encouraging trend in that this had been an under-represented data collection technique. However, the decline in the proportion of studies that are experiments is concerning. It is apparent that there continues to be a need for more experimental studies. Qualitative studies also appear to be somewhat under-represented. While there were no conceptual studies published on the topic of interest published in the set of journals analyzed, this is likely a function of the rigor involved at the journals sampled, and indicative of the expectation of multiple contributions. Hence, it does not appear to be a problematic issue.

Research question 4d posed the question of whether multi-method

Table 1.8   Multi-method study

	Number	Percentage
Yes	9	18%
No	42	82%

Table 1.9   Primary theory base

	Number	Percentage
Cultural	20	39%
Social Science (Consumer Behavior, Psychology, Communications, Sociology)	22	43%
Grounded Theory	2	4%
No Theory Base	7	14%

studies are frequently used in cross-national advertising research. Table 1.8 indicates that nine studies (18 percent) did so. This suggests that, while such studies are not uncommon, there is room for more such studies.

RQ5: Theory Bases

The fifth set of research questions dealt with the theory bases used (see Table 1.9). RQ5a examines which theory bases are most commonly used. Table 1.9 shows that cultural bases are used as the primary basis for hypotheses in 39 percent of the studies, while theories from the social sciences were used 43 percent of the time. A few studies used grounded theory, and seven (14 percent) did not provide a theoretical perspective. Thus, while cultural bases are still commonly used, theories from the social sciences are now being applied more often than in the past, thereby answering RQ5b in the affirmative. Overall, the mix of cultural bases and other theoretical approaches has improved and is likely helping to advance research on global and cross-cultural advertising.

RQ6: Analytical Techniques

The sixth research question examines which analytical techniques are used in cross-national advertising research. Table 1.10 shows that regression was the most common technique (31 percent), followed by t-tests (27 percent), analysis of variance (10 percent), and structural equations modeling (10 percent) and cluster analysis (10 percent). Qualitative techniques and factor

Table 1.10 Primary analytical technique

	Number	Percentage
T-Tests	14	27%
ANOVA/MANOVA	5	10%
Regression	16	31%
Structural Equations Modeling	5	10%
Factor Analysis	2	4%
Cluster Analysis	5	10%
Qualitative Analysis	4	8%

Table 1.11 Use of a translation/back-translation procedure

	Number	Percentage
Yes	25	49%
No	4	8%
Same Native Language/No Need	18	35%
Administered In Non-Native Language	4	8%

analysis were also used as the primary technique in some studies. Thus, it is clear that a wide variety of analytical techniques are being applied to cross-national advertising research. This includes advanced techniques such as various forms of regression, structural equations modeling, cluster analysis and factor analysis. Given an overall trend toward structural equations being used more frequently in many marketing journals, it is somewhat surprising that structural equations are not used in more studies. However, with 10 percent of the studies using this technique, it is at least represented in the literature and suggestive that there may be a trend toward more such studies.

RQ7 and RQ8: Back-translation and Equivalence Tests

As Table 1.11 shows, of the 33 cross-national studies administered in countries where the native language is different, 25 employed back-translation, with four collecting data in another language without a back-translation, and another four collecting data in English from non-native speakers. Thus, more than three-quarters (76 percent) of these studies employed a back-translation, indicative of its status as accepted and normally necessary practice. Just 12 percent did not employ this technique for helping to ensure equivalence and 12 percent more simply administered an English survey everywhere. While it could be argued that the latter practice is

Table 1.12   Use of specific equivalence tests

	Number	Percentage
Configural	9	27%
Scalar	11	33%
Metric	15	45%

Table 1.13   Verification of cultural differences

	Number	Percentage
Yes	11	55%
No	9	45%

acceptable in settings such as graduate students taking their coursework in English or managers who are fluent in English, it is less than ideal in most settings as there is a good chance that information can be interpreted differently in a non-native language. Overall, however, it is clear that most cross-national advertising research is employing back-translations, consistent with the recommendations of Craig and Douglas (2005).

In terms of post hoc equivalence test, Table 1.12 shows that several studies measured configural (27 percent), scalar (33 percent) and metric equivalence (45 percent). While these numbers do not represent a majority, it is nonetheless clear that more studies are running these analyses than was the case in the past. It is also notable that metric equivalence is the most common type of equivalence test run by a significant margin.

RQ9: Verifying the Existence of Cultural Differences

Research question 9 looks at whether studies that propose that cultural variables underlie differences in reaction to advertising in two countries actually verify that these differences are present among the sampled subjects. As shown in Table 1.13, 11 of the 20 studies that used cultural dimensions verified that the cultural differences actually existed in the samples. Thus, while a slight majority of the studies that use cultural dimensions performed such checks, almost half did not.

RQ10: Types of Subject

The final research question examines the relative frequency of student vs. non-student subjects in cross-national advertising studies. As is shown in

Table 1.14   Type of subject

	Number	Percentage
Students	14	27%
Non-Students	18	35%
Students and Non-Students	1	2%
No Subjects	18	35%

Table 1.14, of those studies that used subjects, non-student samples were used in 18 (55 percent) of the studies while students were used in 14 (42 percent), and the remaining study (3 percent) used a combination of students and non-students. These results suggest a substantial increase in the use of non-student subjects. This is perhaps owing to editor and reviewer preferences for more generalizable samples.

CONCLUSION

The content analysis results suggest that considerable progress has been made in cross-national advertising research in terms of accepted procedures for collecting reliable and valid data. A substantial number of studies where cross-national data was collected were found indicative of considerable interest in this topic, which bodes well for advances in academic knowledge. Yet, there is also evidence that additional progress could be made.

Some general observations are summarized as follows:

- Major advertising journals and international marketing journals are the most common outlets for cross-national advertising studies. While this is a positive development, the research would receive a higher profile if more such studies appear in leading general marketing journals.
- A wide variety of countries and regions are being studied. However, relatively few studies that focus directly on issues in Latin America, the Middle East and Africa have been conducted. Moreover, India is a large market on which only a very limited number of comparative studies have been conducted.
- Over time, this body of research has seen improved rationale for the selection of countries.
- More cross-national and cross-functional teams are conducting these studies than was the case in the past, a trend that will likely allow additional insight to be produced from the research.

- Though cultural dimensions are still a commonly used theory base for cross-national advertising research, other theoretical perspectives are now being commonly applied.
- A wide variety of data collection techniques is being used and content analysis does not dominate this area of research to the extent it once did. Content analysis and surveys are now the most common data collection techniques. Experiments lag behind and more experimental studies on cross-national advertising are needed.
- More studies than in the past are taking measures to ensure equivalence both before the data is collected and after it is collected. Still, more studies could run post hoc equivalence tests than are currently doing so.
- Some studies that use cultural dimensions as a basis for hypotheses still do not verify the existence of the cultural difference in the subject population. This is not good practice and such verification should become the norm rather than the exception.
- More studies are using non-student subjects than was the case before, leaving a nice mix of studies that use student and non-student populations.

The above results appear to be somewhat encouraging in terms of the future of international advertising research. Nevertheless, the discipline should recognize the need for both key guidelines to be followed in major studies and encourage a variety of approaches to be used. It appears likely that, in the case of issues such as equivalence testing and verifying that cultural differences apply to the samples, journals are increasingly insisting that these measures be taken. This is a trend that should continue and is likely to do so.

REFERENCES

Alden, D.L., J.E.M. Steenkamp and R. Batra (1999), 'Brand positioning through advertising in Asia, North America, and Europe: The role of global consumer culture', *Journal of Marketing*, **63** (1), 75–87.

Brislin, R.W. (1980), 'Translation and content analysis of oral and written materials', in H.C. Triandis and J.W. Berry (eds), *Handbook of Cross-Cultural Psychology: Methodology*, vol. 2, pp. 389–444. Boston, MA: Allyn & Bacon.

Calder, B.J., L.W. Phillips and A.M Tybout (1981), 'Designing research for applications', *Journal of Consumer Research*, **8**, 197–207.

Chan K., L. Lyann, S. Diehl and R. Terlutter (2007), 'Consumers' response to offensive advertising: A cross cultural study', *International Marketing Review*, **24** (5), 606–28.

Craig, C.S. and S.P. Douglas (2005), *International Marketing Research*, 3rd ed. New York: John Wiley & Sons.

Davila, V. and J. Rojas-Mendez (2001), 'Attitude toward advertising: Does the 7-factor model work in Chile?' *International Journal of Organizational Theory and Behavior*, **4** (1/2), 3–19.

Ewing, M.T., T. Salzberger and R.R. Sinkovics (2005), 'An alternative approach to assessing cross-cultural measurement equivalence in advertising research', *Journal of Advertising*, **34** (1), 17–36.

Ford, J.B., B. Mueller, C.R. Taylor and N. Hollis (2011), 'The tension between strategy and execution: Challenges for international advertising research. Globalization is much more than universal branding', *Journal of Advertising Research*, **51** (1 – supplement), 27–41.

Fam, K. and R. Groh (2007), 'Cultural values and effective executional techniques in advertising', *International Marketing Review*, **24** (5), 519–38.

Han, S. and S. Shavitt (1994), 'Persuasion and culture: advertising appeals in individualistic and collectivistic societies', *Journal of Experimental Social Psychology*, **30** (4), 326–50.

Harkness, J.A., J.R. Fons, J.R. Van de Vijver and P.P. Mohler (2003), *Cross-Cultural Survey Methods*, Hoboken, NJ: John Wiley & Sons.

Hofstede, G. (1980), *Culture's Consequences: International Differences in Work-Related Values*, Newbury Park, CA: Sage.

House, R.J., P.J. Hanges, M. Javidan, P.W. Dorfman and V. Gupta (2004), *Culture, Leadership, and Organizations: The GLOBE Study of 62 Societies*. Beverly Hills, CA: Sage.

Milner, L. (2005), 'Sex-role portrayal in African television advertising: A preliminary examination with implications for use of Hofstede's research', *Journal of International Consumer Research*, **17** (2/3), 73–91.

Miracle, G.E. (1984), 'An assessment of progress in research in international advertising', *Current Issues and Research in Advertising*, **2**, 135–66.

Miracle, G.E. (1988), 'An empirical assessment of the usefulness of the back-translation technique for international advertising messages in print media', in John D. Leckenby (ed.), *Proceedings of the 1988 Conference of the American Academy of Advertising*, RC51–RC54.

Moriarty, S.E. and T.R. Duncan (1991), 'Global advertising: Issues and practices', *Current Issues and Research in Advertising*, **13** (1/2), 313–41.

Okazaki, S. and B. Mueller (2007), 'Cross-cultural advertising research: Where we have been and where we need to go', *International Marketing Review*, **24** (5), 499–518.

Pollay, R. and B. Mittal (1993), 'Here's the beef: Factors, determinants, and segments in consumer criticism of advertising', *Journal of Marketing*, **57** (3), 99–114.

Schudson, M. (1984) *Advertising, the Uneasy Persuasion: Its Dubious Impact on American Society*, New York: Basic Books.

Steenkamp, J.E.M. and H. Baumgartner (1998), 'Assessing measurement equivalence in cross-national consumer research', *Journal of Consumer Research*, **25** (2), 78–90.

Taylor, C.R. (2002), 'What is wrong with international advertising research?' *Journal of Advertising Research*, **42** (6), 48–54.

Taylor, C.R. (2005), 'Moving international advertising research forward: A new research agenda', *Journal of Advertising*, **34** (1), 7–16.

Thompson, C.J. (1997), 'Interpreting consumers: A hermeneutical framework for deriving marketing insights from the texts of consumers' consumption stories', *Journal of Marketing Research*, **34** (4), 438–55.

Yang, C. (2000), 'Taiwanese students' attitudes towards and beliefs about advertising', *Journal of Marketing Communications*, **6** (3), 171–83.

Zinkhan, G.M. (1994), 'International advertising: A research agenda', *Journal of Advertising*, **23** (1), 11–15.

Zou, S. and S.T. Cavusgil (2002), 'The GMS: A broad conceptualization of global marketing strategy and its effect on firm performance', *Journal of Marketing*, **66** (4), 40–56.

2 Understanding the role of culture in advertising

Wei-Na Lee and Jinnie Jinyoung Yoo

INTRODUCTION

Countries around the world today are connected into a global community. Changes that take place in one part of the world almost always impact the rest of the world. These changes can be political. For example, in early 2011, the political uprising that first erupted in Egypt quickly rippled through the mid East with protests in several other countries. Economic changes such as China surpassing Japan as the world's second largest economy in 2010 are felt globally. During the same year, the economic meltdown that started in Greece and triggered domino effects in Portugal, Ireland, Italy and Spain is another prime example of this connectedness. In a globally connected world, countries are increasingly dependent on one another for survival and growth.

In his book titled *The Post-American World*, Fareed Zakaria (2008) alluded to "a great transformation taking place around the world" (p. 1). He remarked that there is a diffusion of power from what used to be a single superpower to many countries around the world and called this the "rise of the rest". In other words, many countries around the world have experienced significant economic growth in recent years. This has resulted in an increase in consumption power for people in many places. Instead of the G-8, we now have the G-20 representing the world's economies. Along with this development is, inevitably, the rise of competition in the global marketplace and changing consumer demands in product offerings, quality, services and benefits.

Business expansion has become a vital tactic for companies to remain competitive both locally and globally. This can be seen through US companies actively pursuing various business development approaches such as brand alliance, venture capital, and mergers and acquisitions (Pekar and Allio 1994; Trendsetter Barometer 2010). The accompanying marketing communication efforts therefore need to focus on engaging consumers who are part of an instantaneously connected global community and world economy.

Since advertising follows business expansion around the world, there is also a similar "rise of the rest" phenomenon in advertising. We can see this by examining advertising expenditures. In 2010, US ad expenditures are estimated to account for less than half of world ad expenditures (Associated Press 2010; Carat 2007). In contrast, prior to the 1950s, global ad spending reflects primarily US advertising spending (Mueller 1998). This shift should not be seen as American advertisers pulling away from advertising. Instead, it is more a reflection of companies from other countries having entered the global marketplace.

Given the above, a major challenge for today's advertising is to understand the role of culture in the process of persuasive communication. Such an understanding will allow us to better communicate with global consumers and help business stay competitive. Therefore, the goal of this chapter is to assess our current understanding of the role of culture in advertising. In the sections below, we first explain advertising from the perspective of persuasive communication. Using the communication framework, we then describe a longitudinal assessment of research on advertising related issues when two or more cultures are the focus of investigation. We also identify the major theoretical underpinnings. We conclude by suggesting areas in need of future research attention.

CULTURE IN THE PROCESS OF ADVERTISING – THE COMMUNICATION MODEL

Culture is the lens through which we see the world (McCracken 1986). It influences the way we think, feel and behave. People within a culture tend to have many things in common. More often than not, they tend to be somewhat different from people in other cultures. The globalization of the marketplace calls for an understanding of similarities and differences between cultures in order to facilitate effective communication with consumers around the world. This sentiment is echoed by Shavitt, Lee and Johnson (2008) when they state, "Cultural distinctions have been demonstrated to have important implications for advertising content, persuasiveness of appeals, consumer motivation, consumer judgment process and consumer response style" (p. 1103). We concur that, since the goal of advertising is to engage consumers, wherever they are, there is a need to examine the role of culture in each step of the communication process.

Advertising has been defined in many ways. Richards and Curran's summary definition (2002) suggests that: "Advertising is a paid, mediated form of communication from an identifiable source, designed to persuade the receiver to take some action, now or in the future" (p. 64). Other than the persuasive intent and paid nature, this definition of advertising describes a process that parallels the traditional view of how communication takes place. It can therefore be argued that advertising is the process of persuasive communication on behalf of a brand.

Communication scholars and theorists have, for years, created, borrowed and adapted models from other disciplines in order to better explain the process of communication and its effects (Casmir 1994; Griffin 1994). One of the oldest models is the S-M-C-R view of communication (Berlo 1960). The key components of this four-segment model are: the source or the sender (S), the message (M), the channel (C) and the receiver (R). The model has been used as a basis for numerous communication studies with varying emphases on one or several of the components (McQuail and Windhahl 1993; Neuliep 1996). Succinctly put, the process of communication is one where senders (S) encode messages (M), verbally or non-verbally, using their choice of channels (C) to receivers (R) who decode them (Berlo 1960). Similarly, in advertising, each of these four components plays an important role in helping achieve the desirable, thus effective, communication outcome. This classic model not only provides a useful framework for conceptualizing the important factors influencing the persuasive communication process (Wilkinson 2005); it also serves as a parsimonious scheme to help us organize our understanding of how culture permeates each step of the process.

THE LONGITUDINAL CONTENT ASSESSMENT

In order to provide a summary assessment of our current knowledge of the role of culture in advertising, we carried out a longitudinal content assessment of cross-cultural advertising research published in four leading advertising journals from 1980 to 2009. The four journals are *Journal of Advertising*, *Journal of Advertising Research*, *International Journal of Advertising Research*, and *Journal of Current Issues and Research in Advertising*. We selected them because of their specific focus on advertising as well as their theoretical and practical orientations toward understanding the practice of advertising. We subsequently identified cross-cultural advertising articles (i.e., articles including two or more cultures in their investigation) and further categorized them according to the four key components of the process of persuasive communication. This approach allows us to find out what aspects of advertising have been examined to what extent and with what theories in a systematic manner.

It should be noted that this content assessment is neither a new nor a first endeavor in the field. Similar efforts with different emphases and time

Table 2.1   Cross-cultural articles by S-M-C-R communication component

Topics	Total Appearance	Articles with Theories
Source	18 (14.3%)	3 (5.3%)
Message	**59 (46.8%)**	**30 (52.6%)**
Channel	11 (8.7%)	7 (12.3%)
Receiver	25 (19.8%)	15 (26.3%)
Others	13 (10.3%)	2 (3.5%)
– Regulation	5 (4.0%)	
– Measurement Issues	5 (4.0%)	
– Accounts & Budgeting	2 (1.6%)	
– Sales Promotion	1 (0.8%)	
Total	**126 (100%)**	**57 (100%)**

frames have been made before (Taylor 2005; Zinkhan 1994; Zou 2005). For example, Taylor (2005) examined the trend of international advertising studies published in the *Journal of Advertising* between 1994 and 2004. He observed that only 12 percent (four articles) of published advertising research dealt with global or multiple countries. More recently, Okazaki and Mueller (2007) carried out a citation analysis of cross-cultural advertising articles published in major marketing and business journals from 1995 to 2006. They summarized countries investigated, topics addressed and research methods employed in those articles. In addition, they discussed the relative contributions of major theories to international advertising and marketing research. These past efforts have yielded important insights. The content assessment we report here should therefore be viewed as a follow-up to supplement previous research.

Between 1980 and 2009, a total of 4292 research articles were published in the four major advertising journals. Among them, 126 (2.9 percent) articles are deemed cross-cultural because they included two or more cultures and studied some aspects of cross-cultural issues in advertising. We classified the main focus of those cross-cultural advertising research articles according to the four components of the S-M-C-R communication model. This resulted in 113 articles with topics related to communication components, while the other 13 articles dealt with topics aside from communication. In addition, whenever possible, we identified up to three theories for each study. Table 2.1 provides a summary of the breakdown according to the S-M-C-R classification.

Our assessment shows that among the 126 cross-cultural articles examined, almost half of them (57, or 45.2 percent) employed at least one theory or a theoretical framework in their investigation. Since each article may have up to three theories identified, we recorded a total of 100 instances of theory use. Among them, the most frequently applied theory is Hofstede's "Dimensions of Culture" (1980, 1983 and 2001) with 36 instances (36 percent). Specifically, individualism and collectivism was the dimension used most often with 31 instances (31 percent). Meanwhile, Hall's postulation of "High vs. Low Cultural Context" (1966, 1976) has 23 instances (23 percent) and is also a frequently consulted theory in cross-cultural advertising research. This confirms observations from previous research on the reliance of few key theories in cross-cultural advertising research.

Below we describe each component of the persuasive communication process and key observations.

The Source

The first part of the advertising process is the source. The source is the place where the message originates (Tyagi and Kumar 2004). Generally speaking, the source component could be one person, a group of people, a company, an organization, or an institution. In advertising, the source of the message could mean the advertiser and/or the advertising agency. Source factors such as different levels of communication skills and knowledge, different cultures and different attitudes toward the audience or the communication situation could influence subsequent components in the communication process and, eventually, the outcome (Tyagi and Kumar 2004). Furthermore, since the source must exist in a socio-cultural environment, various aspects in the society such as values, beliefs, cultures and religions could also exert an influence on the source (Berlo 1960).

Specific to the advertising process, source factors could be examined from two aspects: (1) the cultural background of the source personnel (such as management and the creatives) in terms of how it influences their beliefs, attitudes and behavior; or (2) the larger organizational cultures of the agency and the advertiser and the relationship between the two entities. The extent to which different parties involved in the process coordinate their functions and collaboration is important to our understanding of how communication decisions are made. When cross-cultural advertising is the focus, all of the factors discussed above will need to incorporate the additional layer of culture into their conceptualization.

Table 2.1 shows that among the 126 cross-cultural advertising research articles, 18 (14.3 percent) examined source-related issues. In terms of their specific topic areas, the most frequently researched topic was "advertising agency practice (13 articles)", followed by "company image and management issues (5 articles)". An example of agency practice study could be West's (1993) investigation of the personalities and prevailing processes regarding advertising creativity in the US, Canada and the UK. The study suggests that agency practice between countries tends to vary owing to differences in culture, industrial development, marketing orientation, and the scope and influence of advertising agencies. In addition, there are significant differences in the nature of the creative involvement and execution, and the perceived degree of freedom afforded to copywriters and art directors in the countries analyzed. Another study, for instance, conducted by Kaynak and Mitchell (1981) considered agency practice as it relates to marketing strategies. They compared and contrasted marketing communication practice in advertising agencies in Canada, the UK and Turkey based on the relative stages of economic development, culture and other marketing environmental factors. In addition, Kitchen and Schultz's five-country study (1999) on the implementation of IMC focuses on a specific strategic approach to advertising practice. Research on company image or management issues, on the other hand, has delved into topics such as the use of corporate advertising in different countries (McLeod and Kunita 1994) and the use of corrective advertising on company image (Gural and Kaynak 1984).

Among the 18 articles that focused on source related issues, only three employed theories, with two using either Hofstede's cultural dimensions or Hall's contextuality of culture. Moon and Franke's (2000) study is an example of how Hofstede's cultural dimensions as a theoretical framework is employed to study source-related issues. Their study examined cultural influences on agency practitioners' ethical perceptions between Korea and the US. Four of Hofstede's cultural dimensions were used to determine the relative positions of the two countries, which were then used to explain cross-cultural differences in ethical perceptions and practices.

As can be seen in our assessment of the source component of the communication process, about one-seventh of cross-cultural advertising studies in the four major advertising journals during the past 29 years have focused on agency practice. It appears that the amount of research devoted to this a has been quite limited. No doubt agency practitioners play a crucial role as sources of the advertising message. In this sense, it is reasonable that scholars have been interested in how agency practitioners' communication skills, perceptions, personalities and their managerial practices differ depending on their cultural backgrounds. However, the majority of these studies examined cross-cultural differences without theoretical explanations. This can be problematic because, without a theoretical foundation, we are not able to understand the fundamental reasons for differences that occur. Meanwhile, such studies become a random and oftentimes fruitless exercise to compare and contrast cultures around the world, in combinations of two, three, or four, and report differences.

While many studies that focus on source factors in advertising have examined agency personnel, few have looked into personnel issues on the advertiser's side or the relationship between the agency and the advertiser. Given that the practice of advertising is a collaborative endeavor and that the client has the overall decision-making power, such a relationship is an important one to consider. Unique to cross-cultural advertising, we need to carefully consider the interplay between organizational culture and the larger socio-cultural context. In this vein, the role of culture needs to go beyond that of a tool for sampling and into an integrated part of the overall theoretical formulation.

The Message

The communication message is encoded by the source. It reflects the source's attempt to transmit certain information to the targeted receivers. The message relies on three major factors: the message code, the content, and the treatment (Berlo 1960). Language and culture, for instance, are the code that serves as the broader context to anchor the messages. The content of the message includes the assertions, arguments, appeals and themes. Treatment refers to the way in which the decisions are made about how the message is to be conveyed. Put another way, the treatment of the message involves the decisions that the source makes in selecting and arranging the code and the content. For example, in advertising messages, company executives, managers or creative directors may select content that they think will be interesting to the target audience, words that they think the target audience will understand, or the overall tone and manner of the message deemed appropriate for the target audience. The treatment of the message therefore depends greatly upon the source's communication skills, attitudes, knowledge, and positions in the social systems and cultural backgrounds.

In advertising, a message is the packaging of the creative idea of communication. The success of advertising depends on how well the content of the message is crafted. Advertising messages include a combination of words, pictures, symbols, appeal and other types of communicative elements. Although words have long been considered the key element for an effective message, recent research has shown that other elements, particularly visual factors such as color, illustrations and designs, are equally, if not more, important (Tyagi and Kumar 2004). Advertisers therefore must combine various content elements and arrange them judiciously to achieve success (Tyagi and Kumar 2004). Needless to say, message treatment decisions must come from a thorough understanding of the target consumers, their cultural orientations, ability, lifestyle, knowledge and attitudes.

Our assessment reveals that close to half of the 126 cross-cultural research articles (59, or 46.8 percent) studied message-related issues (see Table 2.1). "Advertising Appeals" (16 articles, or 27.1 percent) is the most frequently researched topic, followed by "Informational and Emotional Contents" (10, or 16.9 percent), "Cultural Values" (7, or 11.9 percent) and "Portrayals" (9, or 15.3 percent). While many articles analyzed the most popular or the most effective advertising appeals from culture to culture and compared them according to consumer perceptions or cultural values (e.g., Lepkowska-White, Brashear and Weinberger 2003), several articles focused on one advertising appeal and examined how it is used differently across cultures (e.g., Weinberger and Spotts 1989).

Over half (30, or 52.6 percent) of the articles that examined message-related factors employed theories to support their investigation. Nineteen of those articles employed Hofstede's cultural dimensions as the major theoretical framework. Instead of simply using cultural dimensions for sample decisions, Cho et al. (1999), for instance, developed a cross-cultural content analysis framework to examine the underlying cultural dimensions and contextuality, and compared US and Korean television commercials. In addition to Hofstede's framework, many message-related articles (15, or 26.3 percent) also used Hall's classification of high vs. low cultural context as their major theoretical perspective. Taylor, Miracle and Wilson (1997), for example, compared the effectiveness of television commercials with varied levels of information content (high vs. low) in the US and Korea.

Since it has long been the consensus that patterns of communication are closely linked to cultural values and that communication messages in a country tend to reflect its culture, the use of Hofstede's dimensions or Hall's contexts of cultures as theoretical underpinnings to explain advertising appeals, informational and emotional contents and cultural cues in the advertising messages, is expected. For example, advertising messages in individualistic cultures place a high value on individuality, independence, success and/or self-realization and benefits to one's own self (Cho et al. 1999). On the contrary, advertising messages in collectivistic cultures reflect interdependence, family integrity, group well-being, concern for others and group goals (Belk and Bryce 1986; Han and Shavitt 1994; Miracle et al. 1992; Mueller 1987). In addition, Hall's theory helps explain that contextual differences may lead to differences in new product diffusion patterns (Takada and Jain 1991), strategies for brand image creation (Roth 1992) and advertising message strategies (Miracle, Chang and Taylor 1992; Mueller 1987).

Besides the verbal messages, it is also important to note that recent research has focused on non-verbal messages such as visual contents, music, symbols and so on in advertising. In particular, visual messages in advertising have been found to be more easily and quickly processed and more effective in getting attention and stimulating curiosity than verbal messages (Berger 1998; Lester 2000; Wells et al. 2003). Visuals in ads are not only the major form of message delivery, but they are likely to be scanned first and considered as an important criterion for making purchase decisions (Smith 1991). Cross-cultural differences in the presentation of visual contents in advertising have also been studied during the last 10 to 15 years. For example, in our sample of articles, ads in high-context cultures have been found to have indirect, subtle forms of visual presentation such as symbols, metaphors and aesthetic expressions (An 2007; Bulmer and Buchanan-Oliver 2004).

The success of advertising depends greatly on how well the content of the message is created and arranged. This is likely the reason why more than half of cross-cultural research in the four major advertising journals focused on message issues. Although, earlier on, most of the research tends to analyze appeals and verbal contents in advertising, our assessment suggests that scholars have recently started to uncover cross-cultural differences in the uses and effects of more diverse advertising contents including both verbal and non-verbal cues.

The Channel

Communication messages are typically created for delivery through a specific channel or medium. In mass communication, the channel of delivery typically includes various media such as television, radio, newspapers and magazines. Characteristics of the media oftentimes influence the accuracy of and efforts associated with delivering different types of message (Byron 2008). In other words, each media type has its inherent characteristics that make it more or less appropriate for a certain type of message (Daft and Lengel 1986).

In advertising, traditional media such as television, radio, magazines and newspapers have been the commonly used channels for message delivery. However, during the past decade, the Internet has quickly evolved into a major communication channel. The Internet combines the broad reach of mass media with the persuasive characteristics of interpersonal communication by allowing for interaction between the source of the message and the receiver. The Internet possesses greater ability than other mass communication channels ever had in delivering messages that can be acted upon by the receivers quickly (Cassell et al. 1998).

Among cross-cultural advertising research articles published during the past three decades, only 11 (8.7 percent) articles studied channel related issues. Regarding the specific topic areas the articles examined, four articles examined new media issues (i.e., the Internet and SMS) while three articles examined product placement or brand placement in movies. Similar to the two previously mentioned communication components, most channel-related studies also elected to use Hofstede's cultural dimensions or Hall's context of cultures as the underlying theoretical framework. Cho and Cheon (2005), for instance, examined cultural differences in interactive functions on corporate websites in Eastern and Western cultures. Eastern advertisers seem more likely to take advantage of the Internet's capabilities for group discussion and activities among consumers, but are less likely to provide consumers with interactive messages about products or functions to interact with advertisers. La Ferle, Edwards and Mizuno (2002), on the other hand, examined the adoption of the Internet in Japan and the US to understand potential underlying factors in the diffusion process.

It is evident that a very small number of cross-cultural studies in the four major advertising journals examined issues related to the media. Furthermore, when compared to topic areas such as the message and the receiver, the theoretical foundation found in articles dealing with media issues is relatively weak. This is similar to research in the source area. Even when theories are applied, they were mainly used for classification purpose, instead of explanation. If media characteristics make them more or less appropriate for a certain type of message, it seems intuitive that we should have an in-depth understanding of media-related issues. Specifically, the fit between the message and media type as well as cultural factors that influence this fit deserve a closer look. In addition, media in different cultural environments may have distinctive characteristics in terms of availability, control, cost structure, usage pattern and trust. Because of these complex local environment factors, media is likely to be the one among the four components of communication that offers less flexibility for standardization practice. More importantly, since the Internet has become the most important channel for global communication, research into its diffusion, usage, control and various platforms' impact is urgent. Unfortunately, our assessment suggests that our understanding of these issues is very limited. Given the importance of the channel in the overall communication process and the rapid growth of new media, this is definitely an under-researched area with under-developed theories.

The Receiver

Receivers are the final component in the communication process. The receiver could be a person or persons who make up the audience for the message. The receiver may be the intended target or simply someone who is within the receiving range. Receivers attend to, interpret and respond to the transmitted message. Meanwhile, the goal of communication may be to generate awareness, deliver information, create an image for the product, brand and company or enhance the consumers' positive attitudes toward and purchase intention for the product (Tyagi and Kumar, 2004). As such, the goal of communication is considered accomplished when the receiver accepts the sender's message as intended.

Attention and comprehension are the primary means through which the receiver responds to the message. Attention is the process by which the receiver tunes into a message through reading, viewing and listening. The source must create the message in such a way that the receiver's attention is easily gained and retained. In a similar vein, the source must make up message content and treatment that will help the receiver understand the message and facilitate its processing. Once the receiver attends to and comprehends the message content, his or her next task may be to react to the message on at least one of the three levels: cognitive (the receiver accepts the message content as true), affective (the receiver believes that the message is not only true but good) and overt action (the receiver believes the message is true, believes it is good, and takes the appropriate action) (McQuil and Windahl 1993). With the communication goal(s) set, advertisers carefully study the demographic, psychographic, geographic and a number of other considerations of the target audience in order to frame the content and choose the media to transmit the communication appropriately.

Our content assessment reveals that 25 (19.8 percent) articles focused on issues related to the receiver. This can be seen in Table 2.1. The most frequently studied topics in receiver-related research are consumer attitudes toward or perceptions of advertising depending on their cultural values and their ability to understand or interpret advertising messages. Among the 25 articles, more than half (15 articles) incorporated theories. Hofstede's cultural dimensions (nine articles) are the most often used framework, followed by Hall's high vs. low context culture (six articles). Additionally, it is important to note that several articles that examined receiver-related issues used Ward's consumer socialization in conjunction with either Hofstede's or Hall's theory as the theoretical framework.

As expected, quite a few studies examined attitudes and behavior depending on consumers' cultural background. In this case, culture is used to distinguish one group from another. Culturally congruent appeals are generally more effective in terms of attitudes toward the advertisements and the brands. Since a receiver also interprets messages based on his or her communication skills, attitudes, knowledge, and social and cultural system (Lange 2000), a number of researchers have studied consumers' ability to understand and interpret advertising messages and how the ability varies depending on cultural background. The quasi-experimental study conducted by Schiffman and Callow (2002) is a good example. Using subjects from the Philippines and the US, they examined how contextual communication styles influenced the audience's ability to interpret meaning from pictorial advertisements. Hall's contextual typology was then applied to examine how consumers from different countries process visual messages in print advertisements.

An interesting observation on the assessment of receiver-related research is that since there is an abundance of theories that explain consumer response to persuasive messages, cross-cultural advertising research to date appears to be applying them to different cultural contexts to gain comparative understanding. In this way, the gain in knowledge largely lies in finding out how cultural forces affect consumers in the way they attend to, comprehend, process and react to persuasion within the set of cultures examined. In contrast, there is less advancement in terms of theory building or global scale understanding.

SUMMARY OF THEORIES AND SUGGESTIONS FOR FUTURE WORK

Not surprisingly, our content assessment reveals that Hofstede's classification of cultural dimensions and Hall's high vs. low context cultures have been the two major theories frequently employed by studies across all four components of the persuasive communication process. Among Hofstede's five dimensions, individualism and collectivism have received significant attention. Below we summarize the major theories.

Dimensions of Culture: Individualism and Collectivism

One of the highly respected theories in cross-cultural research was developed by Geert Hofstede (1980, 1983). Hofstede (1983) categorized five cultural dimensions: 1) power distance, the extent of tolerance of social inequality in a society; 2) uncertainty avoidance, a culture's attitude towards risk; 3) individualism/collectivism, the extent to which a culture is characterized by either more emphasis on individual self-interest or on collective community interest; 4) masculinity/femininity, a culture's achievement orientation; and 5) long vs. short-term orientation, a society's "time horizon", or the importance attached to the future versus the past and present. Among these five cultural dimensions, individualism/collectivism has been adopted most frequently by researchers in cross-cultural studies (Kirkman, Lowe and Gibson 2006).

According to Hofstede (2001), individualism is represented by autonomous and independent individuals who are more or less detached from a group (e.g., loosely tied to a group). For example, in individualistic cultures such as those in some European countries and North America, individuals prefer independent relationships to each other and individual goals and needs take precedence over group goals (Zhang and Gelb 1996). In contrast, collectivism is focused on group interdependence and cohesiveness. In a collectivistic culture, individual goals and needs are likely to be subservient to or indistinguishable from group goals and needs. In general, people in Asia, Africa and Latin America are assumed to have an interdependent relationship with one another within a collectivity.

In individualistic cultures, self-esteem and self-reliance are encouraged as desirable social values (Triandis 1989). Members of individualistic cultures do not make sharp distinctions between in-group and out-group members, unlike those of collectivistic cultures. Instead, individualistic cultures consider it important to keep an independent and consistent individual identity, regardless of the external situations (Triandis et al. 1988). This orientation encourages individualistic people to develop and reward an individual-oriented focus. In contrast, collectivistic cultures tend to associate individual attitudes with in-groups' norms, values and goals. Accordingly, people in collectivistic cultures acquire a sense of achievement when they fulfill a group goal. One product of collectivistic social values is the self-effacing attitude while conforming to group norms.

Contexts of Culture: High and Low

The context of cultures is another well-recognized concept on culture and communication (Hall 1966, 1976). Context refers to the background and circumstances where a communication event occurs (Cho 2010). Context is commonly assimilated through previous interactions and relationships. A long-term relationship between two communicators heightens mutual knowledge of each other, such as habitual gestures and communication backgrounds, which is hidden rather than being articulated.

Context plays a central role in characterizing communication styles (Hall 1976). Given high context communication styles, communication codes in the absence of context can be incomplete and, accordingly, common experiences and understanding among communicators are often required. Hall (1976) stated that in high context cultures the implicit message might be more important than the spoken and written words. A high context communication or message is one in which most of the information is already in the person, while very little is in the coded, explicit, transmitted part of the message. On the contrary, in low context cultures, meaning is dependent more on external information and rules than on internal information. Accordingly, information and meaning in conversations are applicable to any situation and translatable across contexts. In other words, the mass of the information is vested in the explicit code (Hall 1976). Therefore, high context cultures are intuitive with indirect and ambiguous messages, whereas low context cultures are analytical with explicit, clearly articulated messages (Taylor, Miracle and Wilson 1997).

Compared to individualism and collectivism, Hall's classification of high and low context cultures has been adopted in a much narrower manner (Cho 2010). Given that culture can be comprehensively embedded within an individual's thoughts, values and behaviors, Hall's idea explains only the behavioral pattern in a certain culture. It is occasionally associated with cultural values of individualism and collectivism to clarify why such a behavioral pattern is preferred in a certain culture (Gudykunst et al. 1996). It is often limited to explaining differences in communication styles.

While individualism and collectivism facilitate our understanding of perceptions of the self and others and individuals' values, beliefs and norms about the relationship of self to groups, the high and low context cultural aspect articulates the differing communication styles of each culture (Cho 2010). Low context cultures are characterized by explicit and direct verbal expression. In comparison, high context cultures are depicted as privileging implicit and indirect verbal expression (Ting-Toomey 1988). Hall (1976) stated that people standardize what they pay attention to and what they ignore in interactions based on culture. In high context cultures, much meaning is derived from one's given context or internalized understandings rather than being explicitly articulated or transmitted through verbal communication.

While the theories summarized above are important, it is evident that we have not ventured far or sought to expand on them during the past three decades. Research in other areas might offer some guidance in this regard and help advance our knowledge. Below we suggest a few possibilities for future theoretical development.

Horizontal and Vertical Dimensions of Individualism and Collectivism

The horizontal and vertical aspects of social relationships may be a dimension that can help to further distinguish individualism and collectivism (Triandis 1995, 2001). In essence, both individualism and collectivism may be horizontal or vertical. The horizontal dimension assumes that people see themselves as being essentially equal or similar to others in their social relationships. In contrast, the vertical dimension highlights hierarchy as the key to social relationships. From this conceptualization, four types of culture can be identified: (1) Horizontal Individualism (HI-uniqueness) where people strive to be themselves and be unique; (2) Vertical Individualism (VI-achievement) where people endeavor to be distinguished and the best in competition with others; (3) Horizontal Collectivism (HC-egalitarian) where people value interdependence, harmony and common goals with others; and (4) Vertical Collectivism (VC-deference) where people yield to authorities of the in-group and are willing to sacrifice themselves for their in-group (Triandis 2001; Triandis and Suh 2002). Although all individualistic people share the tendency of being independent and giving more priority to personal goals over group goals, HI people (e.g., Sweden) have little interest in acquiring high status, unlike those in VI (e.g., the US). Likewise, although HC people (e.g., Israeli kibbutz) respect group goals, they do not simply give in to authorities; much different from those in VC (e.g., Korea).

Shavitt et al. (2006) have demonstrated that ads that focused on status, prestige, hierarchy and distinction were more effective at generating consumer response in vertical cultures but not so with consumers of a horizontal orientation. Since congruence between cultural orientation and message content is generally considered most likely to produce the desirable consequent effects among consumers, it would be helpful for scholars to consider testing advertising message effectiveness along the four categories of horizontal/vertical individualism/collectivism.

There is initial empirical evidence to support the viability of this four-way typology in detecting differences across national cultures (Nelson and Shavitt 2002). Unfortunately, it has been noted that the cultures we have studied to date are primarily of the vertical type (Shavitt et al. 2008). Country selection bias is also observed in our content assessment. A great deal of past research tends to be US centered. Other cultures included are likely a function of sampling convenience. Therefore, we have not sampled enough cultures to be able to map out these classifications clearly. Given today's global market, future work needs to seek understanding outside of the US and sample sufficient cultures with various orientations.

Situational Individualism and Collectivism

In Han and Shavitt's (1994) content analysis of magazine ads, Korean ads incorporated a significant amount of individualistic appeals whereas US ads exhibited plenty of collectivistic appeals. It seems that, although the dominant cultural orientation was always observed in each country, it was not to the exclusion of the other cultural orientation. Moreover, in another content analysis study of TV commercials, collectivistic executions such as conversation among people, people in harmony or working together, were observed to a comparable extent in both the US and Korea (Cho et al. 1999). In surveying managing directors of advertising agencies in Taiwan, Shao, Raymond and Taylor (1999) found that "westernized" value appeals were preferred over traditional value appeals. Additionally, "individualistic" appeals were found in a study on magazine ads targeting the X-Generation in China (Zhang and Shavitt 2003). These findings echo Mueller's (1987) remark that "differences observed tend to be differences in degree, not in kind. All appeal types were found in the advertisements of both countries [Japan and the US] but to varying degrees" (p. 57).

From the above observations of advertising messages, it could be that advertisers intuitively know that they have to include both individualistic and collectivistic themes to a varying degree in order to communicate with consumers. If we consider culture as the collective programming of the mind (Hofstede 1980) and advertising as a reflection of the culture, any culture in today's environment is likely to be inclusive to a great extent. This suggests two things. First, individualism and collectivism may coexist in a society. Given today's easy access to news, information and entertainment from cultures around the globe, people are indeed fast becoming citizens of the world. Second, because individualism and collectivism may coexist, given a situation or other environment/contextual factors, a person's individualism or collectivism may become dominant. This could be an important implication for persuasive communication because it is possible for advertisers to prime consumers for a certain type of orientation and still achieve the same desirable outcome. Unfortunately, research to date has not fully considered such a possibility with sufficient evidence.

Individual Variations

In today's fast changing media environment, people rely on multiple frames of cultural reference simultaneously to construct their personal orientations (Lee and Choi 2007). Given these, it appears too simplistic to assume that everyone in the same culture adheres to the same pattern of thinking and behavior. In fact, people's cultural orientations within the same society could vary widely (Campbell 2000).

At the individual level, "idiocentrism" and "allocentrism" refer to personal individualism and collectivism respectively (Yamaguchi, Kuhlman and Sugimori 1995). From this perspective, a person's cultural orientation is not automatically equated to his or her cultural or national membership. In other words, at the individual level, a person's cultural orientation may not necessarily conform to the culture to which he or she belongs. There are those who possess individualistic characteristics (idiocentrics) in collectivistic cultures and those who show collectivistic tendencies (allocentrics) in individualistic cultures (Triandis, McCusker and Hui 1990). Both idiocentrics and allocentrics can be found in any given culture. However, as pointed out by Triandis and Suh (2002), the proportions of the two groups might vary given the dominant national orientation.

Since idiocentrics and allocentrics may be found in any society regardless of the dominant cultural orientation, it becomes more complex when we make comparisons across cultures. While individual differences have always been acknowledged, we simply have not delved into this issue sufficiently. If we consider an individual's idiocentric or allocentric tendency a chronic trait, what does it mean when we make cross-cultural comparisons along individualism and collectivism? Or, as suggested in the previous section, could this be a case indicating that individualism and collectivism are situational? Fundamentally, how do these postulations influence how advertising messages are constructed, transmitted and received by consumers in different cultures?

Understanding cultural similarities and differences is crucial to communicating with world consumers and developing effective cross-cultural advertising campaigns (Hudson, Hung and Padley 2002). Consumers respond favorably to advertising messages that are congruent with their cultural orientations, reward advertisers who understand their culture and tailor ads to reflect its values (Zhang and Gelb 1996). Although we have made great strides in research over the past three decades to untangle the relationship between culture and advertising, there are still more avenues to explore. The three possibilities discussed above are only some suggestions on how we might move forward.

CONCLUDING REMARKS

In this chapter, we set out to understand the role of culture in advertising. We reviewed a communication model that provides a scheme to help us gain a systematic understanding of the persuasive communication process that is advertising. We reported a longitudinal content assessment of cross-cultural advertising articles published in four major advertising journals based on the four-component communication view (S-M-C-R). Between 1980 and 2009, 4292 articles were published in the four advertising journals included in the content assessment. Among them, 126 articles reported advertising research on two or more cultures. Other than 13 articles on issues not central to the communication process, 113 articles were classified into one of the four components of communication. We then examined the topics of those articles and the extent of theoretical support and offered observations of research status under each component. Subsequently, we summarized major theories common across all four components by providing in-depth explanations and suggested additional theoretical development to guide future research.

While 57 (45.2 percent) out of 126 articles supported their investigations with theories, 23 of them used only one, 25 used two, while only nine incorporated 3 or more theories in their conceptualization. As such, theoretical explanations for many studies tend to be general and one-dimensional. Among the theories used, Hofstede's dimensions of culture and Hall's high and low contexts of culture have been used frequently among cross-cultural advertising studies across all four communication components. Oftentimes, theories are used to give rationale for classification of cultures and as a tool for selecting the countries to be included in the study (e.g., the individualism and collectivism dichotomy) instead of incorporating them into theoretical explanations for the phenomena of interest. Although research studies that reach out to theories other than the two major ones are less frequent, they should be worthwhile efforts and more like them should be done. For example, delving into the organizational behavior literature should be very helpful for understanding the intricacies among practitioners within the agency or the advertiser as well as the collaborative and functional relationship between the agency and the advertiser. Furthermore, research that integrates several theoretical perspectives and forms a framework to guide investigation is very much needed to provide more precise explanations.

It is not surprising that over half of the research articles (59, or 46.8 percent) were devoted to advertising messages, as they are the core of persuasive communication. We also observe a positive trend that message research has gradually moved from analyzing content materials to investigating message effectiveness. Studies in this area are also the ones that relied on theories the most compared to those in the other three component areas. Although not as many, articles on target audience constitute a good share of research attention at 22 percent. In contrast, research on communication channels (i.e., media) and sources (agency and/or advertisers) tends to have fewer articles with 11 (9.7 percent) and 18 (15.9 percent) respectively. Given the increasing trend toward globalized communication organizations and business expansion, research on the source of communication and, in particular, on organizational operation seems to be lagging behind. In addition, the rapid development in media technology that propelled the world into a connected community continues to evolve. This warrants significantly more research attention on media than what has been done in the past.

More than half of the cross-cultural research examined in this study (75 articles, or 58.7 percent) employed one or more media in data collection. Television is the most frequently used media, followed by magazines. Only seven (9.3 percent) articles utilized the Internet for their research. While this could be owing to the degree of difficulty in data collection, we need to be mindful of the limitations when television and magazines dominate. In a similar vein, in today's connected world of communication, the scarcity of Internet based investigation appears to be out of date. Future research will need to keep pace with technological innovation.

While there could be more issues to contemplate regarding the relationship between culture and advertising, this chapter provides a starting point. The effort to ascertain our state-of-the-knowledge by way of a content assessment of research during the past three decades gives us the opportunity to explore meaningful advancement.

REFERENCES

Aaker, J. (2000), 'Accessibility or diagnosticity? Disentangling the influence of culture on persuasion processes and attitudes', *Journal of Consumer Research*, **26** (4), 340–57.

An, D. (2007), 'Advertising visuals in global brands' local websites: A six-country comparison', *International Journal of Advertising*, **26** (3), 303–32.

Belk, R. W. and W. J. Bryce (1986), 'Materialism and individualism in U.S. and Japanese print and television advertising', *Advances in Consumer Research*, **13**, 568–72.

Berger, Arthur A. (1998), *Seeing is Believing: An Introduction to Visual Communication*. Mountain View, CA: Mayfield.

Berlo, David (1960), *The Process of Communication: An Introduction To Theory and Practice*. New York: Holt, Rinehart and Winston.

Bu, K., D. Kim and S. Lee (2009), 'Determinants of visual forms used in print advertising: A cross-cultural comparison', *International Journal of Advertising*, **28** (1), 13–47.

Bulmer, S. and M. Buchanan-Oliver (2006), 'Visual rhetoric and global advertising imagery', *Journal of Marketing Communications*, **12** (1), 49–61.

Bulmer, S. and M. Buchanan-Oliver (2006), 'Advertising across cultures: Interpretations of visually complex advertising', *Journal of Current Issues and Research in Advertising*, **28** (1), 57–71.

Bush, A. J., R. Smith and C. Martin (1999), 'The influence of consumer socialization variables on attitude toward advertising: A comparison of African-Americans and Caucasians', *Journal of Advertising*, **28** (3), 13–24.

Byron, K. (2008), 'Carrying too heavy a load? The communication and miscommunication of emotion by email', *Academy of Management Review*, **33** (2), 309–27.

Casmir, Fred L. (ed.) (1994), *Building Communication Theories: A Socio/Cultural Approach*. Hillsdale, NJ: Lawrence Erlbaum Associates.

Cassell, M. M., C. Jackson and B. Cheuvront (1998), 'Health communication on the Internet: An effective channel for health behavior change?' *Journal of Health Communication*, **3**, 71–9.

Campbell, A. (2000), 'Cultural identity as a social construct', *Intercultural Education*, **11** (1), 31–9.

Cho, S. E. (2010), *Cross-Cultural Comparison of Korean and American Social Network Sites: Exploring Cultural Differences in Social Relationships and Self-Presentation*. Retrieved from ProQuest Digital Dissertations (3397528).

Cho, B., U. Kwon, J. W. Gentry, S. Jun and F. Kropp (1999), 'Cultural values reflected in theme and execution: A comparative study of U.S. and Korean television', *Journal of Advertising*, **28** (4), 59–73.

Cho, C. H. and H. J. Cheon (2005), 'Cross-cultural comparisons of interactivity on corporate web sites', *Journal of Advertising*, **34** (2), 99–115.

Church, A. T. and W. J. Lonner (1998), 'The cross-cultural perspective in the study of personality: Rationale and current research', *Journal of Cross-Cultural Psychology*, **29** (1), 32–62.

Daft, R. L. and R. H. Lengel (1986), 'Organizational information requirements, media richness and structural design', *Manage. Sci.*, **32**, 554–71.

de Lange, Rudi (2000), 'Culture: A filtration process during communication in education', http://crm.hct.ac.ae/events/archive/tend/RudLP.html, accessed 5 February 2011.

Deutsch, K. (1952), 'On communication models in the social sciences', *Public Opinion Quarterly*, **16**, 356–80.

Gural, M. N. and E. Kaynak (1984), 'The effects of corrective advertising on company image: A cross-cultural study of the USA and Canada', *International Journal of Advertising*, **3** (2), 113–227.

Hall, Edward T. (1966), *The Hidden Dimension*. Garden City, NY: Doubleday.

Hall, Edward T. (1976), *Beyond Culture*. Garden City, NY: Anchor Press.

Han, S. P. and S. Shavitt (1994), 'Persuasion and culture: Advertising appeals in individualistic and collectivistic societies', *Journal of Experimental Social Psychology*, **30** (4), 326–50.

Hermeking, M. (2006), 'Culture and Internet consumption: Contributions from cross-cultural marketing and advertising research', *Journal of Computer-Mediated Communication*, **11**, 192–216.

Hofstede, Geert H. (1980), *Culture's Consequences: International Differences in Work-Related Values*. Beverly Hills, CA: Sage Publications.

Hofstede, G. H. (1983), 'National cultures in four dimensions: A research-based theory of cultural differences among nations', *International Studies of Management & Organization*, **13**, 46–75.

Hofstede, G. H. and M. H. Bond (1987), 'The Confucius connection: From cultural roots to economic growth', *Organizational Dynamics*, **16**, 4–21.

Hofstede, Geert H. (1991), *Cultures and Organizations: Software of the Mind*. London: McGraw-Hill.

Hofstede, Geert H. (1997), *Cultures and Organizations: Software of the Mind*. New York: McGraw-Hill International.

Hofstede, Geert H. (2001), *Culture's Consequences: Comparing Values, Behaviors, Institutions, and Organizations Across Nations*, 2nd ed. Thousand Oaks, CA: Sage.

Hudson, S., C. L. Hung and L. Padley (2002), 'Cross-national standardization of advertisements: A study of the effectiveness of TV advertisements targeted at Chinese Canadians in Canada', *International Journal of Advertising*, **21** (3), 345–66.

Kaynak, E. and L. A. Mitchell (1981), 'Analysis of marketing strategies used in diverse cultures', *Advertising Research*, **21** (3), 25–32.

Kirkman, B. L., K. B. Lowe and C. B. Gibson (2006), 'A quarter century of culture's consequences: A review of empirical research incorporating Hofstede's cultural values framework', *Journal of International Business Studies*, **37**, 285–320.

Kitchen, P. J. and D. E. Schultz (1999), 'A multi-country comparison of the drive for IMC', *Journal of Advertising Research*, **39** (1), 21–38.

Gerbner, G. (1956), 'Toward a general model of communication', *Audio-Visual Communication Review*, **4**, 171–99.

Griffin, Em (1994), *A First Look at Communication Theory*, 2nd ed. New York: McGraw-Hill.

Gudykunst, W. B., Y. Matsumoto, S. Ting-Toomey, T. Nishida, K. S. Kim and S. Heyman (1996), 'The influence of cultural individualism-collectivism, self-construals, and individual values on communication styles across cultures', *Human Communication Research*, **22**, 510–43.

La Ferle, C., S. M. Edwards and Y. Mizuno (2002), 'Internet diffusion in Japan: Cultural considerations', *Journal of Advertising Research*, **42** (2), 65–79.

Lackman, R. (1960), 'The model in theory construction', *Psychological Review*, **67**, 113–29.

Lee, Wei-Na and S. M. Choi (2007), 'Classifying web users: A cultural value based approach', in Kirk Amant (ed.), *Linguistic and Cultural Online Communication Issues in the Global Age*, pp. 45–62. Hershey, PA: Idea Group, Inc.

Lepkowska-White, E., T. G. Brashear and M. G. Weinberger (2003), 'A test of ad appeal effectiveness in Poland and the United States', *Journal of Advertising*, **32** (3), 57–67.

Lester, Paul M. (2000), *Visual Communication: Images with Messages*. Belmont, CA: Wadsworth.

McClelland, David C. (1987), *Human Motivation*. Cambridge: Cambridge University Press.

McCracken, G. (1986), 'Culture and consumption: A theoretical account of the structure and movement of the cultural meaning of consumer goods', *Journal of Consumer Research*, **13** (1), 71–84.

McLeod, D. M. and M. Kunita (1994), 'A comparative analysis of the use of corporate advertising in the United States and Japan', *International Journal of Advertising*, **13** (2), 137–52.

McQuail, Denis and Windhahl, Sven (1993), *Communication Models*. London and New York: Longman.

Miracle, G. E. (1992), 'Achieving reliable and valid results to support export advertising', *Wergeforschung & Praxis*, **4** (2), 134–41.

Miracle, G. E., K. Y. Chang and C. R. Taylor (1992), 'Culture and advertising executions: A comparison of selected characteristics of Korean and U.S. television commercials', *International Marketing Review*, **9** (4), 5–17.

Moon, Y. S. and G. R. Franke (2000), 'Cultural influences on agency practitioners' ethical perceptions: A comparison of Korea and the U.S.', *Journal of Advertising*, **29** (1), 51–65.

Mueller, B. (1987), 'Reflections of culture: An analysis of Japanese and American advertising appeals', *Journal of Advertising Research*, **27**, 51–9.

Mueller, Barbara (1996), *International Advertising: Communicating Across Cultures*. Belmont, CA: Wadsworth.

Mueller, Barbara (2004), *Dynamics of International Advertising*. New York: Peter Lang.

Nelson, M. R. and S. Shavitt (2002), 'Horizontal and vertical individualism and achievement values: A multimethod examination of Denmark and the United States', *Journal of Cross-Cultural Psychology*, **33** (5), 439–58.

Neuliep, James W. (1996), *Communication Theory: Applications & Case Studies*. Needham Heights, MA: Allyn & Bacon.

Okazaki, S. and B. Mueller (2007), 'Cross-cultural advertising research: Where we have been and where we need to go', *International Marketing Review*, **24** (5), 499–518.

Pekar, P. and R. Allio (1994), 'Making alliances work – guidelines for success', *Long Range Planning*, **27** (4), 54–65.

Richards, J. I. and C. M. Curran (2002), 'Oracles on "advertising": Searching for a definition', *Journal of Advertising*, **31** (2), 63–77.

Roth, M. S. (1992), 'Depth vs. breadth strategies for global brand image management', *Journal of Advertising*, **21** (2), 25–35.

Samovar, Larry A. and Richard E. Porter (1995), *Communication between Cultures*, 2nd ed., Belmont, CA: Wadsworth.

Shavitt, Sharon, Angela Y. Lee and Timothy P. Johnson (2008), 'Cross-cultural consumer psychology', in C. Haugtvedt, P. Herr and F. Kardes (eds), *Handbook of Consumer Psychology*, pp. 1103–31. Mahwah, NJ: Lawrence Erlbaum.

Shavitt, S., A. K. Lalwani, J. Zhang and C. J. Torelli (2006), 'The horizontal/vertical distinction in cross-cultural consumer research', *Journal of Consumer Psychology*, **16**(4), 325–42.

Shannon, Claude E. and Warren Weaver (1949), *The Mathematical Theory of Communication*. Urbana, IL: University of Illinois Press.

Schiffman, L. and M. Callow (2002), 'Implicit meaning in visual print advertisements: A cross-cultural examination of the contextual communication effect', *International Journal of Advertising*, **21** (2), 259–77.

Smith, R. (1991), 'The effects of visual and verbal advertising information on consumers' inferences', *Journal of Advertising*, **20** (4), 13–24.

Stern, B. B. (1994), 'A revised communication model for advertising: Multiple dimensions of the source, the message, and the recipient', *Journal of Advertising*, **23** (2), 5–15.

Takada, H. and D. Jain (1991), 'Cross-national analysis of diffusion of consumer durable goods in Pacific Rim countries', *Journal of Marketing*, **55** (2), 48–54.

Taylor, C. R. (2002), 'What is wrong with international advertising research?' *Journal of Advertising Research*, **42** (6), 48–54.

Taylor, C. R. (2005), 'Moving international advertising research forward', *Journal of Advertising*, **34** (1), 7–16.

Taylor, C. R., G. E. Miracle and R. D. Wilson (1997), 'The impact of information level on the effectiveness of U.S. and Korean television commercials', *Journal of Advertising*, **26** (1), 1–18.

Ting-Toomey, Stella (1988), 'Intercultural conflict styles: A face-negotiation theory', in Y. Y. Kim and W. B. Gudykunst (eds), *Theories in Intercultural Communication*, pp. 213–35. London: Sage.

Barometer, Trendsetter (2010), 'Strategic alliance and joint ventures success rate cited by CEO', http://www.1000ventures.com/business_guide/strategic_alliances_main.html, accessed 20 February 2011.

Triandis, H. C. (1989), 'The self and social behavior in differing cultural contexts', *Psychological Review*, **3**, 506–20.

Triandis, H. C., R. Brislin and C. H. Hui (1988), 'Cross-cultural training across the individualism-collectivism divide', *International Journal of Intercultural Relations*, **12**, 269–89.

Triandis, Harry C. (1995), *Collectivism and Individualism*. Boulder, CO: Westview Press.

Triandis, H. C. (2001), 'Individualism-collectivism and personality', *Journal of Personality*, **69**, 907–24.

Triandis, H. C., C. McCusker and H. C. Hui (1990), 'Multimethod probes of individualism and collectivism', *Journal of Personality and Social Psychology*, **59**, 1006–20.

Tyagi, C. L. and Arun Kumar (2004), *Advertising Management*. New Delhi: Atlantic.

Ward, S. (1974), 'Consumer socialization', *Journal of Consumer Research*, **1** (2), 1–14.

Weinberger, M. G. and H. E. Spotts (1989), 'Humor in U.S. versus U.K. TV commercials: A comparison', *Journal of Advertising*, **18** (2), 39–44.

Wells, William, John Burnett and Sandra E. Moriarty (2003), *Advertising: Principles and Practice*. Englewood Cliffs, NJ: Prentice-Hall.

West, C. D. (1993), 'Cross-national creative personalities, processes, and agency philosophies', *Journal of Advertising Research*, **33** (5), 52–60.

Wilkinson, J. (2005), 'Converging communication, colliding cultures: Shifting boundaries and the meaning of our field', *Proceedings from the Conference on Media Convergence: Cooperation, Collisions, and Change*, October 13–15, Provo, UT.

Wingenbach, Garry J. (2010), 'Communication/diffusion-adoption process', http://agcj.tamu.edu/howto/Communication.htm, accessed 10 February 2011.

Yamaguchi, S., D. M. Kuhlman and S. Sugimori (1995), 'Personality correlates of allocentric tendencies in individualist and collectivist cultures', *Journal of Cross-Cultural Psychology*, **26**, 658–72.

Zakaria, Fareed (2008), *The Post-American World*. New York: W. W. Norton & Company.

Zhang, J. and S. Shavitt (2003), 'Cultural values in advertisements to the Chinese X-generation', *Journal of Advertising*, **32** (1), 23–33.

Zhang, Y. and B. D. Gelb (1996), 'Matching advertising appeals to culture: The influence of products' use conditions', *Journal of Advertising*, **25** (3), 29–46.

3 Adoption of global consumer culture: the road to global brands

Ayşegül Özsomer

INTRODUCTION

The cultural influence of global brands has never been more important. In psychological terms, global brands are perceived as creating an identity, and a sense of achievement for consumers, symbolizing the aspired values of global consumer culture (GCC). Through the process of meaning transfer consumers internalize these values and ideals to their self-concept (McCracken 1986). On one hand, global brands carry the espoused values of the global culture, which reflects mostly the core values of Western societies, including freedom of choice, free market, and individual rights (Gupta and Govindarajan 2004); on the other hand, consumers actively create and add new meanings to global brands through a process of meaning co-creation.

Global brands are defined as brands that have widespread global awareness, availability, acceptance and demand, often found under the same name with consistent positioning, personality, look and feel in major markets enabled by centrally coordinated marketing strategies and programs (Özsomer and Altaras 2008). Global brands with their consistent positioning benefit from a unique perceived image worldwide. Consumers equate consumption of global brands with modernity, consumerism, progress, success, efficiency and a promise of abundance (Holton 2000). Consumers' preferences for global brands are positively associated with the extent to which they believe these brands are available around the world rather than being available only in the local markets (Steenkamp, Batra and Alden 2003). Such a global positioning increases in its strategic appeal as consumers around the world develop similar needs and tastes constituting global consumer segments, such as the affluent and teenagers (Hassan and Katsanis 1994; Özsomer and Simonin 2004; Ter Hofstede, Wedel and Steenkamp 2002).

Multinational corporations (MNCs) are positioned to benefit significantly from developing and leveraging global brands. In fact, many of the strategic actions of MNCs are fueling the growth of global brands. Focusing their marketing efforts on fewer global brands enables MNCs to concentrate resources on a portfolio of leading brands with strong *growth* potential that best meets the needs, aspirations and values of people around the world. For example, since its Path to Growth strategy was launched in 2000, Unilever has reduced the number of brands from 1600 to 400 leading brands and under 250 tail brands (www.unilever.com). Around the same time, P&G has also pruned its brand portfolio in favor of global brands (Pitcher, 1999), while in 2003 Heinz declared its intention to focus on a smaller number of "power brands" and selling many of its local brands. Similarly, Colgate Palmolive has invested a lot in making Colgate Total a global brand name.

These and many other companies are betting their futures on global brands, and consumers around the world from advanced to emerging economies are responding favorably. For example, 23 of P&G's and 13 of Unilever's brands have more than a billion dollars in net annual sales.[1] Similarly, Kraft has 11, Coca Cola 14 and PepsiCo 19 billion dollar brands.[2] The economic clout and success of global brands makes their study relevant for practitioners and academicians alike. The purpose of this chapter is to provide an overview of the relationship between the cultural underpinnings of consumers' attitudes towards global consumer culture and its manifestation in preference for global brands. Various cultural models are applied to consumer adoption of global consumer culture in which global brands are strongly embedded. We adopt a dynamic and reciprocal view of culture in which culture influences the individuals and the individuals influence the culture in which they operate (Hannerz 1992; Kitayama 2002). At the highest level, the global consumer culture influences individuals' values and behaviors, while at the same time individuals also influence the global consumer culture by adding new meaning through a process of identity and meaning co-creation. The combination of this top-down, bottom-up approach to culture's influences is in line with recent conceptualizations (e.g., Erez and Gati 2004; Kitayama 2002).

GLOBAL BRANDING AND CONSUMER CULTURE THEORY

We posit consumer culture theory (Arnould and Thompson 2005) as the common thread that underlies the *cultural* drivers of an individual's response to global brands.[3] Consumer culture theory (CCT) posits that, in a modern world, core identities are defined and oriented in relation to consumption (Holt 2002). Thus, consumer culture has been called "a culture *of* consumption" (Slater 1997, p. 8, emphasis in original). CCT explicates the process by which consumers actively appropriate and recontextualize the symbolic meanings encoded in marketer-generated goods and services to construct individual and collective identities (Grayson and Martinec 2004; Holt 2002; Kozinets 2001). The marketplace provides consumers with a rich palette of cultural and mythic resources to enact and personalize cultural scripts that align their identities with the structural imperatives of a consumer-driven global economy.

Globalization processes have given rise to a new cultural force, the global consumer culture (GCC) (Ritzer 2007; Steenkamp and De Jong 2010). Appadurai (1990) and Hannerz (1990) note that media flows, increased travel, rising incomes and other factors are creating widely understood symbols and meanings reflected in global brands, which in turn communicate membership in the global consumer community and culture (McCracken 1986). Global brands are regarded as symbols of cultural ideals and they not only compete in providing the highest quality but also in delivering cultural myths with global appeal (Holt, Quelch and Taylor 2004). Appadurai (1990, p. 299) argues that the potential for global brands to engender preference and transform meaning may depend on whether consumers believe global brands will enable them to "act out imagined or real participation in the more cosmopolitan global consumer culture communicated by the media" (see also Alden, Steenkamp and Batra 1999; Askegaard 2006). Thus, global brands offer consumers the opportunity to acquire and demonstrate participation in an aspired-to global consumer culture (Alden et al. 1999; Steenkamp et al. 2003) and help create an imagined global identity that they share with like minded people (Holt et al. 2004).

We propose that adoption of global consumer culture is linked to a person's belief in global citizenship and the desire to participate in the global village (Strizhakova, Coulter and Price 2008). As passports to global citizenship, global brands create a belief in a person's association with and participation in the global village (Strizhakova, Coulter and Price 2008). That is, consumers' adoption of global consumer culture increases the importance they associate with brands in general and global brands in particular (Strizhakova et al. 2008).

Recent research indicates that the relationship consumers have with global consumer culture and global brands is quite complex. While some consumers are attracted to the shared consciousness and the cultural meanings produced by globalization (Holton 2000) and appreciate the homogenization of consumer culture around a common set of traits and practices associated with the market economy (Alden, Steenkamp and Batra 1999; Steenkamp and de Jong 2010), others are turned off by the perceived homogenization of meanings and symbols that are regarded as empty and void of a connection to an origin or territory (Steenkamp and de Jong 2010). Still others combine the global and the local giving rise to "glocal" identities of many modern consumers (Strizhakova, Coulter and Price 2008; Ritzer 2004). For example, Kinra (2006) finds that Indian consumers exhibit favoritism for local brands while their evaluations and preferences for global brands are equally positive and strong. Thus, embracing GCC in which global brands are firmly embedded is an important driver of positive attitudes toward global brands (Steenkamp and de Jong 2010).

A further complexity arises from the fact that GCC possesses two contrasting aspects (Tomlinson 1999) for some consumers. On the one hand, there are manifest attractions of creating "'one-world' in the interests of peace . . . of the recognition of our 'common humanity'" inherent in global consumer culture. On the other hand, Tomlinson highlights the association of GCC with hegemony and power, particularly the dominance of Western values, lifestyles and brands in creating the GCC. Hence, consumers may have mixed feelings about GCC, embracing some of the universal values, while rejecting the others. This fragile complexity needs to be studied and developed further.

GLOBAL CONSUMER CULTURE

Why do consumers differ in their adoption of global consumer culture? While the literature proposes a wide array of constructs, we focus on the broadest, highest level and most universal motivational concept of values. Values are cognitive beliefs about desirable goals and modes of conduct to promote these goals, which vary in importance, and serve as standards to guide attitudes and behavior (Schwartz 1992). Schwartz (1992) identified ten different types of value recognized in cultures around the world. The universally-shared meaning of these values warrants their use for cross-cultural comparisons (Schwartz 1992) making them useful in understanding adoption of global consumer culture. Values serve as goal setting, guiding principles in people's lives that vary in importance and are central to self-identity (Eagly and Chaiken 1998; Verplanken and Holland 2002). As with attitudes, values can vary in level of abstractness, depending on the entity being evaluated (Ajzen 2001). According to Rokeach (1973, p. 122), a relatively small number of values "is conceived to underlie many if not all social attitudes; moreover, a given value is conceived to determine several or many attitudes and a given attitude to be determined by several or many values".

Cultures and individuals within cultures differ greatly in how much they have been affected by globalization in general (Arnett 2002) and global consumer culture in particular. Differences in acculturation depend on the

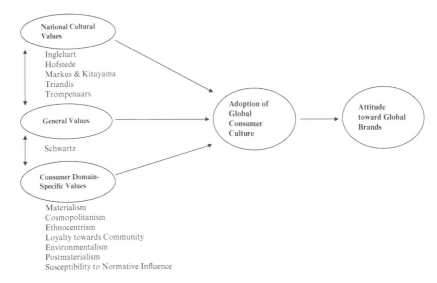

Figure 3.1   Adoption of global consumer culture: the road to global brands

extent to which individuals are attracted to the global consumer culture, and on how deeply they strive to maintain their own cultural identity (Berry 1980). Differences in openness to global consumer culture may be explained by cultural values at the national and individual level. The adoption of global consumer culture in turn manifests itself in the external and visible-level behaviors and artifacts of global consumer culture, such as the purchase and consumption of global brands. Steenkamp and de Jong (2010) distinguish among three levels of values: national cultural, general, and consumer domain-specific (see Figure 3.1). This classification is useful in understanding the adoption of GCC.

NATIONAL-CULTURAL VALUES

National-cultural values "reflect the different solutions that societies evolve to the problems of regulating human activities [and] the different ways that institutional emphases and investments are patterned and justified in one culture compared with another" (Schwartz 1994, p. 92). The shared value emphasis in a country helps shape the reward contingencies to which people must adapt in the institutions in which they spend most of their time (e.g., families, schools, businesses). As a result, the members of each nation share many value-relevant social experiences, and they come to accept similar values (Steenkamp and de Jong 2010, p. 22). Some countries may have higher endorsement of GCC because of systematic differences in their value systems.

Many national-cultural value system frameworks have been developed and proposed by Inglehart, Hofstede, Schwartz, Triandis and Trompenaars. Inglehart's framework (Inglehart and Baker 2000; Inglehart and Wetzel 2005) identifies four clusters of national-cultural values, which are organized in two bipolar dimensions: traditional versus secular–rational values and survival versus self-expression values. Countries low on the traditional/secular–rational dimension emphasize respect for authority, traditional family values and absolute standards. These societies have high levels of national pride and take protectionist and nationalist attitudes. Secular–rational societies' values have the opposite preferences on all these topics. Traditional societies' nationalism and protectionism are closely aligned with a focus on the local element in the consumer culture (Steenkamp and de Jong 2010) and are thus less embracing of the global consumer culture. The polar opposite implies that adoption of GCC should be, on average, higher in secular–rational societies.

Inglehart's second bipolar dimension classifies societies on their relative emphasis on survival versus self-expression values. The contrast between materialist and postmaterialist values is a key component of the survival/self-expression dimension (Inglehart and Welzel 2005). This means that values such as security, affluence and economic well-being are negotiated against values such as subjective well-being, quality of life and protection of the environment. In self-expression societies, "the 'quality of experience' replaces the quantity of commodities as the prime criterion for making a good living" (Inglehart and Welzel 2005, p. 25). Consequently, countries high on self-expression, on average, have a more negative attitude toward consumption of products as a way to bring meaning to life and thus are expected to be less favorable to global consumer culture. Indeed, in a recent 28-country study, Steenkamp and de Jong (2010) find higher attitudes toward global products in countries high on secular–rational values and lower attitudes towards global products in countries high on self-expression.

The Hofstede national-cultural values model (Hofstede 2001; Hofstede and Hofstede 2005) is the most widely used framework in the marketing and advertising literature (e.g., Dawar and Parker 1994; Roth 1995; Steenkamp, ter Hofstede and Wedel 1999). "Applying the model to branding and advertising, which originally sought answers to work-related value differences, needs conceptual insight in the various manifestations" that are relevant to these areas (De Mooij and Hofstede 2010, p. 104). The Hofstede model distinguishes cultures according to five dimensions: power distance, individualism/collectivism, masculinity/femininity, uncertainty avoidance, and long-/short-term orientation. The model provides scales from 0 to 100 for 76 countries for each dimension, and each country has a position on each scale or index, relative to other countries.[4]

While the dimensions have been studied extensively, often it is the *configuration* of dimensions that explains variation (de Mooij and Hofstede 2010). For example, high uncertainty avoidance cultures are low in innovativeness and the wish for change, but, combined with high power distance, appeals like modernity and innovation provide status. Since adoption of GCC implies real or imagined participation in the more cosmopolitan global consumer culture communicated by the media, such cultures (e.g., the Japanese: high power distance/high uncertainty avoidance) can demonstrate more favorable adoption of GCC because of the status signaled by membership in a global community of like-minded, modern people. High scores on masculinity and power distance explain status needs (de Mooij and Hofstede 2010). De Mooij and Hofstede (2010, p. 103) state that "In high power distance cultures, status brands demonstrate one's role in a hierarchy. In masculine cultures, status brands demonstrate one's success." When masculinity and power distance are high simultaneously, success and hierarchy needs are enhanced. This enhanced state could lead to embracing global consumer culture. Furthermore, value paradoxes need to be taken into account when applying the Hofstede model. Since many modern consumers may have a glocal orientation combining the global and local dimensions of values, the adoption of GCC may not be straightforward.

Despite the inherent richness in the Hofstede model, most research has exclusively focused on the individualism/collectivism dimension (Agarwal, Malhotra and Bolton 2010). Markus and Kitayama (1991, 1994) claimed that different conceptions of the self and of the relationship between the self and others constitute the most significant source of differences among cultures. Similar to individualism/collectivism at the national-cultural level, self-construal reflects the extent to which individuals view themselves as separate unique individuals (independent self-construal) or in relationship to other people or social groups (interdependent self-construal; Agrawal and Maheswaran 2005). Research indicates that the independent self-construal is dominant in Western cultures, while interdependent self-construal is dominant in Eastern cultures. Westerners are guided by their inner self, personal preferences, tastes, abilities, personal values, etc. (Wong and Ahuvia 1998). In contrast, Easterners tend to focus more on the collective self and how they are related to others. They identify themselves in terms of their familial, cultural, professional and social relationships.

It is important to note that the independent and interdependent concepts of the self can coexist within the individual (Aaker and Lee 2001; Brewer and Gardner 1996). In this sense, while the individual possesses the two types of self-construal, he or she is likely to rate higher on one of the two aspects of the self (Triandis 1989, 1994). Following this logic, Wong and Ahuvia (1998) argue that, since cultures cannot be considered homogeneous and individuals will vary in the extent to which their self concepts are independent or interdependent, global characterizations of cultures as collectivistic or as individualistic may be too simplistic. Furthermore, the ever-growing influence of the global consumer culture enables people to construct their own elective identities leading to significant within-country heterogeneity (Arnett 2002; Agarwal, Malhotra and Bolton 2010). Hence, the independent–interdependent framework provides a much needed intermediate step combining national-cultural values with individual-level values.

GCC will appeal to both independent and interdependent self-construal individuals but for different reasons. For independent self-construals, participating in the GCC will mean success, achievement and hedonism. For those who have an interdependent concept of the self, participating in GCC will mean status and signal his or her place in society.

Triandis (1994) and Triandis and Gelfand (1998) add to the individualism/collectivism distinction by further distinguishing between societies that are horizontal (valuing equality) and those that are vertical (emphasizing hierarchy) in their cultural orientation, refining the power distance dimension in Hofstede's model. American or British individualism differs from Australian or Norwegian individualism in much the same way that Chinese or Japanese collectivism differs from the collectivism of the Israeli kibbutz. In vertical individualist societies (VI; e.g., the U.S. and the U.K.), people strive to become distinguished and acquire status via competition; whereas in horizontal individualist cultural contexts (HI; e.g., Australia and Norway), people value uniqueness but are not especially interested in becoming distinguished and achieving high status. In vertical collectivist societies (VC; e.g., China and Japan), people emphasize the subordination of their goals to those of their in-groups, submit to the will of authority, and support competition between their in-groups and out-groups. Finally, in horizontal collectivist cultural contexts (HC; e.g., Israeli kibbutz), people see themselves as similar to others, emphasizing common goals with others, interdependence and sociability, but they do not submit to authority.

Triandis's contribution has implications for the adoption of GCC. A vertical individualist (VI) orientation is positively related to the endorsement of power values (Oishi, Schimmack, Diener and Suh 1998). People high in VI orientation give importance to displays of success and gaining of influence and strive to achieve power and status (Torelli and Shavitt 2010). As such, these individuals are more likely to embrace GCC and its consumption focus. Horizontal individualists (HI) value uniqueness but are not especially interested in becoming distinguished and achieving high status. These high HI individuals are particularly concerned with self-reliance and do not give importance to displays of success (Nelson and Shavitt 2002). They would be less likely to embrace GCC and the values, behaviors and symbols that it entails.

A sub-dimension related to national cultural values is the relative importance people in different cultures give to the past, the present and the future. Especially relevant for GCC adoption is "whether our view of time is sequential, a series of passing events, or whether it is synchronic, with past, present, and future all interrelated so that ideas about the future and memories of the past both shape present action" (Trompenaars 1993, p. 107). In cultures that think synchronously about time (e.g., French and South Korean), any lasting relationship combines past, present and future with ties of affection and memory. In these cultures, adoption of GCC is expected to be slower. Furthermore, as global brands stand for modernity and progress (Steenkamp and de Jong, 2010), they need to build long-lasting relationships with consumers using their past heritage, expertise, professionalism and quality as a context for consumers to understand their current (and future) offerings. Present and future opportunities, in these cultures, are connected to the success of the past.

Cultures concerned with sequential time tend to see relationships as more instrumental (Trompenaars 1993). The separation between time intervals tends to separate means from ends (e.g., U.S.). GCC, with its emphasis on materialism and modernization, can be viewed as a means for still more participation in the affluent, cutting edge, high-tech global village. Global brands can be seen as instrumental in this participation.

GENERAL VALUES

General values are powerful, individually held, motivational regula-tors of specific consumer attitudes (Burgess 1992; Smith and Schwartz 1997; Steenkamp, ter Hofstede and Wedel 1999; Steenkamp and de Jong 2010). Schwartz (1992) derives a universal typology of the different con-tents of general values consisting of ten motivationally distinct types of value. Each value type represents a different motivational content and is associated with varying abstract goals. These ten value types can be arranged in a circular order around the perimeter of a circle: universalism, benevolence, conformity, tradition, security, power, achievement, hedonism, stimulation, and self direction. In turn, these are organized into four higher-order value domains: self-transcendence, conservation, openness to change, and self-enhancement. The pursuit of different value types can be compatible or in conflict, depending on how close the value types are in the circular structure. Conflict increases in proportion to the distance between value types, with value types in opposing positions from the center of the structure being in greatest conflict. Since materialism occupies a central position in GCC and since consumers view ownership of global brands as a passport to global citizenship, consumers who value power, achievement, hedonism and stimulation are more likely to endorse GCC. Similarly, consumers who value self-direction and universalism may reject the consumption focus of GCC.

CONSUMER DOMAIN-SPECIFIC VALUES

Consumers acquire more narrowly circumscribed values through experiences in specific domains of consumer activity (Steenkamp and de Jong 2010). These consumer domain-specific values are needed to fully understand and explain consumer attitudes and behavior (Vinson, Scott and Lamont 1977). Many consumer domain-specific values are theoretically relevant for understanding consumers' adoption of GCC and have been suggested and used in previous research. Here, we mention some of the most pertinent ones in influencing the adoption of GCC: materialism, cosmopolitanism, ethnocentrism, loyalty towards community, environmentalism, postmaterialism, and susceptibility to normative influence.

Materialism

Materialism concerns the importance a consumer attaches to worldly possessions and the belief that he/she will derive pleasure and happiness from their ownership (Alden et al. 2006; Richins and Dawson 1992). Materialist consumers should value the central position that consumption and global brands play in GCC (Steenkamp and de Jong 2010).

Cosmopolitanism

Global consumer culture enables people to develop a sense of belonging to a global culture by adopting global values, beliefs, lifestyles and consumption patterns (Arnett 2002). Since cosmopolitans are defined as people who are not influenced by the biases of their local culture (Hannerz 1990) and who view cultural diversity as a fact of life (Cannon and Yaprak 2002), GCC should resonate with cosmopolitan consumers.

Ethnocentrism

As a domain-specific value, ethnocentrism affects the beliefs, attitudes and behaviors of consumers, as well as their consumption choices, and therefore is relevant for their endorsement of GCC. Consumer ethnocentrism "represents consumer beliefs about the appropriateness, indeed morality, of purchasing foreign made products" (Shimp and Sharma 1987, p. 280). Thus, ethnocentric consumers believe that purchasing foreign-made products is wrong because it hurts the local economy. They cherish their own culture and symbols, and therefore may not be favorable towards GCC and its global brands. However, in a recent study, Strizhakova, Coulter and Price (2008) find that more ethnocentric consumers in developed markets with lots of global brands (e.g., the U.S.) view global brands as a vehicle for global citizenship and also as an expression of economic nationalism. While there is extensive research on ethnocentrism and its relation to GCC, foreign and global brands, the relationship is complex and in need of more research.

Loyalty Towards Community

One of the sub-dimensions of the individualism/collectivism dimension relevant to GCC is loyalty towards community. It describes the extent to which individuals feel loyal to their communities and compelled to fulfill their obligations toward in-group members (relatives, clan, organizations) even if in-group members' demands inconvenience them (Aycan et al. 2000). This value orientation is narrower in domain than ethnocentrism, which is a general belief that one's own culture is superior to other cultures.

Environmentalism

The relationships among environmentalism, GCC and global brands are of interest because people who attach greater importance to the well-being of the planet and the environment could reject consumption and its detrimental effects. The "local" movement in many parts of advanced economies could be viewed as anti-GCC by emphasizing the consumption of local produce supporting local farms and farmers (ethnocentrism) and also polluting the environment less by not consuming products that have been transported long distances. In these cases, environmentalism may interact with ethnocentrism, producing stronger anti-GCC attitudes. In other instances, environmentalism may have strong overtones of universalism and the widespread awareness that our common humanity shares our common environment (Tomlinson 1999). This suggests that environmentalism and a shying away from GCC may go together.

Postmaterialism

Inglehart (1990) suggests that a significant number of consumers are likely to exist, especially in societies high in self-expression, that value satisfying higher order needs such as self-expression and quality of life. For these individuals the quality of experience replaces the quantity of material possessions. Yet, this postmodernism should be domain-specific, and different from materialism. That is, consumers may be postmodern in some consumer domains (e.g., clothing, furniture) but exhibit materialistic tendencies in their desire to obtain the latest tech devices (e.g., i-phones, smart phones, latest tablet PCs) and participate in the GCC. That, is materialistic and postmaterialistic values can coexist in modern consumers.

Susceptibility to Normative Influence (SNI)

This construct represents how strongly an individual is influenced by relevant others in "normative" domains (Batra, Homer and Kahle 2001; Bearden, Netemeyer and Teel 1989). Depending on the reference group, high SNI might lead to positive or negative attitudes toward GCC. If the norms of the reference group favor modernization and membership in the global village, high SNI would lead to material possessions as means to impress the reference group and adopt GCC. If the reference group favors local consumption alternatives, the high SNI person would act in a way to fit in and not to differentiate themselves from the dominant consumption norms.

CONCLUSIONS

Global branding has become a very important endeavor in recent decades. In this chapter, a new cultural force, global consumer culture (GCC) (Ritzer 2007; Steenkamp and de Jong 2010), is used as the common thread in presenting major culture theories and value levels. Differences in openness to GCC in which global brands are strongly embedded are explained by cultural values at the national, general and consumer domain-specific levels. The chapter integrates the most influential culture theories that directly or indirectly relate to consumer adoption of global consumer culture and global brands. The interplay between different levels of value, as presented in this chapter, and the dynamic nature of GCC formation (both top-down and bottom-up) makes the understanding of these forces and interactions necessary for effective global brand positioning and communication strategy development and implementation.

NOTES

1. http://en.wikipedia.org/wiki/Procter_%26_Gamble   and   http://en.wikipedia.org/wiki/ Unilever. Retrieved March 16, 2011.
2. http://en.wikipedia.org/wiki/PepsiCo. Retrieved March 16, 2011.
3. In an earlier article, Özsomer and Altaras (2008) present a framework integrating three streams of research: 1) consumer culture theory (Arnould and Thompson 2005); 2) signaling theory from information economics (Tirole 1990; Erdem and Swait 1998, 2004); and 3) associative network memory model (Anderson 1983; Keller 1993, 2003) in theorizing the cultural and economics based drivers of *consumer* attitudes and purchase likelihood of global brands. Here, the emphasis is on culture based drivers.
4. An excellent review of the Hofstede model and its global advertising and branding implications is provided in De Mooij and Hofstede (2010).

REFERENCES

Aaker, Jennifer L. and Angela Y. Lee (2001), 'I Seek Pleasures and "We" Avoid Pains: The Role of Self-Regulatory Goals in Information Processing and Persuasion', *Journal of Consumer Research*, **28** (June), 33–49.
Agarwal, James, Naresh K. Malhotra and Ruth N. Bolton (2010), 'A Cross-National and Cross-Cultural Approach to Global Market Segmentation: An Application Using Consumers' Perceived Service Quality', *Journal of International Marketing*, **18** (3), 18–40.
Agrawal, Nidhi and Durairaj Maheswaran (2005), 'The Effects of Self-Construal and Commitment on Persuasion', *Journal of Consumer Research*, **31** (March), 841–9.
Ajzen, Icek (2001), 'Nature and Operation of Attitudes', *Annual Review of Psychology*, **52**, 27–58.
Alden, Dana L., Jean-Benedict E.M. Steenkamp and Rajeev Batra (1999), 'Brand Positioning through Advertising in Asia, North America, and Europe: The Role of Global Consumer Culture', *Journal of Marketing*, **63** (January), 75–87.
—— and —— (2006), 'Consumer Attitudes toward Marketplace Globalization: Structure, Antecedents and Consequences', *International Journal of Research in Marketing*, **23** (3), 227–39.
Anderson, John R. (1983), *The Architecture of Cognition*. Cambridge, MA: Harvard University Press.
Appadurai, Arjun (1990), 'Disjuncture and Difference in the Global Cultural Economy', *Theory, Culture and Society*, **7**, 295–310.
Arnett, Jeffrey J. (2002), 'The Psychology of Globalization', *American Psychologist*, **57** (October), 774–83.

Arnould, Eric and Craig J. Thompson (2005), 'Consumer Culture Theory (CCT): Twenty Years of Research', *Journal of Consumer Research*, **31** (4), 868–82.

Askegaard, Søren (2006), 'Brands as a Global Ideoscape', in Jonathan E. Schroeder and Miriam Salzer-Mörling (eds), *Brand Culture*, pp. 91–101. London: Routledge Press.

Aycan, Z., R.N. Kanungo, M. Mendonca, K. Yu, J. Deller, G. Stahl and A. Kurshid (2000), 'Impact of Culture on Human Resource Management Practices: A 10-country Comparison', *Applied Psychology: An International Review*, **49** (1), 192–221.

Batra, R., P.M. Homer and L.R. Kahle (2001), 'Values, susceptibility to normative influence, and attribute importance weights: A nomological analysis', *Journal of Consumer Psychology*, **11** (2), 115–28.

Bearden, William O., Richard G. Netemeyer and Jesse E. Teel (1989), 'Consumer Susceptibility to Interpersonal Influence', *Journal of Consumer Research*, **15** (March), 473–81.

Berry, J.W. (1980), 'Social and Cultural Change', in H.C. Triandis and R.W. Brislin (eds), *Handbook of Cross Cultural Psychology*, vol. 5, pp. 211–80. Boston: Allyn & Bacon.

Brewer, Marilynn B. and Wendi Gardner (1996), 'Who Is This "We"? Levels of Collective Identity and Self-Representations', *Journal of Personality and Social Psychology*, **71** (July), 83–93.

Burgess, Steven (1992), 'Personal Values and Consumer Research: An Historical Perspective', in Jagdish N. Sheth (ed.), *Research in Marketing*, vol. 11, pp. 35–79. Greenwich, CT: JAI Press.

Cannon, Hugh M. and Atilla Yaprak (2002), 'Will the Real-World Citizen Please Stand up! The Many Faces of Cosmopolitan Consumer Behavior', *Journal of International Marketing*, **10** (4), 30–52.

Dawar, N. and P. Parker (1994), 'Marketing Universals: Consumers' Use of Brand Name, Price, Physical Appearance, and Retailer Reputation as Signals of Product Quality', *Journal of Marketing*, **58** (April), 81–95.

de Mooij, Marieke and Geert Hofstede (2010), 'The Hofstede Model Applications to Global Branding and Advertising Strategy and Research', *International Journal of Advertising*, **29** (1), 85–110.

Eagly, Alice H. and Shelley Chaiken (1998), 'Attitude Structure and Function', in Daniel T. Gilbert, Susan T. Fiske and Gardner Lindzey (eds), *Handbook of Social Psychology*, 4th ed., pp. 269–322. Boston: McGraw-Hill.

Erdem, Tulin and Joffrey Swait (1998), 'Brand Equity as a Signaling Phenomenon', *Journal of Consumer Psychology*, **7** (April), 131–57.

—— and —— (2004), 'Brand Credibility and its Role in Brand Choice and Consideration', *Journal of Consumer Research*, **31** (1), 191–9.

Erez, Miriam and Efrat Gati (2004), 'A Dynamic, Multi-Level Model of Culture: From the Micro Level of the Individual to the Macro Level of Global Culture', *Applied Psychology: An International Review*, **53** (4), 583–98.

Grayson, Kent and Radan Martinec (2004), 'Consumer Perceptions of Iconicity and Indexicality and Their Influence on Assessments of Authentic Market Offerings', *Journal of Consumer Research*, **31** (September), 296–312.

Hannerz, Ulf (1990), 'Cosmopolitans and Locals in World Culture', *Theory, Culture and Society*, **7**, 237–51.

Hassan, Salah S. and Lea P. Katsanis (1994), 'Global Market Segmentation Strategies and Trends', in Salah S. Hassan and Erdener Kaynak (eds), *Globalization of Consumer Markets: Structures and Strategies*, pp. 47–62. New York: International Business Press.

Hofstede, G.H. (2001), *Culture's Consequences: Comparing Values, Behaviors, Institutions, and Organizations Across Nations*, 2nd ed. Thousand Oaks, CA: Sage Publications.

—— and Hofstede, G.J. (2005), *Cultures and Organizations: Software of the Mind*, 2nd ed. New York: McGraw-Hill.

Holt, Douglas.B. (2002), 'Why Do Brands Cause Trouble? A Dialectical Theory of Consumer Culture and Branding', *Journal of Consumer Research*, **29** (June), 70–90.

——, John A. Quelch and Earl L. Taylor (2004), 'How Global Brands Compete', *Harvard Business Review*, **82** (9), 1–9.

Holton, Robert (2000), 'Globalization's Cultural Consequences', *Annals of the American Academy of Political and Social Science*, **570** (July), 140–52.

Inglehart, Ronald (1990), *Culture Shift in Advanced Industrial Society*. Princeton, NJ: Princeton University Press.

Inglehart, Ronald and Wayne E. Baker (2000), 'Modernization, Cultural Change and the Persistence of Traditional Values', *American Sociological Review*, **65** (February), 19–51.

—— and Christian Welzel (2005), *Modernization, Cultural Change, and Democracy*. New York: Cambridge University Press.

Keller, Kevin L. (1993), 'Conceptualizing, Measuring, and Managing Customer-Based Brand Equity', *Journal of Marketing*, **57** (1), 1–22.

—— (2003), 'Brand Synthesis: The Multi-Dimensionalities of Brand Knowledge', *Journal of Consumer Research*, **29**, 595–600.

Kinra, Neelam (2006), 'The Effect of Country-of-Origin on Foreign Brand Names in the Indian Market', *Marketing Intelligence and Planning*, **24** (1), 15–30.

Kitayama, S. (2002), 'Culture and Basic Psychological Processes – Toward a Systems View of Culture: Comment on Oyserman et al.', *Psychological Bulletin*, **128** (1), 89–96.

Markus, Hazel R. and Shinobu Kitayama (1991), 'Culture and Self: Implications for Cognition, Emotion and Motivation', *Psychological Review*, **98** (2), 224–53.

—— and —— (1994), 'The Cultural Construction of Self and Emotion: Implications for Social Behavior', in S. Kitayama and H.R. Markus (eds), *Emotion and Culture: Empirical Studies of Mutual Influence*, pp. 89–130. Washington, DC: American Psychological Association.

McCracken, Grant (1986), 'Culture and Consumption: A Theoretical Account of the Structure and Movement of the Cultural Meaning of Consumer Goods', *Journal of Consumer Research*, **13**, 71–84.

Nelson, Michelle R. and Sharon Shavitt (2002), 'Horizontal and Vertical Individualism and Achievement Values: A Multimethod Examination of Denmark and the United States', *Journal of Cross-Cultural Psychology*, **33** (5), 439–58.

Oishi, Shigehiro, Ulrich Schimmack, Ed Diener and Eunkook M. Suh (1998), 'The Measurement of Values and Individualism-Collectivism', *Personality and Social Psychology Bulletin*, **24** (11), 1177–89.

Özsomer, A. and S. Altaras (2008), 'Global Brand Purchase Likelihood: A Critical Synthesis and an Integrated Conceptual Framework', *Journal of International Marketing*, **16** (4), 1–28.

Özsomer, Ayşegül and Bernard L. Simonin (2004), 'Marketing Program Standardization: A Cross-Country Exploration', *International Journal of Research in Marketing*, **21** (4), 397–419.

Richins, Marsha and Scott Dawson (1992), 'A Consumer Values Orientation for Materialism and its Measurement: Scale Development and Validation', *Journal of Consumer Research*, **19**, 303–16.

Ritzer, George (2004), *The McDonaldization of Society*. Thousand Oaks, CA: Pine Forge Press.

—— (2007), *The Globalization of Nothing 2*. Thousand Oaks, CA: Pine Forge Press.

Rokeach, Milton J. (1973), *The Nature of Human Values*. New York: The Free Press.

Roth, M.S. (1995), 'The Effects of Culture and Socioeconomics on the Performance of Global Brand Image Strategies', *Journal of Marketing Research*, **32**, 163–75.

Schwartz, Shalom H. (1992), 'Universals in the Content and Structure of Values: Theoretical Advances and Empirical Tests in 20 Countries', in Mark P. Zanna (ed.), *Advances in Experimental Social Psychology*, vol. 25. San Diego, CA: Academic Press.

—— (1994), 'Beyond Individualism/Collectivism: New Cultural Dimensions of Value', in U. Kim, Harry C. Triandis, C. Kagitcibasi, S.C. Choi and G. Yoon (eds), *Individualism and Collectivism: Theory, Method, and Applications*, pp. 85–119. Thousand Oaks, CA: Sage Publications.

Shimp, Terence A. and Subhash Sharma (1987), 'Consumer Ethnocentrism: Construction and Validation of the CETSCALE', *Journal of Marketing Research*, **24**, 280–89.

Slater, Don (1997), *Consumer Culture & Modernity*. Cambridge, UK: Polity.

Smith, Peter B. and Shalom H. Schwartz (1997), 'Values', in John W. Berry, Marshall H. Segall and Cigdem Kagitcibasi (eds), *Handbook of Cross-Cultural Psychology: Social Behavior and Applications*, 2nd ed., pp. 77–118. Boston: Allyn & Bacon.

Steenkamp, Jean-Benedict E.M., Rajeev Batra and Dana L. Alden (2003), 'How Perceived Brand Globalness Creates Brand Value', *Journal of International Business Studies*, **34** (1), 53–65.

—— and Martijn G. de Jong (2010), 'A Global Investigation into the Constellation of Consumer Attitudes Toward Global and Local Products', *Journal of Marketing*, **74** (November), 18–40.

——, Frenkel ter Hofstede and Michel Wedel (1999), 'A Cross-National Investigation into the Individual and National-Cultural Antecedents of Consumer Innovativeness', *Journal of Marketing*, **63** (April), 55–69.

Strizhakova, Yuliya, Robin A. Coulter and Linda L. Price (2008), 'Branded Products as a Passport to Global Citizenship: Perspectives from Developed and Developing Countries', *Journal of International Marketing*, **16** (4), 57–85.

ter Hofstede, F., M. Wedel and J.-B. Steenkamp (2002), 'Identifying Spatial Segments in International Markets', *Marketing Science*, **21** (2), 160–83.

Tirole, Jean (1990), *The Theory of the Industrial Organization*. Cambridge, MA: MIT Press.

Tomlinson, John (1999), *Globalization and Culture*. Chicago: University of Chicago Press.

Torelli, Carlos J. and Sharon Shavitt (2008), 'Culture and Mental Representations of Power Goals: Consequences for Information Processing', *Advances in Consumer Research*, **35**, in press.

Triandis, Harry C. (1989), 'The Self and Behavior in Differing Cultural Contexts', *Psychological Review*, **96** (July), 506–20.

—— (1994), *Our Culture Influences Who We Are and How We View Social Behavior: Culture and Social Behavior*. New York: McGraw-Hill.

—— and Michele J. Gelfand (1998), 'Converging Measurement of Horizontal and Vertical Individualism and Collectivism', *Journal of Personality and Social Psychology*, **74** (1), 118–28.

Verplanken, Bas and Rob W. Holland (2002), 'Motivated Decision Making: Effects of Activation and Self-Centrality of Values on Choices and Behavior', *Journal of Personality and Social Psychology*, **82** (3), 434–47.

Vinson, David E., Jerome E. Scott and Lawrence M. Lamont (1977), 'The Role of Personal Values in Marketing and Consumer Behavior', *Journal of Marketing*, **41** (April), 44–50.

Wong, Nancy and Aaron Ahuvia (1998), 'Personal Taste and Family Face: Luxury Consumption in Confucian and Western Societies', *Psychology & Marketing*, **15** (5), 423–41.

PART II

CULTURE

4 Project GLOBE and cross-cultural advertising research: developing a theory-driven approach

Narda R. Quigley, Mary Sully de Luque and Robert J. House

INTRODUCTION

In their 2007 review, Okazaki and Mueller found that cultural values were the most studied topic in the realm of international and cross-cultural advertising research. Indeed, 36.8 percent of articles meeting their criteria and published between 1995 and 2006 reported studies involving cultural values. Because values 'determine, at a basic level, people's choices and desires . . ., [they] may be one of the most powerful explanations of, and influences on, consumer behavior' (Okazaki & Mueller, 2007, p. 504). Clearly, the extent to which cultural values might influence consumer behavior is quite relevant to advertising research. Given that multinational companies frequently launch worldwide and localized advertising campaigns, the practical implications of this type of research are immense.

This chapter begins by introducing the Project GLOBE study (Global Leadership and Organizational Behavior Effectiveness; House, Hanges, Javidan, Dorfman & Gupta, 2004) and considering the nature of culture at the societal level of analysis. In so doing, we will compare three recent conceptualizations of cultural values (Hofstede, 1980; House et al., 2004; and Schwartz, 2001) and compare and contrast the approaches of Hofstede (1980, 2001) and House et al. (2004). It is worth noting that excellent discussions of this latter comparison can be found in the first published volume of the Project GLOBE study (House et al., 2004), in addition to Hofstede (2006), Javidan, House, Dorfman, Hanges and Sully de Luque (2006), and Okazaki and Mueller (2007). We then build three alternative theoretical models, based on Project GLOBE, linking societal culture to individual perceptions and evaluations of advertising messaging, with implications for future empirical cross-cultural advertising research.

The purpose of this chapter is twofold. First, we hope to introduce the GLOBE study to advertising scholars who may need more information about the study and its findings. Second, we wish to shed light on why the application of GLOBE's concepts, theory and scales hold promise for the field of cross-cultural advertising. In so doing, we hope to respond partly to the call our colleagues in the management and international business realms have made regarding the identification of practical applications of the GLOBE project (e.g., Hofstede, 2006, 2010; Tung & Verbeke, 2010). We ultimately hope to make the reader more familiar with the essential research process, concepts, theory, methodology and findings from the GLOBE research program so as to encourage future cross-cultural advertising researchers to use the advances pioneered by GLOBE.

INTRODUCTION TO PROJECT GLOBE

The idea for the GLOBE project initially arose for the third author of this chapter in 1991, at which time he was exploring the global applicability of charismatic leadership theory. It became apparent early on, after a comprehensive review of the psychology, anthropology, organizational culture and cross-cultural management literatures, that the first step would be a reconsideration of the meaning and dimensions of societal culture. The first phase of the GLOBE project, therefore, was dedicated to the development of research instruments to assess societal culture. The second phase was dedicated to the assessment of nine core attributes of cultures (i.e., nine dimensions). Further, in this phase, the 62 cultures in our sample were ranked according to their mean scores for societal dimensions, and hypotheses were tested about the relationships between these dimensions and other societal, organizational and leadership variables.

More than 170 social scientists and management scholars from countries representing all major regions of the world were involved in the first two phases, and many of these researchers continue to be engaged in GLOBE's long-term, programmatic research goals. The third phase, currently underway, is dedicated to investigating the impact and effectiveness of strategic leader behaviors and styles on top management team attitudes and firm performance (House & Javidan, 2004). The GLOBE team of cross-cultural researchers collected and analyzed data from approximately 17,000 managers from 951 organizations in 62 societies throughout the world. The managers surveyed in each country represented three industries: financial services, food processing, and telecommunications. As noted in House, Quigley and Sully de Luque (2010), research from the GLOBE project has produced two comprehensive volumes (House et al., 2004; Chokhar, Brodbeck & House, 2007) and dozens of journal articles and book chapters written by GLOBE associates (e.g., Den Hartog, House, Hanges, Ruiz-Quintanilla, Dorfman & 170 co-authors,

1999; House et al., 2010; House, Javidan, Dorfman & Sully de Luque, 2006; Javidan & House, 2001; Javidan, House, Dorfman, Hanges & Sully de Luque, 2006; Quigley, Sully de Luque & House, 2005), as well as a number of scholarly responses to the original research (e.g., Graen, 2006; Hofstede, 2006; 2010; Tung & Verbeke, 2010). As of 2004, more than 100 articles and book chapters already had been written on the GLOBE findings (House & Javidan, 2004). While the footprint of the GLOBE study is still to be determined, the idea that societal culture is a critical consideration in business research has gained a great deal of traction in recent years. One example of this is the October/November 2010 issue of the *Journal of International Business Studies*, which became a de facto special issue on the topic of culture and international business (Tung & Verbeke, 2010).

SOCIETAL CULTURE AND VALUES

The comprehensive examination of societal culture in the first two phases of the GLOBE project has led to the development of theoretical and empirical findings relevant to and important for international advertising scholarship (e.g., Diehl, Terlutter & Mueller, 2008; Okazaki & Mueller, 2007; Okazaki, Mueller & Taylor, 2010; Terlutter, Diehl & Mueller, 2005, 2006). In particular, the GLOBE project's focus on clearly defining and measuring societal culture and incorporating past traditions of the study of values as part of culture have important ramifications for global advertising research. Project GLOBE's definition of culture includes 'shared motives, values, beliefs, identities, and interpretations or meanings of significant events that result from common experiences of members of collectives that are transmitted across generations' (House & Javidan, 2004, p. 15). For measuring culture, many prior studies had reflected Hofstede's onion metaphor (e.g., Hofstede, 1980, 2001), in which culture is conceptualized as having invisible and visible manifestations (for example, values and symbols, respectively). Hofstede (2001) further asserted that cultural values drive practices, thus implicitly suggesting that values are the more critical aspect of culture to measure. Indeed, Javidan et al. (2006, p. 899) noted, there is 'general acceptance that the value-based framework for measuring cultures has been helpful in deciphering cultures (Leung et al., 2002; Leung et al., 2005; Smith et al., 2002)'. Project GLOBE, however, went beyond this understanding of the implicit positive relationship between a culture's values and practices (or invisible and visible manifestations). GLOBE researchers attempted to measure *what actually happens* within a culture, in addition to measuring cultural values (*what is desired or wanted*). In this manner, we were able to tease out aspects of the onion metaphor in ways that had not yet been examined (Javidan et al., 2006). Prior to discussing how Project GLOBE measured culture in greater detail, we will provide a brief review of research on individual and cultural values within the social sciences used most commonly in advertising research (Okazaki & Mueller, 2007).

The research begins with a focus on values at the individual or personal level of analysis. A commonly accepted early definition of values was suggested by Rokeach (1968), who defined values as 'an enduring belief that one mode of conduct or end-state of existence is preferable to an opposing mode of conduct or end-state of existence'. Rokeach (1973) provided a new classification system of personal values at two levels: instrumental and terminal, reflecting means and ends, respectively. Instrumental values are 'desirable modes of conduct that help one achieve [certain] end-states', while terminal values are 'desirable end-states, such as a comfortable life, an exciting life, a sense of accomplishment, a world at peace, equality, [and] family security' (Okazaki & Mueller, 2007, p. 504). Later, a revised system (Rokeach, 1973) was simplified by Kahle and Timmer (1983). These scholars developed the LOV scale, consisting of nine values: security, a sense of accomplishment, self-fulfillment, being well respected, a sense of belonging, warm relationship with others, excitement, self-respect, and fun and enjoyment in life. As Okazaki and Mueller (2007) posit, these two approaches have been widely utilized in the areas of international advertising and marketing to link values to consumer behavior (e.g., Goldsmith, Frieden & Kilsheimer, 1993; Kahle, Beatty & Mager, 1994; McEnally & de Chernatony, 1999; Ueltschy & Ryans, 1997). Across social science disciplines, scholars have assessed cultural values, with some researchers strongly labeling 'values' as the foundation of culture (McCarty, 1994). As noted by Samover, Porter and Stefani (1998), these values can be transmitted by a variety of sources (from family to state) and tend to be 'broadbased, enduring, and relatively stable' (Okazaki & Mueller, 2007).

As Okazaki and Mueller (2007) noted, several classification systems of cultural values have been used to date by the cross-cultural marketing and advertising research. The most popular of these have been Hofstede's (1980) typology, Schwartz's (1992, 1994) cultural values, and, most recently, the cultural values classification of the GLOBE study (House et al., 2004). Considered some of the earliest cultural work in the discipline of business, Hofstede's (1980) typology has been an extremely important way to compare cultures. Notably, he defined values as *broad tendencies to prefer certain states of affairs over others* (Hofstede, 1980). Using this definition and a sizable sample of 88,000 respondents of IBM employees reflecting 66 countries gathered in the 1960s, Hofstede identified four dimensions of culture. From his analysis, he advanced that the following dimensions reflected the values of the people within a culture: power distance, 'the amount of inequality between a superior and a subordinate that was both expected and accepted in this society' (Hofstede, 2006, p. 887); uncertainty avoidance, which reveals 'part of respondents' collective anxiety level in view of the unknown and the unfamiliar, expressed for example in the feeling that "what is different, is dangerous"' (Hofstede, 2006, p. 888); individualism, the extent to which a society preferred a group or individualist orientation (Okazaki & Mueller, 2007); and masculinity/femininity, or 'the duality of female vs. male' (Hofstede, 1998, p. 11). Later, based on the results of the Chinese Value Survey given to 23 countries (Chinese Culture Connection, 1987), Hofstede added a fifth cultural dimension: long- vs. short-term orientation. This dimension 'opposed the importance of (mainly) future-oriented life goals to past- and present-oriented life goals: perseverance and thrift on the future side, personal stability, respect for tradition, and reciprocation of favors on the present side' (Hofstede, 2006, p. 888). Remarkably (although seldom noted), while these dimensions were empirically derived from a data set that was collected to address IBM's consulting needs, Hofstede (2001, p. 31) points out that a handbook article by Inkeles and Levinson (1954) provided theoretical rationale for precisely why these four dimensions should have emerged.

As with any study, Hofstede's (1980, 2001) work has a number of limitations (see Erez & Earley, 1993; House et al., 2006; McSweeney, 2002; Schwartz, 1994; and Smith & Schwartz, 1997 for detailed discussions of these issues). One issue is whether his five dimensions capture all possible relevant aspects of culture (Hofstede, 1980). Closely related to this is the fact that Hofstede's data collection effort began as a consulting project for a single company, and all respondents were, in fact, employees of IBM. This may potentially limit the generalizability of the findings, although Hofstede (2006) points out that his data set includes both managers and employees at IBM. While Hofstede's original four dimensions emerged from an analysis of the questions pertaining to values on his surveys, these questions sometimes lacked consistency and face validity with respect to the way they were ultimately labeled (Baskerville, 2003, 2005; Javidan et al., 2006). Additionally, Hofstede's data has also been criticized for its age (Holden, 2002; Okazaki & Mueller, 2007). The data were collected between 1968 and 1972, and the generation of individuals who responded to the survey is likely close to or beyond retirement. While culture is passed from one generation to the next, cultural changes can and do occur over time. Additionally, there is a lack of data on many important parts of the world, including Arab and African countries (with the exception of South Africa).

Despite these limitations, there is no doubt that Hofstede's (1980) work on national culture served as a major advance for the scholarship on culture, as clearly noted by House and colleagues (2004). Hofstede's work, and the 'dimension' paradigm to studying culture, has become the 'normal science' approach to cross-cultural business studies (Hofstede, 2006). This approach, of course, is consistent within much of the cross-cultural marketing and advertising research realm. As Okazaki and Mueller (2007, p. 505) noted, scholars have 'recognized the potential applicability of Hofstede's dimensions to both advertising and marketing research questions' (Albers-Miller, 1996; Bang et al., 2005; Milner & Collins, 2000; Moon & Chan, 2005; Moon & Franke, 2000; Mortimer & Grierson, 2010).

A second approach noted by Okazaki and Mueller (2007) is Schwartz's (1992, 1994) Survey of Values. Using a theory-driven approach based on the empirical, philosophical and religious literature of various cultures, Schwartz identified several values that he believed to be universally relevant (Smith & Schwartz, 1997). He then grouped these into ten categories and developed a theory of how these categories might be interrelated (Hanges & Dickson, 2004). Last, based on his own theory and that of prior researchers (e.g., Rokeach, 1973), Schwartz developed his survey. Collecting data from 41 cultural groups, he ultimately derived seven dimensions of culture: conservatism (the maintenance of the status quo); hierarchy (the legitimacy of an unequal distribution of power); egalitarian commitment (transcendence of selfish interests in favor of promotion of the welfare of others); intellectual autonomy (the right of individuals to pursue their own thoughts and ideas); affective autonomy (the right of individuals to pursue positive experiences); mastery (the quest to actively master and change the world); and harmony (the acceptance of the world as is, rather than attempting to exploit it) (Schwartz, 1992, 1994; Smith & Schwartz, 1997). Despite its strong theoretical base, Okazaki and Mueller (2007) note that Schwartz's cultural values have been used much less in advertising research (see Watson et al., 2002 for an exception).

The above approaches are good ways to examine the effect of values, and we find that these permeate at the individual, personal, and societal culture levels of analysis. Javidan et al. (2006, p. 899) warned against the fallacy of the ecological values assumption, which is the 'conventional wisdom . . . that calculating the respondents' individual values is a sufficient measure of the collective's culture'. Furthermore, a society's culture likely comprises more than just values. Resulting from the qualitative interviews and focus groups, GLOBE researchers chose to take a more holistic view of culture, considering it as both values and practices, or 'actual ways in which members of a culture go about dealing with their collective challenges' (Javidan et al., 2006, p. 899). Moreover, instead of asking respondents about what is desirable to them as individuals, which is the typical approach used in the culture studies reviewed above, the GLOBE questionnaire wording asked individuals about what is desirable in their *societies*. In other words, respondents served as informants reporting on the overall gestalt of their cultures (Javidan et al., 2006), rather than expressing what they personally value as individuals. The assumption we made is that individuals are nested within (and affected by) their societal culture, and therefore they can assess the extent to which the culture espouses certain values.

Project GLOBE developed 735 questionnaire items on the basis of prior literature and our own theorizing based on qualitative research. We used two pilot studies to generate responses to these items; we then analyzed the results of these pilot studies using conventional psychometric procedures such as item, factor, cluster, and generalizability analyses (Hanges & Dickson, 2004). These analyses resulted in the identification of nine major cultural dimensions, operationalized in two forms to reflect both values and practices. Cultural *practices* refer to common behaviors, institutional practices, proscriptions, and prescriptions of a given culture. As noted in House and Javidan (2004), this approach to cultural assessment grew out of a psychological and behavioral tradition that assumed cultures should be studied according to their interpretation and enactment by their members (Segall, Lonner & Berry, 1998). Cultural *values*, in contrast, reflect the respondents' desires concerning cultural phenomenon, as reported by the respondents (House & Javidan, 2004; Kluckholn & Strodtbeck, 1961; Triandis, 1995). Therefore, respondents provided feedback and ratings on the current practices of their society (society 'as is'), as well as the espoused values of their society (society as it 'should be').

OVERVIEW OF THE GLOBE DIMENSIONS OF SOCIETAL CULTURE

The nine dimensions of societal culture and brief descriptions of each dimension from Project GLOBE can be found in Table 4.1, along with a brief comparison of these dimensions with Hofstede's five dimensions.

Many of the GLOBE dimensions drew from Hofstede's (1980, 2001) dimensions, but there are some critical differences. We first review some overall differences with respect to each study, and then discuss the differences associated with each particular dimension. The first critical difference is in the research approach used, which has implications for the dimensions of culture. As noted above, Hofstede's (1980) work began as an IBM consulting study. As such, the constructs and scales that were used

Table 4.1   Comparison of cultural dimensions: Hofstede and Project GLOBE

Hofstede (1980, 2001)	Project GLOBE (2004)

1. Power distance
  • *The degree of equality/inequality between people in a particular society.*
2. Uncertainty avoidance
  • *The level of acceptance for uncertainty and ambiguity within a society.*
3. Individualism
  • *The degree to which a society reinforces individual or collective achievement and interpersonal relationships.*
4. Masculinity/femininity
  • *The degree to which a society reinforces, or does not reinforce, the traditional masculine work role model of male achievement, control, and power.*
5. Short- vs. long-term orientation
  • *A society's 'time horizon', or the importance attached to the future versus the past and present.*
	1. Power distance
	  • *The degree to which members of a society expect and agree that power should be stratified and concentrated at higher levels of an organization or government.*
	2. Uncertainty avoidance
	  • *The extent to which members of a society seek certainty in their environment by relying on established social norms, rituals, and bureaucratic practices.*
	3. Institutional collectivism
	  • *The degree to which organizational and societal institutional practices encourage and reward the collective distribution of resources and collective action.*
	4. In-group collectivism
	  • *The degree to which individuals express pride, loyalty, and cohesiveness in their organizations and families.*
	5. Gender egalitarianism
	  • *The degree to which a society minimizes gender role differences while promoting gender equality.*
	6. Assertiveness
	  • *The degree to which members of a society are assertive, confrontational, or aggressive in social relationships.*
	7. Humane orientation
	  • *The degree to which members of a society encourage and reward individuals for being fair, altruistic, friendly, generous, caring, and kind to others.*
	8. Future orientation
	  • *The degree to which individuals in organizations or societies engage in future-oriented behaviors such as planning, investing in the future, and delaying individual or collective gratification.*
	9. Performance orientation
	  • *The degree to which an organization or society encourages and rewards members for performance improvement and excellence.*

were empirically developed post hoc (McSweeney, 2002). As Hofstede (2006, p. 884) noted, 'The IBM attitude survey questionnaires had been designed as a management tool and developed through open-ended pilot interviews with personnel in nine countries. The surveys were action driven and dealt with issues that IBM employees from different categories and their management considered relevant in their work situation . . . [the] cross-national analysis came years later.' Hofstede's work was important in motivating the Project GLOBE approach to be theoretically-driven. House, Wright and Aditya (1997), House et al. (2004) and House et al. (2010) provide comprehensive details on the theory used to link culture to leadership from the Project GLOBE study. Regarding the scales used, a team of GLOBE researchers were involved in the research design and collaborated to develop the items (House et al., 2004). All survey items were translated and back-translated in each societal culture (Brislin, 1970), to ensure that the essential meaning of the items would be consistent across languages. Hofstede's (1980) scales were not back-translated, creating some concern regarding whether the meaning of the items was parallel across languages (Okazaki & Mueller, 2007). The evidence of the psychometric properties of the GLOBE scales are impressive (Hanges & Dickson, 2004, 2006; Javidan et al., 2006), and the complete GLOBE survey instruments can be freely downloaded at http://www.thunderbird.edu/wwwfiles/ms/globe.

Power Distance

Power distance, as conceived by Hofstede, involves 'how society deals with the fact that people are unequal' (Hofstede, 1983, p. 81). Hofstede based his ideas on those of Mulder and his colleagues (Mulder, 1971, 1976, 1977; Mulder, Ritsema van Eck & De Long, 1971). Hofstede (1983) noted that people are inherently unequal in terms of physical and intellectual capacities, which some societies allow to grow into inequalities in power and wealth. Other societies attempt to 'level the playing field' and minimize these types of inequality as much as possible. Societies with high levels of power distance, in Hofstede's conceptualization, are the most comfortable with inequality and perpetuate it over time; societies with low levels of power distance still exhibit inequalities, but attempt to downplay them. Hofstede's original (1980) scale for this dimension consisted of two to three items (depending on whether the scale was found in the manager or employee version of the survey; Hofstede, 2006).

GLOBE began with Hofstede's original power distance concept, modifying it slightly to be more in line with the GLOBE definition of culture: power distance is 'the degree to which members of an organization or society expect and agree that power should be shared unequally' (Carl, Gupta & Javidan, 2004, p. 517). Consistent with the aim of the GLOBE project to consider both practices and values as reflections of culture, respondents were asked to describe how their culture currently 'is' vs. how it 'should be'. As House et al. (2010) note, a high score on GLOBE's power distance in terms of cultural practices indicates that a given society is more economically, socially, and politically stratified; countries like Russia, Brazil, and India reported scores high on power distance, while countries like the Netherlands reported scores relatively low on power distance practices (Carl et al., 2004). Countries scoring high on this dimension tend to have hierarchical decision making processes with one-way (i.e., top-down) communication processes (Javidan et al., 2006), while countries scoring low on this dimension are less stratified in terms of decision making. To date, no published studies to our knowledge in the areas of cross-cultural marketing and advertising have considered the impact of GLOBE's power distance concept (either values or practices). This may be an important dimension of culture for advertising research to examine, as advertising messaging that emphasizes the stratification of power in a given society may be more or less appropriate given the power distance individuals within the society are comfortable with. The GLOBE study found a negative relationship across all societal cultures with respect to power distance practices and values (-0.43, $p<0.01$); respondents from all cultures seemed to indicate that they desired their culture to have lower levels of power distance in the future. Future advertising research may want to consider this information and explore whether messaging might be more effective if it takes this into account.

Uncertainty Avoidance

The term uncertainty avoidance was originally used at the organizational level by Cyert and March (1963). Hofstede (1980, p. 156) stated that the term represents 'a national syndrome that relates to neuroticism, anxiety, stress, uncertainty avoidance, or whatever we want to call it, that differentiates among modern nations and affected IBM employees as much as anyone else'. Over the years, Hofstede (2006, p. 888) has reinterpreted his uncertainty avoidance index (a three-item measure) 'as revealing part of respondents' collective anxiety level in view of the unknown and the unfamiliar, expressed for example in the feeling that "what is different, is dangerous"'. As defined by GLOBE, uncertainty avoidance 'refers to the extent to which members of collectives seek orderliness, consistency, structure, formalized procedures, and laws to cover situations in their daily lives' (Sully de Luque & Javidan, 2004, p. 603). GLOBE analyses revealed that societal cultures like Switzerland and Germany reported high scores on uncertainty avoidance practices, tending to establish detailed processes, procedures, and strategies. In contrast, societal cultures including Russia and Venezuela reported low scores on uncertainty avoidance practices; these countries tend to prefer simple processes and broad strategies, leaving room for flexibility and risk taking (Sully de Luque & Javidan, 2004). Societies such as the United States, Italy and Brazil reported moderate scores on this dimension.

Like power distance, to our knowledge no cross-cultural marketing or advertising research has included an examination of the GLOBE measure of uncertainty avoidance. As reported in Sully de Luque and Javidan (2004), there is a negative relationship between practices and values with respect to uncertainty avoidance (−0.61, p<0.01). Future cross-cultural marketing and advertising research should consider whether this is an important issue in terms of reaching consumers in messaging; if individuals in societies that highly avoid uncertainty or that seek certainty in their environment (i.e., high uncertainty avoidance practices) would rather be in more fluid, flexible situations (i.e., low uncertainty avoidance values), these individuals might be more likely to appreciate messaging that includes more adventurous elements. The opposite may be true for societies with low uncertainty avoidance practices that say they value more certainty.

Institutional and In-Group Collectivism

There is a long tradition of discussion about the constructs of individualism and collectivism in several fields, including anthropology (e.g., Mead, 1961; Redfield, 1956), psychology (e.g., Hofstede, 1980, 2001; Markus & Kitayama, 1991; Triandis, 1995, 1998; Triandis & Gelfand, 1998) and sociology (e.g., Durkheim, 1933; Parsons, 1949). Hofstede's (1980, 2001) dimension, originally labeled 'individualism vs. collectivism', has had a fundamental impact on cross-cultural psychology, overall being one of the most widely researched dimensions of culture (Earley & Gibson, 1998). He described the dimension as ascertaining the fundamental nature of the relationship between an individual and his or her fellow individuals. As he noted (Hofstede, 1983, p. 79), 'At one end of the scale we find societies in which the ties between individuals are very loose. Everyone is supposed to look after his or her own self-interest . . . At the other end of the scale, we find societies in which the ties between individuals are very tight . . . Everyone is supposed to look after the interest of his or her ingroup and to have no other opinions and beliefs than the opinions and beliefs in their ingroup.' Hofstede's measurement for this dimension was based on IBM employees' scores 'for the importance of various job aspects for describing their ideal job' (Hofstede, 2006, p. 888). After factor-analyzing the job aspects data, Hofstede determined that the first factor 'opposed the importance of time for one's personal life and freedom on the job to training opportunities, physical working conditions, and being able to use one's skills. It was interpreted as opposing an individual's independence from the company to collective things the company did for its employees, and correlations showed it to distinguish individualist from collectivist societies' (Hofstede, 2006, p. 888).

Project GLOBE took cues from Triandis and his colleagues (Triandis, 1995, 1998; Triandis & Gelfand, 1998; Triandis et al., 1986), Realo et al. (1997), and Rhee, Uleman and Lee (1996) to construct scales for individualism and collectivism that reflected both a society's emphasis on family integrity and non-kin components of collectivism (Gelfand et al., 2004). When we analyzed the societal-level scales, it was clear that two dimensions emerged: institutional collectivism and in-group collectivism. With regard to the former, the construct was measured with four items that focused on the extent to which institutional practices at the societal level encourage and reward collective action. Similarly, in-group collectivism was operationalized by a set of four items that assessed the extent to which individuals express interdependence, pride, and loyalty in their families. As with other dimensions, GLOBE included versions of the scales to reflect both practices and values. Countries high on institutional collectivism practices include China, Japan, and Sweden; countries high on in-group collectivism practices include Turkey, Mexico, and India (Gelfand et al., 2004).

We see another opportunity with respect to using the GLOBE dimensions of both institutional collectivism and in-group collectivism for cross-cultural advertising researchers. Although there has been some advertising research using more general measures of collectivism (e.g. Diehl, Mueller & Terlutter, 2008; Diehl, Terlutter & Weinberg, 2003; Diehl, Terlutter & Mueller, 2008), no prior research to our knowledge has examined more specific institutional and in-group collectivism measures in the context of advertising. Yet individuals from societal cultures that are more or less comfortable with collective action and/or family loyalty may react differently to different types of ad campaigns. For example, a campaign focusing on the meaning of family may be extremely effective in societies high on in-group collectivism practices, while a campaign focusing on the meaning of collective effort and country may be extremely effective in societies high on institutional collectivism practices. Interestingly, for institutional collectivism, Project GLOBE found a negative relationship between practices and values (-0.61, $p<0.001$), and a non-significant relationship between practices and values for in-group collectivism (0.21, NS). Future advertising research should examine whether societies that are high in institutional collectivism practices yet are lower on values might actually respond positively to ad campaigns that downplay the role of institutions and emphasize the role of the individual in society vs. ad campaigns that emphasize the role of institutions and downplay the role of the individual.

Gender Egalitarianism

Societies differ in the extent to which they prescribe and proscribe different roles for women and men (Emrich, Denmark & Den Hartog, 2004; Hofstede, 1980). Hofstede (1980, 2001) had conceptualized this difference as the masculinity/femininity dimension. He operationalized the masculinity pole of the dimension with the importance respondents placed on the work goals such as earnings, recognition, advancement, and challenge. For femininity, Emrich et al. (2004) noted that Hofstede's (1980) original dimension included the work values of having a good relationship with one's manager, cooperation among peers, living in a desirable area, and employment security. He selected the masculinity/femininity label for this dimension because it was the only one on which men and women in the IBM sample scored differently (for example, men scored higher on earnings, etc. while women scored higher on cooperation, etc.).

In reviewing the masculinity/femininity dimension, Project GLOBE researchers observed that the dimension likely encompasses at least two distinct aspects of societal culture. First, the dimension seems to address the extent to which the culture emphasizes 'masculine' values such as competition, assertiveness, and success vs. 'feminine' values such as solidarity, nurturance, and cooperation. Second, the dimension reflects differences among societies 'in their beliefs about the behavior that is appropriate for males versus females' (Emrich et al., 2004, p. 344). As a result, GLOBE developed items to reflect both of these aspects of masculinity/femininity, and subsequent statistical analyses revealed that the items grouped into two separate dimensions, which were subsequently called assertiveness and gender egalitarianism. The items that reflected gender egalitarianism were originally written to mirror Hofstede's femininity/masculinity dimension, and as a result there is some interpretive complexity associated with the actual items. For example, a score of four out of seven on some items indicates gender egalitarianism. For one item, however, a score of seven indicates disagreement with the concept that boys are/should be encouraged more than girls to attain a higher education. While there are no societies in the GLOBE sample that exhibited completely egalitarian gender egalitarianism practices, Russia, Sweden, Canada, and England are all examples of countries that scored comparatively high on this dimension. Kuwait and South Korea both fell in the lowest distribution band for gender egalitarianism practices; these two societies were the least gender egalitarian in the GLOBE sample. Interestingly, there is a positive correlation between gender egalitarianism practices and values (0.32, p<0.05). Societies that are more gender egalitarian in practice also value gender egalitarianism.

Gender egalitarianism seems like a particularly relevant scale for advertising research, as it is likely related to how men and women perceive advertising campaigns in different cultures. Again, we know of no current research in the realm of cross-cultural advertising that has examined GLOBE gender egalitarianism as an influence on how individuals may interpret advertising messaging. Additionally, in tandem with Emrich et al.'s (2004, p. 362) call for future researchers 'to construct items that use the full 7-point response scale, with 7 reflecting the greatest degree of gender egalitarianism', we suggest that advertising researchers consider building off the foundational scale from the GLOBE study and developing a new scale to assess gender egalitarianism practices and values.

Assertiveness

As noted above, GLOBE researchers conceptually divided Hofstede's (1980) masculinity/femininity dimension into gender egalitarianism and assertiveness. House et al. (1999) defined assertiveness as the degree to which individuals in organizations or societies are assertive, dominant, tough, and aggressive in social relationships. Items were written to reflect both assertiveness practices and values within each culture. Countries like Germany, Austria, Greece, and the U.S. scored high on assertiveness practices, suggesting that these societies emphasize competition, success and progress over relationships. In contrast, Switzerland, New Zealand, and Sweden scored low on assertiveness practices, suggesting that these cultures emphasize cooperation, people, and tradition (Den Hartog, 2004, p. 405). Assertiveness practices and values at the societal level were found to be significantly negatively correlated (−0.26, p<0.05).

Cross-cultural advertising researchers have begun to examine the impact of GLOBE assertiveness orientation as a cultural dimension. In particular, Terlutter et al. (2005) examined a sample of participants from France, Germany, the U.S., and England, hypothesizing that the level of assertiveness practices and values in each culture would influence the perception and evaluation of an advertising message with an assertive appeal. Terlutter et al. (2006) followed up with more theorizing on how cultural assertiveness may influence whether consumers perceive ads as assertive in nature. We encourage future research to build from these important early studies and develop further the connection between a society's level of assertiveness practices and values and how that might influence an individual's response to an advertising campaign.

Humane Orientation

A third GLOBE dimension that is related to Hofstede's (1980) masculinity/femininity index is humane orientation. GLOBE's definition of humane orientation is 'the degree to which an organization or a society encourages and rewards individuals for being fair, altruistic, friendly, generous, caring, and kind to others (House et al., 1999)' (Kabasakal & Bodur, 2004, p. 569). Five questionnaire items in the GLOBE study were used to assess this dimension. They included the extent to which the culture practised/valued being concerned toward others, sensitive toward others, friendly, tolerant of mistakes and generous. Kabasakal and Bodur (2004) observed that the dimension is similar to one aspect of Hofstede's masculinity/femininity index in that cultures that score low on the index are considered to be relationship-oriented, which is similar to high scores on GLOBE's humane orientation dimension. Countries that score high on humane orientation practices in the GLOBE sample include Malaysia, Thailand, Ireland, and Egypt, while Italy, Poland, Switzerland, Germany, and France scored low. Interestingly, in the GLOBE sample of societal cultures, humane orientation practices and values were negatively correlated (-0.32, $p < 0.05$), suggesting that countries that are lower in humane orientation practices value humane orientation more, and countries that are higher in humane orientation practices value it less.

Examining the concept of GLOBE humane orientation may be a fruitful endeavor for cross-cultural advertising researchers. If cultures are high on humane orientation practices, individuals from those cultures may be more likely to view advertising messaging that emphasizes cooperation and relationships favorably. On the other hand, because there is a negative relationship between practices and values for this dimension, it may be that individuals in societies with high humane orientation practices (hence lower humane orientation values) may be more receptive to advertising that downplays concern for others and other manifestations of humane orientation. Clearly, more research needs to be conducted to explore these ideas.

Future Orientation

As noted above, Hofstede's first inclusion of the concept of time in his cultural dimensions occurred in 1987, after a study across 23 nations using the

Chinese Value Survey (Chinese Culture Connection, 1987). Hofstede and Bond (1988) developed an index of Confucian Dynamism, which Hofstede (2001) later interpreted as long-term orientation. However, the subjective experience of time has been identified consistently as a basic feature of all cultures in the modern era of social science, dating to Kluckholn and Strodtbeck's (1961) work. Building on this research tradition, House et al. (1999) defined future orientation as the extent to which a culture encourages and rewards future-oriented behaviors such as planning and delaying gratification. More specifically, Ashkanasy, Gupta, Mayfield, and Trevor-Roberts (2004, p. 285) defined future orientation as 'the extent to which members of a society . . . believe that their current actions will influence their future, focus on investment in the future, believe that they have a future that matters, believe in planning for developing their future, and look far into the future for assessing the effects of their current actions'. Countries that scored high on the GLOBE measure of future orientation practices include Singapore, Switzerland, Austria, the Netherlands, and South Africa; low-scoring countries include Russia, Poland, and Argentina. There was a moderately strong negative relationship between societal future orientation values and practices (−0.41, p<0.01), suggesting that societal cultures that exhibit lower future orientation practices value it more highly, while those that exhibit higher future orientation practices may actually value it less.

Since part of what influences consumers' intentions to buy is related to whether they want to spend money now or save for the future, it would seem that GLOBE future orientation would be an excellent dimension for cross-cultural advertising researchers to examine. For this particular dimension, there may be a direct effect of the dimension on consumers' perceptions of advertising messaging. However, this dimension may also play a moderating role in the relationship between a consumer's perception of the advertising message and intentions to purchase the product. Individuals from cultures that are more future-oriented may be less inclined to be influenced by the advertising messaging, thus attenuating the relationship between perceptions of the ad and intentions to purchase the product. These types of question carry important practical implications for the advertising field and should be examined empirically in the future.

Performance Orientation

The final dimension included in the GLOBE study is performance orientation. Interestingly, Hofstede's (1980, 2001) study did not conceptualize or measure performance orientation as a separate dimension (Javidan,

2004). Rather, Hofstede (1980, 2001) viewed performance and achievement orientation as aspects of the masculinity/femininity index (Javidan, 2004). Kahn (1979) and Hofstede and Bond (1988) argued that Confucian principles of hard work, perseverance, and skill acquisition are important aspects of Southeast Asian cultures, but neither study specified performance orientation as an independent cultural dimension. Project GLOBE considered performance orientation to reflect 'the extent to which a community encourages and rewards innovation, high standards, and performance improvement' (Javidan, 2004, p. 239). The GLOBE scale that was developed for this dimension included four items assessing practices and four items assessing values. Societal cultures that scored high on this dimension in terms of practices included Switzerland, Hong Kong, Iran, Canada, and the U.S.; cultures that scored comparatively low on this dimension included Greece, Venezuela, Russia, Argentina, and Italy (Javidan, 2004). There was a modest negative correlation for the GLOBE sample in terms of performance orientation practices and values (-0.28, $p < 0.05$), suggesting that countries with high levels of performance orientation practices may value it less, while countries with low levels of performance orientation practices may value it more.

Diehl, Terlutter, and Mueller (2008) was the first study to begin to examine the influence of GLOBE performance orientation as a cultural dimension within the cross-cultural advertising field. Finding partial support for their hypotheses, they concluded that the performance orientation of a culture does influence how an ad incorporating performance-oriented appeals is received, and that this should be taken into account when advertisers are formulating their approaches to a given local market. There is clearly much more work to be done in the advertising literature to examine the influence of performance orientation, particularly since the appeal of many products/services is performance-based. We encourage cross-cultural advertising researchers to continue to explore the ramifications of performance orientation as a dimension of culture.

TOWARD A THEORETICAL MODEL LINKING THE GLOBE PROJECT AND ADVERTISING

In the above discussion, we attempted to briefly juxtapose Hofstede's (1980, 2001) approach and Project GLOBE's (2004) approach to studying societal culture. We believe that the increased specificity of the dimensions and psychometrically validated scales of the GLOBE study will be useful for cross-cultural advertising researchers who wish to examine culture as an antecedent of individual perceptions of advertising messaging. House et al. (2010) developed five research questions that addressed the ways in which the GLOBE study might be applied in future advertising research. In the final part of this chapter, we begin to address the first two of these research questions: 1) What are the cross-level linkages between societal culture, organizational advertising practices, and perceptions of global advertising effectiveness at the individual level? and 2) Would the fit/match between advertising methods, societal expectations regarding communication, and societal culture be an important predictor of advertising effectiveness? We put forth several possible theoretical models that may be used in the future for the development of empirical studies.

Cross-Level Mediated Effects Model

One possible way in which societal culture may influence perceptions of advertising messaging, and ultimately a customer's intention to buy, is through a cross-level mediated effects model. We depict this model in Figure 4.1. The first linkage in the model, labeled as Path A, depicts how individuals are influenced by their societal cultures. The societal culture has certain scores on the nine GLOBE dimensions, and these scores will influence how individuals within that culture perceive the culture. It is important to first spell out this cross-level connection, as we cannot make the assumption that all individuals within a given culture perceive the characteristic dimensions of that culture the same way. Path B depicts the direct effect between an individual's perceptions of his/her societal culture and the perceptions of a given advertising message. These perceptions will directly influence the evaluations they make of the ad (Path C), and those evaluations will subsequently influence individuals' intentions to purchase a given product or service (Path D). Last, Path E depicts the possible direct effect that individuals' perceptions of societal culture may have on their intention to purchase a product. Perceptions of future orientation, for example, may be negatively linked to intentions to buy. In this model, societal culture drives ad evaluation and intention to buy through several mediating mechanisms.

Cross-Level Fit Model

A second possible way societal culture may influence perceptions of advertising messaging is through a cross-level fit model. We depict this model in Figure 4.2. We discussed Path A in the direct-effects model proposed above. In the cross-level fit model, we propose that an individual's perceptions of the advertising message are independent of the effects of societal

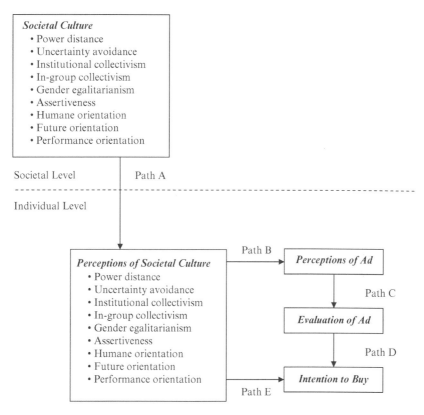

Figure 4.1   Cross-level mediated effects model

culture. However, an individual's perceptions of the advertising message must be consistent (i.e., must 'fit') with their perceptions of their societal culture in order for the perceptions of the advertising message to result in a positive evaluation. Paths B depict this interaction between individual perceptions of the ad's content and individual perceptions of societal culture on evaluations of the ad. Path C depicts the relationship between individuals' evaluation of an ad message and their intentions to purchase the product/service. One potential caveat for examining data with this theoretical approach is that it is not clear at this time whether individual perceptions of cultural practices or values would be more important in determining the strength of the relationship between individual perceptions of the advertising message itself and intention to buy. Exploratory hypotheses may be necessary should cross-cultural advertising researchers want to build on this model.

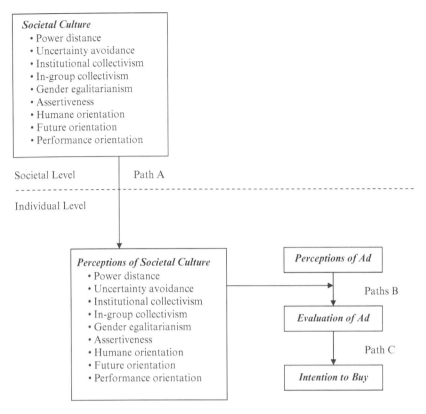

Figure 4.2   Cross-level fit model

Cross-Level Complex Fit Model

The final model we propose is more of an intellectual descendent of Project GLOBE's theoretical approach to leadership. As noted in the first part of this chapter, Project GLOBE was initially developed to examine the relationship between societal culture and leadership (House et al., 2004). As part of this effort, a conceptual model was developed based on an integration of implicit leadership theory (Lord & Maher, 1991), Hofstede's (1980) work, and implicit motivation theory (McClelland, 1985), among other approaches (House & Javidan, 2004; House et al., 1997). We focus here on how implicit leadership theory may be applied in an advertising context. Implicit leadership theory suggests that 'individuals have certain implicit beliefs, convictions, and assumptions concerning attributes and behaviors that distinguish leaders from followers, effective leaders from ineffective

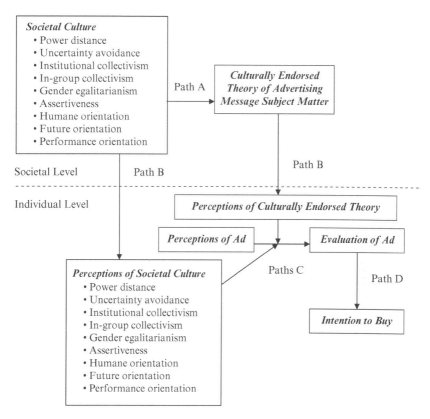

Figure 4.3   Cross-level complex fit model

leaders, and moral leaders from evil leaders' (House & Javidan, 2004, p. 16). In the context of advertising, an implicit theory (whether the subject of the theory is leadership or something else) may be relevant for whatever the particular subject matter of the advertising message is. For example, societal cultures may have very different implicit theories about sex. These implicit theories may be related to the dimensions of societal culture, but they are distinguishable from these dimensions, and may have a separate cultural influence on individual perceptions of a given ad. Our proposed cross-level complex fit model (depicted in Figure 4.3) includes two new variables based on implicit leadership theory: the culturally endorsed theory of the advertising message's subject matter and individual-level perceptions of this culturally endorsed theory.

In the cross-level complex fit model, Path A depicts the relationship between a societal culture's dimensions and its culturally endorsed implicit theory of a given ad's subject matter. Paths B depict the cross-level relationship between cultural characteristics (the GLOBE dimensions of culture and the culturally endorsed implicit theory of the advertising message's subject matter) and individual perceptions of these cultural attributes. Paths C depict both two-way and three-way interactions between individual perceptions of the cultural dimensions, individual perceptions of the culturally endorsed implicit theory, and individual perceptions of the advertising message. In our model, these two- and three-way interactions potentially influence individuals' evaluation of the ad. Ultimately, these evaluations influence consumers' intention to buy the product/service (Path D).

It is important to note that we have proposed the above three models as a starting point for further understanding of the processes by which societal culture influences advertising messaging. Another future research question, which we have not considered here, is the role an *organization's* culture plays in the development of how consumers view ads from that particular organization. There may be more opportunities to use the Project GLOBE scales at the organization level to examine possible congruence between organizational practices and values and individual perceptions of advertising as another possible cross-level influence on how individuals evaluate ad messaging.

CONCLUSION

We hope to have provided international and cross-cultural advertising researchers with a comprehensive introduction to Project GLOBE's approach to societal culture. As several promising early studies and reviews have shown (Diehl et al., 2008; House et al., 2010; Taylor, 2010; Terlutter et al., 2005; Terlutter et al., 2006), the application of Project GLOBE dimensions and scales holds a great deal of promise for this field. We hope to have provided a judicious comparison between Hofstede's (1980, 2001) work on culture and Project GLOBE (House et al., 2004) so as to allow international advertising researchers to make informed decisions about which cultural framework to use. We also hope to have provided a foundation for further theoretical development linking societal culture to individual perceptions and evaluations of advertising. We strongly encourage researchers in this area to adopt a theory-driven approach to data collection; the choice of theoretical framework used with respect to societal culture should be matched appropriately to the research questions being considered in the research.

REFERENCES

Albers-Miller, N.D. (1996), 'Designing cross-cultural advertising research: A closer look at paired comparisons', *International Marketing Review*, 13(5): 59–75.

Ashkanasy, N., Gupta, V., Mayfield, M.S. & Trevor-Roberts, E. (2004), 'Future orientation', in House, R.J., Hanges, P.J., Javidan, M., Dorfman, P.W. & Gupta, V. (eds), *Culture, Leadership, and Organizations: The GLOBE Study of 62 Societies*, pp. 282–342. Thousand Oaks, CA: Sage.

Bang, H.K., Raymond, M.A., Taylor, C.R. & Moo, Y.S. (2005), 'A comparison of service quality dimensions conveyed in advertisements for service providers in the USA and Korea: A content analysis', *International Marketing Review*, 22: 309–26.

Baskerville, R.F. (2003), 'Hofstede never studied culture', *Accounting, Organizations and Society*, 28: 1–14.

Baskerville, R.F. (2005), 'A research note: The unfinished business of culture', *Accounting, Organizations and Society*, 30(4): 389–91.

Brislin, R.W. (1970), 'Back-translation for cross-cultural research', *Journal of Cross-Cultural Psychology*, 1: 185–216.

Carl, D., Gupta, V. & Javidan, M. (2004), 'Power distance', in House, R.J., Hanges, P.J., Javidan, M., Dorfman, P.W. & Gupta, V. (eds), *Culture, Leadership and Organizations: The GLOBE Study of 62 Societies*, pp. 513–63. Thousand Oaks, CA: Sage.

Chhokar, J.S., Brodbeck, F.C. & House, R.J. (2007), *Culture and Leadership across the World: The GLOBE Book of In-Depth Studies of 25 Societies*. Mahwah, NJ: Lawrence Erlbaum.

Cyert, R. & March, J. (1963), *A Behavioral Theory of the Firm*. Englewood Cliffs, NJ: Prentice Hall.

Den Hartog, D., House, R.J., Hanges, P.J., Ruiz-Quintanilla, S.A., Dorfman, P.W. & 170 co-authors (1999), 'Culture specific and cross culturally generalizable implicit leadership theories: Are attributes of charismatic/transformational leadership universally endorsed?' *Leadership Quarterly*, 10: 219–56.

Den Hartog, D.N. (2004), 'Assertiveness', in House, R.J., Hanges, P.J., Javidan, M., Dorfman, P.W. & Gupta, V. (eds), *Culture, Leadership, and Organizations: The GLOBE Study of 62 Societies*, pp. 395–436. Thousand Oaks, CA: Sage.

Diehl, S., Mueller, B. & Terlutter, R. (2008), 'Consumer responses towards non-prescription and prescription drug advertising in the US and Germany', *International Journal of Advertising*, 27(1): 99–131.

Diehl, S., Terlutter, R. & Mueller, B. (2008), 'The influence of culture on responses to the Globe dimension of performance orientation in advertising messages: Results from the U.S., Germany, France, Spain and Thailand', *Advances in Consumer Research*, 35: 269–75.

Diehl, S., Terlutter, R. & Weinberg, P. (2003), 'Advertising effectiveness in different cultures: Results of an experiment analyzing the effects of individualistic and collectivistic advertising on German and Chinese', *European Advances in Consumer Research*, 6: 128–36.

Durkheim, E. (1933), *The Division of Labor*, Chicago: Free Press.

Earley, P.C. & Gibson, C.B. (1998), 'Taking stock in our progress on individualism collectivism: 100 years of solidarity and community', *Journal of Management*, 24: 265–304.

Furnham, A., Kirkcaldy, B.D. & Lynn, R. (1994), 'National attitudes, competition, money, and work: First, second, and third world differences', *Human Relations*, 47(1): 119–32.

Gelfand, M.J., Bhawuk, D.P.S., Nishii, L.H. & Bechtold, D. (2004), 'Individualism and collectivism', in House, R.J., Hanges, P.J., Javidan, M., Dorfman, P.W. & Gupta, V. (eds), *Culture, Leadership and Organizations: The GLOBE Study of 62 Societies*, pp. 437–512. Thousand Oaks, CA: Sage.

Goldsmith, R., Friedan, J. & Kilsheimer, J. (1993), 'Social values and female fashion leadership: A cross-cultural study', *Psychology and Marketing*, 10: 399–412.

Gupta, V. & Hanges, P.J. (2004), 'Regional and climate clustering of societal cultures', in House, R.J., Hanges, P.J., Javidan, M., Dorfman, P.W. & Gupta, V. (eds), *Culture,*

Leadership, and Organizations: The GLOBE Study of 62 Societies, pp. 178–218. Thousand Oaks, CA: Sage.

Gupta, V., Sully de Luque, M.F. & House, R.J. (2004), 'Multisource construct validity of GLOBE scales', in House, R.J., Hanges, P.J., Javidan, M., Dorfman, P.W. & Gupta, V. (eds), *Culture, Leadership, and Organizations: The GLOBE Study of 62 Societies*, pp. 152–72. Thousand Oaks, CA: Sage.

Hanges, P.J. (2004), 'Research methodology', in House, R.J., Hanges, P.J., Javidan, M., Dorfman, P.W. & Gupta, V. (eds), *Culture, Leadership, and Organizations: The GLOBE Study of 62 Societies*, pp. 91–4. Thousand Oaks, CA: Sage.

Hanges, P.J. & Dickson, M.W. (2004), 'The development and validation of the GLOBE culture and leadership scales', in House, R.J., Hanges, P.J., Javidan, M., Dorfman, P.W. & Gupta, V. (eds), *Culture, Leadership, and Organizations: The GLOBE Study of 62 Societies*, pp. 122–51. Thousand Oaks, CA: Sage.

Hanges, P.J. & Dickson, M.W. (2006), 'Agitation over aggregation: Clarifying the development of and the nature of the GLOBE scales', *The Leadership Quarterly*.

Hanges, P.J., Lord, R.G., Day, D.V., Sipe, W.P., Smith, W.C. & Brown, D.J. (1997), 'Leadership and gender bias: Dynamic measures and nonlinear modeling', in R.G. Lord (Chair), *Dynamic Systems, Leadership Perceptions, and Gender Effects*. Symposium presented at the 12th annual conference of the Society for Industrial and Organizational Psychology, St. Louis, MO.

Hofstede, G. (2010), 'The GLOBE debate: Back to relevance', *Journal of International Business Studies*, 41: 1339–46.

Hofstede, G. (1980), *Culture's Consequences: International Differences in Work-Related Values*. London: Sage.

Hofstede, G. (2001), '*Culture's Consequences: Comparing Values, Behaviors, Institutions, and Organizations across Nations*, 2nd edn. Thousand Oaks, CA: Sage.

Hofstede, G. (2006), 'What did GLOBE really measure? Researchers' minds versus respondents' minds', *Journal of International Business Studies*, 37: 882–96.

Hofstede, G. & Bond, M.H. (1988), 'The Confucius connection: From cultural roots to economic growth', *Organizational Dynamics*, 16: 4–21.

Holden, N. (2002), *Cross-Cultural Management: A Knowledge Management Perspective*. Harlow: Prentice Hall.

House, R., Javidan, M., Hanges, P.J. & Dorfman, P.W. (2002), 'Understanding cultures and implicit leadership theories across the globe: An introduction to Project GLOBE', *Journal of World Business*, 37(1): 3–10.

House, R.J. & Hanges, P.J. (2004), 'Research design', in House, R.J., Hanges, P.J., Javidan, M., Dorfman, P.W. & Gupta, V. (eds), *Culture, Leadership, and Organizations: The GLOBE Study of 62 Societies*, pp. 95–101. Thousand Oaks, CA: Sage.

House, R.J. & Javidan, M. (2004), 'Overview of GLOBE', in House, R.J., Hanges, P.J., Javidan, M., Dorfman, P.W. & Gupta, V. (eds), *Culture, Leadership, and Organizations: The GLOBE Study of 62 Societies*, pp. 9–26. Thousand Oaks, CA: Sage.

House, R.J., Hanges, P.J., Javidan, M., Dorfman, P.W. & Gupta, V. (2004), *Culture, Leadership, and Organizations: The GLOBE Study of 62 Societies*. Thousand Oaks, CA: Sage.

House, R.J., Javidan, M., Dorfman, P. & Sully de Luque, M. (2006), 'A failure of scholarship: Response to George Graen's critique of GLOBE', *Academy of Management Perspectives*, 3: 37–42.

House, R.J., Quigley, N.R. & Sully de Luque, M.F. (2010), 'Insights from Project GLOBE: Extending global advertising research through a contemporary framework', *International Journal of Advertising*, 29: 111–39.

House, R.J., Wright, N.S. & Aditya, R.N. (1997), 'Cross-cultural research on organizational leadership: A critical analysis and proposed theory', in Earley, P.C. & Erez, M. (eds), *New Perspectives in International Industrial-Organizational Psychology*, pp. 535–625. San Francisco: New Lexington.

Inkeles, A. & Levinson, D.J. (1954), 'National character: The study of modal personality and sociocultural systems', in Lindzey, G. (ed.), *Handbook of Social Psychology*, (vol. 2), pp. 977–1020. Cambridge, MA: Addison Wesley.

Javidan, M. & House, R.J. (2001), 'Cultural acumen for the global manager: Lessons from Project GLOBE', *Organizational Dynamics*, 29(4): 289–305.

Javidan, M. (2004), 'Performance orientation', in House, R.J., Hanges, P.J., Javidan, M., Dorfman, P.W. & Gupta, V. (eds), *Culture, Leadership, and Organizations: The GLOBE Study of 62 Societies*, pp. 239–81. Thousand Oaks, CA: Sage.

Javidan, M., Dorfman, P.W., Sully de Luque, M.F. & House, R.J. (2006), 'In the eye of the beholder: Cross-cultural lessons in leadership from Project GLOBE', *Academy of Management Perspectives*, February: 67–90.

Javidan, M., House, R.J., Dorfman, P., Hanges, P.M. & Sully de Luque, M. (2006), 'Conceptualizing and measuring cultures and their consequences: A comparative review of GLOBE's and Hofstede's approaches', *Journal of International Business Studies*, 37: 897–914.

Kabasakal, H. & Bodur, M. (2004), 'Humane orientation in societies, organizations, and leader attributes', in House, R.J., Hanges, P.J., Javidan, M., Dorfman, P.W. & Gupta, V. (eds), *Culture, Leadership, and Organizations: The GLOBE Study of 62 Societies*, pp. 564–601. Thousand Oaks, CA: Sage.

Kahle, L.R. & Timmer, S.G. (1983), *A Theory and Method for Studying Values and Social Change: Adaptation to Life in America*. New York: Praeger.

Kahle, L.R., Beatty, S. & Mager, J. (1964), 'Implications of social values for consumer communications: The case of the European community', in Englis, B.G. (ed.), *Global and Multinational Advertising*, pp. 47–64. Hilldale, NJ: Lawrence Erlbaum.

Kahn, H. (1979), *World Economic Development: 1979 and Beyond*. Boulder, CO: Croom Helm.

Kluckholn, F.R. & Strodtbeck, F.L. (1961), *Variations in Value Orientations*. New York: Harper Collins.

Lord, R. & Maher, K.J. (1991), *Leadership and Information Processing: Linking Perceptions and Performance*. Boston: Unwin-Everyman.

Leung, K., Bhagat, R.S., Buchan, N.R., Erez, M. & Gibson, C.B. (2005), 'Culture and international business: Recent advances and their implications for future research', *Journal of International Business Studies*, 36: 357–78.

Leung, K., Bond, M.H., Reimel de Carrasquel, S., Munoz, C., Hernandez, M., Murakami, F., Yamaguchi, S., Bierbrauer, G. & Singelis, T.M. (2002), 'Social axioms: The search for universal dimensions of general beliefs about how the world functions', *Journal of Cross-Cultural Psychology*, 33: 286–302.

Markus, H.R. & Kitiyama, S. (1991), 'Culture and the self: Implications for cognition, emotion, and motivation', *Psychological Review*, 98(2): 224–53.

McCarty, T.L. (1994), 'Bilingual education policy and the empowerment of American Indian communities', *The Journal of Educational Issues of Language Minority Students*, 14: 23–41.

McClelland, D.C. (1961), *The Achieving Society*. Princeton, NJ: Van Nostrand.

McClelland, D.C. (1985), *Human Motivation*. Glenview, IL: Scott, Foresman.

McEnally, M. & de Chernatony, L. (1999), 'The evolving nature of branding: Consumer and managerial considerations', *Academy of Marketing Science Review*, 13(2).

Mead, M. (1961), *Cooperation and Competition among Primitive Peoples*. Boston, MA: Beacon Press.

Milner, L. & Collins, J. (2000), 'Sex-role portrayals and the gender of nations', *Journal of Advertising*, 29: 67–79.

Moon, Y.S. & Chan, K. (2005), 'Advertising appeals and cultural values in television commercials: A comparison of Hong Kong and Korea', *International Marketing Review*, 22(1): 48–66.

Moon, Y.S. & Franke, G.R. (2000), 'Cultural influences on agency practitioners' ethical perceptions: A comparison of Korea and the U.S', *Journal of Advertising*, 29: 51–66.

Mortimer, K. & Grierson, S. (2010), 'The relationship between culture and advertising appeals for services', *Journal of Marketing Communications*, 16(3): 149–62.

Mulder, M. (1971), 'Power equalization through participation', *Administrative Science Quarterly*, 16: 31–8.

Mulder, M. (1976), 'Reduction of power distance in practice: The power distance reduction theory and its applications', in Hofstede, G. & Kaseem, M.S. (eds), *European Contributions to Organizational Theory*. The Netherlands: Van Gorcum.

Mulder, M. (1977), *The Daily Power Game*. Leydem, the Netherlands: Martinus Nijhoff.

Mulder, M., Ritsema van Eck, J.R. & De Long, R.D. (1971), 'An organization in crisis and non-crisis situations', *Human Relations*, 24: 19–41.

Okazaki, S. & Mueller, B. (2008), 'Evolution in the usage of localised appeals in Japanese and American print advertising', *International Journal of Advertising*, 27(5): 771–98.

Okazaki, S. & Mueller, B. (2007), 'Cross-cultural advertising research: Where we have been and where we need to go', *International Marketing Review*, 24(5): 499–518.

Okazaki, S., Mueller, B. & Taylor, C.R. (in press), 'It's all in the execution: American vs. Japanese consumer perceptions of soft sell and hard sell advertising appeals', *Journal of Advertising*, forthcoming.

Parsons, T. (1949), *Essays in Sociological Theory: Pure and Applied*. New York: Free Press.

Quigley, N.R., Sully de Luque, M.F. & House, R.J. (2005), 'Societal culture, corporate responsibility, governance, and responsible leadership: Perspectives from the GLOBE study', in Doh, J.P. & Stumpf, S.A. (eds), *Handbook on Responsible Leadership and Governance in Global Business*, Cheltenham, UK and Northampton, MA, USA: Edward Elgar.

Realo, A., Allik, J. & Vadi, M. (1997), 'The hierarchical structure of collectivism', *Journal of Research in Personality*, 31: 93–116.

Redfield, R. (1956), *Peasant Society and Culture: An Anthropological Approach to Civilization*. Chicago: University of Chicago Press.

Rhee, E., Uleman, J.S. & Lee, H.K. (1996), 'Variations in collectivism and individualism by in-group and culture: Confirmatory factor analyses', *Journal of Personality and Social Psychology*, 71: 1037–54.

Rokeach, M. (1973), *The Nature of Human Values*. San Francisco: Jossey-Bass.

Rokeach, M. (1968), *Beliefs, Attitudes, and Values*. San Francisco: Jossey-Bass.

Samover, L., Porter, R. & Stefani, L. (1998), *Communication between Cultures*. Belmont, CA: Wadsworth Publishing.

Schwartz, S.H. (1992), 'Universals in the content and structure of values: Theoretical advances and empirical tests in 20 countries', in Zanna, M. (ed.), *Advances in Experimental Social Psychology*, pp. 1–65. New York: Academic Press.

Schwartz, S.H. (1994), 'Are there universal aspects in the structure and content of human values?' *Journal of Social Issues*, 50: 19–45.

Schwartz, S.H. (1996), 'Value priorities and behavior: Applying of theory and integrated value systems', in Seligman, C., Olson, J.M. & Zanna, M.P. (eds), *The Psychology of Values: The Ontario Symposium*, vol. 8, pp. 1–24. Hillsdale, NJ: Lawrence Erlbaum.

Segall, M.H., Lonner, W.J. & Berry, J.W. (1998), 'Cross-cultural psychology as a scholarly discipline: On the flowering of culture in behavioral research', *American Psychologist*, 53: 1101–10.

Seijts, G.H. (1998), 'The importance of future time perspective in theories of work motivation', *Journal of Psychology*, 132: 154–68.

Sipe, W.P. & Hanges, P.J. (1997), 'Reframing the glass ceiling: A catastrophe model of changes in the perception of women as leaders', in R.G. Lord (Chair), *Dynamic Systems, Leadership Perceptions, and Gender Effects*. Symposium presented at the 12th annual conference of the Society for Industrial and Organizational Psychology, St. Louis, MO.

Smith, P.B., Peterson, M.F. & Schwartz, S.H. (2002), 'Cultural values, sources of guidance, and their relevance to managerial behavior: A 47-nation study', *Journal of Cross-Cultural Psychology*, 33: 188–208.

Sully de Luque, M.F. & Javidan, M. (2004), 'Uncertainty avoidance', in House, R.J., Hanges, P.J., Javidan, M., Dorfman, P.W. & Gupta, V. (eds), *Culture, Leadership and Organizations: The GLOBE Study of 62 Societies*, pp. 602–44. Thousand Oaks, CA: Sage.

Taylor, C.R. (2005), 'Moving international advertising research forward: A new research agenda', *Journal of Advertising*, 34(1): 7–16.

Taylor, C.R. (2010), 'Toward stronger theory development in international advertising research', *International Journal of Advertising*, 29: 9–14.

Terlutter, R., Diehl, S. & Mueller, B. (2005), 'The influence of culture on responses to assertiveness in advertising messages', in *Advertising and Communication: Proceedings of the 4th International Conference on Research in Advertising (ICORIA)*, pp. 183–92. Saarbruecken.

Terlutter, R., Diehl, S. & Mueller, B. (2006), 'The GLOBE study: Applicability of a new typology of cultural dimensions for cross-cultural marketing and advertising research', in Diehl, S. & Terlutter, R. (eds), *International Advertising and Communication: Current Insights and Empirical Findings*, pp. 420–38. Wissenschaft, Wiesbaden: Gabler Edition.

Triandis, H.C. (1995), *Individualism and Collectivism*. Boulder, CO: Westview Press.

Triandis, H.C. (1998), *Culture and Social Behavior*, New York: McGraw-Hill.

Triandis, H.C., Bontempo, R., Bentancourt, H., Bond, M. et al. (1986), 'The measurement of the etic aspects of individualism and collectivism across cultures', *Australian Journal of Psychology*, 257–67.

Triandis, H.C. & Gelfand, M.J. (1998), 'Converging measurement of horizontal and vertical individualism and collectivism', *Journal of Personality and Social Psychology*, 74: 118–28.

Tung, R.L. & Verbeke, A. (2010), 'Beyond Hofstede and GLOBE: Improving the quality of cross-cultural research', *Journal of International Business Studies*, 41: 1259–74.

Ueltschy, L. & Ryans, J.K. Jr. (1997), 'Advertising strategies to capitalize on Spain's second golden age', *International Journal of Management*, 14: 456–67.

Van de Vijver, F. & Leung, K. (1997), *Methods and Data Analysis for Cross-Cultural Research*. Thousand Oaks, CA: Sage.

Waldman, D.A., Sully de Luque, M.F., Washburn, N., House, R.J. & colleagues (2006), 'Cultural and leadership predictors of corporate social responsibility values of top management: A study of 15 countries', *Journal of International Business Studies*, 37: 823–37.

5 Typologies of cultural dimensions and their applicability to international advertising

Ralf Terlutter, Sandra Diehl and
Barbara Mueller

INTRODUCTION

One important area of cross-cultural research identifies sets of cultural values useful in describing cultures. Resulting frameworks outline a number of cultural dimensions that attempt to explain a significant portion of country-to-country variance. Often, international advertising research draws upon data of cultural dimensions reported in these typologies. We begin with a brief discussion of individual versus societal levels of culture, cultural values versus cultural practices, as well as a comparison of country versus global consumer segments. After this, four typologies of cultural dimensions are highlighted. The first is Hofstede's typology of cultural values, by far the most prominent approach to cultural dimensions in marketing and advertising research. Next, two less frequently applied frameworks are presented: Schwartz's cultural values, and Inglehart's World Values Survey (WVS). Finally, the GLOBE framework is examined. We conclude with a culture-based model of international advertising.

CULTURAL DIMENSIONS IN CROSS-CULTURAL RESEARCH

As the level of global trade increases, corporations around the world have a growing need for knowledge of foreign cultures. Because consumers are increasingly found abroad, advertisers devote a rising percentage of their advertising budgets to foreign markets. For instance, U.S.-based Procter & Gamble, the world's largest advertiser, in 2009 invested two-thirds of measured advertising spendings in non-U.S. markets, generating nearly two-thirds of their revenues from outside the U.S. (Advertising Age, 2010). Netherlands-based Unilever, the second-largest

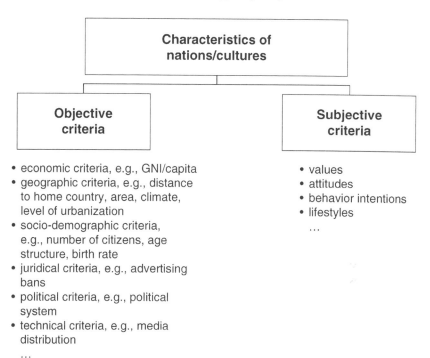

Figure 5.1   Characteristics of nations/cultures

global advertiser, last year devoted over 95 percent of measured advertising spending to non-domestic markets (Advertising Age, 2010). For such companies, a profound knowledge of foreign cultures is vital, in order to effectively communicate with consumers in those markets. Further, data allowing for comparisons between different countries, which provide insights for regional or global marketing and advertising efforts, is of significant value. This article presents four typologies that deliver such a priori data by reporting on the cultural characteristics of a large number of countries.

Information about diverse cultures can be divided into relatively objective, as well as more subjective criteria (Figure 5.1). Objective criteria include economic data such as GNI per capita or purchase power per capita, geographic information such as the level of urbanization, socio-demographic data such as age structure or birth rate, and information on the legal and political system in a country. Subjective criteria, which characterize a nation or culture, include the values, attitudes and lifestyles shared by its citizens.

Among these subjective criteria, in international advertising research, values have received a great deal of attention (Okazaki and Mueller, 2007). Cultural values are considered to be at the core of a culture. They determine the perceptions, the predispositions and the behaviors of the members of a society (Markus and Kitayama, 1991). The theoretical rationale for the analysis of cultural values across nations is that all cultures face similar problems and challenges. These problems and challenges can be dealt with in a variety of ways, reflecting that culture's particular value system. In short, analysis of cultural values is believed to allow for the comparison of similarities and differences between various cultures (Kluckhohn, 1951; Kluckhohn and Strodtbeck, 1961; Parsons and Shils, 1951). Values are implicitly or explicitly shared ideas about what is good, right and desirable in a society and they are expressed in widely shared norms, symbols, rituals, practices and ways of thinking (Sagiv and Schwartz, 2000). They shape how individuals behave in a culture. Members of cultural groups share many value-relevant experiences, and they are socialized to adapt to these shared societal values.

LEVELS OF CULTURE

Cross-cultural research has often emphasized the importance of distinguishing between the influence of culture on an individual level versus on a national or societal level (e.g., Schwartz, 1994; Triandis, 1994, 1995; Singelis and Brown, 1995; Malhotra et al., 1996; Kacen and Lee, 2002). As individuals are socialized through values that are held and behaviors that are practiced in their cultures, it is very likely that they adopt values and practices that are shared among members of their society (Markus and Kitayama, 1991). However, culture is not the sole factor influencing an individual's behavior. Furthermore, societal or culture-level dimensions are not necessarily reflected in the behavior of each and every individual from that culture. Culture-level analyses primarily reflect central tendencies for a country and not necessarily for a particular individual. Thus, the prediction of individual level outcomes based solely on the use of culture-level data may be inappropriate. In short, societal culture-level data and individual level data can be expected to have similar, but not necessarily identical patterns. Individual values are a product of shared culture as well as individual experiences and preferences.

Within societies or cultural groups, individual differences in the importance of values appear, owing to unique experiences, personalities and genetic heritages. However, the general importance that cultures attribute to different values is not affected by these individual differences in the value system (Sagiv and Schwartz, 2000).

CULTURAL VALUES AND CULTURAL PRACTICES

A distinction that is also relevant for cultural typologies is that between cultural values versus cultural practices. Schein (2010), for instance, differentiates between artifacts and espoused values as two unique levels of culture. Artifacts are the visible products, processes and behaviors of a culture. They mainly reflect the current status and how issues are handled in a society and, therefore, the cultural practices. Espoused values are the individuals' or society's sense of what ought to be, as distinct from what is. They primarily reflect how things should be and, therefore, the cultural values. This distinction made between values and practices is similar to DeMooij's (2010) distinction between "desirable" and "desired" values. The "desirable" refers to social norms that are held in a culture and by an individual, whereas the "desired" refers to individuals' choices. Both values and practices can be contradictory in a culture and can therefore be seen as paradoxical values, which are found in many cultures. For instance, a culture or an individual may value healthy foods, but that society's or individual's eating habits may be in direct opposition to this value. Thus, although individuals know that fast food is more or less unhealthy and should not be eaten all too often (values), they nevertheless like it and consume it regularly (practices).

In particular, the GLOBE study explicitly differentiates between cultural values and cultural practices (House and Hanges, 2004) and reports separate data for both dimensions of culture. Neither Schwartz, Hofstede, nor Inglehart explicitly differentiate between values and practices. A closer look at the measurements in these studies reveals that Schwartz's focus is more on values than on practices. He asks respondents to rate the importance of each single value "as a basic principle in my life" (e.g., Schwartz, 1994, p. 99). Hofstede's questions or statements in his instruments are a combination of both practices and values, without analyzing them separately. Inglehart's WVS survey primarily targets values, attitudes and motivations, rather than practices.

The question whether values or practices may be more appropriate for advertising (or other marketing purposes) is essential, given that both values and practices may be contradictory. For example, should an advertisement address the values or the practices of a culture? Should an ad campaign for a fast food restaurant portray people eating fast food (depict practices) or instead address health issues regarding fast food (depict values)?

COUNTRIES VERSUS GLOBAL CONSUMER SEGMENTS AS UNITS OF ANALYSES

Units of analysis in the four typologies described here are territories, that is, countries or geographic areas. Countries or geographic areas are described based on the cultural values and/or practices of their citizens. The dimensions used to describe the countries are identical in all countries. Hence, the typologies focus on those dimensions that can be found (though in differing levels) in all countries, but they leave out those cultural dimensions with a "local" character not found in all countries. However, over the past few decades, it appears that "world cultures" (Hannerz, 1990, p. 237) have emerged, which are not clearly anchored in any single territory, but instead can be found around the globe. A world culture appears to be dependent on people's actual or imagined participation in global consumer segments. Examples might include Facebook or Youtube users who share common wants and needs, which might be independent from their local or countries' cultural preferences. Given the obvious emergence of such world cultures for specific products or product categories, the question arises as to how this development relates to the analyses of typologies of cultural dimensions presented here. We see two main arguments that underline the relevance of such typologies. First, in many corporations, the organizational structure is often related to territorial aspects (e.g., Regions South, East, West, etc.; Regions Asia, Europe, North America, South America; autonomous subsidiaries in the different countries, etc.). Companies may decide to "export to country X or Y", etc. Retailers as well as manufacturers have a multitude of diverse products and sell these goods in a large number of countries. For them, information about countries that allows for comparisons among their customers is of great value. Second, given that the typologies report on the same dimensions in all countries, they might also be useful for products or target groups related to "world cultures". For instance, if the target group is "international business travellers", who are arguably relatively similar across different countries, information related to their values and practices regarding performance orientation or assertiveness – dimensions provided by the GLOBE typology – might be useful. And this information is available for a large number of countries – in the case of GLOBE, for 62 countries. Hence, it is argued that the four typologies presented here may provide useful information for a large number of companies.

EXISTING FRAMEWORKS OF CULTURAL DIMENSIONS

An important category of cross-cultural research identifies sets of cultural values useful in describing cultures. Resulting frameworks outline a given number of cultural dimensions that attempt to explain a significant portion of country-to-country variance. To date, at least four such classification systems exist, which report data from a large number of countries, allowing for cross-cultural comparisons: Hofstede's dimensions (1980, 2001), Schwartz's cultural values (1992, 1994, 1999; Schwartz and Ros, 1995; Schwartz and Bardi, 1997; Smith and Schwartz, 1997; Sagiv and Schwartz, 2000), the World Values Survey (World Values Survey, 1981–2008; Inglehart, 1997; Inglehart, Basañez and Moreno, 1998; Inglehart and Welzel, 2005) and, finally the GLOBE framework (House et al., 2004; Chhokar, Brodbeck and House, 2008). There are other important cultural frameworks that provide useful information as outlined by Hall (e.g., 1966, 1976, 1983), Trompenaars (e.g., 1993) and Kluckhohn and Strodtbeck (1961), which are not highlighted here, in part because they do not report data for a large number of countries.

Hofstede's Cultural Dimensions

Without question, Hofstede (1980, 2001) has developed by far the most influential cultural framework, with over 1100 citations of his work reported in just the decade between 1987 and 1997 (Sivakumar and Nakata, 2001). A number of researchers have recognized the applicability of Hofstede's dimensions to advertising and marketing – Taylor, Miracle and Wilson (1997); Caillat and Mueller (1996); and Diehl, Terlutter and Weinberg (2003), to mention just a few. Hofstede outlined four fundamental problems that all societies face: 1) the relationship between the individual and the group; 2) social inequality; 3) social implications of gender; and 4) handling of uncertainty inherent in economic and social processes. Work-related values and behaviors among matched samples of IBM employees at subsidiaries around the globe were examined. Based on 117000 questionnaires from 88000 respondents in 20 languages reflecting 66 countries, Hofstede delineated four important dimensions useful in characterizing countries: *power distance*, societal desire for hierarchy or egalitarianism; *individualism*, society's preference for a group or individual orientation; *masculinity vs. femininity*, a sex-role dimension; and *uncertainty avoidance*, a culture's tolerance for uncertainty. Later research resulted in the addition of a fifth dimension, *long-term orientation* (Hofstede and Bond, 1988), the cultural perspective on a long-term vs. a short-term basis. Each of these five dimensions is measured on an index scale. Scores indicate relative differences between countries. Combinations of the five scores for each country explain why people and organizations in various countries differ.

According to Hofstede's website (as of February 24, 2011), information is now provided for 74 regions, partly based on replications and extensions of the IBM study on different international populations. Studies validating the earlier results have included commercial airline pilots and students in 23 countries, civil service managers in 14 counties, "up-market" consumers in 15 countries and "elites" in 19 countries. Figure 5.2 depicts a diagram highlighting 50 countries on Hofstede's dimensions of power distance and uncertainty avoidance.

Of late, however, Hofstede's work has come under some scrutiny. The description of countries on mere four or five dimensions is seen as insufficient, with several important dimensions missing. Hofstede (1980, p. 313f.) himself admitted: "it may be that there exist other dimensions related to equally fundamental problems of mankind which were not found . . . because the relevant questions simply were not asked". Further, Hofstede has been criticized regarding measurement of his dimensions, equivalence of the meaning of his values in each of the cultures, as well as the age of his data, which was primarily collected between 1968 and 1972. Because Hofstede measured work-related behaviors and values among employees in large multinational organizations, a transfer of his results to other groups (e.g., consumers) or other areas (e.g., advertising) and the usage of his results to discriminate national cultures, in general, are speculative. Hofstede stated: "The values questions found to discriminate between countries had originally been chosen for IBM's internal purposes. They were never intended to form a complete and universal instrument for measuring national cultures" (Hofstede, 2001, p. 493). De Mooij and Hofstede (2010) discuss some conceptual issues relevant for the application of the Hofstede model to international branding and advertising research.

Despite all criticism, owing to its contribution to understanding cultures, the large pool of country scores for a variety of cultures, as well as the lack of alternative frameworks at the time, Hofstede's typology of cultural values has been applied extensively in cross-cultural research during the last 25 years.

Schwartz's Cultural Values

Schwartz provides another typology of cultural values (1992, 1994, 1999; Schwartz and Ros, 1995; Schwartz and Bardi, 1997; Smith and Schwartz, 1997). Relying on a broad theoretical basis, Schwartz outlined

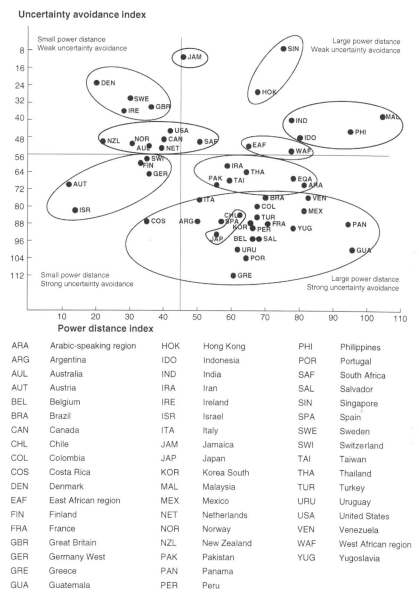

Uncertainty avoidance index

ARA	Arabic-speaking region	HOK	Hong Kong	PHI	Philippines
ARG	Argentina	IDO	Indonesia	POR	Portugal
AUL	Australia	IND	India	SAF	South Africa
AUT	Austria	IRA	Iran	SAL	Salvador
BEL	Belgium	IRE	Ireland	SIN	Singapore
BRA	Brazil	ISR	Israel	SPA	Spain
CAN	Canada	ITA	Italy	SWE	Sweden
CHL	Chile	JAM	Jamaica	SWI	Switzerland
COL	Colombia	JAP	Japan	TAI	Taiwan
COS	Costa Rica	KOR	Korea South	THA	Thailand
DEN	Denmark	MAL	Malaysia	TUR	Turkey
EAF	East African region	MEX	Mexico	URU	Uruguay
FIN	Finland	NET	Netherlands	USA	United States
FRA	France	NOR	Norway	VEN	Venezuela
GBR	Great Britain	NZL	New Zealand	WAF	West African region
GER	Germany West	PAK	Pakistan	YUG	Yugoslavia
GRE	Greece	PAN	Panama		
GUA	Guatemala	PER	Peru		

Source: Geert Hofstede (1990), Institute for Research on Intercultural Cooperation, Maastricht, the Netherlands.

Figure 5.2   Country map based on two of Hofstede's dimensions: power distance and uncertainty avoidance

an exhaustive set of cultural dimensions to describe human variety. He conducted a survey of individual values recognized across cultures (Schwartz, 1992) as a starting point for the development of a framework of cultural values on a societal level. Schwartz (1994) reported survey data from 38 nations representing 41 cultural groups. Data collection took place between 1988 and 1992.

Schwartz identified three basic societal issues: 1) the relationship between the individual and the group; 2) assuring responsible social behavior; and 3) the role of humans in the natural and social world. Cultural adaptations to resolve each of these issues constitute his framework, which consists of seven national-cultural domains, which differentiate cultures. The seven dimensions are: 1) *conservatism*, a cultural emphasis on maintenance of the status quo, propriety, and restraint of actions or inclinations that might disrupt the solidarity of the group or the traditional order; 2) *intellectual autonomy*, a cultural emphasis on the right of individuals to independently pursue their own ideas and intellectual directions; 3) *affective autonomy*, a cultural emphasis on the right of individuals to independently pursue affectively positive experience; 4) *hierarchy*, a cultural emphasis on the legitimacy of an unequal distribution of power, roles and resources; 5) *egalitarian commitment* (or *egalitarianism*), a cultural emphasis on transcendence of selfish interests in favor of voluntary commitment to promoting the welfare of others; 6) *mastery*, a cultural emphasis on seeking to actively master and change the world; and 7) *harmony*, a cultural emphasis on accepting the world as it is rather than attempting to change or exploit it.

According to Sagiv and Schwartz (2000), a total of over 60 000 respondents from 185 samples in 63 nations rated the importance of 57 single values as "guiding principles in MY life". For cross-cultural comparison, only those 45 values with reasonable equivalent meanings across cultures were used for analyses (Schwartz, 1992, 1994, as well as unpublished data referred to in Sagiv and Schwartz, 2000). Subjects were primarily schoolteachers who taught the full range of subjects in grades 3 to 12, in the most common types of school system. Sagiv and Schwartz (2000) argue that schoolteachers constitute a particularly suitable group for such comparison, as they make up the largest occupational group, as well as have a similar educational and socio-economic status relative to the wider population in almost all nations. In addition, they argue that schoolteachers play an explicit role in value socialization in society. According to Sagiv and Schwartz (2000), comparisons of the value hierarchies of schoolteacher samples with the value hierarchies of college student samples in 55 nations as well as with representative or near-representative samples from 12 nations on all five continents reveal that – although representative

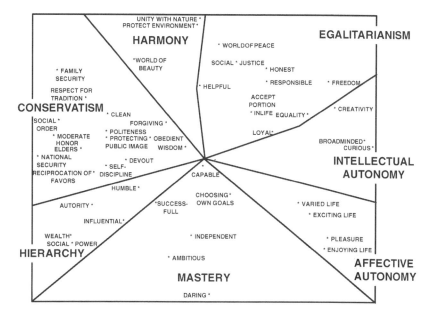

Source: Schwartz (1999).

Figure 5.3   Schwartz's cultural values

samples, students, and schoolteachers differ in their value priorities – the order of nations on the value means of the different groups is quite similar (mean intercorrelations between 0.74 and 0.98). Data collection took place between 1988 and 1997. This data is also available for purchase from the Social Sciences Data Center at the Hebrew University of Jerusalem.

Based on this data, Schwartz hypothesized a structure for the above mentioned seven dimensions (see Figure 5.3.). In this figure, pairs of value types that are in opposition (for example, mastery vs. harmony) emanate in opposing directions from the center. In contrast, compatible pairs of value types are located in proximity to one another. By and large, this structure has been confirmed via Similarity Structure Analysis.

Based on their cultural value priorities, Schwartz arranged countries in a two-dimensional space, presenting meaningful groupings of culturally-related nations (see Figure 5.4). Distances between countries represent the degree of similarity or dissimilarity between them.

The arrow adjacent to the name of each value type indicates the direction of increasing importance of that value type relative to the center of the two-dimensional space. A directional line can thus be drawn through the center of the "map" and the arrow located next to the name of each

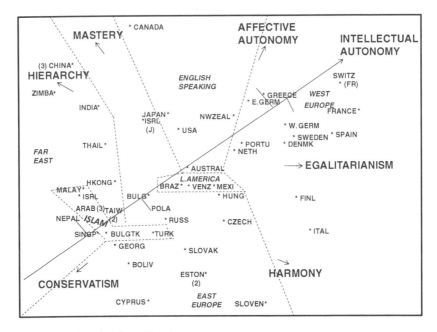

Note: Based on data from 44 nations.

Source: Schwartz (1999).

Figure 5.4   Schwartz's map of countries

value type. Such a line is drawn for intellectual autonomy, extending from the lower left to the upper right in Figure 5.4. This suggests that the farther toward the upper right a country is located, the greater the importance that country attributes to intellectual autonomy values, relative to all other countries. The further toward the lower left, the less importance the country attributes to intellectual autonomy values. As can be seen in this figure, intellectual autonomy is quite important in (the former) West Germany, somewhat less important in Greece, rather unimportant in Poland, and very unimportant in Nepal (Schwartz, 1999). Schwartz suggests the existence of broad cultural groupings of nations, which, though related to geographical proximity, are also based on shared histories, religion, level of development, cultural contact, as well as other factors (such as Western European nations, English-speaking nations, etc.).

Compared with Hofstede's work, Schwartz's typology of cultural values has been less widely applied to advertising. One reason may be the lack of a single comprehensive publication summarizing Schwartz's dimensions for all the multitude of countries examined. Instead, Schwartz's findings are scattered across a number of journals, each focusing on a segment of the total number of cultures explored. Another, perhaps more important, reason may well be that Hofstede's (1980) previously published work had already been widely accepted.

Inglehart's World Values Survey

The third typology of cultural values is the World Values Survey (WVS) (World Values Survey, 1981–2008; Inglehart, 1997; Inglehart, Basañez and Moreno, 1998; Inglehart and Welzel, 2005). The survey provides a standardized cross-cultural measure of people's values and goals, concerning politics, economics, religion, sexual behavior, gender roles, family values and ecological concerns. The WVS in collaboration with EVS (European Values Study) carried out representative national surveys in 97 societies containing almost 90 percent of the world's population. Included in these surveys are countries that range from very poor to very rich, from authoritarian systems to liberal democracies, and include all major cultural zones. There have been five waves of data collection between 1981 and 2008, and over 250 000 people have been interviewed. By conducting the survey in waves, WVS charts how values change, and examines how modernization and tradition interact to shape these changes. These surveys show pervasive shifts in what people want out of life and what they believe. Data is available for download at www.worldvaluessurvey.org.

According to the WVS, there are two basic, broad cultural dimensions that characterize nations. One dimension is survival values versus well-being values. Inglehart, Basañez and Moreno (1998) note that, in post-industrial society, "historically unprecedented levels of wealth and the emergence of welfare states have given rise to a shift from scarcity norms, emphasizing hard work and self-denial, to post-modern values emphasizing the quality of life, emancipation of women and sexual minorities, and related post-materialistic priorities, such as emphasis on self-expression". The second dimension is traditional authority versus secular-rational authority. The authors note that this dimension reflects an emphasis on "obedience to traditional authority (usually religious authority) and adherence to family and communal obligations, and norms of sharing, or, on the other hand, a secular worldview in which authority is legitimated by rational-legal norms, linked with an emphasis on economic and individual achievement". The data reveal that the basic values and beliefs of populations in advanced nations differ significantly from those found in less developed nations.

Based on survey results, countries are plotted on a two-dimensional "map" of nations (see Figure 5.5.). Societies located close to one another on the map reflect relatively similar responses to most of the questions

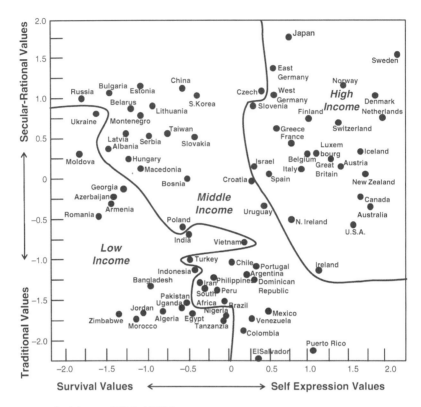

Source: Inglehart and Welzel (2005).

Figure 5.5   Map of countries, based on the WVS

asked in the World Values Survey. For example, while Americans and Canadians are different in many ways, they nonetheless share similar basic values when compared with most other societies. Accordingly, they are located in close proximity on the map. To a remarkable degree, the societies cluster into relatively homogeneous cultural zones, reflecting their cultural heritage. Yet, "socio-economic development tends to shift a society's path on the two value dimensions in a predictable fashion: as the work force shifts from the agrarian sector to the industrial sector, people's world views tend to shift from an emphasis on traditional values to an emphasis on secular-rational values. Subsequently, as the work force shifts from the industrial sector to the service sector, a second major shift in values occurs, from emphasis on survival values to emphasis on self-expression values" (Inglehart and Welzel, 2005, p. 6).

When compared with the work of Hofstede or Schwartz, the World Values Survey has been the typology least often applied to marketing and advertising. Clearly, the theoretical foundation based on social and political science, the magnitude of empirical data and the longitudinal character of the analyses presented are impressive. However, with regard to its applicability to advertising, there are some limitations to the WVS framework, when compared with those of Hofstede, Schwartz, or GLOBE. The two basic dimensions of survival values versus self-expression values and traditional authority versus secular-rational authority used to describe different cultures are quite broad. Hofstede (five dimensions), Schwartz (seven dimensions) and, in particular, GLOBE (nine dimensions, to be addressed next) provide significantly more detailed descriptions of nations than the WVS with just two dimensions. For instance, in investigating cultural differences between France and Greece, the two WVS dimensions would provide very little insight as they indicate that both countries are extremely similar, with minimal variance on the two dimensions. However, the other three frameworks reveal more detailed information and indicate, for instance, that the two countries are, indeed, particularly similar with regard to the dimensions of future orientation, performance orientation and in-group collectivism, but distinct with regard to the cultural dimensions of power distance, institutional collectivism, humane orientation, gender egalitarianism, assertiveness, and especially with regard to the dimension of uncertainty avoidance (based on the GLOBE values, addressed next).

THE GLOBE STUDY

GLOBE (Global Leadership and Organizational Behavior Effectiveness Research Program) (House et al., 2004) offers an alternative to the previous three frameworks of cultural dimensions. The GLOBE project was initially designed to analyze the relationship between societal values and practices, and leadership effectiveness. However, as it provides data on cultural values and practices in different countries, many authors propose that it may prove relevant for advertising purposes, as well (Terlutter et al., 2005; Okazaki and Mueller, 2007; Diehl et al., 2008; House et al., 2010).

Data is provided for 62 cultures, based on a survey of 17 300 middle managers in 951 organizations. Managers were drawn from three industries: financial services, food processing and telecommunications. Given that data collection began after 1994, the GLOBE framework is based on relatively current data, especially when compared with the data provided by Hofstede. In recognizing the work of a large number of cross-cultural researchers, the GLOBE framework aims at providing a broader theoretical foundation for their cultural dimensions.

GLOBE outlined nine cultural dimensions: 1) *assertiveness*, the degree to which individuals in societies are assertive, confrontational, aggressive and straightforward; 2) *uncertainty avoidance*, the extent to which members of a society strive to avoid uncertainty by relying on established social norms and practices; 3) *power distance*, the degree to which members of a society expect and accept that power is distributed unequally; 4) *collectivism I (institutional collectivism)*, the degree to which societal institutional practices encourage and reward collective distribution of resources and collective action, as opposed to individual distribution and individual action; 5) *collectivism II (in-group collectivism)*, the extent to which members of a society express pride, loyalty and cohesiveness in their groups, organizations and families; 6) *gender egalitarianism*, the degree to which a society minimizes gender role differences; 7) *future orientation*, the degree to which members of a society engage in future-oriented behaviors such as planning, investing and delaying gratification; 8) *performance orientation*, the degree to which a society encourages and rewards group members for performance improvement and excellence; and 9) *humane orientation*, the extent to which a society encourages and rewards its members for being fair, altruistic, friendly, caring and kind to others.

The first six GLOBE dimensions are based on Hofstede's (1980) work. GLOBE scales measuring uncertainty avoidance, power distance and collectivism dimensions were designed to reflect Hofstede's (2001) dimensions of uncertainty avoidance, power distance and individualism. However, factor analyses conducted by GLOBE researchers revealed that the dimension of collectivism could effectively be divided into two sub-dimensions: institutional collectivism and in-group collectivism. Whereas in-group collectivism, reflecting the degree to which individuals have pride in and express their loyalty toward their families, is similar to the dimension of collectivism as typically understood in literature (for instance, Hofstede, 1980, 2001; Triandis, 1989, 1995), institutional collectivism, which reflects the degree to which laws, social programs, or institutional practices are designed to encourage collectivistic behavior, is a form of collectivism that has received limited attention to date (House and Javidan, 2004). Further, because Hofstede's masculinity dimension was seen to be confounded by numerous factors judged irrelevant to the concept, and was also seen to be lacking in face validity, GLOBE researchers introduced two new cultural dimensions: gender egalitarianism and assertiveness.

Future orientation has its origins in Kluckhohn and Strodtbeck's (1961) past, present, future orientation dimension, which reflects the temporal orientation of the majority of the population in the society. This dimension has some similarities with, but also some distinctions from Hofstede's (2001) long-term orientation (Ashkanasy et al., 2004). Performance orientation has its roots in the construct of need for achievement (McClelland, 1961). Finally, humane orientation is derived from Kluckhohn and Strodtbeck's (1961) dimension of human nature as good vs. human nature as evil, as well as from work by Putnam (1993) and McClelland (1985).

To the benefit of subsequent investigators, GLOBE researchers describe their methodology in great detail (for instance, pilot studies, double translations, bias testing, and bias elimination). Similarly, reliability and validity measures are tested using multitrait, multimethod approaches (Hanges 2004). In addition, over 170 GLOBE researchers from different cultural backgrounds worked together on construct definition, construct conceptualization and on the measurement of the constructs. In most countries/cultures analyzed in the GLOBE project, data collection was carried out by natives of the country or by researchers with extensive experience in those markets.

GLOBE provides data on the societal level and explicitly differentiates between societal *values* and societal *practices*. The distinction between cultural values and cultural practices was incorporated to correspond with Schein's (2010) concepts of artifacts vs. espoused values as two unique levels of culture (House and Hanges, 2004). As previously noted, this is similar to DeMooij's (2010) distinction between "desirable" and "desired" values. The "desirable" refers to social norms that are held in a culture and by an individual (corresponding to the "should be", or the GLOBE values), whereas the "desired" refers to individuals' choices (corresponding to the "as is", or the GLOBE practices). Both values and practices (the desirable and the desired) are often contradictory in a culture and are therefore seen as paradoxical values, which are found in many cultures. For instance, the GLOBE data reveal a slightly negative correlation between societal values and societal practices for the dimension of *assertiveness* ($r = -0.26$, $p < 0.05$) (Den Hartog, 2004). This negative correlation is in line with the reflections outlined above. It suggests that countries scoring higher on assertiveness practices tend to value assertiveness to a lesser extent, while countries scoring lower on assertiveness practices tend to value assertiveness more strongly.

Given the fact that values and practices in a society may be inconsistent and sometimes even contradictory, it is a major strength that GLOBE clearly distinguishes between both levels of culture. Hofstede (1980, 2001), in particular, often confused values and behaviors (practices) in his dimensions, which is a further weakness of his framework.

While GLOBE provides data on the societal level, it does not do so on the individual level. The items used in the GLOBE project are designed to reflect societal values and practices, not individual values and practices. However, as individuals are socialized through values that are held and behaviors that are practised in their cultures, it is very likely that they adopt values and practices that are shared among members of their society (Markus and Kitayama, 1991). The values held and practices shown by members of a culture influence individual values and practices, as they enable the individual to behave according to social norms and rules and in a manner that is rewarded by other members of that group.

GLOBE offers an alternative perspective to the existing frameworks on cultural dimensions. Compared with the previously discussed frameworks by Hofstede and Schwartz, GLOBE presents the most current data on cultural dimensions and it does so for a large number of cultures (62 cultures). It clearly distinguishes between societal values and practices, recognizing that both levels of culture may, on occasion, even be in conflict. With regard to its theoretical foundation and methodology, GLOBE draws on those dimensions that cross-cultural researchers generally deemed most important in the literature. And, while it draws on previous cross-cultural work (for instance, by adapting five of Hofstede's dimensions with regard to their semantic meaning), it clearly also advances existing frameworks in terms of conceptualization of cultural dimensions (e.g., by splitting up Hostede's masculinity dimension into the two separate dimensions, assertiveness and gender egalitarianism), as well as with regard to the exhaustiveness and measurement of these dimensions.

A major limitation of the GLOBE study is its relatively small sample size, with an average of only about 250 subjects per culture. GLOBE researchers report that the number of respondents ranged from 27 to 1790, though more than 90 percent of the cultures investigated had sample sizes of 75 respondents or greater. While 17 300 total respondents is indeed a large figure, it is still a small sample for describing societal values and practices in 62 different cultures. The previously discussed frameworks are all based on significantly larger samples.

A second limitation is that respondents were middle managers in corporations. As with the Hofstede study (where IBM employees were surveyed) or the Schwartz investigation (where teachers and students were analyzed), a single group within each culture was analyzed in the GLOBE project, as well. Transfer to other groups (for instance, consumers) remains speculative and requires empirical testing. With regard to the sampling of respondents, only the World Values Survey has a more representative sample of the cultures analyzed.

TOWARDS A CULTURE-BASED MODEL OF INTERNATIONAL ADVERTISING

Examples of applications of the GLOBE typology to international advertising are provided by Diehl, Terlutter and Mueller (2008) and Terlutter, Diehl and Mueller (2010). Diehl et al. (2008) analyzed the perception and evaluation of a standardized advertisement incorporating the GLOBE dimension of performance orientation in the U.S., Germany, France, Spain and Thailand. Overall, the proposed conceptual model was supported by the data. The results of this study suggest that, by incorporating a performance-oriented appeal in commercial messages, advertisers can positively influence the evaluation of these messages. As predicted by the researchers, data revealed a significant relationship between the perceived level of performance orientation in an ad and the evaluation of the ad. This proved to be true in every country. Because performance orientation is a positively held value in many countries, it can be seen as an appeal type suitable for cross-cultural standardized advertising campaigns. Results also showed that, overall, a higher individual value of performance orientation increases the strength of the impact of perception of performance orientation and ad evaluation.

Terlutter et al. (2010) analyzed the GLOBE dimension of assertiveness in international advertising and proposed a similar culturally-based conceptual model that explains the perception and evaluation of international advertising. The basic concept behind the model is that a given standardized advertising stimulus is likely to be perceived and evaluated differently in various cultures, dependent upon the level of importance individuals place on a given cultural domain, that is, the individual-level cultural value, and on the practices regarding the given cultural domain in the environment surrounding that individual, that is, the societal-level cultural practice. Hence, the model explicitly differentiates between cultural dimensions on an individual level versus cultural dimensions on a societal level, and also incorporates the differentiation between cultural values and cultural practices. The development of a culturally-based model contributes to the development of a more general theory of culture's impact on advertising, which was identified as a key area for future research in international advertising (Taylor, 2005, 2007, 2010). Figure 5.6 depicts the model proposed by Terlutter et al. (2010) for the cultural dimension of assertiveness. Data from five countries (the United States, Germany, Great Britain, Austria and Argentina) confirmed the model to a large extent. Results indicate that, overall, assertiveness is a favorable cultural dimension for advertising purposes. However, not all relationships in the five countries were fully

Conceptual Model

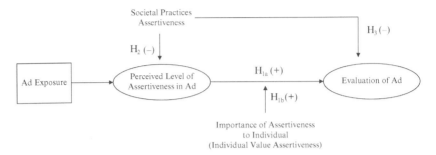

Source: Terlutter et al. (2010).

Figure 5.6 *Conceptual culture-based model of international advertising*

supported and the authors address a number of directions for future research in this area.

Without question, the frameworks and models presented above are invaluable for international advertising researchers. It is hoped that, over time, they will contribute to the development of a more general theory of the impact of culture on advertising in the international setting.

REFERENCES

Advertising Age (2010): Top 100 Global Advertisers See World of Opportunity, http://adage.com/globalnews/article?article_id=147436, accessed February 3, 2011.

Ashkanasy, N., V. Gupta, M.S. Mayfield and E. Trevor-Roberts (2004): Future Orientation, in: House, R.J., P.J. Hanges, M. Javidan, p. Dorfman and V. Gupta (eds): *Culture, Leadership, and Organizations*, Thousand Oaks, CA: Sage, pp. 282–342.

Caillat, Z. and B. Mueller (1996): The Influence of Culture on American and British Advertising: An Exploratory Comparison of Beer Advertising, in: *Journal of Advertising Research*, **36**, 3, 79–88.

De Mooij, M.K. (2010): *Global Marketing and Advertising, Understanding Cultural Paradoxes*, 3rd ed., Thousands Oaks, CA: Sage.

De Mooij, M.K. and G. Hofstede (2010): The Hofstede Model: Applications to Global Branding and Advertising Strategy and Research, in: *International Journal of Advertising*, **29**, 1, 2010, 85–110.

Diehl, S., R. Terlutter and B. Mueller (2008): The Influence of Culture on Responses to the GLOBE Dimension of Performance Orientation in Advertising Messages – Results from the U.S., Germany, France, Spain, and Thailand, in: *Advances in Consumer Research*, **35**, 269–75.

Diehl, S., R. Terlutter and p. Weinberg (2003): Advertising Effectiveness in Different Cultures – Results of an Experiment Analyzing the Effects of Individualistic and Collectivistic Advertising on Germans and Chinese, in: *European Advances in Consumer Research*, **6**, 128–36.

Hall, E.T. (1966): *The Hidden Dimension*, New York: Anchor Books.

Hall, E.T. (1976): *Beyond Culture*, New York: Anchor Books.

Hall, E.T. (1983): *The Dance of Life: The Other Dimension of Time*, New York: Anchor Books.

Hanges, P.J. (2004): Part III: Research Methodology, in: House, R.J., P.J. Hanges, M. Javidan, P. Dorfman and V. Gupta (eds): *Culture, Leadership, and Organizations*, Thousand Oaks, CA: Sage, pp. 91–233.

Hofstede, G. (1980, 2001): *Culture's Consequences: International Differences in Work-Related Values*, 1st and 2nd eds, Thousand Oaks, CA: Sage.

Hofstede, G. and M.H. Bond (1988): The Confucius Connection: From Cultural Roots to Economic Growth, in: *Organizational Dynamics*, **16**, 4, 4–16.

House, R.J., N.R. Quigley and M.S. de Luque (2010): Insights from Project GLOBE, in: *International Journal of Advertising*, **29**, 1, 111–39.

House, R.J. and M. Javidan (2004): Overview of GLOBE, in: House, R.J., P.J. Hanges, M. Javidan, P. Dorfman and V. Gupta (eds): *Culture, Leadership, and Organizations*, Thousand Oaks, CA: Sage, pp. 9–28.

House, R.J. and P.J. Hanges (2004): Research Design, in: House, R.J., P.J. Hanges, M. Javidan, P. Dorfman and V. Gupta (eds): *Culture, Leadership, and Organizations*, Thousand Oaks, CA: Sage, pp. 95–101.

House, R.J., P.J. Hanges, M. Javidan, P.W. Dorfman and V. Gupta (eds) (2004): *Culture, Leadership, and Organizations*, Thousand Oaks, CA: Sage.

Inglehart, R. (1997): *Modernization and Postmodernization: Cultural, Economic, and Political Change in 43 Societies*, Princeton, NJ: Princeton University Press.

Inglehart, R. and C. Welzel (2005): *Modernization, Cultural Change and Democracy: The Human Development Sequence*, New York: Cambridge University Press.

Inglehart, R., M. Basañez and A. Moreno (1998): *Human Values and Beliefs: A Cross-Cultural Sourcebook*, Ann Arbor: University of Michigan Press.

Kluckhohn, C. (1951): Values and Value-Orientation in the Theory of Action: An Exploration in Definition and Classification, in: Parsons, T. and E. Shils (eds): *Toward a General Theory of Action*, Cambridge, MA: Harvard University Press, pp. 388–433.

Kluckhohn, F.R. and F.L. Strodtbeck (1961): *Variations in Value Orientations*, Evanston, IL: Row, Peterson.

Markus, H.R. and S. Kitayama (1991): Culture and the Self: Implications for Cognition, Emotion, and Motivation, in: *Psychological Review*, **98**, 2, 224–53.

McClelland, D.C. (1985): *Human Motivation*, Glenview, IL: Scott Foresman.

Okazaki, S. and B. Mueller (2007): Cross-cultural Advertising Research: Where We Have Been and Where We Need to Go, in: *International Marketing Review*, **24**, 5, 499–518.

Putnam, R.D. (1993): *Making Democracy Work: Civic Traditions in Modern Italy*, Princeton NJ: Princeton University Press.

Schein, E.H. (2010): *Organizational Culture and Leadership*, 4th ed., San Francisco: Jossey Bass.

Schwartz, S.H. (1992): Universals in the Content and Structure of Values: Theoretical Advances and Empirical Tests in 20 Countries, in: *Advances in Experimental Social Psychology*, **25**, 1–65.

Schwartz, S.H. (1994): Are There Universals in the Content and Structure of Values? in: *Journal of Social Issues*, **50**, 19–45.

Schwartz, S.H. (1999): A Theory of Cultural Values and Some Implications for Work, in: *Applied Psychology*, **48**, 1, 23–47.

Schwartz, S.H. and A. Bardi (1997): Influences of Adaptation to Communist Rule on Value Priorities in Eastern Europe, in: *Political Psychology*, **18**, 2, 385–410.

Schwartz, S.H. and M. Ros (1995): Values in the West: A Theoretical and Empirical Challenge to the Individualism-Collectivism Cultural Dimension, in: *World Psychology*, **1**, 2, 91–122.

Sivakumar, K and C. Nakata (2001): The Stampede Toward Hofstede's Framework: Avoiding the Sample Design Pit in Cross-cultural Business Studies, in: *Journal of International Business Studies*, **32**, 3, 555–74 .

Smith, P.B. and S.H. Schwartz (1997): Values, in: Berry, J.W., M.H. Segall and C. Kagitcibasi (eds): *Handbook of Cross-Cultural Psychology*, vol. 3, 2nd ed., Boston: Allyn & Bacon, pp. 77–118.

Steenkamp, J.E.M. (2001): The Role of National Culture in International Marketing Research, in: *International Marketing Review*, **18**, 1, 30–43.

Parsons, T. and E. Shils (eds) (1951): *Toward a General Theory of Action*, Cambridge, MA: Harvard University Press.

Taylor, C.R., G.E. Miracle and R.D. Wilson (1997): The Impact of Information Level on the Effectiveness of U.S. and Korean Television Commercials, in: *Journal of Advertising*, **26**, 1, 1–18.

Terlutter, R., S. Diehl and B. Mueller (2010): The Cultural Dimension of Assertiveness in Cross-cultural Advertising – the Perception and Evaluation of Assertive Advertising Appeals, in: *International Journal of Advertising*, **29**, 3, 369–99.

Terlutter, R., S. Diehl and B. Mueller (2005): The Influence of Culture on Responses to Assertiveness in Advertising Messages, in: *Advertising and Communication*, Proceedings of the 4th International Conference on Research in Advertising (ICORIA), Saarbruecken, 183–92.

Triandis, H.C. (1989): Cross- Cultural Studies of Individualism and Collectivism, in: *Nebraska Symposium on Motivation 1989*, 41–133.

Triandis, H.C. (1995): *Individualism and Collectivism*, Boulder, CO: Westview Press.

Trompenaars, F. (1993): Riding the Waves of Culture: Understanding Cultural Diversity in Business, London: Nicholas Brealey Publishing.

6 Culture and the mind: implications for art, design and advertisement

Takahiko Masuda, Huaitang Wang, Kenichi Ito and Sawa Senzaki

INTRODUCTION

In the last 30 years, cultural psychology – an interdisciplinary field in the intersection of psychology, anthropology, linguistics, history, philosophy and neuroscience – has accumulated abundant evidence that humans are inherently sociocultural beings (Bruner, 1990; Markus & Kitayama, 1991; Miller, 1999; Shweder, 1991). Researchers in cultural psychology have investigated how the mind (perceptions, cognitions, motivations and emotions) is shaped by cultural content (shared meanings, ideas, institutions, practices and norms). These researchers have reported systematic cultural variations in a variety of psychological processes. Their findings cast doubt upon the basic theoretical assumptions of mainstream psychology, which still focuses mainly on the universality of the human mind. Some mainstream researchers regard culture as either playing a minor role in the processes of the human mind, or presenting obstacles to a clear understanding of the mind. However, because of accumulated empirical evidence, the assertions of cultural psychologists have gradually become influential in psychology and even in neuroscience, where researchers investigate the plasticity of the brain (Kitayama & Uskul, 2011). We maintain throughout this chapter that the implications of cultural psychology are not necessarily limited to academia. Rather, findings in cultural psychology have many potential implications for applied research in areas such as mass communication, business and advertising.

The purpose of this chapter is to introduce findings in cultural psychology over the past 30 years to readers who are interested in their application, and to discuss theoretical frameworks and raw sources from cultural psychological research by which the reader can think of the application. We believe that the recent findings we introduce here will eventually stimulate a wide range of audience.

The chapter consists of three parts. First, we will define what cultural psychology is and explain the theoretical assumptions of this field of research. Next, we will describe current findings by referring to cross-cultural comparisons of people's patterns of perception, cognition, motivation and emotion. In particular, we contrast people in East Asian cultures with people in North American cultures from two major research perspectives: *independent vs. interdependent view of self* (e.g., Markus & Kitayama, 1991), and *holistic thought vs. analytic thought* (Nisbett, Peng, Choi & Norenzayan, 2001). We will then review recent empirical works on cultural products (Morling & Lamoreaux, 2008) and discuss cultural variations in aesthetic preference, design preferences for posters and web pages; perspective preferences for video games; and dominant values in advertising messages. Finally, we will reflect on possible applications of this research to the mass communication and advertising industries.

WHAT IS CULTURAL PSYCHOLOGY?

Although the origin of cultural research in psychology can be traced back to the emergence of experimental psychology at the end of the nineteenth century and the beginning of the twentieth, the field has been content with its minor status in psychology. However, in the 1980s and 1990s a handful of researchers rediscovered the importance of culture in psychological processes, and their theoretical framework has since been used by many researchers. Anthropologist Richard Shweder (1991) defined cultural psychology as the study of "the ways subject and object, self and other, the mind and culture, person and context, figure and ground, practitioner and practice, live together, require each other, and dynamically, dialectically and jointly make each other up" (p. 73). This assertion has been supported by a limited number of top-notch researchers in psychology. For example, cognitive psychology researcher Jerome Bruner (1990), in his book *Acts of Meaning*, posited that the main topic of psychology should not be observable behaviour but rather the culturally shared meanings behind the actions. Bruner's assertion strongly resonated with anthropologist Clifford Geertz's (1973) famous statement: "We are in sum, incomplete or unfinished animals who complete or finish ourselves through culture – and not through culture in general but through highly particular forms of it: Dobuan and Javanese, Hopi and Italian, upper-class and lower class, academic and commercial" (p. 49).

We consider Shweder, Bruner and Geertz to be the founders of contemporary cultural psychology. They have strived to assert the dynamic relationships between culture and the mind. Their basic tenet has been that from birth we are surrounded by rich cultural resources, through which we develop our identity. As a member of a given culture, each of us then spreads these cultural resources to our own generation as creator, forerunner and innovator (Sperber, 1996); and later, as parents, caregivers, or educators, we transmit them to the next generation (Tomasello, 1999).

How can we investigate the mutual constitution of culture and the human mind? One of the difficulties of investigating these processes is that cultural difference lives not only in one's internalized psychological processes but also in public representations, and is even embedded in everyday interactions and subtle non-verbal behaviours (Markus & Hamedani, 2007). Therefore, research necessarily targets multiple loci of human–culture interactions (Morling & Lamoreaux, 2008).

First, measuring cultural variation in psychological processes ("culture → the mind") is indispensable. Numerous studies in cultural psychology have documented that actions, motivations, cognitions and emotions differ from culture to culture, and that the systematic cultural variations in these psychological processes are attributable to profound cultural differences in ideas, values, beliefs and meanings. Researchers have devised various concepts for describing the contrasts between two cultures. For example, some researchers investigate East Asians' and Westerners' mentalities in terms of independent vs. interdependent self-view, and others in terms of holistic vs. analytic worldview. Such studies form the most important research strands of cultural psychology (Heine & Norenzayan, 2006).

Second, there is a growing trend toward measuring cultural products ("the mind → culture"). Cultural products can be defined as human-made, tangible, public, shared representations of culture that convey important messages about dominant values, beliefs and meanings in a given culture (Morling & Lamoreaux, 2008). They are vital resources that enable people who are born and raised in a given society to make sense of their lives. Cultural products can have many different forms. Cultural ideas, values and meanings can be *explicitly* conveyed in written forms such as religious texts, books, and magazine and newspaper articles; and visualized forms such as visual arts, movies and TV programs. Important messages can also be *implicitly* embedded in song lyrics, advertisements and popular texts. Although researchers have acknowledged the importance of research into cultural products, it is only recently that this area has been extensively investigated.

In sum, research on culture and the mind simultaneously investigates the two sides of the coin: phenomena inside and outside of the mind. Because of the inseparability of culture and psychology in the research target, cultural psychologists use a wide variety of research methodologies (Cohen, 2007). In focusing on the mind, they have mostly used experimental methods borrowed from empirical research in sciences ("culture → the mind"). Morling and Lamoreaux (2008) maintained that studies that have made creative use of public, shared and tangible cultural products ("the mind → culture") should be added to the methodological repertoire. In the next section, we will begin by introducing two working research frameworks for the mutual construction of "culture → the mind".

EAST VS. WEST: RESEARCH FRAMEWORKS AND EMPIRICAL FINDINGS

Any culture and any population in the world can be a target of cultural psychology. However, much research has focused on two cultural groups – the people of East Asia and the people of North America – and investigated characteristics of these populations under a variety of theoretical frameworks. One reason for focusing on these two groups is that differences in psychological processes between East Asians and North Americans are substantial and systematic, and researchers are able to depict such differences fairly easily. In addition, similarities in the educational systems of these two cultural groups enable researchers to access sufficient numbers of potential participants from the student body and conduct empirical research relatively easily. Two major frameworks of research – *holistic thought vs. analytic thought* (Nisbett, 2003; Nisbett & Masuda, 2003; Nisbett et al., 2001) and *independent construals vs. interdependent construals* (Markus & Kitayama, 1991, 2010) – complementarily explain a variety of social cognitive phenomena.

Analytic vs. Holistic Thought

In this research strand, researchers investigate cultural worldviews that shape people's cognition and perception (e.g., Nisbett, 2003; Nisbett et al., 2001). This framework does not necessarily compete with the view-of-self framework discussed later in this chapter; the two are complementarily related to each other and shed different light on the same phenomena. Nisbett (2003) maintained that the cultural variations in cognition observable in contemporary members of Western and East Asian cultures can be traced back in part to ancient Greek and ancient Chinese civilizations (whose dominant ideologies may in turn have resonated with their own economic or social practices at the time). Aristotelian and traditional Greek philosophy share the worldview that things exist independently, and the characteristics of an object are determined by the object's internal attributes. By contrast, Buddhism, Confucianism and Taoism emphasize the holistic nature of things. This holistic understanding of the world became the foundation of a discourse – shared by contemporary East Asian cultures such as China, Korea and Japan – that affords greater attention to relationships between objects and their contexts. Literature in the humanities and social sciences (e.g., Cromer, 1993; Munro, 1985; Nakamura, 1964/1985; Needham, 1954, 1962) gives credence to Nisbett and colleagues' assertion regarding the systematic cultural differences between psychological processes of people in North American cultures (especially those of European descent) and people in East Asian cultures.

Cognitive aspect

Numerous studies describe how analytic and holistic thought have different influences on people's social cognition. For example, North Americans are more likely to explain an event by referring to internal/dispositional factors of a target individual, whereas East Asians pay more attention to the external/contextual/situational factors that surround the target (Kitayama, Ishii, Imada, Takemura & Ramaswamy, 2006; Koo & Choi, 2005; Lee, Hallahan & Herzog, 1996; Morris & Peng 1994). Similarly, East Asians are more likely to take situational constraints into account when they infer someone's attitude from his/her behaviour (Choi & Nisbett, 1998; Choi, Nisbett & Norezayan, 1999; Masuda & Kitayama, 2004; Miyamoto & Kitayama, 2002; Norenzayan, Choi & Nisbett, 2002; Norenzayan & Nisbett, 2000). Third, North Americans explain the causes of an event by referring to limited numbers of major pieces of information, whereas East Asians refer to more information, some of which is only peripherally important (Choi, Dalal, Kim-Prieto & Park, 2003). Fourth, North Americans are good at detecting specific common attributes among objects, whereas East Asians are good at holistically seeing similarities (Norenzayan, Smith, Kim & Nisbett, 2002) and relationalities among objects (Ji, Peng & Nisbett, 2000). Fifth, East Asians are more likely than North Americans to apply naïve dialecticism, that is, to show greater leniency toward contradictions (Choi & Choi, 2002; Koo & Choi, 2005; Peng & Nisbett, 1999; Spencer-Rogers & Peng, 2004). Finally, North Americans tend to conceptualize the world linearly, whereas East Asians tend to conceptualize the world as a constantly changing field (Ji, 2008; Ji, Nisbett & Su, 2001).

Perceptual aspect

Recent evidence further suggests that systematic cultural differences in cognition are governed by more basic perceptual processes, notably attention (Nisbett & Masuda, 2003; Nisbett & Miyamoto, 2005; Peng & Knowles, 2003). Several studies measuring behavioural patterns during perceptual and cognitive tasks have indicated that East Asians are more likely than North Americans to describe contextual information and remember objects in relation to context (Masuda & Nisbett, 2001), to perform well in a task that requires attention to context (Kitayama, Duffy, Kawamura & Larsen, 2003), and to perform less well in a task that requires attention to focal objects (Ji et al., 2000; Masuda, Akase, Radford & Wang, 2008; Miyamoto, Nisbett & Masuda, 2006). North Americans are good at focusing on focal information while ignoring contextual information; however, they often find it difficult to process information if the contextual information is overwhelmingly complex. By contrast, East Asians are good at coping with complex pieces of information but often find it difficult to ignore contextual information even when asked to do so (Wang, Ito & Masuda, 2011). Other studies directly measured the number and duration of eye fixations during a task; the findings suggest that East Asians are more likely than their North American counterparts to allocate their attention to context, and that the way of allocating attention to specific areas in the field corresponds to cultural patterns of memory (Chua, Boland & Nisbett, 2005; Goh, Tan & Park, 2009) and the observer's style of judging the target's emotional expression (Masuda, Ellsworth et al., 2008).

In sum, much of the cross-cultural research on cognition and attention applied the two different models of thought advocated by Nisbett and his colleagues and demonstrated the usefulness of these models (e.g., Nisbett, 2003; Nisbett et al., 2001). North Americans' mentality is generally analytic and object oriented at the expense of context, whereas East Asians' mentality is more holistic and context oriented. Later in this chapter we will discuss whether it is possible to observe such messages in the dominant cultural products available in each culture.

Independent vs. Interdependent View of Self

Researchers also investigate cultural variations in the human mind from a slightly different angle: the view of self. How culture shapes one's view of oneself is one of the most popular research topics in cultural psychology. Although mainstream psychology has long assumed that the concept of self is the same across cultures, many cultural psychologists challenge this assumption (e.g., Markus & Kitayama, 1991; Shweder & Bourne, 1982). Of the many theoretical frameworks regarding cultural variations in the concept of self, Markus and Kitayama's (1991) models of self-construals – the independent and the interdependent view of self – are the most widely recognized.

The independent view of self is dominant in Western cultures, especially in middle-class European American culture. It defines people as independent agents whose locus is the centre of their world, physically and mentally separated from others. The origin of this view of self can be traced back to modern Western intellectual traditions (Taylor, 1989, 2007). People who share this view of self are highly motivated to actualize themselves by searching for attributes and talents they are proud of, by establishing personal preferences and unique characteristics, and by valuing self-consistency across situations.

In contrast, the interdependent view of self, which is dominant in East Asian cultures such as China, Korea and Japan, defines people as physically separated but mentally interconnected to each other, and surrounded by a complexity of social networks. Buddhism, Taoism and Confucianism are the intellectual traditions that have contributed to generate such a view of self. People who share this view of self are highly motivated to actualize themselves by attuning to social roles expected by important people in their lives in a given social context, by correcting imperfect and insufficient aspects of the self so as to meet the social standard, and by flexibly adapting themselves to the context (e.g., Markus & Kitayama, 1991, 2010). Since the advent of Markus and Kitayama's models of self-construal, these models have been applied to a large number of studies in cognition, motivation and emotion.

Cognitive aspect

As was the case with holistic vs. analytic thought models, empirical evidence regarding the independent vs. interdependent view of self suggests that ways of defining oneself differ systematically from culture to culture. For example, when asked to define themselves, North Americans refer to abstract personal attributes, whereas East Asians describe themselves in terms of social categories and roles (Bond & Cheung, 1983; Cousins, 1989). Furthermore, whereas North Americans are eager to maintain a consistent view of themselves across contexts (e.g., home, school and work), East Asians flexibly redefine and accommodate themselves according to each context (Kanagawa, Cross & Markus, 2001). Further evidence suggests that North Americans are more likely to be motivated by self-consistency and attitude–behaviour consistency (Heine & Lehman, 1997; Kashima, Siegal, Tanaka & Kashima, 1992; Kitayama, Snibbe, Markus & Suzuki, 2004). These differences in self-conceptualization are observable even in patterns of brain activation. When Chinese thought of important people in their lives, the area of the brain that is relevant to self-identification was activated, whereas North Americans activated the same brain area only when they thought of themselves (Han & Northoff, 2008; Zhu, Zhang, Fan & Han, 2007).

Motivational aspect

Culturally influenced views of self are associated with socioculturally expected patterns of motivation. For example, although much research in North American social psychology places importance on the concept of self-esteem and concludes that the motivation to maintain a high level of self-esteem is a human universal, recent findings in cultural psychology indicate that levels of self-esteem are drastically different across cultures, and that such differences can be explained by the view of self. High self-esteem is a desirable characteristic if people are motivated to be proud of and confident in the unique personal attributes that constitute their identity. However, if one is motivated to accommodate and attune to social needs, paying attention to one's insufficiencies is more beneficial than boosting one's self-esteem. In fact, North Americans have higher self-esteem than non-Western individuals (Bond & Cheung, 1983; Heine, Lehman, Markus & Kitayama, 1999). North Americans remember their successes more than Japanese do (Endo & Meijer, 2004) and are motivated by self-enhancement to re-engage in a task they succeeded in, whereas East Asians are motivated by self-criticism/self-improvement to re-engage in a task they failed in (Heine et al., 2001). North Americans tend to believe that their talent and ability is fixed, which motivates them not to persist in activities they are not good at, whereas East Asians tend to believe that their ability is changed by their effort, which motivates them to demonstrate their perseverance and resiliency (Azuma, 1994; Stevenson & Stigler, 1992). Such cultural differences can be observed in motivation to influence vs. motivation to be accommodating to others. In general, when asked to recall their experiences, North Americans can easily recall situations in which they influenced the environment, whereas East Asians can easily recall adjusting to the environment (Morling & Evered, 2006; Morling, Kitayama & Miyamoto, 2002; Weisz, Rothbaum & Blackburn, 1984). North Americans tend to think they are agents at the centre of the world who control the things that surround them; East Asians tend to consider themselves as part of society, so accommodating to the expected role is more important. Finally, a conceptualization of self is also observed in the process of differentiating oneself from others. North Americans strive to express their uniqueness, but this tendency is very weak among East Asians. East Asians are more likely to adopt the dominant or majority patterns of behaviour in a given society (Kim & Markus, 1999). The saying "The squeaky wheel gets the oil" exemplifies North Americans' motivation to assertively actualize themselves, while the saying "The nail that sticks out will get a pounding" nicely depicts the East Asian idea that if you stand out from the crowd, you will invite trouble, and this idea in turn develops the motivation to minimize one's uniqueness.

Emotional aspect

Research on cultural variation in subjective emotional experiences also supports the view of self models. North Americans tend to experience socially disengaged emotions that accentuate the difference between oneself and others, whereas Japanese tend to experience socially engaged emotions that accentuate connections between self and others (Kitayama, Markus & Kurokawa, 2000; Kitayama, Mesquita & Karasawa, 2006; Uchida & Kitayama, 2009). For North Americans, self-esteem is strongly associated with well-being. In East Asia the association is not so strong; rather, the sense of being accepted by others is an important indicator for one's well-being (Diener & Diener, 1995; Uchida, Kitayama, Mesquita, Reyes & Morling, 2008). Such a tendency is observable even in Asian American populations. For example, Asian Americans and Japanese are more likely than their European American counterparts to feel higher life satisfaction when they meet the expectations of important others than when they meet their own personal goals (Oishi & Diener, 2003). Similarly, the emotions of European Americans become more intense when they are reminded of the self, whereas the emotions of Asian Americans intensify when the group is salient (Chentsova-Dutton & Tsai, 2010).

In sum, much of the cross-cultural research on cognition, motivation and emotion supports the two different models of self advocated by Markus and Kitayama (1991, 2010). In general, North Americans' mentality is independence oriented, whereas East Asians' mentality is interdependence oriented. The next section will address the question, "Can we observe such messages in dominant cultural products available in each culture?"

CULTURAL PRODUCTS: DO ART, DESIGN, AND ADVERTISEMENTS CONVEY CULTURALLY IMPORTANT MESSAGES?

Morling and Lamoreaux (2008) maintained that cultural psychologists also need to investigate the "the mind → culture" part of the mutual relationship between culture and psychological processes. In this section, we will review recent findings from research on cultural products. As mentioned previously, culturally important messages that shape one's mind are conveyed through a variety of public, shared and tangible media. These messages can include directly stated values, beliefs and ideas mediated by written forms and visual forms, such as religious texts and icons. But they can also be embedded in secular visual representations such as art, design and advertising. These cultural products are created, maintained and consumed by members of a given culture, so a "culture ← → the mind" mutual construction is taking place. At the same time, however, cultural products that are public, shared and tangible can be investigated as somewhat independent from and external to objects from the mind. Two types of investigation are going on in the field of cultural psychology. First, with regard to cultural variation in attention under the rubric of holistic vs. analytic thought, researchers investigate expressions of fine arts, pictures, posters and web page designs. Second, researchers studying the independent vs. interdependent view of self analyze the perspective of view in video games as well as cultural messages embedded in advertisements.

Holistic vs. Analytic Cultural Products

Previous findings in attention suggest that East Asians are more likely than North Americans to be sensitive to contextual information. For example, Masuda, Ellsworth et al. (2008) asked both Japanese and North Americans to view images of a target figure surrounded by four others, and to judge the target individual's emotion by his or her facial expression. The researchers manipulated the congruency between the facial expressions of the target and the other individuals. In half the scenes, the target and the background figures showed congruent emotional facial expressions (e.g., happy target and happy others); in the rest of the scenes, the figures showed incongruent facial expressions (e.g., happy target and sad others). Since the task was to judge ONLY the target figure's emotions, the target's facial expression should receive the same score in both conditions, and Americans indeed judged the target person's emotion to be the same in both conditions. In contrast, the Japanese ratings of the target emotion were intensified when the target figure was presented with congruent others. In addition, eye-tracking data provided evidence that Japanese allocated their attention to the background figures more often than did Americans, even though they were asked not to do so. Similarly, Masuda and Nisbett (2001) presented 20-second animated vignettes of underwater scenes to Japanese and Americans. The participants were then asked to report what they had seen. Even for such a simple task, there were systematic cultural variations in the reports. That is, Americans tended to spotlight the most important scene (e.g., "I saw three fish swimming around, one of which had red fins"), and Japanese tended to refer to the background ("It looks like a deep sea because the water color was much darker than in the previous video"). The findings suggest that Japanese are prone to include the field and to think about the relationships between objects and fields, whereas Americans are prone to selectively attend to what is the focal and main issue in the scene.

If East Asian and North American patterns of attention are so distinctive, what types of cultural product can be created, disseminated to the same generation, and transmitted to the next generation? We assume that when people are sensitive to context and relationships, their drawings, designs and graphic designs are also likely to set the threshold of relationships among objects low – and therefore to include, rather than exclude, more pieces of information as necessarily and equally important pieces as a whole context. This can be seen as a typical pattern of holistic thought. By contrast, when people have a tendency to selectively attend to a focal object, they are likely to set the threshold of relationships among objects high, and are motivated to clearly differentiate focal objects from peripheral objects, and to exclude, rather than include, peripheral objects.

Several findings give credence to this speculation. For example, Choi et al. (2003) demonstrated that, compared to North Americans, East Asians have a stronger desire to include more pieces of information. The researchers asked Koreans and Americans to read a brief summary of a murder case, in which a professor had been murdered and the chief suspect was a graduate student in the laboratory. Participants were then provided with a booklet containing 97 facts (e.g., the professor had a conflict with the graduate student, the professor's hobby was XX, the graduate student's GPA was XXX), and were asked to exclude the facts they thought to be irrelevant to the investigation. The results indicated that Americans were much more likely to exclude more facts, suggesting that Koreans considered even trivial and slightly relevant pieces of information to be necessary for capturing the whole story, and that Americans thought that the best way to reach the truth was to selectively choose a limited number of important facts while eliminating the noisy peripheral information. Similarly, other research on cultural variation in cognition suggests that East Asians categorize things on the basis of family resemblance and relationship-based processes, whereas North Americans categorize things according to simple rules and shared attributes commonly applicable to all things (Ji et al., 2000; Norenzayan, Smith et al., 2002)

Perspective

If an attentional-cognitive orientation is robustly held by members of each culture, we might reasonably expect to observe this attentional orientation in public, shared and tangible cultural products (Morling & Lamoreaux, 2008) such as artistic expressions. The tradition of artistic expressions in East Asia is completely different from that in Western cultures. The artistic technique known as the *linear perspective*, which has been commonly used for drawing scenery in the West, strongly resonates with Westerners' analytic ideology. The technique of perspective was one of the most notable developments of the Renaissance. Kubovy (1986) described two major functions of this technique. The most obvious is to represent space by providing the illusion of depth. The other is to fix the viewer's standpoint, usually forcing the viewer to occupy the same level as the subject of the work. The amount of field information, moreover, is restricted in classic Western art; painters include field information only to the extent that it can realistically be observed given the perspective within a given scene. East Asian artists, however, have traditionally applied a bird's-eye view, which increases the visible area of the scene, by placing the horizon line high in the upper part of the frame; this aesthetic preference resonates strongly with the holistic cultural ideology. It is therefore reasonable to think that fine arts in the East and West are qualitatively different from each other. To test this possibility with scientific rigor, we analyzed archival data of East Asian and Western fine art masterpieces (Masuda, Gonzalez, Kwan & Nisbett, 2008). The results indicated that the location of the horizon is indeed much higher in East Asian landscape masterpieces than it is in Western art.

Behavioural data analyses by Masuda, Gonzalez et al. (2008) further support this observation by demonstrating that contemporary adult members of East Asian cultures are more likely than their North American counterparts to apply the bird's-eye view when asked to draw a scenic image. Extending this line of research by focusing on socialization processes of aesthetic preferences in landscape drawing, we investigated at what point in the developmental course culturally dominant ways of aesthetics emerge (Senzaki & Masuda, 2011). We examined cultural and developmental differences in the use of holistic and analytic attention styles in artistic expression among young children (ages 6 to 12 years) in Canada and in Japan. We found that the process of learning the concept of horizon was similar across the two cultures, but the children learned the concept in culturally unique manners. That is, the majority of Canadian and Japanese children showed a clear understanding of the concept of horizon by nine years old; however, Japanese children placed the horizon significantly higher and drew a larger number of objects. A similar outcome was observed with college students in Canada and Japan. These findings are consistent with previous indications that cultural differences in lay theories of change (one's tendency to see the world as stable or fluid) became apparent around ages 9 to 11 (Ji, 2008). Similarly, another study suggested that age nine is the critical age for children to become fully acculturated in another country when they move from Eastern to North American cultures (Minoura, 1992). Together, these studies demonstrate that the culture in which we are socialized at a young age significantly influences our cognitive styles, and there seems to be an age range that is significantly important in the socialization processes.

Size of portrait models

Portraiture has been a popular genre in Western societies (Shimada, 1990). Generally, Western portraits depict an individual and fulfill a variety of functions; they can mark the occasion of a particular success or can record the existence of an individual for posterity. Accordingly, Western portraiture seeks to make the subject salient, and the model occupies a major fraction of the space. East Asian portraiture, however, has emphasized the individual in context; the size of the model is relatively small, as if the model is embedded in an important background scene. Sometimes, the open space is filled with much visual information (such as a mattress, a folding screen and a window shade), but sometimes it is filled by comments handwritten by those who evaluated the portraits. Furthermore, a space can be intentionally left empty so viewers can enjoy the sense of *ma* (space). The sense of *ma*, which is highly appreciated in the East Asian arts tradition, serves to soften the salient visual representation (Kenmochi, 1992; Minami, 1983). Although most evidence of obvious cultural differences in artistic representations is still anecdotal, our archival data analysis of art from other historical periods indicated that models in East Asian portraits did tend to be smaller than models in Western portraits (Masuda, Gonzalez et al., 2008).

Further investigations suggest that even contemporary North American and East Asian undergraduates' picture-drawing styles, photo-taking styles and photo selection tasks corresponded to their traditional aesthetic styles. North Americans were more likely than East Asians to exclude context when they took portrait photographs. In addition, East Asians preferred to take portraits with wide backgrounds and small models, whereas North Americans preferred to have the model fill most of the field. These findings suggest that people's aesthetic preference in portraiture has been influenced by the dominant patterns of visual attention developed in their respective cultural worldviews. We maintain that Western analytic thought, which emphasizes the focal object of the scene at the expense of the context, is indeed embedded in a large focal-object-to-frame ratio. In contrast, a small focal-object-to-frame ratio allows East Asian artists to draw more contextual information, which in turn is indicative of the cultural message of context inclusion shared in East Asian holistic thought (Masuda, Gonzalez et al., 2008).

Fuzziness and flatness

Other investigations further support our assertion in terms of cultural variation in artistic expressions. For example, paintings by Westerners are more likely to show contrast between background and foreground (Masuda, Gonzalez et al., 2008). These findings suggest that East Asians are aesthetically habituated to perceive foreground and background boundaries in a more fuzzy manner, allowing them to attend to the background information along with the foreground object. In contrast, Westerners are aesthetically habituated to accentuate the foreground–background contrast. Furthermore, research in fine arts (Azuma, 2000; Gombrich, 1961/2000; Masuda, Gonzalez et al., 2008; Murakami, 2000) indicates that in East Asian pictorial representations the flatness of the representation is emphasized by drawing images two-dimensionally, whereas Western linear perspective allows the audience to perceive three-dimensional texture on the two-dimensional frame. These reports suggest that East Asians are accustomed to seeing the world in a single plane, whereas North Americans are accustomed to seeing the world by perceiving the depth of field of objects.

Complexity
Some findings have indicated that human-made environmental structures of a given culture – such as the structures of cities, towns, and villages – also facilitate the development of specific modes of attention (Miyamoto et al., 2006). Comparisons of the real landscapes of East Asian and North American cities indicated distinctive differences in the complexity of the cities. East Asian landscapes are much more complex than their North American counterparts. Although we have to consider possible confounding variables (e.g., population density) that might differentiate the landscape of these cities, we believe that this finding strongly resonates with research indicating that East Asians' drawings, pictorial collages and cartoons are generally more complex than those produced by North Americans (Masuda, Gonzalez et al., 2008; Wang et al., 2011). Taken together, information disseminated not only through mass media and traditional aesthetic styles (e.g., fine arts) but also through city designs could be important means of conveying dominant messages of a given cultural meaning system. Through exposure to the cultural resources that surround them, people in a given culture internalize certain dominant modes of attention.

These findings further motivated us to investigate the optimal amount of complexity in visual representation. For this purpose, we extended our research to contemporary visual representations such as web page design and conference posters. Our analysis of web pages of federal/provincial governments and major universities (Wang et al., 2011) suggests that East Asians' web page design is characterized by single long frames containing extremely complex pieces of information – showing all the information at once in a single plane – whereas Westerners' web page design is characterized by layered structures of short frames with limited amounts of information per frame, so as not to overwhelm the viewer with the complexity of the information.

Cultural variation in complexity perception can also be observed in conference poster design (Wang et al., 2011). We analyzed 212 electronic versions of conference posters at the 2008/09 Society for Personality and Social Psychology (SPSP) conference. The posters were from both East Asian and North American research institutions. When a single study was presented on a regulation-size (4 feet × 6 feet) poster, no cultural difference in the level of complexity was observed. However, when a poster presented more than one study, presenters dealt with the space constraints in different ways. East Asians retained all the details and complexity of the message, whereas North Americans presented the gist of the studies by sacrificing details and using fewer words. Taken together, these findings suggest that people develop a sense of optimality regarding the amount of information needed, and that their selection and design preferences strongly resonate with the dominant ideology of their culture.

In sum, research on culture and visual representation (actual city design, web page design and posters) has allowed us to identify critical cultural variations in the perspective of landscape, the ratio of model size in portraiture, the fuzziness and flatness of images, and the complexity of visual representation.

Cultural Products and the View of Self

Many researchers have investigated characteristics of cultural variation in cultural products by contrasting independence-oriented self messages with interdependence-oriented self messages. Researchers have investigated how people actively produce and maintain cultural products, and how they consume such cultural products. Overall, as expected, the findings indicated that cultural products from East Asia tend to represent a more interdependent orientation, whereas cultural products from North America tend to represent a more independent orientation (Morling & Lamoreaux, 2008). These studies examine cultural products ranging from media reports and magazine articles to children's books and religious texts. In this section, we will introduce recent empirical research on cultural products in the categories of independent vs. interdependent agency, excitement vs. calm (emotional experience), uniqueness vs. conformity (orientation of the self), and first-person vs. third-person perspective.

Independent vs. interdependent agency
Markus, Uchida, Omoregie, Townsend and Kitayama (2006) examined Japanese and American media coverage of the 2000 and 2002 Olympics.

Although most commentators commented mainly on the performance of sports athletes, Japanese and American accounts differed in their explanations of the nature and source of intentional agency of the action. Japanese commentators tended to interpret an athlete's agency as a mixture of the athlete's personal attributes, social and emotional experience, and the context of the action. By contrast, Americans tended to interpret an athlete's agency as separate from the athlete's background or social and emotional experience. Therefore, in American comments, performance was explained primarily in terms of positive personal characteristics and the characteristics of the other competitors. In addition to analyzing the archival data, Markus et al. asked Japanese and American study participants to select the most important and appropriate pieces of information that they would include if they were to report on winning athletes' accomplishments. Japanese participants selectively preferred information about an athlete's coach and team (e.g., "Her coach has been her most comprehensive advisor, helping her develop strategy and competency"), interdependence-oriented motivation ("After all the help she received from her team, she knew she couldn't let them down"), emotion ("She takes long walks around the city after dinner in order to calm any anxiety she feels about the race") and doubt ("She won despite her worries that the unfamiliar conditions of extreme heat and humidity might hurt her performance"). In contrast, Americans selectively preferred information about the athlete's personal attributes (e.g., "She has been described as a remarkable, interesting, and energetic person, absolutely dedicated to being the best") and uniqueness ("She stood out from the crowd from the start, sticking close to her signature strategies. She showed us all what a world-class champion looks like"). Similarly, other research has indicated that Japanese elementary school textbooks and Korean advertisements commonly use interdependent/collectivistic messages such as relationships with others, whereas American advertisements commonly use individualistic/independent messages (Han & Shavitt, 1994; Imada, in press).

Excitement vs. calm emotional experience

Other researchers have focused more on a specific aspect of independent vs. interdependent contrast: subjective emotional experience. Several studies have targeted specific media – children's books and religious texts – as cultural products that convey the message of culturally expected emotional experiences. For example, Tsai, Louie, Chen and Uchida (2007) analyzed the affective content of pictures in 20 best-selling storybooks for children between 4 and 8 years of age in Taiwan and the United States, respectively. At this range of ages, pictures are more effective than text in conveying affect (Bainbridge & Pantaleo, 1999). Therefore, the facial expressions appearing in storybooks convey culturally important messages. Tsai et al. assumed that, in the North American independent cultural context, assertively expressing oneself would be seen as an important skill for self-actualization and therefore the facial expressions would be more intense. Conversely, in the East Asian interdependent cultural context, harmoniously accommodating with others would be seen as an important skill for self-actualization and the facial expressions would be milder or less intense. Compared to the Taiwanese storybooks, the American storybooks did in fact show more excited expressions, wider smiles and more arousing activities. In a study of practices and written materials pertaining to Christianity and Buddhism, Tsai, Miao and Seppala (2007) examined whether religions differ in the ideal affective states they commonly endorse. Tsai et al. analyzed Christian and Buddhist practitioners' ideal affect, Christian and Buddhist classical texts, and even contemporary self-help books oriented toward either Christianity or Buddhism. The results indicated that, compared to Buddhism, Christianity values high-arousal positive emotional states (such as excitement) more, and values low-arousal positive emotional states (such as calm) less. In another study, Hong Kong residents also reported experiencing positive emotional states that were calm and harmonious rather than excited or intense (Tsai, Knutson & Fung, 2006). In sum, these researchers maintained that culturally shared ideas about the self resonate strongly with the affective states that people ideally want to feel (Tsai, 2007). Thus it is not difficult to see why such culturally dominant messages are observed even in contemporary advertisements (Chim, Moon & Tsai, 2009).

Orientation of the self: Uniqueness vs. conformity
Other researchers have conducted cultural comparisons of advertisements by focusing on cognitive aspects of the independent vs. interdependent contrast. For example, Kim and Markus (1999) coded four types of magazine advertisement (business, social commentary, women's, and pop culture/youth) and found that Korean magazine advertisements use appeals emphasizing conformity, and American magazine advertisements use appeals emphasizing uniqueness. Conformity advertisements emphasized collective values and tradition (e.g., "Our ginseng drink is produced according to the methods of a 500-year-old tradition"), traditional social roles ("Bring a fresh breeze to your wife at home"); harmony, group well-being and group norms ("Our company is working toward building a harmonious society"), popularity ("Seven out of ten people are using this product") and the latest trends ("Trend forecast for spring: Pastel colours!"). By contrast, uniqueness advertisements not only reflected individual values such as freedom ("Inspiration doesn't keep office hours"),

being different from others ("Individualize!") and uniqueness ("The Internet isn't for everybody. But then again, you are not everybody"); they also rebelled against collective values and beliefs by rejecting tradition (e.g., "Ditch the Joneses"), rejecting social roles ("Princess dream. Pony dream. Ready for a kick-butt dream?") and emphasizing personal choice ("Choose your own view").

First-person vs. third-person perspective
Finally, some researchers focus on the perceptual aspect of the independent vs. interdependent contrast. Independent self-construal encourages people in the idea that they are the centre of their social world. In this mode of self-awareness, people tend to take the first-person perspective, that is, seeing the world from their own point of view. Conversely, interdependent self-construal encourages people to see themselves as part of a larger social context, and not necessarily at the middle of it. In this mode of self-awareness, people tend to take the third-person perspective, conceptualizing themselves in context by taking others' point of view (Cohen & Gunz, 2002; Cohen & Hoshino-Browne, 2005; Leung & Cohen, 2007).

Cohen and Gunz (2002) examined cultural variation in Canada. Because the Canadian constitution emphasizes multiculturalism, Canadian immigrants are highly encouraged to maintain their cultural heritage. Cohen and Gunz targeted Canadians of East Asian cultural heritage and Canadians of European cultural heritage. The results indicated that Asian Canadians tended to memorize their experience from the third-person perspective, whereas European Canadians tended to memorize it from the first-person perspective. Perspective taking also shapes here-and-now events. Cohen and Hoshino-Browne (2005) asked Asian Canadians and European Canadians to tap out a tune (such as "London Bridge Is Falling Down") on the table so that another participant might recognize it. They asked participants to estimate how difficult it was for the listener to identify the target song. European Canadians were over-confident about their guesses compared to Asian Canadians, arguably because, from their own first-person perspective, the task was fairly easy. Asian Canadians, who were more likely to apply the third-person perspective, could more accurately guess the constraints on the listener (Cohen & Hoshino-Browne, 2005). Thus it is possible to speculate that cultural products in the Asian tradition tend to take the third-person perspective and those in the Western tradition tend to take the first-person perspective. Although we need to wait for more systematic empirical research to test this possibility, there is at least one report that may support this assumption. Masuda (2010) reported that market research in Japan indicated that video games requiring players to take the first-person perspective (e.g., Call of Duty), which are very popular in the United States, did not catch on in Japan. By 2009, cumulative unit sales for Call of Duty had reached 8 million in the United States, compared to only 230 000 in Japan (http:/www.npd.com/ press/release/press_100203a.html, 2009). However, games that require the player to take the third-person perspective are extremely popular in Japan; cumulative unit sales of Dragon Quest, Pocket Monster, and Final Fantasy video games were 4.1 million, 3.3 million, and 1.6 million (http:// www.famitsu.com/game/news/1231257_1124.html, 2009).

In sum, these findings suggest that in the cycle of "culture ← → the mind", North Americans and East Asians who are exposed to different types of self-relevant cultural products internalize their preference for them, and use that internalized preference to reproduce cultural products containing the same cultural message.

CONCLUSION

This chapter reported two types of research in cultural psychology. First, focusing on the "culture → the mind" path, we reported how East Asians' mentality differs from that of North Americans. Second, focusing on the "the mind → culture" path, we reported that cultural products created and maintained by East Asians entail holistic and interdependent cultural messages, whereas those created and maintained by North Americans entail analytic and independent cultural messages. Practical applications of this research to business have yet to be studied. However, we are confident that these empirical findings, obtained through rigorous scientific methods, will provide a good foundation for thinking about cultural variation in advertisements. To close this chapter, we address the future directions in culture and cognition research, and some caveats for the application of research in culture and the mind.

Investigating Dynamic Processes

Although cross-cultural research on the human mind and on cultural products indicated the constancy in patterns between culture and the mind (e.g., the holistic ideas expressed in East Asian cultural products correspond to East Asians' holistic mentality), the means by which cultural products shape one's mind have not been well investigated. Since the cycle is a dynamic process – culture shapes the mind, and the mind shapes culture – such analyses should be a major part of the research. Our recent work on cultural variation in web page designs attempted to answer this request (Wang et al., 2011). One of the intuitive questions arising from previous findings is, "Why are East Asians not overwhelmed by such a complex organization of information?"

To address this question, we go back to the "culture → the mind" line of research. Wang et al.'s (2011) information search task, using 24 mock web pages, revealed that East Asians' information search speed was much faster than that of European Canadians when participants were presented with complex web pages, although there was no significant cultural difference in performance when using simple web pages. The findings suggest that East Asians are more likely than North Americans to be good at handling complex pieces of information, and to search a target object much more quickly. We concluded that if people are surrounded by complex pieces of information from birth, they develop skills to cope with complex ways of organizing information.

It could thus be said that people are born to attune to the characteristics of available cultural resources. Developmental research under the umbrella of analytic vs. holistic thoughts gives credence to this assertion. These studies suggest that people who are exposed to cultural resources that convey dominant cultural messages become attuned to the values and then transmit them to their own and subsequent generations (e.g., Duffy, Toriyama, Itakura & Kitayama, 2009; Ji, 2008; Senzaki & Masuda, 2011). We believe that more research of this type should be conducted in the future, to better address cultural psychologists' assertion of the "culture ← → the mind" dynamism. Indeed, as Cohen (2007) pointed out, cultural psychologists currently ask whether cultural effects are driven by things "in the head", "out in the world", or some combination of both, and how these causal forces should be measured (p. 200).

The Process of Cultural Transmission and Dissemination: The Caveat

The dominant beliefs, values, ideas and worldview shared by people in a given culture shape those people's minds, and the people in turn reproduce and sustain these cultural messages through cultural products in two ways: by spreading the cultural products (Sperber, 1996) and sharing them with others, and by transmitting the cultural products to the next generation (Tomasello, 1999). Thus, those who are interested in the practical application of cultural psychology cannot help asking the following question: What kind of information is most effectively spread and transmitted to potential customers? After reading this chapter, the reader might expect that messages that fit nicely with the dominant cultural beliefs, values, ideas and worldview would be the most transmittable and disseminable. Or would counterintuitive messages, which are shocking and vivid, influence potential customers more effectively? This is not an easy question, and is obviously beyond the scope of this chapter. Rather, we would like to share one research finding that we find intriguing.

Norenzayan, Atran, Faulkner and Schaller (2006) hypothesized that cultural narratives such as myths and folktales are more likely to achieve cultural stability if they correspond to a minimally counterintuitive (MCI) cognitive template that includes mostly intuitive concepts combined with a minority of counterintuitive ones. To test their hypothesis, they examined whether this template produces a memory advantage, and whether this memory advantage explains the cultural success of myths and folktales. They manipulated the proportions of the intuitive and counterintuitive messages in four ways – totally intuitive messages, mostly intuitive but a few counterintuitive messages, mostly counterintuitive but a few intuitive messages, and totally counterintuitive messages – and asked people to memorize the messages. The results indicated that people can easily memorize messages in which intuitive messages are dominant. This finding suggests that information (or advertising) that includes intuitive messages is the most transmittable and disseminable. However, an interesting phenomenon was observed. Norenzayan, Choi and Nisbett (2002) found that an MCI template produces a memory advantage after a one-week delay, relative to entirely intuitive or maximally counterintuitive cognitive templates. This finding suggests that people easily process culturally dominant messages, but, in the long run, small amounts of vivid or shocking accents increase the likelihood of the message being transmitted and disseminated. We leave the reader to reflect on this example of the complex dynamics of "culture ← → the mind".

REFERENCES

Azuma, H. (1994). *Education and socialization in Japan: A comparison between Japan and the United States* [Nihonjin no shitake to kyoiku – hattatsu no nichibeihikaku ni motozuite]. Tokyo: University of Tokyo Press.

Azuma, H. (2000, January). Sonzaironteki, koukokuteki, superflatteki [Ontological, advertising, and superflat-like]. In *hirokiazuma. com texts*. Retrieved January 6, 2002, from http://www .t3.rim.or.jp/~hazuma/texts/texts.html.

Bainbridge, J. & Pantaleo, S. (1999). *Learning with literature in the Canadian elementary classroom*. Edmonton, Canada: University of Alberta Press and Duvall House Publishing.

Bond, M. H. & Cheung, T. (1983). College students' spontaneous self-concept. *Journal of Cross-Cultural Psychology*, *14*, 153–71.

Bruner, J. (1990). *Acts of meaning: Four lectures on mind and culture*. Cambridge, MA: Harvard University Press.

Chentsova-Dutton, Y. E. & Tsai, J. L. (2010). Self-focused attention and emotional reactivity: The role of culture. *Journal of Personality and Social Psychology*, *98*, 507–19.

Chim, L., Moon, A. & Tsai, J. L. (2009, February). *Beauty is in the culture of the beholden: The occurrence and perception of American and Chinese smiles in magazines*. Poster presented at the 10th Annual Meeting of the Society of Personality and Social Psychology, Tampa, FL, USA.

Choi, I. & Choi, Y. (2002). Culture and self-concept flexibility. *Personality and Social Psychology Bulletin*, 28, 1508–17.

Choi, I., Dalal, R., Kim-Prieto, C. & Park, H. (2003). Culture and judgment of causal relevance. *Journal of Personality and Social Psychology*, 84, 46–59.

Choi, I. & Nisbett, R. E. (1998). The situational salience and cultural differences in the correspondence bias and the actor-observer bias. *Personality and Social Psychology Bulletin*, 24, 949–60.

Choi, I., Nisbett, R. E. & Norenzayan, A. (1999). Causal attribution across cultures: Variation and universality. *Psychological Bulletin*, 125, 47–63.

Chua, H. F., Boland, J. & Nisbett, R. E. (2005). Cultural variation in eye-movements during scene perception. *Proceedings of the National Academy of Sciences of the United States of America*, 102, 12629–33.

Cohen, D. (2007). Methods in cultural psychology. In S. Kitayama & D. Cohen (eds), *Handbook of cultural psychology*. New York: Guilford Press.

Cohen, D. & Gunz, A. (2002). As seen by the other . . .: Perspectives on the self in the memories and emotional perceptions of Easterners and Westerners. *Psychological Science*, 13, 55–9.

Cohen, D. & Hoshino-Browne, E. (2005). Insider and outsider perspectives on the self and social world. In R. M. Sorrention, D. Cohen, J. M Olson & M. P. Zanna (eds), *Culture and social behaviour: The tenth Ontario symposium* (pp. 49–76). Hillsdale, NJ: Laurence Erlbaum.

Cousins, S. D. (1989). Culture and selfhood in Japan and the U.S. *Journal of Personality and Social Psychology*, 56, 124–31.

Cromer, A. (1993). *Uncommon sense: The heretical nature of science*. New York: Oxford University Press.

Diener, E. & Diener, M. (1995). Cross-cultural correlates of life satisfaction and self-esteem. *Journal of Personality and Social Psychology*, 68, 653–63.

Duffy, S., Toriyama, R., Itakura, S. & Kitayama, S. (2009). Development of cultural strategies of attention in North American and Japanese children. *Journal of Experimental Child Psychology*, 102, 351–9.

Endo, Y. & Meijer, Z. (2004). Autobiographical memory of success and failure experiences. In Y. Kashima, Y. Endo, E. S. Kashima, C. Leung & J. McClure (eds), *Progress in Asian social psychology* (vol. 4, pp. 67–84). Seoul, Korea: Kyoyook-Kwahak-Sa.

Geertz, C. (1973). *The interpretation of cultures*. New York: Basic Books.

Goh, J. O., Tan, J. C. & Park, D. C. (2009). Culture modulates eye-movements to visual novelty. *PLoS ONE*, 4(12).

Gombrich, E. H. (2000). *Art and illusion: A study in the psychology of pictorial representation* (2nd ed.). Princeton, NJ: Princeton University Press. (Original work published 1961.)

Han, S. & Northoff, G. (2008). Culture-sensitive neural substrates of human cognition: A transcultural neuroimaging approach. *Nature Reviews Neuroscience*, 9, 646–54.

Han, S.-P. & Shavitt, S. (1994). Persuasion and culture: Advertising appeals in individualistic and collectivistic societies. *Journal of Experimental Social Psychology*, 30, 326–50.

Heine, S. J., Kitayama, S., Lehman, D. R., Takata, T., Ide, E., Leung, C. & Matsumoto, H. (2001). Divergent consequences of success and failure in Japan and North America: An investigation of self-improving motivations and malleable selves. *Journal of Personality and Social Psychology*, 81, 599–615.

Heine, S. J. & Lehman, D. R. (1997). Culture, dissonance, and self-affirmation. *Personality and Social Psychology Bulletin*, 23, 389–400.

Heine, S. J., Lehman, D. R., Markus, H. R. & Kitayama, S. (1999). Is there a universal need for positive self-regard? *Psychological Review*, 106, 766–94.

Heine, S. J. & Norenzayan, A. (2006). Toward a psychological science for a cultural species. *Perspectives on Psychological Science*, 1, 251–69.

Imada, T. (in press). Cultural narratives of individualism and collectivism: A content analysis of textbook stories in the United States and Japan. *Journal of Cross-Cultural Psychology*.

Ji, L. (2008). The leopard cannot change his spots, or can he? Culture and the development of lay theories of change. *Personality and Social Psychology Bulletin, 34*, 613–22.

Ji, L., Nisbett, R. E. & Su, Y. (2001). Culture, change and prediction. *Psychological Science, 12*, 450–56.

Ji, L., Peng, K. & Nisbett, R. E. (2000). Culture, control, and perception of relationships in the environment. *Journal of Personality and Social Psychology, 78*, 943–55.

Kanagawa, C., Cross, S. E. & Markus, H. R. (2001). "Who am I?": The cultural psychology of the conceptual self. *Personality and Social Psychology Bulletin, 27*, 90–103.

Kashima, Y., Siegal, M., Tanaka, K. & Kashima, E. (1992). Do people believe behaviors are consistent with attitudes? Toward a cultural psychology of attribution processes. *British Journal of Social Psychology, 31*, 111–24.

Kenmochi, T. (1992). *Ma no nihon bunka* [The concept of space in Japanese culture]. Tokyo: Chobun-sya.

Kim, H. S. & Markus, H. R. (1999). Deviance or uniqueness, harmony or conformity? A cultural analysis. *Journal of Personality and Social Psychology, 77*, 785–800.

Kitayama, S., Duffy, S., Kawamura, T. & Larsen, J. T. (2003). Perceiving an object and its context in different cultures: A cultural look at New Look. *Psychological Science, 14*, 201–6.

Kitayama, S., Ishii, K., Imada, T., Takemura, K. & Ramaswamy, J. (2006). Voluntary settlement and the spirit of independence: Evidence from Japan's "northern frontier". *Journal of Personality and Social Psychology, 91*(3), 369–84.

Kitayama, S., Markus, H. R. & Kurokawa, M. (2000). Culture, emotion, and well-being: Good feeling in Japan and the United States. *Cognition & Emotion, 14*, 93–124.

Kitayama, S., Mesquita, B. & Karasawa, M. (2006). Cultural affordances and emotional experience: Socially engaging and disengaging emotions in Japan and the United States. *Journal of Personality and Social Psychology, 91*, 890–903.

Kitayama, S., Snibbe, A. C., Markus, H. R. & Suzuki, T. (2004). Is there any "free" choice?: Self and dissonance in two cultures. *Psychological Science, 15*(8), 527–33.

Kitayama, S. & Uskul, A. K. (2011). Culture, mind, and the brain: Current evidence and future directions. *Annual Review of Psychology, 62*, 419–49.

Koo, M. & Choi, I. (2005). Becoming a holistic thinker: Training effect of oriental medicine on reasoning. *Personality and Social Psychology Bulletin, 31*, 1264–72.

Kubovy, M. (1986). *The psychology of perspective and Renaissance art*. New York: Cambridge University Press.

Lee, F., Hallahan, M. & Herzog, T. (1996). Explaining real-life events: How culture and domain shape attributions. *Personality and Social Psychology Bulletin, 22*, 732–41.

Leung, A. K. & Cohen, D. (2007). The soft embodiment of culture: Camera angles and motion through time and space. *Psychological Science, 18*(9), 824–30.

Markus, H. R. & Hamedani, M. G. (2007). Sociocultural psychology: The dynamic interdependence among self systems and social systems. In S. Kitayama & D. Cohen (eds), *Handbook of cultural psychology* (pp. 3–39). New York: Guilford.

Markus, H. R. & Kitayama, S. (1991). Culture and the self: Implications for cognition, emotion, and motivation. *Psychological Review, 98*(2), 224–53.

Markus, H. R. & Kitayama, S. (2010). Cultures and selves: A cycle of mutual constitution. *Perspectives on Psychological Science, 5*(4), 420–30.

Markus, H. R., Uchida, Y., Omoregie, H., Townsend, S. S. M. & Kitayama, S. (2006). Going for the gold: Models of agency in Japanese and American contexts. *Psychological Science, 17*, 103–12.

Masuda, T. (2010). *Bosu dake miru obeijin, minna no kao made miru nihonjin* [North Americans and Westerners see the boss, Japanese see everyone's face]. Tokyo: Kodansha.

Masuda, T., Akase, M., Radford, M. H. B. & Wang, H. (2008). Jokyo yoin ga gankyu undo pattern ni oyobosu eikyo: Nihonjin to Seiyojin no syuken jyoho heno bunkasa no kikaku kenkyu [Cross-cultural research on the pattern of eye-movement: Comparing the level of concentration between Japanese and Western participants]. *The Japanese Journal of Psychology, 79*, 35–43.

Masuda, T., Ellsworth, P., Mesquita, B., Leu, J., Tanida, S. & van de Veerdonk, E. (2008).

Placing the face in context: Cultural differences in the perception of facial emotion. *Journal of Personality and Social Psychology*, *94*, 365–81.

Masuda, T., Gonzalez, R., Kwan, L. & Nisbett, R. E. (2008). Culture and aesthetic preference: Comparing the attention to context of East Asians and European Americans. *Personality and Social Psychology Bulletin*, *34*, 1260–75.

Masuda, T. & Kitayama, S. (2004). Perceived-induced constraint and attitude attribution in Japan and in the US: A case for cultural dependence of the correspondence bias. *Journal of Experimental Social Psychology*, *40*, 409–16.

Masuda, T. & Nisbett, R. E. (2001). Attending holistically vs. analytically: Comparing the context sensitivity of Japanese and Americans. *Journal of Personality and Social Psychology*, *81*, 922–34.

Miller, J. G. (1999). Cultural psychology: Implications for basic psychological theory. *Psychological Science*, *10*, 85–9.

Minami, H. (1983). *Ma no kenkyu: Nihonjin no biteki kankaku* [Studies of the concept of "ma": Aesthetics of the Japanese]. Tokyo: Kodan-sha.

Minoura, Y. (1992). A sensitive period for the incorporation of a cultural meaning system: A study of Japanese children growing up in the United States. *Ethos*, *20*, 304–39.

Miyamoto, Y. & Kitayama, S. (2002). Cultural variation in correspondence bias: The critical role of attitude diagnosticity of socially constrained behaviour. *Journal of Personality and Social Psychology*, *83*, 1239–48.

Miyamoto, Y., Nisbett, R. E. & Masuda, T. (2006). Culture and the physical environment: Holistic versus analytic perceptual affordances. *Psychological Science*, *17*, 113–19.

Morling, B. & Evered, S. (2006). Secondary control reviewed and defined. *Psychological Bulletin*, *132*, 269–96.

Morling, B., Kitayama, S. and Miyamoto, Y. (2002). Cultural practices emphasize influence in the United States and adjustment in Japan. *Personality and Social Psychology Bulletin*, *28*, 311–23.

Morling, B. & Lamoreaux, M. (2008). Measuring culture outside the head: A meta-analysis of individualism-collectivism in cultural products. *Personality and Social Psychology Review*, *12*(3), 199–221.

Morris, M. W. & Peng, K. (1994). Culture and cause: American and Chinese attributions for social and physical events. *Journal of Personality and Social Psychology*, *67*, 949–71.

Munro, D. J. (1985). Introduction. In D. J. Munro (ed.), *Individualism and holism: Studies in Confucian and Taoist values* (pp. 1–34). Ann Arbor: University of Michigan, Center for Chinese Studies.

Murakami, T. (2000). *Super flat visual book*. Tokyo: Madora-sha.

Nakamura, H. (1985). *Ways of thinking of Eastern people*. Honolulu: University of Hawaii Press. (Original work published 1964.)

Needham, J. (1954). *Science and civilization in China: Vol. 1. Introductory orientations.* Cambridge, UK: Cambridge University Press.

Needham, J. (1962). *Science and civilization in China: Vol. 4. Physics and physical technology.* Cambridge, UK: Cambridge University Press.

Nisbett, R. E. (2003). *The geography of thought*. New York: Free Press.

Nisbett, R. E. & Masuda, T. (2003). Culture and point of view. *Proceedings of the National Academy of Sciences of the United States of America*, *100*, 11163–75.

Nisbett, R. E. & Miyamoto, Y. (2005). The influence of culture: Holistic versus analytic perception. *Trends in Cognitive Sciences*, *9*, 467–73.

Nisbett, R. E., Peng, K., Choi, I. & Norenzayan, A. (2001). Culture and systems of thought: Holistic vs. analytic cognition. *Psychological Review*, *108*, 291–310.

Norenzayan, A., Atran, S., Faulkner, J. & Schaller, M. (2006). Memory and mystery: The cultural selection of minimally counterintuitive narratives. *Cognitive Science*, *30*, 531–53.

Norenzayan, A., Choi, I. & Nisbett, R. E. (2002). Cultural similarities and differences in social influence: Evidence from behavioural predictions and lay theories of behaviour. *Personality and Social Psychology Bulletin*, *28*, 109–20.

Norenzayan, A. & Nisbett, R. E. (2000). Culture and causal cognition. *Current Directions in Psychological Science, 9,* 132–5.

Norenzayan, A., Smith, E. E., Kim, B. J. & Nisbett, R. E. (2002). Cultural preferences for formal versus intuitive reasoning. *Cognitive Science, 26,* 653–84.

Oishi, S. & Diener, E. (2003). Culture and well-being: The cycle of action, evaluation and decision. *Personality and Social Psychology Bulletin, 29,* 939–49.

Peng, K. & Knowles, E. D. (2003). Culture, education, and the attribution of physical causality. *Personality and Social Psychology Bulletin, 29,* 1272–84.

Peng, K. & Nisbett, R. E. (1999). Culture, dialecticism, and reasoning about contradiction. *American Psychologist, 54,* 741–54.

Senzaki, S. & Masuda, T. (2011). *When do children internalize a culturally dominant way of seeing things? A developmental and cultural comparison in visual attention in North American and Japanese children.* Unpublished manuscript, University of Alberta.

Shimada, N. (1990). *Kaiga no chisiki hyakka* [Encyclopedia of paintings]. Tokyo: Shufu to Seikatsu Sha.

Shweder, R. A. (1991). Cultural psychology: What is it? In R. Shweder (ed.), *Thinking through culture* (pp. 73–110). Cambridge, MA: Harvard University Press.

Shweder, R. A. & Bourne, E. J. (1982). "Does the concept of the person vary cross-culturally?" In A. Marsella & G. White (eds), *Cultural conceptions of mental health and therapy* (pp. 97–137). Dordrecht, Holland: Reidel. Reprinted in R. A. Shweder (ed.), *Thinking through cultures: Expeditions in cultural psychology.* Cambridge, MA: Harvard University Press, 1991.

Spencer-Rodgers, J. & Peng, K. (2004). The dialectical self: Contradiction, change, and holism in the East Asian self-concept. In R. M. Sorrentino, D. Cohen, J. M. Olsen & M. P. Zanna (eds), *Culture and social behavior: The Ontario symposium* (vol. 10, pp. 227–50). Mahwah, NJ: Lawrence Erlbaum.

Sperber, D. (1996). *Explaining culture: A naturalistic approach.* Oxford, UK: Blackwell.

Stevenson, H. W. & Stigler, J. W. (1992). *The learning gap: Why our schools are failing and what we can learn from Japanese and Chinese education.* New York: Summit Books.

Taylor, C. (1989). *Sources of the self: The making of the modern identity.* Cambridge, MA: Harvard University Press.

Taylor, C. (2007). *A secular age.* Cambridge, MA: Harvard University Press.

Tomasello, M. (1999). *The cultural origins of human cognition.* Cambridge, MA: Harvard University Press.

Tsai, J. L. (2007). Ideal affect: Cultural causes and behavioral consequences. *Perspectives on Psychological Science, 2,* 242–59.

Tsai, J. L., Knutson, B. & Fung, H. H. (2006). Cultural variation in affect valuation. *Journal of Personality and Social Psychology, 90,* 288–307.

Tsai, J. L., Louie, J. Y., Chen, E. E. & Uchida, Y. (2007). Learning what feelings to desire: Socialization of ideal affect through children's storybooks. *Personality and Social Psychology Bulletin, 33,* 17–30.

Tsai, J. L., Miao, F. F. & Seppala, E. (2007). Good feelings in Christianity and Buddhism: Religious differences in ideal affect. *Personality and Social Psychology Bulletin, 33,* 409–21.

Uchida, Y. & Kitayama, S. (2009). Happiness and unhappiness in east and west: Themes and variations. *Emotion, 9,* 441–56.

Uchida, Y., Kitayama, S., Mesquita, B., Reyes, J. A. S. & Morling, B. (2008). Is perceived emotional support beneficial? Well-being and health in independent and interdependent cultures. *Personality and Social Psychology Bulletin, 34,* 741–54.

Wang, H., Ito, K. & Masuda, T. (2011). *Culture and internet environment: Comparing complexity of design between East Asian and North American homepages.* Unpublished manuscript, University of Alberta.

Weisz, J. R., Rothbaum, F. M. & Blackburn, T. C. (1984). Standing out and standing in: The psychology of control in America and Japan. *American Psychologist, 39,* 955–69.

Zhu, Y., Zhang, L., Fan, J. & Han, S. (2007). Neural basis of cultural influence on self-representation. *NeuroImage, 34,* 1310–16.

PART III

RETROSPECTIVE

7 Advertising and consumer culture in Old Shanghai

Russell Belk and Xin Zhao

INTRODUCTION

Benson (1996) notes that there is a striking parallel between the growing momentum of commercial forces in 1930s era Shanghai and the "market socialism" of China today. The late nineteenth and early twentieth centuries were a time of Chinese encounters with foreign products, advertising, and trade that have strong similarities to those that have emerged under the post-Mao "open door" policies of China. In both cases, charges of consumerism, worshipping the foreign, and materialism arose, as well as local accommodations of or confrontations with globalism. Nevertheless, the conditions that surround these two periods of open contact with the West are different. It is also important to avoid simply framing the earlier contact as a "Western-impact/China-response" model, even though "the old 'impact-response' model is perhaps more relevant in [Old] Shanghai than in any other place in the nation" (Lu 1999, p. 18). Among the alternatives to this model is that of localization suggested by Watson (2006) and others. In this case the local response is to transform global brands into something different with specific local meanings. A third model is for the local to dominate the global, as suggested by Cochran (2006), who shows that Chinese brands of patent medicines and pharmaceuticals dominated the market in Old Shanghai and continue to have an important presence in the Chinese market (Zhou and Belk 2009).

A BRIEF HISTORY OF CHINESE FOREIGN TRADE

While China may have had some domestic branded goods as early as the late tenth century (Hamilton and Lai 1989; Moore and Reid 2008), its earliest encounters with foreign goods involved unbranded luxury objects that made their way there along the Spice Route, the Silk Road, and various sea routes. Goods like sugar, spices, and cotton came into China carried largely through Islamic merchants. In exchange, silk, porcelain, nickel, zinc and grain were China's major early exports (Fairbank 1992; Adshead 1995). This trade was part of an early age of "consumption globalization" running from 1400 to 1800 (Adshead 1997; Stearns 2006). Although the Islamic merchants also traded with the Eastern Mediterranean and Europe, the foreign goods that China found most interesting were from West Asia, India, and the Ottoman Empire. Cotton is a prime example. While no one in China wore cotton clothing in 1350, by 1850 it was ubiquitous, even on peasants (Huang 1990). Yet, except for a few novelty fabrics, China proved largely impermeable to European cottons (Adshead 1997, p. 87). China preferred the cotton goods of India and Egypt. When China began to produce its own cotton, it was consistently preferred to European fabrics.

Such resistance contrasts sharply with the enthusiastic embrace of Western fashions and virtually anything Western in Japan after the Meiji Restoration reopened that country in 1853 (Hamilton 1977). Resistance to Western goods characterizes most of China's contact with the West before the twentieth century (Stearns 2001). The causes of this resistance are a matter of debate (Hamilton 1977), but China's belief in the superiority of Chinese civilization to European civilization seems critical.

When some Western goods did enter China in the seventeenth, eighteenth and nineteenth centuries, they too were initially unbranded commodities. They were exported to China in the hope of balancing the trade deficit from Europe's growing appetite for imported Chinese tea. The Dutch East India Company brought tea to the Netherlands from China. They found that they could initially obtain tea cheaply in exchange for borage and sage, which they told the Chinese would cure a variety of ailments and encourage gaiety. After the company had hooked Dutch consumers on tea, they turned to England where tea drinking became fashionable in the mid seventeenth century. By 1740, when tea became the dominant drink in England, the Chinese had found that sage and borage were not as effective as they had been told and they demanded gold and silver bullion instead. This insistence on precious metals became such a drain on the Dutch East India Company that they ceded the Chinese tea trade to the British East India Company.

The British East India Company had little more success than the Dutch in getting the Chinese to accept European goods in exchange for tea. China also restricted foreign tea trade to Canton so that the British never got involved in local distribution the way they had in India. When the head of the British East India Company, Lord Macartney, sailed a 66-gun man-of-war into the Canton harbor in 1793, along with "two escort vessels loaded with examples of British manufacturing technology" (Fairbank 1992, p. 196), the response of the Qing court was to label the goods a "tribute from England". The Chien Lung emperor also sent a message to King George III, stating:

> We possess all things. I set no value on objects strange or ingenious and have no use for your country's manufactures. Our ways bear no resemblance to yours (quoted in Dong 2000, p. 5).

And in 1816, when Lord Amherst tried again to force British goods upon the Chinese, he and his delegation received a rude welcome and were sent back to England. An English merchant described the dilemma, noting that the Chinese, who considered themselves at the center of civilization, seemingly had the best of everything, including "the best food in the world, rice; the best drink, tea; and the best clothing, cotton, silk, fur" (Stearns 2001, p. 85). Although there was a short-term fascination in the Chinese court with imported European clocks (Clunas 1991; Wills 1993), when Chinese brokers in Canton were forced to accept these clocks as payment for tea, they took a considerable loss. Because they were unable to sell them, they ultimately refused the clocks altogether. The clock and Western ways of time-keeping and calendars did not make inroads in China until twentieth-century urban industrialization began (Yeh 1995, 2007). So the British became resigned to buying Chinese tea with silver bullion from the British colonies.

As was the case with the Dutch, the British found that the bullion drain, coupled with the costs of the French Revolution and the Napoleonic Wars, was too much. But unlike the Dutch, the British East India Company found a commodity that was irresistible to the Chinese: opium. The company imported opium from India and left with tea and rhubarb (used in Europe as a laxative to fight child dysentery) from China. In an 1852 report to the British Foreign office, W. H. Mitchell, a local official in Hong Kong concluded that: "We bring the Chinese nothing that is really popular among them . . . Opium is the only 'open sesame' to their stony hearts" (Hao 1986, p. 55). During the height of the British opium trade there were estimated to be 12 million regular users in China (Adshead 1997), or one out of every ten people (Dong 2000). This reversed the flow of silver bullion into China, which had grown to $10 million per year (Fairbank 1992). Opium shipments into Canton harbor grew from 200 chests in 1729 to 4000 in 1790 and over 20000 by 1838. Although opium was previously used by Chinese tea and salt laborers, and was sought as a relief from tuberculosis, opium smoking also became a form of conspicuous leisure and luxury consumption for the Chinese elite (Adshead 1997; Stearns 2001). As opium imports rose from the mid 1820s to the mid 1840s, China lost between a quarter and a half of the silver it had accumulated in the previous 120 years of trade, including virtually the whole stock accumulated from England (Richardson 1999).

When the British East India Company lost its monopoly on China trade in 1834, England sent an official to China to demand free trade. The Qing Emperor of China faced not only a political threat to his power but also the growing realization that opium smoking posed a moral as well as an economic threat to China. Several years of unsuccessful negotiations followed. The Emperor finally sent an incorruptible commissioner (Lin) to Canton. Lin barricaded the foreigners in their factories until they surrendered their current stocks of opium. England responded by sending gunboats and initiating the Opium War (1839–1842). It has been seen as a war about consumption:

> What the Chinese were attacking was not the foreigner or opium per se, but the Canton interest: its business ethos, its multiculturalism, its links with maritime Asia, its ability to corrupt any official sent to govern it. They were attacking it for what it was and for what it might become. When [Chinese Imperial Commissioner] Lin Tse-hsü had those chests of opium destroyed, he was making implicitly a bonfire of all the vanities. In attacking the Canton of the present, he was also attacking the Shanghai and Hong Kong of the future. He was attacking consumerism itself (Adshead 1997, p. 238).

Besides gaining Hong Kong Territory, a substantial reduction in tariffs, most-favored-nation status, five new treaty ports, and freedom from Chinese laws ("extraterritoriality") for British expatriates (Fairbank 1992), the British victory in the Opium War also opened the door for an influx of traders and goods from other European nations and the U.S. As Adshead (1997) suggests, however, it opened the door for rampant consumerism as well. Fairbank (1992) argues that it likely also led to social disruption and psychological demoralization that, together with internal conflicts, shook Chinese faith in the superiority of their civilization over that of the Western imperialists.

Although the opium imports in the first half of the nineteenth century turned the balance of payments against China for a time, by the late 1860s the country showed a surplus again (Richardson 1999). But by the 1890s China had developed a hunger for foreign manufactured and branded goods that again resulted in a growing trade deficit. In the 30 years between 1864 and 1894 China's foreign trade more than doubled, with branded Western consumer goods leading the way (Wang 2000). There was also a qualitative shift in the nature of Chinese trade (Richardson 1999). Previously China's trade was that of an advanced economy with exports of manufactured and processed goods such as silk, tea and porcelain, and imports of barely processed goods (opium). But as China grew more receptive to foreign manufactured goods, it became like an underdeveloped economy. The promotion of newly imported branded merchandise had much to do with the growth of Chinese consumer desire, and eventually the Chinese began to produce branded goods themselves (Hao 1986).

THE INTERNATIONALIZATION OF SHANGHAI

With the end of the Opium War in 1842, Shanghai began a 106-year period of foreign occupation, described as "semi-colonialism" (Wood 1998). In 1849, Britain's International Settlement on the waterfront in Shanghai was joined by France's "French Concession". The British and French were later joined by Americans and Russians within their foreign enclaves. After winning the first Sino-Japanese war in 1895, the Japanese also became a growing, and especially resented, presence. The number of foreigners in Shanghai grew rapidly after the turn of the century, reaching 100 000 by 1930 (Wei 1993). Lee (1999a) saw these foreigners and local Chinese living in two worlds. But, while Chinese were initially excluded from the International Settlement, by 1915, more than 620 000 were living there (Wei 1998).

Prior to the twentieth century (and later under Mao), urban life in China was singled out for criticism by intellectuals (Lu 1999). In Confucian tradition, the countryside and nature are seen as virtuous while urban locales, especially big cities, are seen as depraved and foreign. Because artificial illumination at night was associated with gambling, prostitution and drunkenness, when Shanghai installed electricity, the authorities threatened to punish Chinese who installed foreign lighting (Crow 1940; Chiou 1993). Although anti-urban sentiments never entirely disappeared (Benson 1996), the international milieu of Shanghai proved highly seductive and city life became much more interesting. Shanghai was also the focus of social criticism because it was modern, decadent and wild. It became the emblem of consumerism, materialism, Western influence and cosmopolitanism (Strand 2000).

By 1930, Shanghai was the fifth biggest city in the world. At the end of the nineteenth century, Shanghai had fewer than 1 million people, while by 1937 it had grown to 3.77 million (Shanghai Museum 1998). This meant that most of the population during this boom period were from other places in China or other parts of the world. They were attracted by both jobs and the prospect of living in a thriving and dynamic world city. Even though the largest department stores, Sincere and Wing On, were owned by Chinese entrepreneurs, they featured many foreign luxury goods including clothing, cosmetics, shoes and jewelry (Chan 1998; Ching-hwang 1993). Shanghai became nearly synonymous in China with "modern" – Western style streets, gaslight, electricity, telephones, running water – all made it a metropolis even by Western standards (Lee 1999b). Elevators, sewer systems, air conditioning, department stores, and neon lights all appeared in Shanghai soon after they were introduced in the West (Lu 1999). Shanghai became the Chinese fashion capital as well, with rapidly changing styles of clothes, hairstyles, makeup, dance, music and entertainment.

As a treaty port since the 1840s, Shanghai offered a sharp contrast of old and new, East and West, Chinese traditional and the foreign exotic. It was also a site of contestation for several colonial powers. There was a mix of Western building styles on the Bund – the waterfront area that along with Nanjing Road formed the center of Western commercial culture in the city. Shanghai was also the site of China's confrontations with globalism and cosmopolitanism (Cochran 1999a; Lee 1999b). Leisure locales such as high-rise hotels and golf courses, which largely catered to foreigners, were initially quite alien to the local Chinese and distant from their daily lives. But common people in the city eventually found their own ways of partaking in the new and wondrous world of material consumption. All kinds of consumer goods, from packaged consumer foods to luxurious automobiles, flourished and competed for the attention of Chinese consumers in Shanghai. Western leisure venues such as modern cinemas, dance halls and a horse racing track, as well and many other novel consumer products, became accessible to common people in China for the first time, especially after the fall of the Qing dynasty in 1912.

Old Shanghai was not just a synonym for modernity and an exotic blend of old and new; it was the key exemplar of decadence at the time, with rampant opium, prostitution, corruption, greed and abundant entertainments (Dong 2000). The decadence and consumer culture that characterized Shanghai were no doubt aided by the liminal status of the city: "Half oriental, half occidental; half land, half water; neither a colony nor wholly belonging to China; inhabited by citizens of every nation in the world but ruled by none" (Dong 2000, p. 2). As Bakhtin (1968) has demonstrated in the context of the medieval carnival, both the carnivalesque and the market emerge most strongly within marginal places occupying a liminal betwixt-and-between status; a no-man's-land wherein anything goes. In Shanghai this was aided by the extraterritoriality privileges China granted to the foreign concessions, guaranteeing that Chinese laws did not apply.

Perhaps no other institution of Shanghai captures the carnivalesque and decadent mix of the local and the foreign as well as the great amusement halls that sprung up in the city. When filmmaker Joseph von Sternberg visited Shanghai to make his 1932 movie *Shanghai Express*, he visited the Great World Amusement Center and reported that:

> On the first floor were gambling tables, sing-song girls, magicians, pick-pockets, slot machines, fireworks, bird-cages, fans, stick incense, acrobats and ginger. One flight up were the restaurants, a dozen different groups of actors, crickets in cages, pimps, midwives, barbers and earwax extractors. The third floor had jugglers, herb medicines, ice-cream parlours, photographers, a new bevy of girls, their high-collared gowns slit to reveal their thighs, and under the heading of novelty, several rows of exposed toilets, their impresarios instructing the amused patrons not to squat but to assume a position more in keeping with the imported plumbing. The fourth floor was crowded with shooting galleries, fan-tan tables, revolving wheels, massage benches, acupuncture and moxa cabinets, hot-towel counters, dried fish and intestines, and dance platforms serviced by a horde of music makers competing with each other to see who could drown out the others. The fifth floor featured girls whose dresses were slit to the armpits, a stuffed whale, story-tellers, balloons, peep-shows, masks, a mirror-maze, two love-letter booths with scribes who guaranteed results, "rubber goods," and a temple filled with ferocious gods and joss-sticks. On the top floor and roof of that house of multiple joys, a jumble of tight-rope walkers slithered back and forth, and there were see-saws, Chinese checkers, mahjong, strings of fireworks going off, lottery tickets, and marriage brokers (von Sternberg 1955, in Wood 1998, pp. 237–8).

Other amusement halls also included Shanghai opera, mini-golf courts, skating rinks and in-store hotels (Zhen 2001).

This special climate of hedonism did not arise overnight, and advertising and retailing played important roles in precipitating this dramatic change to a carnivalesque consumer culture. The Shanghai retail landscape included multi-story department stores, with the four most prominent built by overseas Chinese investors. Like the department stores that helped spur consumer culture in the West (e.g., Williams 1982), these stores exuded luxury and enveloped shoppers and window shoppers alike in an aura of rich variety, silver, silk, satins and furs (Chan 1999; Lee 1999a). They offered an array of temptations, including,

> American cosmetics, French truffles, Scotch whiskies, German cameras, American fountain pens, Japanese toys, English leather wallets and shaving kits – alongside a bewildering array of Chinese products (Dong 2000, pp. 96–7).

Many of the free-standing cinemas, theaters, restaurants and hotels of the city were similarly exotic and luxurious in their atmospheres. Tea houses were a popular place for lower- and middle-class men to spend long periods taking in the free story-telling performances (Benson 1996, 1999). Despite the strong tea culture in China, coffee houses eventually eclipsed them in popularity (Lee 2001). While local cuisine is often taken to be one of the most difficult-to-change anchors of culture (Wei 1993; Esherick 2000), Western foods came to be associated with all things chic and elegant (Lu 1999; Yeh 1997). Even milk came to be "the epitome of what it meant to be scientific and modern" (Glosser 1999).

As Wei (1993) demonstrates, many Chinese houses in the foreign settlements emulated the foreigners' homes in wealth and ostentation. A number of these wealthy Chinese were compradors who served as liaisons between foreign firms and local distributors (Bergère 1986). They were necessary, not only owing to the lack of Chinese language by most foreigners, but also as a result of China's policy of allowing little or no direct involvement in distribution by foreigners. Because of their association with Westerners, they were despised by other Chinese as a class. The novelist Wu Chien-jen observed, "To the comprador, even the foreigner's fart is fragrant" (Wood 2000, p. 256). Beneath the wealthy Chinese were a large number of "comfortably well-off" who also lived much as foreigners did.

While newspapers and other forms of advertising were abundant in Shanghai, Crow (1937) estimates that only about 10 percent of Chinese were literate and that less than 5 percent were newspaper readers. Lee and Nathan (1985) suggest considerably higher numbers: 30 to 45 percent male literacy and 2 to 10 percent female literacy. They estimate that one-quarter of urban men read periodicals. Thus, full-fledged participation in the new consumer culture of Shanghai was something which involved only a minority of Shanghai's Chinese residents. Nevertheless, as Lu (1999) documents, few in the city failed to be touched by some aspect of this global consumer culture. Even lowly rickshaw pullers and coolies were likely to wear shoes with British rubber soles, smoke American packaged cigarettes, and light them with Japanese matches (Lu 1999). Esherick (2000) reports that even working-class women from the cotton mills saved to dress up, go to movies and the opera, and go window-shopping with friends. Those who couldn't afford ready-made clothes used less expensive tailors or made their own clothing in the latest styles (Lu 1999). Thus, even though complete adoption of consumer culture was something only a minority of Chinese could afford, there were few, if any, who were untouched by some aspect of global consumption patterns in the city. Moreover, the advertising and consumption that began in Shanghai spread far inland into China as well, although with less intensity (Lee and Nathan 1985).

Lee (2000) argues that a hybridized or creolized culture pervaded city life, as evident in the combination of Western calendars and Chinese lunar calendars on ubiquitous ad posters (*yuefenpai*). As Zhao and Belk (2008a) show, this popular form of advertising was a hybrid that combined US and Chinese traditional forms and initially incorporated Confucian teachings in order to sanction advertising messages. The posters eventually came to focus on displaying Chinese "calendar girls" dressed in the latest qipao and sporting the latest hairdos, like the bobbed hair of the 1920s, as well as showing the latest branded radios, batteries, telephones, cigarettes and medicines. When these models weren't simply luxuriating, they were shown playing golf, at the race track, in Western wedding dresses, and in homes containing Western furniture. Still, all of this was done with a combination of Chinese symbolic elements such as bamboo, plum blossoms, and moon gates. *Yuefenpai* advertising evolved over time and the women employed also changed from being modest and demure to being emblems of modernity and consumer culture (Liang 2004; Shih 2007). This was something that also provoked criticism of Chinese women generally, as will be discussed in the following sections.

THE ADVERTISING ENVIRONMENT

Western missionaries started the first newspaper in China in 1853, the *Chinese Serial*. The next year it began to carry advertising with the express purpose of inciting Chinese to emulate the West (Wang 2000). In 1872 *Shun Bao* (*Shanghai News*) began, and it soon became the largest and most influential newspaper in China, with distribution in other major cities the following day (Lee and Nathan 1985). Both *Shun Bao* and the next leading newspaper in Shanghai, *Sin Wan Pao*, were initially foreign owned, but soon were bought out by Chinese owners (Wang 2000). Newspapers in cosmopolitan Shanghai were published not only in Chinese, but also in English (*North China Daily*), French (*Le Journal de Shanghai*), and Russian (*Shanghai Zaria*).

Magazines circulation also reached its peak in China during the 1920s and 1930s, when it was estimated there were approximately 2000 periodicals on the market with an audience of 30 million readers (Nathan 1985; Xu 1990; Wang 2000). Most magazines carried advertising and had a heavily female readership. Leading titles focused on the home, family, fashion, beauty, movies and shopping (Wang 2000). So significant were these magazines in shaping consumption that Warra (1999) concludes "Artists and Publishers were self-conscious inventors of Shanghai's new-style consumer culture" (p. 87). In addition, corporations published journals to promote their products. British American Tobacco offered *Qing Yan Pao* (a monthly on capitalism), Bayer Pharmaceutical Company published *Tien De* (*God's Virtue*, a medical journal), and Eastman Kodak published *Kodak Photography* (Xu 1990).

Other prominent forms of early twentieth-century advertising in China included billboards, neon signs, posters, calendars, radio and cinema advertising. Shanghai was saturated with outdoor advertising and neon signs that made the city a blazing spectacle at night (Dikötter 2006; Lee 1999a). Retail display in the stores of downtown Shanghai quickly followed European and American trends with big plate glass windows with eye-catching displays and sumptuous arrays of merchandise (Cochran 2000; Lee 1999b).

Shanghai also had approximately half of China's 93 radio stations in 1935 (Lee and Nathan 1985). Radio stations became popular by broadcasting the *tanci*, a traditional story-telling genre popular in tea houses. Advertisers sponsored these shows and writers remade the traditional *kaipan* songs, which the *tanci* included, to address popular topics such as world leaders, soccer stars, movies and divorce, as well as lauding the advertising sponsors (Benson 1996). Unlike the lower class male patrons of *tanci* in the teahouses, the radio *tanci* broadcasts attracted a large and upscale female audience. Prominent among the advertisers who chose to address this radio audience were silk merchants, department stores, jewelry stores, clothing stores, furniture stores and furriers.

By the mid 1930s, Shanghai had approximately 300 movie theaters that could seat 300 000 people (Lee and Nathan 1985). British American Tobacco (BAT) began producing film clips in 1922 using English film crews. Its first ad featured an animated cartoon showing a donkey that refused to move until it smelled the smoke (which spelled out BAT in English) of a cigarette lit by its owner (Cochran 1980, p. 135). Given the predictably poor Chinese response to such advertising, BAT turned to Chinese film makers who were able to employ Chinese language, Chinese actors and actresses, and Chinese theatrical traditions. BAT bought a network of theaters and contracted with others to show their ads. Sometimes packets of its cigarettes were sold at the door as tickets for admission (Cochran 1980). Other advertisers, like medicine companies, also used cinema advertising, based on short films or slide shows (Cochran 2000, 2006).

A special form of advertising in old Shanghai, as noted earlier, was calendar advertising (*yuefenpai*). There is a tradition of hanging up New Year pictures during the Spring Festival (Lunar New Year) period in China. In addition, traditionally lunar calendars with portraits of the kitchen god were purchased and hung at this time of year (Laing 2004). The popularity of New Year Pictures attracted both domestic and foreign businesses. By creating a give-away calendar that was attractive and carried the name and image of their products, they could be assured of a constant presence in numerous Shanghai households. So popular did these posters become that they were also sold on the streets and offered as premiums to attract subscribers to magazines (Laing 2004).

Another special form of advertising in old Shanghai was the cigarette card. So successful was the introduction of foreign cigarettes into Shanghai by American J.B. Duke of British American Tobacco (BAT) that tobacco was called the opium of the twentieth century (Wood 1998, p. 197). The cigarette card is a well-painted small picture with various subjects, inserted in cigarette packages and intended to be a collectible and to promote brand loyalty. The first set of cigarette cards in Shanghai was by British Wales Tobacco in 1894 and included soldiers from the Qing Dynasty Army. American DaMei Tobacco issued a series of cigarette cards and advertised that those who collected 50 of them could send them back to the company and receive a beautiful picture book. China Tobacco Manufacturing Company's Golden Arrow cigarettes were sold with cards that could be exchanged for suitcases, raincoats, watches and radios (Dikötter 2006, p. 70). The subjects of cigarette cards included philosophy, religion, politics, economics, foreign policy, commerce, law, military, geography, history, chemistry, physics, antiques, engineering, agriculture, transportation, art, music, opera, animals, flowers, beauty, famous people, clothing, film stars and more. The cigarette card was so popular that some businesses other than cigarette companies also began to send out printed serial cards as a form of promotion. In the 1930s, cigarette cards reached their peak. Following the second Sino-Japanese war that began in 1937 (Gerth 2003), cigarette cards stopped because of inflation and a prohibition of luxury goods during wartime.

BAT even gave away small rugs for the bottom of rickshaws with their name on them (Chiou 1993). While there were American, British, Japanese and French advertising agencies operating in Shanghai to produce all this advertising (Benson 1999; Cochran 1992b; Xu 1990), of the four largest agencies, two were local (China Commercial Advertising Agency and Consolidated National Advertising Company) and two were owned by foreigners (Carl Crow and Millington). While a detailed comparison of advertising in old Shanghai to that of Europe and America in the same period remains to be done, a cursory look at the media, print ads, retailers and brands of the period suggests that, by the 1930s, Shanghai advertising was as pervasive and sophisticated as its Western counterparts. Many European and U.S. advertisers were striving to sell their brands during this period, called "the golden age for advertising in China" (Xu 1990).

The Western advertisers were not instantly successful in Shanghai, however. Initially, their cultural sensitivity was low. A Hamonter Typewriter ad showed a map of China, but left out parts of the country. Illustrations of Western art masterpieces and German fairytales proved unattractive to Chinese readers (Cochran 1980). Besides inappropriate subject matter, Western art styles used were quite foreign to the Chinese. Similarly, translated slogans like "beauty has a short life" made no sense to many Chinese, who sought to strictly follow the old way of living. Neither did the concept of fashion. When BAT began advertising in Shanghai in 1902, it initially used advertising featuring American landscapes, historical figures such as George Washington and Abraham Lincoln, and, especially, pin-ups featuring American women (Bong, Tong, Ying and Lo 1996; Cochran 1999b). The Chinese, understandably, found such ads confusing, jarring and laughable, referring to them as "foreign pictures" (*yang hua'er*), or "hairy person pictures" (*maozi bian* – a derogatory term for Westerners) (Cochran 1999b). However, it did not take long for BAT to learn to hire local artists and copywriters to produce local advertising forms such as *yuefenpai*. Soon BAT had several highly popular cigarette brands. So successful was BAT that, during World War I, the British Secret Service hired them to create and distribute propaganda in China (Cochran 1999b).

MODERN WOMEN AND CHINESE ADVERTISING

As noted earlier, women became sex objects who appeared in Shanghai's *yuefenpai* early in the twentieth century and were the focus of much Chinese advertising. One function of the *yeufenpai* was to show the latest fashions in Qipao, with changing hemlines, differing slit lengths, differing designs, and increasingly form-fitting and figure-displaying departures from the Qi gowns of the Ming dynasty (Finnane 2008; Roberts 1997). With the end of the Qing dynasty and the birth of the Chinese Republic in 1911, women enjoyed a liberation that included opportunities in education, a formal end of foot binding, and increasing access to new public spaces including stores, transport, restaurants and hotels. In place of foot binding the new torture of high-heeled shoes became all the rage along with the dances, costumes and films of the flapper era of the 1920s. Global fashions prevailed and helped to define the "modern girl" in Shanghai (Barlow 2008; Dong 2008). Hair care products and services, cosmetics, skin lighteners, soaps, insecticides, toothpastes, medicines, feminine hygiene products, foods, lingerie, cigarettes, perfume, wristwatches, furniture and jewelry were among the many products targeted to women and helping to define the modern girl.

As Dikötter (2006) notes, women have long been the focus of critiques of consumer culture. The image of men as producers and women as consumers is an old, if inaccurate, portrait (e.g., deGrazia 1996; Martinez and Ames 1997; Sparke 1995). As Gerth (2003) shows, male fashions were transformed even more fully than women's fashions in Shanghai and were more clearly emulative of Western appearance in Republican Shanghai.

Even a Western hat became an important marker of a republican identity. Despite the ubiquitous qipao (*cheongsam* in Cantonese), women were much more likely than men to adopt hybridized fashions that combined Western and Chinese influences (Dikötter 2006). Nevertheless, it was women who were singled out for criticism not only for being frivolous, compulsive consumers, but also for aping and worshipping the foreign quasi-colonialist occupiers (Shih 2007). As the next section demonstrates, this criticism became all the more forceful during the National Products Movement that arose in Shanghai.

ANTI-FOREIGN PRODUCT BOYCOTTS

At the same time that foreign brands became heavily promoted and highly popular in Shanghai, boycotts of foreign products periodically swept the city and the nation in the first half of the twentieth century. Boycotting was a traditional means used in China by guilds wishing to pressure recalcitrant merchants and corrupt officials (Bergère 1986). But the 1905–1906 anti-American boycott took on a more political character. It was largely directed against the most prominent American consumer goods companies, BAT and Standard Oil. Cochran (1980) characterizes the boycott as an effort "to bring an end to a period of national humiliation . . . from the Opium War of the early 1840s to the Boxer Uprising of 1900" (p. 45). In the treaty ports, and especially Shanghai, this humiliation was provoked daily by the racist condescension of the foreign community in the city (Dong 2000). Anticipating the brand relationship literature that has recently become popular in marketing, one protest song lamented a failed relationship and was sung in the form of a Cantonese love song:

You are really down and out,
American cigarette.
Look at you down and out.
I think back to the way you used to be
In those days when you were flying high.
Who would have rejected you?
Everyone loved you
Saying you were better than silver dollars
Because your taste overwhelms people
And is even better than opium.

. . .
I thought our love affair would remain
Unchanged until earth and sky collapsed.

. . .
Then this movement against the treaty got underway
And spread everywhere.
Because Americans mistreated our Overseas Chinese
Degrading us like lowly oxen and workhorses.
Therefore everyone has united to boycott America,
And that means opposing Americans (quoted in Cochran 1980, p. 47).

While the boycott stimulated local Chinese companies to begin manufacturing cigarettes, they were ultimately overcome by the huge resources of BAT, which faced no serious local competition until 1915.

The anti-American boycott of 1905 and 1906 was followed by anti-Japanese boycotts in 1908 and 1915, as the Japanese pressured China into treaty concessions. When Japan was awarded the former German concession in Shantung province at the end of World War I, Chinese students took to the streets. More massive protests erupted against Japanese products in 1919. Following an incident in which the British police killed Chinese workers in 1925, anti-British boycotts began, with some apparent help from BAT's largest local competitor, Nanyang Tobacco Company (Yeh 1997). While these and other anti-foreign boycotts, lasting into the 1930s, helped shift the fortunes of local and foreign advertisers in China, in Bergère's (1986) assessment they were not so much about patriotism and xenophobia nor "a rejection of the West but, on the contrary, an attempt to come to terms with it both as a model and as a threat" (p. 51). Crow (1937) reports that advertisers were torn between attempting to pass their products off as Chinese and appeal to patriotism, and attempting to claim that their goods were made in England or America and therefore of superior quality. As time progressed, the protests were directed more against Japan. BAT turned this against (Chinese) Nanyang cigarettes by disclosing the company's affiliations with Japan (one of the co-owners had acquired Japanese citizenship in order to facilitate doing business there). Thus, foreign-owned BAT actually used nationalist and anti-Japanese feelings to its own advantage.

The National Products Movement constructed an exposition of Chinese products and condemned merchants who continued to carry foreign products. Although many broadcast *tanci* songs became critiques of the materialistic Shanghai lifestyles and were later used to promote anti-consumption and anti-foreign nationalist movements, advertisers were not deterred and even co-opted these critiques for their own advantage (Benson 1996, 1999). The Lao Jiu He Silk and Foreign Goods Emporium proclaimed that:

The Emporium is deeply aware that promotion of national goods is fundamental to nation building, but among foreign products are articles that China does not produce, and to satisfy the demands of everyone . . . we supplement our silk with foreign merchandise (Benson 1996, p. 160).

Besides critiquing merchants carrying foreign goods, the National Goods Movement was especially critical of women adopting foreign goods. The "modern girl" was highlighted as a symbol of all that was bad about consumer culture (e.g., Bong, Tong, Ying and Lo 1996; Dong 2008; Finnane 2008; Hung, Li and Belk 2007; Jackson 2005). They were called treasonous. In 1934 one participant in the "Women's National Products Year" labeled unpatriotic women prostitutes, claiming that they degraded themselves and their bodies by consuming foreign brands (Gerth 2003, p. 7). Shih (2007) sees this as part of a broader symbolic critique of the colonial power as the dominant male seducing the feminized Chinese consumer with foreign goods and power.

Besides protesting against the foreign presence in Shanghai, the *Guomindang* (GMD) or New Life Movement opposed the tide of consumerism that engulfed the city (Benson 1999). Its slogans were simplicity and economy (Warra 1999). It was a left-wing anti-capitalist movement and part of the forces that eventually led to the Chinese civil war and the establishment of the People's Republic of China. Its particular target was often the new Shanghai woman, who was characterized as self-indulgent, materialistic, and unable to control her love of fashion (Benson 1999). The New Life Movement, using *kaipan* broadcast on the radio in the 1930s, as well as other media, urged women to sacrifice their selfish longings for the latest fashions in the interests of the nation. These appeals were also tied to nationalism in an effort to reduce China's foreign debt and oppose the importation of luxury goods from the West and Japan. The GMD called for buying only national goods and chastised the merchants who stocked foreign silks, perfumes, shoes and other fashion goods. However, as we have seen, these merchants were largely able to claim in their advertising to be supporting the New Life Movement while still advocating consumption of the latest styles and foreign goods (Benson 1996, 1999). Foreign cigarette manufacturers (Cochran 1989, 1999b) and makers of foreign medicines (Cochran 2000, 2006) were also able to turn the nationalist New Life Movement to their advantage via patriotic advertising themes.

CONCLUSION

While these conditions helped shape global versus local emphasis of advertising in Shanghai, they are perhaps not entirely different from today when the West is both a source of admiration and antipathy in China (Belk and

Zhou 2001). Of course, it was not solely the invasion of global brands in Shanghai that precipitated the Chinese civil war that formed the PRC and ROC. The humiliation of Western pseudo-colonization and the occupation by Japan were significant factors as well. But the association of branded promotions with Shanghai, decadence, greed and foreign oppression were significant factors. This opposition continues in contemporary China, despite market socialism. The simultaneous tendencies of foreign brands to insinuate themselves as being local and local brands to pass themselves off as foreign are other practices that continue in contemporary China, especially in large cities (Belk and Zhou 2001; Zhao and Belk 2002, 2009). Just as pre-communist advertisers invoked symbols of Confucianism and Chinese history to introduce the new and foreign into Chinese culture, more contemporary post-Mao advertisers have used symbols of communism in order to do the same for their brands (Zhao and Belk 2008b). It should be remembered, too, that through the 1980s the Chinese government periodically warned against fawning after foreign goods and Western lifestyles. And there is currently a strong government policy of promoting Chinese brands, echoing the National Products Movement in some ways. Other similarities between the two periods can be found in the importance of investments by overseas Chinese, people's love/hate relationships with Western luxury goods, rapid economic growth, rapidly escalating consumerism and cosmopolitanism, corruption and an anything-goes atmosphere, growth of local Chinese brands, individual and national questions about what it means to be Chinese, and backlash against the global (Hooper 2000; Wang 2006; Zhang 1998). And the images and criticisms of the Chinese woman's fashion consumption are not a thing of the past either (Frith and Cheng 2009; Hung, Li and Belk 2007). Although the fashion consciousness of Old Shanghai was eradicated with the Sun Yat-sen uni-sex jackets of the Cultural Revolution, fashion is back today stronger than ever (Finnane 2008; Jackson 2005; Roberts 1997). And men even more than women seem to be demanding new deferential service at retail stores, hotels, restaurants and other opportunities for conspicuous consumption (Davis 2000; Hanser 2008; Wang 2008). So the current encounter with globalizing consumption in China may well have something to learn from Old Shanghai.

Although China remains officially communist, its urban areas are undergoing a wave of rampant consumerism unlike anything during communist China before Deng's 1978 economic reforms. This can be seen in the escalation of consumer desires. The "three bigs" of the 1960s and 1970s were a bicycle, a sewing machine and a wristwatch (Croll 2006). By the 1980s the three bigs had escalated to a color television, a refrigerator and a washing machine. And by the 1990s the most avidly sought goods were cell phones, air conditioners, stereos, VCRs and microwaves (Belk 1989; Croll

2006; Tse, Belk and Zhou 1989). Although the 1980s periodic government attacks on the "spiritual pollution" of Western goods in China indicated a difficult time coming to grips with consumerism, by the end of the decade government propaganda banners that formerly glorified Chinese workers were replaced by banners celebrating the slogan that "to get rich is glorious" (Schell 1984). The world's luxury goods makers already derive much of their profits from Asia and look forward to China soon becoming their biggest market. Although the size of the Chinese luxury market is contested (Chadha and Husband 2006; Lu 2008; Wang 2008), with 1.3 billion people even a small proportion is a huge market.

The Chinese government has largely ceased their opposition to Western-type consumer culture and now relies on domestic demand as well as exports to create much needed jobs and drive the economy. But there is still opposition. The Chinese art movement that is sometimes called cynical realism is devoted to a critique of emerging Chinese consumer culture (e.g., Ilan, Yun and DuPriest 2010; Mallet, Artsi, Zi, Hongmei and Hui 2008; Nuridsany 2004). Artists like the Luo Brothers and Wang Guangyi paint traditional Chinese New Year babies (*nianhua*) holding Big Mac hamburgers and cans or bottles of Coca Cola and Pepsi Cola.

Quite unlike earlier periods in Chinese history when the nation was quite assured of its cultural superiority, it is now struggling to catch up with the West not only in production but more importantly in consumption. It is poised to soon pass Japan and become the world's second largest economy. Forecasts suggest that in just a few decades it will be the largest. As more Chinese consumers bypass their middle-class counterparts in the West in the race of luxury consumption, the old tendency to "worship things foreign" (*chongyang*) (Lu 1999, p. 310) is also accompanied by an increased confidence in Chinese economy, especially when Chinese companies become the owner of global brands (e.g., Volvo). As Belk and Zhou (2001, 2009) demonstrate, this combination of forces has resulted in a simultaneous love/hate relationship with the global/foreign in contemporary China. The Chinese consumer continues as a hybrid, combining the best of Chinese, Asian and Western brands, styles and fashions (Cayla and Eckhardt 2008; Croll 2006; Davis 2000; Wang 2008). However, this time there is far less desire to boycott the foreign or reject the forces of consumerism.

REFERENCES

Adshead, S. A. M. (1995), *China in World History*, New York: St. Martin's Press.
Adshead, S. A. M. (1997), *Material Culture in Europe and China, 1400–1800*, London: Macmillan.

Bakhtin, Mikhail (1968), *Rabelais and His World*, Cambridge, MA: Massachusetts Institute of Technology Press (original 1965).

Barlow, Tani E. (2008), 'Buying In: Advertising and the Sexy Modern Girl Icon in Shanghai in the 1920s and 1930s', in Alys Eve Weinbaum, Lynn M. Thomas, Preti Ramamurthy, Uta G. Poiger, Madeline Yue S. Dong and Tani E. Barlow (eds), *The Modern Girl Around the World*, Durham, NC: Duke University Press, 288–316.

Belk, Russell W. (1989), 'The Benefits and Problems of Market Socialism for Chinese Consumers', *1989 AMA Winter Educators' Conference: Marketing Theory and Practice*, Terry Childers et al. (eds), Chicago: American Marketing Association, 355–9.

Belk, Russell W. and Nan Zhou (2001), 'A Reader Response Analysis of Global and Local Appeals in Chinese Advertising', Salt Lake City, UT: Odyssey Films (21-minute video).

Benson, Carlton (1996), *From Teahouse to Radio: Storytelling and the Commercialization of Culture in 1930s Shanghai*, Berkeley, CA, dissertation, Department of History, University of California.

Benson, Carlton (1999), 'Consumers Are Also Soldiers: Subversive Songs from Nanjing Road', in Sherman Cochran (eds), *Inventing Nanjing Road: Commercial Culture in Shanghai, 1900–1945*, Ithica, NY: Cornell University East Asia Program, 91–132.

Bergère, Marie-Claire (1986), *The Golden Age of the Chinese Bourgeoisie: 1911–1937*, trans. Janet Lloyd, Cambridge: Cambridge University Press.

Bong, Ng Chun, Cheuk Pak Tong, Wong Ying and Yvonne Lo (1996), *Chinese Women and Modernity: Calendar Posters of the 1910s–1930s*, trans. Frank Li, originally *Duhui Modeng: Yuefengpai 1910s–1930s*, 1994, Hong Kong: Joint Publishing Co.

Cayla, J. and M. E. Giana (2008), 'Asian Brands and the Shaping of a Transnational Imagined Community', *Journal of Consumer Research*, 35 (August), 216–30.

Chadha, Radha and Paul Husband (2006), *The Cut of the Luxury Brand: Inside Asia's Love Affair with Luxury*, London: Nicholas Brealey.

Chan, Wellington K. K. (1998), 'Personal Styles, Cultural Values and Management: The Sincere and Wing On Companies in Shanghai and Hong Kong, 1900–1941', in Kerrie L. MacPherson (ed.), *Asian Department Stores*, Honolulu: University of Hawaii Press, 66–89.

Chan, Wellington K. K. (1999), 'Selling Goods and Promoting a New Commercial Culture: The Four Premier Department Stores on Nanjing Road, 1917–1937', in Sherman Cochran (ed.), *Inventing Nanjing Road: Commerical Culture in Shanghai, 1900–1945*, Ithica, NY: Cornell University East Asia Program, 19–36.

Ching-hwang, Yen (1998), 'Wing On and the Kwok Brothers: A Case Study of Pre-War Overseas Chinese Entrepreneurs', in Kerrie L. MacPherson (ed.), *Asian Department Stores*, Honolulu: University of Hawaii Press, 47–65.

Chiou, Jyh-shen (1993), 'Marketing Activities of American Big Business in China: Standard Oil Company and British-American Tobacco Company', in Jeffrey B. Schmidt, Stanley C. Hollander, Terence Nevett and Jagdish N. Sheth (eds), *Contemporary Marketing History: Proceedings of the Sixth Conference on Historical Research in Marketing and Marketing Thought*, East Lansing: Michigan State University, 377–86.

Clunas, Craig (1991), *Superfluous Things: Material Culture and Social Status in Early Modern China*, Urbana, IL: University of Illinois Press.

Cochran, Sherman (1980), *Big Business in China: Sino-Foreign Rivalry in the Cigarette Industry, 1890–1930*, Cambridge, MA: Harvard University Press.

Cochran, Sherman (1999a), 'Commercial Culture in Shanghai, 1900–1945: Imported or Invented? Cut Short or Sustained?' in Sherman Cochran (ed.), *Inventing Nanjing Road: Commercial Culture in Shanghai, 1900–1945*, Ithica, NY: Cornell University East Asia Program, 3–18.

Cochran, Sherman (1999b), 'Transnational Origins of Advertising in Early Twentieth-Century China', in Sherman Cochran (ed.), *Inventing Nanjing Road: Commercial Culture in Shanghai, 1900–1945*, Ithica, NY: Cornell University East Asia Program, 37–58.

Cochran, Sherman (2000), 'Marketing Medicine and Advertising Dreams in China, 1900–1950,' in Wen-hsin Yeh (ed.), *Becoming Chinese: Passages to Modernity and Beyond*, Berkeley: University of California Press, 63–97.

Cochran, Sherman (2006), *Chinese Medicine Men: Consumer Culture in China and Southeast Asia*, Cambridge, MA: Harvard University Press.

Croll, Elisabeth (2006), *China's New Consumers: Social Developments and Domestic Demand*, London: Routledge.

Crow, Carl (1937), *Four Hundred Million Customers*, New York: Harper and Brothers.

Crow, Carl (1940), *Foreign Devils in the Flowery Kingdom*, New York: Harper and Brothers.

Davis, Deborah S. (ed.) (2000), *The Consumer Revolution in Urban China*, Berkeley, CA: University of California Press.

Davis, Deborah S. and Julia S. Sensenbrenner (2000), 'Commercializing Childhood: Parental Purchases for Shanghai's Only Child', in Deborah Davis, *The Consumer Revolution in Urban China*, Berkeley, CA: University of California Press, 54–79.

Dikötter, Frank (2006), *Exotic Commodities: Modern Objects and Everyday Life in China*, New York: Columbia University Press.

Dong, Stella (2000), *Shanghai 1342–1949, The Rise and Fall of a Decadent City*, New York: William Morrow.

Dong, Madeline Y. (2008), 'Who Is Afraid of the Chinese Modern Girl?' in Alys Eve Weinbaum, Lynn M. Thomas, Preti Ramamurthy, Uta G. Poiger, Madeline Yue S. Dong and Tani E. Barlow (eds), *The Modern Girl Around the World*, Durham, NC: Duke University Press, 194–219.

Esherick, Joseph W. (2000), 'Modernity and Nation in the Chinese City', in Joseph W. Esherick (ed.), *Remaking the Chinese City: Modernity and National Identity, 1900–1950*, Honolulu: University of Hawaii Press, 1–16.

Fairbank, John King (1992), *China: A New History*, Cambridge, MA: Belknap Press.

Farquhar, Judith (2002), *Appetites: Food and Sex in Post-Socialist China*, Durham, NC: Duke University Press.

Finnane, Antonia (2008), *Changing Clothes in China: Fashion, History, Nation*, New York: Columbia University Press.

Frith, Katherine T. and Hong Cheng (2009), 'Symbolic Meanings of Advertisements in China', in Hong Cheng and Kara Chan (eds), *Advertising and Chinese Society*, Copenhagen: Copenhagen Business School Press, 191–201.

Gerth, Karl (2003), *China Made: Consumer Culture and the Creation of the Nation*, Cambridge, MA: Harvard University Press.

de Grazia, Victoria (1996), *The Sex of Things: Gender and Consumption in Historical Persepctive*, Berkeley, CA: University of California Press.

Glosser, Susan (1999), 'Milk for Health, Milk for Profit: Shanghai's Chinese Dairy Industry Under Japanese Occupation', in Sherman Cochran (ed.), *Inventing Nanjing Road: Commercial Culture in Shanghai, 1900–1945*, Ithica, NY: Cornell University East Asia Program, 207–33.

Hamilton, G. G. (1977), 'Chinese Consumption of Foreign Commodities: A Comparative Perspective', *American Sociological Review*, 42 (December), 877–91.

Hamilton, Gary G. and Chi-kong Lai (1989), 'Consumerism Without Capitalism: Consumption and Brand Names in Late Imperial China', in Henry J. Rutz and Benjamin S. Orlove (eds), *The Social Economy of Consumption*, Lanham: Society for Economic Anthropology, 253–79.

Hanser, Amy (2008), *Service Encounters: Class, Gender, and the Market for Social Distinction in Urban China*, Stanford, CA: Stanford University Press.

Hao, Yen-p'ing (1986), *The Commercial Revolution in Nineteenth-Century China*, Berkeley: University of California Press.

Hooper, Beverly (2000), 'Globalization and Resistance in Post-Mao China: The Case of Foreign Consumer Products', *Asian Studies Review*, 24 (4), 439–69.

Huang, Philip C. C. (1990), *The Peasant Family and Rural Development in the Yangzi Delta, 1350–1988*, Stanford: Stanford University Press.

Hung, K., S. Y. Li and R. Belk (2007), 'Glocal Understandings: Female Readers' Perceptions of the New Woman in Chinese Advertising', *Journal of International Business Studies*, **38** (6), November, 2007, 1039–51.

Ilan, Lisa, Michael Yun and Bill DuPriest (2010), *East/West: Visually Speaking*, Lafayette, LA: Paul and Lulu Hilliart University Art Museum.

Jackson, Beverley (2005), *Shanghai Girl Gets All Dressed Up*, Berkeley, CA: Ten Speed Press.

Liang, Eleen Johnston (2004), *Selling Happiness: Calendar Posters and Visual Culture in Early-Twentieth-Century Shanghai*, Honolulu, HI: University of Hawaii Press.

Lee, Leo Ou-fan (1999a), *Shanghai Modern: The Flowering of a New Urban Culture in China, 1930–1945*, Cambridge, MA: Harvard University Press.

Lee, L. O. (1999b), 'Shanghai Modern: Reflection on Urban Culture in China in the 1930s', *Public Culture*, **1** (1), 75–107.

Lee, Leo Ou-fan (2000), 'The Cultural Construction of Modernity in Urban Shanghai: Some Preliminary Explorations', in Wen-hsin Yeh (ed.), *Becoming Chinese: Passages to Modernity and Beyond*, Berkeley: University of California Press, 31–61.

Lee, Leo Ou-fan (2001), 'Shanghai Modern: Reflections on Urban Culture in China in the 1930s', in Dilip Parameshwar Gaonkar (ed.), *Alternative Modernities*, Durham, NC: Duke University Press, 86–122.

Lee, Leo Ou-fan and Andrew J. Nathan (1985), 'The Beginnings of Mass Culture: Journalism and Fiction in the Late Ch'ing and Beyond', in David Johnson, Andrew J. Nathan and Evelyn S. Rawski (eds), *Popular Culture in Late Imperial China*, Berkeley: University of California Press, 360–95.

Lu, Hanchao (1999), *Beyond the Neon Lights: Everyday Shanghai in the Early Twentieth Century*, Berkeley: University of California Press.

Lu, Pierre Xiao (2008), *Elite China: Luxury Consumer Behavior in China*, Singapore: John Wiley & Sons.

Mallet, Daphné, Adi Artsi, Fan Zi, Yang Hongmei and Li Hui (2008), *Let's Consume!* Beijing: Xin Dong Cheng Publishing.

Martinez, Katherine and Kenneth L. Ames (eds) (1997), *The Material Culture of Gender; The Gender of Material Culture*, Winterthur, DL: Henry Francis du Point Winterthur Museum.

Moore, Karl and Susan Reid (2008), 'The Birth of Brand: 4000 Years of Branding', *Business History*, 50 (July), 419–32.

Nathan, Andrew (1985), *Chinese Democracy*, New York: Knopf, p. 157.

Nuridsany, Michel (2004), *China Art Now*, Paris: Flammarion.

Richardson, Philip (1999), *Economic Change in China, c.1800–1950*, Cambridge University Press, pp. 26–9.

Roberts, Claire (1997), *Evolution and Revolution: Chinese Dress, 1700s–1990s*, Sydney: Powerhouse Publishing.

Schell, Orville (1984), *To Get Rich is Glorious: China in the 80s*, New York: Pantheon Books.

Shanghai Museum (1998), *Old Fashions of Shanghai*, Shanghai: Shanghai Museum.

Shih, Shu-mei (2007), 'Shanghai Women of 1939: Visuality and the Limits of Feminine Modernity', in Jason C. Kuo (ed.), Washington, DC: New Academia Publishing, pp. 205–40.

Sparke, Penny (1995), *As Long as It's Pink: The Sexual Politics of Taste*, New York: Harper Collins.

von Sternberg, Joseph (1955), *Fun in a Chinese Laundry*, New York: Macmillan.

Sterns, Peter N. (2001), *Consumerism in World History: The Global Transformation of Desire*, London: Routledge.

Strand, David (2000), 'A High Place is no Better than a Low Place: The City in the Making of Modern China', in Wen-Hsin Yeh (ed.), *Becoming Chinese: Passages to Modernity and Beyond*, Berkeley: University of California Press, pp. 98–136.

Tse, D., R. Belk and N. Zhou (1989), 'Becoming a Consumer Society: A Longitudinal and Cross-Cultural Content Analysis of Print Advertisements from Hong Kong, People's Republic of China and Taiwan', *Journal of Consumer Research*, 15 (March), 457–72.

Xu, Baiyi (1990), *Marketing to China: One Billion New Customers*, Lincolnwood, IL: NTC Business Books, p. xxii.

Wang, Jian (2000), *Foreign Advertising in China: Being Global, Becoming Local*, Ames: Iowa State University Press.

Wang, Jian (2006), 'The Politics of Goods: A Case Study of Consumer Nationalism and Media Discourse in Contemporary China', *Asian Journal of Communication*, **16** (2), June, 187–206.

Wang, Jing (2008), *Brand New China: Advertising, Media, and Commercial Culture*, Cambridge, MA: Harvard University Press.

Warra, Carrie (1999), 'Invention, Industry, Art: the Commercialization of Culture in Republican Art Magazines', in Sherman Cochran (ed.), *Inventing Nanjing Road: Commercial Culture in Shanghai, 1900–1945*, Ithica, NY: Cornell University East Asia Program, pp. 61–89.

Watson, James L. (2006), 'Introduction: Transnationalism, Localization, and Fast Foods in East Asia', in James L. Watson (ed.), *Golden Arches East: McDonalds in East Asia*, 2nd edn, Stanford, CA: Stanford University Press, pp. 1–37.

Wei, Betty Peh-T'I (1993), *Old Shanghai*, Hong Kong: Oxford University Press.

Williams, Rosalind (1982), *Dream Worlds: Mass Consumption in Late Nineteenth Century France*, Berkeley, CA: University of California Press.

Wills, John E. Jr. (1993), 'European Consumption and Asian Production in the Seventeenth and Eighteenth Centuries', in John Brewer and Roy Porter (eds), *Consumption and the World of Goods*, London: Routledge, pp. 133–47.

Wood, Frances (1998), *No Dogs & Not Many Chinese: Treaty Port Life in China, 1843–1943*, London: John Murray.

Yeh, W. (1995), 'Corporate Space, Communal Time: Everyday Life in Shanghai's Bank of China', *American Historical Review*, **100** (1), 97–122.

Yeh, W. (1997), 'Shanghai Modernity: Commerce and Culture in a Republican City', *China Quarterly*, 375–94.

Yeh, Wen-hsin (2007), *Shanghai Splendor: Economic Sentiments and the Making of Modern China*, Berkeley, CA: University of California Press.

Zhang, Xudong (1998), 'Nationalism, Mass Culture, and Intellectual Strategies in Post-Tiananmen China', *Social Text*, **16** (2), Summer, 109–40.

Zhao, X. and R. Belk (2002), 'Sinolization: An International Advertising Strategy for China', *Journal of Asia Pacific Marketing*, **1** (1), 3–18.

Zhao, X. and R. Belk (2008a), 'Advertising Consumer Culture in 1930s Shanghai: Globalization and Localization in *Yuefenpai*', *Journal of Advertising*, **32** (Summer), 45–56.

Zhao, X. and R. Belk (2008b), 'Politicizing Consumer Culture: Advertising's Appropriation of Political Ideology in China's Social Transition', *Journal of Consumer Research*, **35**, August, 231–44.

Zhen, Zhang (2001), 'Worldly Shanghai, Metropolitan Film Spectatorship', paper presented at Center for Research in Transitional Economies International Conference on Locating the City, Kemer, Turkey, May 3–6.

Zhou, Nan and Russell Belk (2009), 'Consumer Reactions to Global and Local Advertising Appeals in China', in Hong Cheng and Kara Chan (eds), *Advertising and Chinese Society: Impacts and Issues*, Copenhagen: Copenhagen Business School Press, pp. 111–41.

8 Unearthing insights into the changing nature of Japanese advertising via the grounded theory approach

Shintaro Okazaki and Barbara Mueller

GROUNDED THEORY IN INTERNATIONAL ADVERTISING RESEARCH: BORROWING FROM OTHER DISCIPLINES

While qualitative methodologies are now an accepted feature of marketing and advertising research, their application is still comparatively limited. Taylor (2005) examined articles on international advertising published in the *Journal of Advertising* in the decade between 1994 and 2004, and found that the most common methodological approach was content analysis, representing 34 percent of the studies, followed closely by experiments at 25 percent and surveys at 22 percent. Just 6 percent employed secondary data analysis and only 3 percent used qualitative analysis. Given that content analysis stands at the intersection of qualitative and quantitative methods, simple addition makes clear that quantitative methods dominate. Similar results were found by Okazaki and Mueller (2007) who examined cross-cultural advertising research published during the period 1995 to 2006. Their examination revealed that content analysis also ranked first (35 percent), surveys second (33 percent), and here too qualitative inquiries were practically non-existent.

Nevertheless, "it is fair to say that qualitative research is no longer viewed as merely 'speculative', or 'soft', as was generally held to be the case by many in the past . . . there is increasing acknowledgement, not only in academic circles, but also among practitioners, of the need for the application of qualitative methodologies in their truest and most fundamental sense in order to gain valid insights, develop theory and aid effective decision making" (Goulding, 2005, p. 295). This chapter examines the use of the grounded theory approach in international advertising research. The methodology, developed by Glaser and Strauss (1967), was labeled grounded theory to reflect, as the name suggests, theory that is grounded in the words and actions of those individuals under study (Goulding, 2005). Though traditionally associated with sociology (Glaser, 1998; Strauss and Corbin, 1990), organizational studies (Parry, 1998; Brown,

1995) and nursing and health (Schreiber and Stern, 2001; McCann and Clark, 2003), it has begun to enter the repertoire of marketing and advertising researchers. For instance, Reichert and Ramirez (2000) utilized grounded theory in their analysis of receiver-based definitions of sexually oriented appeals in advertising. More recent examples include Blythe's (2007) grounded theory analysis of the influence of advertising creatives' personalities on the development of brand personality; Palka, Pousttchi and Wiedemann's (2009) examination of mobile viral marketing; and Andronikidis and Lambrianidou's (2010) study of children's understanding of television advertising. Yet, in comparison to other qualitative methodologies, grounded theory is still in its infancy in marketing and advertising research.

As a methodology, grounded theory was specifically designed for the generation of theory – rather than the testing of theory. In *The Discovery of Grounded Theory*, Glaser and Strauss (1967) outline their method of analyzing data that builds theories during data collection, in contrast to testing hypotheses about theories that are determined before data collection has begun. "Consequently, the literature is not exhausted prior to the research, as in many studies, rather it is consulted as part of an interactive, inductive and interactional process of data collection, simultaneous analysis and emergent interpretation" (Goulding, 2005, p. 296). Thus, the researcher essentially sets aside theoretical ideas to allow a "substantive" theory to emerge, while rigorously seeking a plausible relationship between concepts and sets of concepts. The developing theory then directs the researcher to appropriate extant theories and literature. Glaser and Strauss proposed formalized procedures, such as theoretical sampling and coding to provide structure to theory generation (Barnes, 1996). These procedures are designed to develop a well-integrated set of concepts that provides a thorough theoretical explanation of the phenomena under study. Grounded theory seeks not only to uncover relevant conditions, but also to determine how the actors respond to changing conditions and to the consequences of their actions. The data collection procedures involve interviews and observations as well as other sources (Corbin and Strauss, 1990, p. 5). Concepts are developed through *constant comparison* with additional data. This constant comparison constitutes the heart of grounded theory as a method: the process of constantly comparing instances of data that have been labeled as a particular category with other instances of data, to determine if these categories fit and are workable. If they are, and the instances mount up, then we have what Strauss (1987) and Glaser (1992) call "theoretical saturation", which is the ultimate goal of grounded theory. Additional data are collected by theoretical sampling, meaning that researchers seek "people, events, or information to illuminate and define the boundaries and relevance of the categories" (Charmaz, 2006, p. 189). After reaching "theoretical saturation", the final stage of the theory development process is the construction of a core category. "A core category pulls together all the concepts in order to offer an explanation of the phenomenon. It should have theoretical significance and should be traceable back through the data. This is usually when the theory is written up and integrated with existing theories to show relevance, fit and/or extension" (Goulding, 2005, p. 297). Here we apply the grounded theory approach to explore the changing nature of Japanese advertising.

THE CHANGING NATURE OF JAPANESE ADVERTISING

Research has documented that the Japanese have traditionally valued indirect and intuitive communications, whereas Americans tended to value direct, exact, and unambiguous communications (Lazer et al., 1985). Based on advertisements that appeared in Japan during the 1980s, Mueller (1987) suggested that the nature of Japanese advertising was very different from that of American advertising. Her content analysis found that Japanese advertising was far less direct and informative than American-style advertising, and that Japanese ads instead conveyed mood and atmosphere through a beautiful scene, or the development of an emotional story or verse. In short, emotion was emphasized over clear-cut product-related appeals. Japanese ads were characterized as "soft sell" while American advertising was positioned as "hard sell". Her findings were corroborated by a number of cross-cultural advertising researchers, including Mueller (1992), Ramaprasad and Hasegawa (1992) and Lin (1993). However, a replication of Mueller's (1987) study found that ads appearing in Japan in 2005 were significantly more likely to employ product merit and hard sell appeals than earlier ads (Okazaki and Mueller, 2008). This suggests a significant shift in advertising content over nearly three decades – in particular during the "post-bubble" period which has been termed Japan's "lost decade", the ten-year span during the 1990s when economic turmoil overshadowed Japanese society. But, while content analysis enables the detection of changes in manifest content, it does not allow the researcher to identify the "true" causes of such changes. Our focus is to explore whether the "lost decade" impacted Japanese advertising, and whether this was reflected in changes in planning and execution.

There is some evidence, primarily from trade journals, that economic downturns have an impact on advertising. For example, Interbrand suggests: "In a recession, it becomes even more critical for companies to aggressively and tirelessly create a compelling case for their brands. The brand must be perceived as truly special, clearly differentiated, and have attributes that are unique enough to create a strong and lasting value proposition for its customers. Otherwise consumers will just choose not to buy" (Isakovich, 2009). An *Adweek* poll, targeting those in advertising and marketing positions, asked the question, "what is the most effective tone for advertising during a recession?" Selecting from a menu of five choices, respondents gave an outright majority of the vote (52 percent) to "a focus on value". "Empathetic realism" was a distant runner-up at 15 percent (*Adweek* Poll Suggests Ads should Focus on "Value" in a Downturn, June 16, 2009). Clearly, practitioners are suggesting the need to tailor the content of commercial communications in order to succeed in a recession. However, there are virtually no published academic investigations – qualitative or quantitative – which address the relationship between economic conditions and advertising practices. The economic upheaval that Japan experienced before, during and after the "lost decade" provides an excellent opportunity to examine the potential impact of a recession on advertising planning and execution.

In this exploratory investigation, we ask the following questions: Is Japanese advertising today still distinctively Japanese, or has it perhaps become more similar to Western advertising – shifting from a soft sell to a hard sell approach? And, if a shift has taken place, could it have been influenced by the economic downturn experienced during Japan's lost decade? To address these questions, this study adopted a qualitative "grounded theory" approach. In-depth interviews were conducted with Japanese advertising practitioners and the transcripts were analyzed in order to extract significant statements, which were then reduced to essential themes.

This study makes important contributions to the literature in several ways. First, it is one of the few studies that apply the grounded theory approach to advertising. Second, the investigation adds to the scarce body of research focusing on the execution of Japanese advertising and Japanese advertising industry practices. A review of *Journal of Advertising Research* revealed that only two articles focusing on Japan have been published since 1995 (Money, Shimp and Sakano, 2006; Griffin, McArthur, Yamaki and Hidalgo, 1998). Thus, it is necessary and important to update the literature. Third, this study examines how practitioners have responded to changes in consumer behavior as a result of a recession, a topic which has not been covered by the existing literature. Given the worldwide recession, the information provided by this research could prove useful for other markets suffering from economic downturns. Our qualitative exploration provides insights as to whether and how a prolonged economic recession potentially affects advertising planning, execution and evaluation. Fourth, much advertising research focuses on the message (for example, content analyses of commercial messages), or the receivers of these messages (for instance, how consumers respond to certain advertisements). Much less attention has been paid to the senders of commercial communications. This investigation explores practitioners' views regarding shifts in advertising content.

In what follows, we first summarize prior research on Japanese advertising. We then address economic downturns and their impact on advertising with a short description of the lost decade. Next, we explain the interview method employed and outline research questions. A sampling of excerpts from the transcripts is provided. Based on a synthesis of the interviewees' responses, core concepts are presented, and implications are drawn. In closing, some important limitations are recognized, while future research directions are suggested.

PRIOR RESEARCH ON JAPANESE ADVERTISING

Understanding cultural differences is critical to international business success. Hofstede's (1980) model of national culture has been widely used to identify such differences (Sondergaard, 1994). Hofstede initially identified four dimensions of culture that differentiated individuals from various nations in terms of their predominant values: *individualism*, society's preference for group or individual orientation; *power distance*, societal desire for hierarchy or egalitarianism; *masculinity vs. femininity*, a sex-role dimension; and *uncertainty avoidance*, a culture's tolerance of uncertainty. Later research added a fifth dimension, *long-term orientation*, the extent to which a society exhibits a pragmatic future-oriented perspective, rather than a conventional historic or short-term point of view. Hofstede's work revealed that the Japanese tend to be collectivistic rather than individualistic, masculine, above average in power distance, and exhibit strong uncertainty avoidance and a long-term orientation. In contrast, Americans are more likely to rank high on both individualism and masculinity, but are below average on power distance, relatively weak in uncertainty avoidance, and tend to exhibit a short-term orientation.

The concept of high and low context also provides an understanding of different cultural orientations, and explains how communication is conveyed and perceived. Hall and Hall (1987) note that low-context cultures place high value on words, and communicators are encouraged to be direct, exact and unambiguous. What is important is what is said, not how it is said, or the environment in which it is said. In contrast, high-context cultures consider verbal communications only a part of the overall message, and communicators rely much more heavily on contextual cues. Messages in high-context cultures tend to be a good deal more implicit and ambiguous, with communicators relying much more on nonverbal behavior, the physical setting, social circumstances, and the nature of interpersonal relationships. These different communication patterns are said to be reflected in the appeals employed within the advertising created in a given market. According to Martenson (1989), one can rank cultures from high context to low context, starting with the Japanese, the Chinese, the Arab, the Greek, the English, the French, the North American, and ending with the German culture, the most low-context oriented.

A number of investigations have examined the association between cultural values and advertising in Eastern and Western cultures. China has been the focus of a good number of these investigations (e.g., Cheng and Schweitzer, 1996; Lin, 2001; Zhang and Harwood, 2004; Zhang and Shavitt, 2003). Both Taiwanese (e.g., Chang, 2006; Hsu and Hsu, 2007) and Korean (e.g., Cho et al., 1999; Bang et al., 2005) advertising content has also been analyzed. However, comparisons between Japanese and U.S. advertising have been somewhat more limited. In an early investigation, Mueller (1987) outlined a set of values, norms and national characteristics representative of Japanese culture, ranging from the traditional to those more influenced by the West. The prevalent Japanese values, norms and characteristics were operationalized to form both traditionally Japanese appeals (group/consensus appeal, soft-sell appeal, veneration of elderly, status appeals, oneness with nature appeal) and traditionally Western appeals (individual/independence appeal, hard-sell appeal, youth and modernity appeal, product-merit appeal, and manipulation of nature). Content analysis was employed to determine the existence or absence of these appeals in Japanese and American magazine advertisements. Magazines from each country were matched by format, audience demographics and circulation. *Shukan Asahi* and *Newsweek* were selected as representative news magazines in each country. *Katei Gaho* and *Good Housekeeping* were selected as representative women's magazines in each market. The ads were coded for dominant appeal type.

Surprisingly, the data revealed that Japanese ads made less use of group/consensus appeals than did U.S. ads. Also, unexpectedly, Japanese ads were found to make greater use of the typically Western individual/independence appeal than U.S. ads. As expected, Japanese advertising did make significantly greater use of soft-sell appeals than did American commercial messages, and hard-sell themes were a rarity in Japanese ads. More than one in ten of the Japanese ads surveyed stressed tradition or respect for the older generation, but this approach was seldom employed in U.S. ads. The use of youth or modernity appeals showed little difference between the two markets. However, almost twice as many Japanese ads as American ads employed some form of status appeal. The use of product-merit appeals was significantly lower in Japan than in the U.S. Clearly, product-merit appeals are a mainstay of American advertising. Finally, no major differences were found in the use of oneness with nature appeals, and manipulation of nature appeals was almost non-existent in both markets. The investigation revealed numerous differences between Japanese and American advertising, some rather subtle and others quite blatant. Mueller's (1987) categorization of advertising appeals reflecting cultural values has been used extensively in cross-cultural advertising research (see Okazaki and Mueller, 2008 for a review).

Several additional investigations have contributed to the body of literature comparing Japanese and American advertising. Ramaprasad and Hasegawa (1992) compared the advertising styles employed in the television commercials appearing in the two countries. The authors examined the commercials for informational approaches (those presenting factual information) and transformational approaches (those that endow the use of the brand with an emotional experience). No difference was found in the use of informational vs. transformational approaches in the advertising of the two countries. U.S. ads, however, were more likely to employ comparative appeals and hyperbole, while Japanese advertising tended to emphasize mood and nature. Lin (1993) examined the differing levels of informativeness in Japanese and U.S. television ads. Results suggest that Japanese ads are less informative than their U.S. counterparts, reflecting the high-context Japanese culture, in which communication is directed at achieving consensus and harmony in interpersonal relationships. The soft-sell approach dominated in Japanese commercials, and music was employed to set the mood. In contrast, U.S. ads offered more facts and attributes to showcase product superiority.

A recent replication of Mueller's (1986) study suggests that Japanese advertising today has remained much the same in some respects, but has changed in others (Okazaki and Mueller, 2008). Japanese advertising still appeals to the consumer on an emotional level, and attempts to build atmosphere within the confines of the printed page, but this is increasingly blended with significantly more direct communications that highlight the product's features and attest to its benefits. One might argue that Japanese advertising has become somewhat more "American". At the same time, it appears that American advertising may have become significantly more "Japanese", with the use of soft-sell appeals increasing more than eightfold. It is conceivable that these changes in Japanese advertising might have something to do with the drastic economic shift during Japan's "lost decade".

THE BUBBLE ECONOMY AND "LOST DECADE"

Japan has experienced dramatic volatility in its economy over the past three decades. During the late 1980s, Japan enjoyed the boom years of the Bubble Economy (Powell, 2002). Massive inflation of land values and stock prices occurred as a result of cheap capital and financial deregulation. At the height of this boom, Japan became a major exporter of capital and the chief financier of the U.S. federal deficit, purchasing almost 40 percent of U.S. federal bonds issued in 1987 (Bell and McNeill, 1999). However, in 1991, the Japanese bubble burst, and the economy went into a recession. During the following decade, the Japanese economy experienced the longest and most sustained period of economic downturn since World War II – a period that has been termed the Heisei Recession. The Japanese stock market entered a phase of extended decline, with share prices dropping to less than half their monetary value. In December 1993 the government announced a monthly drop in industrial production of 5.1 percent, the worst in post-war history (Bell and McNeill, 1999). Figure 8.1 shows the tremendous economic roller coaster Japan has gone through over the past few decades.

After the dawn of the new millennium, Japan gradually began to recover. In 2002, economic indicators showed signs of cyclical recovery in firms' inventory liquidation and exports (Murashima, 2002). In 2003, Japan achieved real growth of 6.4 percent at an annualized rate in the fourth quarter (OECD, 2004), and this growth continued for a record five consecutive years (Tabushi, 2007). However, in 2007, the tide turned

Note: For Japan, data prior to 1994 are based on the fixed-base year method.

Source: Government of Japan (2007). Percentage change from previous year.

Figure 8.1   Percentage change of real GDP

again, as Japan along with most of the countries around the globe slipped into a recession. Given this background, we attempt to explore whether Japanese advertising practitioners perceived a change in the nature of Japanese advertising over the past three decades.

Economic downturns commonly result in significant changes in consumer behavior. The current recession provides ample evidence of this claim. While academic research in the areas has been more limited, there is a good deal of industry data suggesting massive shifts in consumer behavior as a result of economic contractions. A consumer study conducted by TNS and commissioned by MasterCard, found the most significant shift in European consumer behavior since World War II (MasterCard Europe Study Highlights the Emergence of a New European Consumer, April 29, 2009). The study found more European consumers (69 percent) want to spend only what they can afford, and are actively engaging in bargain hunting (84 percent from 72 percent six months earlier) as a means to make their money stretch as far as possible. This mindset is not unique to Europeans. A series of studies conducted by Datamonitor, exploring the impact of the global economic crisis on consumers in 17 countries, found that, among U.S. consumers, 56 percent feel that their lifestyle has been impacted by the recession. Of U.S. shoppers, 44 percent are now "frequent buyers" of private label products, and for 72 percent of Americans, lower prices have a high degree of influence over where people do their shopping. Among Japanese consumers, 57 percent feel that their lifestyle has been impacted by the recession. One-quarter of Japanese grocery store shoppers are considering changing where they shop for food and drink in order to save money, and over one-third of Japanese shoppers are giving up some of their favorite brands to save money (The Global Economic Crisis: The Impact on Consumer Attitudes and Behavior, Datamonitor, 2009). Consumers are clearly skittish about spending their money, and, in some countries, spending habits appear to have changed permanently. Interbrand, citing a study by management consulting firm Booz & Company (Leinwand, Moeller and Shriram, 2008), noted that consumers in all socioeconomic classes have already made substantial cuts in spending and plan to make even deeper cuts in the future. According to a poll by *Consumer Reports*, spending and saving behaviors adopted during the recession may usher in a "new fiscal conservatism" by American households (Recession Lesson: Consumers Shift Toward Saving, October 5, 2009). The poll found that 44 percent of people said that they will continue to buy only what they absolutely need. And about one-third of consumers think they are going to be spending less on an extended basis.

This shift in consumer behavior has had a direct and dramatic impact on marketers. An Association of National Advertisers survey revealed the top five areas where marketers plan to reduce costs or expenditures in marketing and advertising efforts: departmental travel and expense restrictions (87 percent); reducing advertising campaign media budgets (77 percent); reducing advertising campaign production budgets (72 percent); challenging agencies to reduce internal expenses and/or identify cost reductions (68 percent); and eliminating or delaying new projects (58 percent) (ANA Survey: 77 percent of Marketers Plan to Cut Media Spending, February 12, 2009). According to *Advertising Age* (Emerging from the Great Recession, December 28, 2009), ad spending in 2009 suffered its sharpest drop since the Great Depression (−12.9 percent). This recession also marked the first time since the 1930s that U.S. ad spending declined for two consecutive years. The impact on ad agencies was devastating. The year-to-date agency revenue decline marked the sharpest drop (−9.7 percent) since *Advertising Age* began its agency rankings in 1944. U.S. ad agency staffing in October of 2009 fell to its lowest level (161 500 jobs) since 1995. Media firms were also hard hit. According to Zenith Optimedia, spending on major media in the U.S. dropped a full 12.9 percent in 2009. In total, the advertising and media industry cut 187 500 jobs, or 13 percent of staffing since the start of the recession. It is impossible to examine the ultimate impact of the current recession on advertising, as we sadly have not fully emerged from it. However, the economic turmoil that Japan experienced during its "lost decade" of the 1990s provides an excellent case study.

RESEARCH METHOD

Data Collection

In the case of grounded theory, sampling begins with a "commonsense" process of talking to those informants who are most likely to provide early information. In-depth, in-person interviews were conducted with 18 Japanese practitioners involved in advertising and marketing. The "theoretical" or purposive sampling criterion, "that is sampling for theory construction, not for representativeness of a given population" (Charmaz, 1995, p. 28), was that subjects should have advertising industry experience over a three-decade period – encompassing the bubble economy and the lost decade, as well as the present. Most of the interviewees had at least 30 years of experience in advertising or marketing. Agency executives, creatives and media planners are represented. The selection of the specific interviewees was based on recommendations from advertising agencies, advertising research foundations, research institutes, and academics.

Additionally, subjects were required to be well-respected in industry and/ or academia.

One of the researchers contacted the candidates by e-mail, requesting their participation in the study. A brief summary of the study objectives and background was provided. Candidates were told that the content of the interviews would be used only for academic purposes, and their complete anonymity was guaranteed. Also, they were informed that they could obtain a summary of the study upon its completion. When candidates agreed to the interviews, appointments were scheduled by e-mail. Interviews were conducted in their workplace, with an average duration of 78 minutes.

Interview Questions

Open-ended questions were employed to encourage both a detailed but also flexible discussion of the topics. Non-leading questions are recommended in grounded theory to allow unanticipated statements and stories to emerge (Charmaz, 2006). We aimed for a loosely guided exploration of the topics, while requesting clarification of details as needed to obtain accurate information about the subject's thoughts and views. For example, we addressed the following questions: If a foreigner wanted to understand Japanese advertising, what would you tell them are the most important characteristics of Japanese advertising? How is traditional Japanese advertising the same as, or different from, American advertising? and Do you perceive any changes in the planning, execution and evaluation of Japanese advertising during the 1980s, 1990s vs. today? If so, how would you describe these changes? and so forth.

Coding

Each time an interview was completed, two levels of coding were conducted: initial coding and focused coding. During the first stage of coding, we conducted a "detailed line-by-line analysis (looking for words and sentences in the text that have meaning) necessary at the beginning of a study to generate initial conceptual categories, and to suggest relationships among categories" (Strauss and Corbin, 1998, p. 57). The constant comparison method was used to find similarities and differences in the interviewees' responses to our questions. This comparison led to focused coding. At this level, we attempted to synthesize the initial coding and determine the most significant and frequent categories. We repeated this process – interviews, initial coding, constant comparison, and focused coding – until we reached a theoretical saturation: a point where new interviews no longer brought new insights (Glaser, 1978). Core categories were then constructed. A core

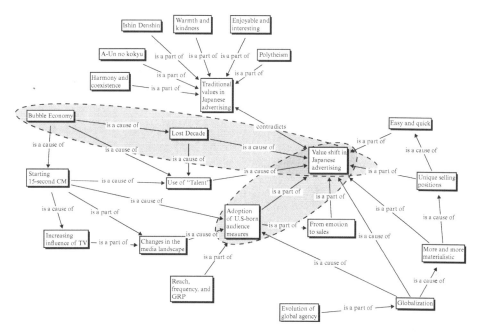

Note: The diagram was created by ATLASti. The dotted circle indicates the core sequence of changes over the past three decades.

Figure 8.2   Network diagram of the text mining results

category pulls together all the concepts in order to offer an explanation of the phenomenon. It is impossible to provide a complete overview of the interviews in this chapter; however, several excerpts from the transcripts have been organized around a number of core themes.

Network Diagramming

Complete transcripts of the in-depth interviews were analyzed using a text data-mining program – ATLASti. Core themes were coded and associated with one another, meaningful relationships noted, and ultimately concepts were pulled together to form an explanation of the phenomenon. Figure 8.2 shows a network diagram reflecting focused coding results created by ATLASti. This diagram consists of numerous nodes, whose relationships were classified into two types: (1) one node is a part of the other node; or (2) one node is a cause of the other node. In this way, we can visually understand the cause–effect relationships, as well as our conceptual categorization (from larger to narrower concepts).

RESULTS

Shifts in Traditional Style Japanese Advertising: Our first question addressed whether traditional Japanese advertising was perceived by Japanese practitioners as different from American advertising. To our surprise, not one Japanese advertising professional employed the terms soft sell vs. hard sell to describe differences between Japanese and American advertising. However, interviewees clearly distinguished between the two styles. Japanese advertising was portrayed as significantly more implicit in nature.

One TV commercial message (CM) planner explained:

> Traditionally, commercials did not have to have any specific message, because we did not try to convince anybody. The most important thing was to make the audience feel close to the advertiser. That's why we wanted to make it so emotional, using visuals and music. We wanted to create something enjoyable and interesting that made them feel good. They didn't have to understand the specs of the product with words. This is the major difference from Western commercials that try to logically persuade the audience. But in Japan, it doesn't sound good if you explain the same thing over and over again. It also appears indecent to try to assert yourself.
>
> We respect and appreciate a sense of a literal telepathic understanding of one another.

This tacit understanding (*Ishin Denshin* in Japanese) is directly related to non-verbal forms of communication, which dominate in high-context cultures, such as Japan (Hall, 1976). Explicit explanations and arguments are still considered to be "rude" in Japanese society. An agency executive (male, 63) provided an explanation for the difference in the two communication styles:

> We, Japanese, believe in polytheism, and respect harmony and coexistence in a relatively closed society. We also use a single language. That's why we prefer non-verbal messages. By contrast, Westerners believe in monotheism, and prefer simple and direct communication. Therefore, the message needs to be verbal.

An agency executive (male, 63) concurred:

> Advertising before the bubble economy had as its mission the transmission of warmth, kindness, humor, wit, happiness, and humanism.

During the period of high economic growth in the1970s and 1980s, many new products were launched in Japan. The main objective of advertising was to communicate this "news" in an entertaining fashion. In contrast, in Western advertising, a sales orientation dominated. Consumers were persuaded via logical arguments. Facts were employed to convey product performance. The U.S. Federal Trade Commission even encouraged advertisers to employ comparative approaches in their commercial messages to provide consumers with sufficient relevant information.

Influence of the bubble economy: Our second question explored changes in the planning, execution and evaluation of Japanese advertising. Many interviewees hinted that changes in Japanese advertising may have occurred not only during the lost decade, but that a shift in the nature of Japanese advertising may have begun even earlier – during the bubble economy. During this economic boom, firms' advertising budgets increased at an astonishing rate, and there was a major shift in ad dollars away from print media and to television. A graphic designer (male, 57) explained:

> TV CM began dominating the media after Expo '70, the first World's Fair held in Japan, because television viewing increased dramatically. This trend accelerated during the bubble economy, and 15-second CM became predominant. Agencies were gaining a lot of power, During this period, commercials began to become more direct and artificial, with too many words.

An agency executive (male, 53) concurred:

> During this period, firms depended too much on advertising. Advertising was considered as a wrapping paper that differentiated their products from competitors. Creative was becoming less and less important, so were firms' primary mission statements. What was important was to get attention quickly by repeating the message within short intervals.

An account planner (male, 54) summarized:

> During the bubble economy, the society was getting richer, but culture was getting thinner. Japanese people's values changed.

Impact of the economic downturn: Practitioners were asked about the impact of the economic downturn in terms of Japanese society, business and advertising. Some interviewees pointed out that, as sales dropped sharply, the level of competition intensified in the market, which produced a drastic shift in advertising objectives – from awareness and liking to ultimate sales – as well as in advertising execution – from mood and atmosphere to a more direct and persuasive approach. A graphic designer (male, 61) explained:

> The very mission of firms, and the overall objective of advertising changed after the recession started in early 1990s. The shift was from emotion to sales.

A TV CM planner (male, 62) explained:

> You need to understand that, during the bubble economy, consumers bought almost everything they wanted. People were becoming more and more materialistic. At the same time, Japanese became so tired of consumption. With the prolonged recession, agencies had to change their advertising strategy. The single most important objective was "sell". Otherwise, their clients could not keep their space in retail channels.

A copy writer (female, 61) pointed out:

> During this period print media became less and less popular. People just stopped buying magazines. This change had an important impact on ad creatives, because we could not use much images or symbols due to space limitation in print media. Selling slogans were becoming much more important.

The interviews also revealed some unanticipated insights. The "lost decade" was apparently much more than an economic recession. It was the decade in which many important social, cultural, technological, as well as economic changes occurred – all of which had an impact on the business of advertising in Japan.

Adoption of numerical audience measures: The drastic economic downturn Japan suffered during the 1990s apparently also influenced how the success of an ad campaign was measured. A copywriter (female, 64) noted:

> During the bubble economy, some US-born media efficiency indices, such as reach and frequency, were introduced to Japan. Agencies expanded the use of these indices during the 1990s because their clients demanded quick and easy explanations regarding the effectiveness of their advertising campaigns. Results became more important than process, because their clients needed to sell more.

Similar comments were heard primarily from graphic designers, less so from agency people. It seems that reach and frequency measures triggered a gradual separation – and an eventual divorce – between the two. For example, a graphic designer (male, 63) noted:

> Agencies started calculating GRP's and began emphasizing reach. Why? An increase in reach meant more TV CMs, and thus greater benefits. Until that time, the most common measure was ad recognition, which became too vague for firms' sales department. So reach, frequency, and GRP quickly became common standards of advertising effectiveness measures.

This was a drastic shift away from traditional feeling-based effectiveness measures, and toward numerical, exposure-based effectiveness measures.

We recognize that it was during this period – the 1990s – that large agencies aggressively expanded their domestic and international networks through mergers and acquisitions (M&A) (Tharp and Jeong, 2001). The evolution of such global agency networks may have influenced this shift in advertising effectiveness measures.

Changes in the media landscape: It appears the Japanese consumer's relationship to television changed during this time period and the shift to shorter television spots also impacted the nature of Japanese television advertising. A TV CM planner notes:

> During the 1970s, the main player of advertising was television. Families watched TV together in their living rooms. It was the most common form of entertainment, because there were so few other options. So the relationship between TV and consumers was very close.

An agency executive (male, 59) explains:

> The influence of television was overwhelming during the 1970s and 1980s. TV was a part of our family, and so close to our life. But when 15-second commercials started, things changed. Our clients wanted more efficiency, with less risky, more logical ads. They thought this type of ad would create greater familiarity with their brands.

According to a TV CM planner (male, 62):

> Ultimately, the relationship between TV and consumers became less and less intimate.

But the shift from indirect to direct commercial messages was also influenced by the introduction of a new medium. A TV CM planner (male, 62) explained:

> Traditionally, Japanese TV CM always respected the relationship between the firm and consumers . . . a CM doesn't have to have any message, because you are not trying to persuade the audience. Advertising is something that made the relationship between the firm and consumers closer, more intimate. CMs needed to be something that made you feel good, or curious, or entertained. Consumers don't have to understand characteristic of goods or services with words. But during and after the bubble economy, everything seemed to have changed . . .

Another advertising executive (male, 59) complained:

> Before the bubble economy, people appreciated advertising that did not talk much. Advertising was kind of "a-un no kokyu" (which means an understanding of one another without exchanging a single word). Therefore, when we

created an ad for a product, showing beautiful scenery was sufficient. Our message was "you know what we mean, right?" But this kind of communication no longer worked after the introduction of Internet. Globalization changed Japan. Speed became more and more important.

Ultimately, messages became more and more to the point.

Use of talent: Apparently the combination of the recession and the shift to shorter format TV spots also had an impact on creative aspects of Japanese advertising. A TV CM planner (male, 61) noted:

> During the bubble economy, as the level of competition was intensified, firms tried to launch as many new products as possible. In doing so, it was increasingly difficult to differentiate their products from the others. Then, they came up with using "talent" (well-known TV personalities) as a differentiation strategy. That is, one "talent" represented one brand. After the 15-second commercials started in mid 1990s, TV commercials got stuck in a rut: simply a combination of "talent" and product.

"Talent" is a uniquely Japanese phenomenon that gained popularity during the bubble economy. They are neither actors nor singers, neither experts nor amateurs. They are simply "present" in a wide range of entertainment programs, as presenters, commentators, or guides. Firms started using talent to differentiate their brands. Unlike in many Western markets, where creative agencies are increasingly compensated via fees, the commission-based remuneration system continues to dominate in Japan, which ultimately results in a lack of creative rivalry. With the shift from TV program sponsorships toward the purchase of 15-second spots, prospects for creativity seemed limited (Kawashima 2006). Given this situation, "talent" was seen as the most practical and economical way to craft a 15-second spot. A copywriter (female, 64) pointed out:

> "Talent" was a common tool employed to generate enjoyment and familiarity among viewers. Firms started to use "talent" as if it were a "symbol" or "icon". They are not actors, but instead entertainers, with whom the audience felt familiar. As the use of talents skyrocketed, eye-catching, attention-getting ads became more and more popular.

IMPLICATIONS

Our research addresses a neglected issue in international advertising: the significant changes that occurred in Japanese advertising during a three-decade period that includes the economic slump called the "lost decade".

This investigation provides several important insights. First, our grounded theory investigation revealed six key trends, namely (1) shifts in traditional style Japanese advertising; (2) the influence of the bubble economy; (3) the impact of the economic downturn; (4) the adoption of numerical advertising effectiveness measures; (5) changes in the media landscape; and (6) the use of "talent". By and large, these key trends help to explain why Japanese advertising went through a significant transition. However, it is likely that the shift in the nature of Japanese advertising primarily stemmed from two of the above: the economic downturn (that is, "lost decade") and the adoption of numerical advertising effectiveness measures. The core sequence of important changes is indicated by dotted circles in Figure 8.2. The "traditional" values and styles of Japanese advertising were forced to change as a result of not only economic factors, but also a structural shift in advertising agencies. During the 1980s, TV dominated, while print media gradually lost its influence. The length of TV spots shrank from 30 seconds to 15 seconds, making traditional story-telling, and emotion-based content less and less feasible. The use of "talent" was in tune with fast-paced, eye-catching, and entertaining TV spots. During the "lost decade", these tendencies simply accelerated: as sales decreased, firms became increasingly dependent upon sales-oriented advertising and effectiveness measures, rather than relying on emotions and story-telling in their commercial messages.

Our qualitative observations also suggest that advertising in Japan was influenced by the worldwide trend toward global agency networks during the 1980s. During this period, a significant change occurred in terms of what firms perceived as "effective advertising". Prior to the bubble economy, effective advertising was defined as that which conveyed mood, curiosity, humor, wit, happiness and humanism. TV spots were crafted to build connections between consumers and firms. However, after the lost decade, firms began focusing on American-style effectiveness measures, such as reach, frequency and GRP. This shift also justified the importance of advertising agencies, which attempted to maximize the number of TV spots aired. As a result, the firms' dependency on its agency drastically increased.

Finally, we feel somewhat tempted to suggest that, as a result of the dramatic changes which took place during a three-decade period, Japanese advertising has moved toward a more hard-sell style. However, here caution must be exercised. Japanese advertising today still does not reflect the true definition of hard sell – fact-based, explicit and direct selling messages. Indeed, the Japanese still do not embrace direct and explicit communication. However, the bubble economy and the subsequent "lost decade" have left their influence on the nature of Japanese advertising. Japanese advertising practitioners appear to have dramatically increased the use of product merit appeals – yet blended them with the traditional soft sell-style (Okazaki and Mueller, 2008). Nearly two decades ago (Mueller, 1992) noted that Japanese advertising "is still far from being Westernized". Our grounded theory investigation shows that, while Japanese advertising practitioners may have adopted product merit appeals, and though Japanese commercial messages are indeed more sales-oriented than they once were, Japanese advertising still remains uniquely Japanese.

LIMITATIONS AND FUTURE RESEARCH SUGGESTIONS

This qualitative study has typical limitations. The findings of this investigation cannot be generalized to the total population of Japanese advertising practitioners. Further, the statements made in relation to the impact of Japan's "lost decade" cannot be generalized to the impact of other recessions (past or current) on the business of advertising. However, the findings are useful in providing insight into the shifts that have occurred in Japanese advertising over the past few decades. A limitation of the grounded theory approach is that it is very resource intensive. In addition, the quality of this type of research relies on the researcher's skills and experience in the analysis and interpretation of qualitative data. Researchers employing the grounded theory approach must be very open and responsive to the emerging data, avoiding any temptation (whether conscious or subconscious) to influence or shape the statements of those interviewed and the concepts ultimately extracted.

Future studies should expand upon our initial results. First and foremost, a broader pool of Japanese practitioners needs to be interviewed to validate the findings of the current investigation – perhaps via an online survey. This would also allow the concepts unveiled in this exploratory study to be further "fleshed out". Once the current recession has ended, it would be worthwhile to return to the Japanese advertising practitioners initially interviewed, to examine whether the shift toward a more direct and assertive form of advertising in Japan has further intensified, or whether the present economic downturn might have had a completely different effect on advertising execution. Regarding the impact of the current recession, it would clearly be of value to explore the perceptions of advertising practitioners in other markets as well. Finally, we encourage future investigators to adopt the grounded theory approach in their examinations of international advertising as a means of responding to Taylor's (2005) call for the development of new theoretical perspectives.

REFERENCES

Adweek poll suggests ads should focus on value in a downturn (2009, June 16). World Federation of Advertisers, http://www.wfanet.org/globalnews.cfm?id=237.

Alden, Dana L., Jan-Benedict E.M. Steenkamp and Rajeev Batra (1999), 'Brand positioning through advertising in Asia, North America, and Europe: The role of global consumer culture', *Journal of Marketing*, **63** (1), 75–87.

ANA Survey: 77 percent of marketers plan to cut media spending (2009, February 12). World Federation of Advertisers, http://www/wfanet.org/globalnews.cfm?id=178.

Andronikidis, A. and M. Lambrianidou (2010), 'Children's understanding of television advertising: A grounded theory approach', *Psychology and Marketing*, **27** (4), 299–322.

Bang, H.K., Mary Anne Raymond, Charles R. Taylor and Young Sook Moon (2005), 'A comparison of service quality dimensions conveyed in advertisements for service providers in the U.S. and Korea: A content analysis', *International Marketing Review*, **22** (3), 309–26.

Barnes, D.M. (1996), 'An analysis of the grounded theory method and the concept of culture', *Qualitative Health Research*, **6** (3), 429–41.

Blythe, J. (2007), 'Advertising creative and brand personality: A grounded theory perspective', *Journal of Brand Management*, **14**, 284–94.

Brown, A. (1995), 'Managing understandings: Politics, symbolism, niche marketing and the quest for legitimacy in IT implementation', *Organization Studies*, **16** (6), 951–69.

Charmaz, K. (1995), 'Grounded theory', in Smith, J.A., R. Harre and L.V. Langenhove (eds), *Rethinking Methods in Psychology*, London: Sage Publications.

Cho, B., Up Kwon, James W. Gentry, Sunkyu Jun and Fredric Kropp (1999), 'Cultural values reflected in theme and execution: A comparative study of U.S. and Korean television commercials', *Journal of Advertising*, **28** (4) (Winter, 1999), 59–73.

Corbin, J. and A. Strauss (1990), 'Grounded theory research: Procedures, canons, and evaluative criteria', *Qualitative Sociology*, **12** (1), 3–21.

Emerging from the great recession (2009), *Advertising Age*, December 28, p. 5.

Glaser, B. (1992), *Basics of Grounded Theory Analysis, Emergence v. Forcing*, Mill Valley, CA: Sociology Press.

Glaser, B. (1998), *Doing Grounded Theory: Issues and Discussions*, Mill Valley, CA: Sociology Press.

Glaser, B. and A. Strauss (1967), *The Discovery of Grounded Theory: Strategies for Qualitative Research*, Chicago, IL: Aldine.

Global consumer confidence, concerns and spending (2009), A Global Nielsen Consumer Report, November.

Goulding, Christina (2005), 'Grounded theory, ethnography and phenomenology: A comparative analysis of three qualitative strategies for marketing research', *European Journal of Marketing*, **39** (3/4), 294–309.

Griffin, Tom, David McArthur, Toshio Yamaki and Pedro Hidalgo (1998), 'Ad agencies' performance and role in providing communication services in Chile, Japan and the United States', *Journal of Advertising Research*, **38** (5), 65–76.

Hayashi, Yuka (2009, May 21), 'Japan's GDP shrinks as consumer spending feels the pinch', *The Wall Street Journal*, http://online.wsj.com/article/SB124280029530738327.html#pringMode. Retrieved January 12, 2010.

Isakovich, Helen (2009), 'Consumer spending in a recession: How brands can capitalize on an economic downturn', Interbrand, www.interbrand.com. Retrieved January 12, 2010.

Kawashima, N. (2006), 'Advertising agencies, media and consumer market: The changing quality of TV advertising in Japan', *Media, Culture & Society*, **28** (3), 393–410.

Lazer, W., S. Murata and H. Kosaka (1985), 'Japanese marketing: Towards a better understanding', *Journal of Marketing*, **49** (2), 69–81.

Leinwand, Paul, Leslie Moeller and K.B. Shriram (2008, September), Consumer spending in the economic downturn: The wide ranging impact on consumer behavior. Results from Consumer Spending Behavior Study, Booz & Company.

Lin, Carolyn (1993), 'Cultural differences in message strategies: A comparison between American and Japanese television commercials', *Journal of Advertising Research*, **21** (5), 40–47.

MasterCard Europe study highlights the emergence of a new European consumer (2009, April 29). MasterCard Worldwide News Release, http://www.mastercard.com/us/company/en/newsroom/pr_mc_europe.

McCann, T. and E. Clark (2003), 'Grounded theory in nursing research: Part 1 – methodology', *Nurse Researcher*, **11** (2), 7–18.

Money, Bruce R., Terence A. Shimp and Tomoaki Sakano (2006), 'Celebrity endorsements in Japan and the United States: Is negative information all that harmful?' *Journal of Advertising Research*, **46** (1), 113–23.

Mueller, Barbara (1987), 'Reflections of culture: An analysis of Japanese and American advertising appeals', *Journal of Advertising Research*, **27** (3), 51–9.

Mueller, Barbara (1992), 'Standardization vs. specialization: An examination of Westernization in Japanese advertising', *Journal of Advertising Research*, **32** (1), 15–24.

Okazaki, Shintaro and Barbara Mueller (2008), 'Evolution in the use of localized appeals in Japanese and American print advertising', *International Journal of Advertising*, **25** (5), 771–98.

Okazaki, Shintaro and Barbara Mueller (2007), 'Cross-cultural advertising research: Where we've been and where we need to go', *International Marketing Review*, **24** (5), 499–518.

Palka, W., K. Pousttchi and D. Wiedemann (2009), 'Mobile word-of-mouth: A grounded theory of mobile viral marketing', *Journal of Information Technology*, **24**, 172–85.

Parry, K.W. (1998), 'Grounded theory and social process: A new direction for leadership research', *Leadership Quarterly*, **9** (1), 85–105.

Ramaprasad, Jyotica and Kazumi Hasegawa (1992), 'Creative strategies in American and Japanese TV commercials: A comparison', *Journal of Advertising Research*, **32** (1), 59–67.

Recession lesson: Consumers shift toward saving (2009, October 5), KOSU Radio News in Business, http://kosu.org/2009/10/recession-lesson-consumers-shift-toward-saving/.

Reichert, T. and A. Ramirez (2000), 'Defining sexually oriented appeals in advertising: A grounded theory investigation', *Advances in Consumer Research*, **27**, 267–73.

Schreiber, R.S. and P.N. Stern (2001), *Using Grounded Theory in Nursing*, Germany: Springer.

Strauss, A. (1987), *Qualitative Analysis for Social Scientists*, New York: Cambridge University Press.

Strauss, A. and J. Corbin (1998), *Basics of Qualitative Research*, Thousand Oaks, CA: Sage.

Strauss, A. and J. Corbin (1990), *Basics of Qualitative Research: Grounded Theory Procedures and Techniques*, London: Sage.

Taylor, C.R. (2005), 'Moving international advertising research forward', *The Journal of Advertising*, **34** (1), 7–16.

Tharp, M. and J. Jeong (2001), ' The Global Network Communications Agency', *Journal of International Marketing*, **9** (4), 111–31.

The global economic crisis: The impact on consumer attitudes and behavior (2009), Datamonitor, http://www.mindbranch.com/listing/product/R313-55074.html. Retrieved January 11, 2010.

9 Twenty years on – retailer advertising during and since the fall of the Soviet Union: Tallinna Kaubamaja, "Estonia's Department Store"

Brent McKenzie

INTRODUCTION

The purpose of this chapter is to use a case study approach (Eisenhardt, 1989) to document the role of retailer advertising in Estonia. The store, Tallinna Kaubamaja ("Tallinn's Department Store" in Estonian) was selected as it is one of the few traditional department stores that opened during the Soviet period (1960), and continued to exist during the re-independence period in the early 1990s and the privatization period in the mid 1990s. The store continues to operate today and is currently the largest department store in the Baltic states.

The case study will align with the various periods of the last 50 years in terms of the types and role of advertising, as it pertains to traditional advertising objectives, as well as its role in retailer brand success. The case findings are drawn from an extensive review of secondary sources, as well as primary research obtained through interviews by the author with current and former employees of Tallinna Kaubamaja. The intent of this case study is both to provide insights as to successful and unsuccessful aspects of a retailer's advertising in a little studied region, and also to provide some historic perspectives as to how advertising as a concept, and in practice, has evolved from the Soviet period.

THE RETAIL SECTOR AND ADVERTISING DURING THE SOVIET PERIOD

The two-prong focus of the Soviet economic system was based upon the agriculture and heavy industry sectors, with a noticeable neglect of retail trade and other service industries. In spite of this, retail trade did have a role to play. As early as 1935 each Soviet Republic capital city was charged with establishing a model department store. The department store was to represent the success of the Soviet economic system and the responsibility that the Soviet consumer played in its overall success (Hessler, 2004). In reality, it was not until 1959, after Premier Khrushchev made a trip to the United States, and thus promised the Soviet people to provide them with a standard of living similar to that in the United States, that the retail sector acquired a significant presence in the Soviet Union (Koshetz, 1959). One reason that has been accredited to this change was the exposure Soviet citizens had to American consumer products in the United States Exhibit in Moscow in 1959. The ordinary Soviet could, for the first time, view dishwashers and other consumer goods that were in short supply, or non-existent, in the Soviet Union at that time (Schwartz, 1960).

During the 1960s, the retail sector in the Soviet Union experienced many performance issues. By 1963 there was official recognition of the fact that many of the consumer goods were in short supply, and that many of those that were available needed to improve in quality. This period saw much of the initial growth of the black market for both these deficit goods, as well as forbidden products from the West (Miller, 1965). It was also interesting to note that, even for those goods that were acknowledged to be of substandard quality, and thus had limited demand, they continued to be produced, as they had higher margins, which was the focus of the producers. Unlike in a free-market economy, production, not retail sales, was the key metric. This issue received greater attention than in the past, because by 1964 consumers in the Soviet Union now had greater knowledge of what types of retail goods could be available. Thus consumers became more selective in their purchases and would no longer just buy whatever was available. One opportunity to alleviate this situation was to explore the possibility of having manufacturers also operate their own retail shops, and that way they could better acquire consumer research as to what products would be best to produce. This area for debate did not appear to go beyond the discussion state, but, at the same time, greater powers were extended to retail shop directors to provide them with more flexibility in terms of merchandise decisions. By taking a more active role in negotiations over product demand forecasts that in the past were just assigned, the expectation was that a better alignment with the actual needs of local markets would result (Miller, 1965).

There can be multiple reasons for advertising (Eng and Keh, 2007), but in the Soviet Union the primary aim of advertising was to mould demand in a particular direction. Advertising, although the staple of the communist propaganda program, was admonished with respect to "creating new artificial needs by persuading people that consumer goods can bring prestige and family happiness" (Misiunas and Taagepera, 1993). The main reason for advertising was to communicate the economic, political, and social aims of the USSR. For instance, in terms of shaping economic activity, there may have been a campaign that heavily advertised the benefits of eating fish, at the expense of promoting the consumption of meat, or poultry. The aim was not to promote the health benefits of eating more fish, but rather as a way to justify the growth of manufacturing of fishing vessels, and the fishing industry. In contrast, more traditional forms of advertising, to position and promote a certain company, brand, or product versus another, were criticized as being both costly, and non-value added activities that were harmful to the Soviet agenda (Hanson, 1974).

For Soviet era retailers, advertising was something that did not align well with the Soviet system. Although the principles of advertising seem to represent a strong fit with the aforementioned propaganda campaigns with the Soviet Union, particularly the use of posters (International Institute of Social History, 2009), it was something that represented the "non-value added" aspects of marketing in general, and a negative impact on consumer behaviour specifically. Furthermore, as noted, since there was little use for advertising in terms of positioning one firm against another in a competitive sense, there was little need for campaigns in this sense.

This was not to say that advertising did not occur. The majority of advertising during the Soviet period was generally in print, specifically in weekly or monthly publications. The plethora of daily newspapers during Soviet times was lightly used for advertising, as each newspaper tended to have the same reader demographics therefore limiting the choice to advertising in all or none of the papers. Little to no radio or television advertising was used, as, beside the high relative cost with respect to a small/fragmented audience, the use of such media was even more strictly controlled (Books LLC, 2010).

The retail networks (the stores) in the Soviet Union were judged to be the best forecasters of consumer demand, which was mainly based on what consumers purchased. This pattern of demand forecasting could be argued to be adequate in the short term (less than six months), but in a free market retailers could rely on the actions of the vendors in terms of advertising and demand stimulation, while also conducting market research to better uncover consumer needs. In the case of the Soviet Union, retailers were also constrained by the fact that, if goods producers reached their predetermined quotas, there was little incentive to increase production even when additional demand existed (Mieczkowski, 1975).

TALLINNA KAUBAMAJA AND ADVERTISING IN SOVIET TIMES

Turning now to the case study, by way of background to the discussion of Tallinna Kaubamaja, and advertising, there is a need to understand the history of retail trade in Estonia. Estonia, particularly its capital city of Tallinn, was an active member in the Hanseatic League, which was an alliance of cities in Northern Europe that was engaged in international trade between the thirteenth and seventeenth centuries (Kasekamp, 2010). Estonia itself, based on its location on the Baltic Sea, was also a key transfer point for international East–West trade (Raun, 2001).

The beginning of Estonia's formalized retail trade started with its period of independence between 1919 and 1940. Because of Estonia's small population and geographic size, the retail networks that developed during this period were mainly small shopkeeper cooperatives. These cooperatives served a dual purpose. Not only were they a source of consumer goods; they also provided a venue through which a strong sense of nationalism could be championed, as well as providing local employment opportunities. By 1929 the cooperatives only represented approximately 6 percent of all retail outlets, but they contributed to 40 percent of all retail trade. Furthermore, many of the funds from the cooperatives were used to support Estonian education goals in terms of language and cultural issues, cementing the role of retail trade and Estonia's growth (Palm, 1989).

By 1940/41 and the first occupation of Estonia by the Soviet Union, the cooperative shops remained the dominant Estonian form of retail trade. Ironically, it could be suggested that the concept of a cooperative would align with the social and economic aims of the Communist system; as was all formal retail trade in the Soviet Union, Estonia's retail outlets were nationalized. Retail trade would now be centrally regulated by the *Central Union of Consumers' Societies in the USSR*, and individual members of cooperatives who were "infected" with Western consumerism were deported to Siberia. The first wave occurred in 1941 and the second wave with the return of Soviet Occupation after 1944 (Aizsilnieks, 1974). In addition, new state owned retail outlets were planned. These retailers would dominate the larger cities for the remainder of the Soviet period, while the cooperative shops did continue to play a role in the rural regions.

In Estonia, the Soviet system resulted in a drop in the overall number of retail outlets. Also during this time, there was forced industrialization within the country, which shifted the historic role that Estonian suppliers had in the consumer goods sector, particularly for locally produced goods, to now having to play the role of suppliers of products to other regions of the Soviet Union. Now a smaller percentage of locally produced goods would remain for sale in Estonia (Kutt, 1968), but, in comparison to other parts of the Soviet Union, Estonians did continue to have better access to consumer goods and better distribution and retail networks than other parts of the USSR. This was one of the reasons that Estonians had an overall higher standard of living compared to the rest of the USSR (Järvesoo, 1978).

As noted above, the decision for each Soviet Republic capital city to build a model department store occurred in 1935, prior to Estonia's annexation into the Soviet Union. So this decision was extended to Estonia's capital Tallinn in 1955. The site chosen for the store was just outside the old walled city of Tallinn. The location was designed to be close to both the city and the inter-city bus stations, which was important as few Estonians owned an automobile and so were reliant on public transportation. The building of the store took approximately five years to complete. The date chosen for its official opening was to be 21 July 1960. This date was specifically selected as it was to coincide with the 20th anniversary of the establishment of the Estonian Soviet Socialist Republic.[1]

On the morning of the 21st, a large crowd had gathered outside the store. As Soviet retailing was predicated upon word of mouth, and a continuous search for consumer products, being able to shop on opening day was expected to provide the best opportunity to acquire scarce, or "deficit" goods (Tamberg, 2009). As the management of Tallinna Kaubamaja were not prepared for such crowds, a decision was made to delay the opening of the store. The "official" reason given was that there was a fear that people would be hurt in a mad rush to buy products. The actual reason was the fear the management had that the crowds would be able to steal products during the mayhem, as well as breaking the displays and products. Thus the crowd outside the store was informed that the store would not open that day. No further information was provided. The employees were also not specifically told when the store was to open but were told to come to work the next day and be at their stations for 8 a.m. Therefore, in reality, the central Estonian department store, Tallinna Kaubamaja, actually opened on 22 July. There was to be no fanfare, and in fact only a few customers came by in the morning and asked if the store was open. When they were told it was, word quickly spread, and large crowds again descended upon the store (Joost, 2009a).

As noted, all Estonian retailers, including Tallinna Kaubamja, had to deal with the central authorities in Moscow who oversaw retail trade. The representatives of Tallinna Kaubamaja were generally well received, partially because of the fact that Estonia's small geographic size and high degree of urbanization (Estonia was the most urbanized

Soviet Republic) made it an ideal market for the testing of new planning and management techniques (Szporluk, 1975). If the ideas did not pan out, the impact on the overall USSR would be small; and if these pilot projects with Tallinna Kaubamaja were successful, they would then be rolled out into other regions of the Soviet Union. Tallinna Kaubamaja, although a "Soviet department store", had a very high level of respect within Tallinn, and was viewed as a favoured source of employment (Tamberg, 2009). In addition to having greater priority access to consumer goods, Tallinna Kaubamaja was an exemplar of a self-contained Soviet enterprise. It had its own doctor, nurse, and employee vacation property (Joost, 2009b).

In terms of advertising practice, Tallinna Kaubamaja played a significant role in the development of "Western" styled advertising in the Soviet Union. The norm at this time was to heavily depend upon in-store advertising, as shopping (although not necessarily purchasing) was a very popular leisure activity in Estonia. This was often the only effective way in which Estonian shoppers knew what products were available. In terms of marketing strategy Tallinna Kaubamaja would use advertising as a way to control sales quotas they were required to meet. They would be cautious in this practice as they had disincentives if they exceeded the pre-established sales targets. Published results (which must be viewed with a degree of scepticism as were most documents during the Soviet period) showed that throughout its first 25 years of operation, from 1960 to 1985, Tallinna Kaubamaja reached its turnover plans in all years as well as reaching other internal performance measures (Tallinna Kaubamaja, 1985). In reality, the majority of the advertising was used to get rid of obsolete, sub-standard goods, with the result being that Soviet consumers would continue to associate advertised goods with poor style or quality (Hanson, 1974).

Other potential venues for advertising included radio and television. Broadcast media in Estonia fell under two main groups, ER ("Eesti Raadio") and ETV ("Eesti Televisioon"). In terms of using these media for advertising during this period, it was generally not supported. There was a particular concern by the Soviet authorities based on Estonia's geographic proximity to Finland (only 90 km across the Baltic Sea). There was a fear that these, or any, broadcast messages would be used for political (i.e., anti-Soviet) purposes, or worse, the airwaves would be "hijacked" and substitute images of Western capitalist programming (Hixon, 1998).[2] The main form of advertising during its first two decades of operation (and continues today) by Tallinna Kaubamaja was by way of the store window displays. Tallinna Kaubamaja utilized extensive campaigns based on the displays in the windows, regardless of

Source: By permission from the Estonian Economic Museum, Tallinn, Estonia.

Figure 9.1   Tallinna Kaubamaja storefront windows during Soviet times

the availability of such products, including both product advertising, as well as lifestyle advertising (see Figure 9.1). There was a challenge in such practice as when there were product shortages; the result was that mannequins in the store windows were "dressed" in aluminum foil (Tamberg, 2009).

Tallinna Kaubamaja also utilized signage, and included their name on their delivery trucks (see Figure 9.2). They also engaged in some joint advertising with another well-known Estonian brand, "Baltika". The Baltika group, which began in 1928 manufacturing raincoats (Baltika Group, 2010) and continues to exist today, could be found on the wrapping paper used at Tallinna Kaubamaja, and even beside the "Kaubamaja" name at a cycling track (see Figure 9.2).

A common question asked when examining retail advertising during the Soviet period was what the value would have been of creating advertising campaigns, as there were no true profit incentives, and no direct competition (i.e., Tallinna Kaubamaja was the only department store in Tallinn, and in fact would be the source of many products for other small retail shops). The reason why, in the case of Tallinna Kaubamaja, was that, as in other areas of Soviet society, competitions were a staple of Soviet society. From awards competitions for sport, education, and culture, there were also competitions for the best advertising. Thus Tallinna Kaubamaja took an active role in developing campaigns with the sole aim of winning awards (Joost, 2009). This may be another reason for an inherent distrust (together with the aforementioned Soviet use of propaganda) of Estonians towards advertising.

Source: By permission from the Estonian Economic Museum, Tallinn, Estonia.

Figure 9.2   Other forms of advertising: Top: Tallinna Kaubamaja joint advertising with the clothing company Baltika; Bottom: Store signage advertising, and delivery truck

THE INTERESTING STORY OF HARRY EGIPT

Although not someone who focused on Tallinna Kaubamaja advertising specifically, a leading example of Soviet television advertising in Estonia was the commercials of Harry Egipt (Egipt, 2008). In fact, the work of Harry Egipt represents one of the few existing collections of Soviet era television advertising. Beginning in 1967 the first commercials for Estonian television were produced by the Estonian Commercial Film Producers (Eesti Reklaamfilm). This government body lead the creation of over 300 commercials and short films, which for a population the size of Estonia was quite large. Although there were a number of producers/directors of these films/commercials, the most popular advertisements were by Harry Egipt.

Harry Egipt was the author, director and producer of these commercials, and was also involved in the hiring of crew and casts. There was even a so-called "Egiptean-style", which was best defined by its editing style, original music (although it should be noted there was also liberal "borrowing" of songs from the West including those by the Beatles and Rolling Stones), and his use of attractive actors.

Perhaps in contrast to Estonian culture in general, and Soviet culture of the time, these commercials were easily identified by the positive attitude that was portrayed. Examples of advertisements for Estonian produce, accordion shops and trade schools, included smiling, happy actors, but there was little support that these commercials had any actual effect upon the "brands". Unlike the traditional television commercials of the time, these commercials were viewed as being of similar production quality to the West, but were strong reminders that they were Soviet advertisements. There was no focus on the comparative quality of the products being advertised, and definitely no mention of the product's superiority to its competitors. This latter point was another one of the reasons attributed to the success of the advertisements as they were in marked contrast to the official Soviet advertising of the time. Harry Egipt's commercials won first place awards at five consecutive advertising film festivals, and in 1990 Harry Egipt's anti-smoking commercial "Young Smoker" was chosen as one of the three best films at the advertising film festival in Moscow (Egipt, 2008).

ADVERTISING DURING TRANSITION – NEW RETAIL COMPETITION: 1991–2000

With the end of the Soviet period and Estonia's return to independence in August of 1991, retail practice, and the role of shopping itself changed dramatically. In a free-market economy retail trade represented the most evident example of the end of the Soviet period. Retailers could now openly focus on the buying and selling of goods for profit. This period also highlighted the lack of comfort with and knowledge by most retailers of the established marketing and retailing practices of the West. In terms of social change, for the younger shoppers, their ability to purchase goods was an overt demonstration of their opposition to the communist system. Although the similar pleasure of the shopping experience itself could be viewed as a general youth trait, those trying to rid themselves of their ties to the previous political and economic structure could see that being a "consumer" helps to speed this process (Drakulic, 1992). Advertising itself was an important educational tool for consumers to now learn about products and brands that were previously unheard of, or strictly prohibited (Good et al. 1996).

Instilling both an interest and a passion for the field of marketing in general within Estonia was a challenge. Advertising, though, helped to play a significant role in the growth of marketing knowledge. The ability to overcome the mentality that advocated "marketing as just sales and advertising" was both a result of the narrow focus of most of those working in the industry, or at minimum their experiences in studying business at the numerous institutions that sprang up after 1991 (McKenzie, 2006). Thus, besides finance and accounting courses, marketing courses were some of the most heavily subscribed programs that developed in the numerous new institutions of higher education that sprang up in Estonia.

The other aspect of advertising in Estonia was the ethnic Russian population. Approximately one-third of the Estonian population speaks Russian as their first language, and the great percentage of these do not speak Estonian. This has been an ongoing political and social issue. For Russian language advertising media, there are a number of Russian language magazines and newspapers, and one Russian language television station. There has also been research conducted that suggests Russian consumers in Estonia are more open to the advertising of certain brands (Kann, 2005). The challenge for Estonian retailers has been how much advertising should be created specifically for the Russian market? The constraints are both in cost for funding duplicate campaigns, as well as tailoring of advertising for Estonian versus Russian consumers. There also still exists concern expressed by certain retailers as being too closely aligned with the Russian consumers. Generally, most large Estonian retailers will have a Russian language option on their website, or include Russian text on their print advertisements, but often in a much smaller font (McKenzie, 2010).

These different stages in the economic history of Tallinna Kaubamaja brought different media into play. During the mid 1990s Tallinna Kaubamaja, as was the case for many former government owned industries and businesses, was subject to privatization. Retailing practice, from a Western perspective, was still in its infancy in the early 1990s. Only reluctantly did Estonian retailers begin to offer sales discounts and promotions. And even at that the actual discounts being made were in the 5 to 10 percent range (the exceptions were the summer/winter end of season sales). One of the possible explanations for this hesitation to offer discount incentives was the widely held Estonian belief that by offering my product at a lower price, you as a customer were "insulting" me in that you do not believe that I am offering the product at a "reasonable" price. Nowhere was this trait more evident than at the "turg" where vendors selling products on a blanket outside the "turg", or out of the trunk of their car, would charge the same prices as those selling the exact same goods inside (McKenzie, 1998).

In terms of the Soviet era stores such as Tallinna Kaubamaja, they could now carry name brand (Western) goods. But in order to continue to position themselves as local stores (and by extension protectors of local

Source: B. McKenzie.

Figure 9.3   Tallinna Kaubamaja outdoor signage – August 1998

culture), advertising of the new brands was conducted in conjunction with the brand of the store itself (Good et al. 1995). For example, Tallinna Kaubamaja advertised itself as "Estonia's Department Store", and during the 1990s continued to rely heavily on the colour blue, which is one of the three colours of the Estonian flag. There were also large posters attached to the two main outside corners of the store (see Figure 9.3), and tag lines such as "Alati põhjust tulla" (Always a reason to come in).

During the 1990s it was very important for Tallinna Kaubamaja to attempt to develop customer loyalty as new foreign-based retailers, such as Stockmann and SOKOS from Finland, were opening stores in Tallinn.[3] These foreign retailers also had an advantage over stores such as Tallinna Kaubamaja as they could utilize their already established supplier networks from their home markets (Dawson and Henley, 2001). In addition, these stores were viewed as new and exciting, and had none of the negative ties to the Soviet period that were possessed by Tallinna Kaubamaja. An example was the fact that Stockmann was the first shop with an escalator in Estonia, and people would come just to "ride it" (McKenzie, 1998), although Tallinna Kaubamaja later was the first to install a glass elevator (see Figure 9.3).

At this time, there was a specific marketing strategy of lowering, or downscaling the brand image of Tallinna Kaubamaja, as this was in conjunction with, and an attempt to deal with the economic fall-out in Estonia from the Asian and Russian economic crises of the later 1990s, as well as the dot.com bust beginning in the early twenty-first century.[4] In terms of advertising strategy, the focus for Tallinna Kaubamaja was on daily newspapers and price communications. This was implemented in order to position Tallinna Kaubamaja as the department store of the Estonian people ("rahvakaubamaja"), in comparison to the "foreign" department stores, Stockmann and SOKOS. In order to do this there was a discontinuation of several higher end brands, and thus a shift to promoting entry level products. This re-positioning, and related advertising, continued on until 2003 when the planning for a new and more upscale Tallinna Kaubamaja store began. A key part of this strategy was to hire new interior designers, and advertising agencies (Parel, 2011).

In terms of the advertising industry in Estonia, 1998 saw the establishment of the Estonian Association of Advertising Agencies – ERAL ("Eesti Reklaamiagentuuride"). The members of the group were the most well known and largest advertising agencies in Estonia, and its intent was to apply code and rules regulating advertising content (ERAL, 2011). As stated, the purpose of ERAL was to protect common interests and secure the rights of members of the association, to regulate professional ethics, and to promote advertising-related activity, although to this day the group has still not established the actual mandate of an enforceable self-regulation mechanism. The other advertising related function for ERAL was the continuation of the aforementioned advertising awards program, but now the focus was on giving awards to the advertising firms versus the retailer. The most well known is the Golden Egg program ("Kuldmuna"), which as it pertains to Tallinna Kaubamaja is discussed below.

TALLINNA KAUBAMAJA, ADVERTISING AND EUROPEAN UNION ACCESSION: 2001–2006

The start of the twenty-first century saw the Estonian economy again begin to grow, and the term "Baltic Tiger" was coined to indicate this success (McKenzie, 2009). By late 2003, and with Estonia to join the European Union the following year, Tallinna Kaubamaja completed an extensive renovation of the store. In conjunction with the store renovations, a new corporate visual identity was introduced. This was heavily promoted through various advertising media. A key focus was the change to print advertising using coated paper, to create a sustained image of a higher end retailer. At this time Tallinna Kaubamaja was part of the holdings of the NG Investment Group (NG Investeeringud, 2010) and took advantage of creating a media pool with other companies that were part of the holdings. In a market the size of Estonia, the result was a significant reduction in media cost, particularly for television commercials, and thus a more active television campaign was developed (Parel, 2011).

The results of these changes, which included the elimination of the

Source: B. McKenzie.

Figure 9.4   Tallinna Kaubamaja 2003, 2007, 2010, 2011

traditional colour of blue for the store, and the introduction of orange, also saw the "Kaubamaja" logo itself removed the name to a stylized T and K (see Figure 9.4). These changes received a lot of recognition, particularly from the aforementioned Golden Egg competition. In its review of these changes, the Golden Egg awards stated that Tallinna Kaubamaja made a significant institutional change to its image, by way of "strong emotion, and controversy, giving rise to a distinct character" (ERAL, 2011). Tallinna Kaubamaja's advertisements were finalists in the television commercials, outdoor advertising, and consumer advertising categories in 2004.

The new store opened in April, and Estonia joined the EU in May, with the expectation that sales would receive a boost owing to rapid growth in visitors from other EU countries, and with that had to ensure that many of its advertising regulations and acceptable practices now aligned with those of the EU. Although this did not seem to be a great burden to Tallinnna Kaubamaja, this did represent a period of transition in terms of its retail brand image

The following year represented a significant renovation and expansion of the store to the adjacent shopping mall, Viru Keskus. No longer was Tallinna Kaubamaja a stand-alone department store, but it now stretched from the original building across into the new shopping mall by way of an over the street bridge. This move necessitated a change in how Tallinna Kaubamaja advertised. They now focused on both the store itself, but as also being part of the new shopping mall as well. This opportunity allowed Tallinna Kaubamaja to physically move from its past as a central Soviet department store to being a modern destination shop.

Tallinna Kaubamaja began to exhibit typical department store advertising activities, not dissimilar to other mid-range department stores in the region. One change in practice was the move to more outdoor media (beyond the store outdoor wall posters; Figure 9.4). This was particularly effective for seasonal fashion campaigns, as the large billboards helped to promote coming season fashions. Tallinna Kaubamaja also developed its own special shopping promotions, one being the twice a year, January and July, sales campaign ("SAH" – see Figure 9.4), aimed at moving out seasonal stock. The other campaign copied that of Stockmann's "Hullud päevad" (Crazy Days), which is a massive sales promotion predicated on developing shopper hysteria in search of deep discounts. Tallinna Kaubamaja named theirs "Osturalli" ("Sales Rally"), and developed multimedia advertising campaigns to promote it (see Figure 9.5).

The challenge with these programs has been the negative press reports that comment on how this type of overt focus on consumerism is detrimental to the Estonian culture (Koovit, 2008). Finally, there was also a launch of a partner's discount/savings card in 2006, which provided shoppers with special discounts at both Tallinna Kaubamaja as well as other NG Group partners.

ADVERTISING TODAY AND IN THE FUTURE: 2007–2011

The worldwide economic crisis of 2008 did not spare the Estonian economy, or Tallinna Kaubamaja. This period resulted in a freeze on any significant changes to Tallinna Kaubamaja's existing business strategy, which unlike in the late 1990s did not result in repositioning the store as the "people's store" (i.e., from an Estonian standard, Tallinna Kaubamaja was to remain an upscale department store). There was a conscious effort not to promote the more expensive brands, but to introduce more modest priced brands for seasonal goods. These products were given a prominent position at the front of the store entrances to help convey the image that Tallinna Kaubamaja was making changes to help its customers (Parel, 2011). Print advertising continued, but price promotions in newspapers were reduced, but the overall media campaigns were not changed

Source: B. McKenzie.

Figure 9.5   "Osturalli" (sales rally) city poster advertisements – 2007

significantly. This was directly related to the fact that media prices dropped substantially, thus allowing for the same amount of advertising exposure at a lower cost.[5]

This period saw a change in the types of advertising media used. Effectively, the majority of print advertising was discontinued, with a switch to online advertising on the Internet versions of the print publications, particularly daily newspapers (for example www.postimees.ee, Estonia's largest circulation newspaper). The other change from print advertising was a direct result of the creation of an in-house quarterly publication, "Hooaeg" (Season). The magazine became the most widely read magazine in Estonia. It was both a source of advertising about the products sold at the store, as well as general interest stories.[6] There was a move towards more electronic media (excluding radio), as Tallinna Kaubamaja began increasing television and online advertising. Like other retailers, they have established their own website, http://www.kaubamaja.ee, which provides advertising and information in the Estonian, English, and Russian languages.

Source: B. McKenzie.

Figure 9.6   50th anniversary campaign – 2010

Television advertising continued to be an economical media choice as there were still few Estonian language broadcasters, each of which could be seen throughout the entire country. The driving force for this change is that, as in other parts of the world, Estonians have also rapidly increased their television and online use, and Estonia had the ninth highest Internet penetration rates in the EU (International Institute of Social History, 2009).

Tallinna Kaubamaja has continued to be a successful and profitable retailer, and in 2010 celebrated its 50th anniversary. There were a number of advertising campaigns in celebration, including in-store displays, the commissioning of a book on its history, "50 Aastat Kaubamaja" (50 Years as a Department Store), and a celebratory party where any former employee of the store was invited (see Figure 9.6).

In terms of a specific advertising strategy, Tallinna Kaubamaja does not view the need to have a formal one. The basis for this is that, as the times and media keep changing in a country the size of Estonia, there really is only time to create a yearly plan, and to react in terms of tactics as the year progresses (Parel, 2011). For the future, the expectation is to use advertising to concentrate on image building, using fewer print ads and more televison and the Internet. Also, depending upon other retail constraints, such as logistics and distribution, there may be an opportunity to launch an online store, further cementing Tallinna Kaubamaja's online presence.

The other online potential is social media. It appears that Tallinna

Kaubamaja plans to go slow in this area, particularly for a market such as Estonia, where access to reliable, relevant benchmarks is challenging. This venue will most likely be tied with any future online selling opportunities, thus limiting the investment at this time, although Tallinna Kaubamaja does have a presence on Facebook and Twitter (www. kaubamaja.ee). The website also has a link using Flikr, which provides an outlet to display current Tallinna Kaubamaja fashion collections (http:// www.flickr.com/photos/kaubamaja). These media portals allow Tallinna Kaubamaja to monitor and respond to blogs and forums as they relate to the brand, and will serve as an outbound communication tool if an online store is created.

DISCUSSION

The focus of this research was not to serve as a promotional vehicle for Tallinna Kaubamaja, or even as a recommendation of its advertising practices as stellar examples of what retailers/department stores competing in emerging markets should do. Rather, this chapter has provided a better understanding of the historical role that advertising can play in future retail success. There were two major thrusts of the role of advertising as it pertained to Tallinna Kaubamaja. The first was to examine the role of retail advertising that took place during the Soviet period, and how advertising could, and often had to, serve a number of often contradictory purposes. The second aim was to highlight the advertising strategies and practices of the same retailer during periods of social and political change, as well as confronting both internal and external economic challenges. Thus, this chapter provides both a historic and a contemporary perspective on the role of retailer advertising in a little studied market. In general, although these findings have presented a case study of one department store, in one country that has experienced significant change, it also provides the reader a greater understanding of the evolutionary nature that retail advertising can take.

Although Estonia is a small country, the findings can be of use by both researchers and practitioners involved in the retailing and advertising sectors in similar types of countries. As per any case study, care should be taken in terms of extending these findings into other markets, but it does provide a template for understanding. Tallinna Kaubamaja is somewhat unique as it was established during the Soviet period, and has continued to exist and grow today, and therefore can also serve as an exemplar for greater interest in examining the role that a variable such as advertising can play in overall retail success.

NOTES

1. The content of this section is heavily drawn from interviews conducted by the author with Jaagup Joost (Joost, 2009a, 2009b). Mr. Joost worked for Tallinna Kaubamaja from its opening in 1960, for over 30 years, until his retirement.
2. It is interesting to note that part of Tallinna Kaubamaja's 50th anniversary television advertising campaign, in 2010, showed shoppers from the Soviet period.
3. Estonians were familiar with SOKOS and Stockmann even during Soviet times in the 1980s, as many Estonians in Tallinn could receive Finnish television.
4. The content of this section is heavily drawn from the invaluable insights provided through interviews conducted with Tallinna Kaubamaja's Director of Marketing, Enn Parel (Parel, 2011).
5. Estonian Public Broadcasting, ERR (Eesti Rahvusringhääling), was created in 2007 as an amalgamation of Estonian radio and Estonian television.
6. It is interesting to note that the Estonian media has referred to "Hooaeg" as a "propaganda" tool (Parel, 2011).

REFERENCES

Aizsilnieks, A. (1974), 'Sovietization of consumers' cooperation in the Baltic states', *Journal of Baltic Studies*, **I** (1), 40–50.
Baltika Group (2010), 'History', http://www.baltikagroup.com/index.php?page=113&, accessed 22 December 2010.
Books LLC (2010), *Soviet Media*, Memphis, TN: Books LLC.
Dawson, J. and S.J. Henley (2001), 'Internationalisation of retailing in Poland: The economics of scarcity', in S.D. Arnold, P. Chadraba and P.R. Springer (eds), *Marketing Strategies for Central and Eastern Europe*, Aldershot: Ashgate, pp. 173–93.
Drakulic, S. (1992), *How We Survived Communism and Even Laughed*, New York: Norton Press.
Egipt, H. (2008), 'Harry Egipt: Reklaamfilmid' (World Famous TV Commercials by Harry Egipt), DVD.
Eisenhardt, K.M. (1989), 'Building theory from case study research', *Academy of Management Review*, **14** (4), 532–50.
Eng, L. and T. Keh (2007), 'The effects of advertising and brand value on future operating and market performance', *Journal of Advertising*, **36** (4), 91–100.
ERAL (2011), 'History of ERAL', *Eesti Reklaamiagentuuride Liidu (Estonian Association of Advertising Agencies)*, http://www.eral.ee/index_eng.php, accessed 4 January 2011.
Good, L.K., P. Huddleston and L. Stoel (1995), 'Ethnocentrism of Polish and Russian consumers: Are feelings and intentions related?' *International Marketing Review*, **12** (5), 35–48.
Hanson, P. (1974), *Advertising and Socialism*, New York: Macmillan Press.
Hessler, J. (2004), *A Social History of Soviet Trade*, New Jersey: Princeton University Press.
Hixon, W.L. (1998), *Parting the Curtain: Propaganda, Culture and the Cold War*, New York: St. Martin's Griffin.
International Institute of Social History (2009), 'Soviet posters', http://www.iisg.nl/exhibitions/chairman/sovintro.php, accessed 10 January 2011.
Järvesoo, E. (1978), 'The postwar economic transformation', in. T. Parming and E. Järvesoo (eds), *A Case Study of a Soviet Republic: The Estonian ESSR*, Boulder, CO: Westview Press, pp. 131–90.
Joost, J. (2009a), Telephone interview with the author [recording in possession of author], Tallinn, Estonia, September 16, 2009.
Joost, J. (2009b), Personal interview with the author [recording in possession of author], Tallinn, Estonia, December 9, 2009.

Kann, E. (2005), 'Russian like to buy the advertised products', *Äripäev (Business Day)*, November 22, 21.

Kasekamp, A. (2010), *A History of the Baltic States*, Basingstoke, UK: Palgrave Macmillan.

Koovit, K. (2008), 'Tallinna Kaubamaja brings special sales week forward', *Baltic Business News*, March 10.

Koshetz, H. (1959), 'The merchant's view', *New York Times*, September 13, F10.

Kutt, A. (1968), 'Reflections on Baltic economies under Soviet management', *The Baltic Review*, **35** (Aug), 18–26.

McKenzie, B. (1998), Author's research field notes – retailing research, Tallinn, Estonia, August 1998.

McKenzie, B. (2006), Author's research field notes – teaching at the Stockholm School of Economics Riga, Riga, Latvia, May 2006.

McKenzie, B. (2009), 'Baltic Tiger or Wounded Lion – Retail Trade and Shopping Behaviour in Estonia, Latvia, and Lithuania', in S. Singh (ed.), *Handbook of Business Practices and Growth in Emerging Markets*, Singapore: World Scientific Publisher, pp. 181–200.

McKenzie, B. (2010), Author's research field notes – retailing research, Tallinn, Estonia, February 2010.

Mieczkowski, B. (1975), *Personal and Social Consumption in Eastern Europe: Poland, Czechoslovakia, Hungary, and East Germany*, New York: Praeger.

Miller (1965), *Rise of the Russian Consumer*, London: Merritt & Hatcher Ltd.

Misiunas, R. and R. Taagepera (1993), *The Baltic States: Years of Dependence, 1940–1990*, Berkeley, CA: University of California Press.

NG Investment Group (2010), http://www.nginvest.ee/en, accessed 10 December 2010.

Palm T. (1989), 'Perestroika in Estonia: The cooperatives', *Journal of Baltic Studies*, **XX** (2), 127–48.

Parel, E. (2011), Personal interview with the author (Mr. Parel is Marketing Director of Tallinna Kaubamaja), Tallinn, Estonia, January 2011.

Raun, T. (2001), *Estonia and the Estonians*, California: Hoover Institution Press.

Schwartz, H. (1960), 'The Russian consumer wants more', *New York Times*, May 29, SM10.

Szporluk, R. (1975), *The Soviet West and the USSR*, New York: Praeger.

Tallinna Kaubamaja (1985), 'Tallinna Kaubamaja majandualiskud näitajad 1960–1985' (Tallinn Department Store Economic Indicators 1960–1985), ESSR Ministry of Commerce, Tallinn Municipal Agency of Markets.

Tamberg, L. (2009), Personal interview with the author (Ms. Tamberg was Deputy Head of the children's sports department, 1971–1977 at Tallinna Kaubamaja) [recording in possession of author], Tallinn, Estonia, December 11, 2009.

PART IV

RESEARCH METHOD

10 International advertising research: conceptual and methodological issues
C. Samuel Craig and Susan P. Douglas

INTRODUCTION

International advertising research is research that takes place in two or more countries and is designed to facilitate the creation, refinement and evaluation of advertising. It involves respondents and researchers from different countries and cultures and is more complex to undertake and more difficult to interpret than research carried out in a single country (see Craig and Douglas 2005 for a comprehensive treatment of international marketing research). International advertising research may be conducted simultaneously in multiple countries or sequentially over a period of time. In some cases, international advertising research also involves collection of information in a single country, with a view to understanding differences and similarities with regard to the firm's home market. In some instances, international advertising research may focus on studying the habits and attitudes of the entire population in a country. In others, it may focus on examining a specific segment, for example, young adults or women.

Based on the understanding gained in the initial research, the advertiser is able to formulate strategies that can be turned into concepts and rough advertisements which can be tested and refined. This process can be done in-house, but is often conducted by research organizations that specialize in testing advertisements. Once the ads are run, the emphasis shifts to evaluating whether the campaign generated the desired results. While increased sales are the ultimate goal, often intermediate measures related to communication effectiveness are taken. While there are some specialized techniques and challenges associated with conducting international advertising research, in most respects it is no different than other types of multi-country marketing research. Hence, the focus of this chapter is on the general issues involved in obtaining reliable, valid and meaningful results that can help advertisers make better decisions in international markets.

At the same time it is important to point out what this chapter is not about. There is a large and rich literature on international advertising research (see Taylor 2005 and special issue of the *International Journal of*

Advertising 2010). There is a large body of research conducted by academics that examines advertising in different countries. Much of the research is comparative in nature and examines advertisements in two or more countries. For example, various studies have examined the type of advertising appeals used in individualistic vs collectivistic societies (Han and Shavitt 1998; Cho et al. 1999; Zhang and Neelankavil 1997). Often the research examines differences in dominant themes or how a particular group of individuals is portrayed, e.g. women (Gilly 1988). Research has also examined the use of celebrities in different countries (Cutler and Lee 1998) and advertising directed toward children (Abramsky and Gunter 1997). Some of the academic research has an institutional thrust and examines the practices of large advertising agencies (Gould, Lerman and Grein 1999; Grein and Ducoffe 1998). There is an even larger literature that deals with cross-cultural differences and differences in consumer behavior. Much of this looks at differences in values and attitudes and is strongly rooted in basic disciplines such as psychology and cross-cultural psychology. While all of these are rich and very valuable streams of research, they are not examined here. Rather, the focus of the present chapter is on the methodological issues that are common to all multi-country investigations. The goal is to provide a framework to help international advertising researchers think about the critical issues as they conduct research.

This chapter examines the challenges that organizations and individuals face when conducting advertising research in multiple countries. First, the purpose of international advertising research is considered. Second, the general issues that make international advertising research different from domestic advertising research are examined. Third, issues related to establishing equivalence of the constructs examined and how they are measured is covered. The remainder of the chapter is devoted to issues related to research implementation. Consideration is given to selecting the most appropriate research technique and effective use of qualitative research. Issues related to instrument design and instrument translation are covered as well as sampling, survey administration techniques, and data analysis. There are concluding remarks regarding the importance of sound research to guide international advertising strategy.

PURPOSE OF INTERNATIONAL ADVERTISING RESEARCH

Advertising is practiced to some degree in virtually all countries around the globe. Firms spend significant amounts of money to advertise their products and services in both their home market and in foreign markets.

Given the sizable sums spent on advertising, firms are vitally interested in designing advertisements that will be most effective. At the outset, the firm has to decide whether it will have a common strategy for all countries in which it conducts business or develop separate advertising campaigns for each country or region. In order to make this decision, it will have to conduct extensive research in multiple countries to assess similarities of needs and aspirations to determine whether consumers are likely to respond similarly to advertising appeals. Generically, this research can be referred to as *strategy development* research and shares elements with other types of multi-country research. This research provides insights and direction as to whether the same strategy can be used everywhere or whether there needs to be adaptation to different countries or regions. Even if the same strategy can be used in multiple countries, the advertisements may have to be modified to be able to effectively implement the same strategy in different countries. This is the most important research as it establishes the overall direction for the advertising.

The second type of research is *advertising development* research and is research aimed at providing a deeper understanding of the appeals that are relevant in different countries. Broadly, this is research that facilitates the creation and refinement of advertisements. It involves research that tests concepts and evaluates different ad appeals. Research used to develop concepts and appeals for advertisements is more likely to be qualitative in nature, particularly in the initial phases. Qualitative research does not impose a specific framework on the respondents and can be very helpful in eliciting insights into what is relevant and meaningful in a particular country or culture. Quantitative research is also used in copy development and testing, particularly when there is interest in how a new advertisement compares to category norms for a particular testing procedure. Often the services of research firms that specialize in pre-testing are utilized in this phase. They not only have extensive experience in doing this type of research, but they also have developed category benchmarks that are often helpful in determining how well a particular execution is performing.

The third type of research is *advertising effectiveness* research. This type of research focuses on answering the question, did the advertisement or advertising campaign have the desired effect? This typically focuses on determining whether the advertisements effectively communicate the intended message to the target audience. This would involve some sort of survey research or tracking study. Alternatively, the firm may focus exclusively on sales response. The methodological issues associated with assessing communication effectiveness are the same as those encountered in the first two stages. In assessing the effectiveness of an entire campaign, sales are ultimately the most important metric, but assessment of the communications results provides a useful diagnostic, particularly if sales target were not reached. However, regardless of the type of research, the issues that must be addressed are essentially the same, although there is added complexity when the research is carried out in multiple countries.

ISSUES IN INTERNATIONAL ADVERTISING RESEARCH

While the fundamental principles underlying the conduct of advertising research are the same in both domestic and international markets, there are a number of conceptual and operational issues to consider in international advertising research that do not arise, or at least not to the same degree as in domestic advertising research. The diversity of international contexts with multi-cultural and multi-linguistic environments and the need to establish comparability and equivalence of data collected in these different environments pose major challenges.

Complexity of Research Design

Designing research for international advertising decisions is more complex than when a single country is concerned. Conducting research in different countries requires attention to problem definition and whether it is similar in structure and relevant parameters, for example, whether the product being advertised serves the same function or appeals to a similar segment across countries. While the same advertisement can be tested in multiple countries, there is no guarantee that the results will be meaningful. An ad that tests well in one country may test poorly in another. However, the poor results in the second country may simply be an artifact of the method rather than reflecting a true difference.

Similarly, the relevant respondent may differ from one country to another. While in the US and many European countries, children play an important role in decisions related to the purchase of candy or cereals, in other countries which are less child-oriented, the mother may be the relevant decision-maker and hence the advertisements need to be designed to convince mothers rather than children. Equally, the role of women in financial and insurance decisions or traditional male purchases such as automobiles may vary from country to country. While in Western societies women often have a key role and in some cases may be sole purchasers of such items, in Arab societies this is rarely the case.

Difficulties in Establishing Comparability and Equivalence

Considerable difficulties are likely to be encountered in establishing comparability and equivalence of research in different countries. Comparability is the more general term and indicates whether two or more objects or constructs, measurement instruments, or research techniques can be compared as similar or different between countries. Equivalence can be used as a synonym for comparability, but more typically it is used to refer to a more precise, in some cases statistical evaluation of comparability.

Many of the concepts, measurement instruments, and procedures for primary data collection were developed and tested in the US and Western Europe. Their relevance and applicability in other countries is far from clear. This is increasingly a problem as large multinationals in search of growth are expanding their operations into emerging market countries such as India and China. The implicit assumption, that is, that concepts and measurement instruments are universal, is typically termed "etic". Where this is inappropriate, it introduces what is termed a "pseudo etic" bias (see Berry 1989; Craig and Douglas 2005). Explicit administrative and analytic procedures for modifying concepts and measures developed in one country, and testing their relevance in another, should be incorporated into the research design (Douglas and Craig 2006). In addition, such procedures should enable identification of "emic" concepts, that is, constructs and measures unique to a specific country or culture (Berry 1989).

Establishing the comparability of data administration procedures poses further difficulties. In one country a certain method of data collection, for example mail questionnaires, may be known to have a given level of reliability. In another country, personal interviews rather than mail questionnaires may have an equivalent level of reliability in terms of response rate, accuracy, completion, etc. Levels of reliability associated with comparable research techniques differ and suggest the desirability of using techniques with equivalent levels of reliability, rather than techniques that are strictly comparable.

Coordination of Research and Data Collection across Countries

Research in multiple countries not only adds to the complexity of research design and data collection, but also gives rise to a number of issues relating to the organization and administration of research in different countries. Concern with the coordination, design and execution of research across different countries implies that agreement has to be reached with regard to research design in every country where research is conducted. The research instruments and data collection procedures also have to be harmonized. This adds to the cost and the time required to complete the research.

Ideally, the organization of international advertising research should strike a delicate balance between centralization of research from the central administrative unit and local input in research design and implementation. Too much centralization may result in lack of attention to specific local idiosyncrasies that are not readily apparent, but too much local autonomy may lead to research and data that are not comparable across countries. While coordination of research across countries is essential to ensure comparability and equivalence of data, input from local operating units is critical to ensure their cooperation.

Choosing a Research Supplier

Choice of a research supplier is an important step as it is unlikely that many companies have the expertise in-house to design and, still less, to implement all the types of research required in all markets. The need for familiarity with the local research environment and for multiple linguistic competences is typically critical for effective field research. Choice of organizations or type of service depends to a large extent on the type of research required and the number of countries in which research is to be conducted. Where the research is exploratory in nature or a firm is concerned with identifying changes in consumer needs and preferences, qualitative research by firms specializing in this type of research may be appropriate. If more extensive ad hoc market surveys are required, use of one of the large international research organizations with offices and experience in the countries to be investigated is desirable. Similarly, if highly specialized research is required, such as in pharmaceuticals, use of organizations specializing in the product market is essential.

For international advertising research there are organizations that offer specialized services in multiple countries around the world. For example, IPSOS ASI ad testing has offices in 55 countries (www.ipsos.com/asi/) and is able to provide a range of services including: pre-testing, copy testing, persuasion testing, and tracking. In addition they offer specialized services for testing print and television advertising. Their offices are primarily in North America, South America and parts of Asia. Coverage of Africa, India, Russia and the former USSR is very limited. The lighter coverage in emerging markets is consistent with current business activity, but it is a potential hindrance as firms seek to expand in these markets.

In developing international advertising strategy, a general international marketing research organization may be helpful. For example, Millward Brown is part of Kantar (WPP's group of research and consulting companies) and has 77 offices in 53 countries (www.millwardbrown.com). Millward Brown offers a range of services, including custom research, copy testing, tracking and campaign assessment. The advantage of using research organizations with extensive operations and established procedures is that they should have worked through most of the threats to reliability and validity. More importantly, they also have established norms and benchmarks that can be used to assess the relative performance of the advertisements being tested. With pre/post shifts on persuasion measures, it is important to know how the ad being tested compares with others, particularly those in the same category.

Selection of research suppliers is greatly facilitated by the information that is available on the Web. Information about local research suppliers around the world can be obtained from the websites of marketing research associations. The New York Chapter of the American Marketing Association publishes the *Greenbook*, which is available online at www. greenbook.org. The online version allows searches based on country, industry specialties, computer programs used in research, and trademarks/ service marks. Under Advertising Research, users can look for full service suppliers, those that provide advertising effectiveness and tracking services, as well as response modeling and communication strategy research. Industry expertise can be specified and, more importantly, searches can be refined to focus on specific countries or cities within a country. The *Greenbook* can also be searched for copy testing services that specialize in print, television, online, outdoor or radio. The European Society for Opinion and Marketing Research (ESOMAR) also provides online access to information about research firms at www.esomar.org. The site is very flexible and allows the user to refine and narrow the search as well. For example, under the broad category of Advertising Research, users can specify a country, and the types of service offered. Both websites provide quick and easy means of locating advertising research suppliers anywhere in the world.

PLANNING INTERNATIONAL ADVERTISING RESEARCH

The best approach to international advertising research depends on the situation and task facing the advertiser. The firm may be dealing with a new product or an existing product. The product may be advertised in a new country or an existing country. New products require extensive marketing research to guide their development and advertising to support their launch. As part of this process, insights should have been obtained regarding motivations for purchase and appeals that may be useful in stimulating interest in the product. Additional international advertising research will be necessary to form these basic ideas into useful concepts and advertising copy. The most challenging situation is when the advertiser wants to introduce a new product into a new country, that is, one in which the organization has no or limited experience in marketing. Here it is extremely important to develop a thorough understanding of the physical and cultural context in which advertising will take place. Some of this understanding would have been developed when the product was being developed and can be incorporated into the planning and development of the advertisements. The issues of equivalence and comparability assume paramount importance and come into play. The more experience that a firm has in a particular country, the less necessary preliminary research will be. However, preliminary research is essential when a new product is being introduced or a new advertising campaign is being considered.

Preliminary research might involve some desk research based on secondary data. In determining likely market potential, investigation of trends in different countries, for example, growth in GNP, political or financial stability, may be useful. Secondary data can also provide valuable insights into the type of media infrastructure that is available for advertising. Information on media penetration and availability, such as television sets per 1000 inhabitants, number of cable TV subscribers and newspaper circulation per capita, are available. Qualitative research, personal or in-depth interviews, focus groups, or observational research may also be conducted to determine relevant questions to be examined in subsequent phases of research. In introducing new products or repositioning products in a given country or set of countries, qualitative research can provide some initial indication as to likely customer response, as well as insights into how products are evaluated, and different scenarios in which products might be used. In addition, qualitative research may be useful in determining the relevant competitive product set, in defining the target market, and in suggesting relevant appeals. The time and effort devoted to such exploratory research depends on the research budget, as well as experience in conducting research in a given country environment.

Introducing an existing product into a new country poses slightly different challenges, but they can be even more problematic. With an existing product comes a pre-existing advertising campaign and notions of how the product should be advertised. It is critical that adequate development and testing be done to ensure that a campaign is developed that will be successful in the new country. In a more general sense, research is necessary to determine whether the same strategy and execution can be used or whether an entirely new strategy and execution is necessary, beyond the obvious language adaptations. Where the advertiser is in a large number of countries outside its home market, there is also the issue of whether a global campaign is appropriate. The obvious appeal of a single strategy and similar executions is the cost savings, efficiency and benefits of a uniform image worldwide. However, the benefits may be somewhat illusory, if in fact research reveals that a uniform image is not appropriate worldwide. The research necessary to determine whether a global campaign is likely to be effective is expensive and time consuming, but necessary. Without adequate research the international advertiser runs the risk of embarking on an elaborate and extensive campaign that is effective in some countries and ineffective in others.

An advertiser interested in introducing a new product into a country where it already conducts business still requires research to develop the campaign. The advertiser has a much better idea of what the cultural context is and has knowledge of what has been successful previously. Also, the advertiser knows what has not worked in the past. This knowledge provides a good starting point for developing the advertising and undertaking the research necessary to determine whether it is effective or not. The key here is, despite in-country experience, research is still necessary to develop advertising that will be impactful.

The least complex situation an international advertiser faces is introducing an existing product, that is, one that is currently being sold in other countries, into a country in which the firm has an established presence. The advertiser has knowledge of how the product has done in other countries and the extent to which similar conditions and purchase motivation prevail suggests that a similar strategy can be used. The main danger here is that the advertiser will assume that everything is the same and not conduct adequate research to make that determination. If things are actually the same, then the campaign is likely to be successful. However, if things are not the same, sales will be disappointing. Research could have confirmed market similarities and differences and guided development of advertising strategy and execution.

Collection of primary data is important for many strategic and tactical advertising decisions. It is essential in testing new concepts, determining relevant appeals or testing advertising copy. In conducting such research, different types of data collection techniques may be used, ranging from qualitative data collection techniques such as focus groups, or in-depth interviews, which require small sample sizes, to survey data collection techniques, which entail large sample sizes.

Qualitative data collection techniques are useful in the initial phases of research since they enable identification of constructs, product class definitions, or relevant attitudes and behavior to be examined in subsequent phases of research. In international advertising research this is advantageous insofar as the researcher may be unfamiliar with the market environment. Qualitative research avoids the direct imposition of a cultural bias, since the researcher imposes no prespecified conceptual model a priori. While the use of an interview guide or use of concepts entails an implicit cultural structure, a skilled local moderator should be able to probe potential sources of cultural bias. On the other hand, the burden of interpretation is placed on the researcher, resulting in potential for cultural bias insofar as she may interpret findings in terms of her own cultural referent (see Craig and Douglas 2005, pp. 170–74 for a more complete discussion).

Where more precise estimation is required, survey research is necessary. Survey research is the most commonly used method of data collection in global marketing research and has the advantage that data can be collected and processed from large samples. Use of the survey in international advertising research is fraught with a number of difficulties, arising from collection of data in a range of diverse sociocultural and linguistic environments. Consequently, considerable care needs to be exercised in instrument design to avoid errors of interpretation on the part of respondents, particularly among those with low levels of literacy or education. Sampling and survey administration procedures need to be designed to avoid bias arising from non-response or respondent–interviewer interaction.

ESTABLISHING DATA EQUIVALENCE

To make meaningful inferences about advertisements in different countries it is important to be certain that the ads, themes, or potential strategies that consumers are reacting to are equivalent. It is critical to have data that are comparable from one country to another and suggests that equivalence needs to be carefully monitored at all stages of the research process. The three main types of equivalence are: 1) *construct* equivalence, ensuring that the constructs are equivalent in all contexts and cultural settings; 2) *measure* equivalence, ensuring that operational measures are equivalent in all research settings; and 3) *method* equivalence, ensuring that data collection procedures are comparable and equally reliable in all contexts studied.

Construct Equivalence

Construct equivalence has three distinct aspects. First, the advertiser must assess *functional* equivalence, whether a given concept or behavior serves the same function from country to country. The second type of equivalence is *conceptual* equivalence and requires the advertiser to determine whether the same concepts or behaviors occur in different countries and whether the way in which they are expressed is similar. Finally, the advertiser must assess *category* equivalence to determine whether the concept belongs to a specific class of objects or activities. This is likely to be more important in the preliminary research to determine who the likely competitors are.

Functional equivalence

Concepts, objects, or behaviors studied may not necessarily be functionally equivalent, that is, they may not have the same role or function in all countries studied (Berry 1989). For example, in the US bicycles are predominantly used for recreation; in The Netherlands, China, and in other countries they provide a basic mode of transportation. This implies that the relevant competing product set must be defined differently. In the US it will include other recreational products such as tennis rackets and golf equipment, while in The Netherlands or China it will include alternative modes of transportation, such as public transportation. In addition to determining the competitive set, understanding functional equivalence also helps identify objects or behaviors that should or should not be incorporated into ads in particular countries.

Seemingly similar activities may also have different functions. In some countries, regular exercise or participation in sports is considered a key element in staying healthy. In other countries, exercise and sports are primarily viewed as leisure activities. Objects may also have different significance in different countries or cultures (Belk and Ger 1999). In the US, car ownership is ubiquitous and no longer confers status, although, in certain circles, makes such as Mercedes-Benz still carry prestige. In emerging market countries, ownership or non-ownership of a car is still an important indicator of status. In parts of rural Africa, ownership of a radio or bicycle by a young male is an important status symbol – reputed by some sources to ensure that the owner will have little difficulty in finding a wife.

Conceptual equivalence

Functional equivalence is concerned with the role of objects and behavior in society at a macro-cultural level, while conceptual equivalence is concerned with the interpretation that individuals place on objects, stimuli, or behavior, and whether these exist or are expressed in similar ways in different countries and cultures (Sears 1961). The focus is on the measurement of attitudes and behavior at the individual level. Individual values such as materialism, or concepts such as "the self" may not be relevant or not construed in the same way in different countries or cultures. For example, "saving face" is a concept prevalent in Chinese society and is an important element dominating behavior in relation to others (Mao 1994). Construals of the self and others are also strikingly different between Asian and Western societies (Markus and Kitayama 1991). In Western cultures, the individual or self is viewed as an independent, self-contained entity with a unique set of traits, abilities, motives and values. Behavior is largely directed to maintain independence from others and to express and reinforce their own unique attributes. In many Asian cultures, on the other hand, emphasis is placed on the fundamental interconnectedness of human beings to each other. An understanding of an individual's role in society and how the individual relates to others is important in structuring advertisements.

Category equivalence

The category in which objects or other stimuli are placed can vary from country to country. In the beverage market, for example, what is considered a soft drink as well as forms of soft drinks such as canned or bottled sodas, mineral waters, fruit juices, iced tea and powdered and liquid fruit concentrates vary from one culture to another. In The Netherlands, milk is commonly consumed with meals and viewed as a soft drink, whereas in many other countries it is used primarily as an additive for hot or cold drinks or as a beverage for children. Variation in categories between countries creates different completive sets and can influence advertising strategy.

Measure Equivalence

Once the advertiser is confident that the constructs are equivalent, or has determined where there is divergence, the next step is to examine the equivalence of the measures used. Construct and measure equivalence are interrelated as the measure is an operational definition of the construct. Measure equivalence has three main dimensions: 1) the calibration system used in measurement; 2) the translation of the research instrument; and 3) the metric equivalence of the instrument (Mullen 1995)

Calibration equivalence

In developing a research instrument, equivalence has first to be established with regard to the calibration system used in measurement. This includes not only equivalence with regard to monetary units and measures of weight, distance, and volume, but also other perceptual cues, such as color, shape, or form, which are used to interpret visual stimuli. For advertising studies, it is the more subtle differences in instrument calibration that are likely to be more problematic. Advertising stimuli are complex and contain a large amount of information. They contain subtle perceptual cues such as color, pictorial form, or shape. Studies in cognitive and cross-cultural psychology suggest that a substantial degree of commonality exists with regard to the manifestations of these in different countries and cultures (Russell et al. 1997). However, ability to interpret, differentiate among, and develop gradations in these schemata appears to differ. Often this is linked to schooling, language and the physical environment.

Translation equivalence
Translation of the instrument so that it is understood by respondents in different countries and has equivalent meaning in each research context is a critical step (Douglas and Craig 2007; Harkness 2003). The need for translation of questionnaires and other verbal stimuli where research is conducted in countries with different languages is readily apparent. The need to translate non-verbal stimuli that are part of the instrument to ensure that they evoke the desired image and to avoid problems of miscommunication is less widely recognized.

Translation equivalence is a central issue in the establishment of construct equivalence, since this is the stage in the research design at which the construct is defined in operational terms. The translation procedure thus frequently helps to pinpoint problems with regard to whether a concept can be measured by using the same or similar questions in each cultural context, and whether a question has the same meaning in different research contexts (Douglas and Craig 2007). If different questions are used, then issues arise with regard to the minimal level of equivalence necessary for two questions to be considered the same, and what criteria for equivalence can be established.

Metric equivalence
In establishing metric equivalence there are two main issues: 1) equivalence of the scale or scoring procedure used to establish the measure; and 2) equivalence of response to a given measure in different countries (Mullen 1995). The greater the emphasis placed on quantitative measurement in data interpretation, the more important the establishment of metric equivalence becomes. Metric equivalence in scale and scoring procedures is of particular relevance as different scales or scoring procedures may be most effective in different countries and cultures. This often depends on what type of scales or scaling procedures are commonly used in schools. While in English-speaking countries, use of a 5- or 7-point scale is common, in other countries 20-point or 10-point scales are more common. Similarly,

use of non-verbal response procedures requires consideration of the comparability of these across countries and cultures.

A second aspect of metric equivalence concerns the interpretation of a score obtained on a measure, or scalar equivalence. The question arises as to whether a score obtained in one research context has the same meaning as in another context (Steenkamp and Baumgartner 1998). For example, on an intentions-to-purchase scale, the top two boxes, commonly used to predict the proportion of likely buyers, may not indicate a similar likelihood of purchase from one country to another. In many Middle Eastern countries, and equally in Southern Europe, respondents have been found to give significantly higher top box ratings than in other countries (van Herk 2003).

In contrast to other types of equivalence, metric equivalence can be examined only once the data have been collected. Prior experience or examination of similar types of measures in the relevant country or culture may provide some guidelines as to appropriate scales and typical response patterns. This may suggest the types of data analysis and statistical procedures that are most appropriate in view of typical response patterns. Different measures that have different potential biases may be applied, and the results compared to establish equivalence (Cohen and Neira 2004).

IMPLEMENTING INTERNATIONAL ADVERTISING RESEARCH

Development of international advertising strategy needs to be guided by research that is valid and reliable and that will provide adequate direction for the formulation of advertising strategy. The firm needs to determine whether the same strategy can be used effectively in multiple countries. Closely related to this is answering the question whether the same execution, with minor modifications such as language, can be used in multiple countries. Answering these questions involves collection of primary data from respondents who are representative of the target market or from a broader group of respondents to help define the target market. In addition the primary data collection may occur in more controlled settings such as mall intercept facilities, focus group facilities, or other facilities where respondents are invited to attend, including online environments. Research instruments suitable for use in all the countries or cultures have to be developed, sampling procedures determined, and appropriate administration procedures selected. Once the data have been collected, they have to be analyzed and the findings need to be presented in a form that can be clearly understood by management.

When using a major research supplier to conduct ad testing, the supplier will have or arrange for facilities to conduct the research. The key challenge researchers face, particularly in emerging market countries is the poorly developed advertising research infrastructure. As indicated earlier, major research organizations may have offices in over 50 countries worldwide and can provide a range of services. Also they are familiar with the local cultural context and should be sensitive to idiosyncratic local issues that would impact the validity of the research. In situations where the scope of the planned research is more limited, the *Greenbook* and ESOMAR can be used to locate research suppliers on a market-by-market basis. The main drawback to this approach is that coordination and control issues are shifted back to the advertiser or its agency.

Choice of Research Techniques

Based on the specific problem facing the advertiser, it must decide whether to conduct a survey, collect qualitative data, or use some combination of these. Selection of appropriate research techniques gives rise to a number of questions about their comparability and cost effectiveness in different countries and cultural contexts and appropriateness to specific research problems.

Survey research is widely used in multi-country research and provides a means of quantifying concepts which have been identified in qualitative research as, for example, customer attitudes and response patterns as well as likely and actual purchase behavior. Use of a survey assumes the existence of a population with a certain minimal level of education, able to understand and respond to oral or written questions or pictorial stimuli. Where a national or representative sample is required, it also requires the availability of sampling lists or profile data from which to draw samples. These conditions are not always met, particularly in emerging markets. Further, among largely illiterate populations and in certain cultures, considerable ingenuity may be required in devising research instruments and procedures to overcome potential communication and comprehension problems. Similarly, survey administration procedures will need to be adapted to the availability and reach of the marketing research and communications infrastructure, for example, levels of telephone or personal computer ownership, Internet access, etc.

Qualitative research techniques such as observational and projective techniques and focus groups help the advertiser gain insights into what types of appeal are likely to be effective. They help reveal how consumers think and explore subconscious feelings and need states. They also can be used to bring to light day-to-day actions, routinized behavior patterns and ingrained habits that do not immediately spring to mind (Branthwaite and Cooper 2001). In some cases, qualitative research alone may be adequate, as, for example, in exploring the meaning of brands and brand names, providing insights into the role of in-store stimuli, or generating ideas for advertising, new products, or promotional appeals. Qualitative research avoids some of the problems associated with survey techniques since it does not impose any pre-structured frame of reference on respondents, which may reflect the specific cultural referents of the researcher. On the other hand, the lack of structure implies that the onus of data interpretation lies on the researcher, and hence cultural bias may occur at the analysis stage.

Qualitative Research

Qualitative research techniques can be used in a number of different ways in international advertising research. They can be used in exploratory research in order to formulate and define the problem more clearly and to identify language or terms used by consumers. It is important to cover emotional as well as rational issues in order to ensure as wide a range of coverage as possible. Qualitative research plays a major role in pre-testing advertisements, packaging, and product concepts, both to generate ideas to be pre-tested and to explore relations with these concepts. Finally, qualitative techniques can be used in exploratory research to probe deeply into attitudes towards product classes, brands, shopping situations and trends in behavior. This is particularly valuable in helping to formulate advertising appeals and uncover purchase motivations.

Qualitative research is used to generate improved understanding of the attitudes and behavior of specific market segments such as teenagers or children, or to understand the patterning of attitudes and cognitions, the meaning of brands and brand associations. It can also provide insights into the role of in-store stimuli, or to generate ideas for new products, advertising or promotional appeals, etc. (Barnard 1997). Here, investigation of relevant issues on a small sample of carefully selected respondents may be adequate.

The various types of qualitative data collection techniques differ primarily in terms of (1) the degree of structure imposed in data collection; (2) whether data are collected while the respondent is in a real world or simulated shopping situation; (3) potential reactivity, that is, the extent to which the respondent is aware of being studied, and hence may behave differently; (4) the introspectiveness of data, that is, whether the individual respondents talk about themselves and their inner feelings, or rationalize their behavior; (5) the subjectivity of the analysis, that is, whether analytic and interpretation procedures and coding schemata are developed prior to data collection, or alternatively are established post hoc by the researcher based on examination of the data; and (6) the sample size, that is, the number of respondents from whom it is feasible to collect data, given typical time and budget constraints.

Projective techniques

Projective techniques typically require the respondent to perform a specific task such as word association or sentence completion, or to respond to specific stimuli such as photos or drawings. For example, respondents might be asked which of a set of pictures they feel best expresses their feelings about a brand. Unless a standardized set of stimuli is used, the equivalence in meaning of these stimuli across cultures needs to be established. With more widespread Internet access, it has become increasingly feasible to administer projective techniques over the Internet enabling use of a mix of qualitative and quantitative techniques (Pawle and Cooper 2002). In some cases, respondents may be asked to interpret the actions of others. Here, it is assumed that respondents project their own feelings and reactions in their interpretation. There is little potential for reactivity or introspection among respondents. Analysis can either be subjective or pre-structured, depending on the extent to which the initial task is structured. Generally, small to moderate sample sizes are used, and the procedure is not overly time-consuming.

Depth interviews and focus group

Depth interviews and focus group techniques typically emphasize verbalization of opinions and are useful for obtain consumers' reactions to concepts, and rough and finished ads. Both types of interviews are generally conducted in an in-home or laboratory situation and have low potential for reactivity. Depth interviews can become introspective, though this is less likely to occur with focus groups. The primary limitation of focus groups is that respondents may tend to express socially acceptable views and to avoid opinions or responses that may be controversial. The development of appropriate coding and analytic procedures as well as interpretation is complex and requires an experienced researcher. The interviewer/moderator should not only be trained in group interviews, but should also be familiar with the language, culture and patterns of social interaction in the country. Difficulties may also be encountered in comparing results across countries, especially insofar as they reflect the specific cultural environment or context. Sample sizes are small and are not randomly selected. It is advisable to conduct them over a range of geographic areas and with different moderators. If the results begin to converge, then greater confidence can be placed in the findings.

In-depth interviews   In-depth interviews can either be conducted on an individual, one-on-one basis or in small groups. In contrast to survey methods, in-depth interviews are unstructured, as the interviewer attempts to probe in-depth attitudes and perceptions about a particular brand, concept, or advertisement to stimulate group discussion. In international advertising research, in-depth interviews are suited to situations where the interviewer aims to gain understanding of customer attitudes and behavior or feelings and associations about a topic, or the language and terms used in discussion of that topic. The unstructured nature of the interview enables the interviewer to probe and does not require the imposition of a pre-structured format or questions that may reflect a specific cultural background or bias. On the other hand, interpretation of data, especially when researchers come from different research traditions, is subjective and, as with other qualitative techniques, variability in moderator skills can impact consistency of data and comparability across countries.

Focus groups   Focus groups are group discussions conducted with individuals who are representative of the target market(s) in an informal setting. The discussion is "moderated" by an interviewer who plays a key role in stimulating discussion about feelings, attitudes and perceptions relating to the topic being studied, and in centering this interchange on relevant issues. As in the case of other forms of qualitative research, there tend to be differences in approach and emphasis in the conduct of focus groups in different countries, notably between the US and Europe. These stem in part from differences in the underlying philosophy of qualitative research, as well as client interest and focus. In the US, focus group moderators emphasize direct questioning and specific issues and more direct interpretation. In Europe, focus groups are more open-ended and make greater use of projective techniques, especially in France and Italy. Focus groups are successfully used in all parts of the world, even in countries such as Japan or South Korea, where social norms restrict frank and open discussion of personal or emotional issues, or expression of controversial opinions. Typically, some adaptation by the moderator to local conventions and sensitivity to social norms is required.

Focus groups are suited to generating and testing ideas for ad concepts, product concepts, and product positioning; studying response to packaging and advertising themes; and assessing and tracking customer needs and interests and detecting new trends. As in the case of individual in-depth interviews, use of focus groups in multi-country research poses a number of problems, especially with regard to comparability of method and data. In the first place, the role of the moderator is crucial to success. Consequently, trained bilingual moderators, conversant with the appropriate language and also patterns of social interaction in each country or culture, are required. This can pose problems, particularly in emerging countries such as Eastern Europe or parts of Asia, particularly China, where the research infrastructure is not well established. Secondly, as in the case of other types of qualitative research, interpretation and analysis of focus group data is subjective and requires considerable skill and experience. In cross-cultural research, understanding not only verbal data but also non-verbal cues, such as voice intonation, gestures, and expressions used in other countries and cultures, is often a key to successful interpretation of findings.

Focus groups can also be conducted in different locations in the world using videoconferencing technology, so that participants can interact with each other (Miller 1991). This does require that participants share a common language, and also that time differences can be accommodated. This places an increased administrative burden as two or more focus groups have to be coordinated simultaneously in real time. The high cost means this approach is most effective in business-to-business studies or for high-end products. Group support systems can also be conducted in multiple locations using electronic technology. Participants sit at computers and type in responses to questions posed by the facilitator. Contributions to the discussion are processed in parallel so that everyone can "talk" at once. This avoids the difficulties associated with certain participants dominating the group. Ideas and opinions are anonymous.

Chat rooms on the Internet can also provide a valuable source of ideas for management about new products, product endorsement, promotional campaigns and other marketing activities as well as a conduit for identifying current and future trends. Chat rooms can be started by consumers or marketers and are typically product or interest specific, for example relating to biking, a particular genre of music, gardening or baby products. These can be avatar or more commonly text based (Zanasi 2003) and can be monitored and content analyzed to obtain information relating to customer interests, needs complaints, and other concerns. Again language constraints typically limit the scope and type of participant in a chat room, but rooms in different languages can be set up and monitored.

Instrument Design

One of the areas that is often neglected, but one that can have a tremendous impact on the quality of the results, is creation of the instrument used to collect data. Instrument design is an important consideration in both qualitative and survey research. However, it assumes greater significance in survey research where structured data collection techniques and large sample sizes are involved. It is important to ensure that the research instrument is adapted to the specific national and cultural environment and that it is not biased in terms of any one country or culture (Harkness, van de Vijver and Mohler 2003). In particular, it is important to try to avoid potential problems of miscommunication between respondents and researcher. This is also an area where the client/user of the research results can have tremendous impact since the tasks are in some respects the least technical aspects of the research process. If the research instrument is not properly designed, then the results will be at best incomplete and at worst misleading.

Questions need to be formulated in such a way to obtain the desired information from respondents and also avoid miscommunication between the researcher and respondent. In multi-country research, one issue is the extent to which questions are formulated in precisely the same terms (Smith 2003). This is more likely to be feasible for questions relating to demographic and other background characteristics and most difficult for attitudinal and psychographic data, and particularly reaction to complex stimuli such as advertisements.

Respondent comprehension can be increased considerably by the use of non-verbal stimuli such as show cards, pictures and photos. These can also be used to provide a check on bias arising from miscomprehension of verbal questions. It is, however, important to note that visual stimuli can be misinterpreted as well and need to be translated into the relevant idiom to ensure they are correctly interpreted. Instruments also need to be designed to avoid potential sources of bias arising from the topics covered in the questionnaire, the interaction between the interviewer and respondent, or alternatively the respondent's response style or socio-economic or demographic origins.

Extreme response style can influence results in domestic advertising research and is even a greater problem in international advertising research (Clark 2001). Different types of response bias, such as yea-saying, nay-saying, social acquiescence, or cultural stereotyping, need to be assessed and accounted for (Baumgartner and Steenkamp 2001). This has been found to vary significantly by country. In Europe, for example, the further south the region within the EU, the more extreme the response style (van Herk 2003). While there are statistical procedures to adjust for response bias (Fischer 2004), it can also be reduced by careful design of the research instrument and use of different response formats, since different types of format tend to be prone to different types of response bias. This is apt to be particularly important when the researcher is trying to gauge the response to advertisements that are being tested. If extreme response is more prevalent in one country being tested, it may give the firm the mistaken belief that the advertisement is going to be highly effective. However, the response may be normal for that particular culture and not reflect any superiority.

Instrument Translation

A procedure commonly used to test the accuracy of translation in multi-country research is back translation (Brislin 1970, 1980). Following this procedure a questionnaire is translated into the target language by a bilingual native of the target country. It is then translated back into the source language by a bilingual native speaker of the source language. The original and back-translated versions are then compared for differences and similarities. The accuracy of the back-translated version is considered to be an indicator of the accuracy of the target translation. Back translation was initially developed for situations where the researcher was not familiar with the target language, but wanted some assurance that respondents were in fact being asked the same question in that language (Harkness 2003). Either there was no one available to review the translation, or the procedure was felt to provide insights into potential errors.

Recently, use of parallel or double translation (i.e., two translated versions) has been advocated as a preferred method of achieving equivalence in meaning (Hambleton 1993, 1994; van de Vijver and Hambleton 1996). This can be used in conjunction with a committee approach to review the meaning and equivalence of translations and select the "best" translation (Harkness 2003; Harkness and Schoua-Glusberg 1998). Extensive checking and pre-testing of the translation is also viewed as essential to ensure that a reliable and accurate translation is obtained.

The complexity of translation, the subjective character of translation assessment, as well as the multiple skills required, that is, linguistic ability, as well as skills in questionnaire development, implies that a team-based approach to translation is desirable. In the social sciences, this has been found to provide the richest output in terms of alternative translations as well as a balanced critique of alternative versions (McKay et al. 1996; Harkness and Schoua-Glusberg 1998). A team can bring together the mix of skills as well as the disciplinary expertise required. They need to have knowledge of the study and of questionnaire design, as well as the cultural and linguistic skills to translate into appropriate versions of the target language(s) where necessary.

Issues related to achieving equivalence also relate to the types of data being collected. International surveys typically involve one or more of three different types of data: socio-economic, behavioral, and attitudinal data. Socio-economic data is usually the easiest to translate, as similar or equivalent categories can typically be identified. Behavioral categories require identifying similar types of behavior, which are equivalent. This may be more problematic especially where the relevant behavior is cognitive rather than physical. Most difficulties are likely to occur with attitudinal data where the construct expressed may differ from one language to another. Consequently, it is not just linguistic equivalence that needs to be considered, but also other equivalence issues, such as category equivalence, functional equivalence, and construct equivalence.

Socio-demographic questions are most likely to raise questions of category equivalence relating to employment, position with the firm, marital status, etc. Here it is important to ensure that categories are equivalent, have similar status and perform similar functions in each context examined. For example, the tasks performed by a lawyer in America would be performed in the UK by either a barrister or solicitor. Questions relating to lifestyle and behavior are most likely to raise issues of functional equivalence. For example, questions relating to washing or doing the laundry will need to take into consideration the mode and circumstances of washing, for example whether hot water is available, whether washing machines are typically used, or whether washing is commonly done by domestic help or services outside the home. Similarly engaging in sports may be viewed as a purely social activity or alternatively as a means of gaining exercise and improving health.

Attitudinal or abstract questions are most likely to raise issues of conceptual equivalence. The linguistic equivalent of words such as *happiness* may, for example, have different connotations and tap other related constructs (Smith 2003). Equally, the apparently equivalent word may reflect different levels of intensity. Use of multiple indicators that are linguistically distinct may help to resolve this problem (Przeworski and Teune 1966) but only if different terms do not replicate the same distinctions.

Use of non-verbal scales, such as visual or numerical scales, can aid in avoiding some of the difficulties in establishing linguistic equivalence of response scales. However, they do not completely eliminate translation issues as the instructions for using the scale have to be translated, as well as the meaning of the scale, and the end points with numerical scales. Non-verbal and numeric scales are also subject to their own problems of differences in meaning and equivalence across cultures. Extensive research has shown that respondents in different countries do not use positions on a scale similarly (see van Herk 2003). Japanese respondents, for example, tend to use positive ends of a scale. Response set bias such as social acquiescence bias or nay-saying bias has also been found to vary across European countries (van Herk 2000). Consequently, scale designs suitable for one population may not be suitable for another. Use of dichotomous scales with responses such as yes/no, favor or disapprove, agree or disagree, which have equivalents across languages, can help minimize these issues. This, however, assumes the feasibility of writing a question with a dichotomous response, which may not necessarily be easy with attitudinal questions. It also requires establishment of an equivalent "no opinion" or "indifferent" category and also a "don't know" category. Response scales can also be calibrated so that the strength of verbal scales used is equivalent across languages. Here two cases may be identified. The first is where only the ends of the rating or ranking scale are labeled. This typically poses fewer problems than where each position on the scale needs to be translated. However, difficulties may be found in finding translations of points, such as strongly agree, strongly disagree, somewhat agree, somewhat disagree, which capture the same level of intensity across languages.

In conducting international advertising research, translation is a critical issue is the development of a valid and effective data collection instrument. While the starting point for any research project is the underlying issue or conceptual framework being investigated, the vehicle that drives the investigation is the questionnaire. International advertising research of necessity involves different countries where different languages or language variants are spoken. It is critical to ensure that, where questions are translated, they have equivalent meaning in each context, are devoid of cultural bias, and can be clearly understood by all respondents. Back translation in isolation is inadequate. While helping to ensure that a correct literal translation is achieved, it does not help in assessing whether the questions have equivalent meaning or are devoid of cultural bias. Even in catching errors, much depends on the back translator's understanding of a question and its purpose. Further, mechanistic applications of back translation, without adjustments, are unlikely to result in an instrument that will produce reliable and valid results. Instrument translation is a crucial element in the conduct of international advertising research. Researchers need to employ an iterative approach to ensure that valid and reliable multi-country instruments are developed (see Douglas and Craig 2007 for more detailed information on instrument translation).

Sampling and Survey Administration Techniques

Once a research instrument has been designed to collect the required data, the next step is to develop appropriate sampling and survey data collection procedures. In developing a sampling plan for a particular target population, decisions first have to be made with regard to the appropriate sampling frame, for example, the world, country groupings, countries or units within countries. Next is the choice of sampling procedures. In the case of global and regional samples, the main problem is to find procedures that ensure representativeness of the target population (Reynolds, Langerak and Diamantopoulos 2003). Since few comprehensive global and regional sampling frames are available, judgment or convenience sampling are often more practical and considerably less expensive than random sampling. They are also more likely to provide reliable and accurate data. This particularly tends to be the case in business-to-business research, where the absolute population may be relatively small and known. In the case of national sampling units, in addition to finding an appropriate frame, researchers also have to consider whether the use of equivalent procedures for each sampling unit will yield comparable results. Differences in the availability and coverage provided by sampling frames or lists suggest that in some cases using different sampling procedures for each unit may provide better representation and be more cost effective (Hader and Gabler 2003).

A decision then has to be made as to how the survey should be administered. As in domestic research, four major alternatives can be identified: mail, telephone, personal interview, and electronic, that is, e-mail or the Internet. The latter method is becoming increasingly popular in Europe and the US as e-mail lists and panels become more widely available. It also enables the use of pictorial and photographic stimuli, for example, products or advertisements, as well as facilitating use of a combination of qualitative and quantitative techniques.

Whatever the method used, the question of whether equivalent procedures from one country to another will yield comparable results has to be assessed. This, in turn, depends on the availability and adequacy of sampling frames for the target population. Mail surveys require the availability of a mailing list, and telephone surveys a list of telephone numbers or sufficient density of telephone ownership to allow random digit dialing. Personal interviewing provides greater flexibility in that where convenience or quota sampling is used, a list of the target population is not required. Use of e-mail or the Internet, on the other hand, requires an adequate base of e-mail or Internet subscribers in the target population. The final sample, whether global, regional, national or within a country, should be as representative as possible of the target population and, in the case of national and within-country sampling units, as comparable as possible across units. Cost considerations and sampling difficulties may, however, limit the feasibility of obtaining representative samples.

The absence of population lists and other lists commonly used as sampling frames means that it can be difficult to use random sampling techniques in many countries (Reynolds et al. 2003). Consequently, use of non-random procedures may be preferable and more cost efficient. Sampling procedures, such as random walk, cluster, or area sampling, vary in reliability and accuracy from one country to another, and a mix of different procedures may be needed in order to obtain comparable samples.

Data collection techniques such as mail or telephone surveys and personal interviewing also vary in relative cost, feasibility, and coverage of the population from one country to another. In some countries, low levels of literacy may preclude the use of mail surveys and low levels of telephone ownership, telephone surveys. Often, especially outside industrialized countries, heavy reliance may be placed on personal interviewing. This requires the availability of trained interviewers fluent in the relevant language.

Increasingly, questionnaires are being administered via the Internet. This has the advantage that product details, pictures of products, brands and shopping environment can be provided as well as links to other sites. Graphics, sound and video can also be integrated. The whole process is automated from the posting of the questionnaire to response, thus minimizing recording errors. However, electronic surveys suffer from a number of limitations, especially in terms of identification of a representative sample. This can be particularly problematic with multi-country research where Internet penetration and usage differ between countries. Valid results will be generated only if an appropriate sampling frame is available, all members respond to the questionnaire, and there is no non-response bias. Response rates are typically quite low (less than 2 percent) so, consequently, a large number of potential respondents need to be contacted to obtain a large enough sample to analyze. Increasingly, research organizations are establishing Internet panels to help increase response rates and representativeness and mitigate some of the problems.

Data Analysis

Once procedures for collecting data have been determined using either survey or non-survey methods, the next step is the choice of appropriate techniques and procedures for data analysis. These two steps (data collection and data analysis) are interrelated as certain types of analysis, for example, multidimensional scaling, require collection of specific types of data. For non-survey research, data analysis is typically qualitative. Survey research requires some type of quantitative analysis. When research is conducted in a single country, these issues are the same as in domestic research. In multi-country research, the issues become more complex owing to the existence of multiple units of analysis. While, in domestic marketing research, decision problems and analysis typically relate to a single national sample, in multi-country research management is concerned not only with developing advertising strategy or tactics relative to a single national market, but also with assessing the extent to which such strategies or tactics can be standardized across different geographic areas. This poses a number of issues with regard to the level of aggregation and procedures used to analyze data.

The multi-tier character of international advertising research suggests that it may be desirable to follow a sequential procedure in analyzing multi-country data. Data are examined first for each country or other relevant unit independently, and cultural biases are identified. It may also be necessary to normalize or standardize data, to adjust for differences in cultural reference points and response biases in different countries. This is important for attitudinal and opinion variables where tendencies for specific response set biases are prevalent. Where scales are developed to measure specific constructs, certain additional steps beyond those followed in domestic research need to be followed, to ensure construct and measure equivalence.

Once equivalence has been examined, the next step is comparison of results across countries. Here the analysis can focus on either the differences in the *level* of variables or the *structure* of variables (Van de Vijver and Leung 1997). The majority of analyses focus on answering the first question: is there a significant difference in variable X between country A and country B? This type of analysis is generally straightforward and employs techniques that are easy to use and interpret such as t tests, Chi square tests, analysis of variance, etc., although more complex multivariate techniques can also be used. Typically, if no significant difference is found, the researcher concludes that the variables are the same in both contexts. If a difference is found, then the researcher seeks to identify the factors underlying this difference.

When addressing structural issues, the researcher asks a more complex research question: is there a difference in the relation of variable X to variable Y between country A and country B? Answering structural questions requires the use of sophisticated statistical techniques such as confirmatory factor analysis, covariance or structural equation modeling, which are more difficult to interpret (Myers, Calantone, Page and Taylor 2000). The relationships between variables often represent complex patterns. Some of this complexity is simply the result of the number of variables being considered and some is owing to the inherent difficulty of making cross-national comparisons of patterns or relationships between variables.

CONCLUSION

Once research has been used to help develop the parameters of the international advertising strategy, ads need to be developed to implement the strategy. Development of the ads is likely to be highly centralized, if the same strategy is to be used in all markets. Local input should be incorporated and local testing conducted to be certain that the same strategy can in fact be used in all markets. On the other hand, in situations where there is considerable diversity and each market requires location-specific ads, then the development process will be highly decentralized. In the latter case it is important that there is some centralized review to be certain that the ads are consistent with the brand's core meaning, particularly since, increasingly, ads are seen outside a specific locale.

One of the biggest challenges is to find research organizations that can provide similar services in different countries throughout the world. If it is the same advertising research supplier and they have standard services there is a greater likelihood that they have the knowledge and ability to ensure that results are comparable across countries. If different research organizations have to be relied upon, then the techniques may not produce comparable results and may be misleading. This is less of an issue with research aimed at concept development and testing, particularly where qualitative techniques are employed.

International advertising research offers tremendous promise as a means to expand knowledge about consumption and purchase behavior and the impact of the market environment and marketing activities on that behavior in other contexts and cultures (see Craig and Douglas 2001; Nakata and Huang 2002). Equipped with this understanding, international advertisers are then able to develop concepts and appeals that form the basis for advertising in different countries. Once the advertisements are developed, research is used to determine whether the advertisements are effective. However, in making this assessment, considerable care is needed to ensure comparability and equivalence across the various countries, measurement instruments, and sampling and data collection procedures employed, so that research results can be meaningfully interpreted and ultimately provide valuable input into international advertising decisions and strategy. Technological advances continue to have a dramatic impact not only on how advertising research is conducted, but also on how results are disseminated and particularly in terms of the speed with which data can be collected and incorporated into management decisions. Yet, at the same time, consumer preferences and behaviors are changing ever more rapidly, making high-quality international advertising research more important, but at the same time more difficult to design and execute.

REFERENCES

Barnard, P. (1997), 'Global Developments and Future Directions in Market Research', MSI Seminar, *Globalization at the Millennium: Opportunities and Imperatives*, Brussels.

Baumgartner, H. and J.-B. E.M. Steenkamp (2001), 'Response Styles in Marketing Research: A Cross-National Investigation', *Journal of Marketing Research*, **38** (May), 143–56.

Berry, J.W. (1989), 'Imposed Etics, Emics and Derived Etics: The Operationalization of a Compelling Idea', *International Journal of Psychology*, **24**, 721–35.

Branthwaite, A. and P. Cooper (2001), 'A New Role for Projective Techniques', *Proceedings of ESOMAR Qualitative Research Conference*, ESOMAR, Budapest.

Brislin, Richard W. (1970), 'Back Translation for Cross-Cultural Research', *Journal of Cross-Cultural Psychology*, **1** (3), 185–216.

Brislin, Richard W. (1980), 'Translation and Content Analysis of Oral and Written Material', in H.C. Triandis and J.W. Berry (eds), *Handbook of Cross-cultural Psychology*, vol. 1, Boston: Allyn and Bacon, pp. 389–444.

Cho, Bongjin, Up Kwon, James W. Gentry, Sunkyu Ju and Fredric Krupp (1999), 'Cultural Values Reflected in Theme and Execution: A Comparative Study of U.S. and Korean Television Commercials', *Journal of Advertising*, **28** (4), 59.

Clark, I. III (2001), 'Extreme Response Style in Cross-Cultural Research', *International Marketing Review*, **18** (3), 301–24.

Cohen, S. and L. Neira (2004), 'Measuring Performance for Product Benefits Across Countries', *Excellence 2004 in International Research*, ESOMAR, Amsterdam, 1–22.

Craig, C.S. and S.P. Douglas (2005), *International Marketing Research*, 3rd ed. London: John Wiley & Sons.

Craig, C.S. and S.P. Douglas (2001), 'Conducting International Marketing Research in the 21st Century', *International Marketing Review*, **18**, 1.

Cutler, Bob D., G. Javalgi Rajshekhar and Lee Dongdae (1995), 'The Portrayal of People in Magazine Advertisements: The United States and Korea', *Journal of International Consumer Marketing*, **8** (2), 45.

Douglas, S.P. and C.S. Craig (2006), 'On Improving the Conceptual Foundations of International Marketing Research', *Journal of International Marketing*, **14** (1), 1–22.

Douglas, S.P. and C.S. Craig (2007), 'Collaborative and Iterative Translation: An Alternative Approach to Back Translation', *Journal of International Marketing*, **15** (1), 30–43.

Fischer, R. (2004), 'Standardization to Account for Cross-cultural Response Bias: A Classification of Score Adjustment Procedures and Review of Research in JCCP', *Journal of Cross-Cultural Psychology*, **35**, 263–82.

Furnham, Adrian, Staci Abramsky and Barrie Gunter (1997), 'A Cross-Cultural Content Analysis of Children's Television Advertisements', *Sex Roles*, **37** (1/2), 91.

Gilly, Mary C. (1988), 'Sex Roles in Advertising: A Comparison of Television Advertisements in Australia, Mexico, and the United States', *Journal of Marketing*, **52** (2), 75–85.

Gould, S.J., D.B. Lerman and A. Grein (1999), 'Agency Perceptions and Practices on Global IMC', *Journal of Advertising Research*, **39** (1), 7–20.

Grein, A and S.J. Ducoffe (1998), 'Strategic Responses to Market Globalization Among Advertising Agencies', *International Journal of Advertising*, **17** (3), 301–19.

Hader, S. and S. Gabler (2003), 'Sampling and Estimation', in J.A. Harkness, F.J.R. Van de Vijver and P. Ph. Mohler (eds) (2003), *Cross-Cultural Survey Methods*, Hoboken, NJ: John Wiley & Sons.

Hambleton, R.K. (1993), 'Translating Achievement Tests for Use in Cross-National Studies', *European Journal of Psychological Assessment*, **9**, 57–65.

Hambleton, R.K. (1994), 'Guidelines for Adapting Educational and Psychological Tests: A Progress Report', *European Journal of Psychological Assessment*, **10**, 229–44.

Han, Sang-Pil and Sharon Shavitt (1998), 'Persuasion and Culture: Advertising Appeals in Individualistic and Collectivistic Societies', *Journal of Experimental Social Psychology*, **30**, 326–50.

Harkness, J.A. (2003), 'Questionnaire Translation', in J.A. Harkness, F.J.R. Van de Vijver and P. Ph. Mohler (eds) (2003), *Cross-Cultural Survey Methods*, Hoboken, NJ: John Wiley & Sons.

Harkness, Janet A. and A. Schoua-Glusberg (1998), 'Questionnaires in Translation', in Janet A. Harkness (ed.), *ZUMA – Nachtrichten Spezial no. 3*, Cross-Cultural Survey Equivalence.

Harkness, J.A., F.J.R. Van de Vijner and P. Ph. Mohler (eds) (2003), *Cross-Cultural Survey Methods*, Hoboken, NJ: John Wiley & Sons.

International Journal of Advertising (2010), **29** (1), 9–140.

Mao, L.R. (1994), 'Beyond Politeness Theory: "Face" Revisited and Renewed', *Journal of Pragmatics*, **2**, 451–86.

Markus, H.R. and S. Kitayama (1991), 'Culture and the Self: Implications for Cognition, Emotion, and Motivation', *Psychological Review*, **98**, 224–53.

McKay, R.B., M.J. Breslow, R.L. Sangster, S.M. Gabbard, R.W. Reynolds, J.M. Nakamoto and J. Tarnai (1996), 'Translating Survey Questionnaires: Lessons Learned', *New Directions for Evaluation*, **70**, 93–105.

Miller, C. (1991), 'Anybody Ever Hear of Global Focus Groups?' *Marketing News*, 27 May, 14.

Mullen, M.R. (1995), 'Diagnosing Measurement Equivalence in Cross-National Research', *Journal of International Business Studies*, **26** (3), 573–96.

Myers, M.B., R.J. Calantone, T.J. Page Jr. and C.R. Taylor (2000), 'An Application of Multiple-Group Causal Models in Assessing Cross-Cultural Measurement Equivalence', *Journal of International Marketing*, **8** (4), 108–21.

Nakata, C. and Y. Huang (2002), 'Progress and Promise: The Last Decade of International Marketing Research', *AMA Educators' Proceedings: Enhancing Knowledge Development in Marketing*, vol. 13, W.J. Kehoe and J.H. Lindgren Jr. (eds), Chicago: American Marketing Association, 306–7.

Pawle, J.S. and P. Cooper (2002), 'Using Web Research Technology to Accelerate Innovation', *Excellence in International Research* 2002, ESOMAR, Amsterdam.

Przeworski, A. and H. Teune (1966), 'Equivalence in Cross-National Research', *Public Opinion Quarterly*, **30**, 551–68.

Reynolds, N.L., F. Langerak and A. Diamantopoulos (2003), 'Theoretical Justification of Sampling Choices in International Marketing Research: Key Issues and Guidelines for Researchers', *Journal of International Business Studies*, **34**, 80–89.

Russell, P., J. Deregowski and P. Kinner (1997), ' Perception and Aesthetics', in J.W. Berry, Y.H. Poortinga and J. Pandey (eds), *Handbook of Cross-Cultural Psychology*, vol. 2, Ally & Bacon, Boston, pp. 109–43.

Sears, R.R. (1961), 'Transcultural Variables and Conceptual Equivalence', in B. Kaplan (ed.), *Studying Personality Cross-Culturally*, Evanston, IL: Row, Peterson, & Co., 445–55.

Smith, Tom W. (2003), 'Developing Comparable Questions in Cross National Surveys', in J.A. Harkness, F.J.R. Van de Vijer and P. Ph. Mohler (eds), *Cross-Cultural Survey Methods*, Hoboken, NJ: John Wiley & Sons.

Steenkamp, J.-B.E.M. and H. Baumgartner (1998), 'Assessing Measurement Invariance in Cross-National Consumer Research', *Journal of Consumer Research*, **25** (June), 78–90.

Taylor, C.R. (2005), 'Moving International Advertising Research Forward', *Journal of Advertising*, **34** (1) 7–16.

Van de Vijver, Fons and R.K. Hambleton (1996), 'Translating Tests: Some Practical Guidelines', *European Psychologist*, **1**, 89–99.

Van de Vijver, F.J.R. and K. Leung (1997), *Methods and Data Analysis for Cross-Cultural Research*, Thousand Oaks, CA: Sage.

van Herk, H. (2003), *Equivalence in a Cross-National Context: Methodological and Empirical Issues In Marketing Research*, Tilburg: Tilburg University Press.

Zanasi, A. (2003), 'Email, Chat Lines, Newsgroups: A Continuous Opinions Survey Source Thanks to Text Mining', *Excellence in International Research 2003*, ESOMAR, Amsterdam.

Zhang, Yong and James P. Neelankavil (1997), 'The Influence of Culture on Advertising Effectiveness in China and the USA: A Cross-Cultural Study', *European Journal of Marketing*, **31** (2), 134.
www.esomar.org
www.greenbook.org
www.ipsoc.com/asi
www.millwardbrown.com

11 Sampling in international advertising research

Louisa Ha

IMPORTANCE AND CHALLENGES OF SAMPLING TO INTERNATIONAL ADVERTISING RESEARCH

International advertising is a field that focuses on finding the differences or similarities in advertising across different nations and how advertising from one country affects the other. In the process of finding examples or collecting data, a key issue is sampling. The topic of sampling is seldom discussed in the international advertising literature, but it is a crucial issue that determines the validity of the study and whether it can be generalizable to the populations under study. International advertising sampling typically has three levels. First is the selection of country to be studied. Second is the type of subjects to be studied such as consumers, advertisers or media advertising content. Third is the time period of the study. In this chapter, I will first explain why it is particularly important for international advertising researchers to pay special attention to sampling in international advertising studies and the problems of sampling in current international advertising research, and then I will show the various applications of different sampling methods in international advertising. I will conclude with some suggestions that can improve sampling in the field of international advertising research.

The term "international advertising" is about advertising in different nations and between nations. But what constitutes a nation? Is it a country with national borders, a race or ethnicity, or is it a culture? This is a unit of analysis issue. Most "international advertising" studies use "country" as the unit to represent a nation. But in the real world, there are different "countries" that have one nation with the same cultural, language and ethnic heritage: North Korea and South Korea, Mainland China and Taiwan. When a study refers to Korean advertising, most likely it is about advertising in South Korea and can only be generalizable to the Koreans in South Korea. A country can represent many different variables for use in international advertising research. Some common ones are political system, legal system, economic system and advertising development, history, cultural norms and customs, and language. Within a country, there are different socio-economic classes, ethnic and demographic groups. Hence when comparing advertising in different countries, if the researchers do not specify the unit of analysis clearly, it is not sure which variable they want to study and to which population in the country the results can infer upon. If the unit of analysis is a culture using categories such as low-context and high-context culture (Hall, 1976), then the choice of country is extremely important because the country is chosen to represent that culture. There can be many choices of countries to represent a certain culture. Culturally similar countries may still exhibit dissimilar advertising practices because of other factors. A study of advertising content in three Arabic countries (Egypt, Lebanon and the United Arab Emirates) shows specific differences in ad elements in a culturally similar setting with socio-economic differences among nations (Karande, Almurshidee and Al-Olayan, 2006). Culturally normative ad content, such as the depiction of women consistent with societal norms, is predominantly culture driven, and standardization is appropriate, regardless of socio-economic differences, but product-related content such as information content, the use of hedonic vs utilitarian appeals, and the provision of price information are influenced by both cultural and socio-economic factors.

Alber-Miller's (1996) study of paired comparisons of advertising values in 11 countries suggests that there are at least three possible reasons for the prevalence of significant results in cross-cultural research – meaningless differences in advertising content detected by overly powerful statistical tests, meaningful differences in advertising resulting from variation in target audience or communication style, and meaningful differences in advertising resulting from genuine cultural difference. The proper sample design will minimize the meaningless difference and highlight the meaningful difference. Another good example of using multiple factors in addition to country culture, illustrating much more of the similarities and differences in advertising strategy use, is Nelson and Paek's (2008) study on nudity of female and male models in TV advertising in seven countries (Brazil, Canada, China, Germany, South Korea, Thailand and the United States). It reveals that cultural values (masculinity/femininity) and advertising regulation play only minimal roles in explaining the degree of nudity in TV advertising. Congruent product category appears to be the most significant predictor, supporting a match-up hypothesis and congruency theory. By adding non-cultural factors in cross-national comparison, the results will be more robust and the predictive power of the results will be much stronger than a study that is limited to cultural factors only.

International advertising studies can be single country studies or multiple country studies. The sampling issue is simpler in single country studies because they can follow basically the rules established for sampling especially when the study is just about advertising practice or issue in a country other than the U.S. (I don't want to sound U.S.-centric. Unfortunately, the current definition of international (or foreign) in mainstream journals published in the U.S. or even the United Kingdom is just another country not U.S. or U.K. Ironically, to U.S. journals, British advertising is categorized as international advertising.) But then within single country study such as how U.S. advertising affects Chinese consumers' perception of the U.S., there are two countries involved and so the sample should well-represent U.S. advertising in China and Chinese consumers respectively. When the study becomes multiple country studies, then the issue of equivalence and logistics of sampling in different countries pose a complex challenge to international advertising researchers.

Sampling is the process of using a smaller number of units from the population to represent the whole population. It offers a cost-effective way to get the same results without the need to include everyone in the population. However, this power of generalization is based on statistical inference and probability theory. There are three critical issues in sample design (Henry, 1990). First is the population definition. Researchers should be concerned about the consistency of the target population and the study population because the study population can yield biased results by including members not in the target population or omitting members who should be in the target population. Second is the sampling method. When some population members (countries or demographic groups) are more likely to be selected than others, the results will also be biased. Third is the precision of the estimate. We have to understand that all samples yield only estimates, not the exact number. There are sampling errors that we need to bear in mind when drawing conclusions from the results. There is a difference between sample and response or participation. Samples are those that you try to collect information from. To identify the sample, you need a sampling frame or a list of people, media entities, companies or countries to represent your population. Responses or participants are those that are willing to participate. Usually there is a discrepancy between the sample and the responses/participants because data are either not available or the sample cannot be reached or they do not want or refuse to participate. Sampling errors can be controlled and estimated, unlike non-response bias that the researchers can only make efforts to minimize but have no control over (Lastovicka, 1985).

In international advertising research, population definition is usually defined at the country or ethnic group level or at the subgroup of students or adolescents. Whether the country is representing a larger concept such as Western or Eastern culture and is to be generalized as such, may not be clear. Although there is a tendency to implicitly conclude the results as the characteristics of the culture, because of the judgmental nature of country selection, authors should be cautious not to generalize the results to the population of countries in that culture. Owing to data accessibility, sampling methods chosen by the international advertising researchers are more likely to be non-probability-based than probability-based. Without a probability-based sample, it will be hard to compute the sampling error with precision.

SAMPLING DECISIONS IN INTERNATIONAL ADVERTISING RESEARCH

Sampling inevitably involves four principal questions: 1) How should the sample be selected? 2) How large should it be? 3) How should the population characteristics be estimated? 4) How reliable are these estimates? (Tryfos, 1996). To answer the first question of how the sample should be selected, let us review the six common approaches to sampling (Maisel and Persell, 1996):

1. Census and pseudo-census: Every member in the population is included in the study. So it is not using any sample. For example, a census of advertising agencies is all registered advertising agencies in the country you want to study. Usually it is very costly to conduct a census unless the population is small when it cannot take advantage of the saving from sampling. But not everyone will participate or be accessible in the study. When you are not able to reach everyone but you attempted to reach them, such as the U.S. Census, then it can be considered as pseudo-census. So the bias that you will get in a census is not sampling bias, but non-response bias. It is very rare if not impossible in international advertising research that a census is used to collect data.
2. Self-selected sample: Samples are obtained via a public announcement either in mass media such as television or newspapers or some public forum or e-mail list. Anyone willing to respond will be accepted as participants. It can be alternatively called volunteer sample. The bias you will get in this type of sample is the self-selection bias. Only those who volunteer themselves will be included in the data.
3. Convenience sample: A sample of cases that is most easily accessible by the researcher such as those people living in the neighborhood or students of the researcher's class. Because of the ease of obtaining consent and participation, most of the student samples in international advertising studies are a convenience sample.

4. Typical case: This is a very deliberate choice of choosing one or a few "typical cases" judged by the researcher meeting the criteria for the study. For example, China is chosen as a "typical" Communist country to study or Iran is chosen as a Muslim country to study. Unfortunately, most international advertising studies' typical case is taken for granted more by convenience or accessibility to the researcher than it being the best representation of the variable.

5. Quota sample: A set number of samples with specific established criteria, and the recruitment of samples being stopped after that number of samples was achieved. For example, 50 advertising practitioners from each country were set as the quota to complete the study. So even though more than 50 wanted to participate, only the first 50 responses were accepted.

6. Probability sample: This is a sample selected by a randomized procedure so that every member of the population has an equal chance of being selected, that is, known probability or non-zero probability for everyone in the population. To create a probability sample, the population must be well-defined and the sampling frame is complete to allow for a random procedure to draw the sample. So if the study is about comparing broadcast television advertising in the U.S. and China, then a probability sampling will be to select a time period (e.g., a randomly selected week out of a randomly selected month or a constructed week) to represent broadcast TV advertising in the U.S. and China, then within that time period, a random selection of national TV networks or local stations (or just limited to national broadcast advertising), then a particular hour of commercials on those selected TV networks or stations to be recorded and analyzed.

The question of sample size is a question of both cost constraint and desired accuracy level. It is well-known that the larger the sample (if they are probability-based samples), the lower the sampling error and people tend to give more credibility to a larger sample. But researchers always have budget limits and many have to carry out projects with little or no funding. The ideal sample size should be "large enough" to yield accurate results and represent the population and to avoid making wrong decisions and inferences by detecting the falsity of the basic hypothesis, but also at an affordable cost to the researcher. Hence an efficient sample size for a descriptive study must provide a sufficient level of precision needed for the estimate. In analytical studies with relationship inferences, the sample size must be large enough to detect the size of the effect. This would require a statistical power analysis. Most efficient sample size estimation is based on a simple random sample design (Henry, 1990). If the sample design deviates from simple random sampling, the efficient sample size will change. For example, cluster sampling will increase sampling variability while stratified sampling will decrease sampling variability. Readers interested in the degree of sample design effect in affecting efficient sample size can refer to Henry's (1990) book on sampling.

The characteristics of the population are both a conceptual and factual challenge to researchers. A successful sample captures the estimates of the variables and attributes of interest among the population. Some of those population characteristics are known to the researcher in advance, such as gender and education based on census data. If those characteristics are already known, then it is a matter of fact checking by comparing the sample's distribution with the population data. But, more often, the variables that researchers are studying have no available prior population estimates. Then it will be up to the researcher to clearly identify what characteristics of the population they need to examine or control. The more comprehensive is the list of the variables of interest in the population that may affect the result of the study, the more able is the researcher to explain the results obtained from the sample and estimate the bias the sample has on those variables. In international advertising, one major difference that researchers must be aware of is the difference in media ownership and control system. In some countries, television stations are state owned or publicly owned, but in other countries, the television stations are commercially owned and profit-driven. When comparing the advertising practices in these populations, then state ownership becomes an important population characteristic to be taken into consideration.

The reliability of the sampling estimate to represent the population estimate is not perfect, even if it is based on the probability sample, because of the various sampling and non-response errors. However, one can identify the margin of error with probability statistics if one uses a probability sample. In international advertising studies, the choice of sample is multi-leveled. The first level is the choice of countries to be studied. Usually the number of countries selected is so small that it is more a typical case than anything else. To justify the countries selected as a typical case is more qualitative than quantitative. Yet the inherent assumptions or variables of interest still need to be reported so that one can judge if the country is the best representation of the variables to be studied. Second is the choice of the subjects, which may be advertising content or consumers or advertisers/agencies. It is at this level that sampling estimates makes the most sense and the researcher can strive to get a good estimate through an appropriate sample design with an efficient sample size.

FOUR MAJOR CHALLENGES TO SAMPLING IN INTERNATIONAL ADVERTISING

Before we discuss different sampling strategies and their applications in international advertising, I want to address the four major challenges in international advertising: 1) language barriers, 2) cost to collect data and cross-country project coordination, 3) equivalency in sampling frame and population definition, 4) accessibility of data, especially if synchronous data information is required. The difference in languages used by different countries is a well-known problem in international advertising. Most cross-cultural research emphasizes the importance of achieving equivalency in translation of research questions to respondents of different countries (Harkness, Vijver and Mohler, 2003). Otherwise, the difference may be an artifact of the language used, not the real difference in the subject matter. In addition, if incorrect translation is used, the respondent may misunderstand the question and is not able to give a valid answer to the question. But, in sampling, the language poses a severe limitation because researchers know only a limited number of languages and have to rely on the local native researchers for translation and access to the data (e.g., foreign ads) and recruitment of subjects or participants. The extra effort to do the translation or reliance on local native researcher availability (many of them are international graduate students who may not have as sophisticated a research level as the researcher) led to a preference of either English-language speaking countries in the sample (e.g., the U.S., Australia, Canada, the U.K.) or mother language of the researchers/co-researchers (e.g., Chinese, Korean, Spanish, etc.).

The cost to collect data across countries is generally higher than domestic research. Just the high shipping cost of research materials and supplies (if one is doing the old fashion print ad comparison for example). International long-distance phone calls are much more expensive than local calls especially in the developing countries. In addition, there are also time zone differences and language differences. Hence there are almost no international phone surveys in international advertising research. Multi-local phone surveys, however, are more feasible. Sampling internationally is more likely to be geographic clusters in the countries accessible to researchers.

Intracountry variation (Ewing, Salzberger and Sinkovics 2005; Leonartowicz, Johnson and White, 2003) is another important factor affecting sampling equivalency. Let us use the example of college students as student samples. In developing countries, college education is for elites only and they represent the brightest and most privileged class in the country. In industrialized countries such as the U.S., a substantial portion of the population has access to higher education and college education is not limited to the top 2 to 3 percent of the country. Their worldview will be quite different from those who are the elites in their country. The elitist college students, who are more likely to be more critical of the society and have high self-esteem, are not as likely to be influenced by advertising as those of their general college student counterparts in an industrialized country. So the researchers must be cautioned on the inferences drawn from college student samples in different countries on subjects such as their attitudes toward advertising. The sample design can compromise the validity of the results unless the researchers can show the equivalency of the college student sample.

Another intracountry factor is the geographical subcultures in a country. Sparkman (1996) notes that advertising content variation occurs at a sub-national level. He suggests that local ads be distinguished from national ads in content analysis especially in television when national ads and local ads appear at the same time in prime-time television. His study of 163 published articles on U.S. media ad content shows that 97 percent of them contain both local/regional and national ads but most of them claim to represent the national U.S. advertising. In addition, there is also variation at the societal/national level versus individual cultural values. Terlutter, Diehl and Mueller's (2010) five-country study also shows the difference between national and respondents' individual perceived assertiveness in each country. The difference in societal and individual values on assertiveness is very high in Austria and Argentina, while the difference in societal and individual values assertiveness is low in the U.S., the United Kingdom and Germany.

As Koslow and Costley's (2010) recent multifaceted analysis on an international advertising data set of cross-country responses to humor in advertising shows, individuals within countries accounted for much more variance than countries could account for. Person differences are up to six times larger than country differences. They concluded that both between- and within-country heterogeneity should influence international advertising strategies. They pointed out that comparing means between two culturally heterogeneous countries can be misleading when the means cannot reflect the characteristics of the subgroup, especially if there are high subgroup variations. By only focusing on national differences, researchers could easily rush to the conclusion to favor localization strategies.

Hence to establish equivalency in population and sampling frames, the researchers must understand well the difference that may affect the results of the study even if the population is supposed to be equivalent. Apart from the college student sample discussed above, ethnic minority is another problematic population to compare across countries. Different countries have different policies toward their ethnic minorities and the reasons why the minority exists (by voluntary immigration or by annexation of neighboring countries or by colonial heritage) play a role in how the minority is treated and perceived in the country of study. For example, in China, the ethnic minorities are a result of annexation throughout the history of China. But in the U.S., the ethnic minorities are created through legal or illegal immigration, slavery, and the conquering of the natives of the U.S.

Another important factor to be considered in the selection of countries is the advertising industry standards and regulations. When a study focuses on these variables, they are analyzed carefully by the researchers. However, when these variables are not examined, they become potential confounds that affect the results of the study. For example, if a researcher compares the advertising strategies of different countries or how multinational advertisers choose standardization or localization strategies without controlling and examining the advertising industry standards of those countries or regulations, the differences may be artifacts of those factors rather than culture, the choice of the strategies or the perceived effectiveness of the strategies. In addition, many regulations are rooted in the history of the country and its advertising industry development. Those contextual factors must be taken into consideration when conclusions are made on those strategies.

The decision of sampling is a trade-off between the purpose of a study, its costs, and its potential for error. As explained earlier, if we are clear on the unit of analysis and the variables to study, then we can develop a sampling strategy appropriate to the study. This is true for a single domestic country study or any comparative studies. But in international advertising, the problems are exacerbated because of the inaccessibility of data, limited country expertise of the researchers, and the costs of coordinating an international data collection.

A previous study on communication research on Greater China showed that country studies on China were dominated by ethnic scholars originally from that China (Ha and Pratt, 2000). The familiarity, home country ties and accessibility factors play a very important role in shaping the productivity of the research on international advertising. In another Asian advertising review study (Ha, 2010), I also illustrated the importance of ethnic scholars in Asian advertising research. The country distribution in Asian advertising studies can be mainly attributed to the number of ethnic scholars in the field, not in terms of advertising expenditure of that country. Hence the ethnic scholar factor then shapes the sampling of countries in international advertising research. Other than the United States, the regions that are over-sampled in international advertising research are

Asia and Europe, as shown in reviews of international advertising research published in the *Journal of Advertising* (Taylor, 2005) and *International Marketing Review* (Okazaki and Mueller, 2007). Notwithstanding international advertising as a subfield, authors of five major advertising journals (*Journal of Advertising, Journal of Advertising Research, Journal of Current Issues and Research in Advertising, International Journal of Advertising* and *Journal of Marketing Communication*) from 1998 to 2007 were also predominantly from U.S. institutions (Polonsky and Carlson, 2009).

One other item is the equivalence of the time period of the study. In a multi-country study, the same time may not be equivalent. The summer months in the northern hemisphere are not the same as those of the southern hemisphere. Different countries have different holidays and festivities that will affect the advertising practices of that time. As a researcher, do we want to find the peak (atypical) season or the low season to study the advertising practice of the country? If we want the results to be generalizable across the year, then one may want to avoid both the peak and low seasons to be the typical case. The constructed week is a good method to create a time frame that is less subject to seasonal fluctuation and meet the probability sampling (it is explained in more details in my discussion on content analysis in subsequent sections).

The final challenge I would like to address is the accessibility of data especially if synchronous data information is required. The impact of a global advertising campaign, for example, will definitely require synchronous data because global effect across different countries is expected. The coordination of different countries to collect data is complex and it requires careful planning to obtain support from various countries' research teams. Currently there is little mechanism that exists to facilitate international collaboration except individual researchers' own networks to conduct such studies. To truly internationalize advertising studies so that synchronous data can be obtained and multiple country data can be comparable, it is necessary to establish mechanisms that facilitate the process.

SAMPLING APPLICATIONS IN DIFFERENT RESEARCH METHODS

Although not much has been written in international advertising sampling, we may be able to learn from other sampling research in the advertising field in general. Below are the sampling problems and solutions that can be applied in the three most common research methods in international advertising: 1) Survey, 2) Content Analysis, and 3) Experiment.

1. Survey

Finding a good sampling frame poses the greatest sampling problem to survey research. There are different types of population posing different problems. Industry professionals are one type of population. Kaldenberg and Becker's (1990) study shows that inappropriate use of the sampling frame is a problem in the 22 studies on professionals' attitudes toward advertising they examined. The key question is: Are all members of a profession equally represented? Non-membership in professional associations is quite common among the younger, non-private practice professionals. Their study comparing different sampling frames of dentists shows significant differences in demographics and attitudes toward advertising between the dentists who are members and those who are non-members of dentist professional associations, and those who are and are not listed in the phone book. Ideally, when one begins doing a survey, one should obtain a list that includes everyone in the population. If a complete list is not available, the researcher may consider the appropriateness of narrowing the scope of the analysis (and resulting generalizations) to fit the list available to the researcher.

In international advertising, the availability of equivalent lists in different countries to sample is a great problem. Many times the researcher has to be creative in compiling their own lists from multiple sources from scratch. Rather than criticizing the researcher for not having an authoritative list covering the entire population, we should examine how the list was compiled and what kind of bias might exist from such a compilation, and interpret the results with those compilation limitations in mind. We can follow the same rule above by narrowing the scope of generalization with a non-complete list.

Consumers are another common population for international advertising research. Telephone surveys are a common way to collect data from consumers. Apart from the sample list, another sampling frame issue in telephone surveys arose from the origin of the telephone numbers. It can be from a telephone directory or by computer-generated random digit numbers. The study by Segal and Hekmat (1985) shows that random dialing samples can produce a higher response rate than the conventional telephone directory sample. In addition, the telephone directories-based random digit numbers produce a higher percentage of non-working numbers and non-residential numbers when compared to computer-generated random digit dialing procedures. The demographic difference is substantial: A higher proportion of random digit dialing samples were younger in age, single and low income as compared with their counterparts in the conventional telephone directory sample. The increasing penetration of mobile phones creates another problem for telephone survey research. Should and can mobile phone users be reached for survey research? Omitting mobile phone users will pose severe problems for younger consumers. Before deciding on using phone surveys, researchers should examine the mobile phone penetration in the countries under study and estimate how many of the population will be omitted by using regular phone surveys.

Lastovicka (1985) recommends a disproportionate stratified sample rather than a simple random sample in surveys of advertisers and agencies because, by grouping these entities into strata, researchers can estimate the sampling error based on the homogeneity of each stratum. Those strata such as larger advertisers and agencies that have high variability on the variable that researchers are interested to study should be over-sampled, while those strata such as small advertisers and agencies that are homogeneous should be under-sampled. Applying such principles to international advertising, large multinational advertising agencies may need to be over-sampled while local ad agencies should be under-sampled to obtain a full picture of advertising practices in different countries.

A recent study on consumer ethnocentrism by Puzakova, Kwak and Andras (2010) can illustrate how one can estimate sampling error with a convenient sample of college students in a single country study but having a cross-national perspective. Russia was selected by the researchers as a representative of a transitional economy. Their study examined consumer ethnocentrism's negative influence on Russians' attitudes towards foreign products and their frequency of purchase of foreign products. The researchers compared their consumer ethnocentrism score with the findings of previous studies on consumer ethnocentrism in Russia and also another 19 countries. They put the comparison in context without the need to conduct a multi-country study. The increase in ethnocentrism of Russian consumers is evidence to the proposition that, as a country is moving towards a more developed economy and domestic products are improving in quality, consumers will have higher levels of ethnocentrism. The relationship between consumer ethnocentrism and frequency of purchase of foreign products is moderated by consumers' exposure to television and foreign product advertising. Ethnocentric consumers with higher exposure to television will tend to purchase foreign products more frequently than ethnocentric consumers with lower exposure to television. Although the sample is a convenient sample – undergraduate college students in one university in Russia – because the authors consulted other literature to put the consumer ethnocentrism (CE) score in that study in context with other Russian market studies and other countries, they could examine how far off the students' scores were in comparison with other studies.

The five-country study by Ralf Terlutter, Sandra Diehl and Barbara Mueller (2010) on responses to a standardized advertising message with assertiveness showed how respondents are recruited by convenience but they are comparable and equivalent for the purpose of their study. Their sample consisted of 714 non-student respondents from the U.S., Germany, the U.K., Austria and Argentina. In all countries, participants were drawn from mid-sized cities and represented a broad spectrum of professions. Respondents were recruited on public property such as public streets, at the entrance to walking/jogging parks, on public transportation (trains), as well as in cafés. Although they could not claim to generalize the results to the entire population for each country, because they were an equivalent sample, they could achieve their goal of comparing the values and the generalizability of the effectiveness of an assertive standardized advertising message.

Another way to obtain a representative national sample without incurring a high cost is to incorporate the study in an omnibus survey of international market research firms. Millan and Mittal's (2010) survey of a national sample of Czech consumers' attitudes toward advertising is such an effort so that they can obtain costly face-to-face interview data to represent the national population.

2.   Content Analysis

In advertising content analysis, one issue is the geography of the ads being sampled. This is particularly important in international advertising research where geography is the key variable. Sparkman (1996) points out that a majority of the advertising information content analysis studies were misrepresented as national studies as their samples were based on limited geographic areas. Laband (1989) contends that the difference between Dowling's (1980) results for Australian ads with Resnik and Stern's (1977) study of U.S. ads was partly caused by their high proportion of regional content.

In television advertising content analysis, the sampling problem will be identifying the object in the video and counting the occurrence of a certain image. Anandathirtha et al. (2009) proposed the sampling of video objects using enhanced experiential sampling method. The method entails taking into account temporal continuity in video, various visual cues and the dynamic nature of video. For each frame, some statistical samples following attention density, called *attention samples*, are determined. Only those objects in the attention samples will be detected. This method results in 6 times faster average time used and 50 times fewer samples needed to get the same result as the frame-based method.

Another important sampling problem for content analysis is the time period to be selected for analysis. Constructed week is a way to sample the time period of media content or advertising which is probability based. The basis of constructed week is that available media content and advertising fluctuates on different days of the week (Riffe, Aust and Lacy, 1993). To have a better representation of the advertising for the whole time period such as the year of 2010, it is better to randomly select one of each day of the week in the year, so that Monday, Tuesday, Wednesday, Thursday, Friday, Saturday and Sunday are all included but they are not in the same week. The constructed week was originally developed for newspaper analysis. But it is equally applicable to other media as well because the amount and type of advertising varies on different days of the week. To utilize this time period sampling method, the international researcher must plan in advance on the chosen period, construct the week with specific dates and obtain support from local field workers to collect data on different days rather than consecutive days. This will be more complex than a convenient sample of consecutive days but it will yield more a representative result of the time period under study rather than a snapshot of one time.

The recent content analysis of TV commercials in four Asian countries (Australia, Hong Kong, Singapore and Malaysia) conducted by Lwin, Stranland and Williams (2010) is a good example of sample design for content analysis of international TV advertising. In their study, a random sample of television commercials aired over the same ten-day period in each country, while avoiding important holidays or special events, were used to prevent a large amount of ads with symbols specific to a particular culture which might bias the sample. Two hours of non-prime-time programming and two hours of prime-time programming were videotaped daily, based on the rotation principle developed to ensure that the commercials collected were representative of network, day and time segment. Overall, 4218 commercials were collected from 200 hours of programming time. Repeated commercials for the same brand were eliminated in order to avoid bias commercials for the same brand that differed in more than 50 percent of the content. All non-commercial and station announcements were removed. The final sample consisted of 973 commercials. The selection procedures resulted in less than one quarter of the commercials collected. But the selected commercials were a valid sample to use to analyze the use of country symbols for the purpose of the study.

3. Experiments

Experiment is a common method to test the effect of advertising. In international advertising when advertisers try to create a standardized message across countries, it is even more important to conduct a pre-test using experiments to increase the chance of success. In a study of sample size for ad copy pre-test, Dalal and Srintvasan (1977) demonstrated that, as the sample size is increased, sampling variations decrease so that the pre-test has a better chance to correctly identify the truly most effective ad. They proposed a minimizing maximum loss approach to compute the optimal sample size which explicitly considers opportunity and sampling costs and the number of ad versions to be compared. The fewer the number of versions needs to be compared, the smaller the opportunity cost. When the sample cost is higher, the lower the optimal sample size the researcher should expect.

Sometimes, examination of the effect of culture does not require collecting samples from multiple countries, especially if the variable is about the effect of specific cultural elements of the advertising content. For example, Shen and Chen's (2006) lab experiment on Taiwanese college students' responses to cultural congruity by mixing Eastern and Western music and ad message in shampoo advertising is a simple way to gauge whether a cultural approach to the ad needs to be consistent or can be different between ad message and music. Subjects were randomly assigned music-congruent vs. the music-incongruent conditions and they also measured students' attention to the ads. They found that an ad with culturally incongruent background music strengthens consumer memory of the ad when compared with the same ad containing culturally congruent music. This incongruity effect on memory is more pronounced in high-attention consumers than in low-attention consumers. But they also note the backlash effect of incongruent message-music causing negative attitudes towards the ad despite a higher memory. For researchers with limited resources and no access to foreign collaborators, lab experiments with a good cultural-related variable can provide great insights for international advertising strategy decision. Another example can be found in how to advertise to bilinguals, and understanding the code-switching, the alternation between two or more languages in the same conversation, is another challenge to international advertising. The experiment by Bishop and Peterson (2010) examined how code-switch should be used to appeal to the dual identities of bilinguals through the use of two languages. It showed that the language of the medium where the code-switch ad was placed affects the effectiveness of the ad. Their study's sample was a convenience sample. Individuals of Mexican descent ages 18 to 30 who were literate to some degree in English and Spanish were recruited to participate in the study. Subjects came from three youth groups, one Mexican-American group, and two local fund-raisers. Because the study focuses on the code-switch process and the effect of the language of the medium on bilinguals, rather than whether Hispanic American population code-switches bilingual ads, the sample was appropriate for the study.

In addition, online experiments are a good method to recruit technology-savvy subjects simultaneously across countries at a low cost. If the research topic is about response to online advertising, then online experiments should overcome the external validity threat of a lab setting and eliminate the cost of asking subjects to come to the lab to do the experiment. The sample size will be larger and can span across many different countries easily. The key is then to establish the adequate credibility of the researcher to recruit subjects from different countries online. The log data that online media and tracking software automatically generates can provide additional accuracy of records for the use of the researcher.

HOW TO CREATE A MORE BALANCED SAMPLE IN INTERNATIONAL ADVERTISING RESEARCH

As discussed above, one of the fundamental problems in sampling in international advertising research is the accessibility of data to researchers. To improve the sample design in international advertising, I recommend three solutions: 1) establish an international researcher registry for conducting research across nations and especially encourage researchers from developing countries to participate; 2) clarify the "international" variables that researchers want to study and identify the equivalent population in each unit; and 3) take advantage of the online medium if it is important to obtain synchronous data and the Internet is your target of study.

Because of data accessibility and the cost of international advertising research, it is much more feasible to conduct a multi-local study and involve researchers from different countries to provide local insights and access to local information. Nonetheless, the current unequal development in advertising research naturally favors certain countries (English-speaking countries and those home countries of advertising researchers residing in the Western world). To correct this imbalance, the research community should establish an international advertising research registry where researchers interested in international advertising all over the world can register. Researchers in the developing countries can benefit from collaborating research with scholars in the Western world so that they can get access to their expertise and publication opportunities in mainstream research publications. Each scholar can provide their research interest, location, and their vita online. Users can identify potential collaborators through the registry by searching for location and topic interest. Successful partnership can lead to co-authorship of research publications.

Co-authorship criteria can be established in the registry. With a win–win mutual beneficial relationship, such a registry can facilitate the collaboration of researchers across the world. With the increasing access to the Internet by the academic community around the world, such a registry can be very handy to researchers and be easily updated. Advertising associations such as the American Academy of Advertising, the Advertising Division of the Association for Education in Journalism and Mass Communication (AEJMC), or the International Advertising Association can play an active role in facilitating the establishment of such a registry. To encourage scholars to register themselves in the registry, it should be a free service and be well advertised among the advertising research community all over the world, especially in developing countries. One easy way to facilitate this process is to put the members of the American Academy of Advertising, Advertising Division members of AEJMC and the International Advertising Association automatically to the registry with an opt-out option so that a large database can be built immediately for the registry. It will serve as a publicity service for those who are registered because their works are showcased to researchers around the world. All research articles published by members of the registry as a result of the international collaboration will be featured on the website.

To illustrate how such a registry may work and improve sample design, let us use a hypothetical case. A researcher in the United States would like to study how foreign advertising (especially from Western countries) affects consumers in Arabic countries. He or she first outlines his ideal sample of Arabic countries and Western countries, and does not need to restrict himself/herself on which country he or she has contacts in. Two Arabic countries (one from the Middle East and one from North Africa) will be chosen to represent Arabic countries. Based on population size, Egypt and Iran are chosen as the country sample. Two Western countries (the U.S. and France) will be chosen based on the high advertising spending of these countries in the selected Arabic markets. This U.S. researcher has contacts in Iran but no contact in Egypt, then he/she can post a call for a collaborator or look under the registry to see if there is any researcher in advertising from Egypt who is already in the registry, and directly contact the Egyptian researcher. If the U.S. researcher is not very familiar with French multinational advertising, then the researcher can also do the same procedure to find a research collaborator from France. Then the collaborators can decide how best to obtain an equivalent probability sample or convenience sample for the market. If TV commercials are determined as the best for studying the impact, because TV is the most important medium, then the collaborators can work on a good sampling period for the two countries which includes time and dates to be collected, knowing that the periods and times are equivalent in the two countries. In addition the TV channels to be recorded can be based on the popularity or ratings (if available). Data collection will be done by researchers in Iran and Egypt locally where videotaping is easy to do.

During the collaboration, the U.S. researcher will develop the coding scheme with input from the local collaborators. The coding could be completed in Iran and Egypt and the U.S. researchers can just use the coding sheets for data analysis. Coders can be native graduate students or researchers. Coder reliability can be computed after a random sample of the collected commercials was chosen for double coding. Or to be safe, the researchers in Iran and Egypt can send some of the video recordings to the U.S. researcher and French researcher for checking. The U.S. and French researcher can write up the findings and do the data analysis, and obtain local insights from the local collaborators in Iran and Egypt. These four collaborators will share authorship, with the U.S. researcher being the lead author because the original idea for the research and design and primary writing is done by the U.S. researcher. The rest of the authorship should be based on the contribution from each collaborator in the study. For the same project, if the initiator is the researcher from Iran who also contributed the most to the study, the same process applies (i.e., the Iranian researcher finds collaborators in the U.S., France and Egypt) but then the Iranian researcher will be the lead author for any resulting publication.

To clarify the "international" variables that researchers want to study and identify the equivalent population in each unit, one way to do it is to identify some common variable such as culture, which may draw from standardized schemes such as Hofstede's (1980) cultural dimensions or House et al.'s (2004) GLOBE (Global Leadership and Organization Behavior Effectiveness Research Program) cultural framework. Other unique variables such as economic development may use GDP per capita or advertising expenditure per capita and then place difference countries on the scale measure. After clearly defining the international variable you are interested to study, then select the countries that either best represent those variables (judgmental) or are available to the researcher (convenient). The next challenge is to find the equivalent group in each country. For example, in comparing college students in the U.S. versus those in India, it must be noted that it is much more competitive for Indian students to be in college, and their status as college students puts them as the elite class in their society, unlike U.S. colleges that are more commonplace and accessible to the general population. To make the sample equivalent, the choice of universities in each country should represent similar student profiles in order to draw meaningful apple to apple comparisons. One way to achieve equivalency can be comparing elitist students in India with elitist universities in the U.S., such as the Ivy League schools. Researchers should document such equivalency in their description of sampling and make no assumption that all college students around the world are equivalent.

In studying advertising standardization, cultural and geographic proximity is a common variable to explain the choice of the standardization strategy. The definition of cultural and geographic proximity will allow a list of options available and the researcher has to justify why a country was selected to represent cultural or geographic proximity to the host or home country among all possible options. Accessibility of data to the researcher is certainly a good justification, but the researcher should also note whether the omission of other countries may affect the result with confounding factors such as country population size, economic power, etc.

Studying international advertising online can overcome some of the problems I discussed above. Simple random sample of countries is possible by the domain name of the website. With the increasing popularity of webcasting and broadband in many developed countries, it is also possible to research on the television (video) on the Web. In essence, the world is in the researcher's hand if the researcher is interested in online advertising or online advertising behavior. Without the physical barrier of geographic border, the researcher can collect online advertising around the world at the same time and make direct comparison without additional cost. As long as the researcher possesses knowledge about the population, such as how to identify the leading websites in the country of study, the researcher can conduct a multi-country advertising comparison easily. So the choice of sample can be greatly widened to any country in which the researcher is able to understand its language, and is not restricted to countries in which the researcher has close ties. Certainly, the knowledge and interest about the country will be a factor in the country's choice. But at least it is possible for a researcher to conduct a study on the U.S., Brazilian and Korean online advertising strategy with ease and look at how the same multinational advertiser presents itself in several countries at the same time.

Online advertising not only presents a good opportunity to do a cross-national content analysis, but is also an easy way to incorporate an online experiment or online survey across countries as well. For example, the researcher can place different variations of an online banner ad campaign for a multinational advertiser on websites in many countries, and see the click-through rates or other measures of advertising responses to determine if certain advertising appeals or creative strategies will work for certain countries. Or the researcher can place an online survey using different local languages in prominent websites of targeted countries/markets to gauge responses on advertising topics such as attitudes toward advertising in general or for specific products. If the population is defined as English proficient online users of the countries under study, a uniform English language online survey can be administered instead of a multi-language survey, because English is the most common second language in the world. Even though all online data collection will be limited to the online population of the countries under study, as long as the study defines the population as online users of the countries and a probability sample was used, then the results can be representative of the country.

To conclude, emphasizing the issue of sampling in international advertising research is not to erect more barriers to studying international advertising, but to enhance the quality and inferential power of the data in international advertising research. With proper sampling design, international advertising research is well positioned to contribute more robust theories that can be applicable to more countries, reveal the true differences and similarities of advertising across countries and explain the process of how one nation's advertising affects other nations.

REFERENCES

Albers-Miller, Nancy D. (1996), 'Designing cross-cultural advertising research: A closer look at paired comparisons', *International Marketing Review*, **13** (5), 59–75.

Anandathirtha, Paresh, K.R. Ramakrishnan, S. Kumar Raja and Mohan S. Kankanhalli (2009), 'Experiential sampling for object detection in video', in A. Divakaran (ed.), *Multimedia Content Analysis, Signals and Communication Technology*, NY: Springer, pp. 175–206.

Dalal, Siddhartha R. and V. Srintvasanj (1977), 'Determining sample size for pretesting comparative effectiveness of advertising copies', *Management Science*, **23** (12), 1284–94.

Dowling, Grahame R. (1980), 'Information content in U.S. and Australian television advertising', *Journal of Marketing*, **44**, 34–7.

Millan, Elena S. and Banwari Mittal (2010), 'Advertising's new audiences: Consumer response in the new free market economies of central and Eastern Europe – The case of the Czech Republic,' *Journal of Advertising,* **39** (3), 81–98.

Ewing, Michael T., Thomas Salzberger and Rudolf R. Sinkovics (2005), 'An alternate approach to assessing cross-cultural measurement equivalence in advertising research', *Journal of Advertising*, **34** (1), 17–36.

Ha, Louisa (2010), 'Advertising research on Asian countries and ethnic groups: A twenty-year trend analysis and state-of-the-art review', *Dimensions*, **1** (1), 13–20.

Ha, Louisa and Cornelius B. Pratt (2000), 'Chinese and non-Chinese scholars' contributions to communication research on Greater China, 1978–98', *Asian Journal of Communication*, **10** (1), 95–114.

Hall, E.T. (1976), *Beyond Culture*, New York: Doubleday.

Harkness, Janet A., Fons J.R. Van de Vijver and Peter Ph. Mohler (2003), *Cross-Cultural Survey Methods*, Hoboken, NJ: John Wiley.

Henry, Gary T. (1990), *Practical Sampling*, Newbury Park, CA: Sage.

Hofstede, G. (1980), *Culture's consequences: International differences in work-related value,* Beverly Hills, CA: Sage.

House, R.J., P.J. Hanges, M. Javidan, P.W. Dorfman and V. Gupta (eds) (2004), *Culture, Leadership, and Organizations*, Thousand Oaks, CA: Sage.

Kaldenberg, Dennis O. and Boris W. Becker (1990), 'Research on attitudes of professionals toward advertising: A methodological caveat', *Journal of Advertising Research*, **30** (June/July), 17–23.

Karande, Kiran, Khalid A. Almurshidee and Fahad Al-Olayan (2006), 'Advertising standardization in culturally similar markets: Can we standardize all components?' *International Journal of Advertising*, **25** (4), 489–512.

Koslow, Scott and Carolyn Costley (2010), 'How consumer heterogeneity muddles the international advertising debate', *International Journal of Advertising*, **29** (2), 221–44.

Laband, David N. (1989), 'The durability of information signals and the content of advertising', *Journal of Advertising*, **18** (1), 13–18.

Lastovicka, John L. (1985), 'Sampling designs for sample surveys of advertisers and agencies', *Current Issues and Research in Advertising*, **7**, 89–94.

Leonartowicz, Tomasz, James P. Johnson and Carolyn T. White (2003), 'The neglect of intracountry cultural variation in international management research', *Journal of Business Research*, **56** (12), 999–1008.

Lwin, May O., Andrew J.S. Stranland and Jerome D. Williams (2010), 'Exporting America usage of symbols in international advertising under conditions of consumer ethnocentrism and US-focused animosity', *International Journal of Advertising*, **29** (2), 245–77.

Maisel, Richard and Caroline Hodges Persell (1996), *How Sampling Works*, Thousand Oaks, CA: Pine Forge Press.

Nelson, Michelle R. and Hye-Jin Paek (2008), 'Nudity of female and male models in prime-time TV advertising across seven countries', *International Journal of Advertising*, **27** (5), 715–44.

Bishop, Melissa M. and Mark Peterson (2010), 'The impact of medium context on bilingual consumers' responses to code-switch advertising', *Journal of Advertising*, **39** (3), 55–67.

Okazaki, Shintaro and Barbara Mueller (2007), 'Cross-cultural advertising research: Where we have been and where we need to go', *International Marketing Review,* **24** (5), 499–518.

Polonsky, Michael and Les Carlson (2009), 'Is there global inclusion of authors in the five leading advertising journals? A regional comparison 1998–2007', *International Journal of Advertising*, **28** (4), 691–714.

Puzakova, Marina, Hyokjin Kwak and Trina Larsen Andras (2010), 'Mitigating consumer ethnocentrism via advertising and media consumption in a transitional market: A study from Russia', *International Journal of Advertising*, **29** (5), 727–64.

Resnik, Alan and Bruce L. Stern (1977), 'An analysis of information content in advertising', *Journal of Marketing*, **41**, 50–53.

Riffe, Daniel, Charles Aust and Stephen Lacy (1993), 'The effectiveness of random, consecutive day, and constructed week sampling in newspaper content analysis', *Journalism and Mass Communication Quarterly*, **70** (1), 133–9.

Segal, Madhav N. and Firooz Hermat (1985), 'Random digit dialing: A comparison of methods', *Journal of Advertising*, **14** (4), 36–43.

Shen, Yung-Cheng and Ting-Chen Chen (2006), 'When East meets West: The effect of cultural tone congruity in ad music and message on consumer ad memory and attitude', *International Journal of Advertising*, **25** (1), 51–70.

Sparkman, Richard (1996), 'Regional geography, the overlooked sampling variable in advertising content analysis', *Journal of Current Issues and Research in Advertising*, **18** (2), 53–7.

Taylor, Charles (2005), 'Moving international advertising research forward: A new research agenda', *Journal of Advertising*, **34** (1), 7–16.

Terlutter, Ralf, Sandra Diehl and Barbara Mueller (2010), 'The cultural dimension of assertiveness in cross-cultural advertising: The perception and evaluation of assertive advertising appeals', *International Journal of Advertising*, **29** (3), 369–99.

Tryfos, Peter (1996), *Sampling Methods for Applied Research*, New York: John Wiley & Sons.

12 Using partial least squares path modeling in advertising research: basic concepts and recent issues

Jörg Henseler, Christian M. Ringle and Marko Sarstedt

INTRODUCTION

Structural equations modeling (SEM) with latent variables has become a quasi-standard statistical method for empirical studies on management and marketing research (Hair et al. 2011a) as well as international advertising research. The desire to test complete theories and concepts is one reason for authors to embrace SEM (Bollen 1989; Henseler et al. 2009). For many marketing and international advertising researchers, SEM is equivalent to carrying out covariance-based structural equation modeling (CB-SEM; e.g., Bagozzi 1994; Diamantopoulos and Siguaw 2000; Rigdon 1998) analyses as supported by statistical software packages such as AMOS, EQS, LISREL, Mplus, and others. In CB-SEM, to estimate a set of model parameters, the difference between the theoretical covariance matrix, implied by the structural equations system for the specified model, and the empirical covariance matrix is minimized. The results permit empirically testing the theoretically developed hypotheses. However, model estimation in CB-SEM requires a large set of assumptions to be fulfilled (i.e., the multivariate normality of the data, the minimum sample size, and others), limiting the approach's applicability in many research situations.

SEM also needs to be thought of as including another unique, and very useful, approach – partial least squares path modeling (PLS; Lohmöller 1989; Wold 1982). Unlike CB-SEM, PLS focuses on maximizing the endogenous latent variables' explained variance rather than on reproducing the theoretical covariance matrix. If CB-SEM's premises are violated or if the research objective is prediction rather than comparing competing theories, researchers seem to favor the variance-based PLS approach (Hair et al. 2011a; Reinartz et al. 2009; Ringle et al. 2009).

PLS's various beneficial statistical properties have increasingly disseminated its application in marketing and management research (e.g.,

Hair et al. 2011b). In the 30 years between 1981 and 2010, for example, 204 studies in the 30 top ranked marketing journals (Hair et al. 2012) used PLS. PLS is particularly appealing in research situations in which CB-SEM provides no or, at best, questionable results. Likewise, the availability of easy-to-use PLS software with a graphical user interface, such as Smart-PLS (Ringle et al. 2005), has widely contributed to the method's dissemination among applied researchers. International advertising research has also been strongly affected by these developments. PLS studies in international advertising address topics such as joint advertising effects, synergies, and advertising effectiveness (Ehrenberg et al. 1997; Jagpal 1981; Martensen et al. 2007; Naik and Raman 2003; O'Cass 2002; Schwaiger et al. 2010), online and mobile advertising (Jensen 2008; Naik and Raman 2003; Okazaki et al. 2009), selling practices (Okazaki et al. 2010b), and multinational/cross-national advertising practices (Okazaki et al. 2010a).

Despite the growing number of studies using PLS in international advertising research, journal editors, reviewers, and readers are not always familiar with its characteristics. There are researchers who even dismiss the use of PLS when other techniques fail to support hypothesized relations (Marcoulides and Saunders 2006). More recent articles, however, conclude that PLS can indeed be a "silver bullet" – if correctly applied (Hair et al. 2011a).

Against this background, our chapter provides insights into PLS's current state of the art by merging contributions from the statistical, management, marketing, and international advertising literatures into a more general picture. The overall aim is to encourage the *appropriate* use of PLS in empirical research by not only describing the approach's goals, requirements, and strengths, but also discussing potential weaknesses and problematic issues of which researchers need to be aware. Thus, we call for a more balanced and informed opinion of and attitude toward the application of PLS in international advertising research and other disciplines.

The section that follows gives a brief introduction to the PLS algorithm and its most important features. We subsequently focus on PLS's important characteristics, including their beneficial and critical aspects. Finally, the study concludes by providing guidelines for the use of PLS and by proposing directions for future research.

SHORT INTRODUCTION TO THE PLS ALGORITHM

In general, a structural equation model with latent variables consists of measurement models describing the relationships between latent variables and their observed indicators, and a structural model of the relationships between the latent variables. In the PLS context, measurement and structural models are frequently called outer and inner models. Measurement models can comprise formative or reflective indicators (e.g., Diamantopoulos and Winklhofer 2001; Jarvis et al. 2003), whereby only one type of relationship is possible per latent variable, although different latent variables in the structural equation model may use different types of measurement models. Reflective indicators are seen as functions of the latent variable. Changes in the latent variable are reflected by changes in the associated indicator variables. In contrast, formative indicators are assumed to cause a latent variable, that is, changes in the indicators imply changes in the latent variable's value.

Figure 12.1 shows an example of a simple PLS path model, which includes one endogenous latent variable (y_3) and two exogenous latent variables (y_1 and y_2). The term "exogenous" is used to characterize latent variables with no preceding ones in the structural model. In contrast, the term "endogenous" characterizes latent variables that are explained by others in the structural model. This differentiation is clear-cut in the case of the PLS example in Figure 12.1. However, if the model had included a fourth latent variable (y_4) with a relationship between y_3 and y_4, both y_3 and y_4 would have been endogenous.

PLS requires the structural model to be recursive, which excludes the use of causal loops in the relationships between the latent variables (there would be a causal loop in the model in Figure 12.1 if there were relationships between y_1 and y_2, y_2 and y_3, and y_3 and y_1). The latent variables y_1 and y_2 are measured by means of formative indicators and y_3 by reflective indicators. It is important to note that PLS measurement models consist of one or more indicators. Each indicator can be assigned only once within a measurement model.

The basic PLS algorithm – originally developed by Wold (1975) as NIPALS (non-linear iterative partial least squares) and later extended by Lohmöller (1989) – follows a two-stage approach. This approach consists of the estimation of latent variable scores via the iteration of four steps in the first stage, and the final estimation of outer weights/loadings and path coefficients in the second stage (Box 12.1).

Figures 12.2 to 12.5 illustrate the PLS algorithm's progress. Each figure shows the PLS path model, the data matrix of the indicator and latent variables, the measurement model specification with its relevant coefficients, and, lastly, the structural model specification with its relevant coefficients. The grey shaded areas show the specific data or coefficients computed in Steps 1.1 to 1.4.

In Step 1.1 (Figure 12.2), the outer proxies of the latent variable scores

Case	x_{11}	x_{12}	x_{21}	x_{22}	x_{31}	x_{32}	x_{33}	y_1	y_2	y_3
1	x_{111}	x_{121}	x_{211}	x_{221}	x_{311}	x_{321}	x_{331}	y_{11}	y_{21}	y_{31}
...	...	...	...	...	...	...	...	...	...	...
n	x_{11n}	x_{12n}	x_{21n}	x_{22n}	x_{31n}	x_{32n}	x_{33n}	y_{1n}	y_{2n}	y_{3n}

Data for Indicator Variables and Latent Variables

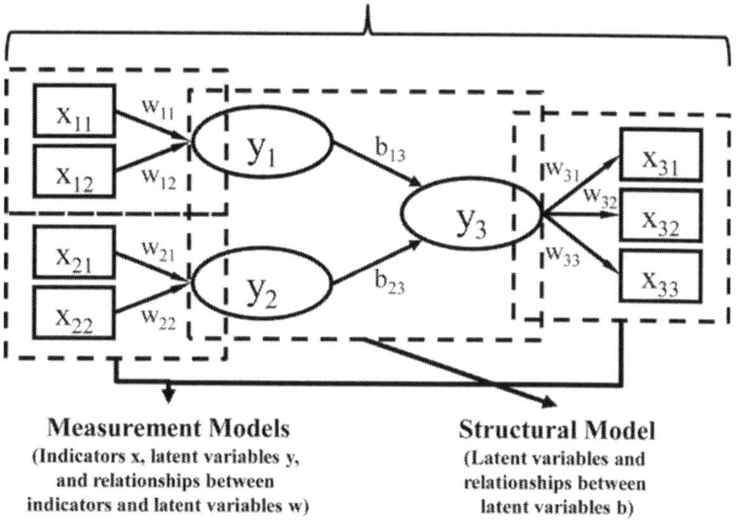

Measurement Models
(Indicators x, latent variables y, and relationships between indicators and latent variables w)

Structural Model
(Latent variables and relationships between latent variables b)

	y_1	y_2	y_3
x_{11}	w_{11}		
x_{12}	w_{12}		
x_{21}		w_{21}	
x_{22}		w_{22}	
x_{31}			w_{31}
x_{32}			w_{32}
x_{33}			w_{33}

	y_1	y_2	y_3
y_1			b_{13}
y_2			b_{23}
y_3			

Figure 12.1 PLS example – initial set-up

are computed as the assigned indicators' weighted sums. The weights are either predetermined (usually in the first iteration) or estimated. For the initial iteration, any non-trivial linear combination of indicators can serve as a latent variable's outer proxy. In practice, equal weights are a good

---

BOX 12.1   KEY STEPS OF THE BASIC PLS ALGORITHM

Stage 1:   Iterative estimation of the latent variable scores.
   Do Loop
      Step 1.1: Outer approximation of the latent variable scores.
      Step 1.2: Estimation of the inner weights.
      Step 1.3: Inner approximation of the latent variable scores.
      Step 1.4: Estimation of the outer weights.
   Until Convergence
Stage 2:   Final estimation of outer weights/loadings and path coefficients through (single and multiple) ordinary least squares (OLS) regressions.

---

choice for the standard initialization of the latent variable scores (Henseler 2010). Later iterations use the weights obtained from the previous iteration's Step 1.4.

In Step 1.2 (Figure 12.3), the PLS algorithm provides so-called inner weights, which quantify the strength of the relationships between the latent variables' outer proxies. Three different weighting schemes are available: the centroid, factor, and path weighting schemes (Henseler et al. 2009). We recommend using the *path weighting scheme* for standard use. This scheme has favorable features in that it yields well-predicted latent variable scores (Fornell and Cha 1994) that maximize the final R^2 value estimations of endogenous latent variables (Lohmöller 1989). Furthermore, the path weighting scheme can be applied to all kinds of PLS path models, including hierarchical component (i.e., second-order) models, which does not apply to the centroid scheme. A weight of zero is assigned to all non-adjacent latent variables in all inner weighting schemes.

The computation of the latent variable scores' inner proxies follows in Step 1.3 (Figure 12.4) as linear combinations of their respective adjacent latent variables' outer proxies (from Step 1.1), using the previously (Step 1.3) determined inner weights.

In Step 1.4 (Figure 12.5), the outer weights are calculated as either the covariances between the inner proxy of each latent variable and its indicators (in reflective measurement models), or as the regression weights resulting from the ordinary least squares (OLS) regression of each latent variable's inner proxy on its indicators (in formative measurement models).

Data for Indicator Variables and Latent Variables									
Case	x_{11}	x_{12}	x_{21}	x_{22}	x_{31}	x_{32}	x_{33}	y_1	y_2	y_3
1	x_{111}	x_{121}	x_{211}	x_{221}	x_{311}	x_{321}	x_{331}	y_{11}	y_{21}	y_{31}
...	...	...	...	...	...	...	...	...	...	...
n	x_{11n}	x_{12n}	x_{21n}	x_{22n}	x_{31n}	x_{32n}	x_{33n}	y_{1n}	y_{2n}	y_{3n}

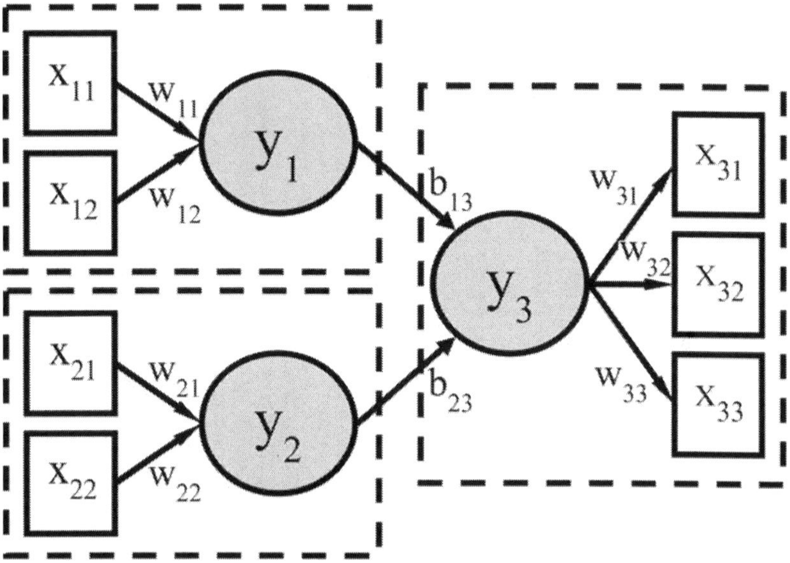

Measurement Model			
	y_1	y_2	y_3
x_{11}	w_{11}		
x_{12}	w_{12}		
x_{21}		w_{21}	
x_{22}		w_{22}	
x_{31}			w_{31}
x_{32}			w_{32}
x_{33}			w_{33}

Structural Model			
	y_1	y_2	y_3
y_1			b_{13}
y_2			b_{23}
y_3			

Note: Grey shaded areas show which data or coefficients are computed.

Figure 12.2 Outer approximation of the latent variable scores (Step 1.1)

The four steps in Stage 1 are repeated until the sum of the outer weights' changes between two iterations is sufficiently low and drops below a predefined limit. We recommend a threshold value of 10^{-5} to ensure that the PLS algorithm converges at reasonably low levels of latent variable

Data for Indicator Variables and Latent Variables									
Case	x_{11}	x_{12}	x_{21}	x_{22}	x_{31}	x_{32}	x_{33}	y_1	y_2	y_3
1	x_{111}	x_{121}	x_{211}	x_{221}	x_{311}	x_{321}	x_{331}	y_{11}	y_{21}	y_{31}
...	...	...	...	...	...	...	...	...	...	...
n	x_{11n}	x_{12n}	x_{21n}	x_{22n}	x_{31n}	x_{32n}	x_{33n}	y_{1n}	y_{2n}	y_{3n}

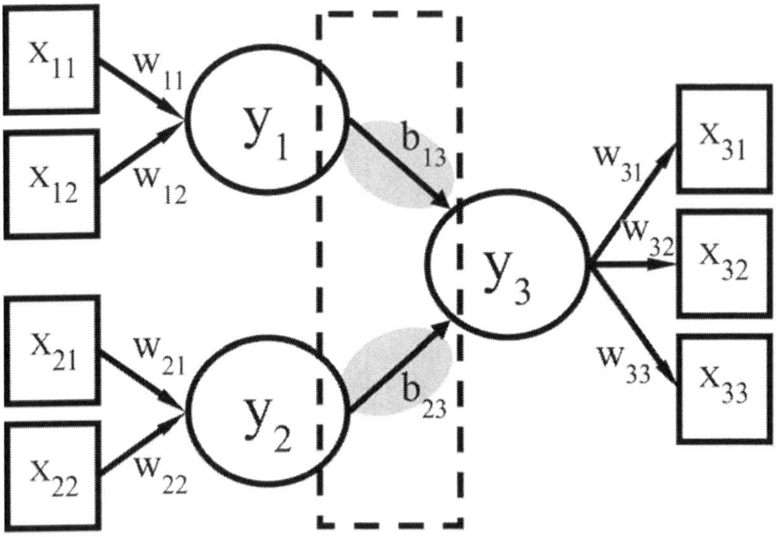

Measurement Model			
	y_1	y_2	y_3
x_{11}	w_{11}		
x_{12}	w_{12}		
x_{21}		w_{21}	
x_{22}		w_{22}	
x_{31}			w_{31}
x_{32}			w_{32}
x_{33}			w_{33}

Structural Model			
	y_1	y_2	y_3
y_1			b_{13}
y_2			b_{23}
y_3			

Note: Grey shaded areas show which data or coefficients are computed.

Figure 12.3   Estimation of the inner weights (Step 1.2)

scores' iterative changes. Upon the algorithm's convergence after Step 1.4, the final outer weights are used to compute the final latent variable scores in Step 2. These scores are used to run OLS regressions to determine estimates for the relationships in the structural model.

Data for Indicator Variables and Latent Variables									
Case	x_{11}	x_{12}	x_{21}	x_{22}	x_{31}	x_{32}	x_{33}	y_1	y_2	y_3
1	x_{111}	x_{121}	x_{211}	x_{221}	x_{311}	x_{321}	x_{331}	y_{11}	y_{21}	y_{31}
...	...	...	...	...	...	...	...	...	...	...
n	x_{11n}	x_{12n}	x_{21n}	x_{22n}	x_{31n}	x_{32n}	x_{33n}	y_{1n}	y_{2n}	y_{3n}

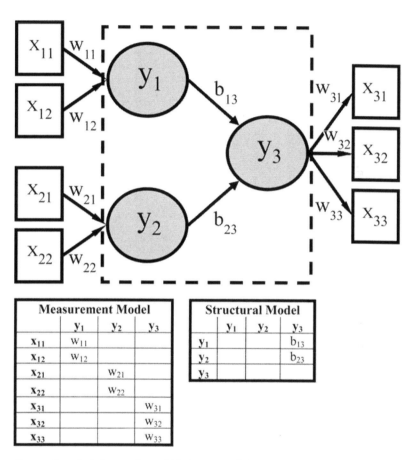

Measurement Model			
	y_1	y_2	y_3
x_{11}	w_{11}		
x_{12}	w_{12}		
x_{21}		w_{21}	
x_{22}		w_{22}	
x_{31}			w_{31}
x_{32}			w_{32}
x_{33}			w_{33}

Structural Model			
	y_1	y_2	y_3
y_1			b_{13}
y_2			b_{23}
y_3			

Note: Grey shaded areas show which data or coefficients are computed.

Figure 12.4   Inner approximation of the latent variable scores (Step 1.3)

Data for Indicator Variables and Latent Variables									
Case	x_{11}	x_{12}	x_{21}	x_{22}	x_{31}	x_{32}	x_{33}	y_1	y_2	y_3
1	x_{111}	x_{121}	x_{211}	x_{221}	x_{311}	x_{321}	x_{331}	y_{11}	y_{21}	y_{31}
...	...	...	...	...	...	...	...	...	...	...
n	x_{11n}	x_{12n}	x_{21n}	x_{22n}	x_{31n}	x_{32n}	x_{33n}	y_{1n}	y_{2n}	y_{3n}

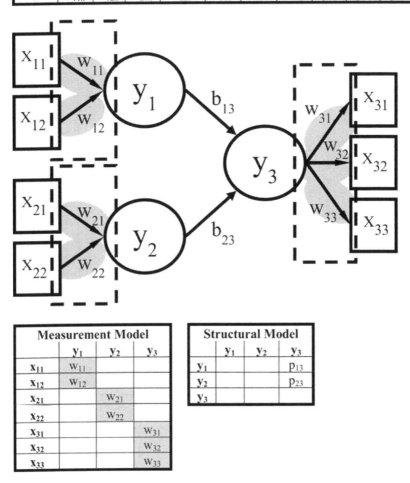

Measurement Model			
	y_1	y_2	y_3
x_{11}	w_{11}		
x_{12}	w_{12}		
x_{21}		w_{21}	
x_{22}		w_{22}	
x_{31}			w_{31}
x_{32}			w_{32}
x_{33}			w_{33}

Structural Model			
	y_1	y_2	y_3
y_1			p_{13}
y_2			p_{23}
y_3			

Note: Grey shaded areas show which data or coefficients are computed.

Figure 12.5   Estimation of the outer weights (Step 1.4)

KEY CHARACTERISTICS OF PLS

Methodological literature on and applications of PLS often refer to a set of characteristics that distinguish the approach from CB-SEM (e.g., Hair et al. 2012; Henseler 2010; Henseler et al. 2009). This section does not aim at comparing PLS and CB-SEM but focuses on PLS characteristics for applications (e.g., in the field of international advertising research). Nevertheless, certain characteristics require such a comparison since many characteristic features of SEM estimation techniques have their roots in "CB-SEM versus PLS" discussions in prior literature (e.g., Fornell and Bookstein 1982; Goodhue et al. 2007; Schneeweiß 1991). More recent publications have turned from a "versus" perspective to a complementary understanding of the two well-established statistical methods for estimating SEM with different objectives and properties (Hair et al. 2011a, 2012; Henseler et al. 2009).

PLS's statistical properties have important features associated with the characteristics of the data and model used. Likewise, PLS's properties also impact the model evaluation. Consequently, we focus on the following four critical issues relevant to SEM: statistical properties, data characteristics, model characteristics, and model evaluation. Table 12.1 provides an overview of PLS's features, which we discuss in greater detail in the following sections.

Statistical Properties

Primarily, PLS is a non-parametric regression-based estimation method whose focus is on prediction by means of a specific set of hypothesized relationships maximizing explained variance in more or less the way that OLS regression does. Since the focus is much more on prediction rather than explanation, PLS is particularly beneficial for success driver studies in marketing theory and practice (Albers 2010; Hair et al. 2011a).

One of PLS's most important features relates to the nature of the latent variable scores. In contrast to CB-SEM, which initially estimates model parameters and then latent variable scores by regressing them on the set of all indicators (Dijkstra 1983), computing these is an inherent part of the PLS algorithm. Specifically, scores are estimated as exact linear combinations of their associated manifest variables (Fornell and Bookstein 1982), and PLS treats these scores as perfect substitutes for the manifest variables capturing the variance that can explain the endogenous latent variables. This approach is based on the implicit assumption that all the measured variance in the model's manifest variables is useful and should be explained. Consequently, the "correctness" of the model is partly

Table 12.1   Features of PLS

Statistical properties

Latent variable scores	• Estimated as linear combinations of their indicators • Used for predictive purposes • Can be used as input for subsequent analyses • Not affected by data inadequacies
Parameter estimates	• Structural model relationships underestimated (PLS bias) • Measurement model relationships overestimated (PLS bias) • Consistency at large • High levels of statistical power

Data characteristics

Sample sizes	• No identification issues with small sample sizes • Generally achieves high levels of statistical power with small sample sizes • Higher numbers of cases are partly beneficial to move toward consistency at large
Distribution	• No distributional assumptions
Scale of measurement	• Works with metric, quasi-metric (ordinal) scaled data, and – within certain boundaries – with binary coded variables • Limitations when using categorical data to measure endogenous latent variables
Philosophy	• Soft modeling

Model characteristics

Number of items in each measurement model	• Handles constructs measured with single-and multi-item measures
Relationships between latent and manifest variables	• Incorporates reflective and formative indicators
Model complexity	• Handles complex models with many structural model relationships • Higher numbers of indicators are partly beneficial to move toward consistency at large
Model set-up	• No loops in the structural model allowed (only in recursive models)

Table 12.1   (continued)

Model evaluation	
Evaluation of the overall model	• No global goodness-of-fit criterion • Model correctness is partly determined by the strength of the structural model relationships
Evaluation of the measurement models	• Systematic evaluation of estimates addresses the measures' reliability and validity according to criteria associated with reflective and formative measurement models
Evaluation of the structural model	• R^2, effect size f^2, predictive relevance Q^2, observed and unobserved heterogeneity
Significance testing	• Traditional parametric techniques for significance testing are not appropriate • Use of resampling procedures for statistical inference

determined by the strength of the structural model relations between the latent variables.

It is important to note that the latent variable scores' distributions are not affected by inadequacies such as multicollinearity in the inner and outer models, skewed data, and misspecification of the structural model (e.g., Cassel et al. 1999; Reinartz et al. 2009). However, because latent variables are aggregates of manifest variables, this leads to a fundamental problem as manifest variables always involve some degree of measurement error. This error is present in the latent variable scores and, finally, is reflected in the path coefficient estimates, which must therefore be considered inconsistent. More precisely, the true inner model relationships are frequently underestimated, while the outer models' parameters are usually overestimated (Dijkstra 1983). This property is frequently called "PLS bias". Even though the "CB-SEM versus PLS" discussion strongly emphasizes that PLS is less accurate in terms of parameter recovery, simulation studies show that the differences between CB-SEM and PLS values are oftentimes negligible (e.g., Reinartz et al. 2009).

Nevertheless, while the estimates resulting from PLS are generally biased, they also exhibit a lower degree of variability than those produced by CB-SEM (e.g., Reinartz et al. 2009; Ringle et al. 2009). This important feature holds specifically for research situations in which maximum likelihood-based CB-SEM typically exhibits inflated standard errors (Sosik et al. 2009) and the method's premises are violated (e.g., small sample size, non-normal data, and high model complexity). This increased parameter estimation efficiency is manifested in PLS' higher level of statistical power than CB-SEM offers (Reinartz et al. 2009). Consequently, despite PLS's exploratory character, it can and should be used in confirmatory set-ups if the purpose is to test whether a certain relationship does or does not exist.

However, it is important to note that, unless the number of indicators per latent variable is also large, the PLS bias does not disappear as the sample size increases. Only when the number of observations *and* the number of indicators per latent variable increase do the latent variable case values approach their true values and the PLS bias disappears. This feature is commonly referred to as "consistency at large" (Lohmöller 1989). Merely increasing the sample size will reduce the variance of the parameter coefficients' distributions, with the larger source of error at some point becoming the PLS bias and not the distribution's variance (Haenlein and Kaplan 2004).

Researchers using PLS are therefore well-advised to use a larger number of indicators to operationalize the constructs, especially when working with small sample sizes (Reinartz et al. 2009). This obviously leads to a trade-off between the PLS method's statistical necessities and the relevant constructs' psychometric properties. Besides practical problems such as higher non-response rates (e.g., Fuchs and Diamantopoulos 2009; Sarstedt and Wilczynski 2009), increasing the number of indicators per construct will also increase the error term correlations and, thus, reduces the incremental value that each additional item provides (Drolet and Morrison 2001).

While the strong reliance on latent variable scores has its drawbacks, it also has certain advantages as researchers may use latent variable scores in subsequent analyses. For example, in their experimental study, Schwaiger, Sarstedt and Taylor (2010) use differences in the latent variable scores of reference and follow-up PLS measurements to reveal significant differences between control and treatment groups regarding reputation assessments in an international advertising research context. Furthermore, recent methodological advancements utilize latent variable scores for further analysis of PLS results (e.g., importance–performance matrix analysis, finite mixture partial least squares), which we will introduce in the model evaluation section.

Data Characteristics

Some of the most often used arguments for applying PLS are related to data characteristics such as the analysis of small sample sizes, non-normal data, and the use of data with different types of scale (Henseler et al. 2009). While some of the arguments suit the method's capabilities, others do not and, thus, fostered some skepticism against PLS. The sample size argument is probably the most critical argument in the context of applying PLS.

Since the PLS algorithm consists of OLS regressions for separate subparts of the focal path model, the overall model's complexity hardly influences the sample size requirements. However, only a few studies have systematically evaluated PLS's performance when the sample sizes are small (e.g., Chin and Newsted 1999; Hui and Wold 1982; Reinartz et al. 2009). The most recent study by Reinartz et al. (2009) shows that PLS is a very sensible methodological choice if the sample size is restricted. Specifically, PLS has higher levels of statistical power in the complex model structures usually encountered within the marketing discipline compared to its covariance-based counterpart. This result is inherent in the PLS algorithm's statistical properties, which we discussed above. Nevertheless, authors seem to believe that sample size considerations do not play a role in PLS. This idea is fostered by the often cited "ten times" rule (Barclay et al. 1995), according to which the sample size should be equal to the larger of: (1) ten times the index with the largest number of formative indicators, or (2) ten times the largest number of structural paths directed at a particular latent variable in the structural model. Likewise, considerations regarding theoretical minimum sample sizes (Tenenhaus et al. 2005), as well as simulation and empirical study results (e.g., Chin and Newsted 1999; Wold 1989) – which take statistical specifics into account rather than research reality – foster the persistent belief that PLS is the ultimate solution for coping with small sample sizes. While the previously mentioned "ten times" rule provides a rough guideline of minimum sample size requirements (Hair et al. 2011a), PLS, like any statistical technique, requires researchers to consider the sample size against the background of the model and data characteristics. Specifically, the required sample sizes should be determined by means of power analyses based on the part of the model with the largest number of predictors. While some authors use PLS's small sample misapplications to argue against the PLS method and its properties (e.g., Marcoulides and Saunders 2006), others state that, if correctly applied, PLS can indeed be a silver bullet with small samples (e.g., Hair et al. 2011a).

The use of method is straightforward regarding the other two key arguments for using PLS that are related to data characteristics (i.e., scales and distribution). PLS offers greater flexibility, especially in situations where it is difficult or even impossible to meet more traditional multivariate techniques' strict assumptions (e.g., distributional assumptions). This characteristic is emphasized by the label "soft modeling" coined by Wold (1982). Within this context, "soft" is only attributed to distributional assumptions and not the concepts, models or estimation techniques (Lohmöller 1989). PLS's statistical properties provide very robust model estimations both with data that have normal and extremely non-normal distributional properties (Reinartz et al. 2009; Ringle et al. 2009). Thus, PLS can also be used when distributions are highly skewed (e.g., Beebe et al. 1998; Cassel et al. 1999; Tenenhaus et al. 2010), especially when formative measurement models are included (Ringle et al. 2009).

Finally, the PLS algorithm principally requires metric data for the indicators in the measurement models. However, the method also generally works with ordinal scales with equidistant data points – that is, quasimetric scales (Mooi and Sarstedt 2011) – and with binary coded data. In the latter case, when using both metric and dummy variables, one must account for the role of dummy coded variables in regressions (Hair et al. 2011c), or the specific considerations provided by Lohmöller (1989) for PLS model estimations that draw solely on dummy coded variables.

Model Characteristics

PLS is also very flexible regarding the modeling properties. The only premise is connected to "predictor specification" (i.e., the systematic portion of all OLS regressions is equal to the dependent variables' conditional expectations; Haenlein and Kaplan 2004). In accordance, the inner model must be a causal chain system with uncorrelated residuals and an endogenous latent variable's residual being uncorrelated with the corresponding predictor latent variables. Thus, the PLS algorithm requires all models to be recursive, which means that no loops are allowed in the structural model. While non-recursive models are hardly seen in marketing research, this characteristic limits PLS's applicability in certain research situations. Other model specification issues that are relevant for CB-SEM (Diamantopoulos and Siguaw 2000) are not pertinent in the PLS context.

In fact, measurement model difficulties are one of the major obstacles to obtaining a solution with CB-SEM. For instance, the estimation of comparably complex models with many latent variables and/or indicators confronts researchers using CB-SEM with vast problems in terms of getting the model identified. Furthermore, when a researcher is attempting to test a model with single item measures, PLS is an option, as it is uninhibited by identification concerns. Researchers have therefore routinely included single item measures in PLS path models (e.g., Ahuja et al. 2003; Arnett et al. 2003; Sarstedt and Schloderer 2010). Nevertheless, one has to keep in mind that – in addition to conceptual and psychometric concerns (Sarstedt and Wilczynski 2009) – the utilization of single item measures is contrary to the consistency at large concept.

PLS is also considered the primary approach when the hypothesized model incorporates formative measures (Diamantopoulos and Winklhofer 2001). These are a common occurrence in managerial research, as illustrated by Jarvis, MacKenzie and Podsakoff (2003), who show that a substantial number of constructs in top-tier marketing and consumer research studies inappropriately specified formative measures as reflective. Likewise, Albers (2010) argues that indicators of success factor studies should be actionable and should be measured formatively. This follows the argument provided by Rossiter (2002) in his initial presentation of the C-OAR-SE procedure. More recently, Rossiter (2011) has rejected the reflective model specification altogether, suggesting that all abstract attributes now follow the formative model. However, not surprisingly, this dogmatic adherence to a single model has triggered off some criticism (Rigdon et al. 2011).

CB-SEM can generally accommodate formative indicators researchers, but to ensure model identification they must follow specific complex rules such as the 2+ emitted paths or the exogenous X rule (Bollen and Davies 2009), which require researchers to modify or impose constraints on the model and often contradict theoretical considerations. In contrast, similar model specification requirements do not arise in PLS (Henseler et al. 2009). This algorithm suits SEM equally well with either reflective and/ or formative measurement models. The only problematic issue is the manifest variables' critical level of multicollinearity in formative measurement models, which may be resolved by the recommendations given by Hair et al. (2011a).

PLS is also a sensible choice in research situations where few observations are used to estimate complex models with many manifest variables. This holds especially true when formative measures are involved (besides the potential identification issues discussed above). Formative measurement models are often more capacious, as formative constructs should be represented by all relevant indicators that form them to ensure content validity (Diamantopoulos et al. 2008). Thus, PLS can be a useful way of quickly exploring a large number of variables to identify sets of latent variables that can predict some outcome variable, underlining the approach's exploratory character.

Model Evaluation

Contrary to CB-SEM, PLS does not optimize any global scalar function; it therefore lacks an index to globally validate the model (such as χ^2 and related measures, see Hair et al. 2010). In essence, this statistical property renders the derivation of a global PLS goodness-of-fit measure impossible.

It is important to note that there is a proposal for a goodness-of-fit criterion (GoF) as a single measure to evaluate PLS path modeling results, computed as the geometric mean of the average communality index and the average R^2 value (Tenenhaus et al. 2004). However, the GoF does not indicate the level of fit between a theoretical and an empirical covariance matrix and, thus, is not a goodness of model fit measure as is found in covariance-based approaches. Moreover, this criterion is applicable only to PLS path models that include only reflective measurement models.

Although PLS does not minimize a total residual (co)variance, the estimation is coherent in the sense that all residual variances are minimized separately. Nevertheless, PLS's lack of a global scalar function and its consequent lack of a well-defined measure of global goodness-of-fit are certainly a limiting factor. Instead of optimizing a global scalar function, parameter estimates are obtained from the ability to minimize dependent (latent and observed) variables' residual variances. An assessment of these PLS results comprise evaluations of partial model structures using well-known criteria from the psychometric and methodological literatures (Chin 1998). Henseler et al. (2009) and Hair et al. (2011a) describe a two-step process that involves (Step 1) assessing the measurement models and (Step 2) the structural model. Specifically, criteria associated with reflective and formative measurement models assess the measures' reliability and validity in Step 1 (Table 12.2). Cenfetelli and Bassellier (2009) and Kim et al. (2010) provide a recent discussion of approaches with which to validate formative measurement models.

If this assessment of the measurement models provides evidence of the latent variables' reliability and validity, the structural model estimates need to be evaluated in Step 2 (Table 12.3). The key evaluation criteria for the structural model are the R^2 values and the level and significance of the structural model relationships. Since PLS aims to explain the endogenous latent variables' variance, the endogenous latent variables' levels of R^2 should thus be high. The R^2 level assessment depends on the specific research discipline. While R^2 results of 0.25 are considered high in disciplines such as consumer behavior, R^2 values of 0.75 would be perceived as high in success driver studies (e.g., in international advertising research). In general terms, however, in the structural model, R^2 values of 0.75, 0.50, or 0.25 for endogenous latent variables can be regarded as substantial, moderate, or weak (Hair et al. 2011a).

Since a key characteristic of PLS is its extraction of latent variable scores, this method is particularly useful for additional analyses that employ these scores. Höck, Ringle and Sarstedt (2010) (e.g., see also Völckner et al. 2010) propose an importance–performance matrix analysis for PLS, which contrasts the inner model total effects and rescaled latent variable scores to

Table 12.2 Assessing measurement models

Criterion	Description
Reflective measurement models	
Composite reliability (ρ_c)	Measure of internal consistency. Critical level: The composite reliability should be higher than 0.7.
Indicator reliability Convergent validity	Critical level: The absolute values of standardized outer (component) loadings should be higher than 0.7. The average variance extracted (AVE) is a common measure to assess convergent validity. Critical level: The average variance extracted should be higher than 0.5.
Discriminant validity	The Fornell-Larcker criterion is a measure to evaluate discriminant validity. The AVE of each latent variable should be higher than the squared correlations of all the other latent variables. Each latent variable therefore shares more variance with its own block of indicators than with another latent variable representing a different block of indicators. Cross-loadings are another measure of discriminant validity. If an indicator has a higher correlation with another latent variable than with its associated one, the model's appropriateness should be reconsidered.
Formative measurement models	
Relationships between latent and manifest variables	Carry out a confirmatory tetrad analysis routine (e.g., CTA-PLS; Gudergan et al. 2008) to empirically confirm the formative mode of the measurement model.

Table 12.2 (continued)

Criterion	Description
Significance of weights	The estimated weights of formative measurement models should be significant. If a large number of formative indicators are used and some have non-significant weights, the indicators should be grouped into two or more distinct constructs, provided there is theoretical support for this step.
Co-occurrence of negative and positive weights	Examine the correlations between the indicators to investigate the possibility of suppressor effects. Suppression occurs when an indicator shares more variance with another indicator than with the formatively measured construct.
Absolute versus relative indicator contributions	Interpret the indicator loadings to evaluate an indicator's absolute importance to its construct. If both the weight and loading are non-significant, there is no empirical support for retaining the indicator, and its theoretical relevance should be questioned.
Multicollinearity	Indicator variables in a formative measurement model must be tested for multicollinearity by means of the variance inflation factor (VIF). VIF values of 10 and above allude to a severe multicollinearity problem. VIF values of 5 already indicate a potential multicollinearity problem, which necessitates the reconsideration of the model set-up. Eigenvalues that significantly depart from 1.00 may also be indicative of multicollinearity.
Heterogeneity	Indicator weights should be examined to determine if they are affected by (observed or unobserved) heterogeneity, which results in significantly different group-specific coefficients. If theory supports the existence of alternative groups of data, carry out multi-group or moderator analyses (Sarstedt et al. 2011b). If no theory or information is available on the underlying groups of data, finite mixture PLS should be used to assess unobserved heterogeneity's existence (FIMIX-PLS; Hahn et al. 2002; Sarstedt et al. 2011a; Sarstedt and Ringle 2010).

Table 12.3   Assessing structural models

Criterion	Description
R^2 of endogenous latent variables	R^2 values express the proportion the endogenous latent variables' explained variance. In the structural model, R^2 values of 0.75, 0.50, or 0.25 for endogenous latent variables can be regarded as substantial, moderate, or weak.
Path coefficients	The parameter estimates of the path relationships in the structural model can be interpreted as standardized regression coefficients.
Effect size f^2	$f^2 = (R^2_{included} - R^2_{excluded})/(1 - R^2_{included})$; values of 0.02, 0.15, and 0.35 can be viewed as a gauge of whether a predictor latent variable has a weak, medium, or large effect at the structural level.
Predictive relevance (Q^2 and q^2)	Use the blindfolding procedure to estimate the cross-validated redundancy Q^2. Make sure that the number of valid observations is not a multiple integer of the omission distance d. Choose values of d between 5 and 10. Q^2-values above zero are indicative of the exogenous latent variables' predictive relevance. Also consider the relative cross-validated redundancy q^2 (computation and interpretation analogous to f^2).
Observed and unobserved heterogeneity	If theory supports the existence of alternative groups of data, carry out PLS multi-group or moderator analyses. If no theory or information is available on underlying groups of data, FIMIX-PLS should be used to assess the existence of unobserved heterogeneity.

highlight significant areas for improvement of management activities. PLS's importance-performance analysis results permit the identification of determinants that have a relatively high importance (i.e., high total effects) and a relatively low performance (i.e., low unstandardized latent variable scores) in respect of a certain criterion. Likewise, finite mixture PLS (FIMIX-PLS; Hahn et al. 2002; Sarstedt et al. 2011a), which allows for the treatment of unobserved heterogeneity in inner model path estimates and whose capabilities have been illustrated in several numerical experiments (e.g., Ringle et al. 2010b; Ringle et al. 2010c), as well as empirical studies (e.g., Navarro et al. 2011; Rigdon et al. 2011; Ringle et al. 2010a; Sarstedt and Ringle 2010), builds on the latent variable score estimates by means of the standard PLS algorithm. Lastly, various approaches to analyzing interaction effects between latent variables rely on latent variable scores (Henseler and Fassott 2010). As some of these approaches are difficult to implement in a CB-SEM context, the strong reliance on latent variable scores in PLS proves advantageous in this context. However, researchers need to control for changes in a latent variable between two moderating conditions, if the changes are owing to respondents perceiving the meaning of the construct as differing in each of the moderating conditions (gamma change), as opposed to a true change in the latent variable (alpha change) (Haenlein and Kaplan 2011).

DISCUSSION

International advertising research and practice progressively more often builds on empirical studies and the application of multivariate analysis tools. SEM in general and, more specifically, PLS path modeling represent one of the key tools for conducting empirical research in international advertising, especially when focusing on sources of competitive advantage or strategic success driver analyses (Henseler et al. 2009).

This chapter presents PLS as a ready-to-use statistical technique for the analysis of SEM models. PLS's objective is to explain variance in the target constructs (prediction orientation), which makes the method useful for a wide range of topics in international advertising research and practice. Studies on the sources of competitive advantage that aim at explaining international advertising success, as well as international advertising's contribution to overall firm success (e.g., Okazaki et al. 2010b), benefit specifically from the PLS method's effectiveness for this kind of research objective. Correspondingly, studies on advertising effectiveness (e.g., Martensen et al. 2007; Schwaiger et al. 2010), selling practices (Okazaki et al. 2010b), or online and mobile advertising (e.g., Jensen 2008; Okazaki et al. 2009), successfully applied PLS.

Given recent research efforts to analyze moderating effects by means of PLS (Rigdon et al. 2010), its application in multinational/cross-national advertising research (e.g., Okazaki et al. 2010a) – as being well established from a cultural perspective in the brand management field (Henseler et al. 2010) is a particularly fruitful field for the method's future applications (e.g., with regard to its capabilities to analyze moderating effects; Henseler and Fassott 2010). More generally, PLS's characteristics fit the challenges of empirical marketing, (strategic) management, and international advertising research perfectly. If researchers correctly apply PLS by closely considering the purpose of the analysis, the data requirements, the evaluation and interpretation of the results, PLS is indeed a silver bullet for many SEM research purposes across a wide range of model and data constellations (e.g., in terms of complexity and/or representative samples of small sizes) (Hair et al. 2011a). Consequently, we anticipate a substantial increase in the use of PLS in international advertising research.

REFERENCES

Ahuja, Manju K., Dennis F. Galletta and Kathleen M. Carley (2003), 'Individual Centrality and Performance in Virtual R&D Groups: An Empirical Study', *Management Science*, **49** (1), 21–38.

Albers, Sönke (2010), 'PLS and Success Factor Studies in Marketing', in Vincenzo Esposito Vinzi, Wynne W. Chin, Jörg Henseler and Huiwen Wang (eds), *Handbook of Partial Least Squares: Concepts, Methods and Applications* (Springer Handbooks of Computational Statistics Series, vol. 111). Heidelberg, Dordrecht, London, New York: Springer, pp. 409–25.

Arnett, Dennis B., Debra A. Laverie and Amanda Meiers (2003), 'Developing Parsimonious Retailer Equity Indexes Using Partial Least Squares Analysis: A Method and Applications', *Journal of Retailing*, **79** (3), 161–70.

Bagozzi, Richard P. (1994), 'Structural Equation Models in Marketing Research: Basic Principles', in Richard P. Bagozzi (ed.), *Principles of Marketing Research*, Oxford: Blackwell, 317–85.

Barclay, Donald W., Christopher A. Higgins and Ronald Thompson (1995), 'The Partial Least Squares Approach to Causal Modeling: Personal Computer Adoption and Use as Illustration', *Technology Studies*, **2** (2), 285–309.

Beebe, Kenneth R., Randy J. Pell and Mary Beth Seasholtz (1998), *Chemometrics: A Practical Guide*, New York: John Wiley.

Bollen, Kenneth A. (1989), *Structural Equations with Latent Variables*, New York: Wiley.

Bollen, Kenneth A. and Walter R. Davies (2009), 'Causal Indicator Models: Identification, Estimation, and Testing', *Structural Equation Modeling. An Interdisciplinary Journal*, **16** (3), 498–522.

Cassel, Claes, Peter Hackl and Anders H. Westlund (1999), 'Robustness of Partial Least-Squares Method for Estimating Latent Variable Quality Structures', *Journal of Applied Statistics*, **26** (4), 435–46.

Chin, Wynne W. (1998), 'The Partial Least Squares Approach to Structural Equation Modeling', in George A. Marcoulides (ed.), *Modern Methods for Business Research*, Hillsdale, NJ: Lawrence Erlbaum Associates, pp. 295–336.

Chin, Wynne W. and Peter R. Newsted (1999), 'Structural Equation Modeling Analysis with Small Samples Using Partial Least Squares', in Rick H. Hoyle (ed.), *Statistical Strategies for Small Sample Research*, Thousand Oaks: Sage, pp. 307–42.

Diamantopoulos, Adamantios, Petra Riefler and Katharina P. Roth (2008), 'Advancing Formative Measurement Models', *Journal of Business Research*, **61** (12), 1203–18.

Diamantopoulos, Adamantios and Judy A. Siguaw (2000), *Introducing LISREL*, Thousand Oaks: Sage.

Diamantopoulos, Adamantios and Heidi M. Winklhofer (2001), 'Index Construction with Formative Indicators: An Alternative to Scale Development', *Journal of Marketing Research*, **38** (2), 269–77.

Dijkstra, Theo K. (1983), 'Some Comments on Maximum Likelihood and Partial Least Squares Methods', *Journal of Econometrics*, **22** (1/2), 67–90.

Drolet, Aimee L. and Donald G. Morrison (2001), 'Do We Really Need Multiple-Item Measures in Service Research?' *Journal of Service Research*, **3** (3), 196–204.

Ehrenberg, Andrew, John Scriven and Neil Barnard (1997), 'Advertising and Price', *Journal of Advertising Research*, **37** (3), 27–35.

Fornell, Claes and Fred L. Bookstein (1982), 'Two Structural Equation Models: LISREL and PLS Applied to Consumer Exit-Voice Theory', *Journal of Marketing Research*, **19** (4), 440–52.

Fuchs, Christoph and Adamantios Diamantopoulos (2009), 'Using Single-Item Measures for Construct Measurement in Management Research: Conceptual Issues and Application Guidelines', *Business Administration Review*, **69** (2), 197–212.

Goodhue, Dale, William Lewis and Ronald Thompson (2007), 'Statistical Power in Analyzing Interaction Effects: Questioning the Advantage of PLS with Product Indicators', *Information Systems Research*, **18** (2), 211–27.

Gudergan, Siegfried P., Christian M. Ringle, Sven Wende and Alexander Will (2008), 'Confirmatory Tetrad Analysis in PLS Path Modeling', *Journal of Business Research*, **61** (12), 1238–49.

Haenlein, Michael and Andreas M. Kaplan (2004), 'A Beginner's Guide to Partial Least Squares Analysis', *Understanding Statistics*, **3** (4), 283–97.

—— (2011), 'The Influence of Observed Heterogeneity on Path Coefficient Significance: Technology Acceptance within the Marketing Discipline', *Journal of Marketing Theory and Practice*, **18** (2), 153–68.

Hahn, Carsten, Michael D. Johnson, Andreas Herrmann and Frank Huber (2002), 'Capturing Customer Heterogeneity Using a Finite Mixture PLS Approach', *Schmalenbach Business Review*, **54** (3), 243–69.

Hair, Joseph F., William C. Black, Barry J. Babin and Rolph E. Anderson (2010), *Multivariate Data Analysis*, 7th ed. Englewood Cliffs: Prentice Hall.

Hair, Joseph F., Christian M. Ringle and Marko Sarstedt (2011a), 'PLS-SEM: Indeed a Silver Bullet', *Journal of Marketing Theory and Practice*, **18** (2), 139–51.

—— (2011b), 'The Use of Partial Least Squares (PLS) to Address Marketing Management Topics: From the Special Issue Guest Editors', *Journal of Marketing Theory and Practice*, **18** (2), 135–7.

Hair, Joseph F., Mary Wolfinbarger Celsi, Arthur H. Money, Phillip Samouel and Michael J. Page (2011c), *Essentials of Business Research Methods*, 2nd ed. Armonk: Sharpe.

Hair, Joseph F., Marko Sarstedt, Christian M. Ringle and Jeanette A. Mena (2012), 'An Assessment of the use of Partial Least Squares Structural Equation Modeling in Market Research', *Journal of the Academy of Marketing Science*, forthcoming.

Henseler, Jörg (2010), 'On the Convergence of the Partial Least Squares Path Modeling Algorithm', *Computational Statistics*, **25** (1), 107–20.

Henseler, Jörg and Georg Fassott (2010), 'Testing Moderating Effects in PLS Path Models: An Illustration of Available Procedures', in Vincenzo Esposito Vinzi, Wynne W. Chin, Jörg Henseler and Huiwen Wang (eds), *Handbook of Partial Least Squares: Concepts, Methods and Applications* (Springer Handbooks of Computational Statistics Series, vol. 111). Heidelberg, Dordrecht, London, New York: Springer, pp. 713–35.

Henseler, Jörg, Csilla Horváth, Marko Sarstedt and Lorenz Zimmermann (2010), 'A Cross-Cultural Comparison of Brand Extension Success Factors: A Meta-Study', *Journal of Brand Management*, **18** (1), 5–20.

Henseler, Jörg, Christian M. Ringle and Rudolf R. Sinkovics (2009), 'The Use of Partial Least Squares Path Modeling in International Marketing', in Rudolf R. Sinkovics and Pervez N. Ghauri (eds), *Advances in International Marketing*, vol. 20. Bingley: Emerald, pp. 277–319.

Höck, Claudia, Christian M. Ringle and Marko Sarstedt (2010), 'Management of Multi-Purpose Stadiums: Importance and Performance Measurement of Service Interfaces', *International Journal of Services Technology and Management*, **14** (2/3), 188–207.

Hui, Baldwin S. and Herman Wold (1982), 'Consistency and Consistency at Large of Partial Least Squares Estimates', in Karl G. Jöreskog and Herman Wold (eds), *Systems Under Indirect Observation, Part II*, Amsterdam: North Holland, pp. 119–30.

Jagpal, Harsharanjeet S. (1981), 'Measuring Joint Advertising Effects in Multiproduct Firms', *Journal of Advertising Research*, **21** (1), 65–9.

Jarvis, Cheryl B., Scott B. MacKenzie and Philip M. Podsakoff (2003), 'A Critical Review of Construct Indicators and Measurement Model Misspecification in Marketing and Consumer Research', *Journal of Consumer Research*, **30** (2), 199–218.

Jensen, Morten B. (2008), 'Online Marketing Communication Potential: Priorities in Danish Firms and Advertising Agencies', *European Journal of Marketing*, **42** (3/4), 502–25.

Lohmöller, Jan-Bernd (1989), *Latent Variable Path Modeling with Partial Least Squares*, Heidelberg: Physica.

Marcoulides, George A. and Carol Saunders (2006), 'PLS: A Silver Bullet?' *MIS Quarterly*, **30** (2), III–IX.

Martensen, Anne, Lars Grønholdt, Lars Bendtsen and Martin J. Jensen (2007), 'Application of a Model for the Effectiveness of Event Marketing', *Journal of Advertising Research*, **47** (3), 283–301.

Mooi, Erik A. and Marko Sarstedt (2011), *A Concise Guide to Market Research: The Process, Data, and Methods using IBM SPSS Statistics*, Berlin: Springer.

Naik, Prasad A. and Kalyan Raman (2003), 'Understanding the Impact of Synergy in Multimedia Communications', *Journal of Marketing Research*, **40** (4), 375–88.

Navarro, Antonio, Francisco J. Acedo, Fernando Losada and Emilio Ruzo (2011), 'Integrated Model of Export Activity: Analysis of Heterogeneity in Managers' Orientations and Perceptions on Strategic Management in Foreign Markets', *Journal of Marketing Theory & Practice*, **19** (2), 187–204.

O'Cass, Aron (2002), 'Political Advertising Believability and Information Source Value During Elections', *Journal of Advertising*, **31** (1), 63–74.

Okazaki, Shintaro, Hairong Li and Morikazu Hirose (2009), 'Consumer Privacy Concerns and Preference for Degree of Regulatory Control: A Study of Mobile Advertising in Japan', *Journal of Advertising*, **38** (4), 63–77.

Okazaki, Shintaro, Barbara Mueller and Charles R. Taylor (2010a), 'Global Consumer Culture Positioning: Testing Perceptions of Soft-Sell and Hard-Sell Advertising Appeals Between U.S. and Japanese Consumers', *Journal of International Marketing*, **18** (2), 20–34.

— (2010b), 'Measuring Soft-Sell Versus Hard-Sell Advertising Appeals', *Journal of Advertising*, **39** (2), 5–20.

Reinartz, Werner, Michael Haenlein and Jörg Henseler (2009), 'An Empirical Comparison of the Efficacy of Covariance-Based and Variance-Based SEM', *International Journal of Research in Marketing*, **26** (4), 332–44.

Rigdon, Edward E. (1998), 'Structural Equation Modeling', in George A. Marcoulides (ed.), *Modern Methods for Business Research*, Mahwah, NJ: Lawrence Erlbaum Associates, pp. 251–94.

Rigdon, Edward E., Kristopher J. Preacher, Nick Lee, Roy D. Howell, George R. Franke and Denny Borsboom (2011), 'Avoiding Measurement Dogma: A Response to Rossiter', *European Journal of Marketing*, **45** (11/12), 1589–1600.

Rigdon, Edward E., Christian M. Ringle and Marko Sarstedt (2010), 'Structural Modeling of Heterogeneous Data with Partial Least Squares', in Naresh K. Malhotra (ed.), *Review of Marketing Research*, vol. 7. Armonk: Sharpe, pp. 255–96.

Rigdon, Edward E., Christian M. Ringle, Marko Sarstedt and Siegfried P. Gudergan (2011), 'Assessing Heterogeneity in Customer Satisfaction Studies: Across Industry Similarities and within Industry Differences', in Marko Sarstedt, Manfred Schwaiger and Charles R. Taylor (eds), *Advances in International Marketing*, vol. 22, Bingley: Emerald.

Ringle, Christian M., Oliver Götz, Martin Wetzels and Bradley Wilson (2009), 'On the Use of Formative Measurement Specifications in Structural Equation Modeling: A Monte Carlo Simulation Study to Compare Covariance-based and Partial Least Squares Model Estimation Methodologies', in METEOR Research Memoranda (RM/09/014): Maastricht University.

Ringle, Christian M., Marko Sarstedt and Erik A. Mooi (2010a), 'Response-Based Segmentation Using Finite Mixture Partial Least Squares: Theoretical Foundations and an Application to American Customer Satisfaction Index Data', *Annals of Information Systems*, **8**, 19–49.

Ringle, Christian M., Marko Sarstedt and Rainer Schlittgen (2010b), 'Finite Mixture and Genetic Algorithm Segmentation in Partial Least Squares Path Modeling: Identification of Multiple Segments in a Complex Path Model', in Andreas Fink, Berthold Lausen, Wilfried Seidel and Alfred Ultsch (eds), *Advances in Data Analysis, Data Handling and Business Intelligence*, Berlin-Heidelberg: Springer, pp. 167–76.

Ringle, Christian M., Sven Wende and Alexander Will (2010c), 'Finite Mixture Partial Least Squares Analysis: Methodology and Numerical Examples', in Vincenzo Esposito Vinzi, Wynne W. Chin, Jörg Henseler and Huiwen Wang (eds), *Handbook of Partial Least Squares: Concepts, Methods and Applications* (Springer Handbooks of Computational Statistics Series, vol. 111). Heidelberg, Dordrecht, London, New York: Springer, pp. 195–218.

Ringle, Christian, Sven Wende and Alexander Will (2005), 'SmartPLS 2.0 (Beta)'. www. smartpls.de.

Rossiter, John R. (2002), 'The C-OAR-SE procedure for scale development in marketing', *International Journal of Research in Marketing*, **19** (4), 305–35.

— (2011), Marketing Measurement Revolution: The C-OAR-SE Method and Why it Must Replace Psychometrics, *European Journal of Marketing*, **45** (11/12), 1561–88.

Sarstedt, Marko, Jan-Michael Becker and Christian M. Ringle (2011a), 'Uncovering and Treating Unobserved Heterogeneity with FIMIX-PLS: Which Model Selection Criterion Provides an Appropriate Number of Segments?' *Schmalenbach Business Review*, **63** (1), 34–62.

Sarstedt, Marko, Jörg Henseler and Christian M. Ringle (2011b), 'Multigroup Analysis in Partial Least Squares (PLS) Path Modeling: Alternative Methods and Empirical Results', in Marko Sarstedt, Manfred Schwaiger and Charles R. Taylor (eds), *Advances in International Marketing*, vol. 22, Bingley: Emerald.

Sarstedt, Marko and Christian M. Ringle (2010), 'Treating Unobserved Heterogeneity in PLS Path Modelling: A Comparison of FIMIX-PLS with Different Data Analysis Strategies', *Journal of Applied Statistics*, **37** (7–8), 1299–318.

Sarstedt, Marko and Matthias Schloderer (2010), 'Developing a Measurement Approach for Reputation of Non-Profit Organizations', *International Journal of Nonprofit and Voluntary Sector Marketing*, **15** (3), 276–99.

Sarstedt, Marko and Petra Wilczynski (2009), 'More for Less? A Comparison of Single-Item and Multi-Item Measures', *Business Administration Review*, **69** (2), 211–27.

Schneeweiß, Hans (1991), 'Models with Latent Variables: LISREL versus PLS', *Statistica Neerlandica*, **45** (2), 145–57.

Schwaiger, Manfred, Marko Sarstedt and Charles R. Taylor (2010), 'Art for the Sake of the Corporation: Audi, BMW Group, DaimlerChrysler, Montblanc, Siemens, and Volkswagen Help Explore the Effect of Sponsorship on Corporate Reputations', *Journal of Advertising Research*, **50** (1), 77–90.

Sosik, John J., Surinder S. Kahai and Michael J. Piovoso (2009), 'Silver Bullet or Voodoo Statistics? A Primer for Using Partial Least Squares Data Analytic Technique in Group and Organization Research', *Group & Organization Management*, **34** (1), 5–36.

Tenenhaus, Michel, Silvano Amato and Vincenzo Esposito Vinzi (2004), 'A Global Goodness-of-Fit Index for PLS Structural Equation Modeling', in *Proceedings of the XLII SIS Scientific Meeting*, Padova: CLEUP.

Tenenhaus, Michel, Vincenzo Esposito Vinzi, Yves-Marie Chatelin and Carlo Lauro (2005), 'PLS Path Modeling', *Computational Statistics & Data Analysis*, **48** (1), 159–205.

Tenenhaus, Michel, Emmanuelle Mauger and Christiane Guinot (2010), 'Use of ULS-SEM and PLS-SEM to Measure a Group Effect in a Regression Model Relating Two Blocks of Binary Variables', in Vincenzo Esposito Vinzi, Wynne W. Chin, Jörg Henseler and Huiwen Wang (eds), *Handbook of Partial Least Squares: Concepts, Methods and Applications* (Springer Handbooks of Computational Statistics Series, vol. 111). Heidelberg, Dordrecht, London, New York: Springer, pp. 125–40.

Völckner, Franziska, Henrik Sattler, Thorsten Hennig-Thurau and Christian M. Ringle (2010), 'The Role of Parent Brand Quality for Service Brand Extension Success', *Journal of Service Research*, **13** (4), 379–96.

Wold, Herman (1989), 'Introduction to the Second Generation of Multivariate Analysis', in Herman Wold (ed.), *Theoretical Empiricism: A General Rationale for Scientific Model-Building*, New York: Paragon House, pp. 7–11.

— (1975), 'Path Models with Latent Variables: The NIPALS Approach', in H.M. Blalock, A. Aganbegian, F.M. Borodkin, R. Boudon and V. Capecchi (eds), *Quantitative Sociology: International Perspectives on Mathematical and Statistical Modeling*, New York: Academic Press, pp. 307–57.

— (1982), 'Soft Modeling: The Basic Design and Some Extensions', in Karl G. Jöreskog and Herman Wold (eds), *Systems Under Indirect Observations: Part I*, Amsterdam: North-Holland, pp. 1–53.

PART V

THE DIGITAL
INFORMATION AGE

13 International advertising theory and methodology in the digital information age
Carolyn A. Lin

INTRODUCTION

Over the past few decades, scholars have developed and refined a raft of theoretical frameworks and research methodologies to help provide empirical evidence of effective international advertising strategies. As a result, a rich body of literature and research convention has been established to help inform our foundational understanding of how advertising works at the international or global level. Even so, not unlike other fields of social scientific research, there have been ongoing debates about the strengths and weaknesses of both the theories and methodologies adopted to predict consumer behavior and marketing outcomes across national boundaries (e.g., Taylor, 2010). These vibrant intellectual exchanges have invigorated further theorizing efforts and methodological advances amidst a rapidly changing international advertising environment in the digital information age.

The underlying issues of these scholarly debates were thoughtfully captured by Taylor (2002), who poignantly highlighted the tendencies of international advertising research to apply global advertising theories to study disparate consumer markets and explain cross-cultural consumer phenomena with empirical evidence of limited scope and duplicability. Taylor's follow-up elaboration (2005, 2010) provided a summary of the advances that were made in international advertising research, in addition to promising new research directions and emerging theoretical developments.

As the pace of development and diffusion of Internet technology continues to accelerate, this unstoppable tidal wave has revolutionized how people access and share product information, obtain product knowledge and seek media and entertainment options as well as communicate with each other around the world. Consequently, consumer expectations have also changed, as they often anticipate finding and receiving product information online that could help inform purchase decisions (Jansen, 2010; Nielsen Research, 2010a).

Conventional advertising practice places its messages separately on a printed page, a location-based space, a voice on the air or a moving image on a TV monitor; it is designed to attract the attention of a relatively "passive audience" in a discontinuous fashion, where the audience action resulting from message exposure is often delayed. Digital advertising placement can integrate the display of different types of messages on the same virtual space; it can be devised to elicit the interest of a relatively "active audience" in a continuous manner, where the audience reaction to the advertising message can be instantaneous. The potential differences in the nature of a "passive" and "active" audience (Kenyon, Wood and Parsons, 2008; Lin, 1999) – particularly within a one-way vs. two-way advertising platform comparison – could have important implications for consumer cognitive response toward advertising messages, in addition to how, when and where such messages could be presented.

The ubiquitous, freewheeling and unpredictable nature of the online communication environment can present both opportunities and challenges to international advertisers and researchers alike. As international advertising in the digital information age remains an emerging research topic, this chapter intends to review the existing theories and methodologies as the basis for exploring and introducing a set of conceptual and empirical approaches that could help advance the research agenda in this new digital frontier.

International Advertising Theories

In general, the theories that we have applied to study international advertising broadly fall into the following categories – macro-, hybrid- or micro-level theories. The macro-level theories are often used to explain consumer behavior based on cultural values, societal conventions or economic systems factors (e.g., GNP or GDP) of a nation or multiple nations in relation to international advertising (De Mooij, 2003; Okazaki, Taylor and Zou, 2006). For instance, Hofstede's (1980) *theory of cultural dimensions* is an excellent example of a macro-level theory, one that has been widely adopted to provide interpretations of consumer behavior across cultures. Other examples of notable macro-level cultural theories include Berry's (1979) notion of *time orientation* differences between Western and Eastern cultures as well as Hall's (1976) typology of *high vs. low context cultures*.

The hybrid-level theories often approach national or consumer cultures from a perspective that considers the increasingly interconnected economic development and massification of media and entertainment options as well as popular fashion, products and brands across different countries in the world. Major hybrid-level theories that have been utilized in advertising research include Schwartz's (1992) ten-dimension human value inventory. Schwartz's contention that human values are more similar than dissimilar across cultures is rooted in an individual's motivational goals associated with specific human values and the larger cultural contexts (Schwartz and Boehnke, 2004). Another example of hybrid-level theory is the *theory of global consumer culture* (Levitt, 1983), which suggests that development in new media technologies would lead to the growth of homogenization of global consumer culture, as consumers prefer goods and services with higher quality and lower prices.

Other researchers expanded this globalization perspective to include the parallel significance of heterogeneous variability within and between global consumer cultures (e.g., House, Quigley and de Luque, 2010; Merz, He and Alden, 2008). Additional theorizing endeavors further operationalized the conception of a globalized consumer culture to reflect certain micro-level aspects. For instance, Alden, Steenkamp and Batra (1999) proposed capturing consumer perceptions of the *local, foreign or global* cultural meanings *of* a global brand. Steenkamp, Batra and Alden (2003) later suggested the concept of *perceived brand globalness* to elucidate consumer perceptions of brand image.

By contrast, micro-level theories and constructs usually examine the factors that influence an individual consumer's motivation, cognition, emotion, attitude, intention and behavior in relation to the effects of international advertising. Research testing micro-level advertising theories and concepts often strived to extract the cognitive and behavioral variability and intersections between consumers within a subgroup and between subgroups in the context of one or between two or more national cultures. For instance, a number of studies have investigated message appeal effectiveness (e.g., Bjerke, Rosendahl, Gopalakrishna and Sandler, 2005; Karande, Almurshidee and Al-Olayan, 2006), psychological needs fulfillment (e.g., Roth, 1992), self-schema construction (e.g., Wang, 2000), emotional involvement (e.g., Lichtlé, 2007; Poels and Dewitte, 2006), product diffusion patterns (e.g., Dwyer, Mesak and Hsu, 2005), information processing (e.g., Aaker and Maheswaran, 1997) as well as theory of reasoned action and theory of planned behavior (e.g., Kang, Hahn, Fortin, Hyun and Eom, 2003).

International Advertising Research Methodologies

Parallel to the debate of whether a standardized, localized or a hybridized strategy would be most cost-efficient and effective, there is also ongoing dialogue on whether to treat each individual nation or the subcultural variations within a nation as the unit of analysis. A number of researchers argued that by not considering the national culture as a continuum, important variations that are useful to explain consumer behavior that may diverge from core national cultural values as well as sub-cultural values within a country could be missed (Oyserman, Daphna, Coon and Kemmelmeiet, 2002; Lenartowicz, Johnson and White, 2003). For instance, Koslow and Costely's (2010) study of three industrialized nations – France, Germany and New Zealand – discovered that the within-country differences were larger than the between-country differences in consumer evaluation of advertising appeals.

Researchers also commented on the over-abundance of descriptive studies, the lack of accumulative theory-driven research and the extensive literature on the standardization debate (Taylor, 2002). For instance, the most popular topical areas covered by international advertising research in the last decade, according to Zou (2005, p. 103), were "standardization" (27.87 percent) and "consumer response" (21.31 percent), followed by "advertising content" (14.75 percent), "social issues" (13.93 percent), "cultural values" (11.48 percent), "campaign management" (7.38 percent) and "agency" (3.28 percent). Taylor's (2005) analysis of methodological trends during the similar period shows that the most commonly used data collection methods were content analysis (34 percent), experiment (25 percent) and survey (22 percent), followed by conceptual (9 percent), secondary data analysis (6 percent) and qualitative (3 percent). Combined, these authors (Taylor, 2002; Zou, 2005) maintained that more explanatory studies and greater data-comparison equivalence reliability as well as cross-national and interdisciplinary collaborations among academic researchers and practitioners are needed.

A number of past studies have endeavored to improve methodological approaches to international advertising and marketing research. For instance, Sharma and Weathers (2003) explored the methods of assessing cross-cultural measurement scale equivalence by comparing confirmatory factor analysis (Steenkamp and Baumgarter, 1998) and generalized (G) theory (Rentz, 1987); their empirical tests showed that the G theory can complement the CFA procedures and both should be utilized to verify measurement scale equivalency.

Tellis and Chandrasekara (2010) found that differences in cross-cultural social desirability response biases resulted in unreliable self-reporting of consumer innovativeness and new product adoption rates across 15 countries in a survey of 5569 respondents; they concluded that negatively valenced items could help reduce such response biases. Their findings updated and confirmed similar methodological concerns discussed in other earlier work (e.g., Van de Vijver and Leung, 1997). Yaprak (2003) summed up these methodological concerns under a "problem umbrella" and emphasized the need for researchers to be mindful of establishing construct equivalence, measure equivalence, data collection and research administration equivalence as well as instrument and measurement reliability across countries and cultures. He further stressed the importance of observing a broader set of socio-cultural contexts, changing consumer behavior in emerging economies and potential biases in cross-cultural research settings.

Craig and Douglas (2000) contend that cross-cultural biases in consumer response to international advertising research can include social acquiescence, social desirability, unique cultural traits, idiosyncratic respondent characteristics, the nature of the research topic and the non-response tendency for certain types of questions across countries and subcultures. Douglas and Craig (1997) suggested three research designs for studying cross-cultural consumer behavior, namely 1) multiple site study design to account for the cultural pluralism within each site; 2) external cultural influence study design to examine consumers' direct and indirect exposure to external influences; and 3) transitional study design to measure consumer transition from one macro-culture to another.

Summary

Unlike advertising research that focuses on domestic consumers, international advertising research could involve additional logistical difficulties in sampling, language translation, data collection and measurement equivalency. As complying with all of the systemic rules associated with conducting scientific empirical research across different countries could be challenging, researchers have been cognizant of setting a reasonable scope for their studies. As a result, international advertising research has yet to fully test a wider range of theories and constructs to amass a broader set of empirical findings to explain and predict consumers' motivational, cognitive, affective and behavioral responses to international or global advertising strategies.

With the increased importance of digital advertising as part of the marketing strategy, would the theoretical debates and methodological challenges associated with traditional international advertising parallel with those of digital international advertising? As the digital media channels that deliver international advertising messages are also the same outlets for consumers to search product information, communicate their product reviews and conduct product purchases, this type of advertising paradigm – which is no longer sender/advertiser centric – has opened up a new set of theoretical and methodological challenges and possibilities. The following discussion will explore the theoretical and methodological approaches that could be effective in conducting digital international advertising.

THE DIGITAL ADVERTISING AGE

In the digital information age, the Internet is the true gateway to a *virtual global village* – one characterized by one-on-one, one-to-many, many-to-one and many-to-many communication – much like the scenario where villagers can freely meet one on one, in groups or in a town hall setting in the offline world. In particular, the Internet has enabled all online villagers in the world to see, hear, experience, witness, share and/or discuss the memorable village moments – memories that they have come together to share – one villager at a time. The same phenomenon is also true with digital international advertising, where the *virtual global village* has provided advertisers a ready and all-encompassing platform to reach their consumers around the world.

Past work has developed a set of definitions to delineate the conceptual meanings of interactive advertising, online advertising, e-commerce, shopping sites (Ha, 2008) as well as international, multinational, global and transnational marketing (De Mooij, 1994). However, digital advertising research would most likely not be bounded by these conventional distinctions. Digital international advertising could take up a number of digital formats and are most likely accessible on the Internet via different media formats. Hence, the concepts of "supranational" and "media spillover" (Roberts and Ko, 2001) would better reflect the nature of international advertising in digital forms, which transcends definitional and national boundaries.

Digital International Advertising Research

According to Ha's (2008, p. 37) review of online advertising research, advertising researchers have applied theoretical frameworks such as product involvement theory, information processing theories and psychological theories. For instance, the elaboration likelihood model was found to have contrary results in predicting online advertising information processing, where one study supported the ELM's basic typology (Cho, 1999), and the other study suggested that the cognitive process for accessing online and offline information may differ (Karson and Korgaonkar, 2001). Rossiter and Bellman (1999) found that consumer web navigation ability and expertise as well as their product needs and situational restraints (e.g., time pressure) could affect their ad schema.

As the theoretical scope and implications for the relations between advertisers and consumers on digital international advertising remain unclear, the communication phenomenon that integrates different aspects of this advertising modality could be seen from the perspectives of *transmissive, social, mobile* and *inter-media communication.* The following discussion will explore this tri-dimensional concept of digital advertising culture and review the relevant empirical studies that fall under these conceptual dimensions.

Transmissive communication
When an advertising message, image and/or video is posted on the Internet, except for those who live within the boundaries of countries that practise system-wide censorship, every Internet user from around the world could have the ability to see and/or hear that message, image and/or video. One question that immediately comes to mind is whether advertisers should generate separate marketing strategies that independently target domestic and international audiences/consumers. As the growth of a *global consumer culture* and a *global youth culture* continues to climb (Kjeldgaard and Askegaard, 2006; Steenkamp, Batra and Alden, 2003), products that have a universal appeal and cut across cultural barriers could perhaps be positioned to target a worldwide audience with an integrated global advertising strategy. For those products whose brand appeal may be more closely tied to certain geographic regions or cultural-linguistic diasporas, the branding strategy could consider adding that extra targeted cultural flavor through an integrated approach to capture the acceptance and liking of both domestic and international consumers.

By implication, if separate domestic, international and global advertising strategies are being adopted to market a particular product or brand on the Internet, the advertisers need to be mindful of preventing any conflicts in those separate advertising strategies to avoid confusing, deluding or damaging the image or equity of the brand/product. More importantly, online advertising messages should be formulated to express a form of *transmissive communication* that reflects a relatable and accessible audience lifestyle and consumer culture across international boundaries. As defined herein, *transmissive communication* permits the transmission of communication meanings across cultures through the use of cross-culturally recognized, accepted, liked and preferred symbols, images, portrayals, activities, consumer values, lifestyle attributes, etc. If these advertising messages could excel in engaging in this type of transmissive communication to connect with and touch the lives of their audiences and consumers both domestic and international, then a standardized advertising strategy could prove to be a practical and cost-efficient way to market an international or global product/brand.

Empirical research efforts that tried to dissect this complex phenomenon have provided preliminary confirmation for the assumption of *transmissive communication* introduced herein. For instance, a study that assessed the cross-cultural validity of web-usage-related lifestyles between the U.S. and Belgium found the structure and meanings of the lifestyle dimensions related to web usage were the same across both cultures (Bregman, Geuens, Weitjers, Smith and Swinyard, 2005). Kwak, Zinkhan, Pan and Andras (2011) investigated cross-cultural attitudes toward online advertising among online chatters and found that there was no difference in consumers' information-seeking tendency and attitude online toward advertising. They contended that the Internet could potentially be a medium that is free from cultural boundaries and can help create a global village.

Social communication
The rise of the social media phenomenon, which has evolved into the largest type of virtual community, reflects a natural outgrowth of the established but disparate virtual communities within the *virtual global village*. In the U.S., social networks accounted for 22.7 percent of the time spent on the Internet, topping all other major Internet-use activities (Nielsen Research, 2010c). Facebook display advertising accounted for about 9.5 percent of the display advertising spending online in 2010 (Flower and Steel, 2010). Twitter usage was reported at 8 percent, whereas young adults, African-Americans and Latinos as well as urbanites, tweeted more than their respective counterparts (Smith and Rainie, 2010). As the U.S. led the 22 nations polled with 46 percent of its adult population using social networking sites, Poland and Britain (each at 43 percent) had the most social network users in Europe and South Korea (40 percent) topped the Asian countries in the number of social networkers (Pew Research, 2010). While Brazil had the highest percentage of South American social networkers (33 percent), Turkey (26 percent) and Jordan (24 percent) were the most socially networked near-East and Middle-East countries. Kenya reported the top percentage of social networking activities (19 percent) among the African nations.

Depending on user preference and communication purposes, consumer-use activity and cognitive involvement associated with these virtual social networks may vary. The social communication that is being conducted via these virtual social networks – including sharing product information and user-generated content about products – can also have an effect on consumer activities in the offline social networks. This is because online social communicators often belong to more than one online and offline social networking group. If a new brand or product idea has been plugged into the online social communication networks, it is likely that the relevant online communication discourse could have a second life in the offline social communication networks (e.g., families, friends, co-workers, other contacts, etc.) as well.

Trusov, Bodapati, Anand and Bucklin (2010) examined the network connections on a social network site and found that their statistical models were able to correctly identify the influential users or influencers on the network. Mulhern (2009) pointed out that research on household buying behavior has always shown that social networks play a role in consumer behavior; today's Internet network environments have provided advertisers with the ability to extract the content of such social communication to help construct their consumers' profile.

It is not surprising that the influence of word-of-mouth (WOM) marketing that takes place among consumers in social communication networks has become an important component of today's digital advertising strategy. Trusov, Bucklin and Pauwels (2009) reported that WOM referrals had a strong effect on increased new consumer traffic and there was a 20-to-1 ratio for the long-term elasticity of consumer signups between WOM and typical marketing events. Additional studies also showed that positive word-of-mouth product reviews could impact consumer attitudes (Lee, Rodgers and Kim, 2009) and facilitate product recommendations (Lee and Youn, 2009). Hung and Li (2007) tested the WOM phenomenon via a Chinese newsgroup and found that online exchanges were seen as good social capital sources to help facilitate their product knowledge and consumer reflexivity.

Mobile communication

As mobile phones rapidly swept across most regions in the world, mobile Internet use has also been on the rise. For instance, there were over 855 million and 604 million mobile phone subscribers in China and India in 2010, respectively, compared to over 186 million mobile phone subscribers in Brazil and another 181 million in Russia (Elkin, 2010). Even though the advertising revenues via the mobile Internet modality remains relatively conservative (e.g., $223.2 million in China in 2010), revenue growth is expected across the board. As the cost of acquiring mobile services is relatively lower than other forms of digital communication technologies in emerging economies, a disruptive growth pattern showing a reverse innovation model with these emerging economies spearheading the mobile advertising success ahead of developed economies will likely take place (Bala, 2010).

While many consumers consider the use of their mobile phones an indispensible part of their daily life, these phones have become a true personal medium. Hence, it is not uncommon to see people keeping their mobile communication devices on and constantly checking them during all waking hours (Tanaka and Terry-Cobo, 2008). For those advertisers who wish to take advantage of this always-on and on-demand communication medium, the question of what people do with and where their eyes roam on their mobile communication devices is an important one. Compared to advertising on the Internet media outlets and the social media platform, tailored mobile communication advertising could be a nimble way to target those consumers who are on the go and likely to indulge in more impulsive purchase behavior. At the same time, as mobile phones are seen as a private and personal device for work, play and much more, consumers could also be more resistant to advertiser intrusion into their personal and personalized digital space.

Preliminary work has addressed several conceptual dimensions related to mobile advertising, including consumer preference, receptivity, attitudes and purchase. For instance, Tsang, Ho and Liang (2004) studied a Taiwanese sample and found that, while entertainment was a major factor influencing consumer attitudes toward mobile advertising, consumers were also concerned with their privacy and could be irritated by the advertising stream on their mobile phone. A study conducted in Australia by Haghirian, Madlberger and Tanuskova (2005) suggested the following: 1) mobile advertising content development should be mindful of the available display space and perhaps be integrated with other media advertising in the marketing mix; 2) consumer attitudes did not influence the perceived value of mobile advertising; and 3) mobile phones and the messages received on them are seen as both private and personal.

A study of Japanese consumers by Okazaki, Li and Hirose (2009), likewise, reported that there was a strong causal relation between consumers' privacy concerns and perceived risk associated with mobile advertising. Similarly, in a New Zealand study, consumer trust of mobile ads that passed the filter of the mobile service and featured personally relevant products were both important factors in determining positive consumer perception and attitude toward a brand (Carroll, Barnes, Scornavacca and Fletcher, 2007). The only cross-cultural study in the literature revealed that, while perceived informativeness and value of the mobile ads was more important for Korean than American college students in determining purchase intention, both groups had a favorable attitude toward the entertainment and trustworthy aspects of mobile advertising (Choi, Hwang and McMillan, 2008).

Inter-media communication
The increasing significance of cross-media synergy between traditional and online digital advertising in the corporate bottom line around the world is obvious. For instance, 58 percent of Americans surveyed did searches about the products and services that they considered purchasing

in 2010 (Jansen, 2010). Online product reviews were ranked as the third most trusted source of information for making a purchase decision on consumer electronics, cosmetics and cars – following family and friends – by a study conducted in nine countries in the Asian Pacific region, including Japan, Korea, China, Taiwan, Hong Kong, Singapore, India, Australia and New Zealand (Nielsen Research, 2010a). Sixteen percent of the United Kingdom consumers who visited the top 200 e-commerce sites turned their online shopping visits into actual purchases (Nielsen Research, 2010b).

The Internet's unique capability for allowing users to obtain and then share information with others on the same reception and delivery channel has set the Internet apart from all other traditional media as an advertising and marketing venue. Past work has established that the synergy stemming from *inter-media communication* between new digital media and traditional media content and delivery modalities could be determined based on their relative content superiority, technical superiority, and cost efficiency as well as their social attribute and lifestyle characteristics (Lin, 2004).

Tsao and Sibley (2004) discovered a complementary and reinforcement relationship between Internet and traditional media advertising (increase–increase) effects but displacement effects between the Internet and newspapers. Okazaki and Hirose (2009) also reported a complementary effect between consumer attitudes toward traditional media, PC-based Internet, and mobile Internet. Their findings also suggest that consumer satisfaction with one medium could influence the gratification opportunities for other media and mobile PC users will reinforce their information search via PC-based Internet for a high-involvement product. Lin (2011) contends that a compensatory relationship could exist between digital media and traditional media to produce an outcome of media supplementation, complementarity and/or displacement, depending on how the audience wishes to compensate for their lack of access to and/or satisfaction with a certain media resource by securing an attainable alternative to optimize their media-use goals.

Other researchers have also suggested that competition from online media has helped traditional media flourish to better serve the audience with their particular brand of content (Kwak, Zinkhan, Pan and Andras, 2011). Since no research has investigated cross-cultural media substitution phenomena between online and traditional advertising changes, additional research is needed to establish which digital international advertising vehicles could be best utilized to displace, supplement or complement traditional media as a global advertising venue for which types of products/brand.

Theorizing Digital International Advertising

Operating under the conceptual umbrella of transmissive, social, mobile and inter-media communication, the following discussion will explore a set of emerging and existing theories that could be useful for studying the phenomenon of digital international advertising. This proposed set of theoretical frameworks could be considered as an addition to the aforementioned corpus of theories relevant to international advertising research.

From the perspective of transmissive communication, a theory of *global digital consumer culture* (GDCC) that can cut across national and cultural boundaries to reflect the age of a virtual global village needs to be developed. This theory will describe, explain and predict the content, structure as well as the system-interactivity and user-interaction dynamics of the digital advertising environment, in addition to the consumer characteristics and behaviors from a virtual global village. This theory will need to describe the shared linguistic basis, message construction principles, visual presentation styles, persuasive communication appeals, etc. that help shape the global digital advertising phenomenon. In developing this GDCC theory, it will also be necessary to establish the substantive similarities and dissimilarities between digital consumer culture, national culture, national consumer culture and global consumer culture. Past work on defining different types of cross-cultural marketing (Akaka and Alden, 2010; de Mooij, 1994; Levitt, 1983) provides a good starting point for the undertaking of this likely complicated and arduous theorizing endeavor.

In addressing the *social communication* phenomenon characterizing a global advertising environment, several existing theories could help us better understand how consumers use the social media. The *uses and gratifications perspective* is one such example (Eighmey, 1997; Katz, Blumler and Gurevitch, 1974; Korgaonkar and Wolin, 1999; Lin, 1999; Roberts and Ko, 2010), where explicating the various user needs met by social media uses and gratifications could help inform researchers on where advertising and consumption may fit in within the social communication context. A recent study of Canadian college students illustrated that, while peer pressure, social connectivity and curiosity were the primary gratifications sought for joining the Facebook network, passing time, sociability and sharing social information were the primary gratifications obtained from their Facebook activity (Quan-Haase and Young, 2011). Hence, the following sample consumer motivations – including surveillance, entertainment, information seeking, information sharing, cognitive stimulation, social identity, personal expression, social presentation, companionship, passing time and voyeurism – could all be relevant factors that will help explain digital social media use and how consumers may process advertising messages displayed on such social media networks.

Other established theories that have been widely utilized to explain social network phenomena could also be useful in exploring the relations involving interpersonal and group dimensions online. For instance, *social network theory*, which has been applied to study the formation of and interactions within interpersonal networks characterized by strong ties and weak ties (Haythornthwaite, 2000), could be a promising framework to help identify the social communication grouping patterns. By the same token, *social capital theory* (Coleman, 1988; Nahapiet and Ghoshal, 1998) could help explicate the social network dynamics and consumer perception/attitude toward the social affordances offered by their social networks that could be used to capitalize their social communication activities – one of which could involve product referral and purchase actions.

As the *mobile communication* culture is still emerging and its popularity relies on the accessibility to mobile Internet connection, it is possible that theory building could be a daunting task. This was evidenced in the limited existing literature, which cast a broad conceptual net by applying a number of theories from different social science disciplines without finding any robust theoretical implications. For instance, a case study review conducted by Park, Shenoy and Salvendy (2008) proposed a typology that helps classify a set of existing domestic mobile advertising cases into advertisement (design), audience (involvement) and environmental (context) factors to help guide future research on mobile advertising consumer behavior. Sullivan Mort and Drennan (2007) tested the concepts of involvement, innovativeness and self-efficacy in consumer use of mobile services; their findings suggest that the first two variables were significant predictors, but not the last.

Kolsaker and Drakatos (2009) examined consumer receptivity to mobile advertising from the perspective of emotional attachment and found that users regarded their mobile devices as an essential part of their daily life at an emotional level. Moreover, the more strongly, emotionally attached users had a more favorable response to mobile advertising interruptions, but other users considered such intrusions irritating. Based on the thesis of theory of reasoned action, Xu, Oh and Teo (2009) tested their empirical models to explain consumer attitude and intention associated with the use of location-based advertising applications. They reported that multimedia location-based advertising was seen as both an irritant as well as a facilitator for enhancing the information and entertainment value of such advertising application; multimedia location-based advertising was also found to have a positive influence on consumer attitude and intention toward a purchase.

As the existing literature has not shown any clear directions for how to explicate *mobile communication* behaviors, it is useful to conceptualize this phenomenon as a user-centric behavior by reviewing the communication activities that consumers carry out with their mobile devices. Hence, focusing on consumer need for cognition (e.g., information) and simulation (e.g., entertainment) – as well as their need for association (e.g., social identity) and social connection (e.g., companionship) – could be a good starting point. Existing theoretical typologies – including the uses and gratifications perspective (Lin, 2006; Roberts and Ko, 2010) or mood management (Zillman, 1988) – could be useful frameworks for examining how mobile advertising could target those consumer needs. The flow construct, which measures consumer online shopping experience from a utilitarian vs. hedonic perspective, could also be another useful construct for theorizing consideration (Novak, Hoffman and Young, 2000).

The conceptual meaning of an *inter-media communication* culture may need to be revisited and updated in the near future, so that its operational definition could reflect the evolving Internet-enabled TV systems (e.g., Apple TV and Google TV) that are threatening to replace the traditional TV-viewing culture as we know it. When the Internet eventually becomes the major delivery platform for all media and mediated entertainment products, the inter-media communication concept will need to guide the understanding of both the content delivery mechanisms (e.g., mobile vs. non-mobile) and the interrelations between different media vehicles (e.g., *American Idol* and Facebook) that play a role in influencing consumer attention, motivations and interface with digital advertising.

The *media substitution hypothesis*, which can help assess the *compensatory functions* between online and offline media use, should also provide another useful approach to study social communication in relation to media use and digital advertising exposure (Lin, 2004, 2011). Other potentially useful theories that could help explain the symbiotic or predatory relations between competing forms of digital advertising media can include niche theory (Hutchinson, 1957), which defines the niche as a hyperdimensional space where different species can co-exist in a finite amount of space through self-transformation or elimination of their competition (Wilson, 1992). The principle of functional equivalence (Himmelweit, Oppenheim and Vince, 1958) could also be another useful concept to help explain how audiences/consumers may reallocate their time spent with digital media and advertising to manage their fixed availability of leisure time (McCombs and Nolan, 1992; McCombs, 1993).

Measuring Digital International Advertising

In a digital advertising environment where inter-media communication may characterize the ways that consumers access media and advertising information, the concept of "audience" will become increasingly difficult to define, as will the metrics that advertisers use to measure audience activity. Similarly, when a two-way interactivity mechanism becomes fully embedded in a digital media environment, the nature of audience activity and hence consumer behavior would also need to be reconceptualized. In an environment where the audience could be the content-generators and the consumer could also be the "designer" of his/her preferred product features (e.g., automobiles or fashion), the audience is by nature an active participant in the digital media platform and the consumer is an initiating collaborator in product marketing.

As such, the strategy that digital advertisers will adopt to target the audience/consumer should treat the audience/consumer as a partner who could help define the measurement methodology and carry out the collection of audience/consumer behavior data. In other words, the concept of "the consumer as researcher" could become useful, if digital advertising vehicles can include a "user-generated question" mechanism and the commonly applied "user-feedback" feature to turn the advertising space into a market data collection vehicle or consumer behavior measurement tool.

Specifically, in measuring the audience/consumer units in a digital international advertising environment, we could add the following exemplars to the methodological discussion and innovations presented above.

Sampling
The difficulties involved in drawing and securing a sample for international advertising research have been many and usually rely on collaboration from researchers who are physically located on site in different nations. The digital advertising environment could change that standard practice by securing international samples through the sampling populations that are provided by the consumers themselves across the world, assuming that the digital advertising strategy follows the transmissive communication principle and can attract sizable consumer segments to patronize the advertising message delivery platforms. Based on the digital tracking data, international advertising researchers could segment the consumers into such categories as browsers, likely adopters, occasional adopters, repeated adopters, regular adopters, loyal adopters, etc., when determining the sampling purposes.

Research methods and procedures
The validity and reliability of online surveys has long been verified and established by past research, when compared to other types of self-reported survey methods (Morris, Woo and Cho, 2003). When conducting and distributing online advertising research surveys in the digital

advertising environment, researchers could consider having the study participants/consumers create their own survey questions with the use of a ready-to-use survey program template for themselves and other study participants to answer. In a similar vein, other traditional research methods such as field data collection could also include this type of interactive research procedure by offering study participants/consumers the opportunity to create their own questions for themselves and others to answer. This type of dualistic approach, which includes researcher-generated and consumer-generated questions, then puts the concept of consumer as researcher into practice.

In terms of controlled experiments, the on-site researcher monitoring of a true experimental design that studies digital international advertising effects should be strictly observed. If the study involves a quasi-experimental design, which is often the case in advertising research, then other types of experimental control approaches could be adopted to alleviate the needs for strict on-site researcher monitoring. For instance, a stand-alone or built-in web video camera could be set up to monitor the experimental condition, if study participants are to interact with the experimental treatment one at a time and their privacy could be protected. As long as the data collection is done via the Internet channel, distributing participant incentives post study could also be easily accomplished via an electronic gift card that is redeemable online.

Depending on the theory and the best research design (as determined by the researchers) to test the theory, experimental research for digital advertising could perhaps rely more heavily on collecting field experiment research data than laboratory-based controlled-experimental data. This is because the digital research environment has a built-in internal control mechanism, one that is characterized by the minimal artificiality in the research setting where the study participants could be interacting with *real* ads in a real-life controlled setting (e.g., their own home) without the unwanted distractions (which have been precluded in the study design and research execution). Robinson, Wysocka and Hand (2007), for instance, found that, compared to a controlled experiment with participant incentives and animation features, banner ad click-through rates did not increase in a field experiment. This outcome is probably what would have actually occurred in a real-life non-experimental setting.

Measurement and analysis

Measurement issues associated with digital international advertising are highly complex, as digital advertising tends to take on a variety of vehicles across media delivery modalities that go beyond the scope of the traditional display and classified ads. Bhat, Bevans and Sengupta (2002) provided a review of the following aspects – exposure or popularity, stickiness (and quality of user relationships), usefulness of content, co-marketing success, and targeting efficiency – to aid researchers in their evaluation of web measurement metrics. They contend that advertisers need to match their consumer research objectives with the most appropriate research methodologies, as there is no one single best way to achieve web measurement effectiveness. Rodgers, Wang, Rettie and Alpert (2007) conducted a cross-cultural validity study of a web motivation inventory; their findings suggest that the cross-culturally neutral scale included in the original inventory was valid and reliable and the extended inventory resulting from their own study could enhance the unidimensionality as well as the validity and reliability of the original inventory.

Other researchers who examined different ways of measuring web audience did not find conclusive measurement metrics for reliably assessing web traffic. For instance, the length of data collection period could easily alter the sample size and site-visit measures needed to take into consideration cumulative audience ratings as well as the measurement units, whether they be unique visitors or visit frequency (e.g., Lee and Leckenby, 1999). Coffey (2002) contrasted three web audience measurement methods – metered user exposure panels, user recall surveys and log file analysis – and documented a set of problems associated with defining the sampling universe and sample recruiting, among other concerns.

Other different preliminary methodologies developed to measure the marketing effectiveness of online social networking sites also represent a useful entry to help guide the continuing pursuit of establishing valid and reliable measurement metrics. For example, Ansari, Koenigsberg and Stahl (2008) proposed a methodological approach to model and map the multiple relationships that exist among different types of social network users of a social networking site. Dholakia, Bagozzi and Pearo (2004) presented two group-level determinants to help explicate group norms and social identity in virtual community participation and activity. Murdough (2009) presented a set of systematic procedures and dimensions for assessing social media measurement, which includes the approach to handle the data from different data sources (i.e., Enterprise listening platform, text mining partners and platform application programming interface) as well as to assess the measurement outcomes involving reach, discussion and site analytics outcomes.

Above and beyond the complex measurement issues and potential methodological solutions cited above, the methodological concerns that arise with digital international advertising loom large, as they could multiply by the number of consumers measured across different regions, countries, cultures, subcultures and linguistic types. While a consensus on adopting a standard set of metrics for measuring digital advertising audience activity is unlikely to arrive in the near future, it would be good practice for all industry researchers (e.g., the IAB) to develop methodologies that observe fundamental social scientific principles and be vigilant in reporting validity and reliability problems. For academic researchers, the biggest challenge will be to scientifically gain a fuller understanding of the motivations, beliefs, attitudes, intentions, habits, norms, and behaviors as well as the socio-cultural, economic and lifestyle moderators associated with global digital consumer culture (GDCC), before empirically affirming the best practice, valid measurement and reliable methodologies for assessing the effectiveness of digital international advertising.

CONCLUSION

It is likely that this chapter has only scratched the surface of the potential complexity, problems and opportunities associated with international advertising research in a digital information age. In the current digital media environment, marketers have the capability to target niche, micro and macro segments of consumers with tailored advertising strategies. Consumers have the freedom to make use of the product information received through digital channels by sharing and discussing the information with others, sending queries and feedback to advertisers, placing purchase orders and redeeming sales promotion rewards, post consumer-generated content (e.g., product reviews), etc. As such, this new digital marketing frontier and its yet-to-be discovered potential are emerging amidst the growth of a global awareness of popular consumer products, which has been permeated by the progressively expanded reach of a global media culture and hastened by the rapid delivery speed of the Internet.

As the online universe is open to all consumers around the world with an Internet connection and information transmitted through mobile communication technologies is much harder for government censors to control, the affordances that digital media technologies offer to marketers and consumers across the national boundaries can be both bountiful in volume and rich in substance. It is possible that the emerging virtual global village described herein is the first true global village in human history (Kwak, Zinkhan, Pan and Andras, 2011). More importantly, this virtual global village is currently fostering a set of global consumer cultures that is being sought, shared and shaped through the exchanges of images, ideas and information from consumers around the world, sidestepping the diversities and differences in other conventional cultural settings (e.g., religion and language).

Lastly, the Internet is the most public mass medium in terms of its ubiquitous reach of users and vast amalgam of social media networks. It is also the most intimate personal medium, as it enables consumers to create information for, seek and retrieve content from as well as make use of such content to accomplish their personal surveillance, entertainment, information, communication and socializing needs for work and play. Hence, an effective digital international advertising strategy will need to take both the public and private nature of the Internet medium into consideration and target those consumer expectations in a satisfactory manner. The existing message and media placement strategies as well as advertising effectiveness measurement (for both traditional and digital advertising media) that were crafted based on the familiar theoretical and methodological approaches may also require a reinvention or re-adaptation, in addition to new theoretical and methodological innovations.

In the digital information age, the future is now. The biggest test for both academic and industry researchers alike then remains how to decipher the operational meanings of the current digital international advertising environment, ascertaining a valid framework for strategy development and capitalizing on the synergy between technology, consumer and culture. After all, what is riding on the future now embodies nothing less than the fluid nature of the digital media environment (Lin, 2004) – one that is characterized by its transmutability in digital international advertising platforms, tasks and functions.

REFERENCES

Aaker, Jennifer and Durairaj Maheswaran (1997), 'The effect of cultural orientations on persuasion', *Journal of Consumer Research*, **24** (December), 315–28.

Akaka, Archpru M. and Dana L. Alden (2010), 'Global brand positioning and perceptions: International advertising and global consumer culture', *International Journal of Advertising*, **29** (1), 37–56.

Alden, Dana, Jan-Benedict E.M. Steenkamp and Rajeev Batra (1999), 'Brand positioning through advertising in Asia, North America, and Europe: The role of global consumer culture', *Journal of Marketing*, **63** (1), 75–87.

Ansari, Ansim, Oded Koenigsberg and Florian Stahl (2008), 'Modeling multiple relationships in online social networks', Working Paper, Columbia University, New York City.

Bala, Venkatesh (2010), 'Going global means going mobile in emerging markets', available at http://blog.nielsen.com/nielsenwire/global/going-global-means-going-mobile-in-emerging-markets/ (accessed 17 August 2010).

Berry, Leonard L. (1979), 'The time-buying consumer', *Journal of Retailing*, **55** (Winter), 58–69.

Bhat, Subodh, Michael Bevans and Sanjit Sengupta (2002), 'Measuring users' web activity to evaluate and enhance advertising effectiveness', *Journal of Advertising*, **31** (3), 97–106.

Bjerke, Rune, Tom Rosendahl, Pradeep Gopalakrishna and Dennis Sandler (2005), 'Ad element liking and its relationship to overall ad liking: A European cross-cultural investigation', *Journal of Promotion Management*, **12** (1), 97–127.

Carroll, Amy, Stuart J. Barnes, Eusebio Scornavacca and Keith Fletcher (2007), 'Consumer perceptions and attitudes towards SMS advertising: Recent evidence from New Zealand', *International Journal of Advertising*, **26** (1), 79–98.

Cho, Chang-Hoan (1999), 'How advertising works on the WWW: Modified elaboration likelihood model', *Journal of Current Issues and Research in Advertising*, **21** (1), 33–51.

Choi, Yung Kyun, Jang-Sun Hwang and Sally J. McMillan (2008), 'Gearing up for mobile advertising: A cross-cultural examination of key factors that drive mobile messages home to consumers', *Psychology & Marketing*, **25** (8), 756–68.

Coffey, Steve (2001), 'Internet audience measurement: A practitioner's view', *Journal of Interactive Advertising*, http://jiad.org/voll/no2/coffey/index.htm.

Coleman, James S. (1988), 'Social capital in the creation of human capital', *American Journal of Sociology*, **94**, 95–120.

Craig, Samuel C. and Susan P. Douglas (2000), *International Marketing Research*, 2nd ed. New York: John Wiley and Sons.

De Mooij, Marieke (1994), *Advertising Worldwide: Concepts, Theories and Practice of International, Multinational and Global Advertising*, 2nd ed. Trowbridge: Prentice Hall International/Redwood Books.

De Mooij, Marieke (2003), 'Convergence and divergence in consumer behavior: Implications for global advertising', *International Journal of Advertising*, **22**, 183–202.

Dholakia, Utpal M., Richard P. Bagozzi and Lisa Klein Pearo (2004), 'A social influence model of consumer participation in network- and small-group-based virtual communities', *International Journal of Research in Marketing*, **21** (3), 241–63.

Douglas, Susan O. and Craig, C. Samuel (1997), 'The changing dynamics of consumer behavior: Implications for cross-cultural research', *International Journal of Research in Marketing*, **14**, 379–95.

Dwyer, Sean, Hani Mesak and Maxwell Hsu (2005), 'An exploratory examination of the influence of national culture on cross-national product diffusion', *Journal of International Marketing*, **13** (2), 1–27.

Eighmey, James (1997), 'Profiling user responses to commercial web sites', *Journal of Advertising Research*, **37** (3), 59–66.

Elkin, Noah (2010), 'Looking beyond the staggering mobile stats in the BRIC countries', available at http://www.emarketer.com/blog/index.php/staggering-mobile-stats-bric-countries (accessed 17 March 2010).

Flower, Geoffrey A. and Emily Steel (2010), 'Valuing Facebooks' Ads', available at http://online.wsj.com/article/SB10001424052748703665904575600482851430358.html (accessed 11 November 2010).

Ha, Louisa (2008), 'Online advertising research in advertising journals: A review', *Journal of Current Issues and Research in Advertising*, **30** (1), 31–48.

Haghirian, P., M. Madlberger and A. Tanuskova (2005), 'Increasing advertising value of mobile marketing – An empirical study of antecedents', *Proceedings of the 38th Hawaii International Conference on System Sciences*, **32c**, 10.1109/HICSS.2005.311, Big Island, Hawaii.

Hall, Edward T. (1976), *Beyond Culture*, Garden City, NY: Anchor Books, Doubleday.

Haythornthwaite, Caroline (2000), 'Online personal networks', *New Media and Society*, **2** (2), 195–226.

Himmelweit, Hilde T., A.N. Oppenheim and Pamela Vince (1958), *Television and the Child: An Empirical Study of the Effect of Television on The Young*, London: Oxford University Press.

Hofstede, Geert (1980), *Culture's Consequences: International Differences in Work-Related Values*, Beverly Hills, CA: Sage Publications.

House, Robert J., Narda R. Quigley and Mary S. de Luque (2010), 'Insights from Project GLOBE: Extending global advertising research through a contemporary framework', *International Journal of Advertising*, **29** (1), 111–39.

Hung, Kineta H. and Stella Yiyan Li (2007), 'The influence of eWOM on virtual consumer communities: Social capital, consumer learning, and behavioral outcomes', *Journal of Advertising Research*, **47** (4), 485–95.

Hutchinson, G.E. (1957), 'Concluding remarks', *Cold Springs Harbor Symposium Quantitative Biology*, **22**, 415–27.

Jansen, Jim (2010), 'Online product research', Pew Research Center, available at http://www. pewinternet.org/Reports/2010/Online-Product-Research.aspx (accessed 5 October 2010).

Kang, Hyunmo, Minhi Hahn, David R. Fortin, Yong J. Hyun and Yunni Eom (2003), 'Effects of perceived behavioral control on the consumer usage intention of e-coupons', *Psychology & Marketing*, **23** (10), 841–64.

Karande, Kiran, Khalid A. Almurshidee and Fahad Al-Olayan (2006), 'Advertising standardisation in culturally similar markets: Can we standardise all components?' *International Journal of Advertising*, **25** (4), 489–512.

Karson, Eric J. and Pradeep K. Korgaonkar (2001), 'An experimental investigation of Internet advertising and the Elaboration Likelihood Model', *Journal of Current Issues and Research in Advertising*, **23** (2), 53–72.

Katz, Elihu, Jay G. Blumler and Gurevitch Michael (1974), 'Utilization of mass communication by the individual', in Jay G. Blumler and Elihu Katz (eds), *The Uses of Mass Communications: Current Perspectives on Gratifications Research*, Beverly Hills, CA: Sage, pp. 19–32.

Kenyon, Alexandra J., Emma H. Wood and Anthony Parsons (2008), 'Exploring the audiences' role: A decoding model for the 21st Century', *Journal of Advertising Research*, **48** (2), 276–86.

Kjeldgaard, Dannie and Søren Askegaard (2006), 'The globalization of youth culture: The global youth segment of common difference', *Journal of Consumer Research*, **33** (2), 231–47.

Kolsaker, Ailsa and Nikolaos Drakatos (2009), 'Mobile advertising: The influence of emotional attachment to mobile devices on consumer receptiveness', *Journal of Marketing Communications*, **15** (4), 267–80.

Korgaonkar, Pradeep K. and Lori D. Wolin (1999), 'A multivariate analysis of web usage', *Journal of Advertising Research*, **39** (2), 53–68.

Koslow, Scott and Carooyn Costely (2010), 'How consumer heterogeneity muddles the international advertising debate', *International Journal of Advertising*, **29** (2), 221–44.

Kwak, Hyokjin, George M. Zinkhan, Yue Pan and Trina Larsen Andras (2011), 'Consumer communications, media use, and purchases via the Internet: A comparative, exploratory study', *Journal of International Consumer Marketing*, **20** (3), 55–68.

Lee, Suckkee and John D. Leckenby (1999), 'Impact of measurement period on website rankings and traffic estimation: A user-centric approach', *Journal of Current Issues and Research in Advertising*, **21** (2), 1–10.

Lee, Mira, Shelly Rodgers and Mikyoung Kim (2009), 'Effects of valence and extremity of eWOM on attitude toward the brand and website', *Journal of Current Issues and Research in Advertising*, **31** (2), 1–11.

Lee, Mira and Seounmi Youn (2009), 'Electronic word of mouth (eWOM) – how eWOM platforms influence consumer product judgement', *International Journal of Advertising*, **28** (3), 473–99.

Lenartowicz, Tomasz, James P. Johnson and Carolyn T. White (2003), 'The neglect of intracountry cultural variation in international management research', *Journal of Business Research*, **56** (12), 999–1008.

Levitt, Theodore (1983), 'The globalization of markers', *Harvard Business Review*, **61** (3), 92–102.

Lichtlé, Marie-Christine (2007), 'The effect of an advertisement's colour on emotions evoked by an ad and attitude towards the ad', *International Journal of Advertising*, **26** (1), 37–62.

Lin, Carolyn A. (2011), 'Media substitution: Supplementation, complementarity or displacement? in Arun Vishwanath and George. A. Barnett (eds), *The Diffusion of Innovations: A Communication Science Perspective*, New York: Peter Lang Publishers, pp. 171–92.

Lin, Carolyn A. (1999), 'Online-service adoption likelihood', *Journal of Advertising Research*, **39** (2), 79–89.

Lin, Carolyn A. (2006), 'Predicting webcasting adoption via personal innovativeness and perceived utilities', *Journal of Advertising Research*, **46** (2), 228–38.

Lin, Carolyn A. (2004), 'Webcasting adoption: Technology fluidity, user innovativeness, and media substitution', *Journal of Broadcasting & Electronic Media*, **48** (30), 446–65.

McCombs, Maxwell (1972), 'Mass media in the marketplace', *Journalism Monographs*, **24**, 1–104.

McCombs, Maxwell and Jack Nolan (1992), 'The relative constancy approach to consumer spending for media', *Journal of Media Economics*, **5** (2), 43–52.

Merz, Michael A., Yi He and Dana L. Alden (2008), 'A categorization approach to analyzing the global consumer culture debate', *International Marketing Review*, **25** (2), 166–82.

Morris, Jon D., Chongmoo Woo and Chang-Hoan Cho (2003), 'Internet measures of advertising effects: A global issue', *Journal of Current Issues and Research in Advertising*, **25** (1), 25–43.

Mulhern, Frank (2009), 'Integrated marketing communications: From media channels to digital connectivity', *Journal of Marketing Communications*, **15** (2–3), 85–101.

Murdough, Chris (2009), 'Social media measurement: It's not impossible', *Journal of Interactive Advertising*, **10** (1), http://jiad.org/article127.

Novak, Thomas P., Donna L. Hoffman and Yiu-Fai Yung (2000), 'Measuring the customer experience in online environments: A structural modeling approach', *Marketing Science*, **19**, (1), 22–42.

Nahapiet, Janine and Sumantra Ghoshal (1998), 'Social capital, intellectual capital, and the organizational advantage', *The Academy of Management Review*, **23** (2), 242–66.

Okazaki, Shintaro and Morikazu Hirose (2009), 'Effects of displacement-reinforcement between traditional media, PC Internet and mobile Internet: A quasi-experiment in Japan', *International Journal of Advertising*, **28** (1), 77–104.

Okazaki, Shintaro, Hairong Li and Morikazu Hirose (2009), 'Consumer privacy concerns and preference for regulatory control', *Journal of Advertising*, **38** (4), 63–77.

Okazaki, Shintaro, Charles R. Taylor and Shaoming Zou (2006), 'Advertising standardization's positive impact on the bottom line: A model of when and how standardization improves financial and strategic performance', *Journal of Advertising*, **35** (Fall), 17–33.

Oyserman, Daphna, Heather M. Coon and Marcus Kemmelmeier (2002), 'Rethinking individualism and collectivism: Evaluation of theoretical assumptions and meta-analyses', *Psychological Bulletin*, **128** (1), 3–72.

Park, Taezoon, Rashmi Shenoy and Gavriel Salvendy (2008), 'Effective advertising on mobile phones: A literature review and presentation of results from 53 case studies', *Behaviour & Information Technology*, **27** (5), 355–73.

Pew Research (2010), 'Global publics embrace social networking: Computer and cell phone usage up around the world', available at http://pewresearch.org/pubs/1830/social-networking-computer-cell-phone-usage-around-the-world (accessed 15 December 2010).

Poels, Karolien and Siegfried Dewitte (2006), 'How to capture the hears? Reviewing 20 years of emotion measurement in advertising', *Journal of Advertising Research*, **46** (1), 18–37.

Polyora, Kawpong and Dana L. Alden (2005), 'Self-construal and need-for-cognition effects on brand attitudes and purchase intentions in response to comparative advertising in Thailand and the United States', *Journal of Advertising*, **34** (1), 37–48.

Quan-Haase, Anabel and Alyson L. Young (2011), 'Uses and gratifications of social media: A comparison of facebook and instant messaging', *Bulletin of Science, Technology & Society*, **30** (5), 350–61.

Rentz, Joseph O. (1987), 'Generalizability theory: A comprehensive method for assessing and improving the dependability of marketing measures', *Journal of Marketing Research*, **24**, 19–28.

Roberts, Marilyn S. and Hanjun Ko (2001), 'Global interactive advertising: Defining what we mean and using what we have learned', *Journal of Interactive Advertising*, **1** (2), http://jiad.org/article10.

Robinson, Helen, Anna Wysocka and Chris Hand (2007), 'Internet advertising effectiveness: Effects of design on clickthrough rates', *International Journal of Advertising*, **26** (4), 527 41.

Rodgers, Shelly, Ye Wang, Ruth Rettie and Frank Alpert (2007), 'The web motivation inventory replication, extension and application to internet advertising', *International Journal of Advertising*, **26** (4), 447–76.

Rossiter, John R. and Steven Bellman (1999), 'A proposed model for explaining *and* measuring web ad effectiveness', *Journal of Current Issues and Research in Advertising*, **21** (1), 13–32.

Roth, Martin S. (1992), 'Depth versus breadth strategies for global brand image management', *Journal of Advertising*, **21** (2), 25–36.

Schwartz, Shalom H. (1992), 'Universals in the content and structure of values', in March Zanna (ed.), *Advances in Experimental Social Psychology*, vol. 25, New York: Academic Press, pp. 1–65.

Schwartz, Shalom H. and Klaus Boehnke (2004), 'Evaluating the structure of human values with confirmatory factor analysis', *Journal of Research in Personality*, **38**, 230–55.

Sharma, Subhash and Danny Weathers (2003), 'Assessing generalizability of scales used in cross-national research', *International Journal of Research in Marketing*, **20** (3), 287–95.

Smith, Aaron and Lee Rainie (2010), '8% of Americans use Twitter', available at http://www. pewinternet.org/Reports/2010/Twitter-Update-2010.aspx (accessed 10 December 2010).

Steenkamp, Jan-Benedict E.M., Rajeev Batra and Dana Alden (2003), 'How perceived brand globalness creates brand value', *Journal of International Business Studies*, **34**, 53–65.

Steenkamp, Jan-Benedict and H. Baumgartner (1998), 'Assessing measurement invariance in cross-national research', *Journal of Consumer Research*, **25**, 78–90.

Sullivan Mort, Gillian and Judy Drennan (2007), 'Mobile communications: A study of factors influencing consumer use of m-services', *Journal of Advertising Research*, **47** (3), 302–12.

Tanaka, Wendy and Sarah Terry-Cobo (2008), 'Cellphone addiction', available at http:// www.forbes.com/2008/06/15/cellphone-addict-iphone-tech-wireless08-cx_wt0616addict. html (accessed 16 June 2008).

Taylor, Charles R. (2005), 'Moving international advertising forward', *Journal of Advertising*, **34** (1), 7–16.

Taylor, Charles R. (2010), 'Editorial: Towards stronger theory development in international advertising research', *International Journal of Advertising*, **29** (1), 9–14.

Taylor, Charles R. (2002), 'What's wrong with international advertising research?' *Journal of Advertising Research*, **42** (6), 48–54.

Tellis, Gerad J. and Deepa Chandrasekaran (2010), 'Extent and impact of response biases in cross-national survey research', *International Journal of Research in Marketing*, **27**, 329–41.

The Nielsen Company (2010a), 'Social media dominates Asia Pacific Internet usage', available at http://blog.nielsen.com/nielsenwire/global/social-media-dominates-asia-pacific-internet-usage (accessed 10 July 2010).

The Nielsen Company (2010b), 'One in six online UK retail visits ends in a purchase', available at http://blog.nielsen.com/nielsenwire/consumer/one-in-six-online-uk-retail-visits-ends-in-a-purchase (accessed 24 November 2010).

The Nielsen Company (2010c), 'What Americans do online: Social media and games dominate activity', available at http://blog.nielsen.com/nielsenwire/online_mobile/what-americans-do-online-social-media-and-games-dominate-activity (accessed 2 August 2010).

Trusov, Michael, Randolph E. Bucklin and Koen Pauwels (2009), 'Effects of word-of-mouth versus traditional marketing: Findings from an Internet social networking site', *Journal of Marketing*, **73** (September), 90–102.

Trusov, Michael, Anand V. Bodapati and Randolph E. Bucklin (2010), 'Determining influential users in Internet social networks', *Journal of Marketing Research*, **47**, 643–58.

Tsang, M., Shu-Chun Ho and Ting-Peng Liang (2004), 'Consumer attitudes toward mobile advertising: An empirical study', *International Journal of Electronic Commerce*, **8**, 65–78.

Tsao, James C. and Stanley D. Sibley (2004), 'Displacement and reinforcement effects of the Internet and other media as sources of advertising information', *Journal of Advertising Research*, **44** (1), 126–42.

Van de Vjver, Fons J.R. and Kwok Leung (1997), *Methods and Data Analysis for Cross-Cultural Research*, Sage Publications.

Wang, Charlie C.L. (2000), 'Right appeals for the "right self": Connectedness–separateness self-schema and cross-cultural persuasion', *Journal of Marketing Communications*, **6**, 205–17.

Wilson, Edward O. (1992), *The Diversity of Life*, New York: W.W. Norton.

Xu, Heng, Lih-Bin Oh and Hock-Hai Teo (2009), 'Perceived effectiveness of text vs. multimedia location-based advertising messaging', *International Journal of Mobile Communications*, **7** (2), 54–177.

Yaprak, Attila (2003), 'Measurement problems in cross-national consumer research: The state-of-the-art and future research directions', in Subhash C. Jain (ed.), *Handbook of Research in International Marketing*, Cheltenham, UK and Northampton, MA, USA: Edward Elgar Publishing, pp. 175–89.

Zillmann, D. (1988), 'Mood management: Using entertainment to full advantage', in Lewis Donohew, Howard E. Sypher and E. Troy. Higgins (eds), *Communication, Social Cognition,and Affect*, Hillsdale, NJ: Lawrence Erlbaum Associates, pp. 147–71.

Zou, Shaoming (2005), 'Contributions to international advertising research: An assessment of the literature between 1990 and 2002', *Journal of Advertising*, **34**, 99–110.

14 Online advertising: a cross-cultural synthesis
Yuping Liu-Thompkins

INTRODUCTION

As a new media platform, the Internet has experienced phenomenal growth since its inception. In less than 20 years, it has spread from its US origin to all six major continents, claiming an estimated total of two billion users or 30 percent of the world population as of 2010 (International Telecommunication Union 2010). For developed countries, Internet penetration rates are even higher at an average of 71.6 percent (International Telecommunication Union 2010). Echoing the quick growth of the Internet, advertisers are increasingly using this medium to reach their target audiences. According to IDC, worldwide spending on online advertising is expected to reach $106.6 billion in 2011, reflecting an annual growth rate of 15 to 20 percent from 2008 (Marketing Charts 2008).

The online channel is especially important in the context of international advertising. When a company posts an advertising message online, the message becomes automatically available to a worldwide audience of Internet users. Indeed, it is not an exaggeration to say that online advertising by definition is international advertising. This has facilitated the globalization of business and has reduced the time, cost, and effort required to reach consumers in other countries. Although the Internet is particularly suitable for international advertising, devising and implementing an effective international advertising strategy through the medium is not a simple decision. Similar to traditional advertising, companies need to answer the questions of whether to standardize or localize their messages across geographic boundaries, how to accommodate the large number of languages spoken by consumers in different countries, and how to remain culturally sensitive and at the same time reach international consumers in a cost-effective fashion. More unique to the online channel, advertisers also need to consider the technology capabilities of individual consumers in different cultures, address the wants of online consumers that may or may not be representative of their offline counterparts, and deal with a more dynamic environment where distinct cultures are becoming more fluid and diffuse owing to increasing globalization.

Addressing these concerns, advertising and marketing researchers have been paying more and more attention to cross-cultural issues in online advertising. Dozens of studies have compared the online advertising practice of companies from different countries of origin (e.g., Cho and Cheon 2005; Singh and Matsuo 2004) as well as the practice of the same multinational companies in different target markets (e.g., Okazaki and Skapa 2008; Shin and Huh 2009). The variables examined ranged from information content and graphics, to other design components of online ads. A more limited number of studies have also examined the reaction of consumers from different countries toward online advertising (e.g., Ko, Roberts, and Cho 2006; Luna, Peracchio, and de Juan 2003). These studies investigated international consumers' general perception of and attitude toward online advertising, and examined specific elements of an online ad (e.g., language, interactivity, and local customization) that may render the ad more or less effective among an international audience.

To date, there has been limited synthesis of this body of work. Addressing this gap, the current chapter offers a comprehensive review of research on cross-cultural issues in online advertising. By extracting the key debates and findings from existing research, it aims to provide a systematic picture of current knowledge in this area and to identify significant gaps in the literature that can lead to fruitful research in the future. The following sections start by examining the famous standardization vs. localization debate in the unique context of online advertising. Then a set of theoretical and practical factors that can lead to cross-cultural differences in online advertising is discussed. This is followed by a summary of key findings from this research stream. The chapter concludes with a list of research topics to help guide future research in this area.

STANDARDIZATION OR LOCALIZATION?

With the Internet emerging as an important advertising channel, the old debate on whether standardization or localization is a better business strategy has resurfaced (Cho and Cheon 2005; Laroche et al. 2001). The universal technology platform that enables consumers around the world to connect to the Internet provides a compelling argument for a standardization approach (Ju-Pak 1999; Laroche et al. 2001). Two consequences flow from the instantaneity and easy accessibility of the Internet. First, it offers companies more ready access to the global market. Previously, companies wanting to do business on a global scale needed to possess extensive resources to deal with the intermediaries and complicated logistics involved in doing business with consumers in another country. With the Internet, even small companies can establish a website to sell directly to consumers in other countries. This favors a cost-effective standardization approach to online advertising.

Secondly, the Internet also makes access to information much faster and easier for consumers in different countries. This breaks the cultural boundaries that may have kept individual cultures in an isolated state prior to the Internet age. As Johnston and Johal (1999) argue, the global reach of the online medium can alter local cultures and help form a global village that fuses cultural values from different countries to create a melting pot of a fluid global culture. Adding to this is the tendency among younger consumers to be early adopters of new technology. As younger consumers are less likely to be deeply rooted in traditional cultural values, these consumers are more likely to embrace global cultures or values that did not originate in their home country (Li, Li, and Zhao 2009; Paek, Yu, and Bae 2009; Shin and Huh 2009). This again favors a standardization approach.

Although the above arguments suggest that online advertising may follow a more standardized approach, industry practice and empirical research findings seem to suggest otherwise. Website localization has quickly grown into a multi-billion dollar industry, within which language services alone are predicted to reach $25 billion in 2013 (Common Sense Advisory 2011). Comparison of websites and online banner ads across countries also reveals significant cross-cultural differences in at least some content and design elements (e.g., An 2007; Paek, Yu, and Bae 2009; Singh, Kumar, and Baack 2005). Furthermore, studies of online consumers show that Internet users in different countries represent distinct demographic groups and exhibit diverse online behavior (Riegner 2008), and that their response to a marketing website is dependent on elements of their home culture such as language (Luna, Peracchio, and de Juan 2003). From a theoretical perspective, Hofstede (2002) argues that cultures are relatively stable. While cultural practices may change over time, deeply rooted cultural values remain rather steady. Together, these suggest that online advertising is still subject to cultural influences and that consumers in different countries may still require communication messages that are targeted toward their specific culture.

While the debate between standardization and localization is still ongoing, some researchers adopted a contingency view and argued that the most suitable strategy in a given situation may be dependent on the country of origin, product type, target audience, management style, and competition (Shin and Huh 2009). Furthermore, some elements of an online ad such as logo and layout may need to be standardized to maintain a consistent brand image, while other elements such as content and specific visual cues require more localization (Zhao et al. 2003).

This chapter does not intend to support any particular approach. Instead, it contributes to the conversation by summarizing what we have learned from scholarly research in this area. The section below introduces several potential theoretical and practical bases for cross-cultural differences in online advertising. Then, building on that, the next sections review empirical findings on cross-cultural differences (or the lack thereof) as reflected in online advertising practice and in consumers' reactions to online advertising.

BASES FOR CROSS-CULTURAL DIFFERENCES IN ONLINE ADVERTISING

Potential cross-cultural differences in online advertising come from a variety of sources. On one hand, similar to traditional advertising, online advertising may reflect and reinforce the cultural values embedded in a society (Pollay 1986). It may also manifest the desired or idealized values that represent a more dynamic and futuristic view of a culture (Okazaki 2004). These differences in cultural values and views are further combined with variation in communication styles across different countries to create the unique discourse of advertising. On the other hand, as a departure from traditional advertising, online advertising is based on a new technology platform. As some researchers argue, this new medium has the ability to simultaneously change culture as well as make theories and assumptions based on traditional media become obsolete (Gevorgyan and Manucharova 2009; Kim, Coyle, and Gould 2009; Murphy and Scharl 2007). In examining cross-cultural online advertising, therefore, it is important to consider the underlying technology and how it interacts with cultural values and communication styles to define the similarities and differences found in online advertising across different countries. Combining these forces of influence (i.e., cultural values, communication styles, and technology), this section reviews the theoretical and practical foundations that are often drawn in online advertising research to explain the differences (or the lack thereof) across cultures.

Cultural Values and World Views

The most commonly used cultural value framework is offered by Hofstede (1980). This framework was formulated based on large-scale surveys of IBM employees across the world. It originally consisted of four dimensions: individualism/collectivism, power distance, uncertainty avoidance, masculinity/femininity. Later, a fifth dimension, short-term/long-term orientation, was added to the framework. Research on the applicability of this classical framework in an online advertising context has shown mixed support so far. In a series of studies, Singh and colleagues examined corporate websites in the US, China, Mexico, Japan, France, and Germany on each of the four original Hofstede dimensions (Singh and Baack 2004; Singh, Hongxin, and Xiaorui 2003; Singh, Kumar, and Baack 2005; Singh and Matsuo 2004). Their results were mostly consistent with the framework. However, uncertainty avoidance repeatedly failed to produce significant difference across websites from different countries. Controversy also exists regarding individualism/collectivism. While Sinkovics, Yamin, and Hossinger's (2007) analysis showed expected findings on indicators of individualism, it also revealed the surprising finding that Latin American websites used fewer collectivistic features than more individualistic countries such as the US, the UK, and Germany. Echoing this contradiction, Paek, Yu, and Bae (2009) found that Korean websites contained more individualistic indicators than their US counterparts. Li, Li, and Zhao's (2009) comparison of banner ads in Eastern and Western cultures, on the other hand, showed both country clusters to be more likely to use individualistic appeals, even though Eastern cultures presumably favor collectivism. In another analysis of university websites from eight countries, Callahan (2005) found general support for Hofstede's (1980) framework, but the strength of correlation was rather weak.

Two other cultural value frameworks have also been drawn upon in online advertising research: the monochronic vs. polychronic time orientation proposed by Hall (1976) and the cultural typology by Schwartz (1994). The former concerns the perception and management of time by individuals in a culture, where monochronic cultures tend to view time as a linear progression whereas polychronic individuals view time as a nonlinear term and are more likely to engage in multitasking. Research shows that this time orientation can affect online advertising design such as the use of a linear vs. nonlinear navigation structure and the presence of rich media and animated content, which reflects a polychronic orientation (Kim, Coyle, and Gould 2009; Zhao et al. 2003).

Schwartz's (1994) cultural typology represents a more updated cultural value system. It proposes three higher-order dimensions: autonomy vs. embeddedness, egalitarianism vs. hierarchy, and harmony vs. mastery. These three dimensions in turn encompass seven lower-order cultural values: conservation, hierarchy, intellectual autonomy, affective autonomy, competency, harmony, and egalitarian compromise. Schwartz's own validation of the typology (1994) shows a significant correlation between his cultural values and some of Hofstede's dimensions. Applying this model to online advertising, Baack and Singh (2007) concluded that neither Hofstede's or Schwartz's framework is sufficient in explaining cross-cultural differences in website design. Instead, the two need to be combined to provide best fit to the data.

Whichever cultural value framework is used, these systems all suffer a common criticism in that they represent a rather static view of national culture and do not consider the dialogue both among cultures brought forth by globalization and within a culture as a result of population diversification. This can be especially problematic in the context of the Internet. As enhanced computer technology facilitates global dialogue among individuals from vastly different cultures, it results in unique cultural identities that represent a mixture of multiple cultures (Ess and Sudweeks 2005). These identities are highly fluid and amorphous and defy the definition from traditional cultural value frameworks (Würtz 2005). As a result, applying these frameworks indiscriminately ignores such new identities and may result in stereotyped conclusions that are no longer accurate or suitable for consumers participating in online communication. In a comprehensive discussion of the applicability of classical cultural typologies in computer-mediated communication, Hermeking (2005) sets the boundary conditions for the productive use of these typologies. That is, these classical theories are more suitable if the specific consumption activity is driven by an unconscious mentality-based process. In contrast, if the consumption is the result of conscious choice based on individual identity, classical cultural theories would fall short of the more complicated process that is involved in consumer information processing and decision making.

Language and Communication Style

As an important part of daily discourse, online advertising is also bound by the language and communication style of the target audience. Language is perhaps the first consideration for advertisers intending to reach out to consumers in other countries. The early Internet was dominated by the English language. But as more consumers in non-English speaking countries move online, need for information in other languages increases, and it becomes more important for advertisers to decide whether and how to adapt their messages to the native languages of the target audience. Languages can vary considerably in vocabulary, grammatical structure, and scripting system (Hernandez and Minor 2010). This is further complicated by interaction with other design elements in an ad, product type, country of origin, and individual consumers' cognitive capacity at the time of ad exposure (Luna, Peracchio, and de Juan 2003; Warden, Lai, and Wu 2002). As a result, the modifications needed for proper language adaptation can go way beyond simple translation to reflect the more nuanced differences across languages (Fletcher 2006).

Besides language, *how* people within a certain culture communicate with each other can also lead to cross-cultural differences in online advertising. The most cited framework in this area is the high- vs. low-context communication styles proposed by Hall (1976). Eastern cultures such as China, Japan, and Korea are generally believed to engage in high-context communication, whereas Western cultures such as the US and the UK tend to follow a low-context communication style. The two styles differ in terms of how direct a communication is and how much meaning is derived from the actual message itself vs. other contextual cues such as symbols, social norms, and implicit knowledge about the communicating entities. Research shows that these differences can have a significant impact on the content as well as design elements of online ads (e.g., An 2007; Paek, Yu, and Bae 2009; Singh and Matsuo 2004). It should be pointed out that, although Hall's (1976) model has been frequently used, it is mostly based on qualitative studies of a limited number of countries. This reduces the operational usefulness of the framework and requires additional in-depth qualitative observations of other cultures before it can be applied empirically (Hermeking 2005).

Technological Development Levels

One unique aspect of online advertising is that it builds on a relatively new technology platform that only emerged in the last two decades. Currently, there is still significant difference in Internet penetration rates across the world, both as a result of varying economic and technological infrastructure among nations and as a result of different consumer cultures (Fletcher 2006). This difference in Internet penetration has several important implications for online advertising. First, Internet penetration rate determines the size of the target market that can be reached via online advertising. As a result, online advertising may be applicable to a different extent in different countries.

Second, countries at various stages of Internet development also have different cohorts of Internet users. For countries that are still at relatively early stages of Internet development, online consumers consist mainly of early adopters who tend to be younger, more affluent, highly educated, and more innovative. As Internet penetration rates increase, however, online consumers become more representative of the general population and shift toward the population mean when it comes to demographic and psychographic traits.

Finally, the Internet development level in a country also determines the maturity of online business and subsequently online advertising in that country. Advertisers in newly online countries may still be exploring best ways to communicate with their consumers through the new channel, whereas companies in more technologically advanced countries tend to face more intense competition online and to be more developed and experienced in online advertising strategy and tactics.

With only a few exceptions, most published studies in online advertising compared cultures without taking technological development variation into consideration. Researchers assume that any difference discovered would be a result of cultural value or communication style variations. But without controlling for the technological development level in each country, this conclusion may be misleading. It is possible that the aforementioned consequences from varying Internet penetration rates may be the actual drivers of the differences found instead. This is an issue that needs to be addressed in future research.

CROSS-CULTURAL DIFFERENCES AS REFLECTED IN ADVERTISING PRACTICE

Having discussed the theoretical and practical bases for cross-cultural differences in online advertising, this and the next sections summarize empirical research findings in this area. In the literature, a large number of empirical studies examined online advertisers' practices using the well-established content analysis approach. They typically compare online ads from multiple countries to infer cultural differences (or the lack thereof) reflected in advertising. The findings from this stream of research can be broadly categorized into two areas: information content and creative strategy. The former pertains to *what* is being said in an ad, such as general informativeness, information cues, and types of claim used. The latter relates to *how* things are said, as reflected by the use of symbols, colors, photographs, spokespersons, and other executional and media elements such as ad positioning.

Information Content

A natural question to ask about the information content of an ad is how much information is provided in the ad. Two cultural values provide the basis for this discussion. First is Hofstede's (1980) uncertainty avoidance dimension. Presumably consumers' desire to avoid uncertainty would prompt advertisers to provide more information to reduce the perceived risks associated with the product. The other reasoning comes from the high vs. low context of a culture, as suggested by Hall (1976). In high-context cultures, meanings are often derived from contextual elements outside of a message itself. As a result, the amount of information provided in an ad becomes less critical than in a low-context culture, where the message itself provides most, if not all, meanings to be conveyed.

Interestingly, the above two cultural factors often lead to opposite predictions for a particular culture. Many Eastern cultures such as Japan and Korea are considered high-context cultures, which would lead to low informativeness in online ads. At the same time, these countries also score high on uncertainty avoidance compared with Western cultures such as the US, which would predict a high level of informativeness. This contradiction is reflected in the empirical findings. Consistent with predictions from a high/low-context perspective, two early studies in this area found US companies' websites and banner ads to be more informative than those from Korea (Chung and Ahn 1999; Oh, Chang-Hoan, and Leckenby 1999). Some researchers, however, found no such difference among the US, the UK, and Korea (Ju-Pak 1999; Yoon and Cropp 1999). More recent analyses further show that countries on the extreme ends of the two cultural dimensions (the US and Japan) featured more informative online ads than do countries in a more moderate range (Spain; Okazaki 2004).

To examine the specific types of information provided in online ads, researchers frequently used Resnik and Stern's (1977) information classification system as the analysis tool (Chung and Ahn 1999; Okazaki and Rivas 2002; Pashupati and Lee 2003). The system identifies 14 types of information cue: price-value, quality, performance, components or contents, availability, special offer, taste, nutrition, packaging or shape, guarantees or warranties, safety, independent research, company-sponsored research, and new ideas. Across studies, quality and performance cues were frequently found in online ads regardless of the country of origin. The presence of other information cues is less consistent across studies, however, possibly owing to the varying mixture of product types represented by each study's sample (Ju-Pak 1999). Two content analyses of Japanese multinational companies' websites found that these companies' domestic websites in Japan are more likely to use price-value cues than their adapted versions in the US and Spain (Okazaki 2004; Okazaki and Rivas 2002). Ju-Pak's (1999) comparison of 310 websites from the US, the UK, and Korea found that US websites are more likely to provide price and promotion-related cues than both UK and Korean websites. In a rare study of online advertising in India, Pashupati and Lee (2003) concluded that banner ads on Indian newspaper websites are more likely to feature price and explicit descriptions of the product or service than their Korean counterparts.

Creative Strategy

As creative strategy involves a wide range of decisions, it is impossible to cover all cross-cultural differences in creative strategy here. Instead, this section will focus on one aspect of creative strategy that is unique to online advertising: interactivity. A high level of interactivity is considered a key feature that separates online advertising from advertising in the traditional media (Liu and Shrum 2002). A website can incorporate interactive features (e.g., customization, hyperlinks, feedback form, etc.) that offer visitors more personal control over their browsing experience and engage them in a synchronous two-way dialogue. Yoon and Cropp (1999) and Ju-Pak (1999) were the first ones to examine interactivity in a cross-cultural setting. Comparing Western and Korean websites, Yoon and Cropp (1999) did not find any significant difference between their US and Korean samples in the use of interactive features, whereas Ju-Pak's (1999) results revealed a higher level of interactivity in Korean websites than in their US and UK counterparts. Supporting the latter finding, Kim, Coyle, and Gould's (2009) analysis of 101 Korean websites and 99 US websites showed that Korean websites are more likely to use clickable images, pull-down bars, and hyperlinks. They argue that, as interactive features require active participation and manipulation from a user, they are more likely to be used in cultures that have a polychronic time orientation such as Korea (Hall 1976).

Drawing on the cultural values of individualism/collectivism and power distance, Cho and Cheon (2005) argue that the popularity of an interactive feature depends on the type of interactivity that it represents. Comparing the top 50 advertisers' websites in the US, the UK, Japan, and Korea, they found that websites in the US and the UK are more likely to emphasize consumer-message interaction and consumer-marketer interaction. Websites in Korea and Japan, in contrast, are more likely to feature consumer-to-consumer interaction, presumably because of the collectivistic nature of these Eastern cultures. In line with these findings, Zhao et al. (2003) found that US websites are more likely to use personalization than their Chinese counterparts, owing to the more individualistic nature of American culture.

Two other studies suggest differences in the use of interactive features even within Western cultures. Okazaki (2005) compared the similarity of top US brands' websites in the US, UK, French, German, and Spanish markets and found the similarity level to be fairly low when it comes to the use of interactive features. In a more recent study, Voorveld, Neijens, and Smit (2010) found that the US version of top 100 global brands' websites contained more interactive features than the Dutch version of these websites. This was true for all three dimensions of interactivity: active control, two-way communication, and synchronicity. Such differences among Western countries may reflect both cultural differences and the development level of technology and online advertising in each country.

Methodology Issues

In reviewing the dozens of content analysis studies, it is important to recognize a few methodological choices that may affect the interpretation of some research findings. First, when creating the sample for a study, researchers often followed one of two approaches: inter-firm sampling or intra-firm sampling. In the former approach, researchers select a separate group of companies in each country based on some criteria (e.g., top 100 advertisers), and then compare these groups' online advertising practices (e.g., Cho and Cheon 2005; Singh and Matsuo 2004). The intra-firm sampling approach, in contrast, follows the same group of companies in each country and compares their practices across different target markets (e.g., An 2007; Voorveld, Neijens, and Smit 2010). One potential issue with the inter-firm sampling approach is different sample compositions across countries. For instance, one sample may contain more physical products, and another may have more service goods. As previous literature suggests, advertising practices are often adjusted according to the industry, product category, and market conditions (Abernethy and Franke 1996; Sinkovics, Yamin, and Hossinger 2007). As a result, the differences discovered among cultures may in fact be caused by the various types of companies involved. Supporting this view, Ju-Pak (1999) found that, after controlling for product category, some differences in the use of informational cues among US, UK, and Korean websites were no longer significant. Shin and Huh (2009) further showed that the extent of standardization in online advertising may be dependent on whether the focal product is durable or non-durable goods and whether the product is targeted toward businesses or consumers. Therefore, when using the inter-firm approach, care should be taken to control for product category and industry differences across the samples in various countries.

Second, the unit of analysis may also affect the depth of differences found in a study. With the exception of a few studies that examined banner ads, most researchers content analyzed corporate websites. Some researchers further chose to focus only on the homepage of each website because of the vast amount of information on websites that is often embedded in deep layers of site hierarchy (e.g., Callahan 2005; Gevorgyan and Manucharova 2009; Yoon and Cropp 1999). While this level of analysis remains consistent across samples, it does limit the depth of information captured by the analysis. Similar to banner ads, the homepage of a website contains limited informational and creative cues and may not fully represent the cultural differences that may be revealed throughout the entire website. Furthermore, as the homepage represents the entry way or "face" of a company's website, branding is likely to be a key communication goal. As a result, cultural differences may be sacrificed to ensure consistency in brand image conveyed across different target countries' websites. This could lead to smaller cultural difference than if entire websites had been analyzed.

Finally, the specific variables and coding scheme used in a study can influence the conclusions drawn from the study. For instance, some researchers attempted to verify the relevance and validity of Hofstede's (1980) cultural value framework in the online advertising context (e.g., Baack and Singh 2007; Singh and Matsuo 2004; Sinkovics, Yamin, and Hossinger 2007). A few studies concluded that the uncertainty avoidance dimension was not sufficiently reflected in cross-cultural website design (Baack and Singh 2007; Singh, Kumar, and Baack 2005; Singh and Matsuo 2004), and Paek, Yu, and Bae (2009) further found no difference between US and Korean websites on collectivism. However, these may simply be an artifact of the features used to code each cultural value. In other words, there may be other informational and executional cues not included in the coding scheme that would have reflected a significant difference in uncertainty avoidance or collectivism across countries. A more unified and comprehensive coding scheme needs to be developed in future research, possibly first through qualitative methods, to increase the validity and reliability of such instruments.

CROSS-CULTURAL DIFFERENCES FROM CONSUMERS' PERSPECTIVES

Although content analysis of online ads is useful in understanding how advertising practices differ across cultures, it does not consider consumer responses to these practices. A popular practice discovered through content analysis does not mean that the practice is necessarily effective in persuading consumers. To this end, some other studies have examined the reactions to online advertising from consumers in different cultures. This section reviews the key findings from these studies, starting with consumers' general attitudes toward online advertising followed by consumers' responses to specific executional strategies in online ads.

Attitude toward Online Advertising

Lutz (1985) defines attitude toward advertising as "a learned predisposition to respond in a consistently favorable or unfavorable manner to advertising in general" (p. 52). This general attitude toward advertising can drive a consumer's response to a specific ad, such that a more positive attitude toward advertising in general is likely to make the consumer more receptive to a specific ad. Applied to the current context, consumers from different cultures may possess variable attitudes toward online advertising, which in turn can affect their reactions to specific online advertising implementations.

Several studies indeed point to systematic differences among cultures in general responses to online advertising. Through a survey of 200 Korean college students and 218 American college students, An and Kim (2007) found that both groups possessed a rather negative attitude toward online advertising. However, this is more so for American students than for Korean students. Choi, Huang, and McMillan's (2008) comparison of a similar college student sample suggests that this may be contingent on the specific medium through which online ads are delivered. Focusing specifically on mobile advertising, these researchers showed the opposite finding that US college students felt more positive toward advertising than Korean students. Comparing consumers from the US, China, and Romania, Wang and Sun (2010) concluded that Romanian consumers had a more positive attitude toward online advertising than both US and Chinese consumers.

Möller and Eisend (2010) attempted to generalize these differences to a large number of cultures and to associate the differences with Hofstede's (1980) cultural framework. Their survey of 7775 consumers from 34 countries revealed that individualism led to more negative attitudes toward banner advertising. Uncertainty avoidance, power distance, and masculinity, on the other hand, were associated with more positive attitudes toward banner advertising. More importantly, their results suggest that, when it comes to individual attitudes toward banner advertising, country-level factors explained a majority of the variance (63.15 percent), and individual-level factors such as age, gender, and Internet experience explained only 0.6 percent of the variance. This points to the importance of considering culture of origin when examining consumers' responses to online advertising.

Not only do cultures vary in consumers' general attitudes toward online advertising, but they also differ in what drives attitude. Four drivers, perceived informational value, perceived entertainment values, perceived credibility, and irritation, have been examined in multiple studies (e.g.,

Lee and Choi 2005; Wang and Sun 2010). Consumers from different cultures were found to hold varying perceptions of online advertising along these dimensions. For instance, US consumers perceived higher informational value in online ads than Korean consumers (An and Kim 2007; Choi, Hwang, and McMillan 2008), reflecting the low-context nature of American culture and as a result US consumers' higher motivation to seek information in a message (Ko, Roberts, and Cho 2006). More interestingly, the impact of these drivers on attitude toward online advertising varied across cultures. For US consumers, information was the dominant driver, whereas credibility carried the most important influence among Korean consumers (An and Kim 2007). This latter difference may be attributed to the tendency to avoid uncertainty in the Korean culture. Within the realm of mobile advertising, Choi, Hwang, and McMillan (2008) found that entertainment value and credibility were the dominant drivers in both the US and Korea. However, information value had a significant impact on attitude toward mobile advertising only for the US sample, again suggesting a higher need for information among US consumers. It is worth noting that, in accounting for attitude toward online advertising, the four drivers explained significantly more variance for the US sample (62 percent) than for the Korean sample (36.2 percent) in An and Kim's (2007) study. The gap was not as big in Choi, Hwang, and McMillan's (2008) study, but it still showed the same direction of difference (71 percent for US consumers and 60 percent for Korean consumers). These findings suggest that, in applying advertising theories and models developed in Western cultures to other cultures, researchers may be missing important factors that are unique to those other cultures. From this perspective, a culture-specific emic approach needs to be used in future research (Fletcher 2006).

Response to Specific Online Advertising Implementations

To date, there has been very limited cross cultural research on consumers' response to specific online advertising implementations, possibly owing to the logistic difficulty of constructing valid experimental stimuli and coordinating controlled experiments in multiple countries. The handful of published studies in this area have focused on two questions: does cultural customization lead to more positive consumer response to an online ad? And relatedly, what is the effect of language on consumers' response to online ads?

Cultural customization effect
In a study involving 250 consumers from Taiwan, Brazil, and Germany, Singh et al. (2006a) exposed each participant to nine international websites

from American and Japanese multinational corporations. Their results show that consumers' perceived level of cultural customization in a website positively affected their perceived ease of use of the website and their attitude toward the website. This effect was especially salient for Taiwanese consumers. The limitation of this study is that it linked two self-reported perception measures, which could be affected by common method bias. Addressing this limitation, Singh et al. (2006b) associated consumer response with a website's cultural customization score derived from a separate content analysis. They found that websites with a high cultural customization score led to more positive attitudes and higher purchase intentions than both websites with a low cultural customization score and websites that were not culturally customized at all.

As cultural customization of an online ad can be implemented in various ways, a few studies focused on more specific customization approaches. In a comparison between US and Chinese consumers, Gevorgyan and Manucharova (2009) found that Chinese consumers responded more positively to website features that reflect collectivism than features that reflect individualism, consistent with the more collectivistic nature of Chinese culture. The opposite was true for American consumers, where individualistic features were viewed more favorably than collectivistic features. Also focusing on individualism/collectivism, Sia et al. (2009) examined two different endorsement approaches: one through affiliation with a well-known online portal (Yahoo!) and the other through testimonials from other consumers. They considered the former an out-group reference and as a result likely to be preferred more in an individualistic culture, whereas the latter represents an in-group reference, favored by a collectivistic culture. Supporting their hypotheses, the effect of portal affiliation on trust perception was stronger for their Australian sample than for the Hong Kong sample, whereas the reverse was true for the effect of peer endorsement.

In a unique study that examined not the visible implementation of cultural customization but the behind-the-scenes designer of a website, Faiola and Matei (2005) found that consumers were able to use a website more efficiently if the website was designed by someone from their home culture than if the website was designed by someone from a foreign culture. They argued that a designer's work is affected by his or her cultural background. Consequently, a website from a designer of one's home culture is more likely to be congruent with one's cognitive schema, which explains improved performance. However, their results also showed that this congruency does not affect the quality perception of information on the website.

Although studies in this area seem to point to the superiority of cultural customization, it is worth noting that a simple standardized message may have universal appeals across cultures. For instance, Hynes and Janson (2007) conducted in-depth interviews to investigate consumer reactions to two online cellphone ads, one from Nokia and one from Ericsson. Across consumers from a diverse group of cultures, including the US, Taiwan, China, and India, the simpler and cleaner ad from Nokia, which merely showed a phone image, was considered more appealing and effective. This points to the possibility of an effective standardized online message, especially if the message is kept relatively simple and uses universal appeals.

Language effect

Language can be considered a specific element of cultural customization. One may naturally assume using a consumer's native language to be more effective in online advertising, as processing one's native language requires less cognitive resource, hence leaving more resources for processing the actual advertising message. Even for proficient bilingual consumers, their cognitive schema and emotions tend to be shaped more strongly by their first language (Luna, Peracchio, and de Juan 2003; Nantel and Glaser 2008). As a result, these consumers may still respond better to messages delivered in their first language. In line with these views, Chen et al. (2009) showed that both Taiwanese and Thai consumers reported more positive attitudes toward a website in their local language than to a standardized English website. In another study, Nantel and Glaser (2008) found that this preference for one's first language is persistent even for the language in which a website was originally conceived and which is unknown to consumers. They compared 204 Canadian consumers' responses to a website originally designed in French versus a website originally designed in English. Their results suggest that English-speaking Canadian consumers found the website originally designed in English to be more user-friendly than the one designed in French and then translated into English. For French-speaking Canadians, they preferred the website originally designed in French than the one that was translated from English to French.

While there seems to be a general preference for one's native language, a few studies show that the exact effect may be contingent on the outcome measure used and on other executional elements of an ad. For the Nantel and Glaser (2008) study above, although usability ratings of the two websites differed, there was no significant difference in perceived quality of offers on the two websites. The researchers attributed this to the fact that language plays a less important role in quality perception. In one of the most in-depth studies on language effects in online advertising, Luna, Peracchio, and de Juan (2003) challenged the notion that first language is always preferred to second language. Drawing on the resource matching theory, they argued that, under certain conditions, messages presented in one's first language may be too unchallenging and therefore may be less preferred than messages in a second language. In two lab experiments, these researchers showed that, when the graphics on a website were related to the content of the website (i.e., less cognitive effort was required), using the second language led to more positive attitudes toward the website and the product than using the first language. The reverse was true when the graphics were not related to the website copy (i.e., higher cognitive effort was required). These findings suggest an interaction between language and other design elements of an online ad, which may dilute or accentuate consumers' responses to a specific language.

FUTURE RESEARCH QUESTIONS

From the above discussion, it is clear that advertising scholars have made significant progress in understanding cross-cultural differences in online advertising. At the same time, it is obvious that the field is far from being mature and many questions remain to be answered. Plenty of conflicting results still exist and need to be resolved, and methodological issues in existing studies also threaten the validity of existing research findings. In introducing a special issue of *Journal of Advertising* on international advertising, Taylor (2005) pointed out significant gaps in the literature that need to be filled by future research. Many of the same issues also apply to cross-cultural online advertising research. To further our knowledge in this area, this section suggests four topics that especially deserve attention in future research.

First, similar to the predominant use of content analysis in studying international advertising in traditional media (Taylor 2005), a large number of studies on cross-cultural online advertising have also been based on content analysis. Although this approach represents a useful exploratory observation of cross-cultural differences, it has a number of limitations. One key limitation is its inability to tell whether the differences discovered indeed reflect consumer preference. Another limitation is that it only demonstrates the outcome of advertisers' decisions without an understanding of the behind-the-scenes processes that led to such differences. Are the cross-cultural differences discovered through content analysis an advertiser's conscious choice? Or do they merely reflect unconscious influence from the advertiser's cultural background that may or may not be optimal from a strategic perspective? As research in this area matures, researchers need to move beyond content analysis to examine specific consumer responses to cross-cultural online ads as well as advertisers' decision-making processes when reaching global markets.

Second, while most existing studies point to the superiority of a localization approach, they do not consider the high cost associated with localization. Does the gain in consumer attitude and intentions translate into incremental purchases that can compensate for the high cost? At least two studies reviewed in this chapter seem to suggest otherwise. They show that, although cultural customization by using a designer from one's home country (Faiola and Matei 2005) or by adapting the language (Nantel and Glaser 2008) may improve consumer interaction with the website, it does not affect consumers' judgment of the quality of information or the offers on the website. Luna, Peracchio, and de Juan's (2003) research further concluded that using a non-native language can be more effective if it is properly coordinated with other elements in an online ad. These findings point to a need to better understand the behavioral and financial impact of cultural customization on consumers in different countries. What is the proper trade-off between higher cost and more positive consumer response? What is the ROI associated with cultural customization in online advertising? When is cultural customization optimal and when is it unnecessary?

Third, from a practical standpoint, cultural customization can be implemented in many ways, such as through language adaptation, using the target culture's symbols and images, and modifying message content and emotional appeals. These approaches may differ in cost as well as level of cultural sensitivity and impact. None of the existing studies has compared the relative effectiveness of different cultural customization approaches. This deserves more attention in future research so as to guide advertisers in making sound decisions when reaching out to the global marketplace. Existing studies also suggest potential moderating effects from other ad design elements and from product type, company background, and market conditions (Luna, Peracchio, and de Juan 2003; Shin and Huh 2009). Future research needs to explore these interactions to identify the best approach in a given situation. Relatedly, most published studies in this area have focused on corporate websites. Although website is an important part of online advertising, there are many other choices such as banner advertising, search engine advertising, and more recently social media advertising. These advertising forms allow different amounts of information to be delivered and target consumers at different stages of the decision-making process. A better understanding of how each of these forms should be adapted or standardized in an international context is needed.

Finally, from a theoretical perspective, most existing studies in this area have drawn upon classical cultural frameworks such as Hofstede (1980) and Hall (1976) as the theoretical foundation. However, culture is a dynamic entity and is bound to evolve over time. This is especially a concern for online advertising, as the common Internet platform and easier and faster information access have fostered more interaction among cultures and have potentially led to cultural fusion especially among younger generations of consumers. Classical theories and frameworks developed based mostly on Western cultures may have diminished value in such a context. Already, a few studies have shown that existing theories accounted for significantly less variance in the data from Eastern cultures than those from Western cultures (An and Kim 2007; Choi, Hwang, and McMillan 2008; Sia et al. 2009). Future research needs to follow a more grounded and emic approach to understand how online consumers from different cultures think, feel, and behave. This will bring more accurate knowledge of the new generation of consumers that literally grew up with the Internet, especially those from non-Western cultures.

As Internet technology evolves, online advertising will continue to play a critical role in companies' advertising strategies. As an inherently global medium, it is important to understand how this channel can be utilized effectively and efficiently to reach consumers around the world. Advertising scholars have started to address some key theoretical and practical questions, but much remains to be done. With a better understanding of how consumers from different cultures interact with each other and with advertisers online, this stream of research will eventually contribute back to the broader international advertising literature and reveal how technology shapes advertising and cultural processes.

REFERENCES

Abernethy, Avery M. and George R. Franke (1996), 'The Information Content of Advertising: A Meta-Analysis', *Journal of Advertising*, **25** (2), 1–17.

An, Daechun (2007), 'Advertising Visuals in Global Brands' Local Websites: A Six-Country Comparison', *International Journal of Advertising*, **26** (3), 303–32.

An, Daechun and Sang Hoon Kim (2007), 'A First Investigation into the Cross-Cultural Perceptions of Internet Advertising: A Comparison of Korean and American Attitudes', *Journal of International Consumer Marketing*, **20** (2), 49–65.

Baack, Daniel W. and Nitish Singh (2007), 'Culture and Web Communications', *Journal of Business Research*, **60** (3), 181–8.

Callahan, Ewa (2005), 'Cultural Similarities and Differences in the Design of University Web Sites', *Journal of Computer-Mediated Communication*, **11** (1), 239–73.

Chen, Jengchung Victor, William H. Ross, David C. Yen, and Lerdsuwankij Akhapon (2009), 'The Effect of Types of Banner Ad, Web Localization, and Customer Involvement on Internet Users' Attitudes', *CyberPsychology & Behavior*, **12** (1), 71–3.

Cho, Chang-Hoan and Hongsik John Cheon (2005), 'Cross-Cultural Comparisons of Interactivity on Corporate Web Sites', *Journal of Advertising*, **34** (2), 99–115.

Choi, Yung Kyun, Jang-Sun Hwang, and Sally J. McMillan (2008), 'Gearing up for Mobile Advertising: A Cross-Cultural Examination of Key Factors That Drive Mobile Messages Home to Consumers', *Psychology & Marketing*, **25** (8), 756–68.

Chung, Hwi-Man and Euijin Ahn (1999), 'A Content Analysis of Internet Banner Advertising: Focusing on Korean and U.S. Cultural Differences', paper presented at Proceedings of the Annual Meeting of the Association for Education in Journalism and Mass Communication Vol. 82. New Orleans, LA: Association for Education in Journalism and Mass Communication, pp. 56–85.

Common Sense Advisory (2011), 'Facts and Figures: Language Services Market', available at http://www.commonsenseadvisory.com/Resources/FactsandFigures.aspx (accessed February 2, 2011).

Ess, Charles and Fay Sudweeks (2005), 'Culture and Computer-Mediated Communication: Toward New Understandings', *Journal of Computer-Mediated Communication*, **11** (1), 179–91.

Faiola, Anthony and Sorin A. Matei (2005), 'Cultural Cognitive Style and Web Design: Beyond a Behavioral Inquiry into Computer-Mediated Communication', *Journal of Computer-Mediated Communication*, **11** (1), 375–94.

Fletcher, Richard (2006), 'The Impact of Culture on Web Site Content, Design, and Structure', *Journal of Communication Management*, **10** (3), 259–73.

Gevorgyan, Gennadi and Naira Manucharova (2009), 'Does Culturally Adapted Online Communication Work? A Study of American and Chinese Internet Users' Attitudes and Preferences toward Culturally Customized Web Design Elements', *Journal of Computer-Mediated Communication*, **14** (2), 393–413.

Hall, Edward T. (1976), *Beyond Culture*, New York: Anchor Books.

Hermeking, Marc (2005), 'Culture and Internet Consumption: Contributions from Cross-Cultural Marketing and Advertising Research', *Journal of Computer-Mediated Communication*, **11** (1), 192–216.

Hernandez, Monica D. and Michael S. Minor (2010), 'Consumer Responses to East–West Writing System Differences', *International Marketing Review*, **27** (5), 579–93.

Hofstede, Geert (1980), *Culture's Consequences: International Differences in Work-Related Values*, Thousand Oaks, CA: Sage Publications.

Hofstede, Geert (2002), 'Dimensions Do Not Exist: A Reply to Brendan Mcsweeney', *Human Relations*, **55** (11), 1355–61.

Hynes, Geraldine E. and Marius Janson (2007), 'Global Imagery in Online Advertisements', *Business Communication Quarterly*, **70** (4), 487–92.

International Telecommunication Union (2010), 'The World in 2010: Ict Facts and Figures', available at http://www.itu.int/ITU-D/ict/material/FactsFigures2010.pdf (accessed February 13, 2011).

Johnston, Kevin and Parminder Johal (1999), 'The Internet as a "Virtual Cultural Region": Are Extant Cultural Classification Schemes Appropriate?' *Internet Research*, **9** (3), 178–86.

Ju-Pak, Kuen-Hee (1999), 'Content Dimensions of Web Advertising: A Cross-National Comparison', *International Journal of Advertising*, **18** (2), 207–31.

Kim, Heeman, James R. Coyle, and Stephen J. Gould (2009), 'Collectivist and Individualist Influences on Website Design in South Korea and the U.S.: A Cross-Cultural Content Analysis', *Journal of Computer-Mediated Communication*, **14** (3), 581–601.

Ko, Hanjun, Marilyn S. Roberts, and Chang-Hoan Cho (2006), 'Cross-Cultural Differences in Motivations and Perceived Interactivity: A Comparative Study of American and Korean Internet Users', *Journal of Current Issues & Research in Advertising*, **28** (2), 93–104.

Laroche, Michel, V.H. Kirpalani, Frank Pons, and Lianxi Zhou (2001), 'A Model of Advertising Standardization in Multinational Corporations', *Journal of International Business Studies*, **32** (2), 249–66.

Lee, Wei-Na and Sejung Marina Choi (2005), 'The Role of Horizontal and Vertical Individualism and Collectivism in Online Consumers' Responses toward Persuasive Communication on the Web', *Journal of Computer-Mediated Communication*, **11** (1), 317–36.

Li, Hairong, Ang Li, and Shuguang Zhao (2009), 'Internet Advertising Strategy of Multinationals in China', *International Journal of Advertising*, **28** (1), 125–46.

Liu, Yuping and L.J. Shrum (2002), 'What Is Interactivity and Is It Always Such a Good

Thing? Implications of Definition, Person, and Situation for the Influence of Interactivity on Advertising Effectiveness', *Journal of Advertising*, **31** (4), 53–64.

Luna, David, Laura A. Peracchio, and María Dolores de Juan (2003), 'The Impact of Language and Congruity on Persuasion in Multicultural E-Marketing', *Journal of Consumer Psychology*, **13** (1/2), 41–50.

Lutz, Richard J. (1985), 'Affective and Cognitive Antecedents of Attitude toward the Ad: A Conceptual Framework', in Linda Alwitt and Andrew Mitchell (eds), *Psychological Processes and Advertising Effects*, Hillsdale, NJ: Lawrence Erlbaum Associates, pp. 45–63.

Marketing Charts (2008), 'Worldwide Internet Advertising Spending to Surpass $106 Billion in 2011', available at http://www.marketingcharts.com/television/worldwide-internet-advertising-spending-to-surpass-106-billion-in-2011-5068/ (accessed February 13, 2011).

Möller, Jana and Martin Eisend (2010), 'A Global Investigation into the Cultural and Individual Antecedents of Banner Advertising Effectiveness', *Journal of International Marketing*, **18** (2), 80–98.

Murphy, Jamie and Arno Scharl (2007), 'An Investigation of Global Versus Local Online Branding', *International Marketing Review*, **24** (3), 297–312.

Nantel, Jacques and Evelyne Glaser (2008), 'The Impact of Language and Culture on Perceived Website Usability', *Journal of Engineering & Technology Management*, **25** (1/2), 112–22.

Oh, Kyu-Won, Cho Chang-Hoan, and John D. Leckenby (1999), 'A Comparative Analysis of Korean and U.S. Web Advertising', paper presented at Proceedings of the 1999 Conference of the American Academy of Advertising, Marilyn S. Roberts (ed.). Gainesville, FL: American Academy of Advertising, pp. 73–86.

Okazaki, Shintaro (2004), 'Do Multinationals Standardise or Localise? The Cross-Cultural Dimensionality of Product-Based Web Sites', *Internet Research*, **14** (1), 81–94.

Okazaki, Shintaro (2005), 'Searching the Web for Global Brands: How American Brands Standardise Their Web Sites in Europe', *European Journal of Marketing*, **39** (1/2), 87–109.

Okazaki, Shintaro and Javier Alonso Rivas (2002), 'A Content Analysis of Multinationals' Web Communication Strategies: Cross-Cultural Research Framework and Pre-Testing', *Internet Research*, **12** (5), 380–90.

Okazaki, Shintaro and Radoslav Skapa (2008), 'Global Web Site Standardization in the New Eu Member States', *European Journal of Marketing*, **42** (11/12), 1224–45.

Paek, H., J. Yu, and B. Bae (2009), 'Is On-Line Health Promotion Culture-Bound?' *Journal of Advertising*, **38** (1), 35–47.

Pashupati, Kartik and Jeng Hoon Lee (2003), 'Web Banner Ads in Online Newspapers: A Cross-National Comparison of India and Korea', *International Journal of Advertising*, **22** (4), 531–64.

Pollay, Richard W. (1986), 'The Distorted Mirror: Reflections on the Unintended Consequences of Advertising', *Journal of Marketing*, **50** (2), 18–36.

Resnik, Alan and Bruce L. Stern (1977), 'An Analysis of Information Content in Television Advertising', *Journal of Marketing*, **41** (1), 50–53.

Riegner, Cate (2008), 'Wired China: The Power of the World's Largest Internet Population', *Journal of Advertising Research*, **48** (4), 496–505.

Schwartz, Shalom H. (1994), 'Beyond Individualism/Collectivism: New Cultural Dimensions of Values', in Uichol Kim, Harry C. Triandis, Cigdem Kagitcibasi, Sang-Chin Choi and Gene Yoon (eds), *Individualism and Collectivism: Theory, Method, and Applications*, Thousand Oaks, CA: Sage Publications, pp. 85–119.

Shin, Wonsun and Jisu Huh (2009), 'Multinational Corporate Website Strategies and Influencing Factors: A Comparison of Us and Korean Corporate Websites', *Journal of Marketing Communications*, **15** (5), 287–310.

Sia, Choon Ling, Kia H. Lim, Kwok Leung, Matthew K.O. Lee, Wayne Wei Huang, and Izak Benbasat (2009), 'Web Strategies to Promote Internet Shopping: Is Cultural-Customization Needed?' *MIS Quarterly*, **33** (3), 491–512.

Singh, Nitish and Daniel W. Baack (2004), 'Web Site Adaptation: A Cross-Cultural

Comparison of U.S. and Mexican Web Sites', *Journal of Computer-Mediated Communication*, **9** (4).

Singh, Nitish, Georg Fassott, Mike C.H. Chao, and Jonas A. Hoffmann (2006a), 'Understanding International Web Site Usage: A Cross-National Study of German, Brazilian, and Taiwanese Online Consumers', *International Marketing Review*, **23** (1), 83–97.

Singh, Nitish, Georg Fassott, Zhao Hongxin, and Paul D. Boughton (2006b), 'A Cross-Cultural Analysis of German, Chinese and Indian Consumers' Perception of Web Site Adaptation', *Journal of Consumer Behaviour*, **5** (1), 56–68.

Singh, Nitish, Zhao Hongxin, and Hu Xiaorui (2003), 'Cultural Adaptation on the Web: A Study of American Companies' Domestic and Chinese Websites', *Journal of Global Information Management*, **11** (3), 63–80.

Singh, Nitish, Vikas Kumar, and Daniel Baack (2005), 'Adaptation of Cultural Content: Evidence from B2c E-Commerce Firms', *European Journal of Marketing*, **39** (1/2), 71–86.

Singh, Nitish and Hisako Matsuo (2004), 'Measuring Cultural Adaptation on the Web: A Content Analytic Study of U.S. and Japanese Web Sites', *Journal of Business Research*, **57** (8), 864–72.

Sinkovics, Rudolf R., Mo Yamin, and Matthias Hossinger (2007), 'Cultural Adaptation in Cross Border E-Commerce: A Study of German Companies', *Journal of Electronic Commerce Research*, **8** (4), 221–35.

Taylor, Charles R. (2005), 'Moving International Advertising Research Forward', *Journal of Advertising*, **34** (1), 7–16.

Voorveld, Hilde, Peter Neijens, and Edith Smit (2010), 'The Interactive Authority of Brand Web Sites', *Journal of Advertising Research*, **50** (3), 292–304.

Wang, Ying and Shaojing Sun (2010), 'Assessing Beliefs, Attitudes, and Behavioral Responses toward Online Advertising in Three Countries', *International Business Review*, **19** (4), 333–44.

Warden, Clyde A., Mengkuan Lai, and Wann-Yih Wu (2002), 'How Worldwide is Marketing Communication on the World Wide Web?' *Journal of Advertising Research*, **42** (5), 72–84.

Würtz, Elizabeth (2005), 'Intercultural Communication on Web Sites: A Cross-Cultural Analysis of Web Sites from High-Context Cultures and Low-Context Cultures', *Journal of Computer-Mediated Communication*, **11** (1), 274–99.

Yoon, Doyle and Fritz Cropp (1999), 'Cultural Differences in Internet Advertising: A Content Analysis of Internet Advertising between the United States and Korea', paper presented at Proceedings of the 1999 Conference of the American Academy of Advertising, Marilyn S. Roberts (ed.), Gainesville, FL: American Academy of Advertising, pp. 89–96.

Zhao, Wenyong, Brian L. Massey, Jamie Murphy, and Fang Liu (2003), 'Cultural Dimensions of Website Design and Content', *Prometheus*, **21** (1), 75–84.

15 The role of e-WOM in international communication

Salvador Ruiz, María Sicilia, Inés López and Manuela López

INTRODUCTION

Word of mouth (WOM) represents a low-cost and trustworthy channel for acquiring and retaining customers (Villanueva et al. 2008). It is an informal mode of communication between non-commercial parties concerning the evaluation of products and services (Arndt, 1967). Its relevance in evaluation makes it a key element to the exchange process because consumers often rely on others for assistance with purchases, especially for products with high financial or psychic risk (Gershoff and Johar, 2006).

With the fast growth and proliferation of e-commerce, the Web has become an excellent source for gathering consumer opinions about products (Duan et al. 2008). Through product review websites (e.g., epinions. com, rateitall.com, cnet.com), on discussion boards or Usenet via Google Groups, or even in personal blogs (aggregated through various platforms), consumers can express their opinions and experiences about products and brands. This activity has also been propelled by manufacturers and retailers, as they have started to provide online forums that allow customers to express their opinions about the products they sell. This access to online comments is based on consumers' interactions with one another quickly and conveniently, in a new form of word of mouth based on online interpersonal influence known as electronic word of mouth (e-WOM) (Goldenberg et al. 2001). The industry and part of the literature have addressed the classification of common types of WOM marketing activities. Terms such as buzz marketing, viral marketing, grassroots marketing and evangelist marketing have became common in industry to implement e-WOM activities through different techniques, in order to access consumers and to encourage them to transmit information through the Internet.

Two main antecedents can be identified behind this phenomenon: the consumers' search for quality information when purchasing new products and the continuous increase in Internet adoption, with more consumers relying on online sources of information in their decision-making process (Steffes and Burgee, 2009).

The anonymous and interactive nature of cyberspace enables consumers to freely give and seek opinions about the product experiences of peer consumers, who thereby affect consumers' brand choices and sales of many goods and services (Goldsmith and Horowitz, 2006). Moreover, the Internet offers consumers unlimited access to large amounts of information and a massive variety of products (Negroponte and Maes, 1996). In the online context, consumers can easily compare prices and quality and communicate with marketers as well as with other consumers (Negroponte and Maes, 1996). As a result, consumers use the Internet to exchange product-related information and share brand experience in the same way they do offline (Goldsmith and Horowitz, 2006). For marketers, the online context represents a new form of understanding WOM characterized by two features: (a) the use of new actions to influence consumers and opinion leaders; and (b) the acknowledgment that market messages and meanings do not flow unidirectionally, but rather are exchanged among members of consumer networks (Kozinets et al. 2010).

While the selection of the optimal communication strategy is a very difficult task (Delre et al. 2007), little is known about how to use personal influences online to market the product succesfully, as e-WOM marketing is still very experimental in nature (Spaulding, 2010). Furthermore, companies are only starting to integrate mass and interpersonal communication influences into their communication activities (Libai et al. 2010). Even though marketers may not have control over e-WOM communication, they still need to understand how it works in order to manage it (Lim and Chung, 2011). Companies such as Nokia, Dell, Phillips, HP and Microsoft are starting to use e-WOM as a successful communication tool.

The relevance of e-WOM in the international arena is justified by both the worldwide access to the Internet and the globalization strategy implemented by many corporations nowadays. Many multinationals have country-adapted versions of their websites in several languages, which represents the easiest and most cost-effective way of entering emerging markets. Other companies only display their websites in the local language though an additional English version would greatly improve the access to the website. With this international presence, the website is often the first port of call for customers and the relevance of e-WOM is then applicable to these multicultural environments. Comments from consumers are then shown and exchanged internationally. From a managerial standpoint, e-WOM is recognized as an important marketing activity in brand communications. Industry reports have also shown and quantified the relevance of e-WOM. On average, consumers mention specific brands over 90 times per week in conversations with friends, family and co-workers (WOMMA, 2010). And, more interesting for companies, 90 percent of online consumers trust recommendations from people they know and 70 percent trust opinions of unknown users (Nielsen Global Online Consumer Survey, 2009). According to Nielsen, e-WOM effects on different countries further stimulate companies to use e-WOM as part of their communications campaigns. However, marketers should take into account that the effect of this communication process varies across countries. For instance, people from China and Vietnam find e-WOM more trustable and useful than people from other countries such as the US or Finland (Nielsen Global Online Consumer Survey, 2009).

In this chapter we offer a review of the communication processes based on consumer-to-consumer interaction (WOM and e-WOM) and their role in international marketing communication activities. We also tackle the issue of managing e-WOM communication from the company, since this activity is emerging as a new tool for advertisers.

WORD OF MOUTH

Literature on interpersonal influences (usually referred to as WOM) is very extensive. First studies date from the sixties (Dichter, 1966; Arndt, 1967), although in the fifties Katz and Lazarsfeld (1955) published *Personal Influence* in order to explain how this personal influence works. WOM can be defined as "a face-to-face conversation between consumers about a product or a service experience" (Sen and Lerman, 2007, p. 77). It usually occurs in a private conversation, where two parties are identified: the source of WOM information and the receiver (Gilly et al. 1998).

An important WOM characteristic that distinguishes it from other communication activities is the non-commercial interest of the source of information (Smith, 1993). Arndt (1967, p. 291) defines WOM as "face-to-face communication about products or companies between those people who are not commercial entities". More recent definitions take into account that WOM is unbiased. For example, Litvin et al. (2008, p. 460) describe WOM as "the communication between consumers about a product, service, or a company in which the sources are considered independent of commercial influence". In a similar vein, Brown et al. (2007) state that "WOM is a consumer-dominated channel of marketing communication where the sender is independent of the market". Most common WOM sources are friends and relatives, although it can also occur with neighbours and acquaintances (Brown and Reingen, 1987).

Main Determinants of WOM effectiveness: Valence and Tie Strength

Valence and tie strength are among the most important WOM aspects that have been examined. Literature on WOM has established additional determinants of WOM influence such as source expertise (Bansal and Voyer, 2000; Gilly et al. 1998), homophily (Brown and Reingen, 1987), and receiver expertise (Bansal and Voyer, 2000).

Valence captures the nature of WOM messages, whether they are positive or negative (Liu, 2006). Negative WOM prevents the receiver from buying the product whereas positive WOM strongly recommends its purchase. Moreover, the relative influence of positive vs. negative WOM is not the same. According to the traditional literature on interpersonal influences, there is a negative bias and negative information is more diagnostic and helpful than positive information to establish a classification of a product (Herr et al. 1991). Therefore marketers have to be very careful when they observe that some negative WOM appears in consumer conversations.

Tie strength refers to the intensity of the social relationship between consumers (Brown and Reingen, 1987). People can receive WOM from friends and relatives (considered as strong ties) or from neighbours and acquaintances (catalogued as weak ties) (Sen and Lerman, 2007). More frequent and intense relations with strong ties have traditionally shown a greater influence than less frequent and intense relations occurring with weak ties (Bansal and Voyer, 2000). However, weak ties play a crucial role in the flow of WOM information across groups. They display an important bridging function, allowing information to travel from one distinct subgroup of referral actors to another subgroup in the broader social system (Brown and Reingen, 1987).

WOM from the Sender Point of View: The Diffusion of Emotions

Literature has identified several motives for consumers' tendency to engage in WOM communication. Sundaram et al. (1998) demonstrated that consumers spread positive WOM for altruistic, product-involvement and self-enhancement reasons, and negative WOM for altruistic, anxiety-reduction, vengeance and advice-seeking reasons. More recently, Cheung et al. (2007) have found several new motivations such as seeking retaliation, seeking compensation and seeking bargaining power.

Consumers, encouraged by these motives, can transmit to other consumers both cognitive information about a product or service and emotional information about the related consumption experiences.

However, initial attempts to model consumer behavior in traditional literature were biased towards reason (Zaltman, 1997). As a result, the affective side of individuals' behavior was given a relatively minor role for decades. Lately, research in consumer behavior dealing with affect has exploded, making it one of the field's central research topics (Cohen et al. 2008). Supporting its importance, Huang and Barlas (2006) demonstrated that people exchange emotional and recreational information more often than cognitive and utilitarian information in WOM. The first attempts to introduce affect in the literature consisted of conceptualizing emotions as general valence dimensions, such as positive and negative affect (Winkielman and Trujillo, 2008). However, recent literature indicates that discrete similar valence emotions can influence judgment in different ways (Bonifield and Cole, 2007; Zeelenberg and Pieters, 2004). Moreover, consumers do not live in isolation but in society, meaning that they belong to different groups of people (friends, acquaintances, work colleagues, etc.) with whom they may interact. People want (need) to exchange and share emotions about their own experiences (Rimé et al. 1999). Some of these experiences are related to the acquisition and use of products, that is to say, consumers express their consumption-related emotions when communicating with others. In line with this, prior research supports the idea that the specific experienced emotion has an impact on behavioral intentions, including WOM communication and loyalty (Westbrook, 1987; Nyer, 1997; Derbaix and Vanhamme, 2003; White and Yu, 2005).

Different studies have accounted for the relationship between emotions and WOM. Nyer (1997) found that emotional responses (joy, anger and sadness) contribute to positive and negative WOM intentions over and above the predictive ability of satisfaction. Westbrook (1987) found that positive and negative emotions influence the amount of WOM. Similarly, Derbaix and Vanhamme (2003) reported that surprise, negative emotions and positive emotions are all highly correlated with the likelihood of talking to others, whereas Soscia (2007) demonstrated a relationship between gratitude and positive WOM. Additionally, Zeelenberg and Pieters (2004) found a positive impact of regret and disappointment on the extent of negative WOM. Bonifield and Cole (2007) also focused on emotions (particularly, anger and regret) and confirmed that, when consumers blamed the service provider for a service failure, they experienced anger and were more likely to engage in negative WOM. In another study, Sweeney et al. (2005) found that negative WOM is largely emotive and driven by strong negative emotions, such as anger, frustration and exasperation. Schoefer and Diamantopoulos's (2008) results are also in harmony with conceptualizing negative WOM as an emotion-focused coping strategy operating as a venting mechanism and as a means to gain sympathy from others. A recent study by Izawa (2010) demonstrates that people engage in WOM communication not only to exchange information so as to make better choices, but also to establish social connections with others. The author finds that people exchange emotional information more often than cognitive information in WOM.

Regarding the diffusion process of WOM, Heath et al. (2001) found that people tend to pass along stories that elicit a higher level of disgust, a negative emotion. Therefore, it is not only that emotions elicited by the consumption experience push the consumer to spread WOM, but also that those who receive the information show a higher propensity to pass along the story. In this regard, Peters et al.'s (2009) study on social talk looked at how social information that arouses emotion is communicated in everyday conversations. The results revealed that people are more willing to share episodes that arouse interest, surprise, disgust and happiness.

Another important aspect of the relationship between WOM and emotions is associated with the goals consumers pursue when they engage in such a communication process. In a recent paper, Wetzer et al. (2007) identified the most commonly felt emotions in consumption experiences and then related them to different goals. Thus, on the one hand, anger, frustration, irritation, regret, disappointment and uncertainty are particularly relevant in negative WOM situations. On the other hand, systematic connections between specific emotions and specific goals to engage in negative WOM emerge. For example, anger is related to venting and revenge, whereas regret is associated to bonding. These findings suggest that the specific goal that a consumer strives for by talking might be reflected in the content of the conversation and that, subsequently, influences the receiver. The difference in destructiveness of negative WOM depending on the prevailing emotion suggests that marketers should pay special attention to the specific emotion that is felt by a consumer who communicates about a negative experience.

Effects of WOM vs. Other Commercial Sources

WOM is perceived to be more reliable, credible and trustworthy by consumers compared to firm-initiated communications (Arndt, 1967). Grewal et al. (2003) indicated that individuals are more inclined to embrace the information sent through WOM than that sent through commercial promotion, on the ground that WOM information senders are usually believed to have no ulterior motive nor receive incentive for their referrals.

Credibility of WOM, when combined with the premise that a receiver will be more involved in a WOM exchange than in an advertisement, lends itself to the formation of some "informational value" over and above the formal advertising messages provided by the company. Such combinations hold influence over the individual's decision making (Brown et al. 2007).

In a pioneer study, Katz and Lazarsfeld (1955) found that WOM is seven times more effective than print media and four times more effective than personal selling in getting a customer to switch brands. Engel et al. (1969) showed that 60 percent of customers of a new auto-repair centre cited WOM as the most influential factor in their choice. In this vein, Herr et al. (1991) found that WOM communication has a greater impact on product judgments than less vivid printed information.

WOM can even help to counteract negative information. Van Hoye and Lievens (2005) found that positive WOM could enhance organizational attractiveness after negative publicity. WOM communication strategies are therefore very appealing for advertisers because they combine the prospect of overcoming consumer resistance with significantly lower costs and fast delivery (Trusov et al. 2009). WOM effects are also very positive in terms of product loyalty. Money (2004) demonstrated that buyers that consult more WOM sources (at least one or more) in their search will be less likely to switch their industrial service providers than buyers that consult fewer (or no) sources. Customers who use referrals to find a service will likely stay more loyal than those who find the provider themselves. Moreover, customers who self-report having been acquired through WOM add more long-term value to the firm than customers acquired through traditional marketing channels (Villanueva et al. 2008).

However, WOM can also be negative and, then, companies need to be very careful when developing their marketing activity. Smith and Vogt (1995) explored consumers' responses to the integration of advertising and negative WOM. They showed that advertising mitigates the detrimental cognitive effects of negative WOM communication when the ad is processed first, and the detrimental affective and conative effects when the ad is processed last. They also showed that when consumers process both types of information, negative WOM reduces the perceived credibility of advertising and both brand attitudes and purchase intentions decrease.

How WOM Combines with Advertising

WOM has been often mentioned as an alternative to traditional media, yet marketers do not really understand the extent to which WOM complements or substitutes traditional media (Libai et al. 2010). Recent studies have investigated these interactions between advertising and WOM. Hogan et al. (2004) observed that the real value that an ad generates is three times higher than if WOM is taken into account. In their study, WOM is considered as a complement of advertising once some consumers already have product experience. Van Hoye and Lievens (2007) found that positive WOM increased the effect of recruitment advertising on organizational attractiveness. Recently, using the TalkTrack WOM monitoring service, Keller and Fay (2009) have suggested that a notable percentage of WOM conversations include references to advertising, and that such conversations may be more influential than those conversations that do not mention advertising.

Academics have also established the order in which both traditional media (i.e., advertising) and WOM should be used when trying to stimulate product sales. From this perspective, Delre et al. (2007) state that it is of great importance to understand how information starting from mass media (external influence) and travelling through WOM (internal influence) affects the intention to buy a product. Hogan et al. (2004) suggest that it is the initial marketing communication that triggers a customer's initial purchase. As marketing and advertising managers have assumed for many years, WOM complements and extends the effects of advertising (Bayus, 1985). A similar reasoning has been applied to the introduction of a new product. Goldenberg et al. (2001) explain that advertising is the tool that best works at the introduction stage, because WOM needs informed individuals to start the process.

Some well-known companies, aware of the potential synergies, have combined WOM with advertising to improve their results. For example, Nintendo developed an amazing communication campaign to launch Wii at Christmas 2006. In addition to advertising and in order to reach a difficult target audience, Nintendo's aim was to persuade mothers to try to become familiar with the product. The underlying reason was that mothers take part in decision making related to household appliances and, at the same time, show a strong reluctance to accept video games. Nintendo proceeded as follows. The company gathered some tech-savvy housewives in Los Angeles and offered them the possibility of interacting with the device. Nintendo called these mothers "alphamom". They replicated the experiment in other areas across the United States. By the time Wii's "mother tenacious battle" finished, over 200 million units were sold and the product became the best-selling entertainment brand during Christmas 2006.

FROM WOM TO E-WOM

The Internet is changing the way consumers communicate by allowing a common space for sharing opinions (Goldsmith, 2006). Nowadays, social media tools enable consumers to extend their connections and conduct WOM with fewer restrictions. New technologies make it easier for consumers to share product- and brand-related information with each other (Stephen and Lehmann, 2009). The advances of information technology have profoundly changed the way information is transmitted between consumers. They can share their product-related experiences on the Internet through e-mail, bulletin boards, chat rooms, forums, fan clubs, brand and other user groups (Goldsmith, 2006).

Many terms have been used interchangeably to refer to e-WOM, including web of mouse, word of mouse, Internet word of mouth, consumer opinions, web recommendations, or consumers' reviews (Shin, 2007). This communication process is defined as "any positive or negative statement made by potential, actual, or former customers about a product or company, which is made available to a multitude of people and institutions via the Internet" (Hennig-Thurau et al., 2004, p. 39). Litvin et al. (2008, p. 461) also defined e-WOM as "all informal communications directed at consumers through Internet-based technology related to the usage or characteristics of particular goods and services, or their sellers". More broadly, Huang et al. (2009, p. 160) describe e-WOM as "the informal communications through the Internet".

WOM vs. e-WOM

It is not surprising that consumers use the new medium (the Internet) to exchange product-related information in much the same way as they do offline. However, online WOM activity differs from traditional WOM in many aspects, which means e-WOM deserves additional attention as an extension of traditional interpersonal communication into the new realm of cyberspace.

In traditional WOM communication, the information is exchanged in face-to-face conversation, while in e-WOM consumers need only to interact with their computers to post or search consumer reviews (Sen and Lerman, 2007). Sources of information in e-WOM are anonymous individuals who have little or no prior relationship with the information seeker (Xia and Bechwati, 2008). Most e-WOM information comes from strangers who have never met or will in the future (Chaterjee, 2001). In contrast, most offline WOM communication comes from friends and relatives (Sen and Lerman, 2007). This difference allows for confidentiality in e-WOM as consumers do not have to reveal their identities when seeking and giving advice. Thus, as opposed to traditional WOM, the non-commercial focus may not be certain in e-WOM (Chaterjee, 2001; Dellarocas, 2006). Companies can disguise commercial information as consumer reviews (Dellarocas, 2006). These actions may have a great effect in terms of credibility derived from online communication process, because consumers may not be able to judge the e-WOM information the way they do when the advice is obtained from friends or family.

In contrast to traditional WOM, in e-WOM the sender and the receiver of information are separated by both space and time (Stefees and Burgee, 2009). WOM happens in an oral face-to-face conversation, while in e-WOM transmitters write opinions that receivers read. The asynchronous discussions are usually kept for some time to allow other users to participate or read the messages at their own pace (Hoffman and Novak, 1997). The main implication of this difference is the permanence of online messages (Kiecker and Cowles, 2001). This e-WOM characteristic allows consumers to obtain personal information about a product when they need it, without simultaneously meeting with the sender, making international exchanges of information easier.

The communication network in e-WOM is much larger than traditional WOM (Cheung et al. 2007). More contributors and audiences are involved, and the reach of such communication extends beyond small personal connections to the Internet world. E-WOM belongs to a many-to-many communication model in which the information exchanged is more voluminous in quantity compared to information obtained from traditional contacts in the offline world (Hennig-Thurau et al. 2004). Therefore, e-WOM can transmit information faster than traditional WOM and reach far beyond the local community through the Internet (Chatterjee, 2001). E-WOM has transcended the traditional limitations of WOM (Shin, 2007). A summary of the main differences is displayed in Table 15.1.

E-WOM and the Diffusion of Emotions

While traditionally individuals have communicated far more with intimates than with non-intimates (Rimé et al. 1991), the tendency to share experiences with others has recently evolved in an unknown fashion with the advent of the Internet and social networks, which have had a tremendous impact on the way people in general and consumers in particular communicate. Internet-based communication channels connect people, and when they communicate with one another, the personal experience – in addition to the mere exchange of information – involves the elicitation of emotions (McKenna et al. 2002). The online environment just

Table 15.1   Critical differences between traditional WOM and e-WOM

	WOM	e-WOM
Communication channel	Face-to-face	Electronic
Message source	Known	Unknown
Type of message	Oral	Written
Type of communication	Synchronous	Asynchronous
Communication model	One-to-one	Many-to-many
Network size	Small	Large
Scope	Local–geographically restricted	Internet world

represents another form of communication between human beings where emotions, which are inherent to humans, play their role. But of course, a distinction that makes the Internet unique is that the number of people who can be exposed to what one person writes is enormous; the amount of people within the reach of e-WOM is huge. This is forcing marketers to understand what factors contribute to its activation in order to generate positive opinions that will be spread around the globe later.

When a consumer engages in a communication action, some motivations must trigger it. Hennig-Thurau et al. (2004) identified eight motives that push consumers to participate in e-WOM: platform assistance, venting negative feelings, concern for consumers, expressing positive feeling/positive self-enhancement, social benefits, economic incentives, helping the company, and seeking advice. The study revealed that social benefits, economic incentives, concern for other consumers, and expressing positive feeling/positive self-enhancement were the main motives for e-WOM behavior.

The premise to forward a message to a friend or acquaintance is related to emotions (Lin et al. 2006). If the message or the information elicits positive emotions in the receiver, (s)he will be more likely to forward it. Therefore, it is the affective component and not the informational load that leads the subject to pass on the information. Moreover, Chiu et al. (2007) conducted a study to identify the determinants of effective viral campaigns. They concluded that messages with both a higher utilitarian value (i.e., more informative) and a higher hedonic value (i.e., more enjoyable) are more likely to be passed along. In the context of online sharing behavior, Izawa (2010) found that particular emotions, impressions and utilities associated with video content have an impact on people's decision on whether to share the video with others. Particularly, those participants who responded that they had shared or would share the videos shown in the survey reported to feel stronger emotions than those who answered that they had not shared information or messages or would not share the video. The former also reported to find the videos more intense, enjoyable and informative than the latter. In relation to this issue, Phelps et al. (2004) examined consumers' motivations to pass along information and concluded that if marketers aim to get diffusion for their e-WOM campaigns they need to include messages that spark strong emotions such as fear, anger, sadness, or inspiration. Otherwise, e-WOM will not spread the way the firm would like. Let us illustrate the presence of emotions in e-WOM with a real comment posted on www.tripadvisor.co.uk:

> Angry and disappointed – Dishonest Hotel! This is a dishonest hotel – actually we didn't really stay in this hotel. We reserved a room online and received an email confirmation from the hotel. The day we went there we already had a terrible day at Pisa when our flight was cancelled, and when we finally arrived at this hotel at around 9:30pm the man there said the hotel was full! He refused to check his email (of course he wouldn't dare to! and too bad we didn't bring the email along – but what's the use?) and kept saying that it must be a misunderstanding (even though we saw our names on the list and pointed it out to him he still said it was a MISUNDERSTANDING!), and then he called another (shabby) hotel for a room. We had no choice because it was already passed 9:30pm – that shabby hotel's price was higher and took no credit card and this further upset our trip plan. Obviously Hotel des Voyageurs overbooked itself and then sent guests to other "conspired" hotels. We are not rich, it's difficult to get long holidays and had to travel for 10+ hours to Europe, and the experience totally destroyed our hard-earned vacation – we are so angry that we don't think we would visit Paris again!

A quick reading of this e-WOM message reveals that e-WOM also enables consumers to vent their emotions. In fact, emotions make the content more intense and indicate how the consumer felt after the service failure. Marketers should identify the specific emotions that can move their customers, that is to say, they need to find out which emotions can lead customers to engage in the e-WOM campaign initiated by the company. Literature indicates that messages eliciting emotions such as happiness, joy, surprise and fear encourage consumers to share the information.

Effects of e-WOM, WOM and Traditional Media

Although recent research appears to generally confirm the influence of e-WOM on purchase intentions and behavior, the difference between e-WOM and the traditional WOM communications may question some previous results. Both the degree and the scope of influence have to be re-examined. Existing (offline) theory may be inappropriate to describe online WOM and its influence on evaluation and purchase (Brown et al. 2007).

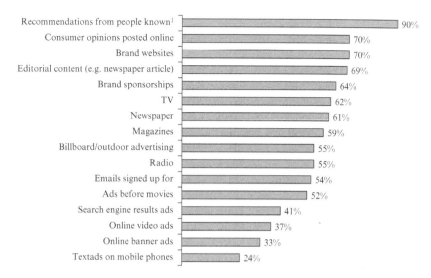

Note: 1. E.g. 90% of respondents trusted "completely" or "somewhat" recommendations from people known.

Source: Nielsen Global Online Consumer Survey.

Figure 15.1 Have some degree of trust in the following forms of advertising

The absence of a face-to-face conversation is critical because consumers do not have to directly meet other people to exchange their opinions and experiences on products, services and trades (Shin, 2007). However, based on principles in social cognition and interpersonal relationship development from social psychology, it seems that, given enough time, individuals can create fully formed impressions of others based solely on the linguistic content of written electronic messages.

According to recent research, the effect of e-WOM on consumers is somehow similar to that of traditional WOM (Hennig-Thurau et al. 2004). Consumers' reviews on products and services have been an influential tool as an information source for consumers (Gogoi, 2007), since it has a direct effect on sales (Dellarocas et al. 2007; Duan et al. 2008; Liu, 2006). As shown in Figure 15.1, 70 percent of Internet users around the world trust e-WOM, being more credible than firm-generated information (Nielsen Global Online Consumer Survey, 2009). Likewise, as traditional WOM, e-WOM is more effective than firm-generated sources on the Internet (Bickart and Schindler, 2001). E-WOM generates more product category interest than exposure to marketing-generated sources of information available on the Internet. In a similar study, Parker (2005) also reports that e-WOM is pervasive and growing. Consumers in this study were approximately 16 percent more likely to be influenced by e-WOM than by traditional advertising media (radio, TV and newspapers).

Regarding effects on time, Trusov et al. (2009) have shown that e-WOM referrals have substantially longer carryover effects than traditional marketing actions, have a strong impact on new customer acquisition and produce substantially higher response elasticities. The long-term elasticity of sign-ups with respect to e-WOM is estimated to be 0.53 (substantially larger than the average advertising elasticities reported in the literature). In addition, those customers who consult referral sources are less likely to switch than those who do not use e-WOM. Given these impacting results, it is not surprising that marketers worldwide are increasingly interested in developing e-WOM campaigns as a potential new communication tool (Kozinets et al. 2010).

MANAGEMENT OF E-WOM

Relevance of the Topic for Managers

The recent resurgence in the use of WOM campaigns, as evidenced by the growing use of referral reward programs, affiliate marketing and Internet-based viral marketing campaigns, emphasizes the need to better understand the value of this important social mechanism (see, for example, Biyalogorsky et al. 2001; Libai et al. 2003).

The marketing practices related to the communication activity of e-WOM are grounded on a basic assumption: the success of e-WOM relies on the fact that consumers engage in this communication process because of its social or psychological benefits. Providing high customer satisfaction is the key to lower-cost future transactions (Anderson et al. 1994), increasing loyalty and retention. Therefore, it is of interest to know and to take into account consumers' motivations to engage in e-WOM before even planning any communication campaign.

Owing to the consumer tendency to participate in interactions on the Internet, online interpersonal influence or e-WOM plays an important role in building strong brands. The customized information available on the Internet also provides opportunities for marketers to implement e-WOM as a permanent communication activity to establish and manage customer relationships (Dellarocas, 2003). Viral marketing, which relies on provocative messages to stimulate peer-to-peer communication of information from identified sponsors, evidently illustrates marketers' attempt to actively capitalize on e-WOM as a marketing tool (Porter and Golan, 2006). Thus, many companies are investing substantial efforts in e-WOM, incorporating this communication activity as part of integrated marketing communications strategies (Stephen and Lehmann, 2009). For example, the impact of e-WOM in the hospitality industry is especially illustrative. Intangibles such as restaurant services cannot be evaluated before the consumption experience; therefore, purchasing intangible products and services brings a higher risk, so customers are more dependent on the interpersonal influence of e-WOM (Lewis and Chambers, 2000). Restaurant customers have both altruistic and selfish motivations for articulating positive e-WOM about restaurants. Their positive comments are based on restaurant experiences with superior food, service and atmosphere (Park and Jang, 2011).

Companies that market their products or services on the Internet are addressing global markets, since consumers all over the world may access their websites and are not constrained by either location or time (Sheth and Sharma, 2005).

How to Develop an e-WOM Campaign

Nowadays, planning e-WOM communication activities has become as essential as any other marketing activity. An e-WOM campaign is also known as a seeding campaign/program (Kozinets et al. 2010; Libai et al. 2009). Marketers try to influence an initial group of consumers, who are called the "seed", in order to activate e-WOM referrals (Libai et al. 2009).

The increasing importance of this communication process online has led to the creation of agencies specialized in WOM marketing. Therefore, each stage can be carried out either by the company or by a WOM agency. We propose four steps to plan an e-WOM campaign (see Figure 15.2): setting of objectives, campaign design (which includes focal message, triggering stimulus, seeding group and channel), implementation, and evaluation of the campaign. Two main types of objective can be associated with e-WOM: direct objectives, such as reach, product and message awareness, brand knowledge, brand image, and customers acquisition; and indirect objectives, such as sales or market share. In a second step, marketers should decide which message they want to send to consumers and how to get it spread. This step also involves related decisions including the triggering stimulus, the seeding group and the communication channels that could be more appropriate to spread the word. Regarding the focal message, marketers have to take into account that the message the company transmits to consumers will not be the message they will pass on. Marketers do not have any control over consumers' opinions.

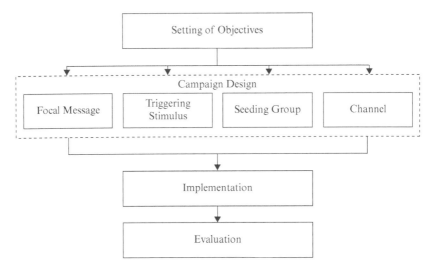

Figure 15.2   e-WOM campaign plan

Therefore, the message should be clearly conceived from the beginning in order to maintain the essential idea behind the focal message. Next they have to decide which triggering stimulus should be used. Companies can provide consumers either with the product, in order to test it and spread their opinions about it, or with a piece of unique information. This unique information may be product-related, company-related or unrelated to them, but interesting enough to consumers. In both cases, product trial and information transmission, marketers should try to be original and transmit emotions along with the main triggering stimulus in order to increase the probability of the word being spread. Next, the marketer has to select the seeding group, which is the initial group of consumers who will later refer the focal message. This decision determines the communication channel used to contact them. Traditional literature has studied the importance of opinion leaders in WOM diffusion (Katz and Lazarsfeld, 1955; Rogers, 1983). In the online environment, opinion leaders have been recently linked to bloggers (Droge et al. 2010; Song et al. 2007), who can be relatively easy to identify and contact through their own blogs. However, companies should be careful when using this seeding group in their e-WOM campaigns. For example, Microsoft sent laptops with its new Windows Vista software to influential bloggers, trying to make them write about the new operating system. However, the resulting online discussion ignored Vista and focused instead on the morality and ethics of accepting gifts from companies wishing to encourage positive e-WOM. In contrast, Nokia was more original and effective. They sent six Nokia N97 Minis in personalized boxes to the leading social media mobile opinion leaders in the UK and New York City, using geo-location and online monitoring tools to surprise them wherever they were. They received the mobile phone accompanied by a Mariachi band playing the famous Nokia ringtone. The campaign was very successful in terms of number of individuals involved and amount of shared information. In sum, marketers should devote more effort when identifying loyal opinion leaders rather than less loyal opinion leaders because they are more prone to generate positive WOM (Godes and Mayzlin, 2009). In addition, less loyal opinion leaders could engage in negative WOM because of negative feelings regarding the company wishes on referring their product. This negative feeling may be the logical consequence of what Dellarocas (2006) called strategic manipulation of e-WOM.

Additionally, marketers should not forget that other types of consumers act as influencers. Consumers are regarded as active co-producers of WOM (Kozinets et al. 2010). On a different campaign, Nokia delivered a new mobile phone (Nokia E72) to people from the US, the United Kingdom, New Zealand and India in a transparent box. The challenge consisted in opening the locked box to get the phone, without any clue about the password to do it. Some consumers uploaded videos to Youtube when trying to open the box with hammers. Other consumers spoke in social networks about it. Even some bloggers posted comments about it. This successful campaign indicates that not only opinion leaders but also general consumers can activate the spread of e-WOM. Companies can contact their customers by using their database information, engaging in conversations in their online communities, or using their own pages in online social networks. In addition, they should even try to influence either less loyal and no customers because their networks represent fertile ground for the generation of incremental sales (Godes and Mayzlin, 2009).

Finally, the e-WOM campaign should be implemented and subsequently evaluated. Each objective should contain particular, relevant evaluative criteria. The choice of criteria will vary across different campaigns, different sectors, the communication tasks needing to be accomplished and the resources available to undertake evaluation and measurement exercises. Campaign results are being evaluated mainly by controlling the volume of e-WOM generated, the number of participants involved in e-WOM and the number of different websites that include opinions. These direct measures should highly correlate with the direct objectives (such as awareness and brand knowledge), which, in turn, may have an effect on sales and market share.

Recommendations for an International e-WOM Campaign

Some differences may appear depending on how WOM is transmitted in several cultures. Research findings on differences in the transmission, decodification and impact of WOM across countries indicate that cultural values moderate the WOM communication process and the relevance customers attribute to WOM (Schumann et al. 2010). In this context, as pointed out by Rowley (2004), the global online audience is less predictable and more diverse than audiences accessed through other communication activities. Therefore, marketers have serious restrictions to prevent unintended audiences from getting access to the message. When firms operate in an international context, they are confronted with cultural differences among countries. These differences may require the adaptation of the message to make it appealing for the target audience. In the particular case of e-WOM, marketers face this challenge too. The reason is that not all societies express and interpret facts and emotions in the same way. On the contrary, there are significant differences that should be observed when creating an e-WOM campaign. Thus, it may be the case that a campaign is very effective and circulates fast through the Internet in a specific geographical area, whereas it is not well received by a different zone. It is important to consider the basic challenges of differing infrastructures, governments and languages around the world. The fact is that, if the company wants to transfer a national campaign globally, it takes people on the ground in each country dedicated to adapting and updating engagement in a way that works for their specific region (WOMMA, 2010).

Promoting e-WOM Worldwide

When marketers aim to develop an international e-WOM campaign, they need to know which cultures are more prone to engage in WOM, as well as what the level of emotional intensity is in their opinions. These differences will be essential when designing an e-WOM campaign. Hofstede (2001) proposed several dimensions to analyze differences across cultures. Most of them (power distance, uncertainty avoidance and individualism/ collectivism) have proved useful for explaining different reactions to WOM. In this vein, Liu et al. (2001) investigated the effects of consumers' cultural values on their intention to spread WOM when the perception of service quality is negative. They demonstrated that customers in large power distance cultures are more likely to spread negative WOM than customers in small power distance cultures, because they consider themselves to have higher power and hence are less tolerant of negative service quality. In addition, customers in high-uncertainty avoidance cultures are less likely to engage in negative WOM messaging than customers in low-uncertainty avoidance cultures. They also found that individuals from a more individualistic culture have a higher intention to spread negative WOM than individuals from a collective culture. In this line, Fong and Burton (2008) examined the content of discussion postings to US and China-based discussion boards and showed that China-based discussion boards engaged in lower levels of information giving. Lam et al. (2009) have recently demonstrated that the more a consumer values individualism, compared with collectivism, the more likely (s)he is to engage in WOM with an outgroup. According to Laroche et al. (2005), collectivistic cultures are less likely to express an opinion that may challenge the opinion of others within the group. In contrast, people from individualist cultures are likely to be more willing to provide information, opinions and recommendations, suggesting that individualist cultures encourage the expression of private opinions. These societies encourage social harmony and bonding within their in-group and also are more likely to exhibit greater trust for their ingroup and to perceive a greater difference between their in- and out-groups (Triandis, 1995).

Moreover, not all the cultures display and share opinions and information with others equally. In the field of social psychology, Mesquita (1993) found that the sharing of emotions occurred in different countries to a similar extent but that the content individuals shared varied when comparing Dutch, Surinamese and Turkish respondents living in The Netherlands. Furthermore, Rimé et al. (1996) collected data in six different locations: four in Asia and two in the Western world. Results confirmed that samples from Asian locations generally reported slightly lower rates of emotion sharing than did samples from Western locations.

Receiving and Actively Seeking e-WOM

E-WOM does not have the same effect in all cultures. Thus, in countries where e-WOM is less effective, managers should complement the campaign with another communication tool. However, another important aspect is how individuals from a culture decode opinions written by individuals from a different culture.

The differences in emotional display can become apparent in terms of emotion recognition; that is to say, there may be subtle differences in expressive style between members of different cultural groups that make it more difficult to decode expressions by cultural out-group members (Elfenbein and Ambady, 2002). For instance, Caucasians are more accurate at recognizing anger, sadness and fear expressions in comparison with Asians (Matsumoto, 1992). These general cultural decoding differences have been attributed to culturally learned display rules (Ekman and Friesen, 1969), that is, the cultural norms that prescribe emotion displays in social situations. Thus, lower recognition accuracy for negative emotions by members of collectivistic cultures, such as Asian individuals, has been associated with a cultural rule against displaying and acknowledging these emotions in others that is prevalent in these cultures (Matsumoto, 1992). In the context of e-WOM, this extent implies that consumers from one country, even if there are no language barriers, may not interpret the content properly. For example, a person from China may engage in e-WOM to express his/her disappointment after a consumption experience but (s)he may display the emotion in such a subtle manner that a person from the United States would interpret that the situation was not so bad. Misinterpretation could also happen in the other direction: an American consumer may express his/her anger in such a vehement and explicit way (in comparison with Asians) that a Chinese consumer would interpret that the situation was pretty bad. The intensity of negative emotions in both situations might be similar but their verbalization interferes with the way in which others interpret them.

Also in relation to emotions, it has been found that people from different countries attach different values to specific emotions. Thus, the Americans value enthusiasm very strongly; the Greeks highly value respect; and the West Indians value respect (Sommers, 1984). The Chinese consider more negative emotions to be useful and constructive than did the three other nations. This leads us to think that the prime emotion present in the advertiser's message should be different depending on the target. Thus, international advertisers need to take all these nuances into account when planning an international e-WOM campaign.

Hofstede's (2001) cultural dimensions also explain cultural differences in the e-WOM-seeking behavior. People in high-power distance cultures share norms for differential prestige, power and wealth, as well as the belief that talents and capabilities are unequally distributed across society (Hofstede, 2001). Therefore, people in low-power distance cultures are more prone to impersonal information acquisition (Dawar et al. 1996). High uncertainty avoidance is associated with a higher level of opinion-seeking (Dawar et al. 1996; Money et al. 1998) behavior. More reliance is then expected on received WOM referral from reliable others who already have experience with or knowledge about the product. Collectivist cultures have been shown to display differences from individualist cultures in information-seeking behavior. For example, in an offline cross-cultural study of information search, Doran (2002) found that Chinese consumers were more likely than American consumers to search for and rely on personal sources of information. In contrast, American consumers did less directed search and relied more on their internal knowledge and personal experience with products. In the same line, Han (2009) showed important cultural differences between Americans and Koreans in terms of the motivations to seek e-WOM. Korean participants, as they belong to a collectivistic culture, showed a higher tendency than Americans to seek e-WOM for social-oriented product information and product usage information.

CONCLUSIONS

The present study analyzes the role of e-WOM on international communication activities. Using and managing e-WOM is associated with higher communication effectiveness and may represent a rational and profit-maximizing solution to the communication problem. The transmission of both information and emotions through e-WOM results in higher efficacy of communication as a way to reach particular goals. The Internet as the platform results in a faster and wider impact than using traditional WOM, meaning that it can be more effective than other communication tools such as advertising or personal selling. Consumers' comments on products and services have a direct impact on sales, as they influence consumer behavior at the very first stages of the decision process. This positive effect is also strengthened by the higher credibility of e-WOM compared to other firm-generated communication activities.

The development of e-WOM campaigns needs to accomplish several decisions (focal message, triggering stimulus, seeding group and channel) that may be critical for its success. Moreover, the implementation of e-WOM campaigns across cultures requires taking into account how cultural differences moderate the e-WOM diffusion process. Cultural differences can influence not only the communication codification–transmission–decodification process, but also the relevance consumers attribute to sharing and shared information. Therefore, the analysis of consumers' motivations and the implementation of a planning process associated with each e-WOM action constitute basic elements to guarantee the success of this new but powerful communication tool.

Acknowledgment

This research was co-funded by the grant ECO2009-13170 from the Spanish Ministry of Science and Technology and FEDER, the grant CSO 2008-02627 from the Spanish Ministry of Science and Technology (more information in www.marcasturisticas.org), and Fundación Séneca-Agencia de

Ciencia y Tecnología de la Región de Murcia, within the framework of the II PCTRM 2007–2010.

This research was also supported by pre-doctoral scholarship AP2009-4125 awarded to the fourth author by the Spanish Ministry of Education.

REFERENCES

Anderson, E., W.C. Fornell and D.R. Lehmann (1994), 'Customer satisfaction, market share, and profitability: Findings from Sweden', *Journal of Marketing*, **58**, 53–66.

Arndt, J. (1967), 'Role of product-related conversations in the diffusion of a new product', *Journal of Marketing Research*, **4**, 291–5.

Bansal, H.S. and P.A. Voyer (2000), 'Word-of-mouth processes within a services purchase decision context, *Journal of Service Research*, **3**, 166–7.

Bayus, B. (1985), 'Word of mouth: The indirect effects of marketing efforts', *Journal of Advertising Research*, **25** (3), 31–9.

Bickart, B. and R.M. Schindler (2001), 'Internet forums as influential source of consumer information', *Journal of Interactive Marketing*, **15** (3), 31–9.

Biyalogorsky, E., E. Gerstner and B. Libai (2001), 'Customer referral management: Optimal reward programs', *Marketing Science*, **20** (1), 82–95.

Bonifield, C. and C. Cole (2007), 'Affective responses to service failure: Anger, regret, and retaliatory versus conciliatory responses', *Marketing Letters*, **18** (1), 85–99.

Brown, J. and P. Reingen, (1987), 'Social ties and word-of-mouth referral behavior', *Journal of Consumer Research*, **14**, 350–62.

Brown, J., A.J. Broderick and N. Lee (2007), 'Word of mouth communication within online communities: Conceptualizing the online social network', *Journal of Interactive Marketing*, **21** (3), 2–17.

Chatterjee, P. (2001), 'Online reviews: Do consumers use them?' *Advances in Consumer Research*, **28**, 129–33.

Cheung, M.S., I. Anitsal and M.M. Anitsal (2007), 'Revisiting word-of-mouth communications: A cross-national exploration', *The Journal of Marketing Theory and Practice*, **15** (3), 235–49.

Chiu, H.C., Y.C. Hsieh, Y.H. Kao and M. Lee (2007), 'The determinants of e-mail receivers' disseminating behaviors on the Internet', *Journal of Advertising Research*, **47** (4), 524–34.

Cohen, Joel B., Michel T. Pham and Eduardo B. Andrade (2008), 'The Nature and Role of Affect in Consumer Behavior', in Curt Haugtvedt, Frank Kardes and Paul Herr (eds), *Handbook of Consumer Psychology*, New York: Psychology Press, pp. 297–348.

Dawar, N., P. Parker and L. Price (1996), 'A cross-cultural study of interpersonal information exchange', *Journal of International Business Studies*, 3rd quarter, 497–516.

Dellarocas, C. (2003), 'The digitization of word of mouth: Promise and challenges of online feedback mechanisms', *Management Science*, **49** (10), 1407–24.

Dellarocas, C. (2006), 'Strategic manipulation of internet opinion forums: Implications for consumers and firms', *Management Science*, **52** (10), 1577–93.

Dellarocas, C.N., N.F. Awad and X. Zhang (2007), 'Exploring the value of online product reviews in forecasting sales: The case of motion pictures', *Journal of Interactive Marketing*, **21** (4), 23–45.

Delre, S., W. Jager, T.H.A. Bijmolt and M.A. Janssen (2007), 'Targeting and timing promotional activities: An agent-based model for the take-off of new products', *Journal of Business Research*, **60** (8), 826–35.

Derbaix C.M. and J. Vanhamme (2003), 'Inducing word-of-mouth by eliciting surprise: A pilot investigation', *Journal of Economic Psychology*, **24**, 99–116.

Dichter, E. (1966), 'How word of mouth advertising works', *Harvard Business Review*, **44** (6), 147–66.

Doran, K.B. (2002), 'Lessons learned in cross-cultural research of Chinese and North American consumers', *Journal of Business Research*, **55** (10), 823–9.

Droge, C., M.A. Stanko and W.A. Pollite (2010), 'Lead users and early adopters on the web: The role of new technology product blogs', *Journal of Product Innovation and Management*, **27**, 66–82.

Duan, W., B. Gu and A.B. Whinston (2008), 'The dynamics of online word-of-mouth and product sales: An empirical investigation of the movie industry', *Journal of Retailing*, **84** (2), 233–42.

Ekman, P. and W.V. Friesen (1969), 'The repertoire of nonverbal behavior: Categories, origin, usage, and coding', *Semiotica*, **1**, 49–98.

Elfenbein, H.A. and N. Ambady (2002), 'On the universality and cultural specificity of emotion recognition: A meta-analysis', *Psychological Bulletin*, **128**, 203–35.

Engel, J.F., R.D. Blackwell and P.W. Miniard (1969), *Consumer Behaviour*, Fort Worth, TX: Dryden.

Fong, J. and S. Burton (2008), 'A cross-cultural comparison of electronic word-of-mouth and country-of-origin effects', *Journal of Business Research*, **61** (3), 233–42.

Gershoff, A.D. and G.V. Johar (2006), 'Do you know me? Consumer calibration of friends' knowledge', *Journal of Consumer Research*, **32**, 496–503.

Gilly, M.C., J.L. Graham, M.F. Wolfinbarger and L.J. Yale (1998), 'A dyadic study of interpersonal information search', *Journal of the Academy of Marketing Science*, **26** (2), 83–100.

Godes, D. and D. Mayzlin (2009), 'Firm-created word-of-mouth communication: Evidence from a field test', *Marketing Science*, **28** (4), 721–39.

Gogoi, P. (2007), 'Retailers take a tip from MySpace', available at http://www.businessweek.com/bwdaily/dnflash/content/feb2007/db20070213_ 626293.html (accessed 24 February 2011).

Goldenberg, J., B. Libai and E. Muller (2001), 'Talk of the network: A complex systems look at the underlying process of word-of-mouth', *Marketing Letters*, **12**, 209–21.

Goldsmith, R.E and D. Horowitz (2006), 'Measuring motivations for online opinion seeking', *Journal of Interactive Advertising*, **6** (2), available at http://jiad.org/article76 (accessed 24 February 2011).

Goldsmith, R.E. (2006), 'Electronic word of mouth', in Mehdi Khosrow-Pour (ed.), *Encyclopedia of E-commerce, E-government and Mobile Commerce*, Hershey, PA: Idea Group Publishing.

Grewal, R., T. Cline and A. Davies (2003), 'Early-entrant advantage, word-of-mouth communication, brand similarity, and the consumer decision-making process', *Journal of Consumer Psychology*, **13** (3), 187–97.

Han, S.M. (2009), 'Motivations for providing and seeking ewom: A cross cultural comparison of U.S. and Korean college students', unpublished doctoral dissertation, Michigan State University.

Heath, C., C. Bell and E. Sternberg (2001), 'Emotional selection in memes: The case of urban legends', *Journal of Personality and Social Psychology*, **81** (6), 1028–41.

Hennig-Thurau, T., K.P. Gwinner, G. Walsh and D.D. Gremler (2004), 'Electronic word-of-mouth via consumer-opinion platforms: What motivates consumers to articulate themselves on the Internet', *Journal of Interactive Marketing*, **18** (1), 38–52.

Herr, P.M., F.M. Kardes and J. Kim (1991), 'Effects of word-of-mouth and attribute information on persuasion: An accessibility-diagnosticity perspective', *Journal of Consumer Research*, **17** (3), 454–62.

Hoffman, D.L. and T.P. Novak (1997), 'A new marketing paradigm for electronic commerce', *Information Society*, **13**, 43–54.

Hofstede, Geert (2001), *Culture's Consequences: Comparing Values, Behaviors, Institutions, and Organizations Across Nations*, 2nd ed. Thousand Oaks, CA: Sage Publications.

Hogan, J.E., K.N. Lemon and B. Libai (2004), 'Quantifying the ripple: Word of mouth and advertising effectiveness', *Journal of Advertising Research*, **44** (3), 271–80.

Huang, C., T. Lin and K. Lin (2009), 'Factors affecting pass-along email intentions (PAEIs): Integrating the social capital and social cognition theories', *Electronic Commerce Research & Applications*, **8** (3), 160–69.

Huang, L. and S. Barlas (2006), 'Sharing of hedonic and utilitarian information in word-of-mouth communications', in APA 114th Annual Convention Program 2006 (Society for Consumer Psychology Annual Conference), New Orleans: American Psychological Association, p. 229.

Izawa, M. (2010), 'What makes viral videos viral? Roles of emotion, impression, utility, and social ties in online sharing behaviour', unpublished doctoral dissertation, The Johns Hopkins University.

Katz, E. and P.F. Lazarsfeld (1955), *Personal Influence*, Glencoe, IL: Free Press.

Keller, E. and B. Fay (2009), 'The role of advertising in word-of-mouth', *Journal of Advertising*, **49** (2), 154–8.

Kiecker, P. and D. Cowles (2001), 'Interpersonal communication and personal influence on the internet', *Conference Proceedings La Londe Seminar: Marketing Communications and Consumer Behavior*, Aix-en-Provence.

Kozinets, R.V., K. de Valck, A.C. Wojnicki and S.J.S. Wilner (2010), 'Networked narriatives: Understanding word-of-mouth marketing in online communities', *Journal of Marketing*, **74** (2), 71–89.

Lam, D., A. Lee and R. Mizerski (2009), 'The effects of cultural values in word-of-mouth communication', *Journal of International Marketing*, **17** (3), 55–70.

Laroche, M., M. Kalamas and M. Cleveland (2005), 'I versus WE: How individualists and collectivists use information sources to formulate their service expectations', *International Marketing Review*, **22** (3), 279–308.

Lewis, R.C. and R.E. Chambers (2000), 'Marketing leadership in hospitality', *Foundations and Practices*, III, New York: Wiley.

Libai, B., E. Biyalogorsky and E. Gerstner (2003), 'Setting referral fees in affiliate marketing', *Journal of Service Research*, **5** (4), 303–15.

Libai, B., E. Muller and R. Peres (2009), 'The social value of word-of-mouth programs: Acceleration versus acquisition', working paper, Tel Aviv University.

Libai, B., R.N. Bolton, M.S. Bügel, Ko de Ruyter, O. Götz, H. Risselada and A.T. Stephen (2010), 'Customer to customer interactions: Broadening the scope of word of mouth research', *Journal of Service Research*, **13** (3), 267–82.

Lim, B.C. and C.M.Y. Chung (2011), 'The impact of word-of-mouth communication on attribute evaluation', *Journal of Business Research*, **64** (1), 18–23.

Lin, C.H., S.C. Chuang, D.T. Kao and C.Y. Kung (2006), 'The role of emotions in the endowment effect', *Journal of Economic Psychology*, **27**, 589–97.

Litvin, S.W., R.E. Goldsmith and B. Pan (2008), 'Electronic word of mouth in hospitality and tourism management', *Tourism Management*, **29**, 458–68.

Liu, B.S.C., O. Furrer and D. Sudharshan (2001), 'The relationship between culture and behavioral intentions toward services', *Journal of Service Research*, **4** (2), 118–29.

Liu, Y. (2006), 'Word-of-mouth for movies: Its dynamics and impact on box office revenue', *Journal of Marketing*, **70**, 74–89.

Matsumoto, Y. (1992), 'Japanese banks in Southeast Asia: The political economy of banking in Indonesia and Thailand', working paper, Cornell University.

McKenna K.Y.A., A.S. Green and M.J. Gleason (2002), 'Relationship formation on the Internet: What's the big attraction?' *Journal of Social Issues*, **58** (1), 9–31.

Mesquita, B. (1993), 'Cultural variations in emotion: A comparative study of Dutch, Surinamese and Turkish people in the Netherlands', unpublished doctoral dissertation, University of Amsterdam, The Netherlands.

Money, R.B. (2004), 'Word-of-mouth promotion and switching behavior in Japanese and American business-to-business service clients', *Journal of Business Research*, **57** (3), 297–305.

Money, R.B., M.C. Gilly and J.L. Graham (1998), 'Explorations of national culture and word-of-mouth referral behavior in the purchase of industrial services in the United States and Japan', *Journal of Marketing*, **62**, 76–87.

Negroponte, N. and P. Maes (1996), 'Electronic word of mouth', *Wired*, 4.10 (October).

Nielsen Global Online Consumer Survey (2009).

Nyer, P.U. (1997), 'A study of the relationships between cognitive appraisals and consumption emotions', *Journal of Academic Marketing Science*, **25** (4), 296–304.

Park, J. and S. Jang (2011), 'Psychographics: Static or dynamic?' working paper, Purdue University.

Parker, P. (2005), 'Reach "ad skippers" via online word-of-mouth', available at http://www.clickz.com/news/article.php/3551611 (accessed 24 February 2011).

Peters, K., Y. Kashima and A. Clark (2009), 'Talking about others: Emotionality and the dissemination of social information', *European Journal of Social Psychology*, **39** (2), 207–22.

Phelps, J.E., R. Lewis, L. Mobilio, D. Perry and N. Raman (2004), 'Viral marketing or electronic word-of-mouth advertising: Examining consumer responses and motivations to pass along email', *Journal of Advertising Research*, **44** (4), 333–48.

Porter, L. and G. Golan (2006), 'From subservient chickens to brawny men: A comparison of viral advertising to television advertising', *Journal of Interactive Advertising*, **6** (2), 30–38.

Rimé, B., B. Mesquita, P. Philippot and S. Boca (1991), 'Beyond the emotional event: Six studies on the social sharing of emotion', *Cognition and Emotion*, **5**, 435–65.

Rimé, B., C. Finkenauer and O. Luminet (1999), 'Social sharing of emotion: New evidence and new questions', *European Review of Social Psychology*, **9**, 145–89.

Rimé, B., M. Yogo and J.W. Pennebaker (1996), 'Social sharing of emotion across cultures', unpublished raw data.

Rogers, E.M. (1983), 'Diffusion of innovations', 3rd ed. New York: Free Press.

Rowley, J. (2004), 'Online branding', *Online Information Review*, **28** (2), 131–9.

Schoefer, K. and A. Diamantopoulos (2008). 'The role of emotions in translating perceptions of (in)justice into postcomplaint behavioral response', *Journal of Service Research*, **11** (1), 91–103.

Schumann, J.H., F.V. Wangenheim, A. Stringfellow, Z. Yang, V. Blazevic, S. Praxmarer, G. Shainesh, M. Komor, R.M. Shannon and F.R. Jiménez (2010), 'Cross-cultural differences in the effect of received word-of-mouth referral in relational service exchange', *Journal of International Marketing*, **18** (3), 62–80.

Sen, S. and D. Lerman (2007), 'Why are you telling me this? An examination into negative consumers reviews on the Web', *Journal of Interactive Marketing*, **21** (4), 76–94.

Sheth, J.N. and A. Sharma (2005), 'International e-marketing: Opportunities and issues', *International Marketing Review*, **22** (6), 611–22.

Shin, K.A. (2007), 'Factors influencing source credibility of consumer reviews: Apparel online shopping', unpublished doctoral dissertation, Oregon State University.

Smith, R.E. and C.A. Vogth (1995), 'The effects of integrating advertising and negative word-of-mouth communications on message processing and response', *Journal of Consumer Psychology*, **4** (2), 133–51.

Smith, V.L. (1993), 'When prior knowledge and law collide helping jurors use the law', *Law and Human Behavior*, **17**, 507–36.

Sommers, Shula (1984), 'Adults evaluating their emotions: A cross-cultural perspective', in Carol Z. Malatesta and Carol E. Izard (eds), *Emotion in Adult Development*, Beverly Hills, CA: Sage, pp. 319–38.

Song, Y., Y. Chi, K. Hino and B.L. Tseng (2007), 'Identifying opinion leaders in the blogosphere', Proceedings of the sixteenth ACM conference on Conference on information and knowledge management.

Soscia, I. (2007), 'Gratitude, delight, or guilt: The role of consumers' emotions in predicting postconsumption behaviors', *Psychology & Marketing*, **12**, 871–94.

Spaulding, T.J. (2010), 'How can virtual communities create value for business?' *Electronic Commerce Research and Applications*, **9** (1), 38–49.

Steffes, E.M. and L.E. Burgee (2009), 'Social ties and online word of mouth', *Internet Research*, **19** (1), 42–59.

Stephen, A.T. and D.R. Lehmann (2009), 'Why do people transmit word-of-mouth? The effects of recipient and relationship characteristics on transmission behaviors', working paper, Columbia University.

Sundaram, D.S., K. Mitra and C. Webster (1998), 'Word-of-mouth communications: A motivational analysis', *Advances in Consumer Research*, **25**, 527–31.

Sweeney, J.C., G.N. Soutar and T. Mazzarol (2005), 'The difference between positive and negative word-of-mouth emotion as a differentiator', Proceedings of the ANZMAC 2005 Conference: Broadening the Boundaries, 331–7.

Triandis, Harry C. (1995), 'Motivation and achievement in collectivist and individualistic cultures', in Martin L. Maehr and Paul R. Pintrich (eds), *Advances in Motivation and Achievement: Culture, Motivation and Achievement*, 9, London: JAI Press, pp. 1–30.

Trusov, M., R.E. Bucklin and K. Pauwels (2009), 'Effects of word-of-mouth versus traditional marketing: Findings from an internet social networking site', *Journal of Marketing*, **73**, 90–102.

Van Hoye, G. and F. Lievens (2005), 'Recruitment-related information sources and organizational attractiveness: Can something be done about negative publicity?' *International Journal of Selection and Assessment*, **13**, 179–87.

Van Hoye, G. and F. Lievens (2007), 'Social influences on organizational attractiveness: Investigating if and when word of mouth matters', *Journal of Applied Social Psychology*, **37** (9), 2024–47.

Villanueva, J., S. Yoo and D.M. Hanssens, (2008), 'The impact of marketing-induced versus word-of-mouth customer acquisition on customer equity growth', *Journal of Marketing Research*, **45** (1), 48–59.

Westbrook, R.A. (1987), 'Product/consumption-based affective responses and postpurchase processes', *Journal of Marketing Research*, **24**, 258–70.

Wetzer, I.M., M. Zeelenberg and R. Pieters (2007), 'Never eat in that restaurant, I did! Exploring why people engage in negative word-of-mouth communication', *Psychology & Marketing*, **24** (8), 661–80.

White, C. and Y. Yi-Ting (2005), 'Satisfaction emotions and consumer behavioral intentions', *Journal of Services Marketing*, **19** (6), 411–20.

Winkielman, Piotr and Jennifer L. Trujillo (2008), 'Emotional influence on decision and behavior: Stimuli, states, and subjectivity', in Kathleen D. Vohs, Roy F. Baumeister and George Loewenstein (eds), *Do Emotions Help or Hurt Decision Making?* New York: Russell Sage, pp. 69–91.

Word of Mouth Marketing Association Summit (2010).

Xia, L. and N.N. Bechwati (2008), 'Word of mouse: the role of cognitive personalization in online consumer reviews', *Journal of Interactive Advertising*, 9 (1), available at http://jiad.org/article105 (accessed 24 February 2011).

Zaltman, G. (1997), 'Rethinking market research: Putting people back in', *Journal of Marketing Research*, **34**, 424–37.

Zeelenberg, M. and R. Pieters (2004), 'Beyond valence in customer dissatisfaction: A review and new findings on behavioral responses to regret and disappointment in failed services', *Journal of Business Research*, **57** (4), 445–55.

PART VI

CROSS-CULTURAL COMPARISON

16 A comparative study of corporate reputation between China and developed Western countries
Yang Zhang and Manfred Schwaiger

INTRODUCTION

Corporate reputation has been enthralling academics as well as top executives for quite a while. Corporate reputation is one of the most valuable intangible assets, as it is extremely hard to imitate by competitors. As an effective management tool, corporate reputation helps firms to achieve sustainable competitive advantages. A fine reputation not only increases customer confidence in products, services and advertising claims but also lowers cognitive dissonance, as it acts as a surrogate for information (Eberl 2006; Fombrun and van Riel 1998; Goldberg and Hartwick 1990; Lafferty and Goldsmith 1999). Via better customer retention (Caminiti 1992; Preece et al. 1995; Rogerson 1983) firms can achieve price premiums and higher purchase rates (Klein and Leffler 1981; Milgrom and Roberts 1986).

Companies showing a strong reputation have better access to capital markets, which decreases capital costs (Beatty and Ritter 1986; Wiedmann and Buxel 2005). Moreover, private investors' stock buying and holding behavior is affected by a company's reputation, whereby effects are intensified in stock market crises (Schütz and Schwaiger 2007).

Several studies (e.g., Caminiti 1992; Dowling 1986; Eidson and Master 2000; Nakra 2000; Preece et al. 1995; Turban and Cable 2003) report higher recruiting and employee retention rates among companies with stronger reputations, thus helping a company to win the war for talents.

Finally, a good reputation pays off in terms of general advantages in conducting negotiations with suppliers (Schwalbach 2000) and other stakeholder groups (Brown 1997; Cordeiro and Sambharya 1997; Deephouse 1997; Fombrun 1996; McMillan and Joshi 1997; Roberts and Dowling 1997; Srivastava et al. 1997).

Given the impact of reputation on performance relevant outcomes, it is obvious that a company's market value *ceteris paribus* should grow with a better reputation. Eberl and Schwaiger (2005) as well as Roberts and Dowling (2002) show that corporate reputation supports the persistence of above-average profits and has a positive impact on net profit.

Summarizing, in accordance with both the scientific community and the majority of practitioners, we may consider corporate reputation as an intangible asset that is scarce, valuable, sustainable and difficult for a competitor to imitate.

Owing to the topic's significance and attractiveness, a rapid increase has been witnessed in relevant studies in recent years. Conducting a survey of present literature, we can easily find ample research on corporate reputation ranging from its formation to measurement to management practice. However, there is still a lack of valid comparative studies among different countries with different cultures, which prevents CEOs in multinational enterprises from managing corporate reputation in a more efficient – that is, culture-specific – way.

Although some obstructive factors are well known, the trend of economic globalization is irreversible. As relations have become unprecedentedly close between countries and economic entities, most companies start to conduct business overseas and, consequently, are forced to adapt strategic management decisions to local conditions. It can be imagined that reputation management is a challenge for multinational companies, involving coping with different economic cultures, multinational environments and numerous regulations. Successful management practices or effective marketing strategies in one place can hardly be replicated at another place within a different cultural setup. Thus, there is need for comparative studies on corporate reputation in different countries or cultures, guiding the CEOs to do the right things at the right place.

This chapter aims to make a contribution to this topic by studying the differences of corporate reputation among three Western countries (Germany, the USA and the UK) and China. Schwaiger (2004) presented a new measurement and explanation model for corporate reputation, which has been empirically proven to work in European countries and the USA. The strong explanation power of the corporate reputation model triggered us to test this model in different cultures. Therefore, we did another empirical study in China in March 2008 (Zhang and Schwaiger 2009) demonstrating that the two-dimensional structure of reputation is valid in collectivistic cultures as well.

Now that we have data available from four countries on drivers and outcomes of reputation, we will provide a thorough comparative study allowing meaningful management implications to be drawn.

Our study consists of two main parts. In the first part, the measurement model is briefly introduced and the main descriptive results for China are provided. In the second part, the method we used to conduct multi-group comparisons is introduced, followed by a detailed analysis procedure and thorough discussion of the results obtained.

MEASUREMENT MODEL AND EMPIRICAL EVIDENCE FROM CHINA

Although research on corporate reputation sprang up all over the world, academic as well as practical contributions have failed to reach agreements on both its definition and measurement methods. Various types of definition differ from one another with regard to the different groups' point of view, focusing on numerous aspects of reputation. Since a comprehensive review of present definitions and measurements has been made in previous papers (e.g., Schwaiger 2004), we will describe only the measurement model we used in this paper and the definition on which the model is based.

Measurement Model

Based on attitude theory, Schwaiger (2004) put forward a two-dimensional measurement model, which comprises both an affective and a cognitive component. While 6 endogenous indicators are needed to measure reputation (see Table 16.1 – Measurement Construct), 18 explanatory items were chosen to identify the drivers of corporate reputation, obtained from open-ended expert interviews. The model development was in line with Rossiter's C-OAR-SE procedure (Rossiter 2002).

By means of principal component analysis, four factors – quality, performance, corporate social responsibility (CSR) and attractiveness – were identified to have impact and indices were successfully constructed for them (see Table 16.1 – Driver Construct).

The estimation results of the statistical analysis have shown a good fitness of this model among Western cultures (Schwaiger 2004), which made us check the model's two-factor structure in rather collectivistic cultures as well. Therefore, in March 2008, we did an empirical study in China and detected that the two measurement dimensions, named competence and likeability, can be considered as prevalent in China, too (Zhang and Schwaiger 2009). This finding allows us to use the full model, consisting of the measurement and the explanation part, to check whether reputation is built in similar ways in both China and Western cultures.

Data

In order to test the applicability of our model in a Chinese context, the data collection was done in China using the questionnaire depicted in Table 16.1. Owing to language and cultural differences, the questionnaire was translated into Chinese using the translation/back-translation method (Douglas and Craig 1983; Malholtra et al. 1996). With the same

Table 16.1   Constructs and measurement items

Constructs		Items
Measurement Construct	Likeability	. . . is a company I would regret more if it didn't exist any more than I would with other companies. . . . is a company I can identify with better than with other companies. I regard . . . as a likeable company.
	Competence	I believe that . . . performs at a premium level. As far as I know . . . is recognized world-wide. . . . is a top competitor in its market.
Driver Construct	Quality	The products/services offered by . . . are of high quality. I think that . . .'s products/services offer good value for money. The services . . . offers are good. . . . seems to be a reliable partner for customers. Customer concerns are held in high regards at . . . In my opinion . . . tends to be an innovator, rather than an imitator.
	Performance	. . . is an economically stable company. I assess the business risk for . . . as modest compared to its competitors. I think that . . . has growth potential. In my opinion . . . has a clear vision about the future of the company. I think . . . is a very well managed company.
	Corporate Social Responsibility (CSR)	I have the feeling that . . . is not only concerned about profit. I have the impression that . . . is forthright in giving information to the public. . . . behaves in a socially conscious way. . . . is concerned about the preservation of the environment. I have the impression that . . . has a fair attitude towards competitors.
	Attractiveness	I like the physical appearance of . . . (company buildings, branch offices). In my opinion . . . is successful in attracting high-quality employees.

questionnaire, face-to-face interviews were done at ten places in China including both urban and rural areas.

Before starting the evaluation of companies, respondents were asked the following two questions: "Are you involved in household decisions?" and "Do you know the companies BMW, Siemens, Haier Group and China Mobile at least by name?" in order to make sure that our respondents were qualified to evaluate these companies. The questionnaire was administered to 100 respondents at each place, which led to a total of 1000 respondents' evaluations of the four companies mentioned above.

After ruling out 21 questionnaires that failed to provide complete information, we applied an optimization algorithm in order to draw a subsample almost perfectly matching sociodemographic means from the sample and the corresponding means in the Chinese population. This resulted in a quasi-representative database of the Chinese population containing 302 respondents' questionnaires. By restructuring the original data, we finally got a sample of 1208 company evaluations.

A descriptive analysis of all items with arithmetic means and standard deviation was done first and correlations for all pairs of variables were examined in SPSS, including both 18 explanatory items and 6 endogenous items. For brevity's sake, these results are not presented here in detail. Principal Component Analysis was done to check if the model structure identified in previous studies would still be valid for China. Table 16.2 indicates that the concept of splitting up corporate reputation into an affective and a cognitive component still holds in a Chinese context. Table 16.3 shows that again we can extract the four factors – quality, performance, responsibility and attractiveness – from the 18 explanatory items, explaining 65 percent of the original information.

Since our focus is placed on the explanation of an endogenous construct, variance-based methods like Partial Least Square (PLS) analysis are preferred. Another reason to adopt this approach is that PLS can deal with both formative and reflective constructs, which was helpful in our case. Contrary to covariance-based structural equation models, which attempt to reproduce the observed covariance matrix using a maximum-likelihood function, PLS understands the latent variable as weighted sums of their respective indicators (Chin and Newsted 1999; Fornell and Cha 1994) and attempts to predict values for the latent variables (component scores) using multiple regressions (Chin 1998a; Chin and Newsted 1999; Fornell and Bookstein 1982; Fornell and Cha 1994).

PLS-model estimation was performed using Smart**PLS**. Since the item scales are comparable, a standardization of the data is not necessary. Therefore, the model estimation was performed using the original data (Chatelin et al. 2002). To test whether the path coefficients differ

*Table 16.2   Principle component analysis result for the endogenous
variables*

Items	Components	
	Likeability	Competence
. . . is a company I would regret more if it didn't exist any more than I would with other companies.	0.870	0.213
. . . is a company I can identify with better than with other companies.	0.834	0.300
I regard. . . as a likeable company.	0.770	0.347
. . . is a top competitor in its market.	0.225	0.839
I believe that . . . performs at a premium level.	0.246	0.825
As far as I know . . . is recognized world-wide.	0.422	0.655
Variance explained	38.9%	34.8%

Extraction Method: Principal Component Analysis.
Rotation Method: Varimax with Kaiser Normalization.

significantly from zero, t-values were calculated using a bootstrapping procedure (Chartelin et al. 2002; Chin 1998a). Contrary to the default of 100 cases and 100 samples in Smart**PLS**, we calculated 1208 cases and 500 samples to get more stable results. This is in line with Gould and Pitblado (2005) who suggested choosing a sample size of the bootstrapping procedure that is equal to the number of cases in the original data set, because the standard error estimates are dependent on the number of observations in each replication.

The final coefficients estimated by Smart**PLS** are shown in three parts (see Tables 16.4, 16.5 and 16.6). All coefficients are presented with t-values given in parentheses.

The results of the reflective part of the model in Table 16.4 show that all factor loadings exhibit values of above 0.8, indicating a strong goodness of fit. Composite reliabilities of each component are uniformly higher than 0.8, while the Cronbach's α are located around 0.8, thus meeting the stipulated thresholds (Nunnally and Bernstein 1994). In order to examine the discriminant validity, the Fornell and Larcker (1981) criterion is applied, where the square root of each endogenous construct's Average Variance Extracted (AVE) is compared to its bivariate correlations with all opposing endogenous constructs (cp. Hulland 1999; Grégoire and Fisher 2006). The result shows that the square root of AVE is greater than the variance shared between likeability and competence. Thus, we

Table 16.3 Principal component analysis for the explanatory items

Items	Factors			
	Qual-ity	Perfor-mance	CSR	Attractive-ness
. . . seems to be a reliable partner for customers.	**0.749**			
Customer concerns are held in high regards at. . . .	**0.737**			
The products / services offered by . . . are of high quality.	**0.698**			
The services . . . offers are good.	**0.693**			
I think that . . .'s products / services offer good value for money.	**0.689**			
In my opinion . . . tends to be an innovator, rather than an imitator.	**0.648**	0.300		
. . . is an economically stable company.		**0.770**		
I think that . . . has growth potential.		**0.724**		
I assess the business risk for . . . as modest compared to its competitors.		**0.670**		
. . . has a clear vision about the future of the company.	0.303	**0.660**		
. . . is a very well managed company.	0.415	**0.582**		
I have the feeling that . . . is not only concerned about the profit.			**0.842**	
. . . behaves in a socially conscious way.	0.340	0.308	**0.629**	
I have the impression that . . . is forthright in giving information to the public.	0.421		**0.548**	0.330
I have the impression that . . . has a fair attitude towards competitors.	0.490		**0.465**	
. . . is concerned about the preservation of the environment.			**0.465**	0.537
I like the physical appearance of . . . (company buildings, branch offices).	0.431			**0.699**
In my opinion . . . is successful in attracting high-quality employees.	0.505	0.350		**0.482**
Variance explained	23.8%	17.1%	12.9%	11.2%

Extraction Method: Principal Component Analysis.
Rotation Method: Varimax with Kaiser Normalization. Loadings< 0.3
suppressed.

Table 16.4   Coefficients and quality criteria of the measurement constructs

	Components	
	Likeability	Competence
[1] . . . is a company I miss more than other companies when it doesn't exist anymore.	0.876 (90.304)	
[2]. . . is a company that I identify more with than with other companies.	0.892 (90.716)	
[3] I regard . . . as a likeable company.	0.860 (82.317)	
[4] I believe that . . . performs at a premium level.		0.838 (67.033)
[5] As far as I know . . . is recognized world-wide.		0.811 (48.740)
[6] . . . is a top competitor in its market.		0.845 (66.028)
R squared	0.5934	0.5317
Composite Reliability	0.908	0.870
Communality	0.768	0.691
Average Variance Extracted (AVE)	0.7677	0.6916
Cronbach's α	0.8487	0.7768
Correlations of latent variables	0.5885	0.5885

can assume discriminant validity for both the likeability and competence component.

The t-values generated by bootstrapping can be interpreted as measures for the stability of the path coefficients. In those exogenous constructs, we can see that there are formative indicators, which turned out to be insignificant according to the cutoff level of 1.96.

The PLS coefficients in Table 16.6 clearly show that responsibility, quality, attractiveness and performance exert a positive influence on both likeability and competence. The t-values generated by bootstrapping indicate that attractiveness does not have a significant influence on likeability, whereas all other coefficients turn out to be significantly different from zero in a statistical sense. So far, we could demonstrate the applicability of our model in the Chinese context. Thus, we will focus on the comparative study among countries in the following part.

COMPARATIVE ANALYSES BETWEEN CHINA AND WESTERN COUNTRIES

The aim of the comparative study is to find out the differences in structural relations of corporate reputation in different countries with different

Table 16.5   Estimated PLS parameters for the driver constructs

Items	Performance	CSR	Attractiveness	Quality
[7] . . . is a very well managed company.	0.615 (15.519)			
[8] I think that . . . has growth potential.	0.061 (1.790)			
[9] . . . is an economically stable company.	0.156 (4.083)			
[10] I assess the business risk for . . . as modest compared to its competitors.	0.167 (4.590)			
[11] . . . has a clear vision about the future of the company.	0.210 (5.428)			
[12] I have the impression that . . . has a fair attitude towards competitors.		0.351 (8.269)		
[13] . . . behaves in a socially conscious way.		0.392 (8.324)		
[14] I have the feeling that . . . is not only concerned about the profit.		0.014 (0.277)		
[15] I have the impression that . . . is forthright in giving information to the public.		0.262 (5.891)		
[16] . . . is concerned about the preservation of the environment.		0.225 (4.795)		
[17] I like the physical appearance of . . . (company buildings, branch offices).			0.433 (8.825)	
[18] In my opinion . . . is successful in attracting high-quality employees.			0.530 (11.966)	
[19] The products / services offered by . . . are of high quality.				0.251 (4.403)
[20] I think that . . .'s products / services offer good value for money.				0.209 (4.003)
[21] The services . . . offers are good.				0.182 (2.928)

Table 16.5   (continued)

Items	Performance	CSR	Attractiveness	Quality
[22] . . . seems to be a reliable partner for customers.				0.287 (4.046)
[23] Customer concerns are held in high regards at. . ..				0.099 (1.840)
[24] In my opinion . . . tends to be an innovator, rather than an imitator.				0.280 (6.188)

Table 16.6   *Estimated PLS parameters of the inner model*

	Coefficients	
	Likeability	Competence
Performance	0.404 (10.74)	0.42 (11.079)
Responsibility	0.246 (5.897)	0.209 (4.906)
Attractiveness	0.052 (1.222)	0.077 (2.005)
Quality	0.152 (3.573)	0.091 (2.095)

cultures in order to calibrate corporate reputation management to specific conditions in terms of locality, culture and, consequently, improve the process of generating competitive advantages for corporations.

Methodology

In 2005, Eberl made a comprehensive review of present available methods in order to analyze moderating effects in path models and to provide an application of PLS in multi-group analysis (Eberl 2005). To examine the difference in structural relations across cultural clusters, we adopted multi-group comparison analysis, which is especially useful for discrete moderator variables. Since we have ruled out CBSEM in the previous part, the multi-group comparisons will be applied in PLS (Chin 2000; Keil et al. 2000). As Chin suggested, the path coefficients between two countries could be compared at a time by treating estimates of the re-sampling in a parametric sense via t-tests (Chin 2000). In this paper, the path coefficients were compared pairwise to examine the difference of the four drivers' impact on the two dimensions of corporate reputation in four countries.

According to Chin, some assumptions have to be made before using this approach. First, the acceptable goodness of fit is required to make sure the following comparisons are meaningful. Then the two samples being compared should be "not too non-normal". Furthermore, there is an assumption that the underlying weights in the formation of constructs for each cluster are approximately equivalent, which means there should be measurement invariance (Chin 2000). The approach uses the re-sampling estimates for the standard errors of the structural paths in two samples under consideration gained from the bootstrapping procedure usually used for model evaluation (Chin 1998b). Differences between path estimators are tested for significance with the following test. If the standard errors of the path estimators are assumed equal, the test statistic is computed as follows (Chin 2000):

$$t = \frac{path_{sample1} - path_{sample2}}{\sqrt{\frac{(m-1)^2}{(m+n-1)} * s.e._{sample1}^2 + \frac{(n-1)}{(m+n-2)} * s.e._{sample2}^2} * \sqrt{\frac{1}{m} + \frac{1}{n}}} \sim t_{m+n-2}$$

Where:

$path_{sample1}/path_{sample2}$ denote the original sample estimate for the path coefficient in the respective sample

m number of cases in sample 1

n number of cases in sample 2

$s.e. sample$ 1/2   standard error of path coefficient in subsample1/2 (gained from the re-sampling procedure implemented in PLS).

If the variances of the two samples are assumed to be different, a Smith-Satterthwait test can be applied (Chin 2000):

$$t = \frac{path_{sample1} - path_{sample2}}{\sqrt{s.e._{sample1}^2 + s.e._{sample2}^2}}$$

Unless the sample size is large, the degrees of freedom (df) can be calculated as follows:

$$df = \text{round to nearest integer} \left[\frac{(s.e._{sample1}^2 + s.e._{sample2}^2)^2}{\left(\frac{s.e._{sample1}^2}{m+1} + \frac{s.e._{sample2}^2}{n+1} \right)} - 2 \right]$$

Since we could not collect original data in four countries owing to the limited financial resources, we decided to use data from previous market research activities. Because the data structure in the Chinese sample has already been described, we will provide a brief overview of the data collection in Germany, the UK and the USA.

A series of three computer-assisted telephone interview studies was conducted in Germany, Great Britain and the United States by GfK market research, Nuremberg. The survey was administered to 300 respondents in each of the three countries for a total of 900 respondents, evaluating three (USA) or four (Germany, UK) companies: Allianz (financial services and insurance), BMW Group (car manufacturer), E.ON (power supplier) and Lufthansa (airline). Potential respondents were screened by asking the questions "Are you involved in decisions concerning your household?" and "Do you have at least a bachelor's degree?" both of which had to be answered with "yes". Moreover, the selected respondents had to know the companies at least by name. Thus, we got a sample of 1200 company evaluations in each country. A descriptive analysis of all the items is given in Table 16.7 showing the arithmetic means and standard deviation (SD) in each country.

As discussed before, the method of a multi-group comparison with t-test suggested by Chin (2000) is subject to several assumptions: (1) each sub-model considered has to achieve an acceptable goodness of fit; (2) the data should not be too non-normal; and (3) measurement invariance should be assumed.

To check the model's goodness of fit in each country, R^2 is the only criterion we can rely on, since there is no other overall parametric criterion in Smart**PLS**. All R^2 values of two endogenous constructs in four countries are presented in Table 16.8, where we can see that most of the values are acceptable within the usual boundaries of interpretation. A relatively low value for the likeability construct in Germany does not make our following comparisons unreasonable.

Another assumption of this approach is the requirement of normality. Since we used a symmetric seven-point rating scale to collect data, visual inspections seem appropriate when dealing with quasi-metric scales (Brosius 2002). We visually inspected the normality of 24 variables in each country by means of QQ-plots. None of the 24 variables used in the analysis was found to have a strong deviation from the distributional assumption.

Levene's F-test with the null hypothesis of variance homogeneity was used to check the equality of standard errors gained from bootstrapping procedures implemented in PLS. As long as the variance homogeneity can be assumed according to the F-test, t-tests may be applied to test the significance of the differences between two groups. Otherwise, the Smith-Satterthwait test would be appropriate.

The final prerequisite for multi-group comparisons is measurement invariance, assuming that the loadings and weights of the constructs'

Table 16.7 Descriptive statistics by country

Items	Germany		UK		USA		China	
	Mean	**SD**	**Mean**	**SD**	**Mean**	**SD**	**Mean**	**SD**
[Q1] . . .is a company I miss more than other companies when it does not exist anymore.	5.73	1.029	5.16	1.5	4.81	1.721	5.64	1.467
[Q2] . . .is a company that I identify more with than with other companies.	5.97	1.016	5.59	1.527	5.15	1.693	5.59	1.405
[Q3] I regard . . . as a likeable company.	6.33	0.933	6.01	1.552	5.8	1.669	5.73	1.410
[Q4] I believe that . . . performs at a premium level.	5.33	1.273	5.04	1.637	4.91	1.748	5.75	1.399
[Q5] As far as I know . . . is recognized world-wide.	5.2	1.604	3.86	1.971	3.66	2.035	5.75	1.453
[Q6] . . . is a top competitor in its market.	4.58	1.695	4.64	1.811	4.04	1.966	5.85	1.346
[Q7] . . . is a very well managed company.	5.59	1.136	5.11	1.565	4.62	1.846	5.69	1.360
[Q8] I think that . . . has growth potential.	5.23	1.335	5.18	1.554	4.96	1.75	5.55	1.503
[Q9] . . . is an economically stable company.	5.72	1.163	5.11	1.561	4.9	1.72	5.70	1.346
[Q10] I assess the business risk for . . . as modest compared to its competitors.	5.36	1.165	4.9	1.501	4.37	1.718	5.69	1.228
[Q11] . . . has a clear vision about the future of the company.	5.84	1.053	5.12	1.548	4.64	1.779	5.80	1.265
[Q12] I have the impression that . . . has a fair attitude towards competitors.	5.16	1.191	4.88	1.505	4.65	1.726	5.63	1.349
[Q13] . . . behaves in a socially conscious way.	4.98	1.248	4.73	1.513	4.27	1.788	5.51	1.367

Table 16.7 (continued)

Items	Germany		UK		USA		China	
	Mean	SD	Mean	SD	Mean	SD	Mean	SD
[Q14] I have the feeling that . . . is not only concerned about the profit.	3.85	1.673	4.33	1.824	3.92	1.837	5.29	1.469
[Q15] I have the impression that . . . is forthright in giving information to the public.	4.85	1.397	4.85	1.492	4.35	1.788	5.33	1.442
[Q16] . . . is concerned about the preservation of the environment.	4.81	1.423	4.58	1.64	4.1	1.832	5.43	1.414
[Q17] I like the physical appearance of . . . (company buildings, branch offices).	5.32	1.291	5.02	1.659	4.18	1.856	5.66	1.301
[Q18] In my opinion . . . is successful in attracting high-quality employees.	6.02	1.028	4.94	1.579	4.5	1.787	5.65	1.322
[Q19] The products / services offered by . . . are of high quality.	5.8	1.113	5.22	1.612	5.01	1.716	5.84	1.280
[Q20] I think that . . .'s products / services offer good value for money.	4.82	1.386	4.84	1.567	4.68	1.732	5.60	1.321
[Q21] The services . . . offers are good.	5.59	1.186	5.06	1.532	4.7	1.792	5.60	1.361
[Q22] . . . seems to be a reliable partner for customers.	5.65	1.118	5.17	1.501	4.76	1.743	5.66	1.324
[Q23] Customer concerns are held in high regards at	5.41	1.193	5.02	1.531	4.57	1.82	5.56	1.338
[Q24] In my opinion . . . tends to be an innovator, rather than an imitator.	5.64	1.164	5.19	1.554	4.93	1.762	5.62	1.341

Table 16.8   Goodness of fit of the models by country

	Germany	USA	UK	China
	R^2	R^2	R^2	R^2
Competence	0.568	0.501	0.596	0.535
Likeability	0.411	0.495	0.504	0.592

measurement models do not differ significantly within the model. This is to ensure that the paths compared in the test are comparable in terms of the causal relationships that they represent. In our study, the measurement invariance of the constructs is also compared by means of pairwise t-tests. The PLS estimation results for the four countries are presented in Table 16.9 and the t-values testing the measurement invariance of the four exogenous constructs are given in Table 16.10. At the 5 percent error level, the majority of these t-tests do not reject the null hypothesis, stating that there is no significant difference between two tested countries. Most of the t-values are below significance thresholds.

However, there are still some exceptions. For example, look at the comparison between the UK and China: the path coefficient of one performance indicator shows significant differences between these two countries; the corresponding t-value is 0.00044. Having a grasp on the original path coefficients in each country, we can find the absolute difference for two coefficients being equal to 0.2118 and to be considered relatively large. But we can not draw a final conclusion so far; in order to test if there is measurement invariance of the construct of "performance" a further statistical test is required. Hence, we applied a Fisher's combined probability test to test the construct's measurement invariance by considering all its indicators as a whole (Shipley 2002). From Table 16.9, we can see that items 7 and 8 show their particularities because the t-test of each indicator is significant in each pairwise comparison. By comparing the original path coefficients of this path, we can see a relatively high coefficient in the Chinese data, clearly reflecting the significance of the given t-test indicator. Although there are several significant t-values, in total they amount only to a small fraction of all tests and mainly focus on the same one or two indicators. Therefore, we would argue that there is measurement invariance of this model from country to country, which allows us to make further comparative analyses.

Results and Discussions

Estimated results of the structural relations within the four countries are presented in Table 16.11. Judging from the values of both path

Table 16.9   PLS estimation results by country (outer loadings/weights)

	Germany		UK		USA		China	
	Outer load-ings/ weights	t-value	Outer load-ings/ weights	t-value	Outer load-ings/ weights	t-value	Outer load-ings/ weights	t-value
Q01 <- Competence	0.853	80.032	0.859	94.196	0.860	89.193	0.837	67.994
Q02 <- Competence	0.884	93.249	0.915	150.390	0.869	88.299	0.846	61.108
Q03 <- Competence	0.816	45.819	0.865	77.162	0.802	47.394	0.812	50.699
Q04 <- Likeability	0.877	123.508	0.861	109.274	0.830	86.406	0.860	84.631
Q05 <- Likeability	0.819	52.622	0.792	52.078	0.777	49.614	0.876	93.153
Q06 <- Likeability	0.867	94.151	0.865	81.333	0.835	72.306	0.892	99.416
Q07 -> Performance	0.339	7.163	0.404	8.080	0.170	2.952	0.615	15.569
Q08 -> Performance	0.241	5.971	0.198	4.116	0.385	8.571	0.061	1.785
Q09 -> Performance	0.235	5.618	0.034	0.685	0.330	6.668	0.156	3.779
Q10 -> Performance	0.334	9.318	0.204	4.333	0.236	5.199	0.167	5.232
Q11 -> Performance	0.178	3.719	0.311	6.345	0.217	4.637	0.210	5.216
Q12 -> Responsibility	0.327	5.721	0.406	10.094	0.212	4.122	0.351	8.023
Q13 -> Responsibility	0.317	5.987	0.357	7.509	0.316	5.117	0.392	7.786
Q14 -> Responsibility	0.082	1.360	0.081	2.502	0.294	5.097	0.014	0.293
Q15 -> Responsibility	0.397	8.110	0.275	6.980	0.356	5.949	0.262	6.146
Q16 -> Responsibility	0.172	3.177	0.239	6.749	0.180	3.017	0.225	4.796
Q17 -> Attractiveness	0.611	14.858	0.591	16.625	0.485	6.831	0.535	11.265
Q18 -> Attractiveness	0.605	14.429	0.518	14.515	0.691	11.101	0.587	12.769
Q19 -> Quality	0.332	8.173	0.196	4.257	0.234	5.894	0.251	4.480
Q20 -> Quality	0.169	5.543	0.225	5.144	0.285	6.625	0.209	4.434
Q21 -> Quality	0.121	2.773	0.035	0.765	0.155	3.687	0.183	3.352
Q22 -> Quality	0.256	5.913	0.241	4.976	0.297	7.330	0.217	4.346
Q23 -> Quality	0.181	5.270	0.092	1.930	0.141	3.449	0.099	2.057
Q24 -> Quality	0.263	5.871	0.397	10.283	0.214	5.433	0.280	5.898

coefficients and t-values, we can clearly see that the four drivers of cor-porate reputation – attractiveness, performance, CSR and quality – show different levels of importance in driving the two dimensions of corporate reputation in each country. Thus, different strategies are recommended to foster reputation in different countries. Differences between China and the other three countries are presented in Table 16.12 with the results of corresponding statistical t-test and p-values, clearly pointing to the specific significant differences between each tuple of two countries.

As can be seen from Table 16.11, the impact of performance on com-petence was found to be significant in all four countries. It was also identified to be stronger than its impact on likeability, which points out

Table 16.10 Differences in path coefficients between two countries

	GER–CHN				USA–CHN				UK–CHN			
	Differ-ences	Pooled s.e	T	P	Differ-ences	Pooled s.e	T	P	Differ-ences	Pooled s.e	T	P
Q07 -> Performance	-0.273	0.056	-4.856	0.000	-0.442	0.066	-6.715	0.000	-0.208	0.063	-3.330	0.000
Q08 -> Performance	0.177	0.054	3.283	0.001	0.321	0.056	5.747	0.000	0.135	0.061	2.206	0.014
Q09 -> Performance	0.080	0.061	1.308	0.095	0.175	0.064	2.723	0.003	-0.121	0.063	-1.923	0.027
Q10 -> Performance	0.167	0.050	3.345	0.000	0.069	0.054	1.282	0.100	0.037	0.054	0.690	0.245
Q11 -> Performance	-0.032	0.062	-0.524	0.300	0.007	0.062	0.109	0.457	0.101	0.063	1.621	0.053
Q12 -> Responsibility	-0.023	0.071	-0.327	0.372	-0.137	0.065	-2.099	0.018	0.057	0.056	1.008	0.157
Q13 -> Responsibility	-0.078	0.074	-1.048	0.147	-0.078	0.074	-1.053	0.146	-0.037	0.063	-0.590	0.278
Q14 -> Responsibility	0.065	0.076	0.852	0.197	0.278	0.069	4.035	0.000	-0.098	0.057	-1.716	0.043
Q15 -> Responsibility	0.140	0.070	1.992	0.023	0.099	0.071	1.391	0.082	0.018	0.056	0.330	0.371
Q16 -> Responsibility	-0.054	0.068	-0.793	0.214	-0.046	0.070	-0.657	0.256	0.013	0.055	0.241	0.405
Q17 -> Attractiveness	0.078	0.060	1.293	0.098	-0.048	0.075	-0.639	0.261	0.058	0.061	0.956	0.170
Q18 -> Attractiveness	0.018	0.060	0.302	0.381	0.105	0.075	1.401	0.081	-0.069	0.060	-1.135	0.128
Q19 -> Quality	0.081	0.068	1.188	0.118	-0.017	0.070	-0.241	0.405	-0.055	0.068	-0.810	0.209
Q20 -> Quality	-0.037	0.057	-0.654	0.257	0.079	0.067	1.164	0.122	0.019	0.065	0.290	0.386
Q21 -> Quality	-0.059	0.067	-0.870	0.192	-0.024	0.068	-0.355	0.361	-0.144	0.074	-1.958	0.025
Q22 -> Quality	0.040	0.067	0.590	0.278	0.080	0.072	1.117	0.132	0.025	0.075	0.331	0.370
Q23 -> Quality	0.078	0.062	1.263	0.103	0.038	0.066	0.577	0.282	-0.011	0.070	-0.152	0.440
Q24 -> Quality	-0.017	0.066	-0.254	0.400	-0.066	0.062	-1.072	0.142	0.117	0.065	1.805	0.036

Table 16.11   PLS estimation results by country (inner model)

	Germany		UK		USA		China	
	Path coe.	t-value	Path coe.	t-value	Path coe.	t-value	Path coe.	t-value
Attractiveness -> Competence	0.188	3.085	0.095	1.166	0.031	0.425	0.119	3.684
Attractiveness -> Likeability	0.065	0.824	0.090	1.009	−0.064	1.013	0.020	0.358
Performance-> Competence	0.310	4.335	0.345	3.864	0.306	2.945	0.424	10.674
Performance -> Likeability	0.082	0.874	0.089	0.910	0.066	0.775	0.409	10.870
Quality -> Competence	0.416	5.187	0.384	4.254	0.476	5.048	0.077	1.742
Quality -> Likeability	0.287	3.037	0.133	1.289	0.429	4.878	0.165	3.946
Responsibility -> Competence	−0.111	1.831	0.000	0.001	−0.076	1.099	0.195	4.458
Responsibility -> Likeability	0.274	3.743	0.443	5.011	0.286	4.005	0.258	6.454

Table 16.12   Multi-group comparison results

	Germany–China			UK–China			USA–China		
	Differ- ences	t- value	p- value	Differ- ences	t- value	p- value	Differ- ences	t- value	p- value
Attractiveness -> Competence	0.069	1.578	0.057	−0.024	−0.455	0.325	−0.088	−1.914	0.028
Attractiveness -> Likeability	0.045	0.784	0.217	0.070	1.155	0.124	−0.083	−1.496	0.067
Performance -> Competence	−0.114	−2.102	0.018	−0.079	−1.332	0.091	−0.119	−1.869	0.031
Performance -> Likeability	−0.327	−5.490	0.000	−0.321	−5.474	0.000	−0.343	−5.583	0.000
Quality -> Competence	0.339	5.948	0.000	0.307	4.899	0.000	0.398	6.219	0.000
Quality -> Likeability	0.122	2.041	0.021	−0.032	−0.516	0.303	0.264	4.532	0.000
Responsibility -> Competence	−0.306	−5.814	0.000	−0.195	−3.287	0.001	−0.271	−4.757	0.000
Responsibility -> Likeability	0.016	0.285	0.388	0.184	3.123	0.001	0.028	0.507	0.306

performance as a strong driver of competence regardless of places and cultures. However, the results of the Chinese data exhibit particularities in two ways. First and foremost, China is the only country where performance was found to be also a strong driver of the affective component of corporate reputation (likeability). In Western countries, performance does not show a significant impact on likeability. This does not necessarily imply a lack of importance but rather shows that performance is not a suitable driver of likeability, as opposed to quality and CSR.

Second, even though the impact of performance on competence was found to be significant in all four countries, according to Table 16.11, significant differences were proved to exist between China and the three other countries. For example, performance exerts a much stronger influence on competence in China than it does in Western countries. Hence, we can conclude that performance plays the most important role in driving corporate reputation in China both affectively and cognitively, pointing to the direction and focus of reputation management work in China.

Similar to the factor of performance, CSR shows a significant impact on reputation, but, as opposed to performance, CSR affects likeability in all four countries more heavily than competence. Apparently, CSR is a driver of likeability rather than a driver of competence and significance levels vary across different countries. Special attention should be paid to Germany and China: contrary to the other three countries, CSR shows a negative impact on competence in Germany, which was proved to be significant and matches well with earlier analyses' results (Schwaiger 2004). Therefore, we may rule out a methodical influence owing to the application of MIMIC models (LISREL) instead of Smart**PLS**. Being a good corporate citizen, taking social responsibility and taking care of environmental issues makes the company likeable, but it does not necessarily make it a target for investors in Western countries. In China, CSR pays off in terms of higher competence as well because it turns out to be the second most important driving force of the cognitive component of corporate reputation.

Contrary to the factor CSR, attractiveness is obviously of minor importance for reputation, except for Germany. If at all, it exhibits a larger impact on competence than on likeability. From Table 16.11, we can see that the path from attractiveness to competence is significant only in Germany and China, while from a statistical point of view, it does not have a significant influence on likeability at all.

When examining the function of quality, an obvious and significant difference could be found between China and Western countries. In European countries and the USA, quality always plays the most important role in driving competence. In China, though, quality is the least important driver of competence with a rather small path coefficient of 0.0774. This is quite counterintuitive because usually a company providing high quality or service is supposed to be more competent in its market. One possible explanation could be the immaturity of the Chinese market and the low purchasing power of consumers compared to developed countries.

Having a closer look at the items forming the driver construct, the following aspects seem to be noteworthy. Both quality and attractiveness items seem to have a pretty much identical impact in all surveyed countries. Performance assessment in China is more based on the notion of management quality, whereas in the USA the growth potential seems to be more important. As far as the CSR construct is concerned, fairness seems to be quite unimportant, whereas social behavior is more important in China. "Not only thinking about the profit" has significant impact only in the USA.

Through these comparisons we can see that the pattern of reputation management in China substantially differs from patterns examined in other countries. In China, corporate reputation management is well advised to focus on companies' performance and CSR because investments in these two drivers should result in significantly higher levels of both cognitive and affective reputation dimension. Besides that, quality should not be left aside because of its low path coefficient, as the perception of quality could be rather homogenous with respect to the companies evaluated in the Chinese sample. The lack of variance in the corresponding items might be another reason for the poor predictive power of the quality construct.

LIMITATIONS AND FURTHER RESEARCH

Though having applied sophisticated methods with care, the present study might be suffering from shortcomings in data quality. First of all, we used a convenience sample in China and decided to match the sample structure with the population structure by means of a weighting scheme. Even if we believe that this sample is adequate for the purpose of the research goal, from a statistical point of view the results cannot be generalized to the Chinese population in total. Nevertheless, even professional market research companies are having a hard time drawing "true" random samples in China.

A second shortcoming addresses the time of data collection. As data were sampled in the first half of the 2000s in Western countries, the Chinese data were obtained no earlier than 2008. And, finally, only one company (BMW) was evaluated in all samples.

Therefore, further research should focus on drawing a multinational sample in several individualistic as well as collectivistic cultures, examining the same set of companies. Until a better database is available, we hope to provide useful insights for those interested in managing the reputation of a multinational enterprise.

REFERENCES

Beatty, R. and J. Ritter (1986), 'Investment Banking, Reputation, and the Underpricing of Initial Public Offerings', *Journal of Financial Economics*, **15** (1/2), 213–32.

Brosius, F. (2002), *SPSS 11*, Bonn: mitp.

Brown, B. (1997), 'Stock Market Valuation of Reputation for Corporate Social Performance', *Corporate Reputation Review*, **1**, 76–80.

Caminiti, S. (1992), 'The Payoff from a Good Reputation', *Fortune*, **125** (3), 49–53.

Chatelin, Y.M., V.E. Vinzi and M. Tenenhaus (2002), 'State-of-art on PLS Modeling Through the Available Software', available at http://www.hec.fr/var/fre/storage/original/application/d713bfa13eff075210485ada1a2f7c48.pdf (accessed 23 February 2011).

Chin, W.W. (1998a), 'Issues and Opinion on Structural Equation Modeling', *MIS Quarterly*, **22** (1), 7–16.

Chin, W.W. (1998b), 'The Partial Least Squares Approach for Structural Equation Modeling', in G.A. Marcoulides (ed.), *Modern Methods For Business Research*, Mahwah, NJ: Lawrence Erlbaum Associates, pp. 295–336.

Chin, W.W. (2000), 'Frequently Asked Questions – Partial Least Squares & PLS-Graph', availble at http://disc-nt.cba.uh.edu/chin/plsfaq.htm (accessed 6 October 2005).

Chin, W.W. and P.R. Newsted (1999), 'Structural Equation Modeling: Analysis with Small Samples Using Partial Least Squares', in R.H. Hoyle (ed.), *Statistical Strategies for Small Sample Research*, Thousand Oaks, CA: Sage, pp. 307–41.

Cordeiro, J.J. and R. Sambharya (1997), 'Do Corporate Reputations Influence Security Analyst Earnings Forecasts', *Corporate Reputation Review*, **1**, 94–8.

Deephouse, D. (1997), 'The Effects of Financial and Media Reputations on Performance', *Corporate Reputation Review*, **1**, 68–72.

Douglas, S.P. and C.S. Craig (1983), *International Marketing Research*, Hoboken: John Wiley & Sons.

Dowling, G.R. (1986), 'Managing Your Corporate Images', *Industrial Marketing Management*, **15** (2), 109–15.

Eberl, M. (2005), 'An Application of PLS in Multi-Group Analysis: The Need for Differentiated Corporate-Level Marketing', in T. Aluja, J. Casanovas, V. Esposito, A. Morrineau and M. Tenenhaus (eds), *PLS and Related Methods – Proceedings of the PLS '05 International Symposium*, Barcelona, pp. 203–10.

Eberl, M. (2006), *Reputation und Kundenverhalten*, München: Deutscher Universitäts-Verlag.

Eberl, M. and M. Schwaiger (2005), 'Corporate Reputation: Disentangling the Effects on Financial Performance', *European Journal of Marketing*, **39** (7/8), 838–54.

Eidson, C. and M. Master (2000), 'Top Ten . . . Most Admired . . . Most Respected: Who Makes the Call?', *Across the Board*, **37** (3), 16–22.

Fombrun, C.J. (1996), *Reputation: Realizing Value from the Corporate Image*, Boston: Havard Business School Press.

Fombrun, C.J. and C. van Riel (1998), 'The Reputational Landscape', *Corporate Reputation Review*, **1**, 5–14.

Fornell, C. and F.L. Bookstein (1982), 'Two Structural Equation Models: LISREL and PLS Applied to Consumer Exit-voice Theory', *Journal of Marketing Research*, **19** (4), 440–52.

Fornell, C. and J. Cha (1994), 'Partial Least Squares', in R.P. Bagozzi (ed.), *Advanced Methods of Marketing Research*, Cambridge, MA: Blackwell Business, pp. 52–78.

Fornell, C. and D.F. Larcker (1981), 'Evaluating Structural Equation Models with

Unobservable Variables and Measurement Error', *Journal of Marketing Research*, **18** (1), 39–50.

Goldberg, M.E. and J. Hartwick (1990), 'The Effects of Advertiser Reputation and Extremity of Advertising Claim on Advertising Effectiveness', *Journal of Consumer Research*, **17** (2), 172–9.

Gould, W. and J. Pitblado (2005), 'Guidelines for bootstrap samples', available at http://www.stata.com/support/faqs/stat/reps.html (accessed 23 February 2011).

Grégoire, Y. and R. Fisher (2006), 'The effects of relationship quality on customer retaliation', *Marketing Letters*, **17** (1), 31–46.

Hulland, J. (1999), 'Use of Partial Least Squares (PLS). Strategic Management Research: A Review of Four Recent Studies', *Strategic Management Journal*, **20** (2), 195–204.

Keil, M., B.C.Y. Tan, K.-K. Wei, T. Saarinen, V. Tuunainen and A. Wasenarr (2000), 'A Cross-Cultural Study on Escalation of Commitment Behavior in Software Projects', *MIS Quarterly*, **24** (2), 299–325.

Klein, B. and K.B. Leffler (1981), 'The Role of Market Forces in Assuring Contractual Performance', *Journal of Political Economy*, **89** (4), 615–41.

Lafferty, B.A. and R.E. Goldsmith (1999), 'Corporate Credibility's Role in Consumers' Attitudes and Purchase Intentions When a High versus a Low Credibility Endorser is Used in the Ad', *Journal of Business Research*, **44** (2), 109–16.

Malholtra, N.K., J. Agarwal and M. Peterson (1996), 'Methodological Issues in Cross-cultural Marketing Research: A State-of-the-art Review', *International Marketing Review*, **13** (5), 7–43.

McMillan, G.S. and M.P. Joshi (1997), 'Sustainable Competitive Advantage and Firm Performance: The Role of Intangible Resources', *Corporate Reputation Review*, **1**, 81–6.

Milgrom, P. and J. Roberts (1986), 'Price and Advertising Signals of Product Quality', *Journal of Political Economy*, **94** (4), 796–821.

Nakra, P. (2000), 'Corporate Reputation Management: "CRM" with a Strategic Twist', *Public Relations Quarterly*, **45** (2), 35–42.

Nunnally, J. and I. Bernstein (1994), *Psychometric Theory*, New York: McGraw-Hill.

Preece, S.B., C. Fleisher and J. Toccacelli (1995), 'Building a Reputation Along the Value Chain at Levi Strauss', *Long Range Planning*, **28** (6), 88–98.

Roberts, P.W. and G.R. Dowling (1997), 'The Value of a Firm's Corporate Reputation: How Reputation Helps Attain and Sustain Superior Profitability?' *Corporate Reputation Review*, **1**, 72–6.

Roberts, P.W. and G.R. Dowling (2002), 'Corporate reputation and sustained superior financial performance', *Strategic Management Journal*, **23** (12), 1077–94.

Rogerson, W.P. (1983), 'Reputation and Product Quality', *The Bell Journal of Economics*, **14** (2), 508–16.

Rossiter, J.R. (2002), 'The C-OAR-SE procedure for scale development in marketing', *International Journal of Research in Marketing*, **19** (4), 305–35.

Schütz T. and M. Schwaiger (2007), 'Der Einfluss der Unternehmensreputation auf Entscheidungen privater Anleger', *Kredit und Kapital*, **40** (2), 189–223.

Schwaiger, M. (2004), 'Components and Parameters of Corporate Reputation – An Empirical Study', *Schmalenbach Business Review*, **56** (1), 46–71.

Schwalbach, J. (2000), 'Image, Reputation und Unternehmenswert', in B. Baerns and J. Raupp (eds), *Information und Kommunikation in Europa – Forschung und Praxis. Transnational Communication in Europe – Research and Practice*, Berlin: Vistas, pp. 287–97.

Shipley, B. (2002), *Cause and Correlation in Biology: A User's Guide to Path Analysis, Structural Equations and Causal Inference*, Cambridge: Cambridge University Press.

Srivastava, R.K., T.H. McInish, R.A. Wood and A.J. Capraro (1997), 'The Value of Corporate Reputations: Evidence from the Equity Markets', *Corporate Reputation Review*, **1**, 62–7.

Turban, D.B. and D.M. Cable (2003), 'Firm reputation and applicant pool characteristics', *Journal of Organizational Behavior*, **24** (6), 733–51.

Wiedmann, K.P. and H. Buxel (2005), 'Corporate Reputation Management in Germany: Results of an Empirical Study', *Corporate Reputation Review*, **8** (2), 145–63.

Zhang, Y. and M. Schwaiger (2009), 'An Empirical Research of Corporate Reputation in China', in L.S. Huang and D. Jin (eds), *Proceedings of the American Academy of Advertising 2009 Asian-Pacific Conference*, Beijing, pp. 84–101.

17 Probability markers in Croatian and Belgian advertisements and tolerance for ambiguity

Ivana Bušljeta Banks and Patrick De Pelsmacker

INTRODUCTION

Probability Markers in Advertisements for Different Types of Service

For the last 37 years beer-lovers and their friends have known exactly which beer is *probably* the best in the world. Ever since Carlsberg's "Probably . . ." campaign was launched in 1973, its slogan has been seen in more than 100 versions of commercials and advertisements worldwide, and has become the longest running beer campaign, but also one of the longest running advertising campaigns ever, regardless of product/service category, according to Super Brands (1998) (Figure 17.1, www.creative-criminals.com/images/carlsbergpearl1.jpg).

Carlsberg's advertisements are also probably the best known example of the use of probability markers in advertising. *Probability markers* are specific words or phrases used to signal to which degree is it likely that a given claim or argument is true. Those markers that indicate probable, rather than absolute, truth of a claim are known as *hedges*, whereas the markers that indicate complete commitment to the truthfulness of the claim are known as *pledges*. Hedges, which can be adverbs ("possibly", "probably"), verbs ("can", "may", "help"), particles ("about", "sort of"), or other expressions ("9 out of 10", "85 percent of", etc.), weaken the impact of a claim by allowing for exceptions or avoiding total commitment (Erickson et al., 1978; Wright and Hosman, 1983). Language that contains hedges is considered powerless. Generally, powerless language is marked by frequent use of both non-verbal and verbal hesitations, tag questions, intensifiers, and hedges, and results in negative speaker attributions and evaluations, specifically in regards to speaker credibility, intelligence, and status (Erickson et al., 1978; Bradac and Mulac, 1984).

Pledges, on the other hand, examples of which also include some adverbs ("definitely", "undoubtedly"), verbs ("will", "guarantee"), and other expressions ("have been proven to", "you can be sure"), are absolute in nature and signal total confidence in the truthfulness of the claim

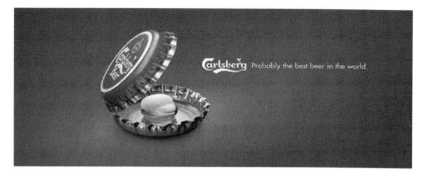

Figure 17.1   Carlsberg commercial from the "Probably. . ." campaign

(Berney-Reddish and Areni, 2005). They are considered markers of powerful language, which is also recognized through the lack of above-listed markers of powerless language. The use of powerful language results in positive speaker attributions in terms of credibility, attractiveness, intelligence, competence, and status (Erickson et al., 1978; Bradac and Mulac, 1984).

Probability markers are frequently used in advertising (Geis, 1982; Areni, 2002). Some well-known examples include the Carlsberg campaign mentioned above, a similar slogan used by a Belgian brand of beer, Delirium Tremens ("Elected as best beer in the world"), numerous drug advertisements (such as a Nutra-Life ad stating: "Nutra-Life Cold and Flu fighter may reduce the severity and duration of colds"), as well as cosmetics ads (such as Oil of Olay stating: "Proven to help you look revitalized"). Despite this, probability markers have been effectively ignored by the great majority of marketing researchers. While some have contributed theoretical insights into the usage and effects of hedges in advertising (Leech, 1966; Geis, 1982; Vestergaard and Schroder, 1985; Cook 1992), empirical studies on the topic of probability markers have been few and far between, concentrated mainly in a study by Harris et al. (1993), and the works of Charles Areni and his associates (e.g. Berney-Reddish and Areni, 2005, 2006).

The few empirical studies that have been conducted on the usage of probability markers in advertising have focused only on the advertising of products, without taking into account the recognized differences between products and services (Zeithaml et al., 1985; Murray and Schlacter, 1990) and the specificities of service advertising (George and Berry, 1981; Kenny and Fisk, 1990; Stafford, 1996; Stafford et al., 2002). Additionally, although it has been well-established that language power acts primarily as a peripheral cue (Areni, 2003; Areni and Sparks, 2005; Sparks and

Areni, 2008), none of the previous studies of the effectiveness of probability marker usage in advertising have included manipulations of the
involvement factor. Another important factor that has not been taken
into account in the existing studies on probability markers in advertising
is that of product or service type, such as the categorization of hedonic vs.
utilitarian, which has been found to play a major role in the effectiveness
of advertising in a number of studies (Stafford and Day, 1995; Wakefield
and Barnes, 1996; Albers-Miller and Stafford, 1999; Stafford et al., 2002;
Bridges and Florsheim, 2008; Geuens at al., 2011).

The present study attempts to partly fill these gaps by, on one hand,
contributing to the theory and body of research on the effects of the usage
of probability markers in advertising, and, on the other, focusing on this
usage in the advertising of different types of services and in situations of
high vs. low involvement.

The Role of Culture

One more potentially important, yet – to this date in the study of the effectiveness of probability markers in advertising – completely overlooked
factor is that of culture and culturally-induced individual differences
among individuals. One of the prevailing debates in the field of international advertising, for the past 50 years, is the one of the standardization
vs. adaptation. While the standardization approach argues that standardized advertising strategy builds and maintains a uniform global image of
the company, the proponents of the adaptation approach point out the
fact that the cultural differences (on the linguistic, religious, historical, and
socio-economic levels) influence the way consumers in different countries/
cultures interpret and react to advertisements, making it difficult, if not
impossible, for a company to merely transfer the exact same advertising
campaign from one country's market to another (Zou and Volz, 2010).
Several recent international advertising studies have demonstrated clear
evidence supporting the effectiveness of the adaptation strategy (e.g.,
Okazaki et al., 2006; Wong and Merrilees, 2007).

The effectiveness, or even basic acceptance, of the use of probability
markers in advertising, owing to their characteristics (such as expression
of powerful vs. powerless language and degrees of certainty vs. ambiguity), could be dependent on culture, as defined by the dimensions introduced by Hofstede (1980) or, more recently, the GLOBE project (House
et al., 2004), particularly the dimension of uncertainty avoidance. The
most often used framework in international management and marketing
research for decades has been the Hofstede model, which differentiates
among cultures on the basis of five dimensions: collectivism/individualism,

femininity/masculinity, power distance, long-/short-term orientation, and uncertainty avoidance (De Mooij and Hofstede, 2010). A more recent development in cross-cultural studies is the Global Leadership and Organizational Behavior Effectiveness Research Program. The GLOBE study developed a set of nine core dimensions of culture, some of which were inspired by Hofstede's dimensions: institutional collectivism, in-group collectivism, power distance, performance orientation, gender egalitarianism, future orientation, humane orientation, assertiveness, and uncertainty avoidance (House et al., 2010).

One of the dimensions both frameworks share is uncertainty avoidance, defined by Hofstede as "the extent to which people feel threatened by uncertainty and ambiguity and try to avoid these situations" (De Mooij and Hofstede, 2010). The GLOBE study offers a very similar definition of the construct – "the extent to which members of a society seek certainty in their environment by relying on established societal norms, rituals, and bureaucratic practices" (House et al., 2010). Since probability markers are linguistic expressions of various degrees of certainty vs. probability or ambiguity (i.e., uncertainty), the question arises whether the cultural dimension of uncertainty avoidance or tolerance for ambiguity could cause higher or lower acceptance of pledges and hedges in different cultures, and, therefore, influence the effectiveness of advertisements containing hedges or pledges on consumers from different country markets. By bringing the factor "tolerance for ambiguity" into the analysis (a frequently studied individual difference variable in consumer behavior), the present study also contributes to the body of research on international advertising, by including the component of culture-related differences.

The choice of countries to be studied is one of the biggest issues facing researchers in cross-cultural research design (Tung and Verbeke, 2010). One of the ways to make useful conclusions on the basis of comparing a rather small number of countries might be to carefully choose those countries that might be representative of specific clusters. One of the major contributions of the GLOBE study, in this respect, is that it provides strong empirical evidence of the existence of ten societal clusters – Anglo, Latin Europe, Nordic Europe, Germanic Europe, Eastern Europe, Latin America, Sub-Saharan Africa, Middle East, Southern Asia, and Confucian Asia (House et al., 2010).

This study is based on a comparison of two countries, Croatia and Belgium. On one hand, they can be viewed as representative of two different societal clusters, Belgium (or more precisely, Flanders) representing the Germanic Europe and Croatia representing Eastern Europe. On the other hand, the two countries score on the two opposite extreme ends of the uncertainty avoidance scale. According to the results of the original

Hofstede study, Belgium, with an Uncertainty Avoidance Index (UAI) of 94 out of a 100 (74 being the European average), scores on the extreme high end of the scale (Hofstede, 2009). Since Croatia as a country did not exist at the time the Hofstede study was carried out, and is now culturally a vastly different society than Yugoslavia was back in 1971, when Hofstede collected the data for his study in a number of former Yugoslav republics, his original UAI score for Yugoslavia is not applicable for Croatia. A recent study (Matic, 2006) conducted mirroring Hofstede's methodology for measuring uncertainty avoidance, found that Croatia scores on the extreme low end of the scale, with a UAI of 13.28. For the two reasons outlined in this paragraph, Croatia and Belgium (Flanders) make an appropriate choice for a cross-cultural study of the effectiveness of probability markers in advertising.

THEORY BACKGROUND AND HYPOTHESES DEVELOPMENT

Studies so far have mostly not been able to prove the existence of any significant positive effects of the usage of probability markers in advertising on claim acceptance. Harris et al. (1993) have tested the effect of hedges (but not pledges) in advertising claims, and have found that they lead, on one hand, to increased claim acceptance, but also, on the other hand, to lower purchase intentions. Berney-Reddish and Areni conducted several studies on probability markers, in which they included pledges, as well as hedges. The results of one show no statistically significant effect of the interaction of the use of probability markers and type of argument in which they are used (inductive or deductive). They do, however, find some significance in the main effects, with pledges resulting in more negative thoughts about the claim in the case of an inductive argument, and hedges in lower levels of claim acceptance in the case of a deductive argument (Berney-Reddish and Areni, 2005). Much along the same lines, in a later study, Berney-Reddish and Areni (2006) found that both pledges and hedges reduce claim acceptance, and that this assertion held true more for men then for women, but their results were only marginally, if at all, significant.

The Role of Involvement

In spite of the abovementioned studies, the question of the impact of probability markers on advertising effectiveness remains. After all, the longevity of the Carlsberg campaign and the frequent occurrences of probability markers in advertisements and commercials (Geis, 1982; Areni, 2002), leads us to believe that, somehow, probability markers must be *working*. One of the possible explanations for the failure of the previous studies to find significant impact of the use of probability markers in advertising can be found in Petty et al.'s (1983) Elaboration Likelihood Model, which differentiates between the central and the peripheral routes to persuasion, and posits that the central route is used in situations of high involvement, while the peripheral route is more conducive to low-involvement situations. In low-involvement situations, therefore, peripheral cues, such as emotions and affect, have a direct impact on consumers' judgments (Geuens et al., 2011).

Language power, just like emotions, has been empirically proven to act as a peripheral cue (Areni, 2003; Areni and Sparks, 2005; Sparks and Areni, 2008). Studies have shown that the impact of language power is more prominent in audio or video stimuli, where the ability for central processing is reduced and recipients must rely largely on peripheral cues, than in written stimuli (Sparks et al., 1998; Blankenship and Holtgraves, 2005). It is, therefore, likely that involvement would act as a moderator to the effectiveness of the usage of probability markers in advertising, namely that the impact of probability markers on advertising effectiveness would be greater in low-involvement situations than in those where involvement is high. This assumption finds support in a previous study (Bušljeta Banks et al., 2011).

Tolerance for Ambiguity

The individual difference of "tolerance for ambiguity" has been at the center of numerous studies in psychology, organizational behavior, management, and cultural studies for over 60 years. It has been used to refer to the way in which individuals or groups of people react to ambiguous, unfamiliar, or incongruent stimuli (Furnham and Ribchester, 1995). On the one end of the tolerance for ambiguity scale, individuals who are averse to thinking in terms of probabilities and show clear preference for concrete, black-and-white situations are considered intolerant to ambiguity (Norton, 1975). Since pledges are the type of probability marker that signifies complete certainty in the claim made, leaving no room for ambiguity, we predict that individuals who are intolerant to ambiguity should prefer claims with pledges over those with hedges and even without probability markers.

Those persons, however, who exhibit characteristics that put them at the other end of the scale, that is, who are tolerant to ambiguity, do not merely tolerate ambiguous, complex stimuli, but also find them interesting and desirable; they, in a way, enjoy the challenge such stimuli provide (Furnham and Ribchester, 1995). We believe that people who are tolerant to ambiguity would, therefore, prefer claims containing hedges over those with pledges or no probability markers, as hedges leave room for ambiguous interpretations of the claim.

In the previous section, we argued that probability markers are expected to have an impact only in low-involvement situations. We therefore expect that the moderating impact of the effect of probability markers on advertising effectiveness will be prevalent only in case of low-involvement services. Hence we posit:

> **H1a:** Compared to high-involvement services, for low-involvement services and individuals higher in tolerance for ambiguity, the use of hedges in advertisements will result in higher brand attitude and purchase intentions than the use of pledges or no probability markers.
> **H1b**: Compared to high-involvement services, for low-involvement services and individuals higher in tolerance for ambiguity, the use of pledges in advertisements will result in lower brand attitude and purchase intentions than the use of hedges or no probability markers.

Product/Service Category: Hedonic vs. Utilitarian

In discussing the drawbacks of their research, Berney-Reddish and Areni (2005) recognize the possibility that the impact of probability markers on advertising effectiveness may depend on the specific product or, as in this study, service being advertised, a notion that they do not specifically test. The difference between the absolute quality of a pledge, as opposed to a more conditional, probabilistic quality of a hedge, we believe, may correspond to the categorization of services into hedonic and utilitarian, frequently used in service advertising research (Stafford and Day, 1995; Wakefield and Barnes, 1996; Albers-Miller and Stafford, 1999; Stafford et al., 2002; Geuens et al., 2011).

Hedonic services, often also referred to as experiential, are characterized by high levels of people orientation, employee contact and customization (Stafford and Day, 1995). The quality of and satisfaction with a hedonic service rely on the sensations derived from the consumption of the service (Voss et al., 2003), and are highly person-specific. As such, they are hard to assess objectively, being dependent on personal, subjective tastes and experiences. Using pledges, markers of absolute certainty, and thus implying universal applicability of the advertising claims, in advertisements of hedonic services might attract the consumers' attention to the inappropriateness of such claims and cause them to question the absolute and categorical conclusion of the truth of the claim. On the other hand, placing a claim with a hedge into a hedonic service advertisement might reduce the tendency of the consumers to counter-argue the claim (Vestergaard and Schroder, 1985) and increase the perceived honesty/ credibility of the advertiser (Areni, 2002).

Utilitarian services are, however, much more pragmatic and practical than hedonic ones. They are characterized by low levels of employee–customer contact, moderate customization and higher product-orientation than hedonic services (Stafford and Day, 1995). All this makes them much less individualized and person-specific, enabling easier objective assessment of service quality and customer satisfaction, which depends mainly on the functionality of their consumption (Voss et al., 2003), based on an almost universal set of characteristics that ensure optimal functionality. Using pledges in advertisements of utilitarian services, therefore, signals the advertisers' full confidence in the truthfulness of the claim (Areni, 2002), thus enhancing its persuasive power. A hedge in an advertising copy for a utilitarian service, on the other hand, might create the impression that the advertiser is not willing to stand behind the claim 100 percent, weakening the claim itself, and undermining the advertiser's authority, credibility, and status (Berney-Reddish and Areni, 2006). This would result in decreased efficiency of the advertisement. We see no reason why the effect of service type on probability marker effects would be different depending on the level of tolerance for ambiguity of the individual. Hence we expect:

> **H2a**: The use of hedges in advertisements of low-involvement hedonic services results in higher brand attitudes and purchase intentions than the use of pledges or no probability markers.
>
> **H2b**: The use of pledges in advertisements of low-involvement utilitarian services results in higher brand attitudes and purchase intentions than the use of hedges or no probability markers.

METHOD

Development of Stimuli

Two (service type: hedonic/utilitarian) × 2 (involvement: high/low) × 3 (probability marker: hedge/pledge/no marker) between-subjects experiments were set up to test the aforementioned hypotheses: one in Croatia, and one in Belgium (Flanders). The two experiments used the same stimuli, albeit that the verbal part was translated into the local languages.

To eliminate possible confounds in the main experiment, two pretests were conducted on two convenience samples of business students (N_1 = 48, N_2 = 27). The first pretest was designed to flesh out the appropriate services to include in the study. First, a list of services that college students regularly purchase and use was compiled by asking several students we came into contact with to state the services they had used recently. The final list included the following 16 services: airline, bank, bar, cable television provider, cinema, copy/print shop, credit card, fitness studio/gym, foreign language school, graduate school, hair salon, Internet service provider, mobile phone service provider, nightclub, sandwich shop, and travel agency. A short questionnaire was developed to test the level of involvement with the service, using Zaichkowsky's (1994) revised PII scale, and the degree to which each of the services was either hedonistic or utilitarian in nature, using an abridged version of the Voss et al.'s (2003) HED/UT scale (the same scales as in the main study were used, see hereafter). The results of the pretests showed that graduate school was the best fit for a utilitarian high-involvement service, copy/printing shop for a utilitarian low-involvement service, bar for a hedonic high-involvement service, and sandwich shop for a hedonic low-involvement service. These four were, therefore, chosen for this study.

Once the appropriate services were chosen, three versions of advertisements were created for each of the four conditions. The advertisements were kept simple and as uniform across services as possible, to avoid any confounding bias. Each advertisement included one visual element (a photograph of a physical element of the service, e.g., a sandwich for the sandwich shop or a copy machine for a copy/print shop), the location of the service provider, and one verbal claim. Within a service, everything was kept constant, except for the verbal claim. Three very similar verbal claims were created (in English). First, the one without any probability markers was created, and then the other two versions were made by inserting either a hedge or a pledge into the original claim, thus keeping the differences between claims to the minimum. The hedges used in the advertisements were "might" and "probably", and the pledges used were "definitely" and "guarantee". These specific hedges and pledges were chosen as simple, archetypal examples of probability markers, which clearly qualify the claim made in the advertisement and sound realistic when inserted into the no-treatment copy (Berney-Reddish and Areni, 2006). Every effort was made to maintain as much uniformity as possible between and within service type, involvement, and probability marker manipulations. Within each service type/involvement manipulation, the sole difference between advertisements was the actual probability marker used, which was added to the control condition claim containing no probability markers, to

Kom...   Relax...

Je zult zeker plezier hebben...

BBBar

Reyndersstraat 37

Antwerpen

*Figure 17.2   Hedonic high-involvement service ad with a pledge (bar) –
Dutch version*

ensure the highest degree of certainty that the results are attributed to the actual effect of the probability markers, without the interference of the other elements of the advertisement.

In Figures 17.2 to 17.5, examples of the stimuli are shown. The 12 completed advertisements were pretested for ad liking to avoid the possibility that the photos, colors, or layout used in making the advertisements would influence the results of the main survey. The pretests showed that there were no significant differences in ad liking between the advertisements. In Table 17.1 the English translation of the verbal parts of each of the advertisement versions are presented.

Procedure

The questionnaire was first created in English, and then translated and back-translated by two teams of marketing experts and translators into Croatian and Dutch. Once the translations were produced, they were uploaded into the online survey software SurveyMaster. The links created by the software were then e-mailed to potential participants.

Each version of the main questionnaire started with a welcome screen, on which the participants were greeted, quickly briefed about the study, and instructed on how to proceed with filling out the questionnaire. The participants were allowed to proceed through the questionnaire at their own pace, and not instructed to spend any more or less time on any one question, in order to simulate as much as possible natural advertisement processing, and not create a forced high-involvement situation. The

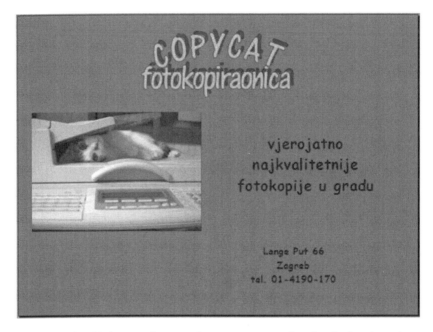

*Figure 17.3   Utilitarian low-involvement service ad with a hedge (copy/
print shop) – Croatian version*

*Figure 17.4   Utilitarian high-involvement service ad with no probability
markers (graduate school) – Dutch version*

Figure 17.5   Hedonic low-involvement service ad with a hedge (sandwich shop) – Croatian version

Table 17.1   Probability marker manipulations by product

Product	Marker	Advertising copy (original English version)
Bar	no pm	Come . . . Relax . . . Have fun
	hedge	Come . . . Relax . . . You might have fun
	pledge	Come . . . Relax . . . You will definitely have fun
Copy/print shop	no pm	Best quality copies in town
	hedge	Probably the best quality copies in town
	pledge	Definitely the best quality copies in town
Graduate school	no pm	Reach your careers goals with an MBA from International Business School
	hedge	An MBA from International Business School might help you reach your career goals
	pledge	An MBA from International Business School guarantees you will reach your career goals
Sandwich shop	no pm	Come to Tace Tee's – your taste buds will thank you!
	hedge	Come to Tace Tee's – your taste buds might thank you!
	pledge	Come to Tace Tee's – we guarantee your taste buds will thank you!

welcome screen was followed first by some warm-up experience-with-the-service questions, and then by a set of questions designed to measure the respondents' tolerance for ambiguity.

After the tolerance for ambiguity questions, the participants were randomly exposed to one of the 12 advertisements representing the 12 conditions of the design. After being exposed to the advertisements, participants were asked whether the ad they had just seen reminded them of any particular brands. Those who answered positively were later eliminated from the analysis, since their answers could have been influenced by their attitude towards those brands. Subsequently, they were asked to score their purchase intention and attitude towards the brand. Finally they had to indicate their age, gender and major. The last screen of the questionnaire included a short message debriefing the participants and thanking them for their participation in the survey.

Measures

The *independent variables* "high/low involvement", "hedonic/utilitarian service" and "hedge/pledge/no probability marker" were determined by the 2 × 2 × 3 design. Zaichkowsky's (1994) revised PII scale, a ten-item (important–unimportant, interesting–boring, relevant–irrelevant, exciting–unexciting, means a lot to me–means nothing, appealing–unappealing, fascinating–mundane, valuable–worthless, involving–uninvolving, needed–not needed), seven-point semantic differential scale was used to measure involvement. The degree to which each of the services was either hedonistic or utilitarian in nature was measured using an abridged version of Voss et al.'s (2003) HED/UT scale also a ten-item (effective–ineffective, helpful–unhelpful, functional–not functional, necessary–unnecessary, practical–impractical, fun–not fun, exciting–dull, delightful–not delightful, thrilling–not thrilling, enjoyable–unenjoyable), seven-point semantic differential scale. The scale used to measure tolerance for ambiguity was developed by Herman et al. (2010), as a 12-item, five-point Likert scale. The items of the scale were as follows: 1) I avoid settings where people don't share my values; 2) I can enjoy being with people whose values are very different from mine; 3) I would like to live in a foreign country; 4) I like to surround myself with things that are familiar to me; 5) The sooner we all acquire similar values and ideals the better; 6) I can be comfortable with nearly all kinds of people; 7) If given a choice, I will usually visit a foreign country rather than vacation at home; 8) A good teacher is one who makes you wonder about your way of looking at things: 9) A good job is one where what is to be done and how it is to be done are always clear; 10) A person who leads an even, regular life in which few surprises or unexpected happenings arise really has a lot to be grateful for; 11) What we are used to is always preferable to what is unfamiliar; 12) I like parties where I know most of the people more than ones where all or most of the people are complete strangers.

With respect to the *dependent variables*, a seven-point Likert scale, based on the one used by Dodds et al. (1991), was used to measure

Table 17.2   Cronbach Alpha's of scale translations

Scale	Cronbach alpha – Croatian	Cronbach alpha – Dutch
Involvement	0.852	0.873
Service type (hedonic, utilitarian)	0.712	0.778
Ad liking	0.733	0.825
Tolerance for ambiguity	0.851	0.929
Purchase intention	0.945	0.939
Attitude towards the brand	0.917	0.915

purchase intention for the service advertised. The scale adopted three out of the seven items included in the original scale (1) If I were going to buy a —— (service), —— (brand) would be one of my choices; 2) The probability that I would buy —— (brand) is very high; 3) I would gladly purchase —— (brand).) A fourth item was added to the scale (I would recommend —— (brand) to my friends). Following the purchase intention measure, a three-item (1) I think the —— (brand) is a very good —— (service); 2) I think the —— (brand) is a very useful —— (service); 3) My opinion of —— (brand) is very favorable), five-point Likert scale (developed by Sengupta and Johar, 2002) was used to measure attitude towards the brand of the service advertised. The Cronbach alphas of all scales used in the pretests and the main study are given in Table 17.2. All alphas are above 0.70 for each of the translated scales.

Participants

The participants in the study were college students from a number of public and private universities in Croatia and Belgium (Flanders). The mailing lists for the study were obtained from the university registrar's offices. Out of approximately 1300 Croatian students who received an e-mail inviting them to participate in the study by filling out the online questionnaire, 448 (just under 35 percent) eventually took part. Once the incomplete responses, as well as those with a positive answer to the question whether the advertisement in the questionnaire prompted associations with an existing brand (in total, 74 of them), were eliminated we were left with a sample size of 374 usable responses ($N_{Croatian}$ = 374). In Belgium, the survey was e-mailed to approximately 1800 students. Ultimately, 343 of them responded (19 percent), out of which 331 were usable ($N_{Belgian}$ = 331), making the total sample size 705 (N_{total} = 705)

The analysis of the sample demographics shows that 44.3 percent of the participants were male and 55.7 percent were female. The majority of them (45.9 percent) were between the ages of 22 and 26. The remainder fell into the following age groups: 33.1 percent between the ages of 18 and 21, 6.7 percent between the ages of 27 and 30, 12.4 percent under 18, and 1.9 percent over 30. Thus, it can be concluded that the sample represents a natural distribution of age and gender for college students.

RESULTS

Since one of the independent variables (tolerance for ambiguity) is a metric variable, linear regressions were conducted to test the hypotheses. H1a and H1b were tested by means of two regressions, one for the attitude towards the brand and one for purchase intention. The independent variables level of involvement was included as a dummy (0 = high, 1 = low). The type of probability marker was represented by two dummies: hedge (1 = hedge, 0 = pledge or no probability marker) and pledge (1 = pledge, 0 = hedge or no probability marker). Tolerance for ambiguity was included as the mean-centered score of the scale. Country of origin (Belgium = 0, Croatia = 1) was added as a control variable. All two- and three-way interaction effects were also included in the model. Both the brand attitude model ($F(14,679) = 12.353$, $p < .001$) and the purchase intentions model ($F(14,679) = 12.749$, $p < .001$) are significant.

The three-way interaction between the level of involvement, hedge and tolerance for ambiguity is significantly positive both in the attitude towards the brand (Beta = .310, p = .001) and in the purchase intention model (Beta = .259, $p < .001$). As the results in Table 17.3 show, more tolerance for ambiguity improves the attitude towards the brand and purchase intention for low-involvement services ads in which hedges are used. This supports H1a. The three-way interaction between the level of involvement, pledge and tolerance for ambiguity is significantly negative both in the attitude towards the brand (Beta = −.276, $p < .001$) and in the purchase intention model (Beta = −286, $p < .001$). More tolerance for ambiguity leads to a lower attitude towards the brand and purchase intention for low-involvement services ads in which pledges are used, in support of H1b. In addition, the country variable has a significant main effect on purchase intentions (Beta = .165, p = .009), and in interaction with the usage of a hedge in the ad both on brand attitude (Beta = .221, p = .003) and on purchase intentions (Beta = .142, p = .051).

To test H2a and H2b, four regression models were estimated, two with the attitude towards the brand and two with purchase intention as the dependent variable. In the models testing H2a (Table 17.4), the

Table 17.3 *Results of the brand attitude and purchase intention linear regression analyses testing the effect of probability marker type, involvement and tolerance for ambiguity*

	Brand attitude		Purchase intentions	
	Beta	Sig.	Beta	Sig.
(Constant)		.000		.000
Hedge	−.129	.098	−.084	.279
Pledge	−.062	.385	.010	.885
Country	.034	.589	.165	.009
Tolerance for ambiguity	−.225	.024	−.256	.010
Involvement	−.118	.054	−.013	.833
Interaction: pledge × country	.022	.746	−.015	.820
Interaction: hedge × country	.221	.003	.143	.051
Interaction: hedge × involvement	−.004	1.000	−.002	.982
Interaction: pledge × involvement	.171	.009	.098	.130
Interaction: tolerance for ambiguity × hedge	−.023	.796	.058	.518
Interaction: tolerance for ambiguity × pledge	.113	.159	.162	.044
Interaction: tolerance for ambiguity × involvement	.088	.373	.038	.702
Interaction: hedge × involvement × tolerance for ambiguity	**.310**	**.001**	**.259**	**.004**
Interaction: pledge × involvement × tolerance for ambiguity	**−.276**	**.000**	**−.286**	**.000**

independent variables were level of involvement (0 = high, 1 = low), hedge (1 = hedge, 0 = pledge or no probability marker), type of service: hedonic (utilitarian = 0, hedonic = 1) and the tolerance for ambiguity. In the models testing H2b (Table 17.5), the independent variables were level of involvement (0 = high, 1 = low), pledge (1 = pledge, 0 = hedge or no probability marker), type of service: utilitarian (utilitarian = 1, hedonic = 0) and the mean-centered tolerance for ambiguity. In all four models, all two-way and the three-way interaction effects were included. Again country of origin (Belgium = 0, Croatia = 1) was added as a control variable. In line with previous research and as indicated in the hypotheses, only the low-involvement cases (sandwich shop and copy/print shop) were used in these analyses.

All models are significant (brand attitude hedonic/hedge F (9, 360) = 22.253, $p < .001$, purchase intention hedonic/hedge $F(9, 360)$ = 22.962, $p < .001$; brand attitude utilitarian/pledge $F(9, 360)$ = 18.599,

Table 17.4 Results of the hedonic/hedge brand attitude and purchase intention linear regression analyses

	Brand attitude		Purchase intentions	
	Beta	Sig.	Beta	Sig.
(Constant)		.000		.000
Hedonic	−.241	.000	−.266	.000
Hedge	−.530	.000	−.448	.000
Country	.095	.079	.149	.006
Tolerance for ambiguity	−.344	.000	−.382	.000
Interaction: hedge × country	.247	.002	.150	.062
Interaction: tolerance for ambiguity × pm: hedge	.377	.000	.357	.000
Interaction: tolerance for ambiguity × hedonic	.039	.611	.000	.999
Interaction: hedge × hedonic	**.481**	**.000**	**.475**	**.000**
Interaction: hedge × hedonic × tolerance for ambiguity	.086	.318	.176	.039

Table 17.5 Results of the hedonic/hedge brand attitude and purchase intention linear regression analyses

	Brand attitude		Purchase intentions	
	Beta	Sig.	Beta	Sig.
(Constant)		.000		.000
Utilitarian	−.185	001	−.151	.007
Pledge	−.096	.233	−.182	.024
Country	.259	.000	.233	.000
Tolerance for ambiguity	.348	.000	.340	.000
Interaction: pledge × country	−.118	.117	−.014	.853
Interaction: tolerance for ambiguity × pm: pledge	−.469	.000	−.522	.000
Interaction: tolerance for ambiguity × utilitarian	−.247	.001	−.277	.000
Interaction: pledge × utilitarian	**.473**	**.000**	**.459**	**.000**
Interaction: pledge × utilitarian × tolerance for ambiguity	.086	.281	.134	.096

$p < .001$), purchase intention utilitarian/pledge $F(9, 360) = 17.835$, $p < .001$). The hedonic/hedge brand attitude and purchase intention models, the summary of which is presented in Table 17.4, provide evidence of a significant positive impact of the interaction between the hedonic type of service and the use of a hedge in the advertisement for such a service (brand attitude: Beta = .481, p < .001; purchase intention: Beta = .475, p < .001). H2b is supported. The three-way interaction of hedonic × hedge × tolerance of ambiguity, for which no significance was expected, was nevertheless significant in the hedonic/hedge purchase intentions model (Beta = .176, p = .039). A higher tolerance for ambiguity reinforces the hedge effect for hedonic services. As in the previous analyses, the country variable significantly interacts with the hedge, at least for brand attitude.

The utilitarian/pledge brand attitude and purchase intentions models fully support H2b, by providing evidence of a significant (brand attitude: Beta = .473, p < .001; purchase intention: Beta = .459, p < .001) positive impact of the interaction between a utilitarian service and the use of a pledge in the advertisement for such a service, as can be seen in Table 17.5. As expected, the introduction of tolerance for ambiguity into the interaction provides no significant results, either for brand attitude (p = .281) or for purchase intentions (p = .096). In these two models, the country variable does not significantly interact with the pledge factor.

The same models were run for high-involvement cases only (bar and graduate school). As expected, no significant effects of the interaction between service type and probability marker usage were found (p > .05) for the high-involvement cases, confirming the expectation that probability markers in advertising do not influence attitude and intention formation of high involvement services.

CONCLUSION

Following the postulates of the Elaboration Likelihood Model, and as expected by H1a and H1b, involvement with the product/service and tolerance for ambiguity moderate the effects the use of probability markers in advertising has on consumers' brand attitude and purchase intentions. More precisely, in low-involvement cases, the higher the consumer's tolerance for ambiguity, the more positive their brand attitude and purchase intentions for services advertised using hedges than for those with ads containing either pledges or probability markers. The reverse was also proven to be true – the higher the tolerance for ambiguity, the lower the brand attitude and purchase intention for services advertised using pledges, when compared to those with ads containing either hedges or no probability markers.

Further analysis of the results concentrated on low-involvement services, and the variable of service type was introduced. Through this analysis, the effects of probability markers, or more precisely, of the interaction between service type (hedonic/utilitarian), and type of probability marker used in the advertising copy (hedge, pledge, no probability marker) on customers' brand attitude and purchase intentions became evident. In line with the expectations of H2a and H2b, different results were found depending on the type of service. For hedonic low-involvement services, which are experiential, subjective, and very person-specific in nature, advertising claims that include hedges have been found to be the most effective, resulting in the highest levels of brand attitude and purchase intentions. It seems that such claims may be inciting heightened perceptions of honesty/credibility of the advertiser in the eyes of the consumer, whereas a claim containing an absolutistic pledge would not only be easy to counter-argue and dismiss, but would also have the opposite effect on the perceived credibility of the advertiser. On the contrary, advertisements for utilitarian low-involvement services seem to work better when they include a claim containing a pledge. Pledges in this case, where the service is much less customized and person-specific, and considerably easier to evaluate objectively (making it also easier to compare its universal functional characteristics to other similar services with certainty), signal the strength of the advertisers' convictions in absolute truthfulness of the claims contained in the advertising copy.

The results of the study also show that the individual difference, "tolerance for ambiguity", plays an important role in developing attitudes and intentions following advertisements with different types of probability marker. In discussing the effect of culture on the response to probability markers, we noted that Croatians have been found to be far less uncertainty avoiding and thus more tolerant for ambiguity than Belgians. This is confirmed in the present study, as Croatian respondents were found to have significantly higher tolerance for ambiguity ($M = 3.208$, $SD = .637$) than Belgian respondents ($M = 2.558$, $SD = 1.053$), t $(702) = -10.033$, $p < .001$. The effect of ambiguity tolerance thus reflects part of the cultural differences between the two countries. However, apart from the effect of tolerance for ambiguity, the country effect in itself (used as a control variable in our analysis) appears to play an additional role in the level of effectiveness of the usage of probability markers in advertisements of services, with Croatian respondents seemingly being more receptive of probability markers than their Belgian (Flemish) counterparts.

The abovementioned results have some interesting practical implications for advertising professionals and executives in both countries. Namely, as Croatian consumers, being in general rather tolerant for ambiguity, seem to react positively to ads containing probability markers, advertising campaigns in Croatia would benefit from inclusion of probability markers into advertising copy. This ought especially to be the case for advertisement for hedonic products or services, for which arguments with hedges have been proven to be the best choice. On the other hand, a comparatively low tolerance for ambiguity of Belgian (Flemish) consumers should cause advertisers in Belgium (Flanders) to be cautious of the use of probability markers in advertising campaigns designed for the Belgian (Flemish) market. An exception to this might be the use of pledges, which leave little room for uncertainty and ambiguity, and which, according to the results of this study, would be especially well-suited to arguments used in advertisements of utilitarian products/services.

To test the effect of other dimensions of culture that may account for this effect, additional research is needed. A future study applying the GLOBE framework, for example, to Croatian and Belgian participants, would not only contribute to the better understanding and explanation of the reasons for cross-cultural differences in the effectiveness of probability markers used in advertising, but would also be beneficial as a way of widening the scope of the GLOBE study through inclusion of new countries. In addition, such a future study should also include a larger number of countries, so that additional comparisons could be made, resulting in stronger, more generalizable conclusions and recommendations.

Each of the treatment conditions in this study was represented by one service only. In addition to that, the brand names used in the stimuli did not represent existing brands. Future research should endeavor to test the conclusions of this study using more than one service per type and existing brand names.

It should also be noted that the results of the present study rely on a sample of undergraduate students. Although every effort was taken to ensure that the services used in the study were appropriate for a student sample, and such homogeneous samples have often been used in past studies to maximize statistical power (Berney-Reddish and Areni, 2005), this comes at the cost of external validity. Generalizations of the findings of the study should, therefore, be made with caution, and additional research might be needed to strengthen the validity of the above reported results for other population contexts.

REFERENCES

Albers-Miller, N.D. and M.R. Stafford (1999), 'International Services Advertising: An Examination in Variation in Appeal Use for Experiential and Utilitarian Services', **13** (4/5), 390–406.
Areni, C.S. (2002), 'The Proposition–Probability Model of Argument Structure and Message Acceptance', *Journal of Consumer Research*, **29** (2), 168–87.

Areni, C.S. (2003), 'The Effects of Structural and Grammatical Variables on Persuasion: An Elaboration Likelihood Model Perspective', *Psychology & Marketing*, **20**, 349–75.

Areni, C.S. and J.R. Sparks (2005), 'Language Power and Persuasion', *Psychology & Marketing*, **22** (6), 507–25.

Berney-Reddish, I.A. and C.S. Areni (2006), 'Sex Differences in Responses to Probability Markers in Advertising Claims', *Journal of Advertising*, **35** (2), 7–16.

Berney-Reddish, I.A. and C.S. Areni (2005), 'Effects of Probability Markers on Advertising Claim Acceptance', *Journal of Marketing Communications*, **11** (1), 41–54.

Blankenship, K.I. and T. Holtgraves (2005), 'The Role of Different Markers of Linguistic Powerlessness in Persuasion', **24** (1), 3–24.

Bradac, J.J. and A. Mulac (1984), 'A Molecular View of Powerful and Powerless Speech Styles: Attributional Consequences of Specific Language Features and Communicator Intentions', *Communication Monographs*, **51**, 307–19.

Bridges, E. and R. Florsheim (2008), 'Hedonic and Utilitarian Shopping Goals: The Online Experience', *Journal of Business Research*, **61** (4), 309–14.

Bušljeta Banks, I., P. De Pelsmacker and N. Purnawirawan (2011), 'Probability Markers in Advertising Have a Different Effect on the Purchase Intention for Hedonic and Utilitarian Low and High involvement Services', unpublished manuscript. University of Antwerp, Antwerp, Belgium.

Cook, G. (1992), *The Discourse of Advertising*, London: Routledge.

Creative & Commercial Communications Ltd (1998), 'Carlsberg Beer', *Super Brands*, available at http://www.carlsberg.co.uk/refrigerator/downloads/superbrands.doc (accessed 25 June 2010).

De Mooij, M. and G. Hofstede (2010), 'The Hofstede Model: Applications to Global Branding and Advertising Strategy and Research', *International Journal of Advertising*, **29** (1), 85–110.

Dodds, W.B., K.B. Monroe and D. Grewal (1991), 'The Effects of Price, Brand, and Store Information on Buyers' Product Evaluations', *Journal of Marketing Research*, **28**, 307–19.

Erickson, B., E.A. Lind, B.C. Johnson and W.M. O'Barr (1978), 'Speech Style and Impression Formation in a Court Setting: the Effects of "Powerful" and "Powerless" Speech', *Journal of Experimental Social Psychology*, **14**, 35–60.

Furnham, A. and T. Ribchester (1995), 'Tolerance of Ambiguity: A Review of the Concept, its Measurement and Applications', *Current Psychology*, **14** (3), 179–99.

Geis, M.L. (1982), *The Language of Television Advertising*, New York: Academic Press.

George, W.R. and L.L. Berry (1981), 'Guidelines for the Advertising of Services', *Business Horizons*, **24**, 52–6.

Geuens, M., P. De Pelsmacker and T. Faseur (2011), 'Emotional Advertising: Revisiting the Role of Advertising', *Journal of Business Research*, **64** (4), 418–26.

Harris, R.J., J.C. Pounds, M.J. Maiorelle and M. Mermis (1993), 'The Effect of Type of Claim, Gender, and Buying History on the Drawing of Pragmatic Inferences from Advertising Claims', *Journal of Consumer Psychology*, **2** (1), 83–95.

Herman, J.L., M.J. Stevens, A. Bird, M. Mendenhall and G. Oddou (2010), 'The Tolerance for Ambiguity Scale: Towards a More Refined Measure for International Management Research', *International Journal of Intercultural Relations*, **34**, 58–65.

Hofstede, G. (1980), *Culture's Consequences: International Differences in Work-related Values*, Beverly Hills, CA: Sage.

Hofstede, G. (2009), 'Geert Hofstede's Cultural Dimensions', available at http://www.geert-hofstede.com/hofstede_belgium.shtml (accessed 30 January 2010).

House, R.J., P.J. Hanges, M. Javidan, P.W. Dorfman and V. Gupta (eds) (2004), *Culture, Leadership and Organizations: The GLOBE Study of 62 Societies*, Thousand Oaks: Sage.

House, R.J., N.R. Quigley and M.S. de Luque (2010), 'Insights from Project GLOBE: Extending Global Advertising Research through a Contemporary Framework', *International Journal of Advertising*, **29** (1), 111–39.

Kenny, J.T. and R.P. Fisk (1990), 'Why Services Promotion Differs from Goods Promotion', in David Lichtenthal et al. (eds), *Marketing Theory and Applications*, Chicago, IL: American Marketing Association, pp. 177–81.

Leech, G.N. (1966), *English in Advertising: A Linguistic Study of Advertising in Great Britain*, London: Longmans, Green and Co. Ltd.

Matic, J.L. (2006), 'The Degree of Uncertainty Avoidance Present in Croatian and American Undergraduate Students: A Comparative Analysis', *Europe's Journal of Psychology*, available at http://www.ejop.org/archives/2006/11/the_degree_of_u.html (accessed 20 January 2010).

Murray, K.B. and J.I. Schlacter (1990), 'The Impact of Services versus Goods on Consumers' Assessment of Perceived Risk and Variability', *Journal of the Academy of Marketing Science*, **18**, 51–65.

Norton, R.W. (1975), 'Measurement of Ambiguity Tolerance', *Journal of Personality Assessment*, **39** (6), 607–19.

Okazaki, S., C.R. Taylor and S. Zou (2006), 'Advertising Standardization's Positive Impact on the Bottom Line', *Journal of Advertising*, **35** (3), 17–33.

Petty, R.E., J.T. Cacioppo and D. Schumann (1983), 'Central and Peripheral Routes to Advertising Effectiveness: The Moderating Role of Involvement', *Journal of Consumer Research*, **10**, 135–46.

Sengupta, J. and G.V. Johar (2002), 'Effects of Inconsistent Attribute Information on the Predictive Value of Product Attitudes: Toward a Resolution of Opposing Perspectives', *Journal of Consumer Research*, **29** (June), 39–56.

Sparks, J.R. and C.S. Areni (2008), 'Style Versus Substance: Multiple Roles of Language Power in Persuasion', *Journal of Applied Social Psychology*, **38** (1), 37–60.

Sparks, J.R., C.S. Areni and K.C. Cox (1998), 'An Investigation of the Effects of Language Style and Communication Modality on Persuasion', *Communication Monographs*, **65**, 108–25.

Stafford, M.R. (1996), 'Tangibility in Services Advertising: An Investigation of Verbal versus Visual Cues', *Journal of Advertising*, **25** (3), 13–28.

Stafford, M.R. and E. Day (1995), 'Retail Services Advertising: The Effects of Appeal, Medium, and Service', *Journal of Advertising*, **24** (1), 57–71.

Stafford, M.R., T.F. Stafford and E. Day (2002), 'A Contingency Approach: The Effects of Spokesperson Type and Service Type on Service Advertising Perceptions', *Journal of Advertising*, **31** (2), 17–35.

Tung, R.L. and A. Verbeke (2010), 'Beyond Hofstede and GLOBE: Improving the Quality of Cross-Cultural Research', *Journal of International Business Studies*, **41** (8), 1259–74.

Vestergaard, T and K. Schroder (1985), *The Language of Advertising*, Oxford: Basil Blackwell.

Voss, K.E., E. Spangenberg and B. Grohmann (2003), 'Measuring the Hedonic and Utilitarian Dimensions of Consumer Attitude', *Journal of Marketing Research*, **11**, 310–20.

Wakefield K.L. and J.H. Barnes (1996), 'Retailing Hedonic Consumption: A Model of Sales Promotion of a Leisure Service', *Journal of Retailing*, **72** (4), 409–27.

Wong, H.Y. and B. Merrilees (2007), 'Multiple Roles of Branding in International Marketing', *International Marketing Review*, **24** (4), 384–408.

Wright, H.J.W. and L.A. Hosman (1983), 'Language Style and Sex Bias in the Courtroom: The Effects of Male and Female Use of Hedges and Intensifiers on Impression Formation', *The Southern Speech Communication Journal*, **48**, 137–52.

Zaichkowsky, J.L. (1994), 'The Personal Involvement Inventory: Reduction, Revision, and Application to Advertising', *Journal of Advertising*, **23** (4), 59–70.

Zeithaml, V.A., A. Parasuraman and L.L. Berry (1985), 'Problems and Strategies in Services Marketing', *Journal of Marketing*, **49**, 33–46.

Zou, S. and Y.Z. Volz (2010), 'An Integrated Theory of Global Advertising: An Application of the GMS Theory', *International Journal of Advertising*, **29** (1), 57–84.

18 Social media usage and responses to social media advertising in emerging and developed economies
Shu-Chuan Chu and Sara Kamal

INTRODUCTION

Researchers have long debated the democratization of digital technologies (Hoffman and Thomas, 1998) advocating that the growth and adoption of information and communication technologies (ICT) will bridge the gap between developed and developing nations, in terms of access of information. In 1981 the International Finance Corporation (IFC) coined the term "emerging markets" for nations with fast developing economies, the features of such an economy including "their transitional character with transitions occurring in economic, political, social and demographic dimensions" (Mody, 2004, p. 4). These economies are said to experience the shared phenomena of quick economic expansion, and influx of international and human capital, coupled by increased technology.

Recent industry reports such as the "Digital Life" survey by *TNS*, a leading global market research firm, provide evidence that consumers in emerging countries are heavily employing the use of social media platforms to keep up to date with the latest information and interacting with their peers (*Financial Times*, 2010a). The volume and level of interaction of social media users has decidedly shifted from developed countries (e.g., the United States, the United Kingdom, France, Germany, and Japan) to emerging markets (e.g., India, China, Brazil, and the United Arab Emirates). Many users in these emerging and newly developed economies are surpassing the penetration and usage rates of their developed counterparts. According to latest industry reports some of the world's most engaged and frequent Internet users hail from countries such as Saudi Arabia, Egypt and China (TNS Digital Life Report, 2010 as cited in *Financial Times* 2010b). These findings can be attributed to a multitude of factors such as the growing youth bulge, leap-frogging technologies as well as growth in discretionary income (Mahajan et al. 2005).

According to eMarketer (2008), advertising spending on social media will reach $2.6 billion worldwide by 2012. As more advertising budget dollars are allocated towards social media, it is critical for empirical studies to examine consumers' perceptions, attitudes and behaviors towards advertising initiatives within social media across different economic development contexts. That is, how do users in newly developed or emerging markets compare and contrast to their counterparts in developed markets such as the United States with respect to their overall responses to social media advertising (hereafter SMADV)?

Limited empirical investigation has examined social media in non-US contexts; undoubtedly as these media grow globally, there is a need for cross-national studies (Boyd and Ellison, 2007). Thus, the aim of the current study is to bridge the gap within the current international advertising research literature. This is particularly important from the standpoint of global advertising strategy. If users have varied levels of interaction, access and usage, this implies that there will be fundamental differences in their cognitive, affective and conative responses towards SMADV.

ECONOMIC DEVELOPMENT AND ADVERTISING

Economic conditions play an important role in shaping the overall context in which marketing systems operate (Dolan, 2000; Swerdlow and Blessios, 1993). In a seminal study on the economic analysis of advertising, Borden (1942a) noted that the effect of advertising on the demand for a product can vary by the nature of the market and the maturity of the product advertised. Specifically, Borden (1942b) argued that in expanding markets and new industries, advertising will have the "greatest influence" on demand (p. 97) and thus, have a positive relationship with economic growth.

Undoubtedly, economic development is an important lens through which marketing communications and media patterns are understood. Past research suggested that, as economic conditions in a given country improve, there is typically an uptake or increase in advertising expenditures (Wurff, Bakker and Picard, 2008). Additionally, the level of a country's urbanization and industrialization has been noted as triggers for growth in advertising levels (Dimmicks, 1997). This is because, as markets experience economic expansion, companies employ advertising to gain new consumers and market demand in an effort to attain their share of the growing economic pie (Chang and Can-Olmsted, 2005).

Yet, there is a lack of research examining the effect of economic conditions on advertising across different media and countries (Wurff et al. 2008). This is particularly true for newly developed or emerging markets where consumers encounter burgeoning foreign and national brands in the marketplace and may look to advertising in getting acclimated to these new brands and products. For example, Tai and Pae (2002) looked at the effects of television advertising in China. These authors noted that Chinese consumers considered advertising as an instrumental tool in developing consumption-relevant information about foreign brands. Furthermore, these authors suggested that advertising not only played a role in building the brand image for advertised product(s) and increasing the overall success for the foreign multinationals, but also served as lifestyle references regarding global consumer culture for users in these new markets. In addition, past research has also underscored that various advertising media possess different characteristics, which allow certain types of media to prove more effective in delivering different advertising messages over others (Lacy and Martin, 2004; Maxwell and Wanta, 2001). These authors contended that advertisers must place on balance the associated media costs and effectiveness in selecting the appropriate media mix.

Taken as a whole, several gaps in the research were noted: 1) the lack of investigation on new advertising media formats (such as social media) in different economic and international contexts; and 2) limited research examining differences in consumer responses towards new advertising media (SMADV) through economic factors. Thus, the aim of this chapter was to compare and contrast beliefs, attitudes, and behaviors towards SMADV among users in a newly developed market, the United Arab Emirates (UAE), and users in a developed country, the United States (US). Specifically, three research questions are proposed: 1) What are the differences in overall social media usage between UAE and US users? 2) What are the differences in beliefs, attitudes, and behaviors toward SMADV between UAE and US users? and 3) What are the relationships among usage, beliefs, attitudes, and behavior toward SMADV? Are there cross-national differences in such relationship between social media users in an emerging market UAE versus a developed market US? It is hoped that answers to these research questions will help bridge the gaps noted in the existing empirical research.

The underlying motivation for the comparison between the US and the UAE is the differences between the two countries with respect to the years and level of economic development, the growth of mass media and ICT, and the advertising business environments. Scholars have long acknowledged that consumers in developing cultures acquire consumption attitudes more rapidly than their Western counterparts and that advertising plays an important role in the process (cf. Belk, 1988). Over the past two decades, the pattern of economic activities in the UAE has significantly changed as a result of globalization. The shift in economic growth has brought about changes in the UAE's population and wealth distributions in favor of the large cities, particularly Dubai and Abu Dhabi, which have became the focus of investment for many multinational companies and international advertising agencies.

In recent years, the UAE has benefited from a surge in economic growth, and is regarded as a leading economic star in the Middle East. Thus while the lag in economic differences between these two nations has quickly evaporated, consumer responses to advertising in the UAE may still differ owing to varying levels of national advertising activity and intensity as well as industry maturity, practices and regulations, as a reflection of each nation's economic development histories. That is, despite the increased levels in typical economic indicators such as GDP, as a newly developed economy the UAE differs from the US with respect to the evolution into consumer society – which undoubtedly shapes the consumer responses within the market (Tse et al. 1989).

ECONOMIC AND SOCIAL MEDIA DEVELOPMENT IN THE UAE

In the past two decades, the UAE has acted as a major trading center for the Middle East and North Africa (MENA) region contributing significantly to the economic development within the Middle East (Business Monitor International, 2009). Recent reports by the International Monetary Fund (IMF) approximated that the aggregate nominal gross domestic product (GDP) for the MENA region increased by 300 percent in the last decade (Eid, 2010). As an emerging market region, MENA provides important growth opportunities for global business (Business Monitor International, 2009), where consumers have experienced an increase in their socio-economic status and discretionary incomes. In fact, owing to its strong economic performance, strategic geographic location and tax-free incentives, the UAE has quickly become a hub for companies targeting consumers across the Middle East, Africa, Central and South Asia, and Eastern Mediterranean regions – a combined population of over 2 billion and GDP of US\$ 6.7 trillion (Dubai eGovernment, 2009).

In terms of economic indicators, the UAE has a per capita GDP of US \$40,200 (Central Intelligence Agency, 2011a). Not only does the UAE population demonstrate high levels of income, but nearly half of the population is under 30 years of age, with a level of literacy rate estimated at 78 percent (Central Intelligence Agency, 2011a). Taken together, these factors make the UAE an attractive prospect for marketers of goods and services. In fact, according to the Nielsen Company, the advertising market in the UAE is estimated at US \$784 million in 2009 (as cited in Arab Media Outlook, 2010). Furthermore, in 2009 Internet advertising grew by approximately 70 percent, representing 2.5 percent of total national advertising spending (Arab Media Outlook, 2010). Advertising revenues are expected to increase; specifically, online advertising is expected to grow "at a CAGR of close to 40%, and to increase its share of total advertising spend to approximately 6% by the end of 2013" (Arab Media Outlook, 2010, p. 117).

In addition, the UAE has been ranked among the countries in the Middle East with the highest level of ICT indicators including PC penetration, and number of Internet, mobile phone and fixed line users (Mardar Research, 2008). Furthermore, in 2000 the UAE Government established Dubai Internet City (DIC), an e-commerce trading free zone, which is the largest ICT cluster in the Middle East (UAE Federal Government Portal, 2010). The establishment of DIC indicates the increasing importance of e-commerce for the UAE economy, and underscores the importance of the UAE as a leader in ICT technologies in the Middle East region.

In terms of social media usage the UAE accounts for over 40 percent of all users in the Middle East (SpotOnPR, 2009) and has the second highest rate of membership of social media worldwide (Synovate, 2008). Additionally, the UAE is the regional leader in terms of Internet usage and penetration rates (Internet World Stats, 2009). A recent survey of social media users in the UAE noted that the majority of users believe that social media is a vital interaction that is quickly replacing personal contact (Menon, 2008). As advertising tends to closely follow economic growth (Telser, 1971) the UAE is posited to be an ideal market within the Middle East to study about advertising growth and trends as it is the regional leader in terms of economic growth (Barkho, 2007). Because of the growing popularity of social media in the UAE, the rapid growth of regional Internet users, and the increased spending power of UAE consumers (Dubai eGovernment, 2009), empirical research in this area is needed. From the managerial viewpoint, the UAE is likely to be one of the first countries within the region to adopt social media advertising owing to the high level of Internet usage (Internet World Stats, 2009) and social media.

ECONOMIC AND SOCIAL MEDIA DEVELOPMENT IN THE US

On the other hand, the US is the world's largest economy with a per capita GDP of $47,400 (Central Intelligence Agency, 2011b). Despite the recent global economic downturn and the mortgage crisis, national personal income increased $166.8 billion for the second quarter of 2010, whereas disposable personal income increased $152.4 billion for the same period (US Department of Commerce, 2010). In terms of global advertising spending, the US represents the world's largest advertising market, with an annual growth rate of 4 percent (Nielsen, 2010). Among the various forms of advertising media in the US, online advertising spending is estimated to grow from $23.4 billion in 2008 to $34.0 billion by 2014 (eMarketer, 2009).

At the same time, academics and policy makers have paid much attention to the economic impact on ICT development (Venturini, 2009). In addition, there has been an agreement that information technology plays a prominent role in the US economic growth, indicating that ICT is a robust determinant of GDP levels (Oliner and Sichel, 2000; Venturini, 2009). More specifically, different patterns of ICT adoption are associated with variables that determine differences in development levels such as GDP, service sector, education, population age, and urban population (Billon et al., 2009). Because ICT diffusion is positively related to Internet accessibility and information availability, the varying degree of economic development between the UAE and the US may have a very different impact on new media usage, and therefore on responses to promotional messages carried in a medium such as social media.

Originated in the US, social media have become one of the most popular online activities among American Internet users in recent years (Madden, 2010). The exponential growth of social media usage has dramatically changed today's media landscape. Social media are essentially self-presenting in that users can construct their identity and share brand experience therein (Steinman and Hawkins, 2010). Recent reports show that approximately three out of four (73 percent) of American teens and 47 percent of online adults use social networking sites (e.g., Facebook) and one-third of online adults use microblogging sites (e.g., Twitter) on a daily basis (Lenhart et al. 2010). Parallel to this usage is the growing popularity of SMADV. According to a recent study conducted by Nielsen and Facebook (Neff, 2010), SMADV has been found to lead to increased advertising recall, awareness and purchase intent. Although growing international advertisers have tapped the potential of social media and designed international advertising strategy to target consumers across the globe, variations in economic development and social environment may lead to differences in usage as well as cognitive, affective and conative responses towards SMADV. In this regard, it is imperative for international advertisers to gain an in-depth understanding of the psychographic characteristics of their consumers and underlying differences for consumer use of social media in different economic contexts.

THEORETICAL FOUNDATIONS

Beliefs towards Social Media Advertising

Consumers' attitudes and beliefs towards advertising across various forms of traditional media have been examined by several notable studies such as Alwitt and Prabhaker, 1994; Karson, McCloy and Bonner, 2006; Shavitt, Lowery and Haefner, 1998; and Wolin, Korgaonkar and Lund, 2002. The aforementioned studies have drawn upon Pollay and Mittal's (1993) seminal model of advertising attitude and belief factors, with respect to mass media outlets such as television and the Internet.

Missing from past empirical research is an investigation of new forms of online media, namely social media. Thus, the goal of the current study was to examine consumer beliefs and attitudes towards SMADV employing Pollay and Mittal's (1993) seven-factor model, which tests four socio-economic factors (Good for Economy, Falsity/No Sense, Materialism, and Value Corruption) and three personal-utility factors (Product Information, Hedonic/Pleasure, and Social Role and Image).

The socio-economic factors within the aforementioned model explored consumer attitudes and beliefs with respect to advertising's ability to contribute to economic development, provide accurate consumption-related information, and instill social values and materialism. With respect to the "Good for Economy" factor in Pollay and Mittal's (1993) model, as e-commerce continues to provide opportunities for global economic growth, it is likely that SMADV will be a natural progression as regional and national e-commerce advances. Further, the economic motivation to seek out information within this medium may be high for users, as social media give consumers access to purchase related information without the restriction of time or location. In addition, consumer economic motivation may be increased by users seeking sales promotions information such as contests, discounts or give-aways. Next, the "Materialism" factor examined consumer beliefs and attitudes towards the importance and role of consumption. Belk (1988) defined materialism as the belief that goods and money are the central path to happiness and social progress. Consumers in emerging markets with increasing discretionary incomes may encounter consumption-related experiences and messages on social media on a constant basis. Similar to Internet usage, these online promotions of commercial content via social media may result in higher materialism among users (Wolin et al. 2002). Because advertising messages on other media have been linked to user values, the "Value Corruption" factor explored users' responses with respect to the fact that SMADV may influence user values, given the frequency and heavy level of usage of the medium. Another factor related to social media is "Falsity/No Sense," which is an important concern for consumers (Ross, 1998). Consistent with other forms of advertising, research shows that Web-related advertising may promote deceptive claims, false or exaggerated information that falls short of consumer experience (Wolin et al., 2002). Therefore, with respect to social media, this chapter examines consumer beliefs towards falsity in SMADV.

On the other hand, the personal-utility factors in Pollay and Mittal's (1993) model encompass consumer attitudes and beliefs with respect to advertising's ability to impart up-to-date product information, and provide entertainment and enjoyment to users, as well as portraying the social role and image of advertised products. The first personal-utility factor is related to "Product Information." Consumers use advertising as a personal source of information (Ju-Pak, 1999); past research found a significant and positive correlation between consumers' value of Web advertising and its informativeness (Ducoffe, 1996). In the same way, social media provides users with marketer-dominated sources of information (e.g., marketer-generated brand information) as well as other consumer-dominated sources of information (e.g., brand comments from personal contacts). The "Hedonic/Pleasure" belief factor looked at SMADV's ability to provide enjoyment and pleasure with usage. Similar to past studies such as Watson, Akselsen and Pitt (1998) it is expected that SMADV is a source of enjoyment to users because it provides content that is relevant, entertaining and motivating to consumers. Advertising through mass media outlets advances social and lifestyle messages to consumers (Pollay and Mittal, 1993). With regard to the last belief factor "Social Role and Image" and SMADV, given its pervasive nature, advertising messages transmitted via social media may possess the ability to convey frequent messages that pertain to the social role and image of its users.

Attitudes towards Social Media Advertising

Past studies in consumer behavior suggest that consumers follow a hierarchal sequence in their behaviors (cf. Lavidge and Stiener, 1961; Palda, 1966). Specifically, these scholars noted that initial consumer responses are typically cognitive in nature, which is when users develop awareness and knowledge. Next, consumers gain affective responses, where they develop liking, preference and conviction. Therefore the current study posits that consumer beliefs about SMADV will be a precursor to their attitudes towards SMADV.

Behaviors towards Social Media Advertising

Past research has established that consumer attitudes are an important antecedent to their responses towards advertising and intention to purchase (Lavidge and Steiner, 1961). Furthermore, research has found that other dimensions of consumer responses such as brand recall and buying intention have been positively linked to advertising attitudes. More specifically, Mehta (2000) found that consumers with higher scores in terms of their attitudes towards advertising had a higher likelihood for brand recall and purchase intention. Applying this logic to the Internet, several studies have sought to analyze the relationship between users' attitudes towards online advertising and shopping behaviors on the Internet. Notably, Stevenson, Bruner and Kumar (2000) found that consumers who had less positive attitudes towards online advertising were less likely to make purchases online. In another study, executed by Korgaonkar and Wolin (2002), the authors found that positive advertising attitudes were significantly related to online consumer spending and higher frequency of online purchases among users. Therefore, it is argued that users with positive attitudes towards SMADV are likely to have higher levels of usage and engagement with advertising messages within social media as well as seek information about the promoted products.

Taken together, this study examines the potential differences in overall social media usage, beliefs, attitudes, and behaviors toward advertising in social media between users in emerging and developed markets, specifically UAE and US social media users.

METHOD

Sample and Data Collection

To examine the proposed research questions, this study used an online survey. College students from major universities located in the metropolitan area of Dubai, UAE and in the Midwest region of the US participated in the study. An invitation email with a survey link was sent to students from introductory business and communication classes in the two countries. Students voluntarily took part in this study and they were offered course credit as compensation for participation. As a result, a total of 637 respondents from the UAE and 347 respondents from the US completed the online survey. After eliminating respondents who showed extreme and consistent high or low rating patterns and incomplete responses,

573 responses and 306 responses constituted the UAE and US samples respectively and were employed in the data analysis. Industry reports show that college students comprise a segment most likely to be active social media users, with more than 70 percent of American Internet users between 18 and 29 years old using social media (Lenhart et al. 2010). A similar demographic profile of social media users was found in the UAE (Menon, 2008). Additionally, past research has suggested that the potential influence of confounding factors on college students are limited given that they are more homogenous on external factors than the general population (Wang et al. 2009), Thus, the use of a college student sample was deemed appropriate. Given the purpose of this study, it is crucial to study college students for an initial understanding of how social media are used across different economic contexts: UAE and US.

The demographic characteristics of the sample, including gender, age, personal income, country of origin (for the UAE) and race/ethnicity (for the US), are provided in Table 18.1. In the UAE, approximately 60 percent (59.5 percent) of the respondents were male and 40.5 percent female. As for the American sample, 42.8 percent were male and 57.2 percent were female. Approximately half (50.3 percent) of the UAE respondents was between 21 and 30 years old, and 49.0 percent were under 20 years of age. Similarly, the American sample was 65.0 percent between 21 and 30 years, 34.3 percent under 20 years, and 0.7 percent over the age of 31 years.

In terms of monthly personal income, more than 40 percent of the UAE respondents indicated a personal income (including family allowance) of more than $1000, while 22.5 percent of the participants reported a personal allowance of between $601 and $1000 and 25.3 percent reported a personal income of between $201 and $600. Only 10.5 percent of the subjects reported a personal income lower than $200. In the US, only 8.8 percent of the American respondents indicated a personal income of more than $1000 and 15 percent of the participants reported a personal income of between $601 and $1000. Approximately 40 percent of the subjects reported a personal allowance of between $201 and $600 and less than $200. With respect to the country of origin breakdown of the sample in the UAE, 16.4 percent were from India, followed by the UAE (12.4 percent), Lebanon (9.3 percent), Nigeria (6.1 percent), and Kazakhstan (5.8 percent). As for race and ethnicity of the American sample, more than three out of four (75.8 percent) were Caucasian, followed by Asian American (11.4 percent), African American (4.2 percent), Native American (3.9 percent) and Hispanic or Latino (3.3 percent).

Table 18.1   Sample demographic characteristics

		UAE (%)		US (%)
Sample	India	16.4	Native	3.9
Composition	UAE	12.4	American	
	Lebanon	9.3	Asian	11.4
	Nigeria	6.1	American	
	Kazakhstan	5.8	African	4.2
	Egypt	5.4	American	
	Syria	4.5	Caucasian	75.8
	Iran	4.0	Hispanic/	3.3
	Palestine	3.7	Latino	
	Jordan	3.5	Mixed/Other	1.3
	Others	28.9		
Gender				
Male		59.5		42.8
Female		40.5		57.2
Age				
Under 20 years		49.0		34.3
21–30 years		50.3		65.0
31–40 years		0.5		0.4
Over 41 years		0.2		0.3
Personal Income				
Less than $200		10.5		37.3
$201–$400		12.0		23.9
$401–$600		13.3		15.0
$601–$800		8.7		8.8
$801–$1000		13.8		6.2
$1001–$1200		10.3		2.9
$1201–$1400		5.6		1.6
$1401–$1600		5.2		1.3
More than $1600		20.6		3.0

Note: UAE n=573; US n=306.

Measures

The self-administered online survey investigated: 1) overall social media usage (LaFerle et al., 2000), absorption with social media activity (Bush and Gilbert, 2002) and social media intensity (Ellison et al., 2007); 2) beliefs, attitudes, and behaviors towards SMADV (Wolin et al., 2002);

and 3) demographic variables such as country of origin, gender, age, education, and personal income. All measurement items were adopted from previous research and were modified when necessary to fit the context of the present study.

Overall social media usage was assessed by asking participants to report the time they spent on social media from the previous day (LaFerle et al., 2000), with a 10-point rating scale ranging from (1) 0 to (10) more than eight hours. Absorption with social media activity was examined using the four items adopted from Bush and Gilbert (2002). Sample items include, "How likely are you to genuinely enjoy the time you spend on social media?" and "How likely are you to feel totally absorbed while you are on social media?" These items were measured on a 5-point Likert scale from (1) unlikely to (7) likely. Lastly, social media intensity (Ellison et al., 2007) assessed use of different types of social media applications or platforms. Specifically, subjects were asked to indicate the time they spent on social networking sites (e.g., Facebook and MySpace), microblogging sites (e.g., Twitter), photo sharing sites (e.g., Flickr and Snapfish), video sharing sites (e.g., YouTube and Hulu), and Wiki sites. For example, items include, "I feel I am part of the social networking site community" and "I would be sorry if social networking sites shut down". The majority of these items were measured on a 5-point Likert scale that ranged from (1) strongly disagree to (5) strongly agree.

In terms of beliefs, attitudes, and behaviors towards SMADV, Wolin et al.'s (2002) measure on beliefs, attitudes, and behavior toward Web advertising was adopted. A total of 31 items was used, including 23 statements for beliefs toward SMADV and four items each for attitudes and behaviors towards SMADV. In particular, the seven underlying belief factors that were originally developed by Pollay and Mittal (1993) were examined: product information, hedonic/pleasure, social role and image, good for the economy, materialism, falsity/no sense, and value corruption. All of these items were measured on a five-point scale such as (1) strongly disagree and (5) strongly agree or (1) never and (5) occasionally. Sample items include, for example, "When I see a social media advertisement on my computer screen, I pay close attention to (behavior toward SMADV)" and "Social media advertisements make you buy things you don't really need (materialism beliefs toward SMADV)".

RESULTS

First, internal reliability was assessed with Cronbach's alpha for each sample. The scales of the major variables exhibited acceptable internal

Table 18.2   Social media usage in the UAE and the US

	Reliability α		M (S.D.)		t
	UAE	US	UAE	US	
Overall Social Media Usage	N/A	N/A	*3.29* (1.82)	*2.38* (1.33)	−7.72***
Absorption with Social Media Activity	.84	.84	*3.09* (.91)	*3.16* (.96)	1.04
Social Media Intensity	N/A	N/A	*2.79* (.78)	*2.39* (.63)	−7.72***
Social networking sites	.85	.85	*3.60* (1.00)	*4.06* (.98)	6.62***
Microblogging sites	.93	.94	*2.44* (1.15)	*1.68* (.92)	−10.00***
Photo sharing sites	.93	.94	*2.36* (1.20)	*1.62* (.92)	−9.39***
Video sharing sites	.90	.91	*2.92* (1.00)	*2.46* (.99)	−6.54***
Wikis sites	.91	.91	*2.63* (.97)	*2.12* (.93)	−7.43***

Note: *Significant at .05; **Significant at .01; ***Significant at .001.

reliability. An index for each variable was created by averaging items measuring the same construct. Second, descriptive statistics and independent sample t-tests were run following the research questions regarding how social media usage and responses to SMADV differ across the UAE and the US. Third, regression analysis was conducted to examine the potential relationships among beliefs, attitudes, and behaviors towards SMADV and identify any differences in such relationships between the two markets. Lastly, a median split and independent sample t-tests were used to determine if levels of social media usage impact users' responses to SMADV.

Research Questions

RQ1: Social media usage
The first research question was designed to examine the effects of economic development on respondents' use of social media. The t-test results in Table 18.2 suggest that UAE participants ($M = 3.29$) had a higher tendency to use social media than their American counterparts ($M = 2.38$) (t (1,877) $= -7.72$, $p < .001$). Specifically, the results indicated that participants in the UAE spent an average of one to three hours on social media on a daily basis, whereas American respondents spent zero to two hours on social media per day on average. In terms of absorption with social media activity, no significant difference was observed between the UAE and the US (UAE: $M = 3.09$ vs. US: $M = 3.16$, t (1,877) $= 1.04$, $p = .30$). When social media intensity was examined, the results suggested that respondents in the UAE were more likely to use micro blogging sites (UAE: $M = 2.44$ vs.

Table 18.3   Responses to social media advertising in the UAE and the US

	Reliability α		M (S.D.)		t
	UAE	US	UAE	US	
Beliefs toward SMADV	N/A	N/A	*3.23* (.45)	*3.08* (.61)	−4.08***
Product information	.82	.89	*3.34* (.82)	*3.17* (.93)	
Hedonic/please	.80	.85	*3.27* (.84)	*2.93* (.92)	
Social role and image	.76	.80	*3.19* (.79)	*2.90* (.87)	
Good for the economy	.70	.64	*3.20* (.77)	*2.91* (.80)	
Materialism	.78	.81	*3.28* (.75)	*3.14* (.77)	
Falsity/no sense	.75	.82	*2.90* (.80)	*3.26* (.77)	
Value corruption	.79	.79	*3.43* (.75)	*3.26* (.77)	
Attitudes toward SMADV	.87	.87	*3.23* (.81)	*3.07* (.85)	−2.70**
Behaviors toward SMADV	.61	.72	*2.75* (.65)	*2.38* (.68)	−8.03***

Note: *Significant at .05; **Significant at .01; ***Significant at .001.

US: $M = 1.68$, t (1,877) $= -10.00$, $p < .001$), photo sharing sites (UAE: $M = 2.36$ vs. US: $M = 1.62$, t (1,877) $= -9.39$, $p < .001$), video sharing sites (UAE: $M = 2.92$ vs. US: $M = 2.46$, t (1,877) $= -6.54$, $p < .001$), and Wiki sites (UAE: $M = 2.63$ vs. US: $M = 2.12$, t (1,877) $= -7.43$, $p < .001$) than their American counterparts. On the other hand, there was a higher tendency to use social networking sites (US: $M = 4.06$ vs. UAE: $M = 3.60$, t (1,877) $= 6.62$, $p < .001$) amongst American respondents compared to those in the UAE. These results indicate there were some differences in social media usage across the emerging and developed markets.

RQ2: Beliefs, attitudes, and behaviors toward SMADV
The second research question investigated whether differences exist in beliefs, attitudes, and behaviors toward SMADV between UAE and US users. Another independent sample t-test comparing the two samples was conducted. As presented in Table 18.3, respondents in the UAE showed a significantly higher level of beliefs (UAE: $M = 3.23$ vs. US: $M = 3.08$, t (1,877) $= -4.08$, $p < .001$), attitudes (UAE: $M = 3.23$ vs. US: $M = 3.07$, t (1,877) $= -2.70$, $p < .01$), and behaviors (UAE: $M = 2.75$ vs. US: $M = 2.38$, t (1,877) $= -8.03$, $p < .001$) toward SMADV than American participants.

RQ3: Relationships among usage, beliefs, attitudes, and behaviors toward SMADV
The third research question explored the potential relationships among usage, beliefs, attitudes, and behaviors toward SMADV and

identified any cross-national differences in such relationship between users in the UAE versus those in the US. In the UAE sample, two regression models were conducted to examine the relationships between advertising beliefs, attitudes, and behaviors in social media. The result showed that the overall regression model was significant (R^2_{adj} = .33), F (1, 571) = 279.28, p < .001. UAE users' beliefs toward SMADV (β = .57, t = 16.71, p < .001) was a significant predictor of attitudes toward SMADV. When examining the relationship between attitudes and behaviors toward SMADV among UAE users, the overall regression model was found to be significant (R^2_{adj} = .12), F (1, 571) = 76.97, p < .001. The results demonstrated that attitudes toward SMADV (β = .35, t = 8.77, p < .001) significantly predicted behavior responses toward SMADV among users in the UAE.

Similarly, attitudes toward SMADV were regressed on beliefs toward SMADV of American users. The result indicated that the overall regression model was significant (R^2_{adj} = .26), F (1, 304) = 109.59, p < .001. That is, beliefs toward SMADV (β = .52, t = 10.47, p < .001) was a significant predictor of attitudes toward SMADV. Next, behaviors toward SMADV were regressed on attitudes toward SMADV. The regression model was found to be significant (R^2_{adj} = .17), F (1, 304) = 64.70, p < .001. American users' attitudes toward advertising on social media (β = .42, t = 8.77, p < .001) significantly predicted their behavior responses toward SMADV. Overall, these results suggested that Pollay and Mittal's model (1993) is applicable across different economic contexts. Table 18.4 presents the regression results.

To further understand how social media usage relates to beliefs, attitudes, and behaviors toward SMADV, a median split was performed to divide the respondents into those with high and low social media usage. First, a series of independent sample t-tests were used to compare beliefs, attitudes, and behaviors between the high versus low usage groups of users in the UAE. The results suggested that high usage respondents reported having a more favorable belief (M_{high} = 3.31; M_{low} = 3.15, t(1,571) = −4.20, p < .001), attitude (M_{high} = 3.42; M_{low} = 3.04, t(1,571) = −5.77, p < .001), and behavior (M_{high} = 2.87; M_{low} = 2.63, t(1,571) = −4.39, p < .001) toward SMADV than did low usage respondents. Thus, when UAE users spent more time on social media, they tended to maintain more favorable beliefs, attitudes, and behaviors toward SMADV.

In the US, users with a higher level of usage reported having more favorable attitudes (M_{high} = 3.23; M_{low} = 2.94, t(1,304) = −3.10, p < .01) and behaviors (M_{high} = 2.53; M_{low} = 2.25, t(1,304) = −3.67, p < .001) toward SMADV than did users with a lower level of usage. Nevertheless, the

Table 18.4   Regression results of beliefs, attitudes, and behaviors toward social media advertising

IV	DV	UAE			US		
		β	R^2_{adj}	F	β	R^2_{adj}	F
Beliefs toward SMADV	Attitudes toward SMADV	.57	.33	279.28***	.52	.26	109.59***
Attitudes toward SMADV	Behaviors toward SMADV	.35	.12	76.97***	.42	.17	64.70***

Notes:
*Significant at .05; **Significant at .01; ***Significant at .001
IV=Independent Variable; DV=Dependent Variable.

results showed no significant difference in beliefs toward SMADV ($M_{high} = 3.13$; $M_{low} = 3.04$, $t(1,304) = -1.42$, $p = .16$). Table 18.5 summarizes these t-tests results.

DISCUSSION AND CONCLUSIONS

The increased use of social media as a tool in digital communication has changed the way consumers interact with brands. Despite the prevalence of social media usage around the world, users' media habits and responses to advertising within the media may vary according to the economic development in a given society. Thus, an examination of SMADV across different economic contexts is timely and necessary. The main objective of this cross-national research is to examine similarities and differences in beliefs, attitudes, and behaviors towards SMADV among users in emerging and developed economics. Drawing from Pollay and Mittal's (1993) framework of advertising attitudes and beliefs, this study attempts to understand the relationship between economic development and consumer response to advertising in social media in the UAE and the US. Overall, differences in social media usage, beliefs, attitudes, and behaviors towards SMADV were found between the two nations, whereas the positive relationships among SMADV beliefs, attitudes, and behaviors hold true across countries.

In terms of differences in social media usage, results indicated that young

Table 18.5   t-tests results of beliefs, attitudes, and behaviors toward social media advertising

	UAE		t	US		t
	High	**Low**		**High**	**Low**	
Overall Social Media Usage	*M* (S.D.)	*M* (S.D.)		*M* (S.D.)	*M* (S.D.)	
Beliefs toward SMADV	*3.31* (.44)	*3.15* (.44)	−4.20***	*3.13* (.63)	*3.04* (.59)	−1.42
Attitudes toward SMADV	*3.42* (.82)	*3.04* (.76)	−5.77***	*3.23* (.87)	*2.94* (.82)	−3.10**
Behaviors toward SMADV	*2.87* (.57)	*2.63* (.70)	−4.39***	*2.53* (.66)	*2.25* (.67)	−3.67***

Note: *Significant at .05; **Significant at .01; ***Significant at .001.

UAE users had a higher level of social media usage compared to their US counterparts. This finding can be best understood by taking into account rapid Internet and broadband penetration rates as well as the high levels of adoption of Smartphones and enhanced data-packages in the region. This expansion has largely been attributed to consumers in the 15 to 35 age groups (Business Intelligence Middle East, 2010). Consumers in emerging markets often "leap frog" to the latest technologies whilst consumers in developed markets tend to systematically upgrade to newer technological advances (Mahajan et al., 2005). For example, in the ME region, Smartphone sales accounted for 13.8 percent of total mobile handset sales in 2009, and are expected to reach 28.8 percent by 2015 (Business Intelligence Middle East, 2010). In fact, in the ME region the UAE has the highest Smartphone penetration rate (Reuters, 2010). Conversely, reports by Mashable, one of the world's leading websites on Internet and social media related news, noted in the North America and Europe region that the Smartphone penetration growth rate in the US still lags behind other countries such as the United Kingdom, Italy, France, and Canada (Mashable, 2010).

Further examination into specific modes of social media usage revealed that UAE users reported a higher usage for microblogging, photo sharing and video sharing compared to US users. This finding may be explained by the need of these young users to employ social media as outlets to express aspects of individualism in society where group-dominated culture is advocated (Piecarge, 2003), as well as to express "multiple perspectives" and disseminate information quickly in a region where many forms of mass media are often controlled (Beckerman, 2007, p. 18).

Overall, these findings suggest that for advertisers SMADV efforts built upon sharing of video and visual content would likely be successful in targeting young UAE users. This may also imply opportunities to integrate existing tactics (such as product placement in films, television advertising commercials, and so on) and adapt these through social media platforms to target younger consumer cohorts. There may also be opportunities for promotions centered on online content sharing (particularly videos and photos) and blogs. Branded social communities, fan pages, Twitter and other SMADV applications that require more active consumer engagement may still take time to develop momentum within the young UAE users given that these platforms are expected to grow further in the future.

More importantly, results showed significant differences between UAE and US users with respect to beliefs, attitudes, and behaviors towards SMADV. Overall the results from the set of analyses suggest that UAE users tended to have more positive beliefs, attitudes and behaviors towards SMADV. The implications of this finding suggest that, for marketers, online advertising formats, particular SMADV, are a sound strategy while targeting consumers within this market, as users are expected to attend and recall messages favorably. Young consumers in the UAE are growing up in a rapidly evolving marketplace, with an influx of global brands; they look to advertising as a positive source of information as they become acclimated towards global consumer culture. In addition, from a cultural perspective, the format of SMADV may be attractive to Arab consumers. As noted by Al-Olayan and Karande (2000), Arab consumers tend to have high appreciation for receiving product information through social sources such as family and friends. Thus, extending this finding to online communications, this may be one of the reasons why UAE consumers showed positive beliefs, attitudes and behaviors towards SMADV.

Another set of findings pertains to the relationships among social media usage, beliefs, attitudes, and behaviors toward SMADV. First, this study found that, in accordance with past empirical research, there is a positive and significant belief, attitude and behavioral link. This finding confirms Pollay and Mittal's (1993) advertising beliefs and attitudes model is applicable across varying economic and international conditions – this finding has both theoretical and practical implications. Understanding how consumers from emerging countries use social media and compare their SMADV responses to consumers from developed countries provides valuable implications for international advertising research and practice, and advances our knowledge of ICT in a global context.

Second, findings of this research further decipher the imperative role that usage plays in consumer responses to promotional efforts in social media. Specifically, the results suggest that, in both countries, users with a higher level of usage maintained more favorable attitudes and behaviors toward SMADV than did users with a lower level of usage. While social media usage is positively related to beliefs toward SMADV among users in the UAE, no significant difference was found in beliefs toward SMADV in the US. Consistent with past research suggesting that increased media usage is positively associated with high levels of advertising responses (Churchill and Moschis, 1979), users' affection and behaviors toward SMADV have been found to link to media exposure. Nevertheless, the non-significant relationship between usage and beliefs toward SMADV in the US may be owing to the fact that consumers in newly developed or emerging markets are more likely to look to advertising for developing product-related information about brands than consumers in developed markets. Thus, the time consumers spend on social media does not affect their existing beliefs toward advertising within social media among US users.

In conclusion, findings from the current study provide relevant implications for theory and practice. From the theoretical perspective, it is important to examine whether existing theoretical frameworks towards advertising beliefs, attitudes and behaviors can be applied to social media users across diverse market conditions, that is, emerging markets and developed markets. From the standpoint of advertising strategy, results provide insight into whether or not differences exist in terms of consumer attitudes, beliefs and behaviors towards SMADV between newly developed and developed markets. If users have varied levels of interaction, access and usage, this would imply differences in their cognitive, affective and conative responses towards SMADV. Thus, it is hoped that the results from the current study will help identify strategies and tactics for consumers within varying economic contexts. Undoubtedly, such findings will have major implications as to the role of SMADV in the overall global advertising campaign strategy as well as its effectiveness in terms of message attendance.

REFERENCES

Al-Olayan, F.S. and K. Karande (2000), 'A content analysis of magazine advertisements from the United States and the Arab world', *Journal of Advertising*, **29** (3), 69–82.
Alwitt, L.F. and P.R. Prabhaker (1994), 'Identifying who dislikes television advertising: Not by demographics alone', *Journal of Advertising Research*, **34** (5), 17–29.
Barkho, L. (2007), 'Advertising resources in oil rich Arab Gulf States – Implications for international marketers', *International Journal of Business Studies*, **19** (2), 1–24.
Beckerman, G. (2007), 'The new Arab conversation', *Columbia Journalism Review*, **45**, 17–23.
Belk, Russell W. (1988), 'Third World Consumer Culture', in Erdogan Kumcu and A. Fuat Firat (eds), *Marketing and Development*, Greenwich, CT: JAI, pp. 103–27.
Billon, M., R. Marco and L.-L. Fernando (2009), 'Disparities in ICT adoption: A

multidimensional approach to study the cross-country digital divide', *Telecommunications Policy*, **33** (10–11), 596–610.

Borden, N.H. (1942a), *The Economic Effects of Advertising*, Chicago, IL: Richard Irwin, Inc.

Borden, N.H. (1942b), 'Findings of the Harvard study on the economic effects of advertising', *Journal of Marketing*, **6** (4), 89–99.

Boyd, D. and N.B. Ellison (2007), 'Social network sites: Definition, history, and scholarship', *Journal of Computer-Mediated Communication*, **13** (1), 210–30.

Bush, V.D. and F.W. Gilbert (2002), 'The Web as a medium: An explanatory comparison of Internet users versus newspaper readers', *Journal of Marketing Theory & Practice*, **10** (1), 1–10.

Business Intelligence Middle East (2010), 'Smartphone penetration in Middle East to increase to 28.8% of total handset sales by 2015', available at http://www.bi-me.com/main.php?id=48860&t=1&c=12&cg=2&mset (accessed 22 January 2011).

Business Monitor International (2009), *United Arab Emirates Business Forecast Report*, ISBN: 1744-8859.

Central Intelligence Agency (2011a), 'The world factbook: UAE economy', available at https://www.cia.gov/library/publications/the-world-factbook/geos/ae.html (accessed 22 January 2011).

Central Intelligence Agency (2011b), 'The world factbook: US economy', available at https://www.cia.gov/library/publications/the-world-factbook/geos/us.html (accessed 22 January 2011).

Chang, B.-H. and S.M. Chan-Olmsted (2005), 'Relative constancy of advertising spending: A cross-national examination of advertising expenditures and their determinants', *Gazette*, **67** (4), 339–57.

Churchill, G.A. and G.P. Moschis (1979), 'Television and interpersonal influences on adolescent consumer learning', *Journal of Consumer Research*, **6** (1), 23–35.

Dimmick, J. (1997), 'The theory of the niche and spending on mass media: The case of the video revolution', *Journal of Media Economics*, **10** (3), 33–43.

Dolan, R.J. (2000), 'Note on Marketing Strategy', Harvard Business School Publishing, 9-598-061, Boston, MA 02163.

Dubai eGovernment (2009), 'Dubai Economy', available at http://www.dubai.ae/en.portal?topic,Article_000239,0,&_nfpb=true&_pageLabel=home (accessed 22 January 2011).

Dubai Press Club (2010), 'Arab Media Outlook 2009-2013', available at http://www.fas.org/irp/eprint/arabmedia.pdf (accessed 22 January 2011).

Ducoffe, R.H. (1996), 'Advertising value and advertising on the Web', *Journal of Advertising Research*, **36** (5), 21–35.

Eid, F. (2010), 'The decade MENA came to be: Middle East and North Africa Outlook', *Arabia Monitor*.

Ellison, N.B., C. Steinfield and C. Lampe (2007), 'The benefits of Facebook "Friends": Social capital and college students' use of online social network sites', *Journal of Computer-Mediated Communication*, **12** (4), 1143–68.

eMarketer (2008), 'Social network marketing: Ad spending update', http://www.emarketer.com (accessed 22 January 2011).

eMarketer (2009), 'US advertising spending', http://www.emarketer.com/Report.aspx?code=emarketer_2000615 (accessed 22 January 2011).

Financial Times (2010a), 'Social networks dominate emerging markets', by Tim Bradshaw, published: 10 October 2010 22:02, available at http://www.ft.com/cms/s/2/5ba84668-d48d-11df-b230-00144feabdc0.html (accessed 22 January 2011).

Financial Times (2010b), 'Chinese and Saudis lead way in internet use', by Tim Bradshaw in London, published: 10 October 2010 22:02, available at http://www.ft.com/cms/s/2/1792f094-d493-11df-b230-00144feabdc0.html (accessed 22 January 2011).

Hoffman, D.L. and P.N. Thomas (1998), 'Bridging the racial divide on the Internet', *Science*, **280** (April 17), 390–91.

Internetworldstats.com (2009), 'United Arab Emirates: Internet usage and marketing report', available at http://www.internetworldstats.com/me/ae.htm (accessed 22 January 2011).

Ju-Pak, K.-H. (1999), 'Content dimensions of Web advertising: A cross-national comparison', *International Journal of Advertising*, **18** (2), 207–31.

Karson, E., S. McCloy and G. Bonner (2006), 'An examination of consumers' attitudes and beliefs toward web site advertising', *Journal of Current Issues and Research in Advertising*, **28**, 77–91.

Korgaonkar, P. and L.D. Wolin (2002), 'Web usage, advertising, and shopping: Relationship patterns', *Internet Research: Electronic Networking Applications and Policy*, **12** (2), 191–204.

Lacy, S. and H.J. Martin (2004), 'Competition, circulation and advertising', *Newspaper Research Journal*, **25** (1), 18–39.

La Ferle, C., S.M. Edwards and W.-N. Lee (2000), 'Teens' use of traditional media and the Internet', *Journal of Advertising Research*, **4** (3), 55–64.

Lavidge, R.J. and G.A. Steiner (1961), 'A model for predictive measurements of advertising effectiveness', *Journal of Marketing*, **25** (6), 59–62.

Lenhart, A., K. Purcell, A. Smith and K. Zickuhr (2010), 'Social media & mobile Internet use among teens and young adults', available at http://www.pewinternet.org/~/media//Files/Reports/2010/PIP_Social_Media_and_Young_Adults_Report.pdf (accessed 22 January 2011).

Madden, M. (2010) 'Older adults and social media', available at http://www.pewinternet.org/~/media//Files/Reports/2010/Pew%20Internet%20-%20Older%20Adults%20and%20Social%20Media.pdf (accessed 22 January 2011).

Mahajan, V., K. Banga and R. Gunther (2005), *The 86 Percent Solution: How to Succeed in the Biggest Market Opportunity of the Next 50 Years*, Upper Saddle River, NJ 07458: Wharton School Publishing.

Mardar Research (2008), 'Middle East ICT use index – 2008', available at http://www.madarresearch.com/ (accessed 22 January 2011).

Mashable (2010), 'Why Smartphone adoption may not be as big as you think', available at http://mashable.com/2010/08/26/smartphone-adoption-trends/ (accessed 22 January 2011).

Maxwell, A. and W. Wanta (2001), 'Advertising agencies reduce reliance on newspaper ads', *Newspaper Research Journal*, **22** (2), 51–65.

Mehta, A. (2000), 'Advertising attitudes and advertising effectiveness', *Journal of Advertising Research*, **40** (3), 67–72.

Menon, V. (2008), 'UAE second in world list for online social networking', available at http://www.arabianbusiness.com/532785-uae-second-in-world-list-for-online-social-networking?ln=en (accessed 22 January 2011).

Mody, A. (2004), 'What is an emerging market?' IMF Working Paper, available at http://www.imf.org/external/pubs/ft/wp/2004/wp04177.pdf (accessed 22 January 2011).

Neff, J. (2010), 'Nielsen: Facebook's ads work pretty well when social ads collide with stated interests, awareness goes up', available at http://adage.com/digital/article?article_id=143381 (accessed 22 January 2011).

Nielsen (2010), 'Global ad spend rebounds 12.5 percent in Q1 2010 driven by spending surge Latin America and Asia', available at http://www.nielsen.com/us/en/insights/press-room/2010/global-ad-spend-q1.html (accessed 22 January 2011).

Oliner, S.D. and D.E. Sichel (2000), 'The resurgence of growth in the late 1990s: Is information technology the story?' *Journal of Economic Perspectives*, **14** (4), 3–22.

Palda, K.S. (1966), 'The hypothesis of a hierarchy of effects: A partial evaluation', *Journal of Marketing Research*, **3**, 13–24.

Piecowye, J. (2003), 'Habitus in Transition? CMC use and impacts among young women in the United Arab Emirates', *Journal of Computer-Mediated Communication*, **8** (2), available at http://jcmc.indiana.edu/vol8/issue2/piecowye.html (accessed 22 January 2011).

Pollay, R. and B. Mittal (1993), 'Here's the beef: Factors, determinants, and segments in consumer criticism of advertising', *Journal of Marketing*, **57** (3), 99–114.

Reuters (2010), 'Qualcomm plans Mideast mobile health rollout', available at http://af.reuters.com/article/investingNews/idAFJOE67004G20100801?pageNumber=2&virtual BrandChannel=0 (accessed 22 January 2011).

Ross, P.D. (1998), 'Interactive marketing and the law: The future rise of unfairness', *Journal of Interactive Marketing*, **12** (3), 21–31.

Shavitt, S., P. Lowrey and J. Haefner (1998), 'Public attitudes toward advertising: More favorable than you might think', *Journal of Advertising Research*, **38** (4), 7–22.

Spot On PR (2009), 'Middle East & North Africa Twitter demographics & user habits survey publication', available at http://interactiveme.com/wp-content/uploads/2009/09/twitter_survey_report_interactiveME.pdf (accessed 22 January 2011).

Steinman, M.L. and M. Hawkins (2010), 'When marketing through social media, legal risks can go viral', *Intellectual Property & Technology Law Journal*, **22** (8), 1–9.

Stevenson, J.S., G.C. Bruner II and A. Kumar (2000), 'Web page background and viewer attitudes', *Journal of Advertising Research*, **20** (1&2), 29–34.

Swerdlow, R.A. and V.I. Blessios (1993), 'A model for predicting advertising expenditures: an inter-industry comparison', *International Journal of Advertising*, **12** (2), 143–53.

Synovate (2008), 'Global survey', available at http://www.synovate.com/news/article/2008/09/global-survey-shows-58-of-people-don-t-know-what-social-networking-is-plus-over-one-third-of-social-networkers-are-losing-interest.html (accessed 22 January 2011).

Tai, S.H.C. and Jae H. Pae (2002), 'Effects of TV advertising on Chinese consumers: Local versus foreign-sourced commercials', *Journal of Marketing Management*, **18** (1–2), 49–72.

Telser, L.G. (1971), *Advertising and Competition*, Bobbs-Merrill reprint series in economics, ECON-305, Indianapolis: Bobbs-Merrill.

Tse, D.K., R.W. Belk and N. Zhou (1989), 'Becoming a consumer society: A longitudinal and cross-cultural content analysis of print ads from Hong Kong, the People's Republic of China and Taiwan', *Journal of Consumer Research*, **15** (March), 457–72.

UAE Federal Government Portal (2010), 'E-Commerce: Fact & figures', available at http://www.government.ae/gov/en/biz/ecommerce/facts.jsp (accessed 22 January 2011).

US Department of Commerce (2010), 'GDP and the economy', available at http://www.bea.gov/newsreleases/glance.htm (accessed 22 January 2011).

Venturini, F. (2009), 'The long-run impact of ICT', *Empirical Economics*, **37** (3), 497–515.

Wang, Y., S. Sun W. Lei and M. Toncar (2009), 'Examining beliefs and attitudes toward online advertising among Chinese consumers', *Direct Marketing: An International Journal*, **3** (1), 52–66.

Watson, R.T., S. Akselsen and L. Pitt (1998), 'Attractors: building mountains in the flat landscape of the World Wide Web', *California Management Review*, **40** (2), 36–56.

Wolin, L., P. Korgaonkar and D. Lund (2002), 'Beliefs, attitudes and behavior towards web advertising', *International Journal of Advertising*, **21** (1), 87–113.

Wurff, R.G., P. Bakker and R. Picard (2008), 'Economic growth and advertising expenditures in different media in different countries', *Journal of Media Economics*, **21** (1), 28–52.

PART VII

SOCIAL INTERACTION

19 Raising the golden arches: advertising's role in the socialization of the world
Jeffrey K. Johnson and Carrie La Ferle

INTRODUCTION

It is claimed that the golden arches of McDonalds are a more recognizable symbol worldwide than the Christian cross (Schlosser 2002) and that Coca-Cola is the second most known word worldwide after 'OK' (Pendergrast 2000). Inarguably, one of the primary reasons that these products have gained such a broad acceptance is their use of advertising. Is this advertising helpful, though, and is the spread of mass culture good for the over seven billion people who inhabit the planet? Depending on the critic, advertising can be viewed as either a creator of economic opportunity or the purveyor of a legion of social ills (Hovland and Wolburg 2010; Jhally 1995; Pollay 1986; Rotzoll, Haefner and Hall 1996). In reality, the truth most likely lies somewhere between these two polar extremes.

However, a large portion of the comments regarding advertising have been negative. Pollay (1986) warns of the unintended effects of advertising leading to materialism, greed, dissatisfaction with self and general lifestyles that are detrimental to people and societies as a whole. Globally, these advertisement-induced changes are said to result in the loss of local values, culture, national identity, language and more (Frith and Mueller 2010; Jhally 1995). In fact, beyond the economic benefits of advertising (Naghshpour 2008), rarely do other potentially positive outcomes rise to the level of public discourse.

Therefore an article suggesting that globalization and the advertising that helps the process can be uniquely effective tools in providing positive global change and stability is important and timely. Beyond the economic benefits, it is argued that global advertising can encourage: 1) the enhanced growth of cultures through cultural exchange rather than simply being seen as a destroyer of culture; 2) peaceful relations and conflict resolution through common understanding versus the instigator of conflict; and 3) a shared culture assisting in the building of support systems and communities beyond simply benefiting its own self-serving purposes. Though these outcomes of global advertising surely have many critics, several of the negative reactions can be muted by an initial change in perspective regarding human nature and the historical development of nations.

Reflecting on the merits of negative commentary and reconfiguring how we frame the discussion provides industry professionals, researchers and students with a more balanced perspective from which to assess the effects of advertising in the globalization of cultures. A more balanced discourse can further enhance public policy decisions. Presenting alternative views using new theories to advertising and new perspectives about globalization can also work to highlight the benefits of such practices. Simultaneously, new research avenues may surface while the negative publicity related to the practice of global advertising may decrease.

REFLECTION AND RECONFIGURATION: PASSIVE OR ACTIVE

Consumers . . . Interdependence?

In recent years seemingly significant groundswells of voices have arisen to protest globalization and cultural interdependency (Frith and Mueller 2010; Mueller 2011). Although the most visible of these declarations was the protest of the World Trade Organization meetings in Seattle in 1999, much has been said or written about the 'new world order' before and since (Ellis 2001). The idea of multinational corporations expanding their markets into new countries and destroying local cultures has often become know as 'McDonaldization'; so named because of McDonalds' extension into over 117 countries serving more than 60 million customers and the repercussions that this is said to involve (aboutmcdonalds.com 2011). Critics claim that companies like McDonalds are responsible for many smaller countries' loss of language, culture and values (Mcdeath.com 2005). Not surprisingly, advertising receives the majority of the blame for spreading the corporate message and homogenizing societies. Concerns that advertisements are enticing foreign consumers to abandon their native culture and become part of a monolithic generic world (Rummel, Goodwin and Sheppard 1990) are often voiced.

However, these arguments hinge on two widely unquestioned assumptions regarding human nature and the historical development of nations. First, they assume that consumers are passive, with low self-efficacy, and will not seek out alternative messages; they will only listen to what is easily available and will conform to these effortlessly accessible points of view (Calfee 1998; Hovland and Wolburg 2010; Rotzoll, Haefner and Hall 1996; Sheehan 2004). Yet, if people are viewed as having a high level of self-efficacy, in other words, if they feel in control and active about their participation and intellect in making decisions, then arguments through this reconfiguration become much less valid (Arthur and Quester 2004).

Second, global advertising critics tend to suggest that most places in the world are divided into rigidly segmented societies with little outside contact. There is a general impression that the recent global business expansion is bringing places together (and not necessarily in a positive way) that have been divided throughout history (Howard-Hassmann 2005). This is a misreading of history. Inarguably, each society has its own unique culture and each of these should be cherished. However, these cultures have not formed within a vacuum and often they were developed as a result of trade and other encounters with outside cultures different from themselves. Very few cultures within the world have formed with little or no outside influence (Benton 1996).

One example of this is Italy; a nation that is very proud of its culture and whose citizens often protest modern day globalization (World Press 2001). Ironically, Italy has historically been a trading port and a society that has interwoven new ideas and notions with old customs. Many historians agree that the Italian Renaissance, an artistic, social and economic movement that revitalized fifteenth- and sixteenth-century Europe, was mainly owing to trade with the East that brought new ideas and ways of life (Jurdjevic 2001).

Additionally, Italians, who are so proud of their food, rarely acknowledge that one of the primary ingredients in many dishes, the tomato, is a North American import dating back to the Columbian exchange (Crosby 2003). Though these are minor examples, they illustrate how interconnected the world has been historically. This is not to contend that Italy, or any other society, does not have a unique and important culture but rather that few cultures developed in isolation (Cateora 2007). When McDonalds advertises in Italy, or any other country, and expands the eating habits of a society, it is in many ways only continuing a tradition of newness and rebirth via the free will and acceptance of the people.

ADVERTISING: ENHANCER OR DESTROYER OF CULTURE?

If we are to believe that the cultures of the world have been historically interconnected for hundreds, if not thousands, of years and that this cultural mixing is in some ways a natural force that happens without any plan or initiative; then should we not be concerned? Will cultural mixing not ring in an age in which one global culture dominates? Will one sterile prepackaged Orwellian lifestyle reign supreme to the detriment of individuality and uniqueness? Although no one can emphatically answer questions about the future, historically interconnectivity has proven to be a boon not a curse. The process is rarely painless when cultures interact, yet traditionally the result is generally beneficial for the majority.

In the mid-nineteenth century an English philosopher named Herbert Spencer applied Charles Darwin's evolutionary theory of natural selection to human social conditions. Spencer proposed that individuals and entire societies work within a 'survival of the fittest' framework in which the most exceptional would prosper. Much like Hegel's dialectic and Marx's class system, Spencer saw the world in a constant conflict, which produced both winners and losers by necessity (Claeys 2000). If Spencer's Social Darwinism can be extrapolated into a cultural context then we arrive at a system in which cultures fight for survival and superiority. The cultures that have the most to offer the greatest number of people develop broadly while others take a more secondary position. This does not mean the death of all cultures except for the most esteemed, though. Cultural Darwinism does not foresee one monolithic culture but rather promotes niche cultures that meet the needs of specific peoples. Things that are helpful and fulfilling are selected no matter where the culture originated. In this model a few widespread ideas, products and even cultures would be shared internationally but most countries would retain the traditions that were seen as valuable (Benton 1996).

International Cultural Darwinism can be illustrated by momentarily returning our focus to McDonalds. There are McDonalds restaurants in over 117 countries and the majority of these countries view fast food as non-traditional to their cultures (McDonalds 2011). Although many studies have been conducted that show McDonalds' negative effect on society, none could be found that proved that the restaurant chain caused people to stop eating traditional cuisine. Certainly McDonald's can have the propensity to change people's eating habits; any new food that was introduced would do that. The fast food chain's cuisine is a supplement, though, and local residents still eat valued national foods (Azaryahu 2000). In the Cultural Darwinism model McDonalds would be a new international culture that rises to a position of high visibility while the national meals retain their niche status and still remain important within the individual nation. In such an example, one can see that, although a global culture may develop, it will not destroy all of the other local cultures, but rather supplement most of them. Within the Social Darwinism model, advertising plays a dominant role in promoting new international cultures by providing facts about new ideas and ways of life. Advertising helps to offer choices that will create dialogues about what is important and what is changeable. Some concepts, values and traditions will change, but in the end the populous of active and participating consumers will decide what they want their culture to be; they will decide, not the multinational corporation (Benton 1996). And in fact, most McDonalds have adapted their food product offerings to better suit local tastes such as the Prosperity Burger in Malaysia and the Majaraja Mac made of Chicken in India and we are seeing this trend increase as we enter in to the second decade of the twenty-first century (de Mooij 2010; Mueller 2011).

ADVERTISING: CREATOR OF SOCIAL PROBLEMS OR CONFLICT REDUCER AND PEACE MAKER?

Although an international culture may not destroy the native cultures that it inhabits, is it not still dangerous because it creates new wants and desires that cause social problems? Is it not harmful to the citizenry to change age-old traditions on a whim? Will societies not face the ill-effects of heightened demand and consumption and will nations not war over natural resources needed to fulfill demand? Pulitzer Prize-winning author Thomas Friedman claims that just the opposite is true.

In his monograph *The Lexus and the Olive Tree* Friedman proposes a theory entitled 'The Golden Arches Theory of Conflict Prevention' in which he states that globalization of culture actually reduces conflict and increases understanding. As his prime example, Friedman has shown that no country with a McDonalds has ever fought a war against another country that also has a McDonalds. Although this has since come into question, the main point he asserts is still worthy in that mutual trade and common culture can result in shared values and ideas that make it far more difficult to go to war. Although it is not impossible to fight against someone with whom you have cultural ties, it is more difficult than if you shared nothing. In other words, according to Friedman international cultural sharing results in a more peaceful and productive planet (Friedman 2000).

Advertising plays a major role in this sharing of cultural bonds and thus providing interconnectivity to the world because it is the voice of the new culture. Advertising's place in society is to present information about new products, ideas and cultures. Not all of these ideas will be accepted and not all of them are good for society but the consumer will make that choice; advertising merely offers the information but it cannot force its acceptance (Calfee 1998). In Friedman's model of conflict prevention it is advertising that spreads the message of global understanding and shared cultures. In various countries in the world advertisements announce the arrival of culture choices that can possibly link together a variety of far-flung nations. If these new cultural paradigms are accepted then all of the places that acquire them share something in common. An example of this is a McDonalds advertising campaign that uses the advertising slogan, 'I'm loving it'. The ad campaign, launched in September 2003, is unique because it uses the same slogan in over 100 counties, but alters the local offerings, promotions and celebrities presented in the campaigns. In past campaigns McDonalds had used diverse slogans for different countries and areas of the world in order to be culturally relevant to each. The 'I'm loving it' campaign acknowledges that, on some level, there is a shared global culture of McDonalds and the understanding that one simple slogan might appeal to those who culturally embrace McDonalds no matter what their nationality (ABC13 2003). In this way, advertising has provided a cultural statement that usurps nationalism and embraces globalism. Although, the three-word slogan's main task is to sell McDonalds' products it also becomes a statement in international sharing and cooperation that embraces globalization that in Friedman's view will also help to promote peace and understanding (Friedman 2000).

A strong case can be made that globalism and the advertising that supports it is a positive force in society. It can provide long-term stability, peaceful relations and cultural understanding. Yet many critics lambaste the creation of an international culture. In fact, it seems to be far easier to find articles that assess the negative aspects than the positive ones. Certainly, many of the critics of global culture have valid concerns and any changes that can be made to make the planet stronger and healthier should be considered. Undoubtedly, though, a significant number of the complaints come from the sheer fact that any kind of change is unsettling to society as a whole. To a large amount of people any kind of newness, no matter how promising, is undesirable because it requires a new mental paradigm and a departure from what is known and safe (Ni Aolain 2005).

Perhaps the most telling historical example is that of the invention of the printing press in Europe. The Chinese had created their own version of the printing press centuries before but Johannes Gutenberg is generally credited with building the first European printing press in 1440. Before the printing press was developed books were copied by hand and were a luxury that only the wealthiest members of society could afford. The invention of mass printing meant that many more books could be produced, and because of this the literacy level rose significantly and education became a more attainable and valued commodity. Printing presses soon spread across Europe and the nations were intrinsically linked through this new era of knowledge. To most twenty-first-century Americans this merely seems like the natural progression of Western society; knowledge increases, it is shared and citizens decide if it is desirable enough to alter their lives with it. In truth, though, many criticized the printing press because it rearranged the society's strata and because of mass uncertainty about its long-term effects. To most people alive today the mass publication of literature is unquestionably a positive thing, but this viewpoint is only in retrospect (Kallen 2001). In the fifteenth and sixteenth centuries such things were not so obvious. Much like the printing press spread literacy and cultural communication, advertising allows for consumer literacy and global cultural contact. Also reminiscent of the earlier era, advertisements promote a new lifestyle that encourages change and promises a bright but more uncertain future. As with any major change, there will be critics who are not ready to take the leap into a new mental and cultural paradigm (Samuelson 2001) but there are also opportunities to be reaped.

ADVERTISING: THE COEXISTENCE OF SELF-SERVING BEHAVIOR AND SOCIAL BENEFITS?

Many critics of advertising will argue that it is by definition a selfish enterprise. They claim that advertising tries to make people buy things that they do not need or cannot afford (Pollay 1986; Sheehan 2004). Whether advertising acts as a mirror or a moulder of society can be argued, but critics are right when they claim that advertising's fundamental purpose is to sell products. Just because this is the desired outcome does not mean that advertising does not benefit society, though. Because advertising wishes to ingratiate its company to the general public it often has to become part of the community and sometimes offers assistance to needy individuals or institutions. This means that advertisers develop ways to help the local society and, although these actions are not entirely for altruistic reasons, the outcome remains the same (Rotzoll 1996).

Cause-related marketing (CRM) initiatives started in the U.S. in the 1980s (Wall 1984) and today are becoming quite standard practices, with American companies spending an estimated $1.51 billion in 2009 to support causes (Cause Marketing Forum 2009). CRM efforts are growing in popularity owing to their ability to build relationships with consumers while garnering goodwill for socially responsible behavior (Cui, Trent, Sullivan and Matiru 2003; Lafferty and Edmondson 2009; Polyorat and Alden 2005).

Globally, McDonalds is once again an excellent example of community building through a social cause and charitable giving. The best known of McDonalds' social cause participation is the Ronald McDonald House programme that provides services to fulfill a variety of medical and educational needs. Established in 1974 the charity has given hundreds of millions of dollars in assistance through chapters in 52 countries (Ronald McDonald House 2011). Advertising plays a key role in the development of this charitable entity because it is doubtful that the organization would exist if not for the advertising that promoted it.

The Ronald McDonald House programme has given a substantial amount of money to the world community but it only exists because it promotes McDonalds. It is not surprising that it has been featured prominently in advertising for years because the two have a symbiotic relationship and the charity, in reality, is an advertisement for the restaurant. This does not mean that the cause is any less desirable or competent but it means that advertising has done something mutually beneficial for both the company and for society (Porter 2001). Another potential social benefit of globalization and the advertising that helps foster a global culture is the lesser discussed concept of 'Third Places'.

ADVERTISING: THE STANDARDIZATION OF THIRD PLACES HURTING OR ENHANCING COMMUNITIES?

It is easy to understand how company-sponsored causes and charitable foundations as well as the advertising that supports them benefit society. What is harder to understand are the advantageous societal lifestyle changes that develop because of advertising's promotional sway. One of these changes is the standardization of places of leisure and comfort. In the mid 1990s, sociologist Ray Oldenburg decried the estrangement of post-World War II life and asserted that society was losing its sense of community. In order to prove this theory he developed the idea of the 'third place' which he defined as 'a generic designation for a great variety of public places that host the regular, voluntary, informal, and happily anticipated gatherings of individuals beyond the realms of work and home' (Oldenburg 1999, p. 16).

Third places are typically the small neighbourhood meeting places that provide a sense of structure and community. Often third places are corner pubs or taverns where friends meet to watch sports and chat, local barbershops that serve as a venue for the exchange of neighbourhood gossip, or 'mom and pop' diners that not only serve food but also provide a physical representation of local values and culture. These third places are generally seen as different from chain stores because they are local and are often considered more authentic. In the world of television the 'Cheers' bar in the sitcom of the same name and the 'Central Perk' coffee house in *Friends* are excellent examples of third places. In Oldenburg's view third places are essential because they provide a place where community bonds can be developed and strengthened and where democracy can be demonstrated on a grassroots level. People meet with one another, share experiences and develop bonds that promote peace, understanding and neighbourliness. He warns, though, that the urban sprawl of post-war suburbia and the growth of the nuclear family have helped to diminish third places to the detriment of society. In other words, if people living in neighbourhoods stop gathering socially then the traditional meaning of a neighbourhood will cease to exist. All that will remain is a group of isolated tenants with no common culture or understanding (Oldenburg 1999).

When Oldenburg and other sociologists write of the death of the third place they fail to take into account the corporatization of the concept. Since the early 1990s there has been a perceivable trend in marketing and advertising to present certain types of business as homey, comfortable and relaxing. Some stores and restaurants are created and marketed with the idea that customers are encouraged to stay for long periods of time, to socialize and relax. These businesses are becoming third places and are often the equivalent of what the local pub was for former generations (Schultz 1999). One of the prime examples of this is the Seattle-based coffee-giant Starbucks, which is well known for its comfortable chairs and open invitation to relax in the store.

Starbucks is performing a valuable service by encouraging people to leave their homes, socialize and use the coffee house as their third place. One of the main reasons that Starbucks is so popular as a third place is that it is consistently clean and safe and the product always conforms to a standard that makes every Starbucks nearly the same (Golway 2005). Even though many Starbucks locations have differences, when a person walks into one of the coffee houses he/she knows what to expect and this comfort level makes the experience very appealing. Historian Brent Simon claims, 'it's a new public space where people can be with each other. It's the corner bar of the 21st century' (Lubrano 2004). It is not just a corner bar; it is the corner bar located in over 17 000 places in 55 countries world-wide (Starbucks 2011). No matter which Starbucks one goes to, the social experience will be replicated as closely as possible and, although everyone will not always know the customer's name, no matter which location one visits she can have her favourite drink and meet people who are looking to socialize. For example, a businessperson could take a trip across Asia, visiting such vastly different places as China, Japan, South Korea, Hong Kong, Taiwan and Thailand, and could sit on an overstuffed sofa, drink a favourite beverage and people-watch in a Starbucks in every country (Starbucks 2011). Although Starbucks serves as a poor substitute for local indigenous culture, it does allow the business traveller to exit her hotel room and socialize in a safe, clean and non-threatening place. She will also have a chance to meet people that value the same things she does and to feel comfortable with her surroundings. In providing such a space, corporations have invented and marketed the idea of an international third place, and society is often the better for it. Some social scientists mourn the death of the third place but a new corporate version of it has been created.

Businesses that market themselves as neo-third places wish to convey a message of familiarity, safety and mass appeal. What they do not want is to be seen as a corporate entity. For third places to be authentic they must be inviting, recognizable and well thought of, but they cannot be plastic and sterile. In other words, advertisers and marketers are trying to produce a non-formulaic formula that allows a chain of restaurants or stores to make each location similar enough to be homey and non-threatening but unique enough to be part of the community. This is important on a global scale because it provides corporate chains the opportunity to embrace local communities and to meld international and native cultures. This means that a network of global third places can be created and propagated that provides the stability of a corporate chain with the connections to the local community that a small business would provide. This mixture of international and local could create an end product that meets the needs of more people and creates a hybrid culture that is neither global nor indigenous but the best of both (Shultz 1999).

In order to expand this new mixed culture advertisers market types of businesses that appeal to mass segments of the population. It appears that one of the most popular types of international third place is restaurants. Because meals are generally viewed as domestic activity, advertisers often try to link eating establishments with concepts of home and community. Two examples of this advertising strategy are advertising for Applebee's and Olive Garden in which the eateries are proclaimed to be part of the neighbourhood or like home. Applebee's, which has almost 2000 restaurants in 15 countries, has a current slogan of, 'There's No Place Like The Neighborhood' and its website promotes that 'the neighborhood wall in every Applebee's celebrates local life'. This refers to the wall at each Applebee's that promotes local people and institutions (Applebee's 2011). The chain has also aired television commercials that promote it as a member of the community. In one ad an Applebee's stays open late in order to feed a local high school football team that has lost the championship game, thus proving that the restaurant is a part of the community and shares its values (Applebee's Ad 2005). The Olive Garden's promotional phrase is, 'When you're here you're Family' and uses the image of the customer being part of the close-knit Italian family that is the restaurant.

In television ads customers are shown laughing and enjoying themselves in an at-home-like atmosphere, which suggests that not only is the Olive Garden a part of the local community but by eating there one can also be part of the restaurant's family and community (Olive Garden 2011). Through advertising, both restaurants draw nearer to the local community while alternatively creating pseudo-communities. In doing so, both companies create new cultures and identities and cause a paradigm shift as to how authentic culture is viewed. As corporate and local cultures merge, the word 'authentic' loses its former meaning and a new culture is born, although, in the end, it is the people who decide what will be accepted, what changed and what will remain the same.

DISCUSSION

Global cultural exchange, and the advertising that encourages it, is a historical phenomenon that at its best encourages a more secure and stable society and promotes better social interactions. Globalization and the advertising that supports it can lead to: 1) enhanced growth of cultures; 2) peaceful relations through economic interdependence and nurturing familiarity; and 3) the establishment of an international community focused on building shared support systems and stronger communities. In the end, cultural globalization is capable of creating positive long-lasting change. Many societies have been historically interconnected and this cultural sharing has created new ideas and ways of life that have actually enhanced the local cultures. Many critics contend that advertisers destroy cultures but in reality they are merely a part of an interconnected world. Advertisements provide a service by making information available that promotes cultural links that make the world more stable and secure (Calfee 1998; Rotzoll, Haefner and Hall 1996: Sheehan 2004). Advertising also creates proactive change by partnering with causes or marketing corporate charities and helping to produce global third places.

Although this article has primarily concerned itself with the positive impacts, it should be noted that not all of the effects of cultural globalization, and the advertising that supports it, are constructive. The list of negatives that surrounds globalization is lengthy and alarming and no one is capable of saying that these changes, as with any in life, are always positive. What should be understood is that a balanced discussion is important and that positive long-term changes can benefit the majority of people and co-exist with criticism. Albeit, it is true that in the short term the process can be potentially destructive and hurtful. As with any enterprise, there will be winners and losers, but, overall, global cultural exchange will benefit the greater good. This fact will offer little solace to those who are displaced by the growing movement but every part of our lives is a product of some cultural decision that benefited the majority but harmed a selected few (Howard-Hassmann 2005).

IMPLICATIONS . . .

The balance between the positive and negative effects of a global society is a constant concern for international advertisers now, and will remain so for the foreseeable future. The implications of social globalization are vast and extremely important to the advertising community, just as they are to the world as a whole. The world market is growing in importance and how advertisers operate within it has become far more sensitive and sophisticated. In times past there has been a certain arrogance by some American companies; American culture was viewed by many of those selling it as superior socially and its products and traditions would sell abroad in the same ways that they did in their home markets (Hassman 2005). Some advertisers conducted insufficient research in foreign markets and launched disastrous products and campaigns because of it. Classic examples of incompetent international ads are: a Pepsi slogan in Taiwan, 'Come alive with the Pepsi Generation', was mistranslated as 'Pepsi will bring your ancestors back from the dead'. Puffs was launched in Germany and then it was revealed that 'puff' in German is slang for 'whorehouse'. Perdue Chicken's slogan, 'It takes a tough man to make a tender chicken', was mistranslated as 'It takes a hard man to make a chicken aroused' (Sivulaka 1998, p. 364). This type of hubris and lack of cultural sensitivity will not be tolerated in the new global culture. American corporations and advertisers can no longer afford not to listen to the wants and needs of a specific international market.

As advertisers become more aware of local needs in global marketing, consumers in turn begin to demand more from those wishing to sell their wares. Individuals trying to strike the proper balance between indigenous culture and global culture will require that companies and advertisers give them the proper mixture of the two. Some places may have a bigger appetite for global culture, while others only want the basics, and each society is intrinsically unique and must be treated as such. Consumers will insist that advertisers respect their cultural norms but offer them something new and enticing. This balance is the heart of social globalization and consumers will stipulate that it be respected and understood. In many ways globalization is merely a modern reflection of Adam Smith's notion of the

Invisible Hand. Consumers and societies will benefit because they make choices that are advantageous. The difference is that now the choices are much more numerous and the effects are global. As a middle class rises in China, India and many parts of the world, consumers in Beijing and New Delhi gain the market importance that their 'Western' brethren have come to expect. This influence will change cultures, individuals and societies in startling, wondrous and terrifying new ways (Howard-Hassmann 2005).

If a writer in 1911 had been asked to predict the social global trends of the next hundred years he would have failed miserably, just as any writer of today will do if he attempts the same task. The unpredictability of the world will undoubtedly make a fool of any current prognosticator as it did his ancestral brethren. Nonetheless, it seems fairly certain that China and India will continue to grow as influential global powers within the next few decades. At the moment about one out of three citizens of the world is from one of these two countries. China is growing economically at a staggering rate and India is developing a large middle class. The United States and other 'Western' countries are outsourcing jobs and the balance of power appears to be shifting (Friedman 2005). As these countries are poised on the brink of global leadership and power one must ask the question, what does this mean for the global society? Scores of pundits debate what China's and India's apparent rise will mean to social globalization and there are as many answers as there are people. One thing is fairly certain: things will change. Although this sounds nebulous and trite, it is an almost certain prediction. Things will change in the coming century and the power bases will shift. No one knows if that is good or bad, but it is necessary. Most likely, global culture will grow and prosper because it provides so much that so many want. Chances are the United States will no longer set the world's cultural standard but will still be a major player within the system. Chinese culture may be the most desirable within 50 years or maybe some other country that no one is thinking about will rise in importance. In the long term, life will get better for more people because globalization will give a voice to many people who have never had one before. In the end, that is all that social globalization really is; a way to provide the populations of the world with a stake in their own destinies. It is not really economics or sales, those are only means to an end, but rather it is a movement towards freedom. The freedom for individuals to choose how they will live their lives.

REFERENCES

30 Seconds Ads (2001), 'Pepsi Ad # One', available at http://www.30sec.net/EN-Soft.htm (accessed 8 March 2005).

ABC13 (2003), 'McDonalds Launches New Advertising Slogan', available at http://abclocal.go.com/ktrk/business/90203_APbusiness_mcdonalds.html (accessed 4 April 2005).

Ackerberg, D. (2003),'Advertising, Learning, and Consumer Choice in Experienced Good Markets: An Empirical Examination', *International Economic Review*, **44** (3), 1007–41.

Applebee's (2011), 'There's No Place Like the Neighborhood', available at http://www.applebees.com (accessed 19 February 2011).

Applebee's Ad (2005), 'Television', 7 April 2005.

Arthur, D. and P. Quester (2004), 'Who's Afraid of That Ad? Applying Segmentation to the Protection Motivation Model', *Psychology & Marketing*, **21** (9), 671.

Azaryahu, M. (2000), 'The Golden Arches of McDonald's: On the "Americanization" of Israel', *Israel Studies*, **5** (1), 41–64.

Benton, L. (1996), 'From the World-Systems Perspective to Institutional World History: Culture and Economy in Global Theory', *Journal of World History*, **7** (2), 261–95.

Bairner, A. (ed.) (2001), *Sport, Nationalism and Globalization: European and North American Perspectives*, Buffalo: State University of New York.

Calfee, J. (1998), 'How Advertising Informs to Our Benefit', *Consumers' Research*, **4**, 13–18.

Cateora, Philip and John Graham (eds) (2007), *International Marketing*, New York McGraw-Hill.

Cause Marketing Forum (2009), 'The Growth of Cause Marketing', available at http://www.causemarketingforum.com/page.asp?ID=188 (accessed 10 February 2005).

Claeys, G. (2000), 'The "Survival of the Fittest" and the Origins of Social Darwinism', *Journal of the History of Ideas*, **61** (2), 223–40.

Crosby, Alfred W. (2003), *The Columbian Exchange*, West Port, CO: Praeger.

Cui Y., E.S. Trent, P.M. Sullivan and G.N. Matiru (2003), 'Cause Related Marketing: How Generation Y Responds', *International Journal of Retail and Distribution Management*, *31*(6/7), 310–22.

de Mooij, Marieke K. (2010), *Global Marketing and Advertising: Understanding Cultural Paradoxes* (3rd edn), Thousand Oaks, CA: Sage Publications, Inc.

Ellis, R. (2001), 'Globalizing the Resistance and Bringing it Back Home', *Social Anarchism*, **1** (12), 11.

FIFA World Cup (2005), 'World Cup 2002', available at fifaworldcup.com (accessed 27 March 2005).

Freidman, T. (ed.) (2000), *Lexus and the Olive Tree*, New York: Anchor Books.

Frith, Katerine T. and Barbara Mueller (eds) (2010), *Advertising and Societies: Global Issues*, New York: Peter Lang.

Garden, O. (2005), 'When You're Here You're Family', available at http://www.olivegarden.com (accessed 12 April 2005).

Golway, T. (2005), 'Like It or Not, the Postmodern Malt Shop', *New York Times*, **12** (15), A16.

Holson, L. (2005), 'The Feng Shui Kingdom', *New York Times*, **4** (25), B1.

Hovland, Roxanne and Joyce M. Wolburg (2010), *Advertising, Society, and Consumer Culture*, Armonk, NY: M.E. Sharpe.

Howard-Hassmann, R. (2005), 'The Second Great Transformation: Human Rights Leapfrogging in the Era of Globalization', *Human Rights Quarterly*, **27** (1), 1–40.

Jurdjevic, M. (2001), 'Virtue, Commerce, and the Enduring Florentine Republican Moment: Reintegrating Italy into the Atlantic Republican Debate', *Journal of the History of Ideas*, **62** (4), 721–43.

Kallen, S. (ed.) (2001), *The 1400s*, San Diego, CA: Greenhaven Press.

Kellert, S. (1996), 'Science and Literature and Philosophy: The Case of Chaos Theory and Deconstruction', *Configurations*, **4** (2), 215–32.

Lafferty, B.A. and D.R. Edmondson (2009), 'Portraying the Cause Instead of the Brand in Cause-Related Marketing Ads: Does It Really Matter?' *Journal of Marketing Theory and Practice*, *17*(2), 129–43.

Lubrano, A. (2004), 'Just the Place for People to Perk Up?' available at http://www.philly. com/mld/philly/entertainment/10426584.htm (accessed 10 April 2005).

Martin, A. and J. Oliva (2001), 'Teaching Children about Money: Applications of Social Learning and Cognitive Learning Development Theories', *Journal of Family and Consumer Sciences*, **93** (2), 26–30.

McDeath (2005), 'McLibel', available at www.mcdeath.com (accessed 21 March 2005).

McDonald's (2011), 'About McDonald's', available at http://www.aboutmcdonalds.com/ mcd/ our_company.html (accessed 19 February 2011).

McSpotlight (2005), 'Stop the Presses', available at www.mcspotlight.com (accessed 19 March 2005).

Moschis, G. (1981), 'Patterns of Consumer Learning', *Academy of Marketing Science Journal*, **9** (2), 110–27.

Mueller, Barbara (ed.) (2011), *Dynamics in International Advertising*, New York: Lang Publishing.

Naghshpour, S. (2008), 'Globalization: Is it Good or Bad?' *Globalization*, **7** (2), 5.

Ni Aolain, F. (2005), 'The Paradox of Transition in Conflicted Democracies', *Human Rights Quarterly*, **27** (1), 172–213.

Oldenburg, R. (ed.) (1999), *The Great Good Place: Cafes, Coffee Shops, Bookstores, Bars, Hair Salons, and Other Hangouts at the Heart of a Community*, New York: Marlowe and Company.

Olive Garden (2011), 'When You're Here You're Family', available at http://www. olivegarden.com (accessed 19 February 2011).

Phillips, Barbara J. (1997), 'In Defense of Advertising: A Social Perspective', *Journal of Business Ethics*, **16**, 109–18.

Pendergrast, M. (ed.) (2000), *For God, Country, and Coca-Cola: The Definitive History of the Great American Soft Drink and the Company that Makes It*, New York: Basic Books.

Pollay, R. (1986), 'The Distorted Mirror: Reflections on the Unintended Consequences of Advertising', *Journal of Marketing*, **50** (2), 18–36.

Polyorat, Kawpong and Dana L. Alden (2005), 'Self-Construal and Need-For-Cognition Effects on Brand Attitudes and Purchase Intentions in Response to Comparative Advertising in Thailand and the United States', *Journal of Advertising*, **34** (1), 37–48.

Porter, D. (2001), 'Interview with Doug Porter', *Advertising & Society Review*, **2** (2), 12–21.

Ronald McDonald House (2011) 'Ronald McDonald House Charities', available at http:// www.rmhc.org (accessed 19 February 2011).

Rotzoll, K., J. Haefner and S. Hall (1996), 'Helpful Perspectives on Advertising as an Institution', in Rotzoll, Haefner and Hall (eds), *Advertising in Contemporary Society*, University of Illinois Press, pp. 57–89.

Plummet, J. (1978), 'A Theoretical View of Advertising Communication', in S. Britt and H. Boyd (eds), *Marketing Management and Administrative Action*, New York: McGraw-Hill, pp. 376–82.

Rummel, A., M. Goodwin and M. Shepherd (1990), 'Self-Efficacy and Stereotyping in Advertising: Should Consumers Want a Change?' *International Journal of Advertising*, **9** (4), 308–17.

Samuelson, R. (ed.) (2001), *Untruth: Why the Conventional Wisdom is (Almost Always) Wrong*, New York: Random House.

Schlosser, E. (ed.) (2002), *Fast Food Nation: The Dark Side of the All-American Meal*, New York: Perennial, p. 4.

Sheehan, K. (ed.) (2004), *Controversies in Contemporary Advertising*, Thousand Oaks, CA: Sage Publications.

Shultz, H. (ed.) (1999), *Pour Your Heart Into It: How Starbucks Built a Company One Cup At a Time*, Boston: Hyperion.

Sivulka, J. (ed.) (1998), *Soap, Sex, and Cigarettes*, Detroit: Wadsworth, p. 364.

Snipes, R., M. LaTour and S. Bliss (1999), 'A Model of the Effects of Self-efficacy on the

Perceived Ethicality and Performance of Fear Appeals in Advertising', *Journal of Business Ethics*, **19** (3), 273–86.

Starbucks (2011), 'Starbucks Company Profile', available at http://assets.starbucks.com/assets/aboutuscompanyprofileq12011final13111.pdf (accessed 19 February 2011).

Steward, I. (ed.) (2002), *Does God Play Dice? The Mathematics of Chaos*, New York: Blackwell.

Wall, Wendy L. (1987), 'Helping Hands: Companies Change the Ways They Make Charitable Donations – "Enlightened Self-Interest" is Used in Selecting Donees; Eyeing Cash Substitutes – Failure of a Worthy Cause', *Wall Street Journal (Eastern edition)*, New York, June 21, 1.

World Press (2001), 'A Death in Genoa', available at http://www.worldpress.org/Europe/236.cfm (accessed 17 March 2005).

20 Transnational trust in advertising media
Martin Eisend and Silke Knoll

INTRODUCTION

It is common knowledge amongst marketers that people have a tendency to mistrust advertising (Calfee and Ringold 1994; Fry and McDougall 1974). Marketers have reasons to be concerned about mistrust in advertising, because the lack of trust harms the persuasiveness of messages conveyed by media and, as a result of this, advertising effectiveness. Previous research has shown that trust in advertising varies over several communication channels. Understanding why consumers (mis-)trust advertising media can help marketers improve advertising effectiveness by choosing the most appropriate channel for communicating with consumers.

In this chapter, we discuss the concept and measurement of trust in advertising media and review previous research on antecedents and consequences of trust in advertising media. We further present empirical results that show how trust in different advertising media depends on and varies between clusters of cultural societies, together with how particular cultural values and practices are related to trust in advertising media. The findings are particularly interesting for international advertising research and the practice of international media choice strategies.

DEFINING TRUST IN ADVERTISING MEDIA

Anderson and Weitz (1989, p. 312) define trust in general as 'one party's belief that its needs will be fulfilled in the future by actions undertaken by the other party'. Trust in advertising is defined by Soh, Reid and King (2009, p. 86) as 'confidence that advertising is a reliable source of product/ service information and willingness to act on the basis of information conveyed by advertising'. Apparently, trust plays a major role when advertising functions as an information source for consumers, that is, when advertising informs consumers about goods and services that are offered by companies and when information conveyed by advertising helps consumers to make better purchase decisions. Only if consumers trust advertising to perform effectively as an information source is advertising able to inform them.

Information sources differ in terms of how much consumers trust them. Such variation in trust is also found between different advertising media (such as newspapers, television, the Internet) that serve as information sources for consumers (Soh, Reid and King 2007). One distinction between different advertising media became a crucial one for advertisers during the recent years: trust towards traditional advertising media (print, TV) and trust towards online advertising media. Soh, Reid and King (2007) showed in their study that consumers trust Internet advertising in general less than traditional advertising media (TV, radio, newspapers and magazines) for which they found no significant differences in trust across the media types. Similar results are provided by Menon, Deshpande, Perri and Zinkhan (2002) and Huh, DeLorme and Reid (2005). They show, however, that there is a positive correlation between trust in information from traditional media and trust in information provided by online media.

Why do consumers show less trust towards online advertising media compared to traditional advertising media? Okazaki, Katsukura and Nishiyama (2007) argue that consumers exhibit mistrust more strongly towards online media compared to traditional advertising media, since content in online media is less liable to governmental or ethical regulation.

A related stream of research that is quite prominent in media studies refers to media credibility as perceptions of believability and trustworthiness of a medium (Kiousis 2001). These studies focus on the role of different media as news channels, not necessarily as advertising channels. Media credibility is a construct closely related to trust in advertising media, but the constructs are not the same. Researchers agree that trust results from trustworthiness (Moorman, Deshpandé and Zaltman 1993). Trustworthiness, defined as the belief that a source (such as particular news media) provides information honestly without the purpose of manipulation or deception (Ohanian 1991), is an important dimension of source credibility next to source competence (Hovland, Janis and Kelley 1953; Ohanian 1990). Hence, source credibility is an antecedent of trust; only if you believe a source can you trust that source (Andaleeb and Anwaar 1996). As for trust in advertising and advertising credibility, Soh, Reid and King (2007, p. 460) argue accordingly that 'credibility may be associated with trust, but may not be sufficient in itself to indicate the nature and scope of trust in advertising'.

MEASURING TRUST IN ADVERTISING MEDIA

Trust in advertising (media) is oftentimes measured with single-item scales (e.g., Menon, Deshpande, Perri and Zinkhan 2002). This is a common approach for studies that compare trust across different media types.

Recently, Soh, Reid and King (2009) have proposed trust as a multi-dimensional construct and have developed a multi-item scale to measure trust in advertising, referring to existing conceptualizations of trust and past research on trust. The authors identify four dimensions of trust in advertising: (1) consumer perceptions of reliability (cognitive dimension); (2) consumer perceptions of the usefulness of advertising (cognitive dimension); (3) consumer affect related to advertising (emotional dimension); and (4) consumer willingness to rely on advertising for decision making (behavioral dimension). The authors develop and validate a 20-item adtrust scale that distinguishes between these four dimensions. Considering trust in different advertising media, Soh, Reid and King (2007) show that their adtrust scale can be applied separately to each medium (TV, radio, newspapers, magazines, and the Internet).

EFFECTS OF TRUST IN ADVERTISING MEDIA

Effects of trust in advertising media have been investigated only sparsely in marketing literature, although there is a long tradition of evidence that persuasion depends on trust (Hovland, Janis and Kelley 1953; Petty and Cacioppo 1986) and trust is an important antecedent of advertising effectiveness (Lutz 1985; MacKenzie and Lutz 1989). Trust correlates with information acceptance, liking, and other information processing constructs (Menon, Deshpande, Zinkhan and Perri 2004).

Menon, Deshpande, Perri and Zinkhan (2002) investigate, in their study, consumers' trust in online prescription drug information and its influence on information search behavior. The authors collected data though 1200 telephone interviews in the United States. They show that trust in drug information from traditional advertising has a positive influence on consumers' trust in drug information from online media. Furthermore, a higher level of trust in online media enhances Internet usage for information search after exposure to prescription drug advertising. Okazaki, Katsukura and Nishiyama (2007) were looking at a mobile advertising campaign in Japan to examine the role of trust in improving attitudes towards and recall of the mobile campaign. A total of 3234 mobile users participated in their survey. Findings show that trust in mobile advertising has a strong impact on attitude toward mobile advertising. In addition, they found that attitude toward mobile advertising is an important antecedent for attitude toward the brand that, in turn, affects recall.

ANTECEDENTS OF TRUST IN ADVERTISING MEDIA

As for antecedents in trust, previous studies have mainly investigated whether trust in different advertising media depends on demographic variables. There are several studies that come up with rather mixed results.

A couple of studies have focused on trust in advertising media as a source for health information. In two nationwide surveys, Gönül, Carter and Wind (2000) have investigated 771 respondents. Their results show that consumers who have been sick recently, older consumers, and more educated consumers are significantly more likely to trust in information given by physicians instead of prescription drug advertising. These results are in line with a study by Menon, Deshpande, Perri and Zinkhan (2002) who found that health status was the only demographic variable predicting trust in online drug information. Healthy consumers exhibit more trust in prescription drug information on the Internet compared to unhealthy consumers. Unhealthy consumers exhibit more trust in information provided by health care professionals, who know about their specific health situation. Consumers with negative opinions toward drug safety are more likely to search online for additional information compared to consumers who have a more positive opinion of drug safety. Except for race, Menon, Deshpande, Zinkhan and Perri (2004) could not support any effect of demographic variables on trust in advertising media considering health information. Huh, DeLorme and Reid (2005) could not find any relationship between trust in online prescription drug information and demographic variables at all. Their study is based on data from 472 respondents in the United States.

Boush, Kim, Kahle and Batra (1993) examine personality variables as correlates of trust in advertising media. The authors obtained data from 663 members of a national panel that is representative for the United States. They show that consumer conformity is positively related to trust in advertising as well as to trust in non-business sources (for example, TV news, friends and relatives). The highest correlations with conformity are found for trust in television advertising and trust in radio advertising compared to other media types. In line with Soh, Reid and King (2007) they show that trust in advertising is negatively related to education level.

Based on data of 122 college students participating in a controlled simulation study, Yoon (2002) found that familiarity and prior satisfaction with e-commerce enhance trust in online media. Aiken and Boush (2006) observe a curvilinear relationship between online experience and consumer trust. The authors assume that at higher levels of online experience, trust decreases, because knowledge about privacy and security problems increases.

Soh, Reid and King (2007) assumed that trust in different advertising media varies by consumer demographics. Their sample consists of 600 adults randomly drawn from the staff of a state university in the United States. The results reveal that variation in consumer trust across different advertising media is associated with education and income, but not with age and gender. Consumers with lower education levels show higher trust in advertising media than consumers with higher education levels. Low-income consumers exhibit more trust in television and newspaper advertising than in magazine and radio advertising. High-income consumers trust radio and magazine advertising more than television and newspaper advertising. While the Internet is the advertising medium least trusted by high- and moderate-income consumers, it is the third most trusted medium (out of five media types) amongst low-income consumers.

All in all these results indicate mixed results and a rather weak impact of individual variables on consumers' trust in advertising media. As there is apparently variation in consumer trust in different advertising media, this might be explained by other variables on an aggregate level, such as cultural values. Using cultural values as predictors seems particularly interesting for international advertising research and practice. A recent study by Möller and Eisend (2010) showed that cultural values are an important antecedent in explaining advertising effectiveness on a national-culture level; cultural values explained considerably more variance than antecedents on the individual level such as age, gender, or media experience. The relationship between cultural values, media use and trust in media is also emphasized by the notion that media are important transmitters for cultural values. Therefore cultural orientation is very likely to influence media preference and also trust in media. Whether trust in different advertising media depends on cultural values has not been investigated, though.

CULTURAL INFLUENCES ON TRUST IN ADVERTISING MEDIA

In order to investigate the cultural influence on trust in advertising media, we use data from the GLOBE project. Countries included in the GLOBE study were grouped by Gupta and Hanges (2004) into a set of ten regional clusters as a result of a detailed conceptual and empirical process, using both cultural practices and nine values that were found by the GLOBE project. Applying discriminant analysis on a set of variables derived from the extant literature on country clusters, Gupta and

Hanges (2004) could support the proposed ten regional clusters and their differentiability. Within each of the ten regional clusters, there are some generalizations that can be made regarding societal cultures. Based on these cultural homogenous groups, we apply a transnational perspective in this study.

A transnational perspective provides an alternative to the dichotomy of standardization versus localization research in the international advertising literature, that is, the question whether advertising strategies and executions should be standardized across national markets or localized to individual national markets. While strategies are often standardized, executions are oftentimes localized (Taylor 2002). Previous research has focused on individual countries to investigate issues of standardization versus localization. Using transnational segments of countries provides another perspective to the research stream. Using clusters of countries instead of single countries seems a particular fruitful approach to investigate trust in advertising media for a simple reason: most of the countries within a cluster share one (or two) common languages (such as Arabic in the Middle East cluster, Spanish and Portuguese in the Latin America cluster, German in the Germanic Europe cluster, and English in the Anglo cluster) and, therefore, media within one cluster can potentially reach all consumers within that cluster, resulting in similarities of media usage patterns within a cluster. This is further supported by the globalization of media culture, driven by globalized online media or transnational TV channels such as MTV. In light of these arguments we ask the following research question:

> RQ 1: (How) does trust in different advertising media, in particular trust in traditional media versus online advertising media, differ across regional clusters?

CULTURAL VALUES AND PRACTICES AS DRIVERS OF TRUST IN ADVERTISING MEDIA

The GLOBE study has identified nine core dimensions of culture. These dimensions (in alphabetical order) and their definitions as described in the literature are as follows (House, Hanges, Javidan, Dorfman and Gupta 2004; House, Quigley and de Luque 2010):

- Assertiveness: The degree to which members in a society are assertive, confrontational or aggressive in social relationships.
- Future orientation: The degree to which individuals in organizations

or societies engage in future-orientated behaviors such as planning, investing in the future and delaying individual or collective gratification.

- Gender egalitarianism: The degree to which a society minimizes gender role differences while promoting gender equality.
- Humane orientation: The degree to which members in a society encourage and reward individuals for being fair, altruistic, friendly, generous, caring, and kind to others.
- In-group collectivism: The degree to which individuals express pride, loyalty, and cohesiveness in their organizations or families.
- Institutional collectivism: The degree to which organizational and societal institutional practices encourage and reward the collective distribution of resources and collective action.
- Performance orientation: The degree to which an organization or society encourages and rewards members for performance improvement and excellence.
- Power distance: The degree to which members of a society expect and agree that power should be stratified and concentrated at higher levels of an organization or government.
- Uncertainty avoidance: The extent to which members of a society seek certainty in their environment by relying on established social norms, rituals, and bureaucratic practices.

GLOBE data comprise measures for both cultural practices ("what is/are common behaviors or actions within a culture") and values ("what should be common behaviors and actions within a culture"). The GLOBE study found that societal practices and values are not always positively related; actually, seven of nine dimensions exhibit even significant negative correlations between practices and values. That is, societies that exhibit high practices wish to exhibit fewer of those practices, and societies that exhibit low practices wish to exhibit more of those practices.

House, Quigley and de Luque (2010) suggested that cultural practices and values might influence consumers in a different way and that practices and values are likely to have differential influences on consumers' interpretation and perceptions of advertising messages. As for trust in advertising media, both cultural practices and values might influence the perception of consumers. For instance, certain cultural practices such as strong advertising regulations in some countries should affect trust in advertising media. On the other hand, values related to individual success and the wish for acknowledgment of success by others might increase trust in advertising media. Therefore we ask the following research question:

RQ 2: (How) do cultural practices and cultural values exhibit different influences on trust in advertising media?

METHOD

Data for our study came from several databases. GLOBE data on countries and country clusters are provided by the GLOBE literature (Gupta and Hanges 2004; House, Hanges, Javidan, Dorfman and Gupta 2004). Data on trust in different advertising channels were provided by Nielsen's 2009 Global Online Consumer Survey (Nielsen Media Research 2009). This survey provides 16 usable measures on trust in advertising media: trust in (1) text ads on mobile phones, (2) online video ads, (3) online banner ads, (4) e-mails I signed for, (5) editorial content such as newspaper article, (6) consumer opinions posted online, (7) brand websites, (8) brand sponsorships, (9) billboards and other outdoor advertising, (10) ads on TV, (11) ads served in search engine results, (12) radio ads, (13) newspaper ads, (14) ads in magazines, (15) ads before movies and (16) ads in general. Each trust item was measured by a four-point scale ranging from "don't trust at all" to "trust completely".

Trust in traditional advertising media was computed as the mean of six items (trust in billboards and other outdoor advertising, ads on TV, radio ads, newspaper ads, ads in magazines and ads before movies; Cronbach's Alpha = 0.98). Trust in online advertising media was computed as a mean of seven items (trust in text ads on mobile phones, online video ads, online banner ads, e-mails I signed for, consumer opinions posted online, brand websites, ads served in search engine result; Cronbach's Alpha = 0.91). Trust in all advertising media was computed as a mean of all 13 items (Cronbach's Alpha = 0.95).

As a control variable for the influence of cultural practices and values on trust in advertising, we applied the 2009 gross domestic product (GDP) per capita in US dollars as provided by Euromonitor International (2009). It is common practice to control for economic development in testing the effects of cultural variables because levels of economic development are strongly related to national cultures (e.g., Chui and Kwok 2008; Franke and Nadler 2008).

The Gallup survey provides trust data for 37 out of 61 countries included in the GLOBE study. Ten additional countries from the Gallup data set that were not amongst the 61 GLOBE countries could be assigned to regional clusters according to the description and approach suggested in the GLOBE literature (Bakacsi, Takáes, Karácsonyi and Imrek 2002; Gupta and Hanges 2004; Gupta, Surie, Javidan and Chhokar 2002;

Kabasakal and Bodur 2002). The final country sample thus included 47 countries that are assigned to nine regional clusters. The tenth cluster (Sub-Saharan Africa cluster) was excluded from further analysis because we had no trust data for any country belonging to the cluster. The following list gives an overview of the countries and regional clusters. Ten countries that were not in the original GLOBE study but assigned by us are marked by an asterisk.

- Anglo: Australia, Canada, England, Ireland, New Zealand, United States
- Latin Europe: France, Israel, Italy, Portugal, Spain
- Nordic Europe: Denmark, Finland, Norway*, Sweden
- Germanic Europe: Austria, Germany, the Netherlands
- Eastern Europe: Czech Republic*, Estonia*, Greece, Hungary, Kosovo*, Latvia*, Poland, Russia
- Latin America: Argentina, Brazil, Chile*, Colombia, Mexico, Venezuela
- Middle East: Saudi Arabia*, Turkey, United Arab Emirates*
- Southern Asia: India, Indonesia, Malaysia, Pakistan*, Philippines, Thailand
- Confucian Asia: China, Hong Kong, Japan, Singapore, Taiwan, Vietnam*

The analytical approach is based on t-tests for comparing trust data across regional clusters. T-tests are robust even for small sample sizes. We test the influence of cultural practices and values using regression analysis with practices or values respectively and GDP as predictors for overall trust in advertising media, trust in traditional advertising media, and trust in online advertising media.

RESULTS

Table 20.1 presents the mean comparisons of each trust variable between country clusters. The results show some variation between media and countries. While in all countries the least trusted advertising media are the same (ads on mobile phones, online video ads, and online banner ads), the most trusted media are either editorial content such as newspaper article (Anglo, Nordic Europe, Germanic Europe, Latin America, Middle East, Southern Asia) or consumer opinions posted online (Latin Europe, Eastern Europe, Confucian Asia). If we look at the ranked media position, some results stick out: direct online communication receives comparatively low trust values in Latin America and Southern Asia. Ads on TV receive comparatively high trust values in Anglo, Latin America, Middle East, Southern Asia, and Confucian Asia. Overall, Latin America, Middle East, Southern Asia, and Confucian Asia show rather high trust values, whereas European and Anglo clusters show lower trust values, with the difference between Nordic Europe and Southern Asia comprising 0.85 scale points on a four-point scale.

When looking at the comparison between trust in traditional versus trust in online advertising media as depicted in Table 20.1, there is some variation between regional clusters, which resembles the same order for both kinds of advertising media. The highest trust in traditional advertising media is found in Latin America and Southern Asia; the lowest values are found in Eastern Europe and Nordic Europe. The highest trust values in online media are found in Latin America, Southern Asia, and Confucian Asia; the lowest values in Nordic Europe and Eastern Europe. If we compare trust in online versus traditional advertising media within regional clusters, five out of nine clusters show significant differences with lower trust values for online compared to traditional advertising media: Anglo ($t = 12.08$, $p < 0.01$), Germanic Europe ($t = 4.74$, $p = 0.04$), Latin America ($t = 17.08$, $p < 0.01$), Southern Asia ($t = 8.33$, $p < 0.01$), and Confucian Asia ($t = 5.39$, $p < 0.01$). The remaining clusters did not show significant differences regarding trust values. Hence the answer to our first research question is:

> Trust in different advertising media, in particular trust in traditional media versus online advertising media, differs over regional clusters. Trust in online advertising media is on average lower than in traditional advertising media for most regional clusters.

Table 20.2 shows the results of the regression analysis. We checked for possible violations of the regression model, particularly for multicollinearity, but did not find any problems with the OLS approach. Since the ratio of the number of predictors to the sample size is rather small, which might make the robustness of the results questionable, we also ran regression models with several smaller subsets of predictors. The results remained stable.

The results show that different cultural practices and values influence trust in advertising media in different ways. Future orientation practices have a positive influence and institutional collectivism practices have a negative impact on trust in advertising media (overall, traditional, and online). Assertiveness values have a positive impact on trust in advertising media (overall, traditional, and online). In addition, power distance values have a negative impact on trust in online advertising media. The results show that practices and values have differential impact, that answers our second research question:

Cultural practices and cultural values exhibit differential influences on trust in advertising media.

Table 20.1 also provides the mean values of the significant predictors for each regional cluster. Future orientation practices reach high scores in Germanic and Nordic Europe and low scores in Eastern Europe. Institutional collectivism practices score high in Nordic Europe and Confucian Asia, and low in Germanic Europe. Assertiveness values reach high scores in Southern Asia and Confucian Asia and low scores in Germanic Europe, Eastern Europe and Latin America. Finally, power distance values have high scores in Anglo, Confucian Asia and Southern Asia and low scores in Latin America.

DISCUSSION

In this chapter, we have discussed the concept of trust in advertising media together with its antecedents and consequences. Trust in advertising media impacts advertising effectiveness to a large extent. Studies that have investigated individual antecedents such as demographic variables came up with mixed results and have provided rather weak evidence in explaining differences in trust in advertising media. Since cultural influences on trust in advertising media have not been investigated so far, we provided results of an empirical study that shows that trust in different advertising media varies over regional clusters. We find several significant differences between regional clusters. The significance of results between clusters is remarkable considering that the underlying sample size of countries in each cluster is rather low. In fact, clusters show high homogeneity and very small within-cluster variance, increasing the heterogeneity between clusters.

The analysis regarding the influence of cultural values and practices on trust in advertising media reveals rather consistent results across online and traditional media. The significant relationships deserve further interpretation. Future orientation practices enhance trust in advertising media. Advertising informs consumers about new products and product features and such information about upcoming products might, therefore, be particularly appreciated by consumers in societies that engage in future-orientated behaviors. These practices are prevalent in Germanic Europe

Table 20.1 Trust in different advertising media along country clusters (mean values)

Trust in	Anglo	Latin Europe	Nordic Europe	Germanic Europe	Eastern Europe	Latin America	Middle East	Southern Asia	Confucian Asia	Overall
. . . text ads on mobile phones	1.85 ᵃ	2.04 ᵇᶜ	1.78 ᵃ	1.83 ᵃᵇ	1.86 ᵃ	2.15 ᵇᶜ	2.17 ᶜ	2.13 ᶜ	2.12 ᶜ	1.99
. . . online video ads	2.15 ᵃᶜ	2.28 ᵃᵈ	2.00 ᵇ	2.17 ᵃᵇᵉ	2.13 ᵃ	2.47 ᶜ	2.37 ᶜᵈ	2.47 ᶜ	2.35 ᶜᵈᵉ	2.27
. . . online banner ads	2.02 ᵃ	2.20 ᵇ	1.95 ᵃ	2.03 ᵃ	2.03 ᵃ	2.52 ᶜ	2.37 ᵇᶜ	2.33 ᵇ	2.33 ᵇᶜ	2.20
. . . e-mails I signed for	2.62 ᵃ	2.56 ᵃᵇᵉ	2.38 ᶜ	2.53 ᵇᶜ	2.33 ᶜᵈ	2.58 ᵃᵇᶜ	2.60 ᵃᵇᵈ	2.63 ᵃᵇ	2.47 ᶜᵈᵉ	2.51
. . . editorial content such as newspaper article	2.75 ᵃ	2.76 ᵃ	2.82 ᵃ	2.73 ᵃᵇ	2.54 ᵇ	3.00 ᶜ	2.87 ᵃᶜ	3.02 ᶜ	2.67 ᵃᵇ	2.78
. . . consumer opinions posted online	2.72 ᵃ	2.78 ᵃ	2.60 ᵃ	2.70 ᵃ	2.71 ᵃ	2.55 ᵇ	2.77 ᵃ	2.82 ᵃ	2.78 ᵃ	2.72
. . . brand websites	2.62 ᵃ	2.68 ᵃᵇ	2.50 ᵃᵇ	2.63 ᵃᵇ	2.58 ᵃᵇ	2.95 ᶜ	2.80 ᵇᶜ	2.88 ᶜᵈ	2.73 ᵃᵇᵈ	2.71
. . . brand sponsorships	2.57 ᵃ	2.52 ᵃᵇ	2.28 ᶜ	2.47 ᵇᶜ	2.41 ᵇ	2.92 ᵈ	2.77 ᵈᵉ	2.85 ᵈᵉ	2.67 ᵃᵉ	2.61
. . . billboards and other outdoor advertising	2.50 ᵃ	2.44 ᵃᵇ	2.20 ᶜᵈ	2.37 ᵇᶜ	2.18 ᵈ	2.72 ᶜ	2.63 ᵉᶠ	2.68 ᵉᶠ	2.55 ᵃᶠ	2.47
. . . ads on TV	2.62 ᵃᵉ	2.48 ᵃᵇ	2.30 ᵇᶜ	2.43 ᵇᶜ	2.25 ᶜ	2.88 ᵈ	2.70 ᵈᵉ	2.85 ᵈ	2.68 ᶜ	2.58
. . . ads served in search engine results	2.17 ᵃ	2.32 ᵇ	2.08 ᵃ	2.20 ᵃᵇ	2.18 ᵃ	2.52 ᶜ	2.37 ᵇᶜ	2.50 ᶜ	2.38 ᵇᶜ	2.31
. . . radio ads	2.60 ᵃᵉ	2.50 ᵃᵇ	2.25 ᶜ	2.43 ᵇᶜ	2.28 ᶜ	2.82 ᵈᵉ	2.60 ᵃᵇᵉ	2.70 ᶜ	2.50 ᵃᵇ	2.52
. . . newspaper ads	2.65 ᵃ	2.50 ᵃᵇ	2.48 ᵇᶜ	2.50 ᵇ	2.31 ᶜ	2.88 ᵈ	2.70 ᵃᵇᵈ	2.85 ᵈ	2.67 ᵃᵇ	2.61
. . . ads in magazines	2.57 ᵃ	2.48 ᵃᵇ	2.35 ᵇᶜ	2.43 ᵇᶠ	2.30 ᶜ	2.87 ᵈᵉ	2.67 ᵃᵉ	2.83 ᶜ	2.63 ᵃᶠ	2.57
. . . ads before movies	2.50 ᵃᵉ	2.42 ᵃᵉ	2.20 ᵇ	2.37 ᵃ	2.15 ᵇ	2.73 ᶜᵈ	2.50 ᵃᵈᵉ	2.65 ᵈᵉ	2.55 ᵉ	2.45
. . . ads in general	2.63 ᵃ	2.56 ᵃ	2.23 ᵇ	2.27 ᵇ	2.50 ᵃᵇ	3.02 ᶜ	3.07 ᶜ	3.08 ᶜ	2.92 ᵈ	2.72
Trust in traditional advertising media	2.57 ᵃ	2.47 ᵃᵇ	2.30 ᵇᶜ	2.42 ᵇ	2.24 ᶜ	2.82 ᵈ	2.63 ᵃᵉ	2.76 ᵈᵉ	2.60 ᵈ	2.54
Trust in online advertising media	2.30 ᵃ	2.41 ᵃᶜᶠ	2.18 ᵇ	2.30 ᵃᶜᶠ	2.26 ᵇᶜ	2.53 ᵈ	2.49 ᶜᵉ	2.54 ᵈᵉ	2.45 ᵈᵉᶠ	2.39
Future orientation, practices	4.07 ᵃ	3.56 ᵇᵈ	4.36 ᵇᶜ	4.42 ᵃ	3.15 ᶜ	3.48 ᵇᶜ	–1	4.04 ᵃᵈ	4.22 ᵃ	3.88
Institutional collectivism, practices	4.43 ᵃ	3.97 ᵇ	4.88 ᶜ	4.16 ᵃᵇᶜ	3.95 ᵃᵇᶜ	3.86 ᵇ	–1	4.44 ᵃᶜ	4.72 ᵃᶜ	4.28
Assertiveness, values	3.92 ᵃᶜ	3.71 ᵃᵇ	3.56 ᵃᵇᶜ	2.99 ᶜ	3.26 ᵇᶜ	3.34 ᵇᶜ	–1	4.58 ᵈ	4.70 ᵈᵉ	3.80
Power distance, values	2.90 ᵃᶜᵈ	2.52 ᵇᶜ	2.55 ᵇᶜ	2.49 ᵃᵇ	2.66 ᵃᵇᶜ	2.37 ᵇ	–1	2.78 ᶜ	3.07 ᵈ	2.68
N²	6/6	5/5	4/3	3/3	8/4	6/5	3/1	6/5	6/5	47/37

Notes: Values within rows with no common superscript differ significantly (*p* < .05).
1. No means are given because only one country provides data for this variable.
2. The first value gives the sample used for the trust variables, the second value the sample used for the cultural variables.

450

Table 20.2 *Impact of cultural practices and values on trust in advertising media (unstandardized coefficients with standard error in parenthesis; n = 36)*

| | Dependent variables | | | | | |
| Independent variables | Trust in all advertising media | | Trust in traditional advertising media | | Trust in online advertising media | |
	Practices	*Values*	*Practices*	*Values*	*Practices*	*Values*
Constant	2.31 (1.08)*	2.14 (1.22)	1.90 (1.39)	1.25 (1.58)	2.66 (.94)**	2.91 (1.04)**
GDP	−.01 (.01)*	−.01 (.01)	−.01 (.01)	.01 (.01)	−.01 (.01)*	−.01 (.01)
Assertiveness	−.10 (.11)	.12 (.04)**	−.12 (.14)	.14 (.05)**	−.08 (.10)	.10 (.03)**
Future orientation	.22 (.09)*	.13 (.08)	.24 (.11)*	.19 (.11)	.21 (.07)**	.07 (.07)
Gender egalitarianism	−.03 (.04)	.09 (.09)	−.03 (.05)	.06 (.11)	−.04 (.03)	.11 (.07)
Humane orientation	.09 (.07)	−.14 (.11)	.15 (.09)	−.18 (.14)	.04 (.06)	−.11 (.09)
In-group collectivism	.01 (.04)	−.09 (.09)	.01 (.05)	−.07 (.11)	.01 (.04)	−.11 (.07)
Institutional collectivism	−.24 (.10) *	.07 (.07)	−.29 (.13)*	.09 (.09)	−.19 (.09)*	.06 (.06)
Performance orientation	.11 (.09)	.08 (.09)	.16 (.11)	.17 (.12)	.07 (.07)	.01 (.08)
Power distance	.08 (.09)	−.20 (.10)+	.11 (.12)	−.19 (.14)	.05 (.08)	−.20 (.09)**
Uncertainty avoidance	−.08 (.08)	−.04 (.05)	−.06 (.10)	−.01 (.06)	−.09 (.07)	−.06 (.04)
R^2	.62	.64	.58	.59	.63	.66
F-value	4.04**	4.36***	3.39**	3.58**	4.16***	4.85**

Note: * p < .05, ** p < .01, ***p < .001.

and Nordic Europe. Institutional collectivism practices reduce trust in advertising media. That is, the more a society emphasizes collective thinking and behavior and the less a society emphasizes individual rewards, as usually fostered in advertising, the more people mistrust advertising media. Low institutional collectivism practices are found in the Latin America cluster. Assertiveness values are positively correlated with trust in advertising media. The more a society wishes for assertive and tough behavior, has sympathy for the strong, and has a can-do attitude (House, Quigley and de Luque 2010), the more people trust in advertising media. Apparently, values related to assertiveness are commonly depicted in advertising. Southern Asia and Confucian Asia are regions with high assertiveness value scores. As for trust in online advertising media, power distance values have a negative influence on trust. The less people wish for a stratified society, the less they trust in online advertising media. Interestingly, power distance is also positively correlated with one-way communication processes (Javidan, Dorfman, De Luque and House 2006), which are rather untypical for the online environment compared to traditional advertising media. That underlines the negative effect of power distance values on trust in online advertising media.

By answering two research questions on the characteristics of transnational trust in advertising media, the study provides preliminary results to the topic. Our approach is rather exploratory and not driven by particular hypotheses. The contribution to the international advertising literature lies mainly in the transnational cluster approach as an interesting candidate for research in the effectiveness of international advertising executions, an approach that also benefits advertising practitioners. Furthermore, the application of GLOBE data that distinguish between practices and values provides further insights into how culture has differential influences on human perceptions and behavior when considering both practices and values separately. This has not been done so far, since previous conceptions have not distinguished between values and practices or have even diminished both concepts (House et al. 2004; Maseland and van Hoorn 2009). An important implication for advertisers is that they should focus on cultural values as provided by GLOBE rather than cultural practices when appealing to consumers' aspirations.

REFERENCES

Aiken, K.D. and D.M. Boush (2006), 'Trustmarks, objective-source ratings, and implied investments in advertising: Investigating online trust and the context-specific nature of internet signals', *Journal of the Academy of Marketing Science*, **34** (3), 308–23.

Andaleeb, S.S. and S.F. Anwar (1996), 'Factors influencing customer trust in salespersons in a developing country', *Journal of International Marketing*, **4** (4), 35–52.

Anderson, E. and B. Weitz (1989), 'Determinants of continuity in conventional industrial channel dyads', *Marketing Science*, **8** (4), 310–23.

Bakacsi, G., S. Takáes, A. Karácsonyi and V. Imrek (2002), 'Eastern European cluster: Tradition and transition', *Journal of World Business*, **37** (1), 69–80.

Boush, D.M., C.-H. Kim, L.R. Kahle and R. Batra (1993), 'Cynicism and conformity as correlates of trust in product information sources', *Journal of Current Issues and Research in Advertising*, **15** (2), 71–9.

Calfee, J.E. and D.J. Ringold (1994), 'The 70% majority: Enduring consumer beliefs about advertising', *Journal of Public Policy & Marketing*, **13** (2), 228–38.

Chui, A.C.W. and C.Y. Kwok (2008), 'National culture and life insurance consumption', *Journal of International Business Studies*, **39** (1), 88–101.

Doney, P.M. and J.P. Cannon (1997), 'An examination of the nature of trust in buyer–seller relationships', *Journal of Marketing*, **61** (2), 35–51.

Euromonitor International (2009), 'Global market information database', available at www.portal.euromonitor.com/portal/default.aspx (accessed 11 July 2010).

Franke, G.R. and S.S. Nadler (2008), 'Culture, economic development, and national ethical attitudes', *Journal of Business Research*, **61** (2), 254–64.

Fry, J.N. and G.H. McDougall (1974), 'Consumer appraisal of retail price advertisements', *Journal of Marketing*, **38** (3), 64–7.

Gönül, F.F., F. Carter and J. Wind (2000), 'What kind of patients and physicians value direct-to-consumer advertising of prescription drugs', *Health Care Management Science*, **3** (3), 215–26.

Gupta, Vipin and Paul J. Hanges (2004), 'Regional and climate clustering of societal cultures', in Robert J. House, Paul J. Hanges, Mansour Javidan, Peter W. Dorfman and Vipin Gupta (eds), *Culture, Leadership, and Organisations: The GLOBE Study of 62 Societies*, Thousands Oaks, CA: Sage, pp. 178–218.

Gupta, V., G. Surie, M. Javidan and J. Chhokar (2002), 'Southern Asia cluster: Where the old meets the new?', *Journal of World Business*, **37** (1), 16–27.

House, Robert J., Paul J. Hanges, Mansour Javidan, Peter W. Dorfman and Vipin Gupta (eds) (2004), *Culture, Leadership, and Organizations. The GLOBE Study of 62 Societies*, Thousand Oaks, CA: Sage.

House, R.J., N.R. Quigley and M.S. de Luque (2010), 'Insights from project globe: Extending global advertising research through a contemporary framework', *International Journal of Advertising*, **29** (1), 111–39.

Hovland, Carl I., Irving L. Janis and Harold H. Kelley (eds) (1953), *Communication and Persuasion. Psychological Studies of Opinion Change*, New Haven, CO: Yale University Press.

Huh, J., D.E. DeLorme and L.N. Reid (2005), 'Factors affecting trust in online prescription drug information and impact of trust behavior following exposure to dtc advertising', *Journal of Health Communication: International Perspectives*, **10** (8), 711–31.

Javidan, M., P.W. Dorfman, M.S. De Luque and R.J. House (2006), 'In the eye of the beholder: Cross-cultural lessons in leadership from project globe', *Academy of Management Perspectives*, **20** (1), 67–90.

Kabasakal, H. and M. Bodur (2002), 'Arabic cluster: A bridge between East and West', *Journal of World Business*, **37** (1), 40–54.

Kiousis, S. (2001), 'Public trust or mistrust? Perceptions of media credibility in the information age', *Mass Communication and Society*, **4** (4), 381–403.

Lutz, Richard J. (1985), 'Affective and cognitive antecedents of attitude toward the ad: A conceptual framework', in Linda F. Alwitt and Andrew A. Mitchell (eds), *Psychological Processes and Advertising Effects: Theory, Research, and Application*, Hillsdale, NJ: Lawrence Erlbaum, pp. 45–63.

MacKenzie, S.B. and R.J. Lutz (1989), 'An empirical examination of the structural antecedents of attitude toward the ad in an advertising pretesting context', *Journal of Marketing*, **53** (2), 48–56.

Maseland, R. and A. van Hoorn (2009), 'Explaining the negative correlation between values and practices: A note on the Hofstede–Globe debate', *Journal of International Business Studies*, **40** (3), 527–32.

Menon, A.M., A.D. Deshpande, M. Perri III and G.M. Zinkhan (2002), 'Trust in on-line prescription drug information among internet users: The impact on information search behavior after exposure to dtc advertising', *Health Marketing Quarterly*, **20** (1), 17–35.

Menon, A.M., A.D. Desphande, G.M. Zinkhan and M. Perri III (2004), 'A model of assessing the effectiveness of direct-consumer-advertising: Integration of concepts and measures from marketing and healthcare', *International Journal of Advertising*, **23** (1), 91–118.

Möller, J. and M. Eisend (2010), 'A global investigation into the cultural and individual antecedents of consumers' responsiveness towards banner advertisements', *Journal of International Marketing*, **18** (2), 80–98.

Moorman, C., R. Deshpandé and G. Zaltman (1993), 'Factors affecting trust in market research relationships', *Journal of Marketing*, **57** (1), 81–101.

Nelson, Phillip (eds) (1974), *The Economic Value of Advertising, Advertising and Society*, Yale Bozen, New York: New York University Press, 43–65.

Nielsen Media Research (2009), 'Nielsen global online consumer survey – trust, value, and engagement in advertising', available at http://hk.acnielsen.com/documents/NielsenTrustAdvertisingGlobalReportJuly09.pdf (accessed 11 July 2010).

Ohanian, R. (1990), 'Construction and validation of a scale to measure celebrity endorsers' perceived expertise, trustworthiness, and attractiveness', *Journal of Advertising*, **19** (3), 39–52.

Ohanian, R. (1991), 'The impact of celebrity spokespersons' perceived image on consumers' intention to purchase', *Journal of Advertising Research*, **13** (1), 46–55.

Okazaki, S., A. Katsukura and M. Nishiyama (2007), 'How mobile advertising works: The role of trust in improving attitudes and recall', *Journal of Advertising Research*, **47** (2), 165–78.

Petty, Richard E. and John T. Cacioppo (eds) (1986), *Communication and Persuasion: Central and Peripheral Routes to Attitude Change*, New York: Springer.

Soh, H., L.N. Reid and K.W. King (2007), 'Trust in different advertising media', *Journalism & Mass Communication Quarterly*, **84** (3), 455–76.

Soh, H., L.N. Reid and K.W. King (2009), 'Measuring trust in advertising: Development and validation of the adtrust scale', *Journal of Advertising*, **38** (2), 83–109.

Taylor, C.R. (2002), 'What is wrong with international advertising research?' *Journal of Advertising Research*, **42** (6), 48–54.

Yoon, S.-J. (2002), 'The antecedents and consequences of trust in online-purchase decisions', *Journal of Interactive Marketing*, **16** (2), 47–63.

21 The relation between gender and cultural orientation and its implications for advertising
*Ashok K. Lalwani and Sharon Shavitt**

INTRODUCTION

Research points to gender differences in individualism and collectivism (e.g., Gilligan, 1982; Kashima et al. 1995; Maccoby, 1990; Singelis, 1994). At the broadest level, women appear to be less individualistic and more collectivistic than do men (Cross & Madson, 1997; Hofstede, 2001; Markus & Kitayama, 1991; Triandis, 1995). For instance, women are more willing and able to care for others (Gilligan, 1982), are more aware of and sensitive to others' needs (Markus & Kitayama, 1991), are more likely to provide social support to others (Wellman, 1992; Wethington, McLeod & Kessler, 1987), view others as more sociable (Marcus & Lehman, 2002) and describe themselves in terms of relatedness to others (Rosenberg, 1989; also see Cramer, 2000), all of which are hallmarks of collectivism. In contrast, men are more likely to focus on themselves than on others (Clancy & Dollinger, 1993), to endorse competitive goals (Gaeddert & Facteau, 1990), and to describe themselves as separate from others (Lyons, 1983), which are characteristics of individualism. These types of gender difference have often been discussed in terms of culturally relevant self-construals. The independent self construal is associated with uniqueness, self-reliance, achievement, and separateness – characteristics that parallel an individualistic cultural orientation; whereas the interdependent self is associated with connectedness, and a focus on social context and relationships – characteristics that parallel a collectivistic cultural orientation (Markus & Kitayama, 1991; Singelis, 1994). Thus, Cross and Madson (1997) noted that gender differences in human cognition, motivation, emotion, and social life may be traced to the distinct independent and interdependent self-construals constructed and maintained by men and women.

However, when it comes to the specific nature of gender differences in individualism and collectivism (INDCOL), results across studies have varied (see Gabriel & Gardner, 1999; Kashima et al. 1995). Some research has shown no gender differences on broad indicators relevant to INDCOL (e.g., Baumeister & Sommer, 1997; Gabriel & Gardner, 1999; Gaines et al.

1997). For instance, across five studies, Gabriel and Gardner (1999) consistently found no gender differences on a variety of tasks and behaviors related to the independent self (e.g., the number of independent thoughts listed on a 20-statement test; Kuhn and McPartland, 1954). Similarly, Gaines et al. (1997) and Baumeister and Sommer (1997) presented evidence that men and women do not differ on individualism, and Kashima et al. (1995) reported no significant gender differences on both collectivism and aspects of individualism (e.g., agency, assertiveness), concluding that gender is linked to relationality, not to INDCOL broadly.

Although the broad constructs of individualism and collectivism have considerable utility, this broad-brush dichotomy is not without limitations, and finer distinctions can afford greater insights into a variety of cultural phenomena (Schwartz, 1990). In that vein, in this chapter we address whether considering different types of individualism and types of collectivism enhances understanding of the link between gender and these cultural orientation categories. We review the literature and then present new findings that support this contention. Finally, we consider implications for advertising.

Recent research suggests that cultures differ significantly on the emphasis given to status and hierarchy (Matsumoto, 2007). In particular, the distinction between the *vertical* and the *horizontal* types of individualism and collectivism highlights differences in the degree to which hierarchy vs. equality are emphasized (Triandis and Gelfand, 1998). This distinction may also track the nature of individualistic and collectivistic orientations that vary by gender, enhancing understanding of the motivational distinctions that characterize men's and women's cultural values. We suggest that considering the horizontal/vertical distinction enables a finer-grained understanding of the relations between gender and INDCOL.

VERTICAL AND HORIZONTAL INDIVIDUALISM AND COLLECTIVISM

People with horizontal cultural values or orientations value equality and view the self as having the same status as others. In contrast, people with vertical cultural values or orientations view the self as differing from others along a hierarchy – they accept inequality and believe that rank has its privileges (Triandis, 1995). This refinement of individualism/collectivism produces four cultural categories: Horizontal Individualism (HI), Vertical Individualism (VI), Horizontal Collectivism (HC), and Vertical Collectivism (VC) (Singelis, Triandis, Bhawuk & Gelfand, 1995; Triandis & Gelfand, 1998).

Table 21.1   *Values characterizing horizontal and vertical individualism and collectivism*

	Horizontal (Self at the same level as others)	Vertical (Self in a hierarchy relative to others)
Individualism	Self-direction	Improving individual status via competition
	Self-reliance	Seeking achievement, power, prestige
	Uniqueness	Standing out
	Being distinct and separate from others	Display of success, status
Collectivism	Maintaining benevolent relationships	Attainment of in-group status via competition
	Common goals with others	Deference to authorities and to in-groups
	Social appropriateness	Conformity
	Sociability	
	Cooperation	Harmony

Vertical individualists tend to be concerned with improving their individual status and standing out – distinguishing themselves from others via competition, achievement, and power. In contrast, horizontal individualists prefer to view themselves as equal to others in status. Rather than standing out, the focus is on expressing their individuality and self-reliance (Triandis & Singelis, 1998). In other words, VI and HI are distinct individualistic motivational profiles that differ in their emphasis on status and hierarchy. Vertical collectivists focus on deference to authorities and on enhancing the cohesion and status of their in-groups, even when that entails sacrificing their own personal goals. In contrast, horizontal collectivists focus on sociability and interdependence with others within an egalitarian framework (see Erez & Earley, 1987). Again, both profiles reflect interdependent, collectivistic values, but differ in the degree to which status/hierarchy motives are emphasized.

The articulation of these horizontal and vertical categories, summarized in Table 21.1, adds an important degree of refinement to the broad individualism/collectivism cultural classifications. Accordingly, research suggests that a consideration of this horizontal/vertical distinction enhances understanding of the link between culture and personal values, persuasion patterns, and self-presentational styles (see Shavitt, Lalwani, Zhang & Torelli, 2006 for a review).

We suggest that the horizontal/vertical dimension may also point to particular types of individualism and collectivism that vary with gender. Specifically, men may be expected to be more VI, but not necessarily more HI, than women. Men emphasize power, and gain social status or dominance through achievement and personal success (Schwartz & Rubel 2005). Men (but not women) also gain satisfying interpersonal connections by achieving status and power over others (Baumeister & Sommer 1997; Maccoby, 1990). However, the emphasis on autonomy and capability that characterizes HI is likely equally relevant to men and women. Although men and women are socialized toward different roles and responsibilities, they both require self-reliance to accomplish the ends valued in their particular spheres. Indeed, prior research suggests that men and women do not differ on values associated with HI (e.g., self-direction; Nelson & Shavitt, 2002; Oishi et al. 1998).

Whereas it is generally accepted that women are more oriented than men toward interdependence and a collectivism, this difference is likely specific to horizontal collectivism (HC). Research indicates that women are more focused than men on sociability and on treating others with benevolence and loyalty (Cross & Madson, 1997). They value interpersonal relationships and their harmony and stability more than do men (Cross & Madson, 1997; Feather, 1984; Gabriel & Gardner, 1999; Schwartz & Rubel, 2005). For instance, Gabriel and Gardner (1999) found that women focus on relational aspects of interdependence more than do men. However, one would not expect women to be higher in focus on deference to authority and in-group status (VC) than men. Indeed, masculine patterns of belongingness, which center on broader social collectivities (Gabriel & Gardner, 1999), may emphasize power hierarchies as a means to organize and lead the activities of those groups (Baumeister & Sommer, 1997). In sum, women's greater tendency toward collectivism may be limited to the horizontal (HC) and not necessarily the vertical (VC) variety.

However, cross-national research points to inconsistent relations between gender and these constructs. Chirkov et al. (2003) found that, in the U.S., men scored higher than women on both VI and VC; in Russia, men scored higher than women on VI only; in Turkey, men scored higher than women on VC only. Nelson and Shavitt (2002) found gender differences in the U.S. in VI (men > women) and HC (women > men) only; in a Danish sample, gender differences emerged in VI (men > women) only. In a Singaporean and Israeli sample, Kurman and Sriram (2002) found women (vs. men) score higher on both HC and HI, and lower on VC.

Our studies attempt to understand these relations at a more phenomenological level. By examining self-rated subjective gender as well as sex differences, across a number of studies conducted with U.S. undergraduates, we offer unique insights on relations between cultural value orientations and masculinity/femininity. Study 1 examines, in multiple samples, gender differences in scores on one of the standard measures of VI, HI, VC, and HC (Triandis & Gelfand, 1998). Study 2 replicates these patterns using other measures of IND and COL that either emphasize status/hierarchy themes (Maslach, Stapp & Santee, 1985; Oyserman, 1993) or horizontal themes (Clark et al. 1987; Oyserman, 1993). Study 3 examines the relationships between subjective assessments of gender and VI, HI, VC, and HC. Study 4 extends the observed relationships to responses on behavioral scenarios relating to HI, VI, HC, and VC.

STUDY 1

Method

Study 1 was conducted on ten different samples of U.S. undergraduates enrolled at the University of Illinois in introductory business courses (total N = 1091; 53% men). Respondents participated in exchange for class credit. Overall, 57 percent of participants were Caucasians, 18 percent were Asians, and 4 percent were African-Americans. Respondents completed Triandis and Gelfand's 16-item scale designed to measure VI, HI, VC, and HC (four items each) on 7-point Likert-type scales with 1 = strongly disagree and 7 = strongly agree. Examples included "I'd rather depend on myself than others" (HI), "It is important that I do my job better than others" (VI), "If a coworker gets a prize, I would feel proud" (HC), and "Parents and children must stay together as much as possible" (VC). This measure has been extensively used in cross-cultural research and has been found to predict a variety of phenomena, including socially desirable responding (Lalwani, Shavitt & Johnson, 2006), regulatory focus (Lee, Aaker & Gardner, 2000), self-enhancement motives (Sedikides, Gaertner & Toguchi, 2003), and personal values (Triandis & Gelfand, 1998). For instance, Triandis and Gelfand (1998) found that VI predicted competitiveness and hedonism, VC predicted family integrity, and both HC and VC predicted sociability. These authors also administered numerous other scales commonly used to measure related cultural orientation categories, and found that their 16-item Likert-type scale correlated as expected with other scales. In addition, Briley and Wyer (2001) found that situationally enhancing cognitions relating to independence led to increased scores on Triandis and Gelfand's (1998) individualism measure, whereas enhancing cognitions relating to interdependence led to increased scores on the collectivism measure. Finally, in a separate data set with 3840 participants, we assessed the factor structure and reliabilities of the four subscales. Results indicated that all items loaded on their respective subscales (all factor loadings > 0.58), and had acceptable reliabilities (e.g., HI: 0.74; VI: 0.76; HC: 0.71; VC: 0.74). Further details on the convergent and discriminant validity of the scale are given in Triandis and Gelfand (1998). Participants in Study 1 also responded to several demographic questions, including their gender, ethnicity, year of birth, and country of birth.

Results

A meta-analysis across the ten samples revealed that the relation between gender (dummy coded 0 = female, 1 = male) and VI (average d = 0.68) as well as that between gender and HC (average d = −0.29) were strong and significant at the 95% confidence interval. In contrast, the relation between gender and HI (average d = 0.11) was non-significant. The meta-analysis also suggested that men scored significantly higher than women on VC (average d = 0.20), although this relationship was weak. The analyses also revealed that 281 (0) additional studies averaging a null effect would be required to render the gender-VI (gender-HI) relationship non-significant and 46 (17) new studies averaging a null effect would be required to render the gender-HC (gender-VC) relationship non-significant. In other words, as expected, robust gender differences exist in individualism, but only for the vertical form, whereas robust gender differences in collectivism appear specific to the horizontal form.

STUDY 2

Although the findings from the ten different samples in Study 1 generally supported the predicted gender differences in cultural orientation, they were all examined using single indicators of HI, VI, HC, VC, and of gender. The subsequent studies were designed to replicate and extend those findings using alternate measures of INDCOL (Study 2) and of gender identity (Studies 3a and 3b). In Study 2, a number of measures were selected to correspond to the motives associated with either the vertical or horizontal forms of individualism or collectivism, in order to determine whether the same pattern of gender differences emerged.

Method

Seventy-eight U.S. undergraduates (40 men), enrolled in introductory courses at the University of Illinois, participated in exchange for class credit. In addition to providing demographic information, they completed several different measures that were selected based on previous research on their convergence with the focal constructs (Triandis & Gelfand, 1998, Study 4) and/or on the face validity of their items. Specifically, to tap motives associated with VI, Maslach et al.'s (1985) 12-item individuation scale ($\alpha = 0.86$) was employed. The individuation scale comprises such questions as, "What is the likelihood you will volunteer to head a committee for a group of people you do not know very well?" and "What is the likelihood you will perform on a stage before a large audience?" All items are measured on 7-point scales with 1 = not at all willing to do this, and 7 = very much willing to do this. We reasoned that responses on this scale, which taps the willingness to be a leader or to gain status and power for oneself, should reflect a particularly vertical form of individualism.

To tap motives associated with HI, Oyserman's (1993, Study 4) 4-item individualism scale ($\alpha = 0.72$) was employed. This scale is comprised of such items as "Self-actualization is one of my highest values" and "It is important to me that I am unique", with responses measured on 7-point Likert-type scales anchored by 1 = strongly disagree and 7 = strongly agree. We reasoned that responses on this scale, which taps the motivation to be a self-directed and unique individual, should reflect a particularly horizontal form of individualism.

To tap motives associated with VC, Oyserman's (1993, Study 4) 5-item collectivism scale ($\alpha = 0.83$) was employed. Example items include, "Whatever is good for my group is good for me" and "My aspirations are the same as those of others in my religion" with responses measured on 7-point Likert-type scales. We reasoned that responses on this scale appear to tap the willingness to subordinate personal goals to the goals of the in-group and show deference to that group's ambitions, which reflects a vertical form of collectivism.

Finally, to tap motives associated with HC, Clark et al.'s (1987) 14-item communal orientation scale ($\alpha = 0.71$) was used. Example items include, "When making a decision, I take other people's needs and feelings into account" and "I don't especially enjoy giving others aid" (reverse scored), measured on a 7-point scale anchored by 1 = very uncharacteristic of me and 7 = very characteristic of me. These items reflect an emphasis on sociability and cooperation, which should reflect a particularly horizontal form of collectivism.

A pretest ($N=110$) indicated that Oyserman's (1993, Study 4) individualism scale, as expected, significantly correlated with HI ($r = 0.38$, $p < 0.001$), but not with VI ($r = 0.17$, $p > 0.08$), suggesting that it taps the horizontal, but not the vertical, aspects of individualism. However, it also correlated with HC ($r = 0.21$, $p < .05$) and VC ($r = 0.29$, $p < .01$), suggesting that it taps collectivism as well. Another pretest ($N=78$) confirmed that Maslach's individuation scale significantly correlated with Triandis and Gelfand's (1998) VI scale ($r = 0.25$, $p < 0.05$), but not with their HI scale ($r = -0.04$, $p > 0.72$), HC scale ($r = 0.07$, $p > .52$), or VC scale ($r = 0.13$, $p > .27$). Oyserman's (1993, study 4) collectivism scale significantly correlated with VC ($r = 0.35$, $p < 0.001$), but not with HC ($r = -0.04$, $p > 0.72$), although it also correlated with VI ($r = 0.27$, $p < .05$) and HI ($r = 0.28$, $p < .05$), suggesting that it taps individualism as well. Finally, Clark et al.'s communal orientation scale significantly positively correlated with HC ($r = 0.31$, $p < 0.005$) but not with VC ($r = -0.09$, $p > 0.41$), VI ($r = -0.12$, $p > .30$) or HI ($r = -0.22$, $p = .06$), a pattern consistent with prior research (Triandis & Gelfand, 1998).[1] Although the intercorrelations for Oyserman's scales suggested that they tapped a broader-than-expected profile of cultural values, at least as captured by Triandis and Gelfand's measure, Oyserman's subscales were somewhat more reflective of the intended cultural value categories than they were of other categories. The findings for Maslach's individuation scale and Clark et al.'s communal orientation scale supported our expectations about the specific hierarchy versus equality themes that they tap.

Results

Our pattern of results indicated that this broader set of scales converged with the pattern reported in Study 1. Independent sample t tests indicated that men scored significantly higher than women on Maslach et al.'s individuation scale (tapping VI; $M_{men} = 4.98$, $M_{women} = 4.50$, $t(76) = 1.88$, $p < 0.05$; Cohen's $d = 0.43$), but not on Oyserman's individualism scale (intended to tap HI; $M_{men} = 5.11$, $M_{women} = 4.88$, $t(76) < 1.00$, *n.s.*; Cohen's $d = 0.22$). In contrast, women scored higher than men on Clark et al.'s communal orientation scale (tapping HC; $M_{men} = 5.15$, $M_{women} = 5.52$, $t(76) = 2.10$, $p < 0.05$; Cohen's $d = 0.55$), but not on Oyserman's collectivism scale (intended to tap VC; $M_{men} = 3.80$, $M_{women} = 2.75$, $t(76) = 3.61$, $p < 0.001$; Cohen's $d = 0.82$). These findings converge with those of Study 1, and are consistent with the notion that the individualism of men (compared to women) in our samples is more characterized by vertical individualism and not by horizontal individualism. In contrast, the collectivism of women (compared to men) in our samples is more characterized by horizontal collectivism and not by vertical collectivism.

STUDY 3

In the next study, we included a subjective measure of masculinity/ femininity (Stern, Barak & Gould, 1987) to examine whether the links between gender and VI and HC observed here reflect distinct masculine and feminine cultural value orientations. If a feminine focus is associated with a type of collectivism that emphasizes cooperation and social relationships (HC), and a masculine focus is associated with an individualism that emphasizes status, power, and prestige (VI), then one would expect a distinct pattern of correlations between VI and self-rated masculinity on the one hand, and HC and self-rated femininity on the other.

Method

One hundred and fifty-eight U.S. undergraduate students (47 percent men), enrolled in introductory courses at the University of Illinois, participated in exchange for class credit. They completed the 16-item Triandis and Gelfand (1998) scale to measure HI ($\alpha = 0.70$), VI ($\alpha = 0.80$), HC ($\alpha = 0.72$), and VC ($\alpha = 0.65$), and demographic measures. They also completed Stern, Barak and Gould's (1987) sexual identity scale ($\alpha = 0.92$), which measures the subjective gender of the respondent by asking them to complete four items on a 5-point scale with 1 representing "very masculine", 2 representing "masculine", 3 representing "neither masculine nor feminine", 4 representing "feminine", and 5 representing "very feminine". The four items are: I FEEL as though I am ——, I LOOK as though I am ——, I DO most things in a manner typical of someone who is ——, My INTERESTS are mostly of a person who is ——. Higher scores on the scale indicate greater femininity (and lower masculinity).

Results

As expected and as shown in Table 21.2, subjective femininity significantly correlated with HC ($r = 0.24$, $p < 0.005$), but not with VC ($r = -0.09$, $p > 0.25$). Moreover, subjective femininity negatively correlated with VI ($r = -0.37$, $p < 0.001$), and to a lesser extent with HI ($r = -0.18$, $p < 0.02$). Further, the partial correlation between VI and femininity controlling for HI was significantly negative ($r = -0.34$, $p < 0.001$), suggesting that the relationship between femininity and VI was independent of HI. In contrast, the partial correlation between HI and femininity controlling for VI was not significant ($r = -0.12$, $p > 0.10$), suggesting that the effect of HI on femininity was owing to its shared variance with VI. Taken together,

Table 21.2   Correlations between subjective gender and cultural orientation in Study 3

	HI	VI	HC	VC
Femininity	−0.18*	−0.37***	0.24**	−0.09

Notes:
The femininity measure used was adapted from Stern, Barak, and Gould (1987). High scores on the measure indicate greater femininity and lower masculinity.
*** $p < 0.001$, ** $p < 0.01$, * $p < 0.05$.

these findings based on self-rated perceptions of one's femininity converge with the previous sex-difference studies in showing that femininity is associated with higher HC and lower VI.

STUDY 4

The previous studies suggested that U.S. men and women differ in specific types of individualism and collectivism. This study was designed to examine implications for the way men and women respond to behavioral scenarios describing situations they may encounter in their day-to-day lives. We examined whether men would be specifically more likely to choose action options that emphasize status and competition (VI), whereas women would be specifically more likely to choose action options that emphasize sociability and cooperation (HC).

Method

Fifty-nine students (24 men, 35 women) at a large university participated in exchange for class credit. Two respondents' data were deleted for failure to follow instructions. Respondents completed Triandis, Chen and Chan's (1998) measure comprising 16 behavioral scenarios. Each of the scenarios presented the participant with an HI, VI, HC, and VC response option, and participants were asked to rank the two best behavioral choices. Examples included the scenarios:

> You and your friends decided spontaneously to go out to dinner at a restaurant. What do you think is the best way to handle the bill? 1) Split it equally, without regard to who ordered what (HC), 2) Split it according to how much each person makes (VI), 3) The group leader pays the bill or decides how to split it (VC), 4) Compute each person's charge according to what that person ordered (HI).

Suppose your fiancé(e) and your parents do not get along very well. What would you do? 1) Nothing (HI), 2) Tell my fiancé(e) that I need my parents' financial support and he or she should learn to handle the politics (VI), 3) Tell my fiancé(e) that he or she should make a greater effort to 'fit in with the family' (HC), 4) Remind my fiancé(e) that my parents and family are very important to me and he or she should submit to their wishes (VC).

Participants also responded to a number of other measures, including demographic items tapping age, country of birth, ethnicity, gender, and year of move to U.S. (if applicable).

Results and Discussion

Independent sample t tests revealed that out of the 16 scenarios, men selected the VI option 8.13 times as one of the two best behavioral choices, whereas women selected it 7.12 times ($t(55) = 2.13$, $p < 0.05$). In contrast, women picked HC behavioral options more often than men did ($M_{men} = 8.17$, $M_{women} = 9.18$, $t(55) = -1.95$, $p < 0.05$). There was no significant difference between men and women in either the number of HI ($M_{men} = 9.83$, $M_{women} = 9.36$, $t(55) = 0.78$, $p > 0.43$) or VC ($M_{men} = 5.88$, $M_{women} = 6.33$, $t(55) = -0.98$ $p > 0.33$) options selected. These findings extend the previous results to choices on behavioral scenarios and are suggestive that men are more likely to endorse actions that characterize vertical forms of individualism but not horizontal forms. In contrast, women are more likely to endorse actions that characterize horizontal forms of collectivism but not vertical forms.

IMPLICATIONS AND CONCLUSIONS

Men and women in our U.S. samples do not appear to differ broadly in individualism and collectivism. Instead, a consideration of the horizontal/vertical distinction yields new insights into the relation between gender and cultural value orientations. Specifically, we find that men (and those high on subjective masculinity) consistently score higher than women on measures of one type of individualism – vertical individualism. That is, the male or masculine form of individualism appears especially focused on status, power, and achievement through competition (VI). Correspondingly, women (and those high on subjective femininity) do not consistently outscore men on collectivism. The female or feminine form of collectivism appears especially focused on sociability, common goals, and cooperation (HC). Our findings replicated across multiple measures of HI, VI, HC, and VC, as well as across multiple gender-identity indicators (including self-rated masculinity and femininity measures).

These findings offer support for the value of the horizontal/vertical distinction by revealing patterns not anticipated in the literature on gender and cultural self-construal. In particular, whereas some have concluded that men and women do not differ in dimensions of self-construal relevant to IND (Baumeister & Sommer, 1997; Gabriel & Gardner, 1999), we find that men consistently score higher than women on VI. Traditional masculine social roles that emphasize achievement and power gained through personal success may contribute to the robust gender difference observed here.

Results also shed light on the motivational underpinnings of gender differences that have been proposed and observed in prior research. Specifically, COL in women appears to emphasize common goals, camaraderie, and cooperation (HC). This is consistent with the relational interdependence identified in previous studies as a characteristically female cultural orientation (Cross, Bacon & Morris, 2000; Gabriel & Gardner, 1999; Kashima et al. 1995; see also Wang, Bristol, Mowen & Chakraborty, 2000). However, women do not appear always to be higher in COL or interdependence. If anything, men report a somewhat greater emphasis on deference to authority and to in-groups, the vertical form of collectivism (VC).

Although cultural value systems can be dimensionalized into a more comprehensive set of categories (Schwartz, 1990), our investigation was restricted to the dimension of individualism/collectivism as it is the most commonly used distinction in cross-cultural research (Triandis, 1995). Moreover, because our samples were U.S. student participants, our findings do not speak to the relation between gender and cultural values in other societies or populations. Nevertheless, this research offers a refinement in our understanding of the relation between gender and a very broadly used classification of cultural orientation.

Future research could examine the degree to which these patterns predict a broader set of judgments and behaviors as a function of gender, as well as the role that qualities of the various orientation scales play in the patterns that have been observed. Overall, broad gender differences in individualism and collectivism may differ depending on whether one is considering the horizontal or vertical varieties of these categories. That is, the horizontal/vertical distinction appears to be important in predicting or qualifying the nature of gender differences in cultural orientation.

ADVERTISING IMPLICATIONS

What does the distinction in horizontal/vertical cultural values among men and women imply for international advertising? Existing studies on advertising and consumer persuasion provide limited insights into the role of status and hierarchy in advertisements targeted to men and women. A straightforward implication of our findings is that men may find advertisements emphasizing improving individual status via competition, seeking achievement, power, prestige, standing out, display of success, and status more persuasive than women. In contrast, women may find ads that emphasize maintaining benevolent relationships with others, pursuing common goals with others, social appropriateness, sociability, and cooperation as more appealing than men.

Wiles, Wiles and Tjernlund's (1996) analysis of magazine advertising in the United States (VI) and Sweden (HI) focused upon the depiction of IND values. Not surprisingly, it thus revealed strong similarities in the values depicted in advertising across these two societies, with predominating themes of leisure, youthfulness, private life, and ideal body shape. However, Nelson (1997) observed that differences in the gender roles depicted by male versus female models in this same data set were consistent with U.S.–Swedish differences in equality of the sexes and, in turn, with cultural differences relevant to the horizontal/vertical distinction. In U.S. ads, women were more likely than men to be portrayed engaging in housework and child care, whereas the reverse was true in Swedish ads. Nelson concluded that, rather than depicting uniformity in the values of these two cultures, the observed differences in gender roles in the advertisements pointed to distinct vertical versus horizontal patterns of individualism, respectively. Nelson's observation appears consistent with content analysis results on inequality in the relationships depicted in humorous ads across cultures (Alden et al. 1993).

We also found relevant evidence in a large-scale analysis of the prevalence of advertising appeals (Shavitt, Johnson & Zhang, in press). A content analysis of 1211 magazine advertisements in five countries (Denmark, Korea, Poland, Russia, and the U.S.) revealed differences in ad content that underscore the value of the horizontal/vertical cultural distinction. Patterns in the degree to which ads emphasized status benefits and uniqueness benefits corresponded to the countries' vertical versus horizontal cultural classification. In particular, the prevalence of status in ad appeals – including depictions of luxury, or references to prestige, impressing others, prominence, membership in high status groups (e.g., Ivy League graduates), endorsements by high status persons (e.g., celebrities), or other distinctions (e.g., "award-winning") – corresponded to the cultural profiles of the countries. Ads in a VI society (the U.S.) and three VC societies (Korea, Russia, Poland) evidenced a greater emphasis on status benefits than did ads in an HI society (Denmark). Indeed, status appeared to be a dominant ad theme (relative to appeals that emphasized pleasure, uniqueness, or relationships) in all of the vertical societies that were examined. In contrast, pleasure appeals dominated in the HI society.

In sum, across studies of advertising content, findings have converged on the notion that advertisements in vertical versus horizontal cultural contexts depict more hierarchical relations or put more emphasis upon status (see Shavitt et al. in press; Shavitt et al. 2006). Future research could examine the degree to which such ads vary in persuasiveness for men versus women. Further studies could address whether, for instance, men would be more persuaded than women by status appeals that are focused on "sticking out" and being admired, whereas women would be more persuaded than men by appeals that are focused on maintaining benevolent relationships with others, sociability, and cooperation.

Interestingly, status appeals have not been a significant focus of cross-cultural research, despite their prevalence in modern advertising. Indeed, the broad INDCOL cultural framework does not lend itself to predictions about the prevalence of such appeals. This further underscores the value of examining the horizontal/vertical cultural distinction, for the development of cross-cultural theory and for the understanding of gender differences.

NOTES

*   This research was supported in part by a Summer Research Grant to Ashok K. Lalwani from the University of Texas at San Antonio. Preparation of this chapter was supported by Grant #1R01HD053636-01A1 from the National Institutes of Health, Grant #0648539 from the National Science Foundation, and Grant #63842 from the Robert Wood Johnson Foundation to Sharon Shavitt.
1.   The hypothesized relationships between gender and HI, VI, HC, and VC were observed in the pretests as well.

REFERENCES

Alden, D.L., Hoyer, W.D. & Lee, C. (1993). Identifying global and culture-specific dimensions of humor in advertising: A multinational analysis. *Journal of Marketing, 57*(2), 64–75.
Baumeister, R.F. & Sommer, K.L. (1997). What do men want? Gender differences and two spheres of belongingness: Comment on Cross and Madson. *Psychological Bulletin, 122*(1), 38–44.
Briley, D.A. & Wyer, R.S. (2001). Transitory determinants of values and decisions: The utility (or nonutility) of individualism and collectivism in understanding cultural differences. *Social Cognition, 19*(3), 197–227.
Chirkov, V.I., Lynch, M. & Niwa, S. (2005). Application of the scenario questionnaire of horizontal and vertical individualism and collectivism to the assessment of cultural distance and cultural fit. *International Journal of Intercultural Relations, 29*(4), 469–90.

Clancy, S.M. & Dollinger, S.J. (1993). Photographic depictions of the self: Gender and age differences in social connectedness. *Sex Roles*, *29*(7–8), 477–95.

Clark, M.S. Oullette, R., Powell, M.C. & Milberg, S. (1987). Recipient's mood, relationship type, and helping. *Journal of Personality and Social Psychology*, *53*(1), 94–103.

Cramer, P. (2000). Development of identity: Gender makes a difference. *Journal of Research in Personality*, *34*(1), 42–72.

Cross, S.E., Bacon, P.L. & Morris, M.L. (2000). The relational-interdependent self-construal and relationships. *Journal of Personality and Social Psychology*, *78*(4), 791–808.

Cross, S.E. & Madson, L. (1997). Models of the self: Self-construals and gender. *Psychological Bulletin*, *122*(1), 5–37.

Erez, M. & Earley, P.C. (1987). Comparative analysis of goal-setting strategies across cultures. *Journal of Applied Psychology*, *72*(4), 658–65.

Feather, N.T. (1984). Masculinity, femininity, psychological androgyny, and the structure of values. *Journal of Personality and Social Psychology*, *47*(3), 604–20.

Gabriel, S. & Gardner, W.L. (1999). Are there 'his' and 'hers' types of interdependence? The implications of gender differences in collective versus relational interdependence for affect, behavior, and cognition. *Journal of Personality and Social Psychology*, *77*(3), 642–55.

Gaeddert, W.P. & Facteau, J.D. (1990). The effects of gender and achievement domain on two cognitive indices of strivings in personal accomplishments. *Journal of Research in Personality*, *24*(4), 522–35.

Gaines, S.O.J., Marelich, W.D., Bledsoe, K.L., Steers, W.N., Henderson, M.C., Granrose, C.S. et al. (1997). Links between race/ethnicity and cultural values as mediated by racial/ethnic identity and moderated by gender. *Journal of Personality and Social Psychology*, *72*(6), 1460–76.

Gilligan, C. (1982). *In a Different Voice: Psychological Theory and Women's Development*. Cambridge, MA: Harvard University Press.

Hofstede, G.H. (2001). *Culture's Consequences: Comparing Values, Behaviors, Institutions and Organizations Across Nations*. Thousand Oaks, CA: Sage.

Kashima, Y., Yamaguchi, S., Kim, U., Choi, S.C., Gelfand, M. & Yuki, M. (1995). Culture, gender, and self: A perspective from individualism–collectivism research. *Journal of Personality and Social Psychology*, *69*(5), 925–37.

Kuhn, M.H. & McPartland, T.S. (1954). An empirical investigation of self-attitudes. *American Sociological Review*, *19*, 68–76.

Kurman, J., & Sriram, N. (2002). Interrelationships among vertical and horizontal collectivism, modesty, and self-enhancement. *Journal of Cross-Cultural Psychology*, *33*(1), 71–86.

Lalwani, A.K., Shavitt, S. & Johnson, T. (2006). What is the relation between cultural orientation and socially desirable responding? *Journal of Personality and Social Psychology*, *90*(1), 165–78.

Lee, A.Y., Aaker, J.L. and Gardner, W.L. (2000). The pleasures and pains of distinct self-construals: The role of interdependence in regulatory focus. *Journal of Personality and Social Psychology*, *78*(6), 1122–34.

Lyons, N.P. (1983). Two perspectives: On self, relationships, and morality. *Harvard Educational Review*, *53*(2), 125–45.

Maccoby, E.E. (1990). Gender and relationships: A developmental account. *American Psychologist*, *45*(4), 513–20.

Marcus, D.K. & Lehman, S.J. (2002). Are there sex differences in interpersonal perception at zero acquaintance? A social relations analysis. *Journal of Research in Personality*, *36*(3), 190–207.

Markus, H.R. & Kitayama, S. (1991). Culture and the self: Implications for cognition, emotion, and motivation. *Psychological Review*, *98*(2), 224–53.

Maslach, C., Stapp, J. & Santee, R.T. (1985). Individuation: Conceptual analysis and assessment. *Journal of Personality and Social Psychology*, *49*(3), 729–38.

Matsumoto, D. (2007). Individual and cultural differences on status differentiation: The status differentiation scale. *Journal of Cross-Cultural Psychology*, *38*(4), 413–31.

Nelson, M.R. (1997). Examining the horizontal and vertical dimensions of individualism within the United States and Denmark. Unpublished doctoral dissertation, University of Illinois, Urbana-Champaign.

Nelson, M.R. & Shavitt, S. (2002). Horizontal and vertical individualism and achievement values: A multimethod examination of Denmark and the United States. *Journal of Cross-Cultural Psychology*, *33*(5), 439–58.

Oishi, S., Schimmack, U., Diener, E. & Suh, E.M. (1998). The measurement of values and individualism–collectivism. *Personality and Social Psychology Bulletin*, *24*(11), 1177–89.

Oyserman, D. (1993). The lens of personhood: Viewing the self and others in a multicultural society. *Journal of Personality and Social Psychology*, *65*(5), 993–1009.

Rosenberg, M. (1989). *Society and the Adolescent Self-Image*. Middletown, CT: Wesleyan University Press.

Schwartz, S.H. (1990). Individualism–collectivism: Critique and proposed refinements. *Journal of Cross-Cultural Psychology*, *21*(2), 139–57.

Schwartz, S.H. & Rubel, T. (2005). Sex differences in value priorities: Cross-cultural and multimethod studies. *Journal of Personality and Social Psychology*, *89*(6), 1010–28.

Sedikides, C., Gaertner, L. & Toguchi, Y. (2003). Pancultural self-enhancement. *Journal of Personality and Social Psychology*, *84*(1), 60–79.

Shavitt, S., Johnson, T. & Zhang, J. (in press). Horizontal and vertical cultural differences in the content of advertising appeals. *Journal of International Consumer Marketing*.

Shavitt, S., Lalwani, A.K., Zhang, J. & Torelli, C. (2006). The horizontal/vertical distinction in cross-cultural consumer research. *Journal of Consumer Psychology*, *16*(4), 325–42.

Singelis, T.M. (1994). The measurement of independent and interdependent self-construals. *Personality and Social Psychology Bulletin*, *20*(5), 580–91.

Singelis, T.M., Triandis, H.C., Bhawuk, D. & Gelfand, M.J. (1995). Horizontal and vertical dimensions of individualism and collectivism: A theoretical and measurement refinement. *Cross-Cultural Research: The Journal of Comparative Social Science*, *29*(3), 240–75.

Stern, B.B., Barak, B. & Gould, S.J. (1987). Sexual identity scale: A new self-assessment measure. *Sex Roles*, *17*(9–10), 503–19.

Triandis, H. (1995). *Individualism and Collectivism*. Boulder, CO: Westview Press.

Triandis, H.C., Chen, X.P. & Chan, D.K. (1998). Scenarios for the measurement of collectivism and individualism. *Journal of Cross-Cultural Psychology*, *29*(2), 275–89.

Triandis, H.C. & Gelfand, M.J. (1998). Converging measurement of horizontal and vertical individualism and collectivism. *Journal of Personality and Social Psychology*, *74*(1), 118–28.

Triandis, H.C. & Singelis, T.M. (1998). Training to recognize individual differences in collectivism and individualism within culture. *International Journal of Intercultural Relations*, *22*(1), 35–47.

Wang, C.L., Bristol, T., Mowen, J.C. & Chakraborty, G. (2000). Alternative modes of self-construal: Dimensions of connectedness–separateness and advertising appeals to the cultural and gender-specific self. *Journal of Consumer Psychology*, *9*(2), 107–15.

Wellman, B. (1992). Men in networks: Private communities, domestic friendships. In P.M. Nardi (ed.), *Men's Friendships* (pp. 74–114). Newbury Park, CA: Sage.

Wethington, E., McLeod, J. & Kessler, R.C. (1987). The importance of life events for explaining sex differences in psychological distress. In R.C. Barnett, L. Beiner & G.K. Baruch (eds), *Gender and Stress* (pp. 144–56). New York: Free Press.

Wiles, C.R.,Wiles, J.A. & Tjernlund, A. (1996). The ideology of advertising: The United States and Sweden. *Journal of Advertising Research*, *36*(3), 57–66.

PART VIII

IMC AND THE GLOBAL MARKET

22 The importance and relevance of integrated marketing communications: a global perspective

Philip J. Kitchen and Marwa Tourky

INTRODUCTION

In the past decade, the concept of integrated marketing communications (IMC) has swept around the globe and become an apparently integral part of the marketing, and even the corporate communication strategies of many companies (Kitchen, 2005; Schultz et al. 2011). IMC is considered a major factor affecting the outcomes of marketing strategy, and can help companies position products/services/brands, reach target markets, and effectively build brand image whether in a national or international context (Hsu et al. 2009) owing to synergies created from interactions between instruments of the marketing or promotion mix (Naik and Raman, 2003; Prasad and Sethi, 2008).

All modern organizations, businesses as well as not-for-profit, use various forms of marketing communications functions, tools or instruments, led by advertising in the business-to-consumer (B2C) sector, to promote their offerings and achieve brand financial and non-financial goals (Shimp, 2008). An accelerating and ongoing integration of political, economic, cultural and technological developments has enabled companies to operate globally and adopt international advertising strategies (see Okazaki and Taylor, 2006). Meanwhile, the recent financial tsunamis sweeping over the global economy have helped companies focus on what matters most – *retaining their existing customers.*

Ongoing polemic in the global arena concerns standardization versus localization of advertising. This topic has been extensively debated in the international advertising literature and seems to be of perennial interest (Melewar et al. 2009). A standardized approach assumes that advertising content and strategy created at home can be effectively implemented in other markets, in translation where appropriate. A localized approach criticizes the standardized assumption for not taking into account the economic, cultural and social aspects of local environs. In recent years, researchers have begun to recognize that decisions to standardize or to adapt cannot be dichotomous, as there are degrees along a continuum to which international advertising may be modified (Vrontis and Kitchen, 2005) based on product typology, consumer characteristics and environmental factors, thus producing a reconciliation or contingency approach. Tharp and Jeong (2001) proposed a solution for global organizations, "glocalisation", which is based on global thinking and local adaptation, as explained by Singh et al. (2005).

Despite the lively debate in international advertising strategy, very few studies have investigated the implications of international advertising on IMC or vice versa, the specific requirements and opportunities of international advertising for implementing IMC (Douglas and Carig, 1996; Reich, 1998), or the applications of global IMC in international advertising (Gronroos, 2004; Johnson and Schultz, 2004; Schultz, 2003). In fact, advertising is one of the few promotional mix elements that can effectively cross cultural barriers, unlike, for example, sales promotion or direct marketing.

This chapter attempts to shed the light on the applicability of implementing global IMC utilizing standardized versus adapted advertising in a global or international context. We commence with the premise that a number of evolutionary trends in various areas of marketing and communications have transformed the application of IMC principles from an alternative option to an absolute requirement (Gurau, 2008). The chapter discusses various conceptualizations of IMC and communication tools with an emphasis on the importance of advertising as the most powerful form of communications in a B2C context (Navarro, 2005) and an essential component of marketing communications strategy. Then, controversy over the standardization of advertising campaigns is discussed from a global perspective in terms of three schools of thought: standardization, localization, and reconciliation. Based on this, the implications of international advertising on IMC are presented, as are the challenges and opportunities created by international advertising relating to implementation of global IMC.

THE INCREASING IMPORTANCE OF IMC

In recent years, integrated marketing communication (IMC) has made its way into the mainstream marketing literature (Duncan and Caywood, 1996; Nowak and Phelps, 1994; Schultz, 2003, 2000b; Schultz and Kitchen, 1997; Schultz et al. 2011; Zahay et al. 2004; Grove et al. 2007).

IMC was introduced in the late 1980s in the United States. However, considerable and widespread interest came from both academics and practitioners in marketing communications (Kliatchko, 2001a) as a result of a number of evolutionary trends in various areas of marketing (Gurau, 2008). These trends include the increased fragmentation and segmentation of markets, relationship marketing and direct marketing (Durkin and Lawlor, 2001; Eagle and Kitchen, 2000); information technology – the development of new communication technologies and database applications (Kitchen and Schultz, 1999; McGoon, 1999; McKim, 2002; Reich, 1998); and the increased fragmentation of media audiences with the concomitant multiplicity and saturation of media channels (Hackley and Kitchen, 1998; Smith, 2002; Shimp, 2008).

Kitchen et al. (2004a) and Schultz (1996b) argued that advances in information technology and the Internet underpinned and were driving forces leading toward IMC. These caused a major tectonic shift from mass marketing and product-centred theories of marketing to the more customer-centred, database driven and interactive measurable approaches of integrated marketing communications (Schultz, 2003) – and undoubtedly hastened the move toward relationship marketing.

The IT revolution in fact fundamentally changed the media landscape, which now includes database systems and sophisticated online facilities (Eagle and Kitchen, 2000; Kitchen, 2003 as cited in Holm, 2006). Technology has provided new and innovative channels of communication as well as making availability, development and management of databases an essential tool in customer management (Schultz and Schultz, 1998). Thus, as a result of the rapidly increasing tempo of communication technologies, the IMC approach can more accurately capture and manipulate data on consumers' empirical behaviour *if* appropriately developed and managed (Schultz and Schultz, 1998), which has sped the movement toward segment and niche marketing and enabled marketers to adopt or adapt to new diverse fragmented communication channels (Kotler and Armstrong, 2005). Moreover, such vast improvements in information technology did diminish the power of traditional marketing and advertising, which simultaneously increased the need for more effective and cost-efficient methods in marketing communications (Kim et al. 2004).

From the organizational side, the rapid movement towards cross-border marketing and increased international competition led many organizations to emphasize efficiency in all their operations, including marketing communications (Kliatchko, 2001a). Organizations are increasingly concerned about cost effectiveness and realizing that advertising in the old traditional ways is not always the most cost-effective way of reaching and influencing markets (Kliatchko, 2001a). This has led to allocation of budgets away from traditional mass media and advertising, which has promoted other promotional elements and IMC in terms of their recognisance and importance for effective marketing (see Holm, 2006).

Other organizational drivers for IMC include greater profitability through improved efficiency, increasing levels of accountability, coordinated brand development and competitive advantage, opportunities to utilize management time more productively, and in providing directionality and purposiveness for employees (Fill, 2003). As an aside here, empirical proof is needed for measured outcomes relating to these drivers.

From the market side, Jackson (2000) argues that the most basic driving force behind IMC were changes in the marketing environment(s) in which business is conducted. It is clear that the marketing communication industry – in terms of the structure of advertising agencies, the relationship between advertising and other agencies, and even the functions of various promotional tools – has undergone dramatic changes in the past two decades, both nationally and internationally. Such changes have resulted in the following seven major marketplace trends, which in turn have necessitated new ways of communicating (Duncan and Caywood, 1996).

Decreasing message impact and credibility: The growing number of commercial messages makes it increasingly difficult for single messages or media to be effective (Duncan and Caywood, 1996; Shimp, 2008). Consumers are no longer easily impressed by, or willing to accept commercial messages that are nothing more than a cacophony of words, visuals and sounds put together for the sake of being creative (Kliatchko, 2001a). Kiely also pointed out that the increase in the number of advertising channels, owing to the introduction of digital communication and other various forms of multimedia, coupled with more diversified and fragmented social change, has resulted in a decrease in the effectiveness of advertising through mass media, which has further eroded the dominance of traditional television advertising (Keily, 1993 as cited in Kim et al. 2004).

Increasing mass media costs: Cost of tri-media advertising, particularly TV advertising, continues to escalate (Duncan and Caywood, 1996; Shimp, 2008). This trend has led ad clients to reallocate, and in many cases shift, proportions of marketing communication budgets to below-the-line promotional efforts (Kliatchko, 2001a).

Increasing media fragmentation: Not only are media vehicles becoming more expensive, they are also becoming more fragmented as more specialized offerings in TV, radio and print, and in offline and online media, emerge and coalesce (Duncan and Caywood, 1996; Kliatchko, 2001a). As markets have increasingly fragmented over the past three decades, marketers have moved away from mass toward micro, or even niche, marketing (Kotler and Armstrong, 2005). Increasingly, targeted marketing programmes are designed to build closer relationships with customers in more narrowly segmented markets (Lee and Park, 2007). It should be noted that these markets are not necessarily geographically based. Thus, the notion of a 'marketplace' is counterpoised, and indeed counterbalanced by the 'marketspace' – space in which relationships can be built and sustained and in which repeated transactions take place (Kitchen, 2012).

Decreasing costs of databases: Currently, consumer databases are more affordable to many organizations than ever before, particularly in developed markets. This, coupled with the increased sophistication of audience segmentation, has provided companies with many new ways to reach target audiences efficiently. For marketing to be practised effectively today, use of consumer databases is mandated (Kliatchko, 2001a).

Increasing audience fragmentation: With the help of computers and more sophisticated research methods, companies have increasingly been able to segment and target specialized audiences more accurately. This has, in turn, placed more emphasis on finding media that can efficiently reach niche markets (Duncan and Caywood, 1996). The point to note here that it is not so much how organizations wish to communicate that is important in the twenty-first century, but how customers want to be communicated with. Thus, the very notion of audience fragmentation, demassification and smudge inexorably and necessarily direct managerial attention to the underlying dynamics of served markets.

Increasing number of me-too products: Because of strong competition within product categories, manufacturers have been able successfully to copy their competitors' products in almost all aspects – product quality, pricing, distribution, and so on. This, however, has also created problems. The result has been a proliferation of almost identical products with very little perceived differentiation (Kliatchko, 2001a; Kitchen, 2012). This means that marketing communication must either create a strong brand image and/or deliver sufficient commercial messages to gain attention and sales (Duncan and Caywood, 1996; Shimp, 2010).

Increasing power of retailers: Giant retailers, because of their size and instantaneous information provided by scanner data, have both the influence and knowledge to dictate to suppliers the kind of products and promotions they want and when they want them (Duncan and Caywood, 1996). The growth of global retail chains such as Carrefour, Walmart and Tesco testifies to the internationalization of retail strategies. Hence, promotional strategies spearheaded by advertising can presumably be replicated in other, similar cultures. In some cases this can be both irritating and annoying, for example, as US voice-overs inform consumers in a recognizable nasal twang of the virtues of multinational brands in other countries. UK-based customers visiting the USA or Canada can hardly fail to recognize the many resemblances to ASDA, while the ubiquity of attempting to create low price consciousness in consumers by global or international retailers spans many countries.

Other market-based drivers for IMC include greater levels of audience communication literacy, stakeholder needs for increasing amounts and diversity of information, the move from transaction-based marketing towards relationship marketing, and the rapid ongoing development of networks, collaboration and alliances (Fill, 2003).

From the consumer side, changes in consumer lifestyles, which have resulted in audience fragmentation, encourage advertisers to develop fast and diverse response communication approaches (Kim et al. 2004).

As seen, consumer markets have splintered into smaller, more diversified segments (Kliatchko, 2001a). Engel et al. (1994) stated that appealing to unidentified individuals in a mass market was becoming a dead end, similar to advertising wedding cakes on confetti. One fundamental consequence of this has been that the traditional emphasis on heavyweight mass communication campaigns (so-called above-the-line campaigns) has been replaced or at least supplemented by more direct and highly targeted promotional activities, ranging from narrowly focused speciality magazines and cable television channels to Internet catalogues and coupon promotions aimed at reaching and influencing the smallest of all target groups, the single individual (Holm, 2006).

However, such a shift from mass to target marketing and the corresponding multiplication of on- and offline communications media and promotion channels have brought in their wake unanticipated serious challenges for marketers. That is, when customers obtain information about a brand or a product from an increasing array of sources, they may also receive confused different or inconsistent messages about the same product or brand. This unexpected development is a result of the fact that marketers tend to neglect the integration and coordination of these various messages and communications channels. In the consumer's mind, information from different media channels all becomes part of many messages about companies, products and brands (Lee and Park, 2007). Conflicting messages from these different sources can create confused brand positions and company images in consumers' minds. Hence, unintegrated approaches lead directly to ambivalence and confusion and oftimes to demotion rather than promotion.

From this perspective, the new paradigm of IMC can be represented as a strategic solution to the social and business conditions of the postmodern society (Gurau, 2008; Proctor and Kitchen, 2002) through the systematic integration and coordination of messages and media or communication channels (Lee and Park, 2007).

However, despite its increasing importance, IMC's further development and strategic conceptualization is considered a fundamental and crucial issue that requires further research involving definitional issues, strategic dimensionality, and empirical in-company evidence (Lee and Park, 2007; Schultz et al. 2011).

THE CONCEPTUALIZATION OF IMC

IMC has become accepted practice and dominates the field of marketing communications (Kitchen 2004a, 2010). An increasing number of advertising executives consider IMC as a key competitive advantage associated with marketing (Kitchen and Schultz, 2000; Kitchen, 2010; Schultz et al. 2011).

Concerning the conceptualization of IMC, the literature reveals a number of studies that have explained its meaning and practice from many different perspectives, providing a useful conceptual and theoretical basis for defining its multidimensionality (Lee and Park, 2007; Schultz et al. 2011).

For instance, Nowak and Phelps (1994) provided early contribution to the understanding of the IMC concept, based primarily on the most fundamental notions of the concept, which were 'one-voice' marketing communications, 'integrated' marketing communications (i.e., advertisements), and 'coordinated' marketing communications (Nowak and Phelps, 1994).

The first concept, 'one voice', suggests a 'clear and consistent image, position, message and/or theme, across all marketing communication disciplines or tools' (Kliatchko, 2005). Nowak and Phelps indicated that sales promotion, direct marketing, brand advertising and public relations should be unified under the one-voice theme to create single positioning of brand identity (Lee and Park, 2007).

Second, the 'integrated' marketing communications concept focuses on the creation of both a brand image and behavioural responses created from marketing communications materials such as advertisements (Kliatchko, 2005). Thus, in a marketing communications campaign, the tools used for creating an image (e.g., image advertisements) and the tools employed to influence consumer actions (e.g., such direct response tools as sales promotions) should be integrated (Lee and Park, 2007).

The third concept, 'coordinated' marketing communications, emphasizes the coordination among various marketing communications tools, such as advertising, sales promotion and public relations, with the aim of producing holistic communications campaigns (Kliatchko, 2005). Coordinated marketing communications associates 'integrated' with the concept of 'coordination'. This refers to the coordination of all marketing communications tools such as, for example, advertising, public relations and direct marketing. The goal is to produce holistic campaigns to achieve synergy, that is, op awareness and build brand image, and at the same time to be able to evoke behavioural response from target audiences (Nowak and Phelps, 1994). This unifying view requires that various communication tools designed to appeal to audiences in different stages of the buying process should converge to maximize the impact of communications.

Unlike the one-voice view, this coordinated view recognizes that multiple brand positioning strategy is necessary for different customer groups in the target market. There is empirical evidence that this view is embraced by IMC practitioners. In practical terms, companies that apply IMC identify multiple customer groups in the target market and direct differentiated communications efforts to each of them (Nowak and Siraj, 1996 as cited in Lee and Park, 2007). Thus, well-coordinated marketing communications campaigns create awareness, images, or beliefs as well as boosting the behavioural responses of diverse customer groups in the target market (Lee and Park, 2007). Notably, this identification approach would work well internationally or globally by adapting messages and media where necessary in relation to target audiences or markets.

Another nascent global conceptualization was suggested by Cathey and Schumann (1996, as cited in Lee and Park, 2007). They identified three important aspects of IMC, which are: integration of messages and media, audience-orientation, and assessment of impact. They emphasized the importance of coordination of messages and media to create the most positive communications experiences for consumers who may be in different stages of the buying process. They also highlighted the importance of customer orientation by pointing out that integration should be designed from the perspective of message receivers, not just from the perspective of the ad agency or its client. Moreover, they stressed the need to objectively evaluate customers' responses to integrated campaigns in order to make IMC a dynamic process instead of a one-time activity. Finally, they indicated that the impact of IMC on marketing practice should be continually assessed (Lee and Park, 2007).

Based on a survey of marketing communication practitioners, Phelps and Johnson (1996) had previously identified five factors underlying the IMC construct: one-voice, coordinated marketing communications, direct marketing, response goals, and increased responsibility. One-voice and coordinated marketing communications concepts are the same dimensions as those identified by Nowak and Phelps (1994). Direct marketing refers to the use of direct communications tools such as mail and telephone calls, customer databases, and direct response promotions. This emphasizes the importance of consumer databases in modern marketing communications. Response goals highlight the increasing emphasis on tangible outcomes (i.e., increased sales and awareness) of marketing communications (Phelps and Johnson, 1996). Increased responsibility implies that managers feel that their responsibility is increasing with the more widespread practice of integrated marketing communications (Lee and Park, 2007).

In the conceptual development of IMC, an important milestone was established by Schultz and Schultz (1998) when they proposed a shift in focus from marketing communication tactics and operations to viewing IMC as a 'business process'. While the view of IMC was previously focused on the tactical aspect of putting marketing messages together with a variety of communication tools to create consistent brand image, in recent years it has shifted toward a more strategic orientation (Tsai, 2005; Kitchen, 2010).

Schultz's call for viewing IMC from the strategic perspective came when he strongly expressed his view that the brand is the *very key* to IMC. Schultz (1998) argued that the brand is supposed to be the centre of what consumers want, need, and consider to be of value. In fact, it is the need or want that the brand is assumed to satisfy that is important. Finding this need or want and persuading consumers that this need can be satisfied is the sine qua non of marketing (Kitchen, 2010). Thus, strategic utilization of IMC should be brought into full play (Tsai, 2005).

Schultz (1998) further explained that brand communication was no longer simply what the organization develops, delivers, and pays for, as in the case with traditional advertising programmes. Rather, it is what the customer or prospect receives about the brand from any source whatever, not only advertising. This includes all aspects, elements, functions and activities of the brand (product) such as performance, distribution, advertising, customer service, after-sales service, and so on. He asserts that a combination of all these elements, combined, is what really defines and differentiates one product or service from the competition. In turn, it is all these elements, activities and functions that need to be integrated in a unified manner (Schultz, 1998; Kliatchko, 2001b; Kitchen, 2010).

This may be achieved by further distinguishing between two types of integration: executional or message integration (which means using the same tone, product benefits, brand character, logo, theme line, and so on, across all channels of communication in order to create consistent communication messages) and planning integration (which refers to maximizing efficiency in communication by using the various marketing communications tools to their best advantage) (Kliatchko, 2001b).

More recently, based on the previous review of the conceptual meanings in the IMC literature, Lee and Park (2007) introduced another conceptualization of IMC, encompassing four-dimensions: 'unified communications for consistent message and image', 'differentiated communications to multiple customer groups', 'database-centered communications for tangible results' and 'relationships fostering communications with existing customers' dimensions'. Although these elements might have been identified in previous studies (e.g., Cathey and Schumann, 1996; Nowak and Phelps, 1994), their approach is more comprehensive than those previously proposed. In addition, it added a newly identified dimension to the growing conceptual base of IMC, which is relationship oriented and thus fosters and deepens communications with existing customers (Lee and Park, 2007).

Nevertheless, this conceptualization of IMC was not based on a comprehensive definition, and could be criticized as lacking validity. However, as IMC definitions are not wholly endorsed, this may be a moot point. Moreover, Lee and Park argued that the concept of IMC was still evolving and expanding (see Cook, 2004); hence, practically any attempt to offer a comprehensive definition of IMC at this time is incomplete at best (Lee and Park, 2007), a point endorsed by Kitchen (2010).

In sum, it could be concluded that IMC is now conceptually old but still relatively new in operational terms given that the concept concerns two fundamental principles: the principle of integration or coordination *and* the principle of consumer orientation. It is also operationally new as current technology has made it possible for marketers to put integration and customer focus into actual practice (Kliatchko, 2005). Whether they do so or not is their decision, but it could be argued that it would be folly not to coordinate all marketing and promotional mix elements, based on a sound understanding of served markets.

IMC TOOLS

All modern organizations, businesses as well as not-for-profit organizations, use various forms of marketing communications functions, tools or instruments to promote their offerings and achieve financial and non-financial goals (Shimp, 2010). These primarily include advertisements (Ogden, 1998; Kitchen and Schultz, 2001), sales people (Shimp, 2000; Yeshin, 1998), direct marketing (Yeshin, 1998; Ogden, 1998), free samples, coupons, publicity releases (Kitchen, 1997; Ogden, 1998; Kitchen and Schultz, 2001), exhibitions (Smith, 2002), point-of-purchase (de Pelsmacker et al. 2001), cyber marketing (Smith, 2002; Ogden, 1998), sponsorship (Shimp, 2000), store signs, displays and product packages (Shimp, 2008) and various other communication devices (Shimp, 2010).

In spite of the proclamations concerning the demise of advertising as a mass media vehicle, advertising today remains a powerful form of communication (Navarro, 2005; Kitchen, 2005, 2010) and an essential component of marketing communications strategy, allowing companies to communicate and disseminate their messages to target audiences. This is vitally important in today's markets as consumers around the world are familiar with global brands. This requires multinational and international companies to communicate with individuals from diverse nations. Yet, globalization has become a marketing reality that is a direct consequence of more open commercial boundaries. In addition, the economies and cultures of different nations have indeed become intertwined, although not necessarily homogenized, necessitating more sophisticated communications (Melewar et al. 2009).

During internationalization/globalization, the mastery of international campaigns has become increasingly important (Gabrielsson et al. 2008). Companies need to decide on elements related to marketing such as advertising (De Mooij, 1994). For example, international marketers are being faced with the issue of whether they should modify their advertising from one country to another, and, if so, to what extent (Melewar et al. 2009). This decision is dependent, however, *upon market understanding*, not just corporate or agency edict.

Message development can be a highly complex and controversial problem for companies marketing their products and services on a global scale. We now pick up the controversy earlier outlined previously, which concerns the use of standardized (universal) versus localized (customized) advertising strategies. A review of the literature reveals a division in both academic and corporate circles regarding the effectiveness of a standardized strategy for international advertising.

Advertising Strategies: Standardization versus Adaptation Revisited

The controversy over the standardization of advertising campaigns, first addressed by Elinder (1961), has focused on the appropriateness of variation in advertising content from country to country (Kanso and Nelson, 2002). As a result, three schools of thought have emerged: standardization, localization, and reconciliation, which are discussed below.

Standardization school of thought
The main argument in favour of standardization was proposed by Levitt (1983), who assumed (erroneously, as it transpired) that markets were driven[1] 'toward a converging commonality' by technology and increased communication owing to forces of globalization, resulting in homogenizing markets everywhere personified by worldwide consumer demand for high-quality, low-cost products. Accordingly, marketers needed to take

advantage of this trend by following a standardized marketing strategy that will result in these products for world markets (Viswanathan and Dickson, 2007). However, Levitt (1983) failed to mention that such a standardized approach was relevant only in the very early stages of new product or market development. In fact, the standardized approach, as propounded by Levitt (1983), was at best a mistake, and at worst would set the marketing clock back to a much earlier stage of evolution.

However, continuing with the theme, proponents of the standardized approach (e.g., Ohmae, 1985) argue that people all over the world share the same basic needs and motivations, and, therefore, advertising campaigns can be constructed around these needs and motivations with a universal approach. Furthermore, such authors believed that, even though people are different, their basic physiological and psychological needs are the same. This view was supported by Link (1988). He argued that more and more marketers have recognized the need to build a global brand image and identity and that the resistance to global advertising should and could be overcome. Another supporter of global advertising was Peebles (1988), who admittedly recognized local differences, but claimed these were not insurmountable obstacles to global campaigns. Over two decades later, these apparently surmountable obstacles are still extant and no doubt problematic to would-be globalizers.

Hence, the standardization school challenges the belief that markets are heterogeneous and that an adaption approach is necessary or desirable (Melewar and Vemmervik, 2004).

Standardized advertisement themes do provide two major benefits: cost reductions, mainly originating from economies of scale and scope, since there is a strong relation between standardized advertisements and centralized advertising functions (Onkvisit and Shaw, 1990; Hite and Fraser, 1990; Kirpilani et al. 1988; Tai, 1997; Van Mesdag, 2000), and consistent brand images worldwide (Kirpilani et al. 1988; Melewar et al. 2000; Onkvisit and Shaw, 1990; Tai, 1997).

Other benefits of standardization include consistent positioning arguments throughout the world (Shoham, 1995), sharing of experience, effective use of advertising budget (Tai, 1997), consistency of communication, less duplication of effort and pre-selling of the company's products (Kirpilani et al. 1988).

The adaptation school of thought
The adaptation school holds the opposite view to the standardization school. Advocates of the localized approach (e.g., Boddewyn et al. 1986; Craig et al. 1992; Fournis, 1962; Schlegelmilch et al. 1992; Shoham, 1995) attested that standardization of advertising campaigns is not possible,

pointing out that, in spite of the forces of globalization, markets continue to be different among countries in terms of culture, stages of economic development, political and legal systems, customer values and lifestyles (Cavusgil et al. 1993). Owing to these differences, advertisers are recommended to tailor their campaigns on a country-by-country basis (Kanso and Nelson, 2002), thus creating differential advantage through local sensitivity and increased communications effectiveness (Hite and Fraser, 1990). Indeed, Boddewyn et al. (1986) argued that the evidence for standardization was weak and that standardization was not a necessity to compete in global markets. Even in markets or countries that are apparently culturally similar, such as in the European Union or the USA and Canada, differences in customer needs persist, and the criteria that influence consumer decisions are not the same (Fournis, 1962; Shimp, 2008). Likewise, Wind and Douglas (1986) questioned the feasibility and benefits of a standardized approach, noting that in many cases the costs of production may not be a significant enough part of the total cost for the firm to enjoy economies of scale. In addition, there are too many differences between countries and too many constraints in different markets for a standardized approach to be feasible (Viswanathan and Dickson, 2007).

Hite and Fraser (1990) also claimed that advertising is more dependent on cultural influence than on other marketing elements. Because of these characteristics, the visual and verbal parts of advertising are, in particular, sensitive, and use of local language, models and scenery increases the probability that the advertisement will be effective. In studies by Kanso and Nelson (2002) and Kanso et al. (2011) on the design and implementation of campaigns for non-domestic markets, it was concluded that advertising themes should not be the same across countries. They also proposed that the use of similar appeals and symbols when targeting overseas markets was ill-advised. For customers in these markets, illustrations and colours should be appropriate in order to satisfy the aesthetic sense of different consumers. Kanso and Nelson (2002) and Kanso et al. (2011) also proposed that integration of local communication expertise is vital to overcome language and cultural barriers in worldwide markets. Hence, these and other proponents of the customization approach claim that advertising is difficult to standardize (see also Melewar and Vemmervik, 2004).

The main benefit of adaptation is to gain differential advantage by adapting an advertisement to achieve maximum effectiveness in terms of response and sales (Onkvisit and Shaw, 1990). Such adaptation is usually linked with a decentralized advertising function. The advantage of a decentralized advertising function is that it allows responsiveness and adaptation to culture, infrastructure and competition. As mentioned previously, the visual and verbal parts of advertising are particularly sensitive to adaptation, and use of local language, models and scenery increases the probability that an advertisement will be effective. Consequently, adaptation of creative presentations and decentralized implementation of campaigns should offer greater benefits than less culturally-tied functions (Hite and Fraser, 1990). Other reasons for adaptation are accurate positioning arguments and price discrimination (Shoham, 1995; Shimp, 2010).

Reconciliation school of thought

This school of thought represents a middle ground between standardization and customization recognizing local differences as well as some degree of advertising standardization (Onkvisit and Shaw, 1990). In these terms, the appropriateness of standardization is situation-specific, based on product type, consumer characteristics and environmental factors. This approach is seen by some authors as a redefinition of the standardization concept (Peebles et al. 1974).

One way to look at the compromise school is to view standardization versus adaptation as a continuum (Onkvisit and Shaw, 1990). For instance, Link (1988) argued that companies can be placed on a globalization continuum. On the left side are companies with highly decentralized, multi-domestic operations and products, while on the right side are the totally integrated and globally advertised brands and companies (Melewar and Vemmervik, 2004). In the middle are companies that increasingly standardize brands or products, but still adapt to local differences. It is clear that the decision to standardize or to adapt cannot be dichotomous because there are degrees along a continuum, to which international advertising is modified (Vrontis and Kitchen, 2005).

Tharp and Jeong (2001) offered 'glocalisation' as a preferred solution for global organizations. As explained by Singh et al. (2005), glocalisation is based on global thinking and local adaptation. Furthermore, Overby et al. (2005) suggest that to operate in international markets, organizations have to build strategies that enable them to address successfully the needs of global markets, although marketing strategies should be designed so that they can be adapted to local needs of customers and consumers.

Onkvisit and Shaw (1994) suggested using advertisements that are both global and local at the same time. This kind of 'glocal' advertising tries to achieve the best of both worlds by combining the efficiency of standardization with the effectiveness of localization. The efficiency is derived from the identification of the common theme and elements whose appeals are suffiently universal to serve as the advertisement's main theme that can be used everywhere. The effectiveness is accomplished by planning in advance for necessary modifications that will make the advertisement more meaningful to each country's customers. As such, a global advertisement recognizes both market homogeneity and heterogeneity (Onkvisit and Shaw, 1999). In support, Gould et al. (1999) 'confirm and amplify the need to seek a balance between global efficiency and responsiveness to local conditions'.

Because of the differences of opinion described above, numerous researchers have turned to examining questions related to whether, and/ or under what conditions it is appropriate, to standardize advertising programmes. This is considered important, as there is a clear need for global companies to engage in effective advertising in order to be successful. Regardless of cultural influences, advertising is effective when it elicits positive customer responses, and when it gains customer attention, creates some empathy and effectively communicates a message (Meyers, 1996).

Thus, given the importance of advertising as a hugely influential communications process and with the rise of both globalization and on- and offline advertising activities, there is a pressing need to understand better the factors influencing the choice of international advertising strategy (Vrontis, 2003).

Factors Influencing Decision

There are several models identifying a variety of external and internal factors that impact the standardization or alternate decision (Chandra et al. 2002), which involve trade-offs between the economic benefits of leveraging a global brand identity via standardized strategies with the performance gains achieved when adapting to local market conditions and consumer preferences (Baalbaki and Malhotra, 1993, 1995; Jain, 1989; Ozomer and Prussia, 2000; Shoham, 1999; Szymanski et al. 1993; Wind and Douglas, 1986).

Harvey (1993) identified six variables that affect the degree of standardization or adaptation of advertising. These variables are: (1) product – the degree of universality of the product; (2) competition – the structure of the competitive environment; (3) organizational experience and control – the level of organizational experience in the corporation; (4) infrastructure – the degree of similarity of the media infrastructure, for instance, media, advertising agencies and production facilities; (5) government – restrictions on mass-communication; and (6) culture and society – the cultural differences between the home and export markets. Essentially, the model implies that there are three variables – product, competition and organization – that influence a company when making the decision to standardize or adapt. In addition, the company needs to consider the legal environment and local culture. The influence of these variables should then be mapped on the primary elements of the advertising process to determine the level of standardization needed for each element.

Papavassiliou and Stathakopoulos (1997) created a framework for standardization or adaptation of advertising strategy based on three areas of influence: local environment, firm environment and intrinsic determinants. Cavusgil et al. (1993) also support the contingency perspective, concluding that promotion adaptations correlate significantly and positively with cultural product specificity, international company experience, market competitiveness and product uniqueness.

Shoham (1999) found that only three environmental factors affected the level of standardization: local government, level of competition and physical environment. The fact that only three environmental factors affect the decision to standardize or adapt is consistent with the theory of bounded rationality, which implies that managers do not collect all available information to make a profound analysis, but rather develop plans from incomplete information and analysis (Shoham, 1999).

Viswanathan and Dickson (2007) developed a framework of standardization that attempts to go beyond the focus on 'consumer homogeneity', while recognizing its importance, by incorporating theories of competition. The framework identifies three complex constructs as critical to the standardization process – homogeneity of customer response to the marketing mix, transferability of competitive advantage, and variation in the degree of market freedom. These three constructs serve as critical drivers of the degree of standardization and also serve as the mediating variables through which other variables impact standardization (Viswanathan and Dickson, 2007).

More recently, Melewar et al. (2009) from a practitioner point of view, studied the variables that affect a firm's decision concerning the degree of standardization and divided them into three categories, namely: (1) macro-environmental determinants; (2) micro-environmental determinants specifically related to the firm and the industry in which it operates; and (3) consumer-related determinants.

This reveals that a middle ground between standardization and adaptation pervades the literature on global marketing and promotion (Peebles et al. 1978). Strategies range on a continuum from high adaptation to high standardization (Banerjee, 1994). Within a given product category and market, some companies may thrive by standardizing while others may do so by adapting (Wolfe, 1991). This leads to a contingency approach, which argues that a wide variety of factors both within and outside the firm determine the appropriateness of different promotional campaigns.

Overall, the models are all similar in the sense that they map external and organizational factors that determine the firm's approach to advertising

(Melewar and Vemmervik, 2004). Moreover, organizational arrangements seem to have a substantial impact on the decision to standardize or adapt international advertising (Mclewar and Vemmervik, 2004).

IMPLICATIONS OF INTERNATIONAL ADVERTISING FOR IMC: TOWARD A CONCLUSION

In a similar manner to advertising, IMC is challenged and challenges companies at a global level. As countries are become increasingly interconnected, the importance of global management has grown considerably (Douglas and Craig, 1996), adding a further level of coordination to IMC. In fact, it suggests that theories of international marketing and strategy need to be combined with IMC to explain and effectively utilize global communications.

Although IMC conceptualizations have been elusive, it has been suggested that the purpose of integrated communications is to coordinate all marketing and promotion disciplines around pre-researched needs so that synergies are created (Novak and Phelps, 1994) to ensure that messages are received and decoded correctly (Schultz, 1991). Communications can also be coordinated synergistically even though multiple audiences are being targeted and multiple themes used (Novak and Phelps, 1994). In this case, the purpose is to avoid unnecessary overlap and confusion in terms of reaching audiences while retaining the ability to adjust messages being presented. Thus, IMC aims to develop a one-voice creative perspective involving one theme and image, as well as coordinating activities across communication disciplines, that is, advertising, publicity and sales promotion both off- and online (Novak and Phelps, 1994; Phelps et al. 1994; Shimp, 2010). However, this does not reflect the complexity of international settings. Douglas and Craig (1996) argue that firms should not only coordinate across communications disciplines, leading to a clear and consistent message, but should also coordinate across countries, thus marshalling towards what has been termed global IMC (GIMC).

Similar to IMC, GIMC may be seen to possess vertical integration, which concerns coordinating various promotions and related marketing disciplines (e.g., advertising, brand management, public relations, and so forth). However, GIMC should possess horizontal integration, which involves coordination of communications not only across the offices/ divisions of a promoting organization (such as an agency) as in IMC but also across countries. Thus, for GIMC, coordination entails the management of the global marketplace as a whole and as a system of component parts each with its own specifications.

Based on this view, Douglas and Craig (1996) introduced GIMC as a system of active promotional management that strategically coordinates global communications in all of its component parts both horizontally, in terms of countries and organizations (target market, market position and organisational factors), and vertically, in terms of promotion disciplines (overall promotion mix, advertising creation and public relations). It contingently takes into account the full range of standardized versus adaptive market options, synergies, variations among target populations and other marketplace and business conditions that underlie the level and nature of coordination across disciplines and countries.

However, regarding organizational factors, particularly coordination and control, Schultz (2000a) viewed structure, the way the firm is put together, as the most difficult problem of integration. He argued that, in new economy firms, the traditional command and control structures should be substituted by a quick-response model. In addition, most problems of integration can be resolved only when management starts to focus on outcomes rather than outputs (Kitchen et al. 2004b).

Also, Gurau (2008) claims that the organizational structure of many companies prevents/restricts the effective implementation of IMC. In reality, IMC does not fit easily into the organizational structure adopted by most firms (Percy, 1997) owing to significant organizational barriers to implementation, such as lack of horizontal communication, functional specialization, decentralization, lack of IMC planning and expertise, budget shortage, lack of database technology, corporate culture, and fear of change (Gurau, 2008).

The potential benefits of GIMC, though, include standardization of advertisements to reduce costs, taking advantage of cross-border communications (such as television broadcasts that spill into other countries), developing a consistent brand name and image so that mobile consumers recognize the product in more than one country, and exploiting knowledge from different country operations for the benefits of all company operations.

Thus, this chapter has indicated that integrated advertising campaigns with a global orientation may often involve designing campaigns for a worldwide audience while allowing for needed individual market modification where necessary (Onkvisit and Shaw, 1987). Such a strategic concept, somewhere between complete standardization and total adaptation, means that GIMC represents a contingency approach to global advertising. Cavusgil et al. (1993) found support for such a contingency approach, suggesting that the degree of standardization for advertising depends on a set of factors, such as the firm's international experience, product uniqueness, product type and competitive intensity. To this we also add the need for integration of messages – media (where possible) underpinned by market knowledge. Therefore, a contingency approach to GIMC argues that it is important to coordinate or integrate world-wide communications programmes, but that the level and nature of this coordination occurs across promotion disciplines and countries varies dependent upon underlying conditions (Douglas and Carig, 1996). However, it is not just about internal contingency elements. Almost all advertising approaches *must depend* for their validity upon understanding the dynamics of served markets and then maintaining that understanding over time. Thus, without denigrating all the variegated terms that international marketers may or may not use, nothing can usurp, overturn or adumbrate this need for understanding. Based on such understanding, integrated approaches can be developed and serve as operationalized marketing or communication where behavioural returns feed back to the organization and a virtuous relational circle develops and continues to turn in economic good times and bad. Integration or IMC is indeed here to stay, but integration led and spearheaded by market knowledge. In the end, company- or agency-led integration *without market-based knowledge* is nothing more or less than sales orientation reborn. Such an old-fashioned orientation is actually a denial of the marketing orientation and a slap across the cheeks of twenty-first-century customers and consumers. In the end, such inappropriate approaches will be met by falling sales, lessening profits, as businesses that could be good or may have been great, relegated themselves to the dustbin of economic history.

NOTE

1. The word 'driven' is an interesting choice, and not necessarily picked up by subsequent commentators on the paper. Converging forces may be drivers, but Levitt pointedly ignores the driving force of import penetration in the USA at that time and a growing deficit in terms of their international balance of trade.

REFERENCES

Baalbaki, I.B. and N.K. Malhotra (1993), 'Marketing management bases for international market segmentation: An alternate look at the standardization/customization debate', *International Marketing Review*, **10** (1), 19–43.
Baalbaki, I.B. and N.K. Malhotra (1995), 'Standardization versus customization in international marketing: An investigation using bridging conjoint analysis', *Journal of the Academy of Marketing Science*, **23** (3), 182–94.
Banerjee, A. (1994), 'Transnational advertising development and management: An account

planning approach and a process framework', *International Journal of Advertising*, **13** (2), 95–124.

Boddewyn, J., R. Soehl and J. Picard (1986), 'Standardization in international marketing: Is Ted Levitt in fact right?' *Business Horizons*, **29**, 69–75.

Cathey, A. and D.W. Schumann (1996), 'Integrated marketing communications: Construct development and foundations for research', Proceedings of the 1996 American Academy of Advertising Conference.

Cavusgil, S.T., S. Zou and G.M. Naidu (1993), 'Product and promotion adaptation in export ventures: An empirical investigation', *Journal of International Business Studies*, **24** (3), 479–506.

Chandra, A., D.A. Griffith and J.K. Ryans Jr (2002), 'Advertising standardization in India: US multinational experience', *International Journal of Advertising*, **21** (1), 47–66.

Cook, W. (2004), 'IMC's Fussy Picture: Break through or break down?' *Journal of Advertising Research*, **44** (1), 1–2.

Craig, S.C., S.P. Douglas and A. Grein (1992), 'Patterns of convergence and divergence among industrialized nations: 1960–1988', *Journal of International Business Studies*, **23** (4), 773–87.

De Mooij, M. (1994), *Advertising Worldwide: Concepts, Theories and Practice of International, Multinational and Global Advertising*, London: Prentice-Hall.

De Mooij, M. and W. Keegan (1991), *Advertising Worldwide: Concepts, Theories and Practice of International, Multinational and Global Advertising*, London: Prentice Hall.

De Pelsmacker, P., M. Geuens and J. Van den Berg (2001), *Marketing Communications*, Essex: Pearson Education Limited.

Douglas, S.P. and C.S. Craig (1996), *Global Marketing Strategy*, New York: McGraw Hill.

Duncan, T. and C. Caywood (1996), 'The concept, process, and evolution of integrated marketing communications', in E. Thorson and J. Moore (eds), *Integrated Communication: Synergy of Persuasive Voices*, Mahwah, NJ: Lawrence Erlbaum, pp. 13–34.

Durkin, M. and M.-A. Lawlor (2001), 'The implications of the Internet on the advertising agency–client relationship', *The Service Industries Journal*, **21** (2), 175–90.

Eagle, L. and P. Kitchen (2000), 'MC, brand, communications and corporate cultures: Client/ advertising agency co-ordination and cohesion', *European Journal of Marketing*, **34**, 667–86.

Eagle, L., M. Warshaw and T. Kinnear (1994), *Promotional Strategy: Managing the Marketing Communications Process*, Burr Ridge: Erwin.

Elinder, E. (1961), 'International can advertising must devise universal ads, dump separate national ones', *Advertising Age*, **27**, 91.

Fill, C. (2003), *Marketing Communications: Contexts, Strategies and Applications*, London: Prentice Hall.

Fournis, Y. (1962), 'The markets of Europe or the European market?' *Business Horizons*, **5** (4), 77–83.

Gabrielsson, P., M. Gabrielsson and H. Gabrielsson (2008), 'International advertising campaigns in fast-moving consumer goods companies originating from a SMOPEC country', *International Business Review*, **17**, 714–28.

Gould, S.J., D.B. Lerman and A.F. Grein (1999), 'Agency perceptions and practices on global IMC', *Journal of Advertising Research*, **39** (1), 7–20.

Gronroos, C. (2004), 'The relationship marketing process: Communication, interaction, dialogue, value', *The Journal of Business & Industrial Marketing*, **19** (2), 99–113.

Grove, S., L. Carlson and M. Dorsch (2007), 'Comparing the application of integrated marketing communication (IMC) in magazine ads across product type and time', *Journal of Advertising*, **36** (1), 37–54.

Gurau, C. (2008), 'Integrated online marketing communication: Implementation and management', *Journal of Communication Management*, **12** (2), 169–84.

Hackley, C. and P.J. Kitchen (1998), 'IMC: A consumer psychological perspective', *Marketing Intelligence & Planning*, **16** (3), 229–35.

Harvey, M.G. (1993), 'Point of view: A model to determine standardization of the advertising process in international markets', *Journal of Advertising Research*, **33** (4), 57–64.

Hite, R. and C. Fraser (1988), 'International advertising strategies of multinational corporations', *Journal of Advertising Research*, **28** (4), 9–16.

Hite, R. and C. Fraser (1990), 'Configuration and coordination of global advertising', *Journal of Business Research*, **21**.

Holm, O. (2006), 'Integrated marketing communication: From tactics to strategy', *Corporate Communications*, **11** (1), 23–34.

Hsu, T., T. Tsai and P. Chiang (2009), 'Selection of the optimum promotion mix by integrating a fuzzy linguistic decision model with genetic algorithms', *Information Science*, **179** (1), 41–52.

Jackson, M.G. (2000), *Systems Approaches to Management*, New York: Kluwer Academic/ Plenum Press.

Jain, S.C. (1989), 'Standardization of international marketing strategy: Some hypotheses', *Journal of Marketing*, **53** (1), 70–79.

Johnson, C.R. and D.E. Schultz (2004), 'A focus on customers', *Marketing Management*, **13** (5), 20–27.

Kanso, A. and R. Nelson (2002), 'Advertising localization overshadows standardization', *Journal of Advertising Research*, **40**, 79–89.

Kanso, A., R. Nelson and P.J. Kitchen (2011), 'Meaningful obstacles remain to standardization of international services advertising: New insights from a managerial survey', *International Journal of Commerce and Management*, **21** (4), forthcoming.

Kim, I., D. Ham and D. Schultz (2004), 'Understanding the diffusion of integrated marketing communications', *Journal of Advertising Research*, **44** (1), 31.

Kirpalani, V.H., M. Laroche and R.Y. Darmon (1988), 'Role of headquarter control by multinationals in international advertising decisions', *International Journal of Advertising*, **7** (4), 323–34.

Kitchen, P.J. (1997), *Public Relations: Principle and Practice*, 1st ed. London: Thomson Business Press.

Kitchen, P.J. (2005), 'New Paradigm-IMC-Under Fire', *Competitiveness Review*, **15** (1), 72–80.

Kitchen, P.J. (ed.) (2010), *Integrated Brand Marketing and Measuring Returns*, Basingstoke: Palgrave-Macmillan.

Kitchen, P.J. (ed.) (2012), *The Dominant Role of Marketing in the 21st Century: The Marketing Leviathan*, Basingstoke: Palgrave-Macmillan. Under development.

Kitchen, P. and D. Schultz (1999), 'A multi-country comparison of the drive for IMC', *Journal of Advertising Research*, **39** (1), 21–38.

Kitchen, P.J. and D. Schultz (2001), *Raising the Corporate Umbrella: Corporate Communications in the 21st Century*, Basingstoke: Palgrave.

Kitchen, P.J., J. Brignell, T. Li and G. Spickett-Jones (2004a), 'The emergence of IMC: A theoretical perspective', *Journal of Advertising Research*, **44** (1), 19–30.

Kitchen, P.J., D. Schultz, I. Kim, D. Han and I. Li (2004b), 'Will agencies ever get (or understand) IMC?' *European Journal of Marketing*, **38** (11/12), 1417–36.

Kliatchko, J. (2001a), 'Driving forces behind IMC (integrated marketing communications)', *Business World*, July, p. 1.

Kliatchko, J. (2001b), 'Weekender: Integration of brand communication programs (integrated marketing communications)', *Business World*, August, p. 1.

Kliatchko, J. (2002), *Understanding Integrated Marketing Communications*, Pasig City, Philippines: Inkwell Publishing.

Kliatchko, J.G. (2005), 'Towards a new definition of integrated marketing communications (IMC)', *International Journal of Advertising*, **24** (1), 7–34.

Kirpalani, V.H., M. Laroche and R.Y. Darmon, (1988), 'Role of headquarter control by multinationals in international advertising decisions', *International Journal of Advertising*, **7**, 323–33.

Kotler, P. and G. Armstrong (2005), *Principles of Marketing*, Englewood Cliffs, NJ: Prentice Hall.

Lee, D. and C. Park (2007), 'Conceptualization and measurement of multidimensionality of integrated marketing communications', *Journal of Advertising Research*, **47** (3), 222.

Levitt, T. (1983), 'The globalisation of markets', *Harvard Business Review*, **61**, 102.

Link, G.L. (1988), 'Global advertising: An update', *The Journal of Consumer Marketing*, **5** (2), 69–74.

McGoon, C. (1998), 'Cutting edge companies use integrated marketing communication', *Communication World*, **16** (1), 15–19.

McKim, B. (2002), 'The difference between CRM and database marketing', Journal *of Database Marketing*, **9** (4), 371–5.

Melewar, T.C., D. Pickton, S. Gupta and T. Chigovanyika (2009), 'MNE executive insights into international advertising programme standardisation', *Journal of Marketing Communications*, **15** (5), 345–65.

Melewar, T.C., S. Turnbull and G. Balabanis (2000), 'International advertising strategies of multinational enterprises in the Middle East', *International Journal of Advertising*, **19** (4), 529–47.

Melewar, T.C. and C. Vemmervik (2004), 'International advertising strategy: A review, reassessment and recommendation', *Management Decision*, **42** (7/8), 863–81.

Meyers, R.D. (1996), 'Consistent advertising evaluation from multi-country inconsistent data sets', *Journal of Advertising Research*, **36** (3), RC2.

Naik, P. and K. Raman (2003), 'Understanding the impact of synergy in multimedia communications', *Journal of Marketing Research*, XL (November), 375–88.

Navarro, P. (2005), 'The well-timed strategy: Managing the business cycle', *California Management Review*, **48** (1), 1–21.

Nowak, G. and J. Phelps (1994), 'Conceptualizing the integrated marketing communications' phenomenon: An examination of its impact on advertising practices and its implications for advertising research', *Journal of Current Issues and Research in Advertising*, **16** (1), 49–66.

Ogden, J. (1998), *Developing a Creative and Innovative Integrated Marketing Communication Plan: A Working Model*, London: Prentice-Hall.

Okazaki, S. and C. Taylor (2006), 'Towards an understanding advertising standardization in the European Union: A theoretical framework and research propositions', in Sandra Diehl and Ralf Terlutter (eds), *International Advertising and Communication*, Deutscher Universitats-Verlag.

Ohmae, Kenichi (1985), *Triad Power: The Coming Shape of Global Competition*, New York: The Free Press.

Onkvisit, S. and S. John (1987), 'Standardized international advertising: A review and critical evaluation of the theoretical and empirical evidence', *Columbia Journal of World Business*, **22** (3), 43–55.

Onkvisit, S. and J.J. Shaw (1990), 'Global advertising: Revolution or myopia', *Journal of International Consumer Marketing*, **2** (3), 97–112.

Onkvisit, S. and J.J. Shaw (1994), 'Standardization versus localization: The need for compromising perspectives', in Salah S. Hassan and Roger D. Blackwell (eds), *Global Marketing: Perspectives and Cases*, Fort Worth, TX: Dryden Press.

Onkvisit, S. and J.J. Shaw (1999), 'Standardized international advertising: Some research issues and implications', *Journal of Advertising Research*, **39** (6), 19–25.

Overby, J.W., R.B. Woodruff and S.F. Gardial (2005), 'The influence of culture upon consumers' desired value perceptions: A research agenda', *Marketing Theory*, **5** (2), 139–63.

Ozsomer, A. and G.E. Prussia (2000), 'Competing perspectives in international marketing strategy: Contingency and process models', *Journal of International Marketing*, **8** (1), 27–50.

Papavassiliou, N. and V. Stathakopoulos (1997), 'Standardization versus adaptation of international advertising strategies: Towards a framework', *European Journal of Marketing*, **31**, 504–27.

Peebles, D.M. (1988), 'Executive insights don't write off global advertising: A commentary', *International Marketing Review*, **6** (1), 73–8.

Peebles, D.M., J.K.J. Ryans and I.R. Vernon (1977), 'A new perspective on advertising standardization', *European Journal of Marketing*, **11** (8), 569–78.

Peebles, D., J.K. Ryans Jr and I.R. Vernon (1978), 'Coordinating international advertising', *Journal of Marketing*, **42** (1), 28–34.

Percy, L. (1997), *Strategies for Implementing Integrated Marketing Communication*, Chicago: NTC Business Books.

Phelps, J. and E. Johnson (1996), 'Entering the quagmire: Examining the "meaning" of integrated marketing communications', *Journal of Marketing Communications*, **2** (3), 159–72.

Phelps, J., J. Plumley and E. Johnson (1994), 'Integrated marketing communications: Who is doing what?' in Karen Whitehill King (ed.), *Proceedings of the 1994 Conference of the American Academy of Advertising*, Athens: University of Georgia.

Prasad, A. and S. Sethi (2008), 'Integrated marketing communication in markets with uncertainty and competition', *Automatica*. In press. www. Elsevier.com/locate/automatic.

Proctor, T. and P.J. Kitchen (2002), 'Communication in postmodern integrated marketing', *Corporate Communications: An International Journal*, **7** (3), 144–54.

Reich, K. (1998), 'IMC: Through the looking glass of the new millennium', *Communication World*, **15** (7), 26–33.

Schlegelmilch, B.B., A. Diamantopoulos and J.P. Du Preez (1992), 'Consumer preferences as barriers to standardized marketing programmes in the single European market: The role of country-of-origin and ecological product attributes', in V.L. Crittenden (ed.), *Developments in Marketing Science*, vol. 15, Chestnut Hill, MS: AMS.

Schultz, D.E. (1991), 'Integrated marketing communications: The status of integrated marketing communications programs in the US today', *Journal of Promotion Management*, **1** (1), 99–104.

Schultz, D. (1998), 'Branding: The basis for marketing integration', *Marketing News*, **32** (24), 8.

Schultz, D. (2000a), 'Structural flows dash marcom plans', *Marketing News*, **43** (18), 9.

Schultz, D. (2006b), 'Definition of internal mktg. Remains elusive', *Marketing News*, **40** (1), 6.

Schultz, D.E. (2003), 'Opinion piece: the next generation of integrated marketing communications', *Interactive Marketing*, **4** (4), 318–19.

Schultz, D.E. and P.J. Kitchen (2000a), *Communicating Globally: An Integrated Marketing Approach*, Basingstoke: Macmillan.

Schultz, D. and P. Kitchen (2000b), 'A response to "Theoretical concept or management fashion"', *Journal of Advertising Research*, **40** (5), 17–21.

Schultz, D. and H. Schultz (1998), 'Transitioning marketing communication into the twenty-first century', *Journal of Marketing Communications*, **4** (1), 9–26.

Schultz, D.E., C. Patti and P.J. Kitchen (eds) (2011), *The Current Status of Integrated Marketing Communications*, London: Routledge. In press.

Shimp, T. (2000), *Advertising, Promotions: Supplemental Aspects of Integrated Marketing Communications*, TX: Dyer Press.

Shimp, T. (2008), *Advertising, Promotions, and Other Supplemental Aspects of Integrated Marketing Communications*, OH: Thomson-Southwestern.

Shimp, T. (2010), *Advertising, Promotion and Other Aspects of Integrated Marketing Communications*, South Western: Cengage Learning, UK.

Shoham, A. (1999), 'Bounded rationality, planning, standardization of international strategy, and export performance: A structural model examination', *Journal of International Marketing*, **7** (2), 24–50.

Shoham, A. (1995), 'Global marketing standardization', *Journal of Global Marketing*, **9** (1/2), 91–119.

Singh, N., V. Kumar and D. Baack (2005), 'Adaptation of cultural content: evidence from B2C e-commerce firms', *European Journal of Marketing*, **39** (1/2), 71–86.

Smith, P. (2002), *Marketing Communications: An Integrated Approach*, London: Kogan Page.

Szymanski, D.M., S.G. Bharadwaj and P.R. Varadarajan (1993), 'Standardization versus adaptation of international marketing strategy: An empirical investigation', *Journal of Marketing*, **57** (4), 1–17.

Tharp, M. and J. Jeong (2001), 'The global network communications agency', *Journal of International Marketing*, **9** (4), 111–31.

Tai, S.H.C. (1997), 'Advertising in Asia: Localize or regionalize?' *International Journal of Advertising*, **16** (1), 48–62.

Tsai, S. (2005), 'Integrated marketing as management of holistic experience', *Business Horizon*, **48**, 431–41.

Van Mesdag, M. (2000), 'Culture-sensitive adaptation or global standardization – the duration-of-usage hypothesis', *International Marketing Review*, **17** (1), 74–84.

Viswanathan, N.K. and P.R. Dickson (2007), 'The fundamentals of standardizing global marketing strategy', *International Marketing Review*, **24** (1), 46–63.

Vrontis, D. (2003), 'International advertising and standardisation in international marketing: The adaptstand modelling process', *Journal of Marketing Management*, **19** (3/4), 283–305.

Vrontis, D. and P.J. Kitchen (2005), 'Entry methods and international marketing decision making: An empirical investigation', *International Journal of Business Studies*, **13** (1), 87–110.

Wind, Y. and S.P. Douglas (1986), 'The myth of globalization', *Journal of Consumer Marketing*, **3** (2), 23–6.

Wolfe, A. (1991), 'The single European market: National or Euro-brands?' *International Journal of Advertising*, **10**, 49–58.

Yeshin, T. (1998), *Marketing Communications Strategy*, Oxford: Butterworth-Heinemann.

Zahay, D., J. Peltier, D. Schultz and A. Griffin (2004), 'The role of transactional versus relational data in IMC programs: Bringing customer data together', *Journal of Advertising Research*, **44** (1), 3.

23 Analysis of the relationship between advertisers and advertising agencies in the global market

Hirokazu Takada, Makoto Mizuno and Ling Bith-Hong

INTRODUCTION

The major tasks for companies operating in the highly competitive global marketplace are to formulate advertising and branding strategies, and to implement them by working together with advertising agencies. In the global market, companies must coordinate these activities across different countries; thus the relationship between companies and advertising agencies becomes highly complex. One of the key questions confronting managers is whether or not to use the same advertising agency or its network for the entire operation across countries to achieve cohesiveness and better coordination of advertising activities. An alternative strategy is to use local advertising agencies to better respond to local needs/wants. Obviously, some companies may choose a combination of both strategies, or a variant of these, e.g., globally networked agencies for key markets along with local agencies for the rest of the markets.

Recently, global advertising agencies have responded to the needs of global companies by building a global network through alliance with other agencies such that these agencies can provide the necessary service whichever country their client company is operating in. Furthermore, a majority of these advertising agencies strictly adhere to the policy that they will work for just one company in the industry; thereby the client and agency can work very closely by sharing a great amount of information between them, and the agency is highly involved not only in daily operations but also in strategic decisions.

It is well known that Japanese advertising agencies, such as Dentsu and Hakuhodo, are taking multiple accounts in the same industry. Recently, in order to better meet the needs of their global Japanese clients in the overseas markets, the Japanese agencies have formed strategic alliances with foreign agencies and have fortified their subsidiary operations. They have also shifted their way of conducting business, from the traditional selling of media space to a more comprehensive marketing partnership with their clients. They are also responding to the growing concerns raised by the foreign companies in Japan, i.e., the demand for better accountability and security of the information. Despite these efforts, fundamental differences still remain between Japanese agencies and Western agencies.

What would be the optimal strategy to achieve the delicate balancing act of allowing flexibility to deal with the local conditions and building the consistent corporate and brand identity in the global market? There is a rich stream of literature in the area of international marketing on this topic that could provide answers to this fundamental question, which confronts not only the automotive firms but also many other multinational corporations. The standardized marketing concept (Buzzell, 1968) was advocated by Levitt (1983) as having advantages such as cost reduction, owing to global economy of scale and scope, and the learning curve effect; better control, improving product quality, and the uniformity of brand image, under the presumption of global customer needs and taste. Since then, numerous articles have been published (Boddewyn et al. 1986; Jain, 1989; Samiee and Roth, 1992; Szymanski et al. 1993; Walters, 1986 and 1989, among others) that present various views on the topic of whether global firms should standardize or customize their corporate and marketing strategies.

Rau and Preble (1987) have focused on a standardized marketing process as the key attribute of global marketing, which means standardizing the way in which country subsidiaries analyze markets and develop marketing plans, and a way of transferring skills and setting high standards for the marketing function. Yip (2003) argues that the standardizing process is merely good multinational practice, and suggests a flexible approach as the global marketing strategy: within each element, some parts can be globally uniform and others less so. The key in global strategy is to find the best balance between local adaptation and global standardization in favor of uniformity. So global marketing is not a blind adherence to standardization of all marketing elements for its own sake, but a different, global approach to developing marketing strategies and programs that blend flexibility with uniformity (Yip, 2003, p. 141). Research shows that brand names need the most uniformity; advertising moderate uniformity; selling and promotion the least (Yip, 1997).

THE CONCEPTUAL FRAMEWORK

We hypothesize and classify the client and agency relationships as depicted in Figure 23.1, which shows the hypothesized typology of client–agency relationship in the global market for the automobile industry as

The U.S./European Model   The Japanese Model

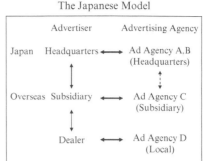

Figure 23.1   Hypothetical relationship between advertisers and agencies

an example. It is readily seen from Figure 23.1 that the U.S./European model hypothesizes that the advertiser hires advertising agency A at its headquarters, and then it also uses the subsidiaries of the same agency in foreign markets as far as the agency's network has coverage in these markets. The advertiser may hire a local agency, if the car dealer has some relationship in the local market. As the bold-faced arrow shows, there is a strong linkage between the headquarters and subsidiaries in terms of communication, transfer of knowledge, and control of marketing and advertising operations, whereas the thin and dotted arrow indicates a weaker linkage, e.g., the case in the Japanese model. The strong linkage in the U.S./European model for the company's relationship with the advertising agency, for instance, implies that the client tends to share detailed information with the agency, such that they work very closely to formulate and implement advertising strategy as partners, rather than the client–agency relationship. The unidirectional arrows from the headquarters to the subsidiary and to dealers/local ad agency for both clients and agency attempt to capture the top-down decision making, i.e., highly centralized and controlled decision making that enables better control of branding and advertising across different markets. The disadvantages of this model would include that the strategies do not necessarily reflect local market needs and wants if the control is exercised excessively.

The Japanese model in Figure 23.1, on the other hand, attempts to capture the traditional relationship between the client and the agency in the Japanese market. Although the client holds a tight relationship with the ad agency as indicated by the bold-faced arrow, the client often works with not just one agency, but with other agencies as well. Toyota Motor Corporation, the heaviest advertiser in Japan for years, is known to work with Dentsu, but also works with Hakuhodo and other advertising

Table 23.1   Advertising accounts of major auto companies

Advertiser Company/ Brand	Agency – Worldwide		Agency – Japan	
	Media	Creative	Media	Creative
Ford	J.W.T.		Hakuhodo	J.W.T
Jaguar	Y&R, etc.		Hakuhodo	Dentsu Y&R
Chrysler(Jeep)	BBDO		I&S BBDO	
Mercedes	BBDO	Springer & Jacoby, etc.	Dentsu	
BMW	Fallon, etc.		ADK	Cove-Ito
VOLVO	MVBMS (Euro RSGC)		Hakuhodo	Dentsu Y&R
GM	(Not disclosed)		McCann-Erickson	
Nissan	TBWA		Hakuhodo G1	
Toyota	Saatchi & Saatchi, etc.		Dentsu, Hakuhodo, Delphys	
Honda	Starcom Motive, etc.	Widen & Kennedy, etc.	Dentsu	
Mazda	JWT (in Europe);	Doner (in U.S.)	Hakuhodo	
VW	DDB, etc.		ADK	DDB/Fallon

Source: AdverTimes, July 14, 2005.

agencies. The unique characteristics of the client–agency relationship in Japan also hold true in the case of the dominant Dentsu and other advertising agencies, as they also work with more than one client in the same industry sector. Dentsu, for instance, is working with Toyota, but also with Honda, and other domestic and foreign automotive companies (Table 23.1). We hypothesize that advertisers make their decisions through consensus building by communicating among the headquarters, subsidiaries, and dealers, rather than using the top-down approach of the U.S./European model. We also suspect that the Japanese agencies have not built a global network, as compared with the Western agencies that have been devoting their continuous efforts to formulate global networks; thus the dotted and light-faced arrow in Figure 23.1 underneath the advertising agency of the Japanese model reflects the agency's relationship between its headquarters and subsidiary being still in its infancy stage. Furthermore, the client in foreign markets does not necessarily rely on the same agency they use in the home market, as indicated by ad agencies A and C in Figure 23.1, whereas ad agency C is any other agency unrelated to the agency located in Japan. It is thus likely that the client's local agency working with its dealer is a local agency denoted as D in Figure 23.1, and not related to the Japanese agency. The report compiled by the Federal Trade Commission of the Government of Japan (2005) illustrates the unique characteristics of the Japanese advertising industry.

WHY DIFFERENT?

Why do these differences emerge between the U.S./European model and the Japanese model? It is readily seen that these differences are caused by structural impediments, i.e., the various macro environments, which include legal and political environments, business practices and customs, and historical reasons, among others, unique to the market, and beyond the control of managers. At the same time, globalization is thought to prompt managers to control branding and advertising strategies across the regions and throughout the organization. The advertising agencies have also responded well to clients' needs, but in different ways.

GOAL OF THE STUDY AND CONTRIBUTIONS

What should be the optimal path for clients and advertising agencies in the future to better survive in the global market? It is the goal of this study to find out the answers to this question. We take a holistic approach to analyzing the problem by looking at the whole spectrum of the relationships at different levels within the organization and in different countries, covering the various stages ranging from strategy formulation to implementation, rather than an ad hoc approach of looking at a specific relationship at a specific time, as employed by previous studies. We will conduct in-depth interviews with the managers of leading automotive manufacturers to analyze their behavior when formulating strategies and implementing advertising plans. This research is unprecedented owing to the scope of the markets covered and the nature of the information to be collected. Therefore, we expect that the study is making a significant contribution to the research of international marketing management and advertising studies.

RESEARCH DESIGN AND QUESTIONS

We observe two different models of managing advertising operations dealing with advertising agencies as depicted in the conceptual framework

Table 23.2   Advertising decision and strategy of advertisers

	Development in individual region			Development that exceeds country border	
	Corporate advertising	Brand advertising	Sales promotion advertising	Corporate advertising	Product advertising
Advertising basic strategy Creation Media					

of our study, namely, the U.S./European model in which Western firms tend to deal with the same advertising agency and its global network so that they can achieve consistency for their advertising activities across different regions; and the Japanese model, in which the Japanese firms tend to delegate responsibilities to local subsidiaries and allow them to deal with multiple advertising agencies so that they can better respond to local needs and wants. The Japanese market is often regarded as an exception in the global landscape of advertising business by the Western firms that are forced to deviate from and modify their global advertising strategy to adjust to the unique conditions in Japan.

Thus, the partnership between the client and agency takes various forms, although the relationship is dictated by the auspices of the client's global strategy. We, however, consider such variations as a result of different adaptation strategies in response to the different environmental conditions in the global marketplace. The objective of this study is to find out how managers will cope with dynamic changes in the business environment in the global marketplace. In light of this objective, we have conducted interviews with managers of German and Japanese global automotive firms with the following specific questions:

Global Marketing and Advertising Strategies and Organization

1. When the firm formulates the global (covering the U.S., Europe, Japan and Asia) advertising strategy at the headquarters and subsidiaries, how does the firm delegate its decision making at each level? Various advertising decisions are summarized in Table 23.2. We attempt to identify how the firm makes a decision for each blank cell in the table, and fill those cells with the

information to be obtained through interviews with managers involved. We are focusing our study on the four specific markets, namely, the U.S., Japan, China and Taiwan. For the overall advertising decision of corporate advertising in a particular market, for instance in China, which corresponds to an upper left cell in the table, we tried to identify whether the corporate head-quarters gets involved in this decision. Alternatively, this decision may be delegated to the management at the local subsidiary in China. On the other hand, we attempt to find out whether the overall corporate advertising decision across the boundaries is made at the headquarters first, and then communicated to the subsidiaries, such as in the case of top-down decision making. Alternatively, this decision may be made through communication between the corporate headquarters and the subsidiaries.

2. For the regional advertising activities, how does the headquarters control or review such activities in the foreign market? How often is this done? Which department is responsible for this?

How Does the Firm Work with Advertising Agencies?

3. When the firm selects the advertising agency in a foreign market, to what extent does the headquarters get involved in this decision? Is the decision made by the headquarters? Or is this decision del-egated to the subsidiary to its full extent? Or is this decision made by both the headquarters and the subsidiary?

4. For the home country and foreign markets, does the firm use sepa-rate advertising agencies for particular products/models, media types, and other functions? Alternatively, is the firm centralizing these advertising operations to a particular agency? When the firm selects these agencies, what kinds of criteria are employed to evalu-ate and review the alternative ad agencies?

5. How does the ad agency get involved in formulating and imple-menting advertising strategies in the home country and foreign markets with respect to the following areas:
   i.   overall advertising strategy (advertising budget alloca-tion by product and brand, targeting, and positioning, among others);
   ii. creative decisions;

iii.   media decisions (including media planning and media buying); and

iv.   advertising research (including target research and measurement of advertising effectiveness).

For each of these activities, we asked managers to choose the appropriate action from among the following alternatives:

i.   The headquarters/regional subsidiaries would make basic decisions and then let agencies implement the decisions.

ii.   The headquarters/regional subsidiaries would work closely with the ad agencies as a team.

iii.   The headquarters/regional subsidiaries provide briefings regarding the basic guideline, and let the agencies work on their own for further details.

iv.   Other forms of the relationship between the headquarters/regional subsidiaries and the agency apply.

6.   If the firm observes any variations or deviations between the headquarters and regional subsidiaries with respect to the way in which the firm conducts advertising management or the way in which the firm manages the relationship with the ad agencies, what would be the reasons for the firm observing such variations or deviations?

7.   If the way of managing advertising as illustrated above is different from other major competitive manufacturers, domestic or foreign, what would be the reasons?

8.   How does a manager foresee the company's global advertising strategy evolving in the future? Does the firm expect that a major shift and adjustment will be required for the firm's strategy to better cope with any possible changes in the global business environment? Or, should the strategy remain much the same in the near future?

Global Brand Management

9.   How does the firm control the corporate brand or model-specific brand management, which covers not only brand names, logos and campaign slogans, but also a more comprehensive image control? How is this brand management organized? Would this be implemented by a particular department or division within the corporate

headquarters alone, or in conjunction with foreign subsidiaries as well?

10. What does a manager think about the extent to which brand management should be implemented in the global sphere? Should the brand be tightly controlled across countries to build a cohesive corporate image? Or should the brand management also take into account regional situations?

EMPIRICAL ANALYSIS

We have conducted an extensive data collection to test the hypotheses presented in the previous sections of the conceptual framework and research design and questions. The scope of the data collection is quite extensive. The automotive industry was selected for this study, because its advertising expenditure is significant, and the advertising decision making involved is highly complex. Among the global automotive manufacturers included in the study are major firms with headquarters, the top four (in terms of total revenue) manufacturers in Germany, and top three in Japan, respectively. These firms have substantial presence in the global marketplace, particularly in the countries we are studying. We have selected four major countries (Japan, the United States, China and Taiwan), because these countries possess strategic importance for the automotive firms. The U.S. market, for instance, is becoming the primary market for the companies in terms of their sales relative to overall sales, especially for the Japanese firms. China is presenting unprecedented opportunities for future growth in this industry. Furthermore, complexities of political and legal environments in China pose various challenges for the firms when making marketing and advertising decisions. Taiwan appears to be an interesting market for this study, since its culture is very similar to that of China, whereas its business practices are similar to Japan's.

In the following section, we will explain the nature of the data and information collected and the results of the empirical hypotheses testing based on the data and information collected.

Data Collection

We have organized this section into secondary data collection and primary data collection, respectively.

Secondary data collection
We collected the secondary data related to the automotive industry and advertising agencies in the four countries from various sources. The specific items in the data set include the following: automotive industry sales data by countries, companies, and models; lineup of major brands across the countries; information on the advertising agencies working with the automotive companies; advertising expenditures of the major automotive companies in the four countries.

Primary data collection
We conducted interviews with the managers of automotive firms who are responsible for each of the markets in Japan, China, Taiwan and the U.S. The Japanese and European companies chosen for this study represent global players with presence in the four major countries. All of these companies fully cooperated with our study. One of the leading companies in Japan, in particular, was generous and gave us full access to the managers in different divisions so that we were able to cover the firm's key areas of operations, including overseas and domestic marketing, and the research division at their headquarters. We contacted Presidents and Chief Executive Officers of European companies in Japan, and all of these companies gave us the opportunity to interview the marketing directors and managers, and provided detailed information on their operations, not only in Japan but also across major regions of the world. We were also successful in conducting interviews with the set of firms in Taiwan.

The interviews lasted for between two and several hours, and covered various topics presented in the research design in great detail. We also conducted interviews with managers in the leading advertising agency in Japan, and with Professor Fujimoto at the University of Tokyo, who is an expert on the automotive manufacturing process.

The secondary data indicate that the Chinese automotive market is experiencing unprecedented growth, and that the major domestic brands and foreign brands, not only of the firms included in this study but also of the U.S. and South Korea, are competing fiercely. We made a field trip to China to gain an understanding of the automotive business environment, in general, and of the advertising and media environment in China. Furthermore, we conducted interviews with the Chinese Advertising Association, academia, and a leading research firm, and collected the data and statistics about the automotive and advertising industries. The majority of the firms in the study have formulated joint ventures with Chinese automotive manufacturers

Hypotheses Testing

The conceptual framework in Figure 23.1 illustrates the hypothesized relationships between clients and agencies across different countries. We tested hypotheses by analyzing the contents of the transcripts and the secondary data we collected. We have organized this section by presenting the test results with respect to each of the research questions.

Global marketing and advertising strategies and organization

The first research question we posed in the interviews deals with fundamental strategic decision processes within the firms under study, in order to identify patterns in their decision-making processes that are generalizable across the firms. The pattern could alternatively be generalizable across firms by region, such as Western and Eastern decision-making processes. The decision-making processes of marketing and advertising strategy formulation and implementation can be broadly classified into the following categories: vertical (top-down or bottom-up), or horizontal decision making. Furthermore, coordination between headquarters and subsidiaries can also be classified into three categories: independent, vertical, or horizontal. Another conceptualization of the coordination between headquarters and subsidiaries is whether it is done only within a particular function, such as marketing, new product development, accounting, and other functions, or whether it takes the form of a matrix structure so that the firm as a whole is involved in the coordination task and functional division also communicates across borders.

Furthermore, these decision-making processes are investigated with respect to specific operational activities, i.e., corporate advertising and regional advertising. For the latter, participating firms have provided information that shows to what extent the headquarters get involved in overseeing regional advertising activities.

The empirical evidence emanating from the information provided by the interviews indicates that Japanese firms tend to allow a great deal of autonomy for regional subsidiaries, such that managers in the regional subsidiaries can make decisions on their own, although they frequently communicate with the headquarters. Considering the fact that major Japanese companies are relying more on the revenue generated from foreign markets, owing to the fact that the domestic Japanese market is getting saturated and is becoming extremely competitive, they are shifting the decision-making responsibilities to overseas subsidiaries, in particular to the United States where Japanese automotives are increasing their market shares. The unprecedented success of the prestige brands such as Lexus, Infiniti, and Accord in the U.S. market, along with the fact that these brands were first introduced in the U.S. market, lends support to their shifting of their decision-making responsibilities to the U.S. subsidiaries; thus those subsidiaries can respond faster to the competitive market, rather than wasting time in seeking and waiting for approvals for daily operations from the headquarters. Therefore it is fair to assess that their decision process is characterized, not as a top-down approach, but more as a bottom-up approach where the headquarters allow the local subsidiaries to make decisions. One executive of the leading firm tacitly stated in the interview,

> subsidiary people know better about their market than the headquarters, and they should feel comfortable about implementing their strategies, rather than being forced to carry out the plan set forth by the headquarters. As far as they are yielding better results with their approach year after year, it does not make much sense for the headquarters to interfere unnecessarily with the regional activities, unless their operation deviates too much from the corporate guideline.

We also found that these firms are coordinating the corporate advertising at the headquarters, by producing the corporate campaign and disseminating the creative materials overseas, so that they can try to maintain a consistent corporate image across different markets. Media purchasing for corporate advertising, however, is often done by the regional subsidiaries to deal with various local conditions. The overall weight of the corporate advertising tends to be much smaller than sales campaign and dealer support or dealer initiated campaigns.

The European firms, on the other hand, exhibit somewhat different behavior from their Japanese counterparts. Although we have observed that marketing directors and managers in Japan, for instance, are enjoying a great amount of autonomy, so that they can formulate their own marketing and advertising strategies, retain local advertising agencies, and work closely with local dealers, they often communicate with the headquarters so as to comply with the guideline. Their advertising campaigns are closely monitored by the headquarters, although they are not required to seek approval for the advertising campaign from the headquarters. They may get a flag from the headquarters if the campaign is not consistent with the global brand image. The advertising campaigns are also shared by other regional offices so that creative ideas and campaigns are often used across different regions for the advertising campaign for the same brands. This approach has clear advantages, i.e., cost savings, building a consistent image for the brand across different regions, and benchmarking the results across regions. We characterize this approach as horizontal, as opposed to the bottom-up or raise fair approach of the Japanese firms, and the top-down approach of the U.S. firms. Furthermore, marketing managers often communicate with engineers and product designers at the headquarters and other regional offices when they face new product development. The relationship is not hierarchical but horizontal, even across different functions. Thus we conclude that their functional structure is defined as being similar to the matrix form as described by Quelch (1986).

How does the firm work with advertising agencies?
In order to further investigate the adaptation versus standardization strategy for specific decisions regarding the advertiser–agency relationship, we have posed the following five questions as listed in the section of the research design and questions:

1. *Involvement of the headquarters for selecting the advertising agency in overseas subsidiaries* U.S. firms often work with the same global advertising agencies both at the headquarters and in overseas subsidiaries, utilizing the agencies' expansive network. The firms we conducted interviews with, however, indicated that their approach is more toward adaptation when they pitch and choose the advertising agency. Managers concur that the advertising agency should be well versed in local culture in order to communicate subtle nuances in creating advertising, and that the agency requires purchasing power and information to secure the appropriate media space. This is particularly true in the case of countries such as Japan, China and Taiwan, whose culture is vastly different from those of Western countries. The firms do report the results of their choice of agency, but the responsibility rests with the local managers.

2. *Use of an exclusive agency or multiple agencies by brand, media types, and other functions* Use of an exclusive agency, or the 'one client, one agency' policy, appears to be a norm for the U.S. multinational firms, since the client works very closely with an agency as a team, and they share proprietary information to formulate strategies and implement them. The recent reshuffle of Volkswagen's advertising agency in the United States stirred a controversy among the news media, because Crispin, Porter + Bogusky, an extremely creative ad agency working with BMW Mini USA, resigned from Mini to take over the VW account (Kiely, 2006). Crispin ended their relationship with their existing client of $30 million to take on the $400 million Volkswagen business.

Crispin's case is extreme, but, as the transcripts indicate, working very closely with an agency is the norm for European and Japanese firms. However, European firms demand more commitment from the agencies as a partner for the daily advertising operations, as opposed to a mere client–agency relationship. The agency is requested to contribute to strategy formulations and other operations more as an insider, and to actively participate in the meetings with the client. We also found the case that part of the agency's fee is tied with the client's business performance, rather than the traditional commission system in which the fee is paid as part of media expenditure.

We must note that agency selection in Japan should take into account the unique business environment, which is best characterized as a quasi-duopoly for the advertising business, traditionally dominated by two gigantic advertising agencies, Dentsu and Hakuhodo. Large advertisers are working with either one of or both agencies, which results in the situation that Dentsu and Hakuhodo hold multiple clients in the same industry. However, they have strict policies to ensure that their accounts are completely separated from each other within the agency. Those agencies usually set up a separate entity to serve solely a particular client. Nonetheless, given that they control a vast majority of media buying, the reality is that clients do not have much choice but to work with either agency to secure the media space.

We have carefully reviewed the document released by the Federal Trade Commission of the Japanese Government regarding this topic. The FTC report tacitly depicts that such problems exist and pose a potential conflict of interest, i.e., the ad agency could represent the interest of media companies rather than the client, which indicates a serious accountability issue, namely, that more clients are demanding clarification for their huge advertising expenditures because of the lack of any documentation for media transactions, and requesting information on the effectiveness of the advertising expenditures. The firms under study expressed deep concern for these issues also during the interviews.

According to the data compiled by Nikkei Advertising Research (2005), the automotive industry in Japan indeed represents the segment that has the heaviest advertising expenditure. Toyota tops the list over ten years as the heaviest advertiser in Japan. Honda is ranked as the second and the third heaviest advertiser (depending on the year), followed by Nissan whose ranking varies from the second to the eighth position from 1995 to 2004.

Japanese firms thus have a somewhat different type of relationship with the agencies. In some cases, the firms attempt to finalize the advertising plan in house, and then seek pitching from alternative agencies. Once they choose the agency, the client and the agency start working very closely, similar to the case of the European firms. However, the extent to which they share proprietary information with the agency appears to be much less than European firms.

However, this is not the case for the Japanese firms in the United States. The good example is Lexus in the United States. As Dawson (2004) illustrated in his book about hugely successful Lexus in the United States, the Lexus Division of Toyota USA is working very closely with Team One, which Saatchi & Saatchi, Toyota's global advertising agency, set up as its special unit. They have been working together as a team since the inception of the Lexus brand in 1989.

3.   *Role of advertising agencies for strategy formulation, creative decisions, media decisions, and research*   Do advertising agencies formulate strategies, make creative and media decisions, and conduct research on behalf of the client? We have found that this is true for European firms in Japan, and we also speculate that the Japanese firms in the U.S. follow the same strategy, where one client, one agency is a norm. The interviews we conducted also suggest that the Japanese advertising agencies attempt to emulate this by providing services to the client during the stage of strategy formulation, such as overall advertising strategy, creative strategy, and media planning.

4.   *Advertising management between the headquarters and subsidiaries*   We asked in our interviews whether the way overseas subsidiaries conduct advertising activities varies from the way the headquarters conducts advertising in the home market. The answers to this question obviously depend on the market in which the firm is conducting business. European firms operating in Japan, for instance, need to adjust their operation according to the unique advertising and media environment as depicted in the preceding sections. The Japanese firms, on the other hand, appear to adjust to a great extent to local conditions. This is in accordance with the findings of the study by Grein, Craig and Takada (2001). They found in their econometric study that Japanese firms are successful in adapting to local conditions by employing the responsive strategy in the European market, whereas the European firms are using the integration strategy. The Japanese firms in the U.S. are behaving more like the firms in the United States, i.e., fully adjusting to the local market.

5.   *The future advertising strategy*   This subject is related to the development of new media technology and the integration of media communication. The key question is how managers foresee the effect of these factors on their advertising strategies in the future. Although mass media such as TV, magazines, and newspapers still dominate their advertising activities as the major

vehicles to reach target audiences, managers express the need to investigate diversification into alternative media vehicles, in particular the Internet. This implies that web pages should be designed to be tied with the contents of TV and other media advertising, so that the target audience will receive the information and brand image consistently across different media.

Global brand management

Marketing and advertising strategy should be formulated to be consistent with the corporate strategy. European firms, especially German firms, are famous for maintaining consistent brand image. This consistency is not only created by the advertising campaign alone, but also by the product development, branding strategy, and other efforts. For example, Kiley (2004) in his book about BMW hails its innovative product design by the head designer Chris Bangel. The *New York Times* article by Patton (2006) echoes his view, and indicates that the raised trunk of the BMW 7 Series drew criticism at first, but is now widely copied by Toyota Camry, Lexus LS 460 and GS 450h, Hyundai Azera, Mercedes-Benz S-Class, and Chrysler Imperial.

European firms have been successful in producing and marketing the same brands, and it is not surprising to see that these firms are successful in building a consistent brand image across different regions, albeit with minor modifications in order to satisfy local needs and wants, and meet local requirements. Therefore, it is plausible to find in the transcripts that managers of the European firms are paying closer attention to enhance a consistent brand image in their marketing and advertising activities.

In comparison, the Japanese firms tend to have a product lineup of completely different brands across regions. It is well known that many models available in Japan are not distributed in other countries. Even the extremely successful global brand is perceived by consumers in a different way, e.g., the brand positioned to the young segment in the U.S. is appealing to the older segment in the European market. It is also true that the successful brands in the U.S. are unavailable in Japan. Managers of both European and Japanese firms concur with the above observations in their interviews. However, we must note that the strategies employed by the Japanese firms for their prestige brands that first appeared in the U.S. seem to reflect their novel approach to building and strengthening a consistent brand image across regions. Dawson (2004) illustrates that Lexus is a good example of successfully implementing this strategy. Ghosn and Riès (2005) also describe the efforts to transform and streamline Nissan's organization into a globalized firm with their tremendous efforts to build a consistent brand identity across markets.

Professor Fujimoto, the automotive production management expert at the University of Tokyo, provided during our interview the explanation

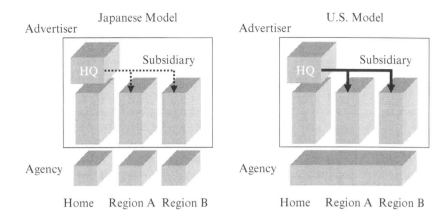

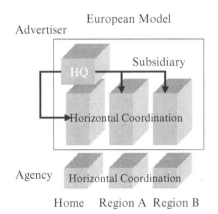

Figure 23.2   New hypothetical relations between advertisers and agencies across regions: Japanese, U.S. and European models

for the flourishing multibrand strategy used by the Japanese firms from the manufacturing perspective. The Japanese firms are capable of producing a smaller number of automobiles with shorter product life cycles, thus capable of introducing more brands into the marketplace. This explanation is indeed quite helpful to understand the rationale behind Japanese firms are employing this strategy. Figure 23.2 summarizes the relationship between advertisers and agencies, which consists of three models for Japanese, U.S., and European firms, respectively. We have derived those models based on the results of empirical results, and updated the previously presented hypothesized relationship in Figure 23.1.

DISCUSSION

In this section, we attempt to derive managerial implications based on the findings presented in the empirical section, along with the literature in international business, marketing, and advertising. The objective is to identify answers to the key question: how should firms coordinate the branding and advertising strategies for their global operation to survive and flourish in the highly competitive markets? Furthermore, are there any optimal strategies that can be derived from the managerial implications?

In order to answer these questions, we review the effect of the unique market environment that confronts managers when formulating strategy. It is evident from the interviews that managers of both Japanese and German firms are working intensely to better respond to various local conditions, which include consumers, dealers, advertising agencies, and the media environment, among others. At the same time, it is true that the basic production process of automobiles is highly standardized and less susceptible to local conditions, much less than such consumer products as food and fashion goods, which are known to be highly sensitive to local preference and culture. This, however, does not imply that the task of marketing managers at the automotive firms can be simply extended to or transferred from one market to the other. Automobiles are among the most highly complex and expensive products, and accordingly consumers' information processing is best described as one of higher involvement by them. Marketing managers expressed their concern during the interviews that automobiles are appealing to the varying segments according to the price range, and it is often the case that buyer behavior varies considerably across segments, e.g., the segment for less expensive cars versus the status-conscious segment for exclusive automobiles, even in a single market. Therefore, their task of properly communicating with these segments with the right product becomes extremely complex, and requires extensive knowledge about the local market conditions. We observe a fairly good degree of consensus for this requirement among the marketing managers of Japanese and German manufacturers. Use of local advertising agencies, in particular, for creative work seems to bode well and solve managers' concern for this requirement. Even a good media agency is chosen based on their buying power in the local market to secure the ideal media space.

Beyond adaptation of marketing and advertising to the local market conditions, the firm should instill the unique brand concept in consumers' minds in the long run, and the brand concept should be consistent and coherent across markets as well. Achieving adaptation to the local market and building a consistent brand image in the long run, thus, seem to contradict each other, since an excessive adaptation to the local market would call for a customization strategy, while the effort of building a consistent image in the global marketplace requires coordination and control for the brand positioning and communication strategy by the firm as a whole. The latter effort can be achieved only by carefully formulating a global strategy and monitoring the various marketing and advertising operations across markets from a long-term perspective.

We observe different behaviors between the Japanese and German companies on this dimension. As illustrated in the empirical analysis, the German companies are paying more attention to building a consistent brand image across markets. Historically, they prefer to use consistent car designs, logos and trademarks, with minor deviations if necessary. The Japanese firms, on the other hand, change car designs more often. They are also very flexible about branding, i.e., introducing new brands frequently and terminating unsuccessful brands at an early stage. This is often done in response to market competition, and dealers also request that car manufacturers refresh and revitalize the brand lineup and make it more attractive to customers, rather than displaying and selling the same old models year after year. In the short run, this strategy of overcustomization bodes well for gaining market shares in a highly competitive market like Japan. However, this sends a mixed signal across markets, and, more importantly, it may work against establishing a consistent corporate and brand image in the long run, besides obvious drawbacks such as higher cost.

It is obvious from the interviews that automotive companies in Japan are frustrated by the lack of accountability including the absence of reliable media research, and possible breach of security within the large advertising agencies. At the same time, they recognize that changing the advertising landscape is far beyond the scope of private firms. The proliferation of small and medium sized agencies with creative minds and further inroads into global advertising agencies are expected to create a healthier and more productive advertising environment for both advertisers and agencies in the future.

CONCLUSION

We developed the conceptual framework for the advertiser–agency relationship for global firms, and conducted an extensive empirical investigation and analysis to test the hypotheses. The empirical analysis involves unprecedented scope of data collection, both of primary and secondary data. For the primary data collection, we conducted interviews with the managers of the leading automotive manufacturers whose headquarters are located in Japan and Germany. Those companies represent a good majority of the global automotive market, in particular, the higher segment of the automotive market. We were fortunate that we were able to obtain full cooperation from the companies we chose for this study. Our data collection covers the important automotive markets in the world, namely, Japan, China and Taiwan for the Asian markets, and the United States representing the Western hemisphere. We analyzed the test results in depth, and concluded that the overall conceptualization framework holds. Based on the empirical results and the literature, we derived the optimal strategies for global firms. We strongly believe that this study makes a significant contribution to the literature, and that the managerial implications should be carefully looked into by the companies for their future strategy development. We shed light on the unique advertising environment in Japan.

The study, however, suffers from some limitations. First, the empirical investigation involves only a single industry, which thus limits the generalizability of the results to other industries. Nonetheless, despite its limitation, we believe that our findings are sufficient to disentangle the advertiser–agency relationships. Second, the study mainly relies on the subjective information collected from the managers. Therefore, validity of the results is subject to the accuracy of the information provided by the managers. However, we conducted individual interviews with these managers on a one-to-one basis, rather than using the survey method that is the prevalent data collection procedure among other studies. A major advantage of the individual interview is that we know the source of the information. The survey method, on the other hand, suffers from the lack of validation, which means that anybody can fill out the questionnaire (Takada et al. 2003). The study of the global auto industry by Grein et al. (2001), on the other hand, relies on quantitative data. Thus, it is fair to suggest that both studies can shed light on the analysis of marketing strategies by European and Japanese automotive firms, from different perspectives, i.e., quantitative and qualitative, or, alternatively, macro and micro insights. The first limitation leads to the implications and suggestions for future studies. Replicating the framework developed in this study to other industries, and other countries, is highly advised to obtain more generalizable results.

REFERENCES

Boddewyn, J.J., Robin Soehl and Jacques Picard (1986), 'Standardization in International Marketing: Is Ted Levitt in Fact Right?' *Business Horizons*, **29** (6), 69–75.

Buzzell, R. (1968), 'Can You Standardize Multinational Marketing', *Harvard Business Reviews*, **46** (6), November–December, 702.

Dawson, Chester (2004), *Lexus: The Relentless Pursuit*, Singapore: John Wiley & Sons (Asia) Pte Ltd.

Fair Trade Commission of Japan (2004), *Report of the Survey on the Current Status of Business Practices in the Advertising Industry* (広告業界の取引実態に関する調査報告), November 8 (in Japanese), p. 71.

Fujimoto, Takahito and Kim B. Clark (1991), *Product Development Performance*, Boston, MA: Harvard Business School Publishing.

Ghosn, Carlos and Philippe Riès (2005), *Shift: Inside Nissan's Historic Revival*, New York: Currency Doubleday.

Grein, Andreas. F., C.S. Craig and Hirokazu Takada (2001), 'Integration and Responsiveness: Marketing Strategies of Japanese and European Automobile Manufacturers', *Journal of International Marketing*, **9**, (2), 19–50.

Jain, Subhash C. (1989), 'Standardization of International Marketing Strategy: Some Research Hypotheses', *Journal of Marketing*, **53** (1), January, 70–79.

Kiley, David (2004), *Driven: Inside BMW, the Most Admired Car Company in the World*, Hoboken, NJ: John Wiley & Sons.

— (2006), 'Getting Creative with Mad Ave: To Find the Right Agency, MINI Cooper Devised a Quirky Trial-by-Immersion', Marketing: New Solutions, *Business Week*, February 6, 80–81.

Levitt, Theodore (1983), 'The Globalization of Markets', *Harvard Business Review*, **61** (3), May–June, 92–102.

Liker, Jeffrey K. (2004), *The Toyota Way: 14 Management Principles from the World's Greatest Manufacturer*, New York: McGraw-Hill.

Nikkei Advertising Research (2005), *Advertising Expenditures by Top 20 Heaviest Companies over 10 Years*, in Japanese.

Patton, Phil (2006), 'A Flood of Imitators Flatter a Once-Mocked Rump', Autos on Monday/Design in the Automobiles, *The New York Times*, February 20, D10.

Quelch, John A. and Edward J. Hoff (1986), 'Customizing Global Marketing', *Harvard Business Review*, **64** (3), 59–68.

Rau, Pradeep A. and John F. Preble (1987), 'Standardization of Marketing Strategy by Multinationals', *International Marketing Review*, Autumn, 18–28.

Roberts, Dexter and Frederik Balfour (2006), 'China: To Get Rich is Glorious', Global Business, *Business Week*, February 6, 46–7.

Samiee, Saeed and Kendell Roth (1992), 'The Influence of Global Marketing Standardization on Performance', *Journal of Marketing*, 56, April 1–17.

Szymanski, David M., Sundar G. Bharadwaj and P. Rajan Varadarajan (1993), 'Standardization versus Adaptation of International Marketing Strategy: An Empirical Investigation', *Journal of Marketing*, **57** (October), 1–17.

Takada, Hirokazu, Takaho Ueda, Yoshiyuki Okuse and Manabu Uchida (2003), *MBA Marketing Research*, Tokyo: Toyo-Keizai.

Walters, Peter G.P. (1986), 'International Marketing Policy: A Discussion of the Standardization Construct and its Relevance for Corporate Policy', *Journal of International Business Studies*, **17** (2), Summer, 55–67.

— and Brian Toyne (1989), 'Product Modification and Standardization in International Markets: Strategic Options and Facilitating Policies', *Columbia Journal of World Business*, **24** (4), Winter, 37–44.

Yip, George S. (1997), 'Patterns and Determinants of Global Marketing', *Journal of Marketing Management*, **13**, 153–64.

— (2003), *Total Global Strategy*, Upper Saddle River, NJ: Prentice-Hall.

Index